MASTERS OF WAR

Latin America and
United States Aggression
from the Cuban
Revolution Through
the Clinton Years

CLARA NIETO

Translated from the Spanish
by Chris Brandt

Foreword by Howard Zinn

SEVEN STORIES PRESS
New York • Toronto • Melbourne • London

Seven Stories Press
140 Watts Street
New York, NY 10013
www.sevenstories.com

In Canada: Hushion House, 36 Northline Road, Toronto, Ontario M4B 3E2

In the U.K.: Turnaround Publisher Services Ltd., Unit 3, Olympia Trading Estate, Coburg Road, Wood Green, London N22 6TZ

In Australia: Palgrave Macmillan, 627 Chapel Street, South Yarra, VIC 3141

Library of Congress Cataloging-in-Publication Data
   [Amos de la guerra y las guerras de los amos. English]
   Masters of war: Latin America and U.S. aggression from the Cuban revolution through the Clinton years / Clara Nieto; translated from the Spanish by Chris Brandt.—A Seven Stories Press 1st ed.
      p. cm.
   Includes bibliographical references and index.
   ISBN 1-58322-545-5 (pbk.)
      1. Latin America—Politics and government—1948–1980. 2. Latin America—Politics and government—1980– 3. Cuba—Politics and government—1959– 4. Cuba—History—Revolution, 1959– Influence. 5. United States—Foreign relations—Latin America. 6. Latin America—Foreign relations—United States. 7. United States—Foreign relations—Cuba. 8. Cuba—Foreign relations—United States. I. Brandt, Chris. II. Title.

F1414.2 .N5313 2001
980.03'3—dc21   2001041071

9 8 7 6 5 4 3 2 1

College professors may order examination copies of Seven Stories Press titles for a free six-month trial period. To order, visit www.sevenstories.com/textbook/ or fax on school letterhead to 212.226.1411.

Book design by Jon Gilbert and India Amos

Printed in Canada.

CONTENTS

CHAPTER IV: "The Backyard"

by Howard Zinn

Anyone who has studied or taught in the schools and colleges of the United States must recognize that Latin America is shamefully neglected as an area of study. I suggest one possible reason for this neglect: to study the United States' relations with Latin America would be embarrassing. Indeed, it might disrupt the naive view fostered by the educational system and the entire culture—the view that the United States is a benign force for democracy in the world.

In 1927 Undersecretary of State Robert Olds wrote a confidential memorandum to his colleagues: "We do control the destinies of Central America. Until now Central America has always understood that governments which we recognize and support stay in power, while those which we do not recognize and support fall."

That statement would be an accurate description of the attitude of the United States government to all of Latin America, from the Monroe Doctrine of 1823 to the present day. It leads to a disturbing thought: that the United States has, throughout its history, been an aggressive, expansionist imperial power, especially in relation to Latin America.

As I write this, there are scattered news items: the United States is giving over a billion dollars to the government of Colombia to suppress a guerrilla movement; an embargo against Cuba, designed to strangle its economy and impoverish its people, remains in force; a high Peruvian official, Vladimoros Montesinos, implicated with corruption, torture, and death squads, turns out to have worked for the CIA.

But the newspapers and television networks that report these items give no historical context that would show they are part of an immense, complex pattern of the United States' domination of Latin America.

This book, by the distinguished Latin American writer Clara Nieto, is exactly what is needed to supply the missing context for the superficial stories we find in the mass media and for the paltry treatment of Latin America we get in our educational system. We in the United States need badly to hear a Latin American point of view, and here we have it from a scholar of international repute.

Ms. Nieto provides us with a sweeping history of United States relations with Latin America. She begins and ends with Cuba, giving it special attention, but she also displays her solid knowledge of the rest of the continent. Her account, based on meticulous research and presented with clarity and grace, will be enormously useful for a long time to come.

HISTORY IN THE PRESENT TENSE

This book covers a cycle of history that divides the American hemisphere in two. It begins with the triumph of the Cuban Revolution on January 1, 1959, and ends with the collapse of the Soviet Union in December 1991, marking the end of the fifty-year Cold War and opening the way for global hegemony by the United States. The book's focal point is the Cuban revolutionary process, a moving force for armed struggle and insurgency on the continent, and the United States' policies designed to undermine the Revolution to keep it from reaching deeper into Latin America and the Caribbean, its natural zone of influence. Such policies have profound repercussions in these countries throughout this period.

In effect, Cuba becomes a factor in the East-West confrontation, in the Cold War, and in worldwide political debate, as well as a flash point of controversy in United States' internal politics. For the first time a Latin American nation—one of the smallest—stood up to the Empire, threw it out of its territory, allied itself with the Soviet Union, and declared itself socialist. Cuba shattered the United States hegemony and threatened its security and continental stability. No other Latin American country has had a greater impact for as long a time in the international arena and in the third world. Havana emerged as the revolutionary epicenter and Fidel Castro and Che Guevara as rebel idols.

Fidel's nationalist and anti-imperialist discourse encouraged the struggle of Latin American people to defend their rights and fight against the national governments and oligarchies allied with Washington. His discourse was a challenge and a threat. During the 1960s, armed pro-Castro movements rose up in dictatorships and democracies, with hopes of repeating the heroic Cuban deed. That insurgency was born out of aberrant and endemic social and economic inequalities, the misery of masses exploited and cheated by the ever-smaller numbers of the powerful, and the violent repression by official forces. The narrowness or absence of democratic channels prevented the people's participation in the decisions made by their governments and parliaments.

The armed groups and the liberation movements of the third world were linked to Havana one way or another throughout these three decades. Havana provided them with political orientation, military training, arms, and advisers. Cuban troops—with help from the Soviet Union—assured the triumph of Angola and Ethiopia against their aggressors. Such aid disappeared in Latin America during the 1970s, when most of its governments reestablished diplomatic relations with Cuba and broke its isolation.

The changes brought about in the Catholic Church by Pope John XXIII, who oriented the church's duties toward helping the poor and promoting social justice, also contributed to this explosion of revolutionary activity. Progressive sectors of the Church educated the poor about their rights, organized their movements, and took part in their struggles. This union of Christians and revolutionaries was enormously important for the Sandinista struggle against the Somoza dictatorship in Nicaragua and for the civil war against the military dictatorships in El Salvador led by the Farabundo Martí National Liberation Front.

Nine American administrations—those of Dwight D. Eisenhower, John F. Kennedy, Lyndon B. Johnson, Richard Nixon, Gerald Ford, Jimmy Carter, Ronald Reagan, George Bush, and Bill Clinton—maintained a policy of greater or lesser aggression against Cuba, aiming to destroy the Cuban Revolution and Fidel Castro. Fearing Cuba's role as an example to other nations and the expansion of international communism throughout the hemisphere, Kennedy reconsidered his policies toward Latin America. He set in motion the Alliance for Progress, a program of economic and social development to serve the immense needs of Latin and Caribbean countries, and gave a radical turn to the United States' hemispheric defense strategies, focusing on counterinsurgency to fight "the enemy within." But strengthening national armies—a cornerstone of that srategy—also strengthened militarism. During the three years of his administration, new military dictatorships overthrew constitutional governments under the banner of anti-Communism. During the 1960s, in the countries of the Southern Cone (Argentina, Brazil, Uruguay, and Chile), military dictatorships planted the doctrine of National Security, with anti-Commmunist and counterinsurgency objectives similar to Kennedy's military strategy.

These decades (1960s–1980s) were marked by violence, civil wars, and confrontations between armed movements seeking radical change and military counter-insurgents trying to obstruct them. Many hundreds of men and women were murdered, tortured, and "disappeared" in what the military called internal wars, and the people called dirty wars. The vast majority were not killed in combat. Never before had the continent seen such brutal, massive, and profound violations of human rights.

By the end of the 1960s the armed movements in the Andean countries (Colombia, Peru, and Venezuela) were virtually eliminated. In the 1980s these movements as well as the neo-fascist dictatorships disappeared from the Southern Cone. The military—decadent, discredited, and harassed by increasing opposition, both internal and international—called for elections. In the 1990s peace finally came to Central America. El Salvador, Guatemala, and Nicaragua's governments signed peace treaties with insurgent movements, which became political parties.

The costs of peace were broad amnesties that the civilian governments conceded to the military and police forces responsible for the dirty wars. They were exempted from appearing before civilian courts to account for their crimes. Such laws, approved by the nations' parliaments and courts—supposed "pillars" of democracy—legitimized impunity.

This volume explores the history of this hemisphere by decade and by country, concentrating only on those that faced insurgent-counterinsurgent conflicts. It also looks at United States policies toward Latin America and the Caribbean since the declaration of the Monroe Doctrine. These policies have formed a coherent interventionist policy—whether open or covert—designed to impede changes that might affect the political or economic interests of the United States.

I will analyze the development of the Cuban revolution, its anti-imperialist and third-world-oriented foreign policy, its role in the international arena, its influence in the third world, its alliance with the Soviet bloc, its actions in response to the aggression of the world superpower, and the impact the collapse of the Communist world has had on the island. This dramatic turn of events, which radically changed the world panorama, leaves Cuba without its principal allies and most important markets. Without Soviet support, the impact of the economic blockade imposed by the United States was much harder and United States aggression much more dangerous. Confronted with this enormous threat, Cuba instituted a set of changes to strengthen the Revolution and assure its survival, and the net result of these efforts has proven favorable.

The disappearance of the Communist superpower and its empire closed this historic cycle, opening a new chapter for the world.

CHAPTER I

MARE NOSTRUM, MARE CLAUSTRUM

THE UNITED STATES: THE DAWNING OF A NEW EMPIRE

For the European colonial powers, the great Caribbean Sea—the mare claustrum—served as the arena for their rivalries and for their capitalist expansion. There "the most striking genocide of the modern world was carried out through the extermination of the indigenous Taíno population from the effects of the foreign, technological-military and economic yoke," wrote Gerard Pierre-Charles, in his book *El Caribe a la hora de Cuba.*

Spain, Great Britain, France, and the Netherlands imposed their dominion on the Caribbean natives, extracting riches from their lands, transporting Africans to the New World as slaves and objects of exploitation, implanting their racial separation—the supremacy of whites over natives and blacks—and establishing the antagonisms between master and slave, oppressor and oppressed. They imposed their cultural, religious, and linguistic patterns and brought their diseases as well. Under such dissimilar influences the Antillean colonial enclaves—already separated by water—became disjointed from each other, as if they were ethnically different. Their common destiny was as satellites of European metropolises, sources of raw materials for European industries (bauxite, petroleum, sugar, cotton, copper, wood, gold and silver, and metals used in the manufacture of weaponry), and captive markets for European products, which the conquerors needed for the extension of their foreign trade, wealth, and power.[1]

The United States began displacing the influence of the European powers in the Caribbean, and by the mid-nineteenth century it was owner and master of its "inland sea." In 1823, in his State of the Union address to Congress, James Monroe (1817–1825) warned the European powers of the Holy Alliance that he would consider their intervention in any country of the Americas as a threat to the peace and security of the United States. Once and for all, he established the boundaries of the new Empire, its predominance in the New World, and its right to intervene in the nations of the Americas when it felt that its interests or security was at risk. The declaration, the Americas for the Americans— or better stated, the Americas for the United States—was codified as the Monroe Doctrine, and it has been the foundation of the United States' foreign policy ever since.

Vigorous expansion—manifest in the Monroe Doctrine—was the expression of the "Founding Fathers'" belief that their mission lay in extending the territorial, economic, and political dominion of the great North American nation and thus "extend[ing] the area of freedom." Thomas Jefferson and James Madison believed expansion to be the key to United States greatness and the foundation of its democracy.[2]

Monroe's successors added other principles, doctrines, and policies that strengthened this expansionist and redemptive vocation. "Manifest destiny" was an expression of their self-professed "ideological and moral superiority" over the rest of the globe. Andrew Jackson (1829–1837) saw the extension of the United States' authority over "semi-barbarous peoples" to bring them civilization and "teaching inferiors to appreciate the blessings they already enjoyed but were inclined to overlook" as the "inevitable historical mission" of the United States.[3]

Theodore Roosevelt (1901–1909) complemented the Monroe Doctrine with his "corollary," extending the United States' "right" to intervene in the internal affairs of these nations when they behaved in "an irresponsible manner" or proved incapable of maintaining internal order. These were "Big Stick" politics. Roosevelt believed that it was inevitable for the United States to protect and regulate the life of the Caribbean republics, since "every expansion of a great civilized power [meant] a victory for law, order, and righteousness."[4] In 1901 Congress imposed the Platt Amendment on Cuba, giving the United States the right to intervene in the island's internal affairs, and in 1903 Roosevelt "took" Panama, converted it into a semicolony, and constructed the Panama Canal. In the Dominican Republic, the United States took over customs and stationed warships along its coasts.[5]

Other expansionist and imperialist policies included the dollar diplomacy of William Howard Taft (1909–1913), supported by military action[6] and the Open Door policy for United States global commerce and investments.[7]

Central American and Caribbean countries endured continual landings by the marines to "protect North American lives and interests,"[8] whenever there were internal disturbances. Thus, the United States impeded changes that did not suit its needs. Such occupations could last days, months, or years. Mexico was the primary victim. In wars provoked by the new empire, it lost 1,500 square miles of its territory, which today make up California, Nevada, Texas, Utah, and the greater part of Arizona, New Mexico, Wyoming, and Colorado.[9]

"THE PEARL OF THE ANTILLES"

To the Founding Fathers, Cuba—the largest of the Antilles Islands and situated a mere 90 miles off the coast of the United States—was irresistibly attractive. Jefferson, assuming that Great Britain wanted to annex the island, was willing to go to war for it. As for John Quincy Adams, who maintained that Cuba was of vital importance to the commercial and political interests of the United States, he saw that geographic determinism and the "laws of political as well as of physical gravitation" would make it fall into his hands like "an apple severed by the tempest from its native tree."[10] Presidents Andrew Jackson, James K. Polk, James Buchanan, Grover Cleveland, and William McKinley all dreamed of annexing "the Pearl of the Antilles," offering to buy it from Spain for $300 million. But Spain declined; it would not sell "the most precious jewel of its crown."[11] Nevertheless, it allowed North American investors to convert it into a commercial dependent of the United States.[12]

For thirty years Cuban patriots fought to get out from under the Spanish yoke. In 1895, organized and directed by José Martí, what became known in Cuba as the Second War of Independence from Spain exploded. The whole island was engulfed by the struggle, and the people joined with the rebel forces. Twice Spain expelled Martí from the island for fanning the flames of rebellion against Spanish domination. In exile he traveled to Spain, France, Mexico, Guatemala, Venezuela, and New York. There he sought recruits and funds for the War of Independence. He founded the Cuban Revolutionary Party to unite the people in the struggle for the independence of their country and to support independence for Puerto Rico. Having returned to Cuba, Martí died heroically on May 19, 1895, in Dos Ríos, brought down by enemy fire.[13]

Given the turmoil in Cuba, Cleveland decided to intervene in this war in order to "save" the island. He announced that he would help pacify the island

and warned that if Spain did not put an end to the conflict soon, the United States would be "obliged to protect its interests and those of its nationals, which coincide with those of humanity and civilization and to restore the blessing of Peace to the Island." The United States' interests, however, were in assuring the defeat of the Cuban patriots.[14]

McKinley, Cleveland's successor, solicited from Congress authorization to send troops, but "not for the exercise of sovereignty, jurisdiction, or control" over Cuba. Important New York businessmen asked that he take immediate and effective measures on the island to stem their tremendous losses and restore "a most valuable commercial field."[15] In January 1898 he sent the battleship *Maine* on a "good will" visit and to protect "North American lives and interests." The ship mysteriously exploded off the Cuban coast. Of the 276 men who died, most of them were black marines.[16]

The United States held Spain responsible for this incident. In April, Congress declared war against Spain, stating that Cuba had "the right to be free and independent of Spain," and authorized McKinley to send military forces. The Cuban War of Independence from Spain became the Spanish-American War, which appeared in American history books as a "brief, glorious, and inexpensive" war.[17] Cuban historians characterized it as "Yankee meddling in the War of '95," maintaining that the action was not to assure Cuba's independence but to protect the United States' monopolies.[18]

It was, in fact, a short war. In April 1898 the United States began its intervention. By August it had signed an armistice with Spain and in December, the peace with the Treaty of Paris. Cuba was not invited to participate in any of the events organized to determine its future. With the defeat of the already weakened Spanish Empire, the United States acquired the Philippines (it paid Spain $20 million for it) and Guam in the Pacific, and in the Caribbean it imposed its dominion over Cuba—despite the Treaty of Paris, which granted Cuba's independence—and Puerto Rico. The United States' flag was the sole banner to rise over the public buildings of Havana and San Juan.

Cuba became a de facto protectorate with the United States imposing its own military governors. In 1901 Congress approved the Platt Amendment, granting itself the right to intervene militarily in Cuba "to preserve its independence." Furthermore, Congress prohibited Cuba from making treaties or conventions with other countries, contracting debts without its consent, and imposed on it the obligation to sell or lease lands for the installation of a Navy base and a coal port. Cuba conceded, leasing Bahía Honda and Guantánamo to the

United States. In 1903 the amendment was incorporated in the permanent treaty signed by both governments.[19]

Congressmen who were not in agreement with the amendment declared that it was a "legislative ultimatum" and an "invitation to intervention" in Cuban politics. When both houses approved it, Havana seethed with indignation. In a contemporary caricature, Cuba appeared crucified between two thieves—United States General Leonard Wood and McKinley—while Senator Orville Platt thrust a lance into its side.[20] A torchlight procession marched before the government palace, where General Wood presided as governor of Cuba.

However, Washington warned that it would not withdraw its troops until the Platt Amendment became Cuban law. The Cuban Assembly, after hectic debates, adopted it with a one-vote majority (15 to 14), and it was written into the first national constitution.[21] Thus, began the era of the so-called Mediated Republic.

With constitutional guarantees allowing the United States to intervene whenever it wanted, the United States permitted the Cubans to elect their own presidents—with its blessings—and pulled out its troops. But these concessions did not signal the end of military interventions. In 1912 during a new revolt against the Cuban president, the marines landed "to protect the lives and interests" of Americans. Nearly 3,000 rebels were massacred.[22] In 1917, when the United States entered the first World War, President Mario García Menocal placed the island at its disposal. A detachment of marines remained in Cuba for five years. Washington continued to send consultants to advise Cuban presidents[23] and meddle in all aspects of Cuban public life, the intrigues of its corrupt politics, internal power struggles, and the selection of those who governed it. With the Cuban ruling class at the service of the Empire, relations between the two countries were excellent.

In 1933 President Franklin Delano Roosevelt repealed the Platt Amendment, though he assured the permanent occupation of the Guantánamo base with a new treaty. The United States' economic penetration in the island, however, kept Cuba in a semicolonial state: the greatest part of its trade was with the United States, and the United States was also the major market for sugar, Cuba's principal product.

For Puerto Rico, the small Caribbean island that Martí wanted to have by his side in his war for independence, the defeat of Spain meant merely a change of masters. The United States lowered the Spanish flag and raised its own over Morro castle. From 1898 to 1917 the island was governed first by a military governor, then by a civilian. In 1917 Congress granted the islanders United States nationality, but without political rights—Puerto Ricans could not vote or run for office. In 1946 the United States permitted Puerto Rico to have its own government under congressional control, reserving the right to veto any constitutional change. Four years later, the United States conferred on the island commonwealth status and granted it "total" independence. Nevertheless, Washington directed its economy, defense, and foreign policies.[24]

THE NEIGHBORS

"All the world thinks of the United States today as an empire, except the people of the United States," wrote *New York Times* columnist Walter Lippman in 1927. "We shrink from the word 'empire,' and insist that it should not be used to describe the dominion we exercise from Alaska to the Philippines, from Cuba to Panama, and beyond." Nonetheless, he added, "we control the foreign relations of all the Caribbean countries; not one of them could enter into serious relations abroad without our consent. We control their relations with each other. We exercise the power of life and death over their governments in that no government can survive if we refuse it recognition. We help in many of these countries to decide what they call their elections, and we do not hesitate, as we have done recently in Mexico, to tell them what kind of constitution we think they ought to have. Whatever we may choose to call it, this is what the world at large calls an empire, or at least an empire in the making. Admitting that the word has an unpleasant connotation, nevertheless it does seem as if the time had come for us to look the whole thing squarely in the face and to stop trying to deceive ourselves."[25]

Woodrow Wilson (1913–1921) was the first American president to suggest abandoning this imperialist policy of intervention. He wanted to approach Latin America to "promote the common interests of the peoples of the two continents by all appropriate and honorable means." But the "crude and violent reality of imperialism" demonstrated otherwise; intervention followed intervention "in apparent obedience to a pathological need to impose on them by force United States democracy."[26]

When Franklin Delano Roosevelt (1933–1945) arrived at the White House, Central America and the Caribbean had already endured more than a hundred military interventions and territorial occupations. The marines spent nine years in Haiti and Nicaragua, and eighteen in the Dominican Republic. With his Good Neighbor policy, Roosevelt suspended interventions, rescinded the Platt Amendment on Cuba, and signed new agreements with Panamanian President

Arnulfo Arias, which excised from the 1903 treaties the clauses and concepts most offensive to the Panamanians: the United States' "right" of intervention, its "perpetual rights" over the Canal, and its "sovereignty" in the isthmus. Moreover he recognized Panamanian sovereignty over the Canal Zone which was under United States "jurisdiction."[27] Under Roosevelt, relations were characterized by equality and cooperation.

According to the Mexican writer Jesús Silva Herzog, Roosevelt exchanged "the big stick for the white glove." Herzog wrote: "Comparing his policies with those of his relative Theodore Roosevelt, the Good Neighbor policy is a change of form rather than content" and "imperialism, an economic phenomenon, the inevitable and legitimate offspring of capitalism, will never cease to be a constant threat and growing evil for the progress of the majority of nations, until capitalist society transforms itself into a new society capable of superseding the bloody civilizations of the merchant."[28]

In 1936 Roosevelt traveled to Buenos Aires to take part in the Inter-American Conference for the Maintenance of Peace. At that point Germany—under the euphoria of Nazi doctrines of racial superiority—had begun occupying lands outside its borders, while Fascist Italy invaded Ethiopia. Hitler and Mussolini proclaimed the Berlin-Rome Axis, and Japan invaded China. These great conflicts, which led to the Second World War, determined that relations between the United States and Latin America would make for a convenient military alliance.

Roosevelt assured political and military solidarity in the hemisphere and collective defense under United States leadership. In Buenos Aires he made important proposals against militarism, which he defined as a "suicidal policy," and indicated that "sacrifices in the cause of peace are infinitesimal compared with the holocaust of war." Roosevelt criticized aggressive dollar diplomacy. He insisted on defending "representative democracy" as the "best instrument for insuring the social, economic, and cultural development in a just and peaceful world."[29] Meanwhile, military dictatorships predominated on the continent.

The Conference adopted the Declaration of Principles for Inter-American Solidarity and Cooperation—a top priority for Roosevelt, given the worldwide upheaval—and created the consultative organ of foreign ministers as a mechanism to coordinate hemispheric defense policies. It also adopted a protocol of nonintervention—a priority for Latin America proposed by Mexico—as a judicial safeguard in the face of United States interventionism. It affirmed respect for the principle of non-intervention, judicial equality of member states, and the right of its members to act freely in accordance with their own laws.[30]

For the occasion Roosevelt made a twenty-eight-day tour of the Southern Cone. It was a resounding success. In Río de Janeiro, Montevideo, and Buenos Aires the people gave him the warmest, largest, and most spontaneous homage any head of state had ever received.

When war broke out in September 1939, the Caribbean colonies of Nazi-occupied France and the Netherlands were considered a threat; thus the Caribbean became vitally important for the security of the United States and the defense of the Panama Canal. In 1940 the second consultative meeting in Havana adopted a resolution on "mutual assistance in the case of threats or acts of aggression on the part of non-American nations" and agreed that member nations would consult on how to handle such cases. Argentina was the only country on the continent that had not broken off relations with the Axis nations.

By June 1941 Germany had invaded every nation from Poland to France, attacked the Balkans and Greece, and mounted an offensive against the Soviet Union. In December of that year Japan bombed the United States fleet at the Pearl Harbor naval base. Declarations of war came one after another: the United States and Great Britain against Japan (which joined the Axis), Germany and Italy against the United States, and the United States against the Axis powers.

After the bombing of Pearl Harbor, the United States officially entered the war. From the start the greatest military and economic power in the world imposed its dominion. Winston Churchill understood that United States priorities and strategic plans differed from those of Europe and that the United States would carry the leadership of the war from that point on.

In 1942, at a gathering in Rio de Janeiro, the Third Consultative Meeting of Foreign Ministers adopted a declaration reaffirming continental solidarity and respect for the principle of nonintervention and created the Inter-American Joint Defense Board, composed of the military high commanders of the hemisphere. Its function was to advise the governments on defense plans in the event of attack.[31]

The United States proceeded to step up its capacity to defend and protect the Panama Canal with new military and naval bases. It took out ninety-nine-year renewable leases on lands in British possessions in the Caribbean: Antigua, Santa Lucía, Jamaica, British Guyana, and Trinidad and Tobago. With bases there, in addition to ones in Panama, Puerto Rico, and Cuba (Guantánamo), the United States enclosed the Caribbean. In 1944 it also installed bases on Turks and Caicos Islands—also British colonies—for which Great Britain received fifty old North American destroyers.[32]

Shortly before Roosevelt died, he, Churchill, and Stalin signed the Yalta Accords, which fixed the conditions for peace and established the respective zones of influence of the three countries. By 1945 Roosevelt was dead, and the war finally ended. Harry Truman assumed the presidency, and the complex postwar era began. The Allies defeated Nazi Germany and Fascist Italy, and the United States defeated the Japanese Empire after having itself suffered a string of defeats in the Pacific. But in the international arena distrust, rivalries, and open confrontation with the Soviet Union, the former ally, were intensifying. Between 1944 and 1948, with Soviet help, Communist governments were installed in Albania, Poland, Romania, Bulgaria, Czechoslovakia, and Hungary.

In a famous 1946 speech Churchill alerted the world to the danger of Soviet expansion, articulating the concept of an Iron Curtain going up between Eastern and Western Europe. The world was divided in two, the great powers confronting one another and their interests in conflict: capitalism vs. communism, democracy vs. totalitarianism.

The following year Truman declared that the United States would defend the "free world"—another new concept—against Communist expansion. "The free countries of the world expect us to help them maintain their freedom. If we fail we could endanger world peace, and we would surely put the welfare of this nation in danger."[33] The Truman Doctrine rationalized Cold War policies and globalized the Monroe Doctrine.

United States society was seized with anti-Communist fervor. Senator Joseph McCarthy and Republican leaders—Congressman Richard Nixon among them—accused the Democratic presidents of having allowed "reds," "the enemy within," and "Russian spies" to infiltrate the State Department, foreign policies, the Armed Forces, radio networks, the press, and the movie industry (Ronald Reagan was one of the testifying witnesses). Congress asked that Albert Einstein—whom legislators called a "red faker"—be deported, and lawmakers accused the scientist Klaus Fuchs of having passed atomic secrets to the Russians. (Fuchs confessed to having done so). The Cold War permeated United States society, and Washington extended McCarthy's "red scare" to Latin America.[34]

Senator William Fulbright dismissed this red hysteria as a Republican strategy for regaining power after five electoral defeats and saw it as a "pernicious" policy based on the supposition that the Soviet Union wanted to take over the world and extend Communist domination. "To save ourselves and go forward," he said, "we must see the world as it is defined in the Truman Doctrine."[35]

Truman tied up the continent politically and militarily. During his administration the most important agreements of the inter-American system were signed. In 1947 the Inter-American Treaty of Reciprocal Assistance, commonly known as the Río Treaty, established the principle of mutual military defense; in 1948 the Ninth Inter-American Conference in Bogotá created the Organization of American States (OAS), approved the OAS Charter, and adopted a resolution on the "Preservation and Defense of Democracy in America."[36] Most of those who signed these agreements were representatives of brutal dictatorships supported by Washington.[37] Truman also signed the Mutual Military Assistance Pacts (MAP)—bilateral military accords—with thirteen countries, most of them Central American and Caribbean. These agreements firmed up military assistance and standardized the military organizations and the forces of Latin America. The United States provided training for officers and weapons for the defense of the hemisphere. The Southern Command was responsible for coordinating the MAPs. (In 1963 it was transferred to the Panama Canal Zone in violation of the Canal Treaties.)

THE PARTY'S OVER

In 1949 the Western Powers created their military alliance, NATO, the Soviet Union exploded its first atomic bomb, and the arms race and nuclear competition began. The Truman doctrine was going full blast. The United States took the first steps in its military involvement in Vietnam (sending thirty-five military advisers to help the French government maintain its colony) and sent troops to Korea to combat communist forces. This war, under the banner of the United Nations, lasted three years. By the 1950s the Cold War was at its most intense.

Truman left the White House and made way for Dwight D. Eisenhower (1953–1960). After twenty years of Democratic administrations, the Republicans returned to power; however, this did not signify a policy change. The country remained in the grip of anti-Communist hysteria. Congress and the administration continued their persecution of "internal enemies," and the secretary of state, John Foster Dulles, a fanatical anti-Communist, maintained an aggressive policy toward the Soviet Union. The Truman doctrine remained in effect until the collapse of the Soviet Union in 1991.

Latin America was not a priority during Eisenhower's administration. The main goal of the administration was hemispheric defense—assured by inter-American treaties—and the stifling of Communism in Latin American governments. Most of these (fifteen to twenty) were military dictatorships allied with Washington. There were important political changes during this time (eight dictators fell), but the one that most concerned and unnerved Washington was the triumph of the Cuban Revolution.

United States intervention throughout the continent was no longer carried out directly (that is, by invasions by the marines); covert operations by the CIA were clearly under way. In 1954 the CIA overthrew the government of Guatemala. It would try to do the same in Cuba.

CHAPTER II

SOME COME, SOME GO

CUBA: THE TRIUMPH OF THE REVOLUTION

On January 1, 1959, news of the triumph of the Cuban Revolution failed to make the headlines of the continent's morning papers, since General Fulgencio Batista's dictatorship had been overthrown at dawn. Without much fanfare, the *New York Times* reported that the state department had informed the Senate that it considered the Cuban regime's position extremely grave but that the United States would remain neutral in the conflict. On an inside page it was reported that Batista's government claimed success in the fight against the rebels in Santa Clara, the capital of Las Villas province.

Neither item reflected actual events. Batista's army could not claim victory over the rebels. Las Villas had fallen to the *comandantes* Ernesto "Che" Guevara and Camilo Cienfuegos: in a decisive attack, 350 soldiers and officers on an armored train surrendered themselves and their supplies to the rebels. And Washington did not remain neutral. On the eve of Batista's fall the military high commands in Havana and Washington met to figure out what to do, faced as they were with the situation of the government in the throes of death.

The news of the collapse of Cuba's regime came as a surprise in Washington. Government circles were disconcerted; they believed that the regime would have been able to resist. On January 2 the *New York Times* reported that the United States government did not particularly lament the ousting of Batista— at the time relations with him were "cool but correct"—it was nevertheless worried about Cuba's future. It predicted a period of "sharp conflicts" between Fidel Castro and "those who believe they can prevent him from reaping the fruits of victory." As a result of the activities of United States ambassadors, the Eisenhower administration assumed that Batista had left in place a civilian-military junta and that conservative sectors in the island would surely mount a resistance.

Judging by his efforts to sustain Batista to the very end, Eisenhower could not have been pleased by his fall. He had given him substantial military aid—including bombers—and kept a mission of military, naval, and aerial advisers on the island. As the rebels' attacks grew stronger, Eisenhower increased the aid. With great pomp and ceremony Batista received the military equipment to demonstrate to his nation and the world that he had Washington's support.

As the Batista government began to sink, the United States revised its policies. The rebel forces advanced toward the center of the country under the command of Che Guevara, Raúl Castro, and Juan Almeida, while evidence appeared of towns and cities destroyed by bombardment by napalm bombs. Uneasy about rebel accusations that Batista was using United States-supplied weapons earmarked for "defense of the hemisphere" in the internal conflict, on March 1958, the United States announced the suspension of arms sales to Cuba.

The rebels claimed, however, that the arms sales continued through Nicaragua and the Dominican Republic, under the dictatorships of Anastasio Somoza and Rafael Leonidas Trujillo, both allies of Washington. They also alleged that Batista's airplanes were still refueling at the Guantánamo military base.

In order to pressure the United States and force Batista to suspend the bombings, Raúl Castro ordered the rebels to capture Americans. They took twenty-five civilian supervisors and employees, and a bus returning twenty-four marines to the Guantánamo base. This action created tremendous tension with the United States. Batista put the bombings on hold for fear of reprisals against the hostages. The United States Consul in Santiago de Cuba went to the Sierra Maestra to negotiate their release. He advised the state department against demanding Batista's "strict compliance" with the accords prohibiting the use of United States arms for any purpose other than "defense of the hemisphere," since there was a "possible Communist influence" among the rebel forces.

Washington denied that the United States was continuing to supply arms, chalking the belief up to a misunderstanding, and claimed that Nicaragua was sending weapons it had bought from Israel.[1] On the airwaves of Rebel Radio, Fidel Castro announced the captured Americans' release. Raúl let them go a few at a time. When the last one was freed, Batista renewed his attacks.

Washington wanted to prevent a rebel triumph. With the help of the CIA,

Ambassador Arthur Gardner and his successor, Earl T. Smith, attempted to unite the civilian opposition and tried to convince Batista to step down and name a civilian military junta, which would later call for "free" elections.[2] Batista refused any formula that required him to abandon power.

The unexpected collapse of the Batista regime took Fidel by surprise. He immediately ordered the rebel army to consolidate control of the territory and commanded Che and Cienfuegos to advance to Havana and seize the barracks of La Cabaña and Columbia, the government's stronghold. Fidel took control of Santiago de Cuba and Oriente Province and announced that he did not accept the cease-fire decreed by Batista, nor would he recognize the junta named by the dictator. He threatened to continue the war and bring it to the capital. He ordered a general strike, which paralyzed the country for four days.[3] Washington's plan failed, and Fidel got the revolutionary government he wanted, with Manuel Urrutia, a liberal and anti-Communist Santiago judge, serving as provisional president.

THE RISE AND FALL OF THE CAUDILLO BATISTA

Revolutionary fervor in Cuba began in opposition to the dictatorship of General Gerardo Machado (1925–1933), one of the most corrupt and brutal in the island's history. Machado had himself reelected by a rigged constitutional assembly, abolished the vice presidency, decreed that his term would extend to six years, and granted himself the title of Illustrious and Exemplary Citizen.

When Franklin D. Roosevelt became president in 1932, the internal situation in Cuba was at fever pitch. Roosevelt was concerned that social and political agitation in the midst of a profound economic crisis could be explosive and lead to revolution. He sent Undersecretary of State Sumner Welles as his ambassador to convince Machado to step down. Machado declined. The United States stationed a naval squadron off the Cuban coast, prepared to intervene. Strikes and violent clashes between demonstrators and police left hundreds dead and thousands wounded, sounding the death rattle of the "machadato." Machado fled with his family to Nassau and later settled in the United States, a nation he had served so well.

Carlos Manuel de Céspedes was named provisional president, with Washington's approval. However, neither he nor the cabinet he named augured change; after a brief respite, the rebellion continued. A conspiracy led by Sergeant Fulgencio Batista, which became known in Cuban history as "the revolt of the sergeants," took only three weeks to oust Céspedes from office.

From that point, Batista was in control of the power for a quarter of a century.

Six days after the coup the sergeants named a provisional governing junta (the Pentarchy) chaired by Ramón Grau San Martín. The United States considered it to be Communist and refused to acknowledge it. In January 1934, Batista, now a colonel and head of the army, overthrew Grau San Martín with Washington's support and placed Carlos Hevia in the presidency. The United States recognized his government at once. Later Batista replaced him with Colonel Carlos Mendieta.

Batista became the power behind the throne, installing and expelling presidents until he was elected in 1940. According to analysts, his first term (1940–1944) was the best government Cuba ever had. Under his "moderate, gentle, and loving rule"—as he himself described it—and favored by the high price of sugar on international markets, he oversaw a broad program of public works: extending roads and highways; strengthening the school system; and constructing electrical generating plants, bridges, and ports. He also made forays into the democratic process, allowing the press certain liberties and not being too harsh on his critics. He satisfied the military with high salaries, cultivated the bureaucracy with good jobs and bribes, and improved workers' wages and working conditions. By making everyone happy, Batista could laugh at the opposition.[4]

Under pressure from Roosevelt, in 1944 Batista called for elections. Ramón Grau San Martín, from the Authentic Party—a party left of center—was elected. Batista settled in Miami "to let him govern." Grau proved even less competent and more corrupt than Machado. Under him more opponents, labor leaders, and members of leftist parties were murdered, while the international Mafia flourished. Hotels, casinos, cabarets, banks, and insurance companies were in the hands of Mafia capos from the United States.

With the election of Carlos Prío Socarrás (1948–1952), the government plunged deeper into corruption, shamelessly looting the public treasury. He persecuted the labor movement, closed down newspapers, perpetuated general repression and political assassinations, and turned the country over to American investors. Prío authorized Batista's return. Not long before the elections Batista—the underdog candidate—toppled him, canceled the elections, suspended the constitution of 1940, and eliminated the office of vice president. Truman immediately recognized his government.[5]

Fidel Castro, a lawyer and candidate for congress, protested that Batista's coup abrogated the electoral process. Years later, in 1966, in a speech delivered on the seventh anniversary of the Revolution's triumph, he described Batista's ascension to power. "He did it with the complicity of the Yankee embassy, of the reactionary clergy, of the dominant economic classes, of a judicial system corrupt to the bone, and of a vast number of venal politicians, through a military coup whose godfathers were imperialism and the exploiting classes, because the exploiting classes found they needed a Batista. A thief? Yes, but that doesn't matter. A felon? Yes, but that doesn't matter. Vicious? Immoral? That did not matter to them as long as the rural police were at the service of the overseers and plantation owners, to cut down the worker who demanded a decent salary or the campesino who demanded land."[6]

Sickened by Prío's corruption and incompetence, the Cuban people welcomed the coup. Two days later, Prío's four-party coalition threw its support behind Batista. In less than a year all the political parties joined with the government. According to Fidel, it proved that Cuban politics was a *cachumbambé* (seesaw) of bandits.[7]

Two years later Batista legitimized his presidency in an undisputed election. His second administration (1952–1959) was a bloody and merciless dictatorship that relied on its secret police and on repression. These were years of police terror, murder, and torture. Many Cubans left for exile. Batista dissolved Congress and closed the University of Havana, the center of the insurrection against his regime led by the young Fidel Castro.

With the treasury flush as a result of high sugar prices, Batista again took up his ambitious program of public works. He constructed new office buildings, highways, and streets, while new hotels, casinos, and upscale buildings rose from the burgeoning private sector. Havana, the epicenter of wealth, became one of the most beautiful and dissolute cities of the continent. Never had the Cuban elite been so rich. But the richest of all was Batista, whose personal and family fortune grew with the millions in commissions he collected from public contracts, the cuts he took from customs, and his percentage from the national lottery. The fortunes of his associates grew as his did. Under his rule, "Cuba [had] everything but freedom."[8]

Batista's relations with Washington were excellent, and Cuba was paradise for its investors. He granted them tax and duty exemptions, and looked the other way when they engaged in dishonest practices to manipulate their capital. The benefits of this policy went both ways with Batista receiving juicy bribes for his favors. Equally important, he also persecuted Communists, cut off diplomatic relations with the Soviet Union, and created institutions similar to those of the American McCarthyites, which cooperated with the FBI.

THE STRUGGLE

There was no organized and cohesive labor or farm workers' movement in Cuba to oppose Batista. Political parties were broken up into factions, with no political directions. The secretary general of the Cuban Workers Federation (CTC), Eugenio Mujal Barniol, was a pawn of the regime, in the service of the employers and foreign business interests. Mujal shattered labor unity; under the pretext of anti-Communism, he persecuted labor leaders who refused to obey his dictates, removed honest ones from office, and replaced them with token leaders loyal to him. He prohibited strikes and did not protest against the repression of the working classes, which included armed assaults on union headquarters.[9]

Fidel denounced the repression and corruption of the regime and its cohorts. The continual student demonstrations resulted in confrontations with the police, leaving hundreds wounded and arrested. Legal avenues of resistance did not exist, and justice was bought and sold. The only alternative to bring about change was an armed struggle. Fidel and a small group of rebels began to obtain arms and to train clandestinely. The group, led by university students and comprised mainly of workers, laborers, and campesinos, grew quickly.

Fidel stepped up his denunciations of corruption, accusing the regime of sharing the spoils and the *vende-patrias* (sell-outs) with converting Cuba into a Yankee semicolony in exchange for millions in bribes. He denounced the press for being bought off by Batista, with swarms of journalists receiving *botellas* (bribes). He also accused the courts of being submissive to the dictator, and he condemned the torture and murder of opposition leaders, students, and unionists and the brutality of the rural police, whose victims were the campesinos.

As in Prío's time, Cuba continued to be a Mafia paradise. The top capos—Lucky Luciano, Meyer Lansky, Santo Trafficante, Amadeo Barletta—owned hotels, casinos, dazzling nightclubs, whorehouses, and popular game arcades. They also owned commercial centers, banks, financial institutions, airlines, radio and television stations, and some newspapers.[10]

As the rebellion grew, repression became more brutal, implacable, and bloody, and many revolutionaries died heroically. In the midst of this extremely violent atmosphere, the rebels prepared for their first big military action: the attack on the Moncada barracks in Santiago de Cuba. The fortification, surrounded by high walls in the center of the city and manned by more than 400

armed men with a large arsenal at their disposal, was the second most important military installation in the country. The rebels' plan was audacious and
prepared with the greatest of care. But because of a lack of money and the vigilance of the police some obstacles proved insurmountable. Little by little, they
gathered weapons at Siboney, a farm they had rented 10.5 miles from Santiago
de Cuba.

The rebels decided to attack on July 26, Santa Ana's Day, when Santiago
de Cuba begins its traditional nationwide carnival; they thought they would
be able to pass unnoticed amid the music, the dancing, and the rivers of rum.
With a total of 165 people—the force could not be larger because there were
not enough weapons—they arrived in small groups, with two women among
them, Haydée Santamaría and Melba Hernández. The operation started at 5:00
AM, with a caravan of eighteen automobiles heading for the Plaza de Marte.
Fidel, Raúl Castro, and Abel Santamaría headed three groups and were responsible for directing the attack.

As always at carnival festivities, the guard was placed on alert to control the
excesses of the crowd. The arrival of the rebels, dressed in military uniforms,
at the barracks confused the guards, but they sounded the alarm almost immediately, and the shooting began. The fight was extremely unbalanced. The barracks were surrounded by troops, and the rebels were caught inside. Eight died
and another eight were wounded, while the soldiers lost nineteen, with another
twenty-two wounded. The discrepancy in the casualties infuriated Batista, for
it showed the rebels' military superiority.

The regime's bloody cruelties against the attackers of Moncada rose to
unprecedented heights. Those who did not die in the battle were captured,
brutally tortured, shot or strangled to death. Others were thrown alive from
the barracks roofs. Batista ordered that their punishment be made an example to others. For a week Moncada was a center for torture and death. Fidel
and two *compañeros* were captured five days later in a sugar-cane field. The
Guardia came upon them exhausted and asleep. They did not kill them
because public disgust at the regime's excesses demanded moderation.

Fidel's trial was heavily guarded and held in secret; Batista knew that the
publicity would go against him. Fidel, who conducted his own defense, made
serious accusations against the regime and set forth a series of revolutionary
laws: reestablishment of sovereignty and of the 1940 constitution—which
had been abrogated by Batista—land and agrarian reform, profit sharing in
all businesses with the workers, nationalization of public utilities, confiscation
of illegally obtained properties, prohibition of the large landed estates known

as *latifundio*, and workers' rights. These were to be the political and ideological foundations for the Revolution.

He also pointed to the country's police repression, the regime's network of spies, and the millions of dollars spent in bribes to informers. In the meantime 600,000 unemployed workers demanded justice, 500,000 campesinos were without land, 400,000 workers were exploited, 30,000 teachers were mistreated and exploited, 20,000 merchants were broken or consumed by debt, and 10,000 professionals seeking employment found every door closed to them.[11]

The intelligence network—the "eyes and ears of the tyrant"—was comprised of the army; the police; the military intelligence service (SIM); the Bureau of Investigation, which also operated outside of Cuba; the Bureau for the Repression of Communist Activities (BRAC), a McCarthy-era mechanism that collaborated with the CIA and the FBI; special groups created to suppress the insurgency; and a mass of spies, informers, assassins, and paid thieves. Anyone could be imprisoned, tortured, and become disappeared on mere suspicion.

Subsequently Haydée and Melba managed to smuggle out the records of Fidel's defense and published them under the title *La historia me absolverá*, translated under the title, *History Will Absolve Me*.

The rebels were taken to the La Rotonda Prison, on the Isle of Pines (rechristened the Isle of Youth by the Revolution). Fidel was sentenced to fifteen years imprisonment, Raúl to thirteen, and the rest to lesser terms. Two years later, pressured by public opinion, Batista conceded an amnesty, freeing them all. Fidel continued his denunciations of the regime in the pages of the daily *La Calle* (The Street), causing Batista to close down the paper and to threaten him publicly.

Six weeks after the amnesty the rebels left for Mexico. There, despite enormous difficulties, they secretly formed the nucleus of the revolutionary army and began training. They were pursued by the Mexican authorities, the FBI, Batista's agents, and spies sent by Trujillo in the Dominican Republic, and they suffered denunciations by infiltrators. Some of them were sent to prison. Nevertheless they persevered. Che Guevara joined the rebel fighters in Mexico, and Fidel went to the United States to organize the resistance and to raise funds.

At dawn on November 25, 1956, eighty-one rebels set sail on the yacht *Granma* from the Mexican port of Tuxpán. Sailing without lights and dangerously overloaded with people and arms, the ship landed on Las Coloradas beach in Cuba on December 1. They were quickly discovered by a coast guard boat, which sent out the alarm. Batista's forces attacked them by land and by air. Four days later, the rebels came face to face with the army in Alegría del Pío. The seventeen survivors regrouped in the Sierra Maestra with the help of campesinos. These survivors of Moncada and the *Granma* founded the July 26 Movement—named to honor the attack on the Moncada Barracks—the first nucleus of the Rebel Army.

On January 17, 1957—a month and a half after the landing of the *Granma*—in the Rebel Army's first battle, Batista's soldiers surrendered. Two soldiers died, five were wounded, and three were taken prisoner. The rebels had no casualties. Campesinos from the Sierra Maestra began to join their ranks, and in Havana and Santiago, urban groups supported them by securing recruits and funds, with political work, and with sabotage.

On March 13, 1957, the Student Directorate, another rebel group, attacked the presidential palace in Havana and occupied the broadcasting station Radio Reloj. Several of the rebels were killed, but, miraculously, Batista escaped. Convinced the rebels had won, José Antonio Echevarría, president of the Federation of University Students (FEU), who had taken over the radio station, announced the death of the tyrant in his "hideout." Shortly thereafter Echevarría was killed on the hill that is the site of the University of Havana.

In 1957 the Rebel Army mounted a series of attacks on military barracks, occupying some and confiscating weapons. The columns commanded by Fidel, Che, and Camilo Cienfuegos inflicted serious casualties and added to their store of arms and ammunition. Little by little, the rebels consolidated their territory; as their military victories mounted, so did their political gains; the rebels kept the people informed by broadcasting the news over their clandestine station, Radio Rebelde (Rebel Radio).

The army, demoralized and corrupt, lacked the motivation to defend with their lives the oppressive and thieving regime. Every day their losses mounted, as did the numbers of soldiers and officers who joined the rebels. An uprising of officers and sailors staged at the Cienfuegos Naval District in September 1957, was Batista's greatest humiliation. The insurgents occupied the Cayo Loco base and gave their weapons to the people.[12] "The war lasted two years, and the revolutionary struggle five years, five months, and five days," Fidel remarked.

BATISTA'S FLIGHT

On December 31, 1958, Havana was calm. The war had worsened to such a degree and the situation had become so unstable that few people dared to leave their homes. At Columbia Camp, where Batista moved his residence when the war mounted, the General and seventy guests—among them a small group of relatives, high government and military officials and their wives, and close friends—were getting ready to celebrate the New Year. It had not been easy for him to gather this group, whom he had invited merely for a toast. Those close to the regime knew that the time was not right for celebration. The atmosphere was tense and depressing, with little talk, wrote United States Ambassador Earl Smith in his memoir, *The Fourth Floor.* Batista was calm as he gave orders and announced his plans for the following day.[13]

As the bells struck midnight, General Eulogio Cantillo Piedra appealed in the name of the armed forces, to the "undeniable patriotism" of the General, and asked him to resign. Batista did so two hours later, delegating military power to Cantillo Piedra, naming a government junta, and appointing the oldest judge of the supreme court, Carlos Manuel Piedra, as the titular president—following the procedures of the 1940 constitution that was no longer in effect, since he himself had suspended it.

Few of those present at the tense New Year's Eve party—so different from the pompous celebrations of years past—suspected that they would witness the end of the Batista dictatorship. Only his most intimate collaborators knew what he was about to do in order to leave the presidency with honor and Cuban territory unharmed. The presidential secretary, Andrés Domingo, and Foreign Minister, Gonzalo Güell, held on to several large manila envelopes; they contained not dollars, as some suspected, but passports issued with the greatest urgency for the top government brass. [14] Batista had not forgotten his closest friends and associates.

Still dressed in their formal attire, Batista; his second wife Marta Fernández; Jorge, one of his eight children; Andrés Rivero Agüero—previously-elected president (in rigged elections)—and his wife; and a group of close advisers—forty in all—flew into exile, landing in Ciudad Trujillo.[15] In two other planes, Batista's older children—Rubén, Mirta, and Elisa—along with various other officials, flew to Jacksonville, Florida; New York City; and New Orleans, respectively. His younger children, Roberto and Carlos, had left two days earlier on "vacation" to New York, accompanied by two governesses, a detective, and Manuel Pérez Benitoa, the chief of customs of Havana, and his family, who were related to Batista through the marriage of their children.

The departure of Batista and his retinue was rather uneventful. They boarded five DC-4s belonging to the Cuban army, which were waiting for them at the Columbia military base. Several suitcases remained behind on the tarmac; someone had managed to have them taken off the plane at gun point to ensure his own passage, wrote one of the travelers.[16] Five wooden cases containing more than eight hundred boxes filled with jewels were later found in Batista's residence; Marta had already sent the best of her gems to New York for safekeeping. This was the first and smallest discovery of Batista's large fortune confiscated by the Revolution. The greater part, however, was already out of the country. Batista and his friends took between $300 million and $400 million in cash with them.[17]

Upon his arrival in Florida, the General's oldest son, twenty-five-year-old Rubén, a Senator-elect, was attacked and beaten by an exiled Cuban. He was the only member of the ousted family to suffer personally from the rage of the people. At a press conference he said he foresaw problems for Cuba, since some of the rebels were militant Communists.[18]

The departure of the dictator and his coterie was kept under tight wraps. The pilots learned that their destination was Santo Domingo only after they were airborne. According to Porfirio Rubirosa, the Dominican ambassador in Cuba, his government was not consulted about Batista's intention to seek asylum in his country.[19]

When the Cuban airplanes touched down at the Dominican military airbase, the Generalissimo's oldest son, Ramfis Trujillo, was waiting to welcome them. Receiving Batista as a "guest of honor," Generalissimo Trujillo set his visitor up in a mansion near the National Palace. Although Trujillo had not forgotten that Batista had snubbed him—he had refused to invite him to Havana, despite Trujillo's numerous hints through diplomatic channels—he had nevertheless sent him a cargo of weapons to fight the rebels. Trujillo was eager to get even with Fidel Castro for having participated in an attempt to invade his country in 1947—an attempt that was literally quashed by Trujillo. Just twenty-one years old at the time, Fidel survived by a miracle.

Trujillo had a few surprises in store for Batista. On the day after his arrival, Trujillo informed Batista that he had at his disposal 25,000 men, along with ships and airplanes, so that he could lead an expedition against Cuba. Batista declined. To undertake such an adventure against Fidel, who was at the height of his power, would have been absurd. Trujillo also presented him with a bill for $900,000 for the last shipment of arms to Cuba. Batista refused to pay, claiming that it was a Cuban national debt and not a personal one. Trujillo continued to demand payment through high-ranking military emissaries, but Batista would not budge. Finally Batista was put in prison, where he was held for a day and a half, until he paid the debt. Trujillo then asked him for another

$1 million to finance anti-Castro activities. This time Batista paid without demur. Fearing that Trujillo would continue to squeeze him, he tried to flee, but Dominican forces detained him at the airport after he boarded a private plane.[20]

Batista had a one-way ticket out of Cuba. His destiny was quite different from that of other Latin American caudillos who had preceded him in the 1950s. Juan Domingo Perón returned to Argentina twenty years later and was elected President with 61 percent of the vote. Marcos Pérez Jiménez, who was extradited to Venezuela in August 1963, during Kennedy's administration, was released from Dade County Prison in Florida and returned home to be incarcerated in San Juan de los Morros Penitentiary.[21] Gustavo Rojas Pinilla returned to Colombia in January 1959 to be tried by the Senate of the Republic, which condemned him for violating the constitution and the laws of the country, deprived him of political rights (to vote and to be elected), and prohibited him from occupying any position in the army. But in the 1970 elections, he was at the threshhold of the presidency.

Such good fortune eluded "Tacho" Somoza, the dictator of Nicaragua, who was assassinated in 1956 by Rigoberto López Perez, a young poet, and the Guatemalan Colonel Carlos E. Castillo Armas, who, in the same year, was assassinated in the Presidential Palace by a conspiracy that, to this day, has not been explained.

THE REBELS ARRIVE

The rebels' triumph produced unprecedented euphoria in Cuba. People streamed into the streets and gathered on balconies. Cuban flags waved everywhere, and caravans of automobiles honked their horns to cheer the fall of the dictatorship and the triumph of the revolutionaries. The rebels came out of hiding with their weapons and their red and black flags—symbol of the rebel movement—to celebrate their victory. Rage and frustration, repressed for a quarter of a century, gave free rein to acts of violence against the symbols of the dictatorship and its "masters." The mobs destroyed casinos—one of Havana's tourist attractions—and sacked businesses, and gun battles broke out between the police and the rebels. Jules Dubois from the *Chicago Tribune* reported that the center of the capital became a battlefield, with many wounded and dead.[22]

On January 8 Fidel's triumphant entry into Havana—after a long, slow crossing of the island—was televised and widely aired by both national and international media. Concerning the people's feverish welcome to Fidel, their greatest hero, Dubois wrote: "In all my years of reporting in Latin America never had I seen a similar tribute to one man."[23]

While the people took to the streets and the rebels assumed power, hundreds of government officials, high-ranking members of the army, security forces, police, politicians, businessmen, and relatives and friends who had gravitated in the regime's privileged orbit, fled the country. On regular and on charter flights, by yacht and on boats stolen from fishermen, they sought their salvation in the United States, Canada, and the Dominican Republic. To halt the flight of those who for obvious reasons feared justice, the Revolutionary Government suspended international air traffic and prohibited Cubans from leaving the island.

The biggest criminals managed to escape, some loaded down with millions of dollars. Many "war criminals" found refuge in the United States, and those who could not put the ocean between themselves and their country sought asylum in Latin American embassies. Protected by foreign flags, the asylum seekers were taken to the airport to board planes that would take them to lives of impunity. The people shouted as they passed: "Traitors, thieves, murderers!"[24]

At ten in the morning of January 1, Cuban television began to air denunciations of the regime by the families of victims. They demanded justice—thousands had been murdered or were made to disappear. From the very first days, the prison doors were opened for hundreds of political prisoners, who came out starving and showing signs of torture.[25] Inmates released from the prisons described the brutal torture and abuse they had suffered at the hands of Batista's henchmen.

With their embassies crammed full of asylum seekers, the ambassadors were fearful of becoming targets of the people's rage. Some, more knowledgeable about the fallen regime's shadowy depths, took advantage of their associates' lack of experience and traded off prominent asylum seekers to lighten their load and reduce the danger. Colombian Ambassador Juan N. Calvo did just that with his Argentine counterpart, sending him ex-Secretary General of the CTC, Eugenio Mujal Barniol, who was deeply hated by the Cuban working class. Calvo also dexterously rid himself of Santiago Rey, the former Minister of the Interior, who was responsible for the brutal repression of the rebels.[26]

The moment of truth came for the Colombian diplomat. Twenty-two revolutionaries armed with machine guns forced their way into the embassy, where former ministers, government officials, and industrialists took refuge.

Their preference for the Colombian embassy as a place of asylum was a dubious homage to Ambassador Calvo for having cultivated the friendship of the top people in the Cuban regime, beginning with Batista himself. The rebels remained there for an hour, searching every corner and interrogating the asylum seekers. "I felt like a prisoner," reported the ambassador to his government. The revolutionaries left them alone—"We're looking for murderers, not thieves." The rebel government in Cuba deplored the incident.[27]

The biggest crooks and criminals saved their skins, since the United States refused to extradite them, but not the thousands of fearful followers of Batista who hid in cities and the countryside. More than 300 former military officers were placed under house arrest while their trials were being prepared. Cantillo Piedra, who enabled the men most sought after by the new regime to escape, was among the thousands arrested. He was saved from the firing squad by pressure from the governments of the United States and Brazil.[28] There were also suicides. One colonel—a well-known torturer—hanged himself, while others blew their brains out to keep from being captured and tried by the rebels.

After a few days flights to Miami were reinstated; Havana and Miami's economies were intimately tied together. The planes left Havana empty and returned filled with hundreds of jubilant exiles. The Venezuelan government provided return passage by air for Cubans within its territory.

Batista's fall and the triumph of the revolutionary July 26 Movement were greeted with immense joy throughout Latin America: Another corrupt, brutal dictator supported by Washington had fallen; it was a new victory for democracy. News of the great deeds by the young heroes from the Sierra Maestra resonated throughout the continent. Masses of people celebrated with tumultuous and fervent demonstrations, and well-known personalities throughout the continent praised the rebels in words that rang with emotion, exalting Fidel as a legendary fighter and hero. Songs paid tribute to a Cuba free of Machados and Batistas, of corrupt Príos Socarrases and Grau San Martíns. Other songs celebrated the rebirth of democracy and the victory over tyrants "torn from their omnipotence by a people reborn to liberty," as described in the Bogotá daily *El Tiempo* on February 4, 1959. Latin America gloried in its lyricism. Everyone wanted to climb onto the triumphal carriage of the Cuban Revolution, spouting flowery verbal solidarity.

But nowhere was the triumph of the Cuban Revolution received with greater jubilation than in Venezuela. Rear Admiral Wolfgang Larrazábal, president of the civilian-military junta that had taken over after the fall of Pérez Jiménez, was the only Latin American head of state who openly supported the

Revolution. During the struggle he allowed representatives of the July 26 Movement to operate in Caracas, and he supplied the rebels with arms.[29] Batista discovered these shipments in 1958 and accused Rómulo Betancourt and Larrazábal of being Communists.[30]

During the final weeks of the struggle Venezuelan radio stations broadcast news of the events in Cuba twenty-four hours a day. Some of these stations warned of the danger of United States military intervention, something the continent had experienced often.[31] President-elect Betancourt stated that the Cuban Revolution was an example of "the invincible passion for liberty on the continent" and criticized the "casual indifference of the Organization of American States (OAS) to Batista's genocidal bombardment of his people.[32] The OAS and its member governments remained silent about these crimes.

EISENHOWER AND THE REBELS

In the matter of recognition for the rebel government, Washington adopted the parctice of "neither first nor last." Six days after the fall of Batista and two days before Fidel arrived in Havana, Dwight Eisenhower recognized the rebel government. The haste of the act—the second recognition after that of Venezuela—was seen as an attempt to repair the bad image stemming from his support for the dictator. Nine Latin American nations followed suit, as well as the Soviet Union, even though Batista had severed diplomatic ties with it in 1952 to ingratiate himself with Washington after his coup against Prío Socarrás.

On January 6, an editorial in the *New York Times* applauded Washington's decision to recognize the revolutionary government, since "it has consolidated its position sufficiently to win widespread international recognition, including that of the United States. It has pledged itself to honor all international obligations, to hold new elections within a maximum of two years, and to protect foreign property and investments." In addition, noted the editors, it had rejected accusations of Communist infiltration among the rebel ranks and had given assurances that it would not establish diplomatic relations with the Soviet Union nor with socialist countries. Nevertheless, added the *Times*, "if there is one blot on its record thus far, it is the summary executions of former opponents and the proposed 'war crimes' trial of hundreds more."

The *paredones*—the "firing squad wall" of revolutionary justice—was the subject of the first major controversy with the United States, and it gave rise to a tenacious campaign to discredit the Revolution. Senator Wayne Morse denounced this "blood bath" and asked his government to exercise political and economic sanctions against Cuba. Relations between Washington and Havana became embittered. The situation became graver when Cuba annulled the absolution granted by a tribunal to several pilots of Batista's air force who had been responsible for the genocidal bombardments of unarmed populations. Fidel stated, "revolutionary justice is based not on legal precepts but on moral convictions." The pilots were sentenced to long prison terms.[33]

Tad Szulc, a *New York Times* correspondent in Latin America at the time, interpreted the disparity between the United States and the Cuban positions on revolutionary justice as the result of a lack of mutual understanding and a vicious circle of misunderstandings, in which each nation judged the other by its own standards.[34] In North American public opinion, these prison sentences did not comply with Western rules of justice. The majority knew nothing of the atrocities committed by the Batista dictatorship, since the media reported little about events on the island, and no one denounced such crimes.

Meanwhile the magazine *Bohemia* published accounts of the crimes, along with photographs of the victims of torture and murder, printing the names of thousands of victims and listing the torturers.

Herbert Matthews, an editor at the *New York Times*, maintained that Fidel's policy of promising justice and asking the population for common sense prevented the rage of the people from erupting into violence. He recalled that when the *machadato* (Machado's dictatorship) fell, the mob had dragged corpses of assassins and torturers through the streets, a process that also had happened with the fall of Marcos Pérez Jiménez in Venezuela. Fidel appealed to reason and promised to bring the war criminals to trial, and the people believed him. The vast majority favored the firing squad as punishment for such crimes, Matthews added.[35] These laws of the revolutionary government were not new, for they had already been applied to rebels of the Sierra.

Fidel accused the United States of a double standard, claiming that it was scandalized by the judgments handed down against a few criminals but not by the atrocities of the Batista regime—crimes that the United States never condemned. In an interview in the January 26, 1959, issue of *Life* magazine, Fidel pointed to United States insensitivity for having provided tanks, napalm bombs, and rifles to the Batista regime to kill the populace, and for its outrage at the execution of war criminals, the most notorious of which had found safe haven in the United States.

Revolución, the official newspaper of the July 26 Movement, recommended an immediate end to the sentences and the executions "to take the principal attack weapon out of the enemy's hands." It lamented the intense and violent continental campaign to discredit Cuba for the decisions of some 400 killers—at that point, 476 people had been executed, and 2,437 more cases were still in court—while the 20,000 crimes committed by the Batista tyranny had received scant attention.

FIDEL FACING THE AMERICAS

Fidel's first trip outside Cuba was to Venezuela, in response to an invitation by the president of the junta, Rear Admiral Larrazábal. Fidel went to show solidarity for the first-anniversary celebration of Pérez Jiménez's overthrow, and to thank the Venezuelan government for the support it had provided the Revolution. His reception by the public was delirious. Close to 100,000 people gathered to hear and cheer him in Caracas' Plaza del Silencio.

In a series of speeches Fidel raised important points about the new hemispheric relations to which the United States "would have to adapt."[36] Speaking of the Revolution, he said, "It is said that revolutions against the military are impossible, or only possible when they originate within it. That where there is no economic crisis and no hunger there will be no revolution. But the Cuban Revolution has shattered these ideas." To some, Fidel's words seemed like a diatribe against the Venezuelan armed forces, which were still practically intact, and against the military throughout Latin America, as well as a call to revolution.

Fidel's formulations of these points did not please the recently elected president, Rómulo Betancourt, who avoided a meeting with the Cuban leader by leaving Caracas. From the start there was a tacit hostility between the two leaders. Betancourt soon became a fierce enemy of the Cuban Revolution and of Fidel. And Fidel, when the Venezuelan guerrilla movement rose up, provided arms, advisers and aid to topple Betancourt.

Venezuela was ripe for revolution, according to Fidel, given the people's open hostility toward Pérez Jiménez's dictatorship, the strength of the civilian movement that led to his fall, and the violent popular demonstrations against Vice President Richard Nixon's visit to Caracas in May 1958. Because of its geographic location, oil wealth, and the United States' involvement in the Venezuelan economy, Fidel felt it was the ideal country to launch a revolution on the continent. Nevertheless, there were great internal differences between Cuba and Venezuela. The armed struggle would be not be against a dictator, as had been the case in Cuba, but against a president democratically elected after decades of dictatorships, who enjoyed enormous national and international popularity.

In April 1959—three months after his triumph—Fidel arrived in the United States, having been invited by the National Association of Newspaper Editors. He was a mere thirty-one years old, and already the prime minister of his country. The visit to the Empire was a trial by fire. He was confronted with the hostility of the American administration and the suspicion of the powerful press.

The young people of the United States, deeply involved in their own revolution against the adult world—opposed to their parents' "American Dream" of peace, prosperity, and well being—and fighting for civil rights, welcomed Fidel with enormous enthusiasm.

The New Left opposed equally Western imperialism and the excesses of Soviet Marxism. Beatnik agitators, Beat poets and pacifists opposed war from an ideological and political position. For the first time, the younger generation erupted with great force to make its voice heard, pointing to capitalism as the culprit responsible for wars, social inequities, and poverty. This generational collision made for profound upset and anxiety in the more advanced Western societies and in the unequal, unjust, and poor ones of the third world.

For these young people, the Cuban Revolution—another generational collision—was an inspiration and an example. Fidel and his rebels were acclaimed by thousands of students at prominent universities—Harvard, Princeton, City College in New York. Some 30,000 youths gathered in Central Park in New York City to hear Fidel. Todd Gitlin, who was one of the young American activists, asked himself twenty years later, "What was I doing cheering a bunch of bearded revolutionaries? What were ten thousand North Americans doing in Harvard Stadium that April, chanting 'Viva! Viva!' to the same Fidel Castro? Why were middle-class children of the fifties looking in such strange places for heroes?" Gitlin wrote that they had seen them on the news, smiling before the crowds that surrounded them with adoration, delirious with enthusiasm.[37]

When Fidel arrived in Washington, he was hampered by the suspicions about Communist infiltration of the Revolution and his participation in the April 9, 1948, "Bogotazo" in Colombia, which, according to United States intelligence services, had been instigated by Communists. In United States and Latin American centers of power, few doubted the Communist sympathies of some of the Cuban commanders, and many feared that Cuba would choose that course.

Fidel's statements throughout his bumpy political career had been suffi-ciently radical. Though he never used such words as "nationalism," "anti-imperialism," or "socialism" in his famous self-defense, *History Will Absolve Me*, his nationalism, anti-imperialism, and socialism permeated the work, according to United States historian Maurice Halperin. Years later, in 1966, Fidel declared that his defense was the seed of all that the Revolution later accomplished, adding, "They can call it Marxist, but perhaps a real Marxist would not consider it so." In fact, the laws he proposed, although radical and of deep social and political significance—perhaps revolutionary for Latin America—were not extremist. "It would not have been intelligent to create an open confrontation," he pointed out. "I think that all radical rev-olutionaries, at certain moments and under certain circumstances, do not announce programs that could create a united front among their enemies."39

From the start this political baggage was augmented by critical statements regarding American policies toward Cuba. Fidel warned that the events of the 1898 War of Independence against Spain would not be repeated. He scorned the United States military mission stationed in Cuba by an agreement between Eisenhower and Batista. He stated: "We do not need it; it trained Batista's sol-diers to lose the war, so we do not want it to teach us anything." The follow-ing day he expelled it from the country. And in a speech at the Rotary Club he repeated that he was not a Communist but noted sarcastically that anyone who refused to sell out is branded a Communist, and "as far as I am concerned," he added, "I will neither sell out to the Americans nor take orders from them."40

In most of the statements and speeches he made in the United States, Fidel tried to calm local fears, reassuring his audiences that neither he nor the Revolution were Communist, nor did he have any intention of letting the "comrades" play a part in the government. He promised that agrarian reform—the First Law of the Revolution, enacted in the Sierra Maestra in 1958—would not expropriate or nationalize American property; it would be carried out on uncultivated lands and be compensated in kind.

In the United States, Fidel displayed an unexpected restraint, though it was not out of keeping with the moderate composition of the revolutionary gov-ernment, which included prominent non-Communist or decidedly anti-Communist figures. He was careful not to offend the great power. Some pundits considered these aseptic pronouncements on American soil a strategy designed to confuse public opinion and gain him time to accomplish his objectives without great controversies.41

Fidel was well aware of the hemispheric realities. He knew that his strug-gle was evolving in the context of a society "deformed" by years of McCarthyism, and anti-Communist ideological indoctrination; any Marxist, Leninist, or anti-imperialist pronouncements would be absurd at such a point. Eight years later, Raúl Castro confirmed what many already knew: The aim of the revolutionary struggle was not only intended to remove Batista and his gang from power, but also "to begin the complete transformation of Cuba's political, economic, and social system, and to put an end to foreign oppres-sion, poverty, unemployment, poor health care, and ignorance, which have been holding our people down."[42]

During his visit to the United States, Fidel proposed new conditions for commercial relations between the two countries: They must be fair. Contrary to what all heads of state did on their first visits to the capital of the Empire— ask for economic aid—Fidel declared, "Many men come here to sell their souls. We want only understanding and sympathy."[43]

Fidel's statements distancing himself from Communism disconcerted the left wing in Cuba, as well as the rest of the continent. The newspaper *Hoy*, a publication of the Cuban Communist Party, carried hardly any news about Fidel's important visit to the United States.[44]

Though his invitation had not been cleared with the State Department, and did not please the government, some United States officials gave Fidel a warm reception. However, Raúl Roa, who was the Cuban ambassador to the OAS at the time (later he would become its chancellor), claimed that this was not the case: "That was the opportunity the United States government lost, after having supported the Batista tyranny for seven years, to make a good-will ges-ture toward the Cuban Revolution."[45]

Eisenhower also avoided a meeting with Fidel. For the five days of the visit, he was at Camp David, playing golf, not realizing that the Cuban Revolution was beginning to divide the history of the hemisphere in two.

After successful visits to the United States and Canada, Fidel went to Buenos Aires in May 1959, to take part in a meeting of the Committee of 21, composed of the Treasury Ministers of the Americas. (The United States was represented by an undersecretary.) He stopped in several capitals along the way, meeting with Eric Williams, prime minister of Trinidad and Tobago; Juscelino Kubitschek, president of Brazil; members of the Uruguayan government; and in Buenos Aires with President Arturo Frondizi. Everywhere he received a hero's welcome.

In Buenos Aires, Fidel presented a harsh analysis of the situation in the hemisphere; he pointed out the social and economic inequalities, claiming that they made "impossible the realization of the democratic ideals that all peoples desire." He proposed the creation of a Latin American common market, and suggested that the continent undertake a regional economic development plan funded by a United States contribution of $30 billion over a ten-year period. Eisenhower characterized these proposals as "ridiculous" and "demagogic." Javier Pazos, a Cuban economist who accompanied Fidel to Buenos Aires (he left Cuba in 1960), believed that at this moment Fidel Castro wanted to keep the United States as a close ally and the sponsor of the proposal he had made, and he saw himself at the head of a "Latin American revolution." For Herbert Matthews, of the *New York Times*, this was the last chance Fidel gave the United States to keep him within a "Western" democratic context and at a distance from Communism.[46]

THE CARIBBEAN IN FLAMES

On April 21, 1959, while Fidel was still in Washington, eighty-five men and two women—most of them Cubans—left Cuba and disembarked in Panamanian territory with the aim of overthrowing the government. This action was extremely embarrassing for Fidel, since it clouded the image of the Revolution.[47] Furthermore, the action caused a major international scandal, since the famous British dancer Margot Fonteyn and her husband, Roberto Arias, a member of Panama's high society, were accused of having instigated it. Fonteyn was arrested and expelled from Panama, and Arias went into hiding.

On a hemispheric scale, the reaction was alarm. Cuba was perceived as a threat, since it was "exporting" its revolution. Fidel quickly condemned the action, which he described as the "deed of adventurers," "harmful" to the Revolution and "inconceivably irresponsible."[48] He denied any involvement of his government in the effort. Influential media in the United States maintained that the invaders could not have left Cuba without the cooperation or knowledge of the Cuban government.[49] Some declared that Raúl Castro must have been behind this action, because of the unscheduled meeting he had with Fidel at the Houston airport (when Fidel was on his way to Buenos Aires for the meeting of the Committee of 21). One member of Fidel's entourage later said that he heard a bitter telephone conversation between the two brothers when Fidel was passing through Boston on one leg of his journey to Buenos Aires.[50]

The Eisenhower administration wanted a hemisphere-wide condemnation of the Revolutionary government for this act. But the greatest source of surprise, frustration, and sense of alarm was the attitude of President Ernesto de la Guardia, against whom the attempted invasion was directed. He did not blame the Cuban government, because Fidel attested that his government had no responsibility in such an undertaking.

At the OAS, where the matter was discussed, the Panamanian representative described the invasion as the action of "Panamanian pirates and adventurers." Panama requested military aid, claiming that it was not able to defend itself. Washington sent arms and deployed planes and ships to the Caribbean to "observe" suspicious movements. Months later the OAS commission assigned to investigate the threat of invasion to Panama exonerated the Cuban Revolutionary government of all responsibility.

From May to August of 1959, groups of Nicaraguan, Dominican, and Haitian revolutionaries left Cuba with the aim of creating *focos*—centers of resistance—to oust their respective dictators: Somoza, Trujillo, and Duvalier. All failed. Although the Cuban government disclaimed all responsibility in these attempted invasions, Washington orchestrated an intense campaign to discredit the Cuban government and accuse it of "exporting its revolution." It portrayed Cuba as a threat to the continent.

"Revolution is not exportable. It is a phenomenon particular to each country. It is its people who make the revolution," declared Fidel. Cuba was not responsible for these invasion attempts; on the contrary, it forbade them, stated the Cuban chancellor Raúl Roa, before the United Nations Security Council in January 1960.[51] In effect, a few days before the attempt to invade Panama news agencies reported that at Pinar del Río, the Rebel Army had arrested and disarmed 100 Nicaraguans who were preparing to launch an attack against Somoza.

The Caribbean was in flames, and the Cuban Revolution advanced with a firm step, opening its doors to rebels, political refugees, and exiles from the dictatorships supported by Washington throughout the continent. It became a veritable Mecca for revolutionaries, to whom it gave refuge and military training.

The old struggle between Fidel and Generalissimo Rafael Leonidas Trujillo fanned the flames of the burning Caribbean. Both—dedicated to increasing their arsenals—launched virulent verbal attacks and threats against each other through the press and the radio and tried to invade each other's countries. In June 1959 an expedition, composed of forty-six Dominicans—"authentic opponents"—and ten Cubans under Cuban command, left Cuba for Santo Domingo. They arrived on a Venezuelan airliner. As in previous attempts, Trujillo crushed the invasion. But this particular attempt, commented Tad Szulc, planted the seed of rebellion against the Trujillo dictatorship.[52]

One month later Trujillo returned the blow and sent his "Anti-Communist Foreign Legion"—composed of Batista supporters, Spanish and German veterans, and Croatian fascists—against Cuba. The operation was planned with Batista, who was still in exile in Santo Domingo, and refugee ex-members of the Cuban National Guard, who trained the mercenary brigade. Both attacks failed. The respective leaders' efficient intelligence services informed them in plenty of time about the "enemy's" plans.

Batista's presence in Santo Domingo and the conspiratorial relations he developed with Trujillo to attack Cuba were a matter of concern for Washington, given the volatile state of the region. The United States wanted to remove Batista by granting him a visa, which up to that point it had refused to do. Faced with criticism from several newspapers over such a possibility, Undersecretary of State for Inter-American Affairs Roy Rubottom denied the stories and assured the public that his government would not permit Batista to enter the United States.[53]

For Washington, the growing tension between President Rómulo Betancourt of Venezuela and Generalissimo Trujillo of the Dominican Republic was also very worrisome. Trujillo's government denied safe conduct to several citizens who sought asylum in the Venezuelan Embassy in Ciudad Trujillo (Santo Domingo), and Betancourt severed ties with the Dominican Republic. His aim was to promote a continental movement against Trujillo, and in the OAS he proposed the creation of a cordon sanitaire against dictatorships and in defense of democracy. He asked for collective measures to eliminate them and to expel them from the organization.

Claiming that Cuba was close to succumbing to Communism, Washington announced the suspension of arms sales to Cuba and the Dominican Republic and asked allied and friendly nations to take the same actions. The United States made this move with a certain reluctance—according to declassified State Department documents—for fear that its own transgressions might come to light, for the United States sold arms to Indonesia in its conflict with Belgium and the Netherlands and to Tunisia in its struggle against France. Washington's allies raised no objections to the request, but in the face of such lucrative business, solidarity did not count for much. Great Britain, Canada, Belgium, Italy, and Spain continued to sell Cuba "defensive" weapons.[54]

The Cuban Revolution was a real problem for the United States. It was tearing hemispheric unity to shreds, it had enormous popular appeal, and some governments, so as to avoid internal problems, were reluctant to support United States policies against Cuba. In several capitals of the continent massive demonstrations were held in support of the Revolution, with anti-imperialist and anti-Yankee slogans; these rallies frequently ended with the burning of the United States flag and the stoning of its embassies. This was a new and worrisome state of affairs for Washington.

Eisenhower understood the necessity of retooling his policies to show greater interest in economic and social problems—major concerns throughout the continent. Up to this point his policies had been limited to military and security questions. In April 1959 the *New York Times* reported on a "supersecret" and "stormy" meeting in El Salvador, convened by the State Department, of United States ambassadors to Central America and the Caribbean. Its purpose was to study "such delicate matters as dictatorships and revolutionists" in the Caribbean region and to give direction to policies concerning the area. Cuba, the main subject of discussion, gave rise to bitter polemics and splits between the career diplomats (headed by Philip Bonsal, the United States ambassador to Cuba), who favored negotiation and concerted action through the OAS, and the political appointees, who wanted direct intervention. Some of those opposed to Bonsal's "soft" line threatened to resign.[55]

The Caribbean situation was explosive. Assistant Secretary of State Roy Rubottom called it critical and urgent and recommended dealing with it immediately through the OAS. The State Department pressured the democratic governments to call a consultative meeting of the OAS. The United States' objective was to condemn Cuba for "exporting the revolution" and violating the nonintervention principle so dear to the continent. Rubottom traveled to Colombia to ask President Alberto Lleras to host the meeting. Lleras agreed to the meeting, but suggested that it be held in Washington. Rubottom did not consider this venue suitable. No government was willing to confront the internal agitation a conference against Cuba would provoke.

Jorge Alessandri, president of Chile, one of the most stable democracies on the continent, offered to host the meeting. Thus, the Fifth Consultative Meeting on the "Caribbean Situation" was held in Santiago, from August 12 to 18, 1959.

The continent was deeply divided and fast reaching the boiling point. The more salient conflicts were between Betancourt and Trujillo (Trujillo attempted to have him assassinated), between Fidel and Trujillo, and between the Central

American dictatorships—spearheaded by Somoza—and Fidel. Most of the countries were under military dictatorships allied with Washington and opposed to Cuba. The presidents of the civilian governments—Argentina, Colombia, Costa Rica, Mexico, Peru and Venezuela—were democratic, anti-Communist, and firm defenders of nonintervention. Only Argentina and Mexico favored the Cuban Revolution.

After hearing the Inter-American Peace Commission's report on democracy, human rights, and Caribbean political tensions, the chancellors issued resounding declarations against Communism, against dictatorships (without naming names), in defense of nonintervention and in favor of "representative democracies." Venezuela proposed collective action by the OAS against the dictatorships, but the majority opposed the motion, declaring that it represented an intervention in the internal affairs of other states. The United States' proposal to create a commission to watch over peace in the Caribbean and to assist governments in resolving conflicts or controversies in defense of the democracies against Communism also failed to pass. It was up to the Inter-American Peace Commission to handle this task, but within set limitations.

The United States did not succeed in its attempt to condemn Cuba, nor did Cuba or Venezuela manage to pass a condemnation of the dictatorships. Nor did Latin America succeed in persuading the meeting to deal with its major concerns—social and economic conditions—because of firm and repeated United States opposition. At the Washington OAS meeting to set the agenda for the Fifth Consultative Meeting, Cuba had proposed the inclusion of the item, "Economic Underdevelopment and Political Instability," since these were the cause of the continent's explosive situation. The United States blocked this proposal, noting that the item "would distract" attention from more important topics. The majority went docilely along.

United States embassies in the various capitals reported official and press reaction to the Fifth Consultative OAS meeting. The governments responded diplomatically, generally favorably, noting that the principle of nonintervention had been upheld, while for the most part the press was critical. A Bolivian daily characterized the OAS as "sluggish and bureaucratic" and demanded energetic action against the dictatorships. A Brazilian paper held that "little or nothing was done to change the attitude of the dictatorial governments." In Costa Rica another newspaper affirmed that "nothing has been achieved by the conference, since Somoza and Trujillo are proceeding as if nothing had happened." Editorials in Venezuelan dailies ranged from a "wait and see" attitude to labeling the meetings as "blah, blah, blah," and the Santiago Declaration as just "another piece of paper."[56]

Raúl Castro, who arrived in Santiago with a group of rebels—a surprise Alessandri hardly appreciated—said upon his return to Havana that the OAS was good for nothing, was dominated by the United States, and was opposed to Latin American interests. He observed that the Santiago Declaration was "so pretty" that it could be signed by representatives of Trujillo, Somoza, and other tyrants, and boasted that because of Cuba's opposition, the "international police force" the United States had requested was not established. The Cuban press headlined the conference as a triumph for Cuba.

THE CONFLICT

The Revolutionary government declared 1959 the "Year of Liberation" and proceeded to eradicate every trace of Batista's dictatorship, of the proimperialist and bourgeois state, and it began the process of economic, political, and military liberation from the United States. In January, before a demonstration the likes never before seen in Havana—the crowd was estimated at 800,000—Fidel announced that Cuba wanted not only political but also economic freedom. In February he ordered the removal of the United States' military mission—army, navy, and air force—that was part of the voluminous aid package Eisenhower had granted Batista to crush the rebel movement.

The "liberation" of Cuba meant its liberation from United States domination, imposed by the "Yankee meddling," in Cuba's War of Independence against Spain in 1898. At the triumph of the Revolution, the Cuban economy was an integral part of the United States economy. United States monopolies controlled key industries—sugar, tobacco, copper, and manganese, as well as important parts of the banking and financial sector. United States corporations owned 40 percent of the sugar cane plantations, almost all the cattle ranches, 80 percent of the public service sector, and 90 percent of the mining sector, and it supplied practically the entire oil industry. Until 1958 Cuba was the fifth most important country for the United States in terms of trade and investment, and 80 percent of Cuba's international transactions were with the United States. The United States was the largest market for Cuban sugar, the island's most important product. The United States' military mission stationed in Cuba was another form of domination.

In May of 1959, when the Agrarian Reform Law (the first law approved by the rebels in the Sierra Maestra), the policy of seizing lands and national resources and the confiscation of underused lands, was put into effect Fidel expropriated United States investments valued at $500 million. Washington issued energetic protests, sending verbal notes and urgent messages through its ambassador. The Cuban government deemed these attempts as intervention in the nation's internal affairs and refused to heed any of the demands or veiled threats.

In September 1959 Cuban Chancellor Roa made the first declaration of the Revolution's foreign policy at the United Nations: Cuba refused to choose between "capitalism, under which the people die of hunger, and communism, which solves economic problems but suppresses the freedoms so dear to mankind." He announced a policy of neutrality concerning Cold War conflicts and stressed Cuba's commitment to the third world.[57]

It became clear to the United States president and the Congress, as well as to the monopolies and investors, that the exceptional relationship with Cuba was a thing of the past; serious conflicts loomed near. The former ambassador, Earl Smith, described the lost paradise to a Senate committee: "[T]he United States, until the advent of Castro, was so overwhelmingly influential in Cuba that the American Ambassador was the second most important man in Cuba, sometimes even more important than the [Cuban] President." Smith also reiterated his fears of Communist infiltration in the rebel ranks.[58]

The United States was not disposed to "tolerate" the fact that this small Caribbean island would threaten its hegemony and leadership of the hemisphere, break its unity, and demolish its interests. Open and covert aggression began at once. According to documents declassified by the United States government in 1990, in March 1959 Eisenhower ordered the CIA to set into motion "Operation Pluto," an extensive effort to subvert the Revolution and overthrow Fidel. Immediately CIA agents began to infiltrate, and terrorist actions and sabotage in commercial and public centers ensued. Pirate aircraft took off from Florida to drop napalm on Cuban sugar refineries and other important economic targets. And the CIA provided arms, money, and equipment to a counterrevolutionary group that was forming in the mountains of Escambray in the central Cuba.

Washington offered employment premiums to stimulate an exodus of professionals and industrialists, so as to weaken the Revolution. Thousands of politicians, businessmen, and professionals—especially doctors—abandoned the island. Most of them were members of the upper middle class. Many who left during those first years left behind families, professions, and fortunes. They did so, not so much for the opportunities the United States offered them, but with the conviction that they would soon be returning home because the

United States would intervene as it had five years earlier in Guatemala, when it toppled Jacobo Arbenz.

Blows were traded, and with each day that passed, the conflict grew increasingly bitter. The United States watched with consternation as Cuba grew progressively closer to the Soviet Union. In February 1960, Anastas Mikoyan, the vice prime minister of the Soviet Union, arrived in Havana to preside at the opening of a Soviet exposition, and the two countries signed a five-year commercial agreement by which the Soviet Union granted Cuba a $100 million credit and agreed to buy a million tons of sugar annually. In May diplomatic relations, broken off by Batista, were resumed.

In April 1960, the first shipment of 300,000 tons of Soviet oil arrived. The United States-owned refineries refused to refine it, and Cuba nationalized them in June. In July the United States suspended the purchase of 700,000 tons of sugar from Cuba—the balance of the year's quota—on which Cuba's economy depended (four days later, the Soviet Union announced that it would buy a million tons). In August the United States declared an economic and commercial embargo on Cuba and asked its European and Latin American allies to join in, threatening them with reprisals if they would not do so. In the same month Cuba nationalized thirty-six sugar plantations, expropriated large industrial enterprises, and nationalized the telephone and electrical utility companies owned by United States investors.[59] The following month, the Cuban government nationalized subsidiaries of the United States' banking industry, in October more sugar mills and 383 industrial, commercial, and financial enterprises, railways, harbor installations, hotels and movie theaters; the total value reached $1 billion. In November, Cuba further expropriated lands and nationalized mining companies, oil refineries, banks, hotels, industrial plants and public services. In December the United States announced that it was going to eliminate its purchase of the Cuban sugar quota altogether.[60]

These measures and mutual reprisals continued overtly. Covertly, the CIA continued Operation Pluto and began preparations for an invasion of the island by anti-Castro Cubans living in the United States.[61] The invasion was to be carried out by proxy.

In February 1961, the Revolutionary Air Force brought down a clandestine airplane, killing a U.S. pilot. The government displayed his corpse as evidence of direct United States responsibility in these acts of aggression.[62] The CIA carried out most of these acts of sabotage using anti-Castro and pro-Batista operatives—"war criminals" living in Florida.

The terrorist acts cost the lives of innocent victims. The worst such instance was the explosion of the French ship *La Coubre* in Havana harbor in March 1960. It carried a shipment of Belgian weapons, the first the Cuban government had succeeded in acquiring. Scores of workers, soldiers, and police were killed and hundreds of people were wounded. Some were permanently disabled. At the victims' funeral Fidel launched the slogan, "*Patria o Muerte*" ("Motherland or Death"). Later he added "*Venceremos*" ("We will win").

In September of the same year, after the detonation of two explosive devices in the midst of a large crowd in Havana's Revolution Square, Fidel created the Committees for the Defense of the Revolution (CDR) to mobilize and unite the populace against the internal and external threats. The CDRs are the most important mass organization in Cuba, the spine of internal security. From that time on they functioned twenty-four hours a day on every block, in all cities and towns, in every factory and workplace, serving as informants for the security and police apparatuses.

In January 1961, after a series of assassination attempts and acts of sabotage in which the long arm of the CIA was evident, Fidel denounced the espionage operations of the United States Embassy in Havana. "The Revolution has allowed a plague of intelligence service agents disguised as diplomats to remain here conspiring and promoting terrorism. But the revolutionary government has decided that within forty-eight hours the United States Embassy shall have not one officer more here than we have in the United States."[63] The United States was supposed to reduce its personnel from 300 to 11. The Cuban people received this news with enormous joy, shouting, "Out! Out!"[64] In reprisal, two weeks before the end of his term, Eisenhower broke off all diplomatic and consular relations with Cuba and prohibited United States citizens from traveling to the island. He had already succeeded in persuading several countries to break off relations with Cuba.

The Cuban government voiced its first denunciation before the United Nations Security Council in July 1960. It accused the United States of aggression against its country, offering protection to pro-Batista "war criminals," and providing facilities for counterrevolutionary elements to attack Cuba. It denounced the flights of clandestine aircraft, which took off from Florida, violating Cuban air space and bombing sugar plantations and other economic targets. The speech pointed out that the economic and commercial embargo imposed on Cuba was intended to strangle its economy in violation of the UN and OAS charters.

On the same day the United States denounced Cuba at the OAS, accusing it of carrying out "an intense and systematic campaign of distortions, half-truths, and outright falsehoods against" the United States, and argued that the UN should not consider the Cuban complaint until the OAS reported on the counterdenunciation. In this way, the United States negated Cuba's complaints before the Security Council.

Washington and influential American newspapers portrayed the Cuban denunciations as "anti-American propaganda," as "vicious" as that of the Soviets.[65] For the first time in its history the United States had come under attack from Latin America, its traditional zone of influence.

The Cuban intelligence services infiltrated agents into the CIA and among the anti-Castro ranks in Miami. In this way the Revolutionary government learned of preparations for an invasion and of the existence of secret camps in Florida and bases in Guatemala where United States military advisers were training anti-Castro forces. Such operations, supposedly covert, were widely known within and outside the United States.

In 1960 Nikita Khrushchev offered Fidel military aid and the support of rockets in case of an attack against his country by the United States. The acceptance of this aid provoked intense diplomatic activity in Washington to convene the consultative organ of the OAS, in order to condemn Cuba for threatening international peace. The United States always counted on the support of a majority of OAS members—Cuban chancellor Roa referred to this coalition as the United States' "colonial ministry."

But at the Seventh Meeting of the Consultative Organ in San José, Costa Rica, in August 1960, for the first time this support was absent and the United States did not have its way. The Final Declaration merely condemned the "interference" of "extracontinental powers" (the Soviet Union and the People's Republic of China) in the internal affairs of Latin America. The name Cuba did not appear in any of the documents from this meeting.[66]

THE FIRST DECLARATION OF HAVANA

Fidel's response to the San José Declaration consisted of the First Havana Declaration, approved by the Cuban people in a massive rally in Revolution Square that was convened as a National General Assembly. The Declaration energetically condemned its San José counterpart "in all particulars" and characterized it as a "document dictated by United States imperialism, an outrage to national self-determination, to sovereignty, and to the dignity of the continent's family of peoples." It condemned "open and criminal intervention," which "for more than a century North American imperialism has exercised against all the peoples of Latin America," and denounced the "miserable submission of traitorous heads of government" who permitted such intervention. It averred that the "spontaneous aid" from the Soviet Union was an act of solidarity, which Cuba accepted with gratitude, and announced that it would establish relations with the People's Republic of China and was rescinding its relations with "the puppet government sustained by the Yankee Seventh Fleet in Formosa."[67]

The United States failed to achieve consensus in the continent. These were new times. No government dared to hoist the anti-Cuban banner for fear of the violent protests of their people who supported the Revolution.

On December 31, 1960, in a letter to the president of the Security Council, Chancellor Roa requested an urgent meeting of the Council to study United States intentions to commit direct military aggression against his country, with the cooperation of some governments and Cuban "war criminals," of which plans, he affirmed, his government had evidence. He said the United States was accusing Cuba of building 17 launching pads for rockets to be used by the Soviet Union, and that it was sending confidential letters to the governments of the continent in an attempt to isolate his country. The Council met for two days, heard the Cuban Chancellor and the U.S. representative, and adjourned without taking any action. The invasion of the Bay of Pigs occurred three months later.

THE PARTY'S OVER

The policy of the United States regarding Latin America had been to support dictatorships. The brutality and corruption bothered neither Eisenhower nor his secretary of state, John Foster Dulles. What mattered to them was that these governments maintained public order, prosecuted Communists, and granted carte blanche to United States transnational companies and investors. Their priorities had been questions of hemispheric security in the context of the Cold War.

Although the weapons provided to the continent "for defense of the hemisphere" were given with restrictions—they were not to be used for any other purpose nor passed on to any third country without previous approval by Washington—such safeguards could be lifted when there was "a clear indication of Communist implication among the opposition forces." The United States sold napalm bombs, useless for defense of the hemisphere but of enormous destructive potential against civilian populations. When it refrained from selling them for fear of scandal, it provided the know-how for their manufacture. Such was the case with Colombia and Peru.

Eisenhower invited, on separate occasions, Batista, Somoza, Pérez Jiménez, and Trujillo to Washington and gave them a state welcome. In turn, Congress applauded them in joint sessions of both houses, a high honor rarely conceded, and the Pentagon decorated them with the Order of Merit, the highest military distinction. Two months after the brutal bombardment of Cienfuegos on September 15, 1957, by Batista's air force, a ranking officer of the United States Air Force visited Havana to decorate Colonel Carlos Tabernilla, head of the Cuban Air Force, who was responsible for those genocidal bombings. The people denounced this gesture.[68] The broad political and military support for dictators, while verbally defending democracy, offended the democratic elements throughout the continent. They accused the United States of a double standard. Washington cynically explained that its policies reflected its "unrestricted respect" for the principle of nonintervention. The people's resentment and growing anti-Americanism and anti-imperialist feelings exploded when Vice President Richard Nixon arrived in Caracas and Lima on a good will tour in 1958. He was greeted with stones, spit, and insults. Dulles was ready to send in the marines to rescue him. Such incidents in friendly nations surprised and bothered Washington and worried members of Congress; they showed the degree of deterioration in relations with the continent and the effect of the Eisenhower administration's lack of interest in and ignorance of Latin America.

In February 1960, during the last year of his administration, Eisenhower undertook an impromptu and futile tour through Latin America. He visited Argentina, Brazil, Chile, and Uruguay. The *New York Times* commented that the trip had gone fairly smoothly with only two incidents that marred the "massive and warm welcome" the President received in all the capitals. This was not the picture of the tour through the Southern Cone painted by Townsend Hoopes, the biographer of John Foster Dulles. In Buenos Aires, Eisenhower was taken by helicopter from the airport to the United States Embassy because of hostile demonstrations, complete with riots and bombs, that had been organized by the Peronistas. In Montevideo anti-Yankee student protests were dispersed with water cannons and tear gas. In Chile student criticism of his policies forced Eisenhower to call an ad hoc press conference to explain them, and in Brazil the fatal airplane accident of the navy band intended to entertain the banquet hosted by Eisenhower in honor of Kubitschek, added a mournful touch to the visit.[69]

At the end of his two terms Eisenhower's image deteriorated as a result of his failures in the international arena. In the context of the harsh confrontation with the Soviet Union, Khrushchev boycotted the summit meeting in Paris attended by Eisenhower, British Prime Minister Harold Macmillan, and French President Charles de Gaulle, and he withdrew an invitation to Eisenhower to visit Moscow because of the downing of a U-2 spy plane over Soviet territory. This incident was strongly criticized by Congress and influential newspapers, since it diminished the chances for a relaxing of tensions with the Soviet Union. Furthermore, while Eisenhower was en route to Tokyo, the Japanese government announced that "much to its regret" it would be unable to receive him because the violent popular demonstrations his visit would provoke rendered it inadvisable.[70]

Eisenhower left office satisfied and convinced that on his watch the Communists had been unable to gain an inch of ground, forgetting that the Communists already had a firm grip on North Vietnam. He did not suspect that Cuba, blazing a revolutionary trail traveled by no other Latin American government, would shortly become the first socialist state in the Americas, allied with the Soviet Union, to break the nearly 150 years of United States hegemony in its zone of influence.

When Eisenhower left the White House in January 1960, the United States' confrontation with Cuba was already irreversible. The Revolution caused profound unrest in the hemisphere; the meetings of the Consultative Organ of the OAS called to condemn Cuba had proven to be a failure, and relations between Cuba, the Soviet Union, and the Communist world were becoming closer every day. As John F. Kennedy assumed the presidency, preparations for an invasion of the island were in full swing.

Cuba was also a cause for concern in Latin America. The Revolution set off deep unrest among its peoples and presented great challenges to its governments. Fidel was poking the wounds of the endemic situations of inequality, social injustice, and enormous unsatisfied needs, and armed movements were beginning to emerge that were intent on following the Cuban example.

The masses applauded Fidel's strong confrontation with the Empire, the way he put an end to dependency, and his policy of giving preference to the Cuban people. Fidel was an icon and a source of inspiration.

CHAPTER III

THE TURBULENT 1960s

THE UNITED STATES: THE WORLD AND CUBA'S CHALLENGE

John F. Kennedy's victory over Richard Nixon in the November 1960 presidential election heralded a domestic rebirth and a favorable change in the tense international atmosphere. Kennedy's victory, by a narrow margin of 118,000 votes out of a total of 68 million, not only returned the Democratic Party to power after eight years of Republican rule, but also ushered in a great generational shift in the White House.

The administration of the beloved hero of the second World War—one of "the bland leading the bland,"[1]—had ended. Gone were "[the] goofy grin and the stack of Zane Grey Westerns on his night table, forever playing golf or fishing, or otherwise treating the White House as a pleasant retirement home," as *Time* magazine put it.

With the vigorous Kennedy team of "the best and the brightest" came the magic of a sophisticated, complex, intellectual, and elegant society, with a progressive program called the New Frontier. Kennedy was the first Catholic and the youngest (ten years older than Fidel Castro) president in United States history. He blew onto the national and international scene of the turbulent 1960s like a breath of hope. He was "gay, charming, irreverent, good-looking, and far from dilligent," said his Harvard professor, John Kenneth Galbraith, but he nevertheless graduated *magna cum laude,* Theodore Sorensen, one of his many biographers, noted.[2]

For the United States, the Kennedy and Johnson years were explosive. Society was divided by profound social conflicts, by the youth rebellion, by the struggle for civil rights, and by the war in Vietnam and the growing internal and international opposition to it.

There was uncertainty among the people of the United States about the direction the country was taking. Young people questioned traditional values, the codes and dogmas of an opulent, white and puritanical America, ultimately dismissing them as banal and obsolete. The young people invented their own codes of conduct, throwing out the traditional family unit, embracing a communal lifestyle and sexual freedom. Gays and lesbians demanded that their civil rights be respected. It was a decade of drugs, sex, meditation, antiwar activism, and emphasis on interior richness. The hippies, with their own style of dress, their long hair, their beards, and their music—the Beatles, Jimi Hendrix, Bob Dylan, Joan Baez, the Rolling Stones, the Doors, and many more who evolved into the soundtrack of the counterculture—became the emblem of a liberated youth opposed to violence, the Vietnam War, and the hypocrisy of their elders. Such slogans as "Make love, not war," Bob Dylan's protest against the "Masters of War," and John Lennon's song "Give Peace a Chance" became the chant for many of the antiwar demonstrations in San Francisco in November 1969.

The 1960s in the United States were bursting with enormous creativity and breakthroughs; it was the time of a cultural revolution with new expressions and conventions in all arts. There was the emergence of avant-garde theater—the *living theater*, and the theater of the absurd—a new antiliterary movement, of abstraction in literature, pop art, op art, abstract expressionism, experimental and underground films. The Christian churches were called on to change as well. Jim F. Heath, a writer in the United States, discussed radical Protestant theologians who proclaimed that "God is dead." He talked about a "gang" of Catholic priests, such as Daniel and Philip Berrigan, who led antiwar movements, and ministers less willing to take great risks who revived the social gospel and participated in demonstrations for human rights, in strikes, and in peace marches. Protestants and Catholics alike pledged to simplify and purify religious services to give them greater significance and make them more accessible to the worshipers.[3]

"TOGETHER LET US EXPLORE THE STARS"

When the Soviet cosmonaut Yuri Gagarin orbited Earth for the first time, in April 1961, the Communist superpower inaugurated the space race, forever changing the dimensions of the world. Eight years later American astronauts

Neil Armstrong, Edwin Aldrin, and Michael Collins landed on the moon. John Kennedy, who had pushed hard for the space program, was long dead when the first interplanetary communication reached Earth. It was Richard Nixon, his opponent, who triumphantly received the astronauts' message from the moon.

In his victory speech, in the State of the Union message, and in front of the United Nations General Assembly in 1961, Kennedy spoke of peaceful cooperation in space between East and West. He did not want space to become a new arena for the Cold War, and he extended a proposal to the Soviet Union: "Together let us explore the stars." But the Soviet Union did not accept, since its space program was far more advanced.[4] Both nations continued their separate explorations of the moon, Venus, and Mars—the United States with the Apollo program, and the Soviets with Vostok, Voskhod, and Soyuz craft. In 1972 however, missions to the moon were suspended. Thirty years later Americans still ask themselves why these flights were abandoned and why they went in the first place. In July 1975, the crews of Soyuz and Apollo first met in space during a joint rescue mission test. From space they spoke to the world, delivering a message of peace.

UPHEAVALS IN THE COMMUNIST WORLD

The Communist world experienced tremendous upheavals with the liberalizing policies of Nikita Khrushchev (1955–1964), and his denunciations of Stalin. At the Twentieth Congress of the Soviet Communist Party (CPSU) in 1956 he made public Stalin's criminal acts of repression and the corruption and distortions of Marxism tolerated by the Soviet state. Digging through thirty years of impenetrable secrecy, he brought to light the horrors of that regime— the crimes, the cult of personality, the abuse of power, and the corruption at the top levels of government in an orgy of privilege and luxury unthinkable in a supposedly egalitarian socialist society. With the abrupt departure of "Uncle Joe" from the Communist pantheon and the subsequent de-Stalinization of the Soviet system—approved by the Soviet Communist Party in 1961—Khrushchev revived the doctrine of "different roads to socialism" (of Marx, Engels, and Lenin), and repudiated the centralization with which Stalin had tried to mold the Communist world in the image and likeness of the Soviet Union. The Soviet Communist Party lost its infallibility and Moscow its hegemony as the Communist epicenter.[5]

In 1960 the break between the Soviet Union and China over ideological differences—which masked geopolitical conflicts—expanded the debate and deepened controversy in the Communist world. Each accused the other of deviating from the fundamental principles of Marxism. The Soviets accused the Chinese of usurping the power of the Communist Party and terrorizing the true Chinese Communists into silence, replacing Marxism with Maoist ideologies, and working toward a social order that had nothing to do with Marxism. The Chinese, in turn, claimed that the Soviet leaders were usurping power with a "palace revolution" and had restored capitalism and become into a new bourgeois caste that oppressed and exploited the people.[6]

With this break grew a heretical and schismatic current that turned the Communist world upside down. The parties sought their own practices, and new Marxist-Leninist movements and parties emerged, some of them pro-China.[7] The Soviet masses, disillusioned by the corruption in the Kremlin, wanted not more doctrine, but "better goulash," said Khrushchev.[8]

JOHN XXIII, PONTIFF OF THE POOR

The Catholic Church was experiencing its own revolution in the 1960s. The ecumenical and reformist direction of the brief and dynamic papacy of John XXIII (1958–1963) marked a liberating moment in the history of a church caught up in doctrinal questions and alienated from the realities and needs of the people. "Our sacred obligation," noted the Pontiff, "is not only to guard the precious treasure [of the Faith] as if we had only to worry about the past, but to dedicate ourselves with joy and without fear to the task of giving this ancient and eternal doctrine a relevance that corresponds to the conditions of our time." After a hundred years of stasis in the Church, John XXIII called the Second Vatican Council (1962–1965), whose purpose was to "work actively so that there may be fulfilled the great mystery of that unity" in accordance with the desires of Christ. In his encyclicals *Mater et Magistra* (1961) and *Pacem in Terra* (1963), the Pope declared that the Church should address the world's problems and place economic and social development "in the moral realm of conformity to the dignity of man and the enormous value which is the life of human beings."[9]

At the 1968 conclave of the Latin American Episcopal Council—Consejo Episcopal Latinoamericano (CELAM)—held in Medellín, Colombia—the most important ecclesiastic event of the decade—the bishops met to study the Second Vatican Council's recommendations with respect to the continental realities. Concluding that the Church's duty was to fight against injustice and institutionalized violence, which was deemed sinful, the clerics broke with the old rules that had governed the Latin American Church.

The Vatican reoriented its attention toward the plight of the poor signaling, like Cuban Revolution, the volatility of social and economic injustice and the misery of the masses. Thus in 1968 Latin America, a continent where the vast majority of people are poor and Catholic, saw the emergence of liberation theology. Its origin was ecumenical, the result of the work of Catholic and Protestant theologians who sought the union of faith with Christian practice of the credo and justice. They questioned the conduct of the rich nations toward the poor ones and the growing gap in the Latin American societies between the small minority privileged families—not eager to lose their advantages—and the vast number of the destitute. They stressed the need to make deep structural changes to correct such injustices.

After Pope John XXIII's death, opposition arose throughout the continent from the hierarchies within the Vatican and the Catholic Church against the liberation theologians. They were seen as dipping dangerously into the stream of Marxism, and their analysis of social reality was considered to be drawn along its doctrine. The radicalized clergy had created Christian grassroots communities in several countries, to work for the poor campesinos and rural marginalized sectors, to raise consciousness of the rights of the poor, to help organize their movements, and to support their struggles. Some joined insurgent groups.

THE UNSTABLE INTERNATIONAL ARENA

The scene in the international arena was changing. The geopolitical power struggle between Washington and Moscow created sharp tensions and the division of the world into two antagonistic blocs led by the superpowers. The emergence of new axes of power—Western Europe, China, Japan and the Nonaligned Movement—weakened the superpowers.

At the beginning of the 1960s the third world was strengthened by the creation of two important political organizations, the Nonaligned Movement (1961) and the Organization of African Unity (1963). The objectives of the Nonaligned Movement were anti-imperialist, anticolonialist, antineocolonialist, and in support of the national liberation movements. The objective of the Organization of African Unity (OAU) was to give political cohesion and unity to the African nations and to establish a power bloc against the rest of the world. With the entry into the United Nations of twenty-seven newly independent and nonaligned African countries, the balance of power in that organization changed. The United States could no longer count on easy majorities. The political weight of Latin America, on which it had always relied, disappeared in the face of the developing power of the Afro-Asian bloc.

The United States, the Soviet Union, China, and Israel sought to extend their influence in these newly independent countries, offering economic and technical assistance to aid in their development. Similarly, Cuba built closer ties to them, sending advisers in various fields, educating thousands of students at no charge in its schools, and supporting African liberation with weapons, military advisers, and training for their combatants.

TENSIONS BETWEEN THE GIANTS

The tensions between Washington and Moscow increased after a U-2 plane was shot down over Sverdlovsk, Russia, in 1959. Khrushchev proved that Eisenhower had lied to him about the plane's mission. It had not been on a meteorological flight, as the President maintained, but had engaged in espionage. In May 1960, at a summit meeting in Paris in which the United States, Great Britain, and France participated, Khrushchev accused Eisenhower of an act of "provocation," walked out of the conference, and withdrew an invitation to Eisenhower to visit Moscow. After this incident, confrontation and mutual distrust clouded the international atmosphere once again.

Khrushchev had declared his policy of "peaceful coexistence among states" before John F. Kennedy was elected president. He proposed that relations between communist and capitalist countries should be respectful, and he admonished the United States for trying to remake the world in its own image. Kennedy's election victory in November 1960 promised to relieve some of the existing tensions. During his presidential campaign, Kennedy questioned the policies that rejected Communism out of hand, and he disapproved of the confrontation with the Soviet Union maintained by Eisenhower and his secretary of state, John Foster Dulles. In his inaugural address, Kennedy stressed that the "enemies" were not the Communists but those who became "adversaries." In a letter to Khrushchev he noted, "What your government believes is its own business; what it does in the world is the world's business."[10] Tensions grew in August 1961, when the Soviets erected the Berlin Wall, a barrier both concrete and symbolic of East-West confrontation.

Kennedy was open to dialogue with the Soviet Union. He made this clear when he said, "Let us never negotiate out of fear, but let us never fear to nego-tiate." He maintained that their differences did not impede dialogue or col-laboration, essential to preventing a third world war.[11] Between April 1961 and December 1962, the two leaders exchanged some forty messages in which they dealt with their bilateral relations and international matters of mutual inter-est: disarmament, nuclear testing, the sensitive situations of Berlin, Cuba, Southeast Asia (Laos and Vietnam), and the situation in the Congo (Leopoldville), whose war was a burning topic at the Unied Nations.

In their first and only summit meeting, held in Vienna in June 1961, two months after the Bay of Pigs fiasco, the two leaders held a tough and open dia-logue but came to no agreement. For Kennedy the experience was enor-mously frustrating. In London, on his way back to Washington, he described the meeting as "somber" but immensely useful.[12]

The most dangerous crisis during Kennedy and Khrushchev's time in office arose from the installation of Soviet nuclear missiles in Cuba in October 1962. It brought the world to the brink of a nuclear conflagration. Kennedy demanded their withdrawal, and Khrushchev acceded. Thereafter the two lead-ers established a direct telephone line between Washington and Moscow—the "red phone"—to avoid errors and situations that would endanger world peace.

THE "BALANCE OF TERROR"

By 1961 the nuclear arms race was speeding up. The Soviet Union exploded its first hydrogen bomb—at 50 megatons, the most powerful to date—and France tested its first atomic bomb. The destructive potential of the super-powers reached a peak with intercontinental ballistic missiles armed with nuclear warheads; now they could destroy not only each other but also the world. For the United States, this "balance of terror" thwarted aggressive action and ensured world peace. Kennedy was uneasy about the entry of new countries into the nuclear club, since it would increase the risk of a confla-gration. In 1962 the United States and Great Britain renewed nuclear testing, striking a hard blow for the slow and difficult negotiations on general and com-plete disarmament. Two years later China tested its first atomic bomb and by 1967 had exploded its first hydrogen bomb.

The net result of Kennedy and Khrushchev's peace efforts was positive. In 1963 the United States and the Soviet Union signed in Moscow the first inter-national limited test ban treaty, prohibiting tests in the atmosphere, the stratosphere, and underwater. Great Britain signed on as well. The great powers, which poisoned the atmosphere with 336 tests in thirteen years, were forced to carry out their tests exclusively underground.

The signing of this important treaty was not the culmination of a process but the first step toward general and complete disarmament, according to Kennedy. Discussion on this point had been stalled in the United Nations General Assembly since 1946. The sticking point had been the United States' demand for inspection and international control of disarmament and the Soviet Union's refusal to accept these terms.

THE CUBAN REVOLUTION BREAKS OUT

When Kennedy assumed the presidency, the Cuban Revolution already posed a serious problem for his country. Cuba's alliance with the Soviet Union was growing stronger and soon after, Fidel announced the socialist nature of the Revolution. The existence of the first socialist state in the hemisphere meant a geopolitical change with enormous negative consequences for the United States, with Cuba becoming a factor in the East-West confrontation.

Kennedy was forced to reformulate his policy toward Latin America and the Caribbean so as to confront the influence of the Cuban Revolution. Fidel had virtually expelled the United States from the island and expropriated and nationalized all American enterprises and large land holdings, and Kennedy worried such procedures might also be implemented in other countries. Fidel's vigorous anti-imperialist and nationalist discourse encouraged the people's armed struggles in defense of their rights and against the dictatorships and oligarchies that exploited them and the domination exercised by the world superpower on Latin America. Armed pro-Castro groups began to arise almost immediately. In effect, the Cuban Revolution was giving a new dynamic to social protest and hope to the peoples burdened with the endemic situation of poverty, social injustice, exploitation, and false promises. Faced with the fact that there were few opportunities along democratic lines, armed struggle seemed to be the only possible way to achieve change.

THE KENNEDY ERA

When Kennedy settled into the White House, the international atmosphere was charged with growing anti-Americanism in different parts of the world. The prestige of the United States was tainted by the mistakes and fiascoes of the last years of Eisenhower's administration.

In the United Nations, the principal forum where Cuba and the United States aired their differences, the Cuban government constantly denounced American acts of aggression against its country, cultivating an anti-Yankee and anti-imperialist discourse. Never before had the United States suffered such a public affront from a nation in its own sphere.

Within the United States, the struggle for civil rights was growing hotter, with protests raging throughout the nation. Its main leader, Martin Luther King Jr., (who was assassinated in 1968) advocated a peaceful struggle, while the Black Power, Black Muslim, and Black Panthers movements declared their right to respond, in self-defense, to violence with violence. In the hot summer of 1963 Kennedy witnessed the most impressive racial protest ever seen in Washington. As many as 200,000 blacks, along with thousands of whites, marched silently through the streets of the capital. At the Lincoln Memorial, King delivered his now-famous "I Have a Dream" speech:

I have a dream that one day even the State of Mississippi, a desert state, sweltering with the heat of injustice and oppression, will be transformed into an oasis of freedom and justice. I have a dream that one day this nation will rise up and live out the true meaning of its creed: "We hold these truths to be self-evident, that all men are created equal."[13]

Also in 1963 the United States saw the first massive student protest demanding the cessation of U.S. intervention in Asia. Between 1961 and 1963 Kennedy had sent 17,000 soldiers to Vietnam—the first combat troops. Vigorous youth movements flooded the streets and university campuses, demanding "Hands off Vietnam."

THE HEMISPHERIC ALLIANCE

Kennedy was severely critical of Eisenhower's policies, which he considered terribly misguided. Latin America had been of secondary importance to Eisenhower's foreign policy; his priorities were military strategy and security, openly supporting dictatorships. Such support, stated Kennedy, had propped up "one of the most bloody and repressive dictatorships in the long history of Latin American repression," referring to Batista's regime in Cuba. "Our action too often gave the impression that this country was more interested in taking money from the Cuban people than in helping them build a strong and diversified economy of their own," he noted. He criticized Eisenhower for not having used the United States' enormous influence to persuade Batista to hold free elections and "let the Cuban people pick his successor instead of letting Castro seize it in what almost amounted to a palace revolution." And, he added, the Soviet ambassador became the second most powerful man in Cuba. He charged Eisenhower with being responsible for the triumph of the Revolution, which he called a "disaster," and he pointed out that the "enemy" was now a mere 90 miles from the United States' coast. "As a Soviet satellite, it will do anything to hasten our fall and it will attempt to spread its revolution throughout Latin America."[14]

For Kennedy, Latin America was the "most critical area of the world." He understood that popular solidarity with the Cuban Revolution signified something more than youthful idealism or revolts instigated by the Communists. He saw Latin America as sitting on a volcano of hunger, sickness, social injustice, and aspirations repressed for decades. Kennedy spoke of strengthening the democracies and supporting the cause of freedom in Latin America. He wanted to differentiate his policies from Eisenhower's, seeing that hemispheric relations should be conducted through the OAS and the Cuban question should be handled as continental policy. He was against unilateral actions, since they awakened strong reactions against "Yankee imperialism." "No continent was more constantly in the President's mind—or had a warmer appreciation of his efforts—than Latin America," wrote Kennedy's biographer Theodore Sorensen.[15]

During his campaign and in his inaugural address, Kennedy proposed that hemispheric relations should represent an alliance for progress. He spoke of a quiet social and economic revolution. The social content of Kennedy's politics ran as deep as Franklin D. Roosevelt's Good Neighbor policy. It was a program of social and economic development, which sought to improve the living conditions of the people of Latin America.

The Alliance for Progress was the first plan for Latin America proposed by the United States in which social and economic themes were considered of equal importance. It was a plan for development within a capitalist and democratic framework, an alternative to Cuba's socialist policy. The United States offered $20 billion in aid over a ten-year period. Some dubbed the Alliance the "Castro Plan," believing that the United States government's change in favor of the continent was a result of Fidel's spreading of unrest throughout the continent.

The Alliance's first priority was to raise the people's standard of living by providing employment, housing, land, health care, and education to all. "Our unfulfilled task is to demonstrate that man's unsatisfied aspiration for economic progress and social justice can best be achieved by free men working within the framework of democratic institutions." said Kennedy.[16] He conceived of the Alliance as a plan for cooperation. Each country should set aside resources to improve the living conditions for its people and to realize the structural reforms necessary to correct existing inequalities.

The Alliance was received with enormous enthusiasm and hope throughout the region. At the opening of the OAS Conference in the resort city of Punta del Este, Uruguay, in August 1961, where the proposal for the Alliance was adopted (over Cuba's vote against), Uruguay's President Víctor Haedo exclaimed that "finally a hope for our millions of hungry" existed. Carlos Sanz de Santamaría, former chancellor of Colombia and later president of the Inter-American Committee for the Alliance (CIAP), called it a program "with a human face."[17] Kennedy considered the Alliance the only alternative that could produce change without violence.

The continent's peoples and democratic sectors recognized Kennedy as an ally, a friend, and a hope for change. On his visit to Colombia in 1961, where he and his wife, Jacqueline, were the guests of President Alberto Lleras, the people gave them a tumultuous welcome. Lleras told Kennedy that this popular enthusiasm was because the people believed him to be on their side and against the oligarchies.[18]

Kennedy's defense strategy in response to the Cuban Revolution gave a completely new direction to the hemispheric defense policies of the Cold War. Its focus was counterinsurgency. Under the Military Mutual Assistance Pacts (MAP), bilateral agreements in force since the 1940s for hemispheric defense, the United States gave weapons and sent its Special Forces to train national armies in martial techniques for combating guerrilla movements, controlling public order, and vanquishing the "enemy within."[19] These new tasks assigned to the armies, which are police functions, were adopted by all governments in violation of constitutional dispositions that assigned the armies exclusively to the defense of national sovereignty.

Kennedy lent more economic resources and greater leadership and imagination to this counterinsurgency strategy than any general in the Pentagon and even than Secretary of Defense Robert McNamara himself. Sorensen writes that the president read Mao Tse-tung's and Che Guevara's texts on guerrilla warfare—sources of inspiration to third world revolutionaries—and recommended them to "certain" military officers, since he was convinced that the Pentagon's own military manuals were uninspiring and inadequate.[20]

To train Latin American officers in counterinsurgency techniques, the Pentagon beefed up the war colleges for jungle warfare, the School of the Americas at Fort Benning, Georgia; the Special Warfare School at Fort Bragg, North Carolina; and the Special Forces Group at Fort Gulick, Canal Zone.

Between 1950 and 1975, more than 70,000 officers from countries in conflict graduated from these schools.[21] In 1962 Kennedy created the Inter-American Police Academy at Fort Davis in Panama to train continental police officers in keeping the public order and in espionage and counterespionage techniques. Between 1962 and 1963, 600 officers from 15 countries were trained at this school.[22]

This training was not only in military and security matters. It also included instruction in anti-Communist ideology and the strengthening of democratic principles. The objective was to prepare a military elite capable of assuming leadership in countries where social and student protests deemed Communist or Communist-leaning had the potential to explode into revolutionary situations. Secretary of Defense McNamara explained to Congress in 1962: "Probably the greatest return in our military assistance investment comes from training selective officers and key specialists at our military schools and training centers in the United States and overseas. . . . They are the coming leaders, the men that will have the know-how and impart it to their own forces." He signaled the importance to the United States "beyond price to us to make friends of such men who will have first-hand knowledge of how things are done and how Americans think."[23]

Kennedy's counterinsurgency strategy and the National Security Doctrine—the work of Brazilian generals—went hand in hand. Both were based on the concept of "Security and Development," were anti-Communist, and gave a preeminent place to the military. According to Alfredo Vázquez Carrizosa, the former Colombian chancellor, such doctrines had vast implications for the future national political and social development, and were a source of inspiration to the military officers on the continent.[24]

WHAT'S HAPPENING IN CUBA?

The conflict in the United States over the Cuban Revolution was a key campaign issue in 1960, crucial in the televised debate of the candidates Kennedy and Richard Nixon. Kennedy severely criticized the policies of the Republican administration, charging that "for the first time in the United States' history an enemy stands poised at the throat of the United States." He also slammed Fidel Castro on September 2, 1960, saying he should be "condemned" for being the source of the "maximum danger," adding that the major task of his government would be to "contain this revolution" and Communism in Latin America.[25]

Arthur Schlesinger, one of the President's advisers, noted that Kennedy was the first president not to hold the misconception that "all Latin American agitation is Communist-inspired—that every anti-American voice is the voice of Moscow—and that most citizens of Latin America share our dedication to an anti-Communist crusade to save what we call free enterprise."[26] Sorensen indicated that in 1963 Kennedy recognized that the great dangers on the continent bore no relation to Cuba or to Communist activity in these countries. But Kennedy maintained that Communist infiltration and subversion must be held in check in order for the Alliance to succeed.[27]

Without sharing Dulles's aggravated anti-Communist stance, Kennedy continued the Cold War policy of containment of international Communism. He put the Cuban problem in this context. He considered Cuba a threat to security in the United States and Latin America. His policies opposing the Revolution were more aggressive than Eisenhower's. Kennedy was determined to crush the Revolution, and get rid of Fidel Castro. He cut off entirely the quota of Cuban sugar, the resource on which the island's economy depended. He extended the economic and commercial embargo and pressured allied and friendly countries—under threat of reprisals and sanctions—to join this embargo and cut diplomatic and commercial relations with the island. By 1964, a year after Kennedy's assassination, all the Latin American countries, except Mexico, had severed relations with Havana.

The CIA intensified the clandestine aircraft flights from Florida—operations mostly carried out with anti-Castro exiles living in the United States— to bombard sugar processing plants and oil refineries. It also stepped up efforts to infiltrate agents who would carry out acts of terrorism and sabotage; their primary objective was to assassinate Fidel and members of the Cuban leadership. Most of these attempts failed. Cuban security forces captured, imprisoned, and exposed the CIA agents to prove United States acts of aggression against Cuba.

Kennedy inherited from Eisenhower secret preparations for invading Cuba with a mercenary brigade of anti-Castro exiles.[28] In spite of his profound reservations —not for ethical reasons, but for fear of failure—Kennedy continued to further this adventurous plan. It was already common knowledge that the United States was responsible for this CIA covert enterprise. Kennedy knew that its failure could strike a severe blow to the United States' prestige as well as to his government and to his chances for reelection.

A month after his inauguration, in February 1961, Kennedy sent Senator George McGovern and Arthur Schlesinger to Latin America to sound out the governments, the political and economic power centers, and public opinion about the Revolution and Fidel. What they learned amounted to a picture of unqualified popular support for the Revolution, Fidel, and Che and fear on the part of governments, which perceived the Revolution as a potential danger. Important democratic leaders expressed themselves in favor of eliminating Castro, calling him the main threat to their democracies. In fact, Raúl Haya de la Torre, the leader of the American Revolutionary People's Alliance (APRA: *Alianza Popular Revolucionaria Americana*)—the main Peruvian popular party—and president of Bolivia Víctor Paz Estensoro, ex-president of Guatemala Juan José Arévalo, and president of Venezuela Rómulo Betancourt, all criticized the Revolution. Betancourt opined that Latin America would unite against Castro just at it had when the OAS discovered that Trujillo had attempted to kill him.[29]

THE BAY OF PIGS

Sorensen wrote that Kennedy inherited not only the plan to invade Cuba but also the planners and, most disquieting, the brigade of Cuban exiles—an armed force under another flag, highly trained at secret bases in Guatemala, with the sole mission of invading the island. He commented that when the CIA informed Kennedy of these plans before his inauguration, he was surprised at its "magnitude and audacity."[30] From the start he harbored profound doubts, which were shared by some members of Congress and the Pentagon. CIA reports were contradictory. Some claimed that anti-Castro forces could count on massive support from the Cuban people, while others warned that time was against them because Castro was growing stronger by the day.

Kennedy did not dare to suspend the "clandestine" operation—its preparations were moving ahead at full speed—since the operation became public almost immediately. Cuban Chancellor Raúl Roa denounced it at the United Nations and the OAS. The *New York Times* and other influential newspapers reported on the preparations and the clandestine bases in Guatemala where United States military advisers were training a brigade of more than a thousand anti-Castro mercenaries. They also revealed that Somoza provided Puerto Cabezas in Nicaragua as a base from which the invasion could set out, along with other training centers in Costa Rica and on the island of Vieques in Puerto Rico.[31] In addition, the anti-Castro forces recruited by the CIA in Miami were telling everything they knew everywhere they went.

This public dissemination of information about United States plans to invade Cuba was embarrassing for Kennedy. He had to define the situation quickly, since problems were mounting. The Guatemalan bases were infested with poisonous snakes and boiling with tension between the gringos and Cuban trainees—they were fed up with the bad food, the inadequate medical services, and the second-class treatment their patrons allotted to them. Some gave up and left. By January 1961, they were on the point of shooting at each other. The Guatemalan army, too, no longer able to tolerate the discriminatory treatment or the subordinate role assigned it by gringos and "mercenaries," confronted them.[32]

The Cuban brigade was becoming unmanageable, not only because of the high tensions at the bases, but also because of the "relief" its members sought off base. They left in droves in search of prostitutes, sometimes going as far away as Mexico. Guatemalan president General Miguel Ydígoras Fuentes informed Washington about this "dangerous" situation and asked for help in resolving it. He had set up a whorehouse near the base stocked not with young Guatemalans but with Salvadoran and Costa Rican women. With so much pillow talk going on, he was afraid that secrets embarrassing to his government and to the United States would be revealed. The CIA refused to allow the contributors' money to be used (at least openly) to satisfy the lusts of the brigade.[33]

On March 11, 1961, at a meeting at the White House that Schlesinger termed "intimidating," the Secretaries of State and Defense, three members of the Joint Chiefs of Staff dressed in uniform and wearing decorations, and numerous assistants and hawkish aides pressed the President to launch the invasion. One of those present warned, "Don't forget that we have a disposal problem. If we have to take these men out of Guatemala, we will have to transfer them to the United States, and we cannot have them wandering around the country telling everyone what they have been doing." They insisted that if the United States demobilized these troops, they could refuse to surrender their arms, and if the United States dispersed them they would tell all of Latin America that the United States had turned its back on them and would provoke other Communist takeovers in the hemisphere.[34] In a press conference a week before the invasion, Kennedy said that United States troops would not take part in any action against Cuba. He wanted to indicate to the public that the coming invasion, which was already common knowledge, was an affair among Cubans.[35]

For Kennedy the situation was irreversible. He reluctantly agreed to send the anti-Castro forces to the destination they had chosen: Cuba. The 2506 Brigade was composed of 1,500 "magnificently" trained men, with uniforms, weapons, tanks and planes, all provided by the United States, with 6 infantry battalions, 1 company of paratroopers, 61 pilots, and a detachment of frogmen.[36]

On April 15, 1961, two days before the invasion, B-26 bombers blasted Havana, San Antonio de los Baños, Santiago de Cuba, and other cities, leaving many casualties and destroying a large part of the Cuban air force. The United Nations General Assembly, meeting in New York, immediately had to address the Cuban denunciation of this new and serious act of aggression by the United States. Washington maintained that the bombardment was an act against Castro's government by deserters from the Cuban air forces, but the Cuban government immediately demonstrated that it had been a clumsy CIA operation. Cuban Chancellor Raúl Roa declared before the Assembly that the type of aircraft used did not exist in Cuba, the planes were painted with false insignias and had taken off from Florida. Adlai Stevenson, the United States' ambassador to the United Nations, vigorously defended the story of "deserters" that the State Department had given him. But he had been fooled and set up to defend a lie before the international community. For a man so respected and admired all over the world for his integrity and intellectual honesty, this was an intolerable situation. Four days later, the defeat of the United States at the Bay of Pigs shamed him deeply. Stevenson had opposed this adventure from the start and had repeatedly said as much to the President. At the funeral for the victims of these bombings—shortly before the invasion—Fidel declared that the Cuban Revolution was indeed a socialist one.

On April 17, 1961, the invasion brigade set out from Puerto Cabezas in Nicaragua, sailing out in seven ships escorted by the United States fleet. It disembarked at dawn in the Bay of Pigs (known as Girón Beach to Cubans), 125 miles from Havana. After seventy-two hours of intense combat, the Cuban army had sunk 4 ships, shot down 5 planes, killed 89 invaders (at a cost of 157 deaths among the defenders), and taken 1,197 prisoners. The decimated flotilla returned to its port. The invasion was Cuba's great triumph and a big fiasco for Kennedy. He admitted his defeat.

The captives, left to their fate, had to face the tribunals of the Revolution. Several Batista-era war criminals, recognized by the people when they were shown on television, were indicted, some put before a firing squad and others condemned to long prison terms. There was a great deal of bitterness and resentment among the prisoners, many of whom claimed that the United States had tricked them and openly regretted their involvement in this dangerous enterprise. Arthur Schlesinger wrote, "Fidel Castro turned out to be a far more formidable foe and in command of a better organized regime than anyone had supposed. His patrols spotted the invasion at almost the first possible moment. His planes reacted with speed and vigor. His police eliminated any chance of sabotage or rebellion behind the lines. His soldiers stayed loyal and fought hard."[37]

Fidel demanded that the United States pay reparations in kind (500 tractors) for the damage done and promised to return more than a thousand prisoners. After long negotiations, according to United States records, Fidel received $53 million dollars worth of food and medicine (donated by the private sector), though Fidel claimed that the donations amounted to no more than $43 million. Cuba returned many of the prisoners to Miami in December 1962, so that they could enjoy the Christmas holiday with their families.[38] They were welcomed as "the heroes of Girón." The rest remained in Cuban prisons.

The United States' defeat at the Bay of Pigs was not only a great military victory for Cuba but a political triumph as well. For Kennedy, it was not only a great national and international fiasco, but an embarrassing situation before the nation; it became clear that the president had lied to the people. Nevertheless, public opinion solidly supported him. A month later, according to a Gallup poll, his approval rating was 82 percent.

Reaction against the United States was vigorous in several parts of the world. Countless mass demonstrations in support of Cuba and in condemnation of "Yankee imperialism" occurred in many cities including New York City, Rome, Milan, Moscow, Montevideo, Warsaw, Bucharest, Buenos Aires, Bonn, Berlin, Recife, Bogotá, Caracas, Tokyo, Guayaquil, and Guatemala City. In several capitals the American embassies were stoned, their flags burned in the streets. Throughout Latin America, congresses, student movements, politicians and intellectuals, and the press condemned this aggressive behavior, alleging that the United States had violated standards of international law and the charters of both the UN and the OAS.

Kennedy took responsibility for the failure, recalling the old adage, "Victory has a hundred fathers, but defeat is an orphan." Later he regretted having persuaded the *New York Times* to drop its denunciations of the preparations for the invasion of Cuba—as he had done by citing reasons of national security. If the newspaper had persisted, he believed, he might have been dissuaded. Kennedy held the CIA responsible for the fiasco and heads began to roll, leading to the fall of CIA Director Allan Dulles and of Deputy Director for Planning Richard Bissell—considered one of the agency's best minds.[39] Kennedy named John McCone the new director (1961–1965), and Richard

Helms as deputy director (1962–1965). Some considered the departure of the old guard, the *Torquemadas* of Cold War anti-Communism, the end of the CIA's Golden Age; for others it marked the end of the agency's most sinister period, characterized by murders, assassination attempts on foreign leaders, and coups d'état in other countries.

Every year on April 19 the Cuban government commemorates its victory in Playa Girón (the Bay of Pigs), the "first defeat of Imperialism in America." On the same day in Miami, Cuban-Americans and veterans of the invasion gather at the monument they erected to honor the "Martyrs of Girón" to celebrate their "heroic deed." They bring floral offerings and make speeches in which "resentments are recited, rosaries of broken promises. Occasions of error are recounted, imperfect understandings, instances in which the superimposition of Washington abstractions on Miami possibilities may or may not have been, in a word Washington came to prefer during the 1980s, flawed," wrote Joan Didion in her book *Miami*. She recalled the melancholic words of Reagan's United Nations Ambassador Jeane Kirkpatrick, at the anniversary event in 1986. "How different would the world have been" if the brigade had triumphed.[40]

"GETTING RID" OF FIDEL

After the Bay of Pigs fiasco Kennedy toughened his policies concerning Cuba, extended the economic embargo, and became even more determined to overthrow Fidel. CIA Director William Colby (1973–1976) claimed that Kennedy had ordered the CIA to use its covert-action capabilities to "get rid of" the Cuban leader, "with all the ambiguity that phrase implies."[41] The CIA set up "Operation Mongoose," the most expansive and costly operation at the time, run by Attorney General Robert F. Kennedy and General Maxwell Taylor. No operation had been as carefully tended to, more secretive, of higher priority, or treated with a greater sense of urgency. The Kennedys wanted quick results. The special group created to supervise the operation scheduled Fidel's downfall for October 1962, believing that the operation could count on Cuban popular support. Its planner could not have been more wrong.[42]

The CIA proceeded to recruit agents to infiltrate into Cuba. Most of these were Cuban exiles. It also recruited foreign businessmen and diplomats. The prime objective was to assassinate Fidel. The Senate commission chaired by Frank Church, which investigated the Watergate scandal in the 1970s, confirmed several of the attempts to assassinate Fidel, some of which were coordinated with the Mafia dons Meyer Lansky, John Roselli, Sam Giancana, and Santo Trafficante, whose businesses in the island were cut off by the Revolution.[43/44] According to a CIA agent, Robert Kennedy was furious when he learned of such agreements, since they could derail the case he was building against Giancana and Roselli. Several agents testified that the Kennedys were keenly aware of their plans to assassinate the Cuban leader.[45]

The CIA installed an enormous espionage apparatus at the University of Miami, "the biggest base ever created on United States territory," code-named JM WAVE. It had an annual budget of $100 million, 600 employees, and more than 3,000 agents.[46] It was equipped with small boats, mother ships disguised as merchant ships, planes (from the CIA front, Southern Air Transport), a huge arsenal, and safe houses and buildings. Between January and August 1961 it carried out 5,780 acts of sabotage and terrorism against Cuba, including attempts on Fidel's life with the cooperation of Mafia.

OAS: THE "COLONIAL MINISTRY"

Washington sought judicial formalities and continental support for the development of its policies regarding Cuba through the OAS, where it could count on easy majorities. As Eisenhower did, Kennedy relied on unconditional solidarity from the Central American and Caribbean dictatorships and from most democratic governments. But in the case of Cuba, he failed to get the backing of the most influential nations.

Washington made active diplomatic efforts to isolate Cuba from the rest of the continent and to expel it from the Inter-American system. The United States succeeded in getting Peru to call the Eighth Consultative Meeting of the OAS, under Article 6 of the Treaty of Rio, which was invoked only in cases of armed aggression. The majority of the OAS members supported the move; few abstained, Mexico voted against it, arguing that Cuba had not committed any acts of armed aggression or territorial violation, and that it was not threatening the independence of any member nation, thus the convocation of this meeting under the Treaty of Rio lacked the necessary legal basis.[47]

In January 1962 the Eighth Consultative Meeting held in Punta del Este, Uruguay, met to consider "the threats to peace and political independence of American states that might result from the intervention of extracontinental powers" and "the incompatibility of the inter-American system with all forms of totalitarianism." This was the argument used to expel Cuba. The Kennedy team obtained the necessary majority by buying Haiti's vote for $43 million

(Haiti had indicated that it would abstain). Cuba was "suspended"—expelled—from the OAS and the Inter-American system. In addition, the meeting decreed a collective break with the Cuban government. Argentina, Brazil, Chile, Mexico, Ecuador, and Bolivia abstained, allegedly on legal grounds, and did not sever relations with Cuba as directed. Brazil, Chile, Ecuador, and Mexico also abstained from a resolution that decreed a suspension of commerce with Cuba. Between 1962 and 1963 Argentina, Bolivia, Brazil, Chile, Ecuador, and Uruguay broke off relations with Cuba after they had fallen under military dictatorships.[48]

This meeting represented another lamentable episode in the history of the regional organization, which always bowed to Washington's dictates. This time it supported Washington in spite of the fact that nothing in the OAS Charter allowed for the expulsion or suspension of one of its member nations. The arguments for the "incompatibility" of the Inter-American system with "any form of totalitarianism" and for the defense of "representative democracy" were unsustainable, since the majority of the Organization's member at this time were dictatorships that had never been challenged by the defenders of democracy.

Fidel responded to the Punta del Este Declaration with the Second Havana Declaration, which was approved, as the first, by a massive concentration of people in the Plaza de la Revolución. The declaration accused the United States and the Latin American oligarchies of being responsible for the misery of their people; what united and incited them against Cuba, he said, was a fear not of the Cuban revolution but of a Latin American revolution in which "workers, campesinos, students, intellectuals, and progressive sectors might take power by means of revolution among the oppressed and hungry peoples exploited by the Yankee monopolies and the reactionary oligarchy of America."[49]

To the accusations that Cuba was exporting its revolution, Fidel responded that revolutions were not exported but made by the people. He also charged that the United States, along with the "reactionary oligarchies," was creating an apparatus to repress the struggles of these people with "blood and fire." He further alleged that the Inter-American Joint Defense Board, the United States military missions on the continent, its schools in the Panama Canal Zone, and the CIA were all training armies in "the subtlest forms of assassination" and turning them into tools for the United States' interests. He exhorted the people to rebel against their oppressors. He asserted that Cuba had set the example: "The duty of every revolutionary is to make revolution!" He concluded with the slogan "*Patria o Muerte, Venceremos*" (Motherland or Death, We Shall

Win)[50] amid thunderous applause and shouts of the people in defense of their revolution and their support of Fidel.

THE OCTOBER CRISIS

In September 1962 the United States administration and Congress, citing the Monroe Doctrine, unleashed a tenacious and belligerent campaign against Cuba. At a meeting of the Senate Foreign Relations and the Armed Services Committees with administration officials on September 17—a meeting that lasted five hours and had standing room only—it was agreed that direct action should be taken against Cuba. Three days later the Senate unanimously passed a resolution recommending that all means, "including the use of force," be used to prevent Cuba from extending its subversive activities to any part of the hemisphere. Six days later the House of Representatives passed a similar bill by a vote of 384 to 7.[51]

That same September, Kennedy ordered a close watch—by air, by sea, and on land—of the island. He intensified surveillance flights. Five U-2 airplanes set off on espionage flights, but bad weather kept them from taking aerial photographs. On September 16, a CIA report on the "latest Soviet military activities in Cuba" stated that the Soviet Union was building eight launching pads for surface-to-air missiles and would "eventually" build twenty-four more. Three days later the CIA reported that the agency did not believe that the Soviet Union intended to place nuclear weapons in Cuba, though to do so would be good military strategy, because of the immense risk it would present.[52] By then thirty Soviet R-12 missiles had arrived in Cuba, and more were on the way.[53]

Washington was alarmed by a report from the Soviet press agency TASS dated September 11 to the effect that the Soviet Union would respond to an attack on Cuba and that such an attack would be tantamount to a declaration of nuclear war. Presidential adviser Theodore Sorensen noted that this announcement stirred up a number of inquiries, for at that given moment an attack "here" could be retaliated "there." That *here* and *there* described a world map on which the two superpowers had sensitive objectives dispersed over several continents. What Washington feared most was an act of retaliation against Berlin. In the transcript of the recordings made in the Oval Office during the crisis, this was the most resonant and constant concern.[54]

In October the CIA informed Kennedy that more than one hundred ships of the Soviet Union and Communist bloc nations were arriving and unloading at Cuban ports; the agency suspected that the cargo consisted of military materials. However, it was not until October 14 that the CIA's aerial photographs detected the presence of Soviet missiles in San Cristóbal in the province of Pinar del Río. The President demanded better proof and more photographs, sufficiently enlarged for the necessary details to be clearly visible. When he confirmed the presence of these missiles, he called a top-secret meeting with the Executive Committee of the National Security Council (ExCom), including the secretaries of state and defense, the director of the CIA, Attorney General Robert Kennedy, and United Nations Ambassador Adlai Stevenson. ExCom's meetings were held in strict secrecy; public awareness of the presence of nuclear weapons 90 miles from the United States would create panic, both domestically and internationally.

On October 18, a date set long before the crisis, Soviet Chancellor Andrei Gromyko had met with President Kennedy. Unaware that Kennedy knew of the presence of Soviet nuclear missiles in Cuba, Gromyko assured him that Soviet military aid to the island solely consisted of defensive weapons. The Soviet troops, he claimed, were there only to train Cubans. The missiles were not mentioned. Kennedy held his tongue, but he was tremendously irritated by Gromyko's hypocrisy; as they spoke, Soviet ships were sailing toward Cuba carrying forty-two nuclear missiles—each more powerful than the Hiroshima bomb—that posed a definite threat to the security of the United States. This was the first time that the Soviet Union had installed nuclear weapons outside its own territory.[55]

ExCom considered a number of options: massive invasion, naval blockade, "surgical" strikes on the launching complexes (though such an attack would run the risk of killing many Cubans and Soviets), pressuring Khrushchev to remove the weapons, proposing a summit meeting, offering to remove United States missiles in Turkey and Italy in exchange for removal of the ones in Cuba, sending secret messages to Castro in an effort to separate him from the Soviet Union, declaring a state of emergency, asking Congress to declare war on Cuba, calling for United Nations and OAS inspection commissions, managing the crisis through secret diplomacy, or doing nothing. The Pentagon advisers suggested inaction, reminding Kennedy that the United States had long been within reach of Soviet missiles and that Khrushchev lived with American missiles on his borders. They counseled the President to deal with the situation calmly, to keep Khrushchev from escalating the tension.[56]

Some ExCom members were in favor of an air attack. Others supported an invasion. Twenty years later Robert McNamara remembered that at that moment they were unaware of the presence of Soviet troops in Cuba, and that an invasion or air attack would have led to a terrible massacre. The Cubans calculated that it would have cost the lives of 100,000 Cubans and Soviets.[57] Kennedy knew that confrontation with the Soviet Union would have unforseeable consequences, including the danger of nuclear conflagration.[58] ExCom worked around the clock for days, calculating the risks of retaliation by Moscow if the United States were to take action against Cuba and the NATO allies' response if there were to be Soviet retaliation against Berlin. It could not allow the Europeans to believe that the United States would put their security at risk in order to protect its interests in the Caribbean, a region foreign to them.

Robert Kennedy was against an attack on Cuba. He thought it would be a "Pearl Harbor in reverse, and it would blacken the name of the United States in the pages of history." He added that an attack by a great power on a small neighbor would affect Latin America and produce new Castros and that the Cuban people would not forgive the United States for decades to come.[59]

While these tense secret meetings were taking place in the White House, military preparations were in full swing. Troops were moved to Florida, defense commandos stationed in the Caribbean and the Atlantic were put on red alert, and 85,000 men and a powerful war machine were mobilized to move on the Caribbean. On October 22 alone there were 368 espionage flights over Cuba.[60]

At 7:00 PM that day, the most serious crisis to threaten humanity since the Second World War broke out. Kennedy informed the United States and the world that his intelligence services had discovered Soviet nuclear missiles in Cuba. He called the installation "a deliberately provocative and unjustified change in the status quo," unacceptable to the United States. President Kennedy announced that he would impose a naval "quarantine" on Cuba to block the arrival of new shipments, and he warned that a nuclear attack on the United States from Cuba would be considered an attack by the Soviet Union, requiring a "full retaliatory response." Never before had the President so carefully prepared a speech.[61]

An hour before the President's speech, Foy Kohler, the United States ambassador to Moscow, delivered a letter from Kennedy to the Kremlin addressed to Khrushchev in which Kennedy accused the Soviet Union of aggression. Along with the letter, Kennedy sent a copy of the speech he would deliver that night.

Kennedy did not want to undertake a naval blockade without Latin American support, an element important both to opponents and to allies. But if he could not gain such support, he would still forge ahead since a blockade was a legitimate act of defense and served the security of the hemisphere.[62] On October 23 he called an urgent consultative meeting of the OAS. The members unanimously approved a resolution authorizing the use of force and the blockade of the island, and they demanded the immediate withdrawal of the missiles. Several countries offered the United States military assistance. Venezuela offered ships, Argentina two destroyers, Honduras and Peru troops, and six countries of the Caribbean region the temporary use of their naval bases.[63] The United States proceeded to blockade Cuba.[63] The Soviet Union objected to the decision by the OAS, arguing that the organization lacked the legal authority to take such action.[64]

The United Nations Security Council met in an urgent session on October 23 to consider the petitions made to the Council president, in separate communications, by the United States, Cuba, and the Soviet Union. The United States was set to take up the matter of "the dangerous threat to world peace and security by the secret placement of nuclear missiles in Cuba on the part of the Soviet Union." Cuba wanted the Council to consider "the unilateral act of war by the United States government in ordering the naval blockade" of its country, and the Soviet Union demanded that the Security Council deal with "the violation of the UN Charter and the threat to peace on the part of the United States" In an attached declaration, the Soviet Union accused the United States of unleashing a worldwide thermonuclear war. Both the Soviet Union and the United States expressed willingness to hold talks on the situation. The United States presented the Security Council with a draft resolution demanding the immediate dismantling of the missiles and asking that the United Nations send observers to Cuba to verify compliance with the resolution. The Cuban representative warned that his government would not accept observers in matters under its internal jurisdiction.[65]

That same evening, on television and radio, Fidel spoke of the blockade as an act of aggression. He said that "Cuba needs to account to no one for the measures it takes in its defense," categorically rejecting the United States' pretensions to inspect Cuban territory and decide what kind of weapons and how many his country may or may not have.[66]

The situation was extremely dangerous. Any incident between the United States air and naval forces and the Soviet ships could set off a nuclear conflict. On October 24 the press services reported that eighteen Soviet freighters had set out for Cuba, escorted by eight submarines. Debate continued at the United Nations. National tension eased when television news in the United States showed the Soviet ships turning back toward their own country—

United States Air Force craft kept them under surveillance all the way back to their ports.[67]

On October 23 Cuba was readying for war. Infantry divisions, antiaircraft artillery, and fighter planes were all put on alert, and 400,000 combatants from the three branches of the armed forces and the popular defense forces were mobilized. Raúl Castro and Che Guevara took political-military command in the provinces of Oriente and Pinar del Río, and Juan Almeida commanded the forces in Santa Clara. And along with the missiles, 43,000 Soviet troops had arrived in Cuba.[68]

On October 25 the Security Council decided to suspend its meetings while United Nations Secretary General U Thant continued negotiating with the three nations involved in the conflict. In communiqués dated October 24, U Thant asked Khrushchev to voluntarily suspend the shipment of arms to Cuba for a period of three weeks, requested that Kennedy lift the quarantine, and asked Fidel to help find solutions to the "impasse" and suspend the installation of the missiles. U Thant offered to serve as mediator, receiving favorable responses from Kennedy and Khrushchev, and an invitation from Fidel to visit Havana to discuss the situation with him in person. U Thant arrived in Havana on October 30, returning the next day. He reported that his talks with Fidel had been "fruitful and cordial." The Security Council did not meet about the crisis again.[69]

Between October 22 and the beginning of December, Kennedy and Khrushchev exchanged more than twenty letters, some published and others kept confidential, in which they accused each other of having set off this explosive crisis. But they also called on each other to exercise prudence. Khrushchev insisted that the weapons he had sent to Cuba were strictly "defensive," intended to confront American aggression, and, in a letter to Kennedy, he accused the United States of meddling in affairs that were the sole concern of Cuba and the Soviet Union. He called the blockade an "act of piracy or, if you prefer, of the insanity of degenerate capitalism." Kennedy saw things in terms of hemispheric security and the balance of forces. In letters to Khrushchev he stated that he would not tolerate any measure that altered the current balance and signaled that secretly providing Cuba with offensive weapons and the "false" declarations of the Soviet government were a threat that merited the "quarantine," which was a "minimal response."[70]

On October 26 the situation began to change, starting with a strange conversation in a Washington restaurant, to which a Soviet Embassy official invited a correspondent from ABC television. The Soviet official told the reporter that the Soviet Union would agree to dismantle the launching pads and pull out the missiles, allow the United Nations to supervise the withdrawal, and commit itself to discontinuing the missile shipments if the United States would publicly promise not to invade Cuba. A few hours later a letter from Khrushchev with the same proposal arrived at the White House.[71]

ExCom had not finished digesting the letter when another arrived in which Khrushchev proposed an exchange of missile withdrawals: the missiles in Turkey for those in Cuba. This proposal worried the White House because it seemed that Khrushchev was raising the ante. Kennedy did not want to make a public commitment, since the withdrawal of missiles from Turkey and Italy would create problems with NATO. ExCom decided to respond to the first letter without mentioning the proposed exchange. The reply merely accepted the basis for the agreement proposed by Khrushchev, but noted that the installation of missiles must be suspended and the missiles rendered inoperative under effective United Nations supervision.[72]

The option of an invasion was still on the table. Kennedy asked the state department to organize a civilian government for the island.[73] In the meantime the construction of ramps for the missiles continued, and Fidel gave the order to fire at the U-2s that were violating Cuban air space with low-level flights. One was shot down over eastern Cuba as ordered by a Soviet general. This news caused consternation in Washington.

Fidel feared that the situation would end horribly. He didn't know that Khrushchev had already offered to dismantle the launching pads and pull out the missiles. On the night of October 26 Fidel went to the Soviet Embassy to send a letter to Khrushchev (it was translated into Russian by Soviet officials on the spot). He foresaw an imminent attack on his country, within the next twenty-four to seventy-two hours. It might come in the form of an aerial attack, aiming for the destruction of certain targets, or an invasion, though he believed the latter less likely, since it would require a large number of forces—"the most repulsive sort of aggression"—and this necessity might deter the United States. In the case of an invasion, he added, "the danger posed to humanity by such an aggressive policy is so great" that the Soviet Union must never allow "the imperialists" to strike the first nuclear blow. "[T]his is the moment to eliminate such danger forever by an act of the most legitimate defense, as difficult and terrible as the solution must be, for there is no other." The letter was delivered at dawn on October 28, Moscow time. Khrushchev was terrified, for he thought Fidel was proposing a preemptive nuclear strike against the United States.[74]

Khrushchev continued dousing the bonfire. In a message broadcast on Radio Moscow that day, he said that he trusted Kennedy's statement in which he accepted the condition that he would not invade Cuba and that the United Nations would oversee the dismantling of the missiles.[75]

This radio message was met in Washington with feelings of great relief. Kennedy sent four officials to New York to ask U Thant to order inspectors to Cuba immediately, since the Soviets were in agreement. U Thant could not accede, stating that such an order exceeded his powers. Kennedy responded the same day in a radio message in which he reiterated his demand for "immediate" United Nations inspection and the dismantling of the missiles so he could lift the blockade. These two letters ended the most dangerous chapter of the crisis. ExCom decided to pressure the Soviet Union to withdraw the IL-28 bombers from Cuba as well, deeming them "offensive" weapons.[76]

When Fidel learned of the agreement between Kennedy and Khrushchev concerning withdrawls, he wrote to U Thant repeating that he would "not permit unilateral inspection, national or international, on Cuban territory."[77] Fidel subjected Khrushchev to the humiliation of having to allow the inspection of his ships on the high seas by United States military personnel. On January 7, 1963, Kennedy and Khrushchev, in a joint letter, thanked U Thant for his efforts, while Fidel told him that these negotiations did not lead to "an effective agreement guaranteeing a permanent peace in the Caribbean, nor do they relieve the existing tensions." He stated that the United States had not "renounced its aggressive and interventionist policies" and still maintained a posture of force in violation of international law.[78]

THE CRISIS FROM A DISTANCE

In 1987 Harvard University called together high Soviet and American officials who were involved in the October missile crisis, to analyze these events, establish their origin, background, development, their lessons, and their consequences. Such conferences continued in Moscow in 1989, in Antigua in 1991, and in Havana in 1992. High Cuban officials participated in the last two of these conferences, and Fidel himself took part in the Havana session.

Participants from the Kennedy team included former Secretary of Defense Robert McNamara, former Security Adviser McGeorge Bundy, former presidential advisers Arthur Schlesinger and Theodore Sorensen, and former Press Secretary Pierre Salinger, as well as high-ranking military officers and advisers. Attendees for the Soviets were Chancellor Andrei Gromyko; Anatoly Dobrinin, the former ambassador to Washington (1962–1986) during the Cold War; the former ambassador to Havana, Aleksandr Alexeiev; Nikita Khrushchev's son Sergei; the son (also named Sergei) of Anastas Mikoyan, a senior envoy; and top military officers and advisers all participated. In addition to Fidel himself, Jorge Risquet, Generals Fabián Escalante and Sergio del Valle, and other high officials joined in the discussion.

They drew important conclusions: that the world had been on the verge of nuclear war, that Washington's and Moscow's evaluations of the situation had not been free of "profound perceptual errors throughout the four decades" of the Cold War. Any small error in calculations or perception, claimed McNamara, might have thrown the world into a state of catastrophe. Sorensen commented that on October 27, Kennedy had told him, "If we are wrong on this occasion, there could be 200 million dead." He believed that Kennedy foresaw the possibility of nuclear war.[79]

Another conclusion was that this crisis had arisen from the aggressive policies of the United States against Cuba and the Soviet government's conviction that the threat of invasion was real, leading to the decision to place nuclear missiles in Cuba for its defense and as a means of dissuasion.[80] Sergei Khrushchev stated that ever since the Vienna Summit in June 1961, his father was convinced that Kennedy, still reeling with anger over the Bay of Pigs, was determined to overthrow Castro. He communicated this impression to Fidel. Fidel in turn believed that the United States' next move would be direct intervention, since Washington could not organize another invasion by mercenaries. He noted that there could not be many people who would be willing to "embark" on such an adventure.[81]

Sergei Khrushchev further commented that in 1961 his father believed that Cuba could not put up greater resistance to the United States-sponsored mercenary invasion then underway. The Soviet leader believed that after the mercenaries landed, the United States would land its own troops. The idea that prevailed in the Soviet Union was that the Cuban Revolution was doomed to failure. "We underestimated the weapons Cuba had and the Cuban determination to resist." The news of the defeat of the United States' adventure was cause for celebration, not only for the Cubans, but for the Soviets as well. "This date marked a change in our relations with Cuba, and it was decided that we can and must send weapons to resist the next United States aggression." In September 1961 Cuba and the Soviet Union signed a military treaty, but it did not mention nuclear arms. This came later. Between 1962 and 1963 the Soviet Union provided Cuba with MIG fighter planes, bombers, helicopters, radio and radar transmitters and receivers, transport vehicles, airport equipment, and repair facilities and ammunition for every class of weapons—enough to resist a limited attack.[82]

Khrushchev made the decision to place nuclear missiles in Cuba during a visit to Bulgaria in May 1962. He was convinced that only nuclear weapons would prevent intervention by the United States. The great distance separating their two countries did not allow the Soviet Union to defend Cuba with conventional arms, as it could in the case of Czechoslovakia or Poland.[83]

On May 29, 1962, an important Soviet delegation led by Sharaf Rashidov in capacity of Deputy Member of the Presidium of the Soviet Communist Party's Central Committee, and including Chief of the Strategic Missile Forces Sergei Beriuzov, Aleksandr Alexeiev (shortly thereafter named ambassador to Cuba), and other high officials, arrived in Cuba. They came under the guise of an agricultural mission, using assumed names, to discuss with the Cuban leaders the possibility of installing the nuclear missiles on the island.[84]

The Cuban leaders studied the proposal, and Fidel did not hesitate to accept it as "an elementary duty of solidarity and internationalism" to fortify the socialist camp, though he recognized that such a measure was not free of risks for Cuba, since it would convert the island into a strategic target.[85]

Fidel suggested that the Soviets include the issue of nuclear missiles in their bilateral military treaty and that the matter be dealt with openly, since the treaty was between two sovereign countries and met the standards of international law. He feared that such a large operation would be discovered sooner or later by United States intelligence, and that the United States' reaction would be violent. The Soviets replied that they would go public only after the missiles had been installed. They argued that the installation had to be done in secret, otherwise Washington would prevent the manuever. They would make it public in November during Khrushchev's visit to Cuba. Raúl Castro, minister of the Revolutionary Armed Forces, went to Moscow in May to discuss the military aspects of the operation.[86]

The text of the treaty was approved after mutual official visits between Havana and Moscow. It included an introduction written by Fidel, listing the political and judicial grounds on which the treaty was based. The document was given the title, "Cuban-Soviet Mutual Defense" Treaty, but because of the crisis it was never signed.

The installation, code-named ANADIR (after a river in Russia), began in early June 1962. By September thirty R-12 missiles and 43,000 troops had arrived in Cuba. It took seventy-six days to transport the missiles from the

Soviet missile center and move them onto their launching sites. This huge military undertaking passed unnoticed by United States intelligence. In October the final thirty R-12 missiles arrived. The R-14s were stopped by the naval blockade. A hundred ships secretly transported the missiles, which were unloaded at night. During these months the United States intelligence services became aware of the unusual movement of Soviet ships and flags of Communist nations into Cuban ports. The Cuban population noticed long convoys of large trucks moving without lights through the island at night, manned by foreign crews, some in uniform and some in plain clothes. Cuba is long and narrow, measuring 75 miles at it widest point and 28 miles at its narrowest, without forests that might conceal such an operation. This situation worried the Cuban leaders. Mistakes on the part of the Soviets made it easier for United States spy planes to detect the convoys. If Cuba had controlled the operation, Fidel affirmed, Cuban air defenses would have fired on such planes.[87]

Sergei Mikoyan recalled that when his father went to Havana after the October crisis and asked Fidel why he had accepted the missiles, Fidel responded, perplexed, that he thought the Soviet Union needed to place them. It was an act of assistance to the Soviet Union, which was surrounded by United States missiles aimed at strategic targets. The transaction arose from a misunderstanding, noted Mikoyan, since "we thought that we were doing it for the Cubans, and the Cubans thought they were doing it for us."[88]

THE PRICE OF THE CRISIS

Kennedy's determination to force the withdrawal of the missiles at any cost left Khrushchev no choice but to yield; withdrawal was the only way to prevent a serious conflict. In the international front, this decision carried a high political price for the Soviet Union—its image was tarnished—and for Khrushchev himself. It was one of the reasons for his political demise. As the missiles began to be withdrawn, the Cuban people chanted, "*Nikita, Nikita, lo que se da no se quita*" ("Nikita, Nikita, what you give you can't take back."). In a profound controversy with the Soviet Union, China openly supported Cuba and accused the Soviets of adventurism and capitulation.

International reaction to the crisis was ambivalent. The British prime minister, Harold Macmillan, told Kennedy that Western Europe, accustomed to living under the "nuclear gun," wondered what all the fuss was about, but he gave his support to the United States. Hugh Gaitskell, head of the British Labor Party, expressed doubts about the legality of the quarantine. France's president, Charles de Gaulle, supported Kennedy without heeding the popular demonstrations of solidarity with Cuba or the influential media critics in his nation. The German leaders Konrad Adenauer and Willy Brandt "did not flinch or complain." European pacifists staged massive demonstrations to protest the quarantine imposed on Cuba without mentioning or questioning the presence of the missiles. The British philosopher Bertrand Russell publicly expressed his forceful objections. "Within a week you will all be dead to please American madmen." He sent a message to Kennedy, calling his action rash, unjustified, and a threat to the survival of humankind, and in another to Khrushchev he remarked, "Your continued forbearance is our great hope."[89]

Press reaction was also ambivalent. The *New York Times* commented that the President's actions constituted the least he could have done. The *New York Post* maintained that Kennedy should first have consulted the United Nations and the OAS. The *Times* of London wondered if there were really any missiles in Cuba to begin with, and the *Guardian* said Khrushchev had given the United States a lesson in "the meaning of United States bases close to the Soviet border."[90]

With the most serious postwar crisis resolved, the protagonists of the drama prepared to ease tensions and overcome resentments. Khrushchev openly justified Kennedy's reasons for demanding the removal of the missiles: "Not to have believed him would have meant war."[91] Kennedy and Khrushchev installed the "hot line" between Washington and Moscow to avoid accidents or costly errors.

In October 1963 the two superpowers met in Moscow and signed the Partial Test Ban Treaty prohibiting nuclear testing in the atmosphere, outer space, and underwater. This treaty represented their biggest step toward disarmament to date.

Khrushchev's management of the crisis was frustrating, offensive, and humiliating to the Cuban leaders, since he made the decision to withdraw the missiles without consulting or even informing them—they learned of the decision through international cables. Fidel argued that Khrushchev should have consulted with Cuba, have negotiated with the United States on the end of the blockade; cessation of all subversive activities; a halt to all "piratical attacks" against Cuba; respect for Cuba's airspace and territorial waters; and on the return of Guantanamo Bay. He told Khrushchev that none of these matters had been resolved and that the causes that led to the crisis remained intact.

Kennedy's promise not to attack Cuba was not enough. Khrushchev explained that the pressure of the situation had left him no time in which to consult with Fidel. Fidel did not accept this explanation; Khrushchev should have demanded a meeting of the Soviets with the Cuban government, and he should have insisted that negotiations be handled by the three parties in question.[92]

The Soviet Union wanted to erase resentments. Anastas Mikoyan arrived in Havana to smooth over relations with Fidel. They did not speak about the past, only about the future. Good relations with the Soviet Union were vital to the Cuban Revolution. The Communist superpower had been a steady and generous ally. After the crisis Cuba also wanted to reestablish cordial relations. Cuba reiterated its gratitude for the assistance the Soviet Union had given it, renewed its expressions of friendship, and reaffirmed the Marxist-Leninist character of the Revolution. At the forty-fifth anniversary of the bolshevik revolution in Moscow, the Cuban national anthem was played—an unexpected and warm gesture to Cuba on so solemn an occasion.

Fidel was a hard pill for the Soviet Union to swallow—the Cuban leader was like none of its other allies. Che recounted that when Mikoyan made his first visit to Havana in 1960 he remarked that the Cuban Revolution "[wa]s a phenomenon Marx did not foresee."[93]

ARE KENNEDY'S POLICIES FAILING?

In 1963 Kennedy's policies regarding Cuba were not working. The economic blockade did nothing to weaken the island, and Cuba's relations with the Soviet Union and the socialist bloc grew closer every day. Operation Mongoose, plotted by the United States to overthrow Fidel, was abandoned after the missile crisis in October 1962. The operation was a costly failure.

Kennedy's vigorous defense of democracies and his criticism of dictatorships, which he had been making since his campaign—the international community believed he would be a defense against coups d'état and dictatorships—also fell apart after an avalanche of military coups was launched against constitutional governments and Kennedy ended up recognizing all these new dictators. In 1962 and 1963 Arturo Frondizi in Argentina, Carlos Julio Arosmena in Ecuador, Manuel Prado y Urgarteche in Peru, Juan Bosch in the Dominican Republic, and Ramón Villeda Morales in Honduras all fell. It was said that the coup against the corrupt and erratic General Miguel Ydígoras Fuentes of Guatemala was carried out with Washington's support.

The new Kennedy administration policy regarding the role of Latin

American military in their governments caused great alarm on the southern continent, as explained in an article by Undersecretary of State for Inter-American Affairs Edwin Martin, published in the *New York Herald Tribune* in October 1963. The article argues that the military must be "helped" to assume a more constructive role in times of peace, to maintain internal security, to work with civilian-military programs, and to formulate national policies. He cited military governments that had, in his opinion, realized important social and economic reforms.[94] This policy, contravening constitutional mandates that assigned the military only the defense of national sovereignty, was one of the most controversial and negative legacies of Kennedy's administration. Participation by the armed forces in matters of internal security and the control of public order with Washington's blessing turned to brutal repression, campaigns of counterinsurgent "pacification," and dirty wars against civilian populations. Three years after Kennedy launched the Alliance for Progress—which the New Frontiersmen considered one of his most important foreign policy initiatives and which could have been an important legacy—he saw it beginning to fail. Kennedy admitted in a public speech that he was "depressed."[95]

The main reasons for the failure of the Alliance was the inefficiency or the reluctance of the governments to carry out the structural and political changes to which they had committed themselves and opposition of powerful economic sectors to such changes, primarily agrarian reform. Fidel praised the Alliance, whose goals were similar to those of the Revolution. He called it an "intelligent strategy," but hopeless because the oligarchies would not allow the reforms.[96] It also failed because of the protectionist laws passed by the United States Congress, which imposed bilateral aid, subject to all sorts of conditions and dependencies, instead of the collective aid agreed upon at Punta del Este.

A LIGHT IS EXTINGUISHED

A brief long-distance exchange between Kennedy and Fidel took place in November 1963, when Kennedy asked Jean Daniel, a reporter for the Paris daily *L'Express*, to come see him—he knew Daniel was going to Havana to interview Fidel. They talked for half an hour on the subject of Cuba. Daniel understood that the President was sending Fidel a message, for as he was leaving, Kennedy said that they would have a more interesting conversation upon his return from the island.[97]

Daniel knew that Kennedy's words about Cuba were unusual for a U.S. president. Kennedy observed that more than any other nation in the world, Cuba had been subjected to economic colonization, humiliation, and exploitation, partly as a result of United States policies regarding Batista's regime. He noted that the United States constructed and enabled Castro's movement without realizing it. "I have understood the Cubans and I approved of Castro's proclamation from the Sierra Maestra and I'll go further: up to a point Batista is the incarnation of a number of United States errors, and now we have to pay for them." Nevertheless, he harshly criticized the Revolution, spoke of Castro's "betrayal" of the promises he had made in the Sierra Maestra, and accused him of becoming a "Soviet agent" in Latin America and bringing the world to the brink of nuclear war.[98]

On November 19, after three weeks of waiting in Havana in hope of meeting with Fidel, just as Jean Daniel was preparing to fly back to Mexico, Fidel sought him out. Over the next three days the two men engaged in a dialogue that lasted some twenty hours. Intrigued by Kennedy's comments on Batista, Fidel asked to hear them again and again. In spite of Kennedy's tenacious harassment and aggression toward Cuba, Fidel admired and respected him. He said that Kennedy had the potential of becoming the greatest United States president, greater even than Lincoln, because he was the first to understand that the coexistence of capitalists and socialists was possible. Since Daniel would be seeing the President again, Fidel asked him to go as "an emissary of peace," telling Kennedy that he, Fidel, neither wanted nor expected anything from the President, but had found positive elements in what Daniel had told him.[99]

They were together in Varadero when the news of Kennedy's assassination in Dallas, Texas, reached them. Profoundly shocked, Fidel repeated several times, "This is bad news. Everything has changed and will change. The United States occupies such a position in the world that the death of its president affects millions of people everywhere. The Cold War, relations with the Soviet Union, Latin America, Cuba, the question of the blacks, everything will have to be rethought. This is a very serious matter, an extremely serious matter." Turning to Daniel, he added: "Look, this is the end of your peace mission."[100]

THE DEATHS OF THREE GIANTS

Kennedy, Khrushchev, and John XXIII, three great figures of the 1960s who fueled great changes, burned brightly and disappeared almost simultaneously. In 1963 the Pope and the President died. The following year brought

Khrushchev's political death. At a plenary session of the Central Committee of the Soviet Communist Party he was "relieved" of his positions in the Party and the government. His downfall was due to accumulated failures and errors, among them his management of the Cuban missile crisis and his responsibility in the break with the People's Republic of China in 1960, which shattered the unity of the Communist world.

As these three giants left the stage, their successors proceeded slowly to close the doors to change and understanding. Paul VI gradually returned the Church to a more conservative line, although his encyclical *Populorum Progressio* followed the trail blazed by the Second Vatican Council, recognizing that the progress of the people was the basis for peace. The changes he introduced, however, were only in liturgy and form. When Vice President Lyndon B. Johnson became president, he abandoned the Alliance for Progress and returned to the hard line of interventionism and "big stick" policies. Leonid Brezhnev introduced the doctrine of "limited sovereignty"—a Soviet Monroe Doctrine—put into effect in 1968 when Soviet tanks and Warsaw Pact troops entered Czechoslovakia to stop a popular liberation uprising: the "Prague Spring." Brezhnev called this brutal intervention "fraternal aid." Ten years later, in 1979, he invaded Afghanistan.

JOHNSON IN THE WHITE HOUSE

Lyndon B. Johnson took the oath of office as the new president of the United States on the plane carrying John F. Kennedy's body to Washington, D.C. He assumed Kennedy's mandate with the tacit promise that he would continue the work of the assassinated president, elevated to the status of hero and martyr.[101]

Kennedy and Johnson could not have been more different. While both were millionaires, Kennedy was an intellectual and a man of the world, while Johnson was a seasoned politician. His manners, his Southern, direct, occasionally crude speech, and his ingenuity made the sophisticated circles of Washington shiver, for they had become accustomed to the courtly style of the Kennedy clan. But Johnson was by turns deeply respected, feared, and admired as a politician. He was the dominant figure in Congress for thirty years. The country trusted his leadership abilities, necessary in those times of grief and confusion.

Aside from the strategic reasons that prompted Kennedy to choose this important Texas politician as his running mate in the election campaign, many were surprised by his choice. But time showed that this choice could not have been better, for they became a charismatic and dynamic duo who complemented each other. Their differences lay not in their politics but in their priorities. Kennedy's preferred field of action was international, and he showed a particular interest in Latin America. The most brilliant advisers of his New Frontier program were experts on Latin American affairs. Johnson's priority concerned national politics, and he demonstrated little or no interest in Latin America.

Kennedy sympathized with Johnson, admired him, and had an attitude of special deference toward him.[102] He knew Johnson as an energetic politician and understood the frustration he must have felt at having so little power in so high an office. He kept Johnson fully informed about the most delicate matters of his administration, turning him into an international figure by sending him as his representative on official visits around the world. Johnson traveled to more than thirty countries in the three years of Kennedy's presidency. Johnson understood and appreciated Kennedy's generosity. The knowledge of the inner workings of the government to which he was made party was fundamental to his ability to maintain continuity during the abrupt transition.

The assassination of the President had a tremendous impact on the American people, yet the transition was seamless. Johnson maintained calm, and he dominated the situation with limitless energy and great dignity, wrote the United States journalist Theodore White.[103] During the early months the New Frontiersmen were grateful for his loyalty to the commitments made by his predecessor. Johnson asked Congress to approve the civil rights legislation for which Kennedy had fought so hard, as the best tribute to his memory. He spoke of national unity and continuity, succeeding in getting Congress to pass a spate of laws on civil rights, tariff reductions, elections, a health program for the elderly, and improved education. Johnson had his own government program, called the Great Society, which summed up the glories of the American Dream of power, prosperity, and equality. He wanted an affluent society, without poverty or injustice and with liberty for all.[104]

"MISSISSIPPI BURNING"

Kennedy and Johnson dedicated themselves to the issue of civil rights and to opposition to racial discrimination more than any other presidents, but during their respective administrations the nation endured the greatest racial violence in its history. "The fires of frustration and discord are burning in every city, North and South, where legal remedies are not at hand," remarked Kennedy shortly before he was assassinated.[105] In several states, including Mississippi, Alabama, Pennsylvania, Maryland, and Massachusetts, blacks marched for civil rights, protesting against school segregation and police brutality.

Students held peaceful marches and demonstrations, uprisings, and violent protests in support of black movements, on university campuses in such cities as Boston and Chicago. In New York some 400,000 students marched in solidarity with the struggle for civil rights. In the face of all this violence and hatred, the Reverend Martin Luther King Jr. led a pacifist movement that sought recognition of black rights and equality in an emphatically nonviolent fashion. His message was one of peace. In 1963 *Time* magazine named him Man of the Year, and in 1964 he was awarded the Nobel Peace Prize.

The deep South—Alabama, Tennessee, and Mississippi—saw the most brutal police violence against black people in the whole country. In 1964 three human rights activists—two white and one black—were murdered in Mississippi at the hands of Ku Klux Klansmen, among them the chief of the state police, who was well known for other atrocious racist acts. This horrendous crime was portrayed in Alan Parker's moving film *Mississippi Burning* (1989), which was nominated for seven Oscars.

The year 1965 was particularly violent. In Selma, Alabama, King was arrested along with 2,000 peaceful demonstrators. In New York the charismatic Black Muslim leader Malcolm X was assassinated. In Watts, Los Angeles, a six-day riot—the first racially-fueled rebellion of its kind—left thirty-four black people dead, 1,000 wounded, and more than 4,000 arrested; fires caused several millions dollars worth of damage.

The assassination of Malcolm X shook up the black movements and alarmed many. His message exalted and promoted black pride, and black separatism. His denunciations of the atrocities the white people perpetrated against his race frightened the country. The New York police department thought he had "too much power"—that the black movement followed him to a man. Many feared that Malcolm X was killed by the police and that this would provoke more riots; however, it was soon learned that his former mentor, Elijah Muhammad, ordered his assassination because he felt that Malcolm had betrayed the Nation of Islam. The former youth activist Todd Gitlin later wrote, "Malcolm had been left unprotected by the police; how could we fail to wonder whether there was a government claw in his death?"[106] Malcolm X became a martyr and a hero, like Che Guevara, to the New Left and the youth movement.

In 1965 Congress passed the Voting Rights Act, the culmination of many years of the Reverend King's struggle and his great triumph. On March 25 King led a 50 mile march through Alabama, from Selma to Montgomery, where 25,000 demonstrators gathered to celebrate the victory. Selma was renowned for its violent opposition to civil rights for blacks because the state's Republican governor, George Wallace, and the town sheriff, Jim Clark, were racists. They accused blacks of being Communists and of waging guerrilla warfare in the streets.

Racial tensions ran deep. Two years later, in 1967, violent black riots broke out in Detroit; Harlem in New York City; Rochester, N.Y.; and Birmingham, Alabama. King's assassination in 1968 in Memphis, Tennessee, brought much horror and grief both to blacks and to whites who respected his nonviolent approach to achieving civil rights. They feared that the nonviolence he had preached would be buried with him.

THE "BIG STICK" ONCE AGAIN

Latin America was of no interest to Johnson. Border Texan that he was, he envisioned a continent of miserable people, "wetbacks" entering the country illegally and staying in Texas in search of work and better luck. Shortly after coming into the presidency, he commented bitterly to a group of reporters that "these Latin Americans," barefoot and hungry, would "take" everything until someone stopped them.[107]

Johnson disagreed with Kennedy's policies regarding Latin America, but he held his tongue during White House discussions. As president he made it clear that he would tolerate neither new Cubas nor Communist activities on the continent.[108] He returned to the support for military coups to prevent the "Communizing" or "Cubanizing" of other nations, brandishing the "big stick" like some of his predecessors. In 1964 he recognized General René Barrientos, who had overthrown Bolivia's constitutionally elected president, Víctor Paz Estenssoro. Johnson openly supported the military coup in Brazil against Joao Goulart, another constitutionally elected president; the CIA, the United States ambassador, and Johnson's military attaché, Colonel Vernon Walters, conspired with the Brazilian military officers to effect the change. Johnson also sent a naval squadron that was prepared to intervene. Walters, a member of army intelligence—he was later named assistant director of the CIA—was a friend of Marshal Humberto Castelo Branco, the leader of the coup. They had met twenty years earlier at Fort Leavenworth, Kansas, where Walters was Castelo Branco's military instructor.[109] Castelo Branco installed a brutal neo-fascist dictatorship—the first of the "National Security" doctrine—and maintained very close relations with Washington. By the end of his term more than 25,000 people had been assassinated or disappeared.

Johnson's first international crisis occurred in Panama in January 1964, when American students, in violation of the agreement between John F. Kennedy and Roberto Chiari of 1963, raised only the United States flag in their secondary school. The agreement dictated that, in recognition of Panamanian sovereignty, the flags of both nations were to fly side by side over public buildings in the Zone. Panamanian students responded to the provocation by raising their own flag, but the gringo students tore it down. The dispute, which began with stones and Molotov cocktails, quickly escalated into a pitched three-day battle with United States troops firing at the demonstrators. Twenty-four Panamanians and three American soldiers died, more than 300 were wounded, and hundreds were arrested. American businesses were torched and the United States Embassy was stoned. The crisis continued with diplomatic confrontations in the United Nations and the OAS; Panama broke off relations with the United States.[110]

The Panamanian government complained to the United Nations Security Council, claiming that the aggressive behavior of the United States armed forces stationed in the Canal Zone against Panamanian citizens constituted a threat to world peace. Panama also requested a meeting of the Consultative Organ of the OAS under the Río Treaty. Such a request, which was invoked only in case of military aggression against one of its members, had never before been invoked against the United States. The United States ambassador denied the charges, claiming that his country respected the precepts of international law and complied with the obligation to guarantee the security of the free world and to defend the canal. Latin America rallied behind Panama—Chile was the sole abstention.[111]

The United States ambassador to the United Nations, Adlai Stevenson, expressed his government's deep concerns and reported that President Johnson had called on President Chiari to take steps to stem the violence. The Security Council tabled the debate on Panama's complaint, and the impasse was resolved in direct negotiations. Chiari proposed "complete renegotiation" of the Canal treaties and Johnson agreed to "discuss" a revision, but he refused to "negotiate."[112] When Johnson finally did agree to negotiate with the new Panamanian president, Marco Aurelio Robles, he announced that the United States would build a new canal elsewhere and would return the canal to Panama when the new one was finished. United States citizens found this violent incident in Panama to be an embarrassment; they criticized Johnson for his management of the situation. Robert Kennedy called it clumsy.[113]

Johnson's second major crisis occurred in April 1965, when he invaded the Dominican Republic. Rebel forces that favored the defeated President Juan Bosch attempted a coup against the military junta to reinstall him. Johnson saw this movement as the beginning of a revolution. He sent 400 marines to "save endangered American lives" and followed almost immediately with 40,000 infantry soldiers to occupy the country. Johnson claimed the deployment of troops had been necessary to stop an attempted revolution led by Communists. The United States Ambassador Tapley Bennett had sent a hysterical communiqué to the state department alleging that the lives of United States citizens were in danger and requesting that troops be sent to insure their evacuation. On May 3 Johnson "read" Bennett's missive to the nation. In this address to the people Johnson requested the immediate deployment of troops to prevent the risk of American blood running in the streets. In a press conference on June 17 Johnson described horrific, bloody scenes that had taken place before the deployment; he claimed that before any troops had been deployed, 1,500 innocent people had been murdered and decapitated and six Latin American embassies had been set on fire. United States journalists who were covering the conflict, however, witnessed a different picture: no embassies were in flames, no decapitations had occurred, and no United States citizens were dead or wounded.[114]

Johnson was strongly criticized throughout Latin America and at the United Nations and the OAS for this new violation of the principle of nonintervention, of international law, of the United Nations' and the OAS charters, and for his return to "big stick" policy. The United Nations Security Council and the OAS demanded the immediate withdrawal of the troops. At the Tenth Consultative Meeting of the OAS in Washington, called to deal with this crisis, the United States won the necessary majority to recast its intervention as a collective action and created an Inter-American peacekeeping force. Chile, Ecuador, Mexico, Uruguay, and Peru voted against that resolution, and Venezuela abstained. In May the contributions of Latin American countries to the peacekeeping forces began to arrive in Santo Domingo; the majority were Central American soldiers. Johnson was frustrated and annoyed by such scant support on the part of the Latins.[115]

Stevenson did not succeed in preventing the Security Council from dealing with the Dominican crisis (it dedicated twenty-eight meetings to it), nor could he avoid the Secretary General's intervention; he appointed Venezuelan José Mayobre as his representative to go to Santo Domingo and report on the situation. Mayobre severely criticized the military intervention and the activities of the occupying United States troops.

With imperial arrogance Johnson kept the troops and special advisers in place and intervened in the country's affairs at his whim, including placing former president Joaquín Belaguer once again in the presidency; living in exile in New York, Belaguer had served as an adviser to Johnson during the invasion.[116]

The invasion was nothing short of a scandal. Alberto Lleras, the former president of Colombia and one of the mainstays of United States policy regarding Latin America, was afraid that the United States' new acts of aggression would turn the Cold War into a hot one.[117] President Raúl Leoni of Venezuela sent Johnson a message condemning the invasion as a "violation of the principle of non-intervention." The Peruvian chancellor maintained that it was the most severe blow of the past few years to the inter-American system of laws. The *New York Times* called the presence of the marines in Santo Domingo unjustifiable.[118] Robert Kennedy thought it was just plain scandalous.

Though both citizens and outsiders condemned the invasion, public opinion polls indicated that the immense majority in the United States supported their President, satisfied with the way in which he crushed this new upsurge in revolutionary activity.[119]

A messianic and interventionist fever gripped the majorities in the United States Congress. In September 1965, by a vote of 312 to 54, the House of Representatives approved a resolution authorizing the government to intervene in the affairs of other nations, including armed intervention, where there was a risk of Communist subversion, thus legitimizing the Johnson Doctrine.

Fear of the United States imperialist arrogance and its crusaders in Congress was forcefully expressed by governments, media, congresses, politicians, parties, and intellectuals throughout Latin America. They saw a new threat of intervention at their doorstep. But the Johnson Doctrine aroused enormous enthusiasm in the dictatorships of the Southern Cone and the high military commands of Latin America. These considered the moment a propitious one to coordinate their policies against "Communist penetration" in their countries and in Latin America.[120]

IS THE ALLIANCE DEAD?

When Johnson appointed Thomas Mann to be Assistant Secretary of State for Inter-American Affairs and Special Adviser, supporters of the New Frontier feared for the future of the Alliance for Progress. Mann, a Texan who had previously served as ambassador to Mexico, was a reactionary free-trade fanatic, favorably disposed toward any anti-Communist government. The New Frontiersmen were sure that he would abandon the Alliance's goals of social and economic reforms. In effect, Mann directed it toward economic development and the traditional protection of investors. He opted for "selective and concentrated" aid to the most stable countries and the most rational social structures, ignoring the most underdeveloped ones, though the Alliance recommended these for help.[121]

At the Conference of American Presidents at Punta del Este, Uruguay, in which Johnson participated, many concluded that the Alliance was retreating from its agreed objectives. For former Dominican president Juan Bosch, the "vitality and spirit" with which Kennedy had imbued it "died with him in Dallas."[122] Robert Kennedy traveled throughout Latin America in 1965 to observe the results of the Alliance. "I saw much progress and much retrogression as well," he reported. He singled out "the military coups, the stagnating economies, unchecked population growth, and the tiny islands of enormous privilege in the midst of awful poverty. These, and the smarting wound caused by the United States intervention in the Dominican Republic, posed serious threats to the Alliance's bold hope."[123]

Carlos Sanz de Santamaría, President of the Inter-American Committee on the Alliance for Progress (CIAP), maintained that Johnson took favorable measures concerning Latin America. He supported the proposal of converting the Inter-American Development Bank into a great financial institution. He asked Congress to augment substantially the resources for aid to the region, and he sought to improve conditions of credit for development and to eliminate commercial barriers. He also supported programs for education, health, and agriculture. If Johnson's policies failed, it was for lack of support from Congress, not from him, Santamaría commented.[124]

WHAT'S HAPPENING IN CUBA?

The "Cuban problem" was not a priority for Johnson. He could not intervene because Kennedy had promised Khrushchev that the United States would not invade Cuba. Nevertheless, he ordered a review of Kennedy's policies to determine their effectiveness. While he did not change the policies, he maintained Cuba's isolation, he intensified the embargo and increased pressure on allies and friendly countries to join it, and he continued to send spy planes over the island. He did not share the Kennedys' animosity toward Fidel, and he claimed to know nothing of the CIA's plans to assassinate him. Nevertheless, Leon

Janos, a Johnson adviser, recounted the President's comment to him, "We've been running a damned branch of Murder, Inc. in the Caribbean."[125] Cuba's minister of the interior, Ramiro Valdés, told the former *New York Times* correspondent Tad Szulc of about thirty attempts on Fidel's life in 1964 and 1965, during Johnson's administration. Needless to say, Fidel lost all hope of improving relations with the United States after the violent incident in Panama and the invasion of Dominican Republic.

JOHNSON'S AUTUMN

Johnson's political future ran aground with the Vietnam War, his great obsession. It was the highest priority of his foreign policy. It was an unpopular war— the longest in United States history—and it damaged the country's image among allies, friends, and enemies, and was profoundly offensive to many North Americans. Besides which, it was clear that the United States was losing the war.

The future of this distant Asian country was of no great importance to public opinion; instead, people were appalled by the great loss of human lives for a cause that few accepted and many failed to understand. "How many kids have you killed today?" antiwar protesters yelled at Johnson, who sent over half a million soldiers to Vietnam. The price to the United States were tens of thousands dead, thousands crippled, and many millions of dollars. The United States dropped more explosives on Vietnamese territory than the entire tonnage dropped on all fronts in the Second World War.[126] Johnson's obsession was not to "lose" Vietnam, not to be the president who "let go" of Asia, as Roosevelt and Truman had "lost" China.

Worn out by the military failures, by the great numbers of young people sacrificed to the war effort, by the massive antiwar protests both at home and abroad, Johnson announced a peace offensive in December 1965. Hanoi did not respond. He renewed the bombing with greater intensity, hoping to force the Vietnamese to negotiate. He suspended it in 1968 to continue the Paris talks, but these went nowhere. In the larger cities and on university campuses the demonstrations against the war and military recruitment and the protests for civil rights—more than a hundred between 1964 and 1967—were an expression of the general and growing national discontent with Johnson's policies and of his administration's shrinking prestige. He was no longer the popular figure elected in 1964 with 61 percent of the vote (16 million more votes than his Republican rival Barry Goldwater). According to the Gallup Polls that year, he had a 70 percent approval rating. Four years later his rating was at 36 percent, the lowest since Harry Truman.

Johnson undermined his own image and destroyed his credibility. His exuberant personality and limitless imagination led him to commit grave errors in relation to the public and the press. His clumsy handling of information about matters of the utmost importance to the nation, such as the war in Vietnam, was evident. He presented facts as he wished them to be, often misleading the country. People said that the only way you knew he was not lying was when his lips were shut.[127] In March 1968 he announced that he would not seek reelection. He knew very well, as did the whole country, that he would lose badly.

THE PARTY'S OVER

For the United States the 1960s ended with the beginning of Richard Nixon's presidency. His administration was successful in the international field: the tempering of tension with the Soviet Union, the opening of relations with the People's Republic of China, and the end of United States intervention in Vietnam. Convinced that this war could not be won, he pulled the troops out. Another important event was the moon landing by four United States astronauts.

Under Nixon the country also experienced one of the most traumatic incidents in its history, the Watergate scandal. Nixon's administration came to an abrupt end with his forced resignation and a small group of his advisers sent to jail. The Watergate events were seen as the most unscrupulous abuse of power by any United States president.

In relation to Latin America, in the first year of his term Nixon ordered the CIA to increase its operations in Cuba. Nevertheless tensions with that country decreased. A month after his inauguration Nixon sent a commission of inquiry, headed by Nelson Rockefeller, to take the pulse of the explosive situation in Latin America. Fourteen nations—the majority—were under military dictatorships, and the "dirty war" was on the march. When Nixon arrived at the White House, most of the armed rebel groups in the Andean countries had disappeared. The strongest—the Tupamaros in Uruguay and the Montoneros and the People's Revolutionary Army (ERP: Ejercito Revolucionario del Pueblo) in Argentina—were still quite active. That same year, Nixon started to keep an eye on Chile, determined to prevent Salvador Allende, the Socialist candidate, from being elected to the presidency. Later on he started to interfere.

CHAPTER IV

"THE BACKYARD"

THE UNITED STATES AND CENTRAL AMERICA

Central America, the narrow strip of land comprised of five small republics—
El Salvador, Nicaragua, Costa Rica, Guatemala and Honduras, the United
States' "backyard"—endured the longest and harshest political, economic, and
military dependence on the United States of any nation on the continent. No
leader came to power or remained in power without the United States' consent. They became its faithful allies and obsequious servants, and were most
generous with their national sovereignty. Their geographic location between
two oceans and their proximity to the Panama Canal were the reasons for
repeated military intervention in these nations.[1]

Until the wars of liberation of the 1970s and 1980s the history of Central
America—with the exception of Costa Rica—was a succession of brutal,
inept, and corrupt military dictatorships, military coups, electoral fraud, and
violence. Their feudal societies were static, stratified, and based on deep
inequalities. Power was in the hands of the military, allied with the oligarchies,
and supported by the hierarchy of the Catholic Church. The "fourteen"
Salvadoran families, the "twenty" in Guatemala, the few in Honduras, and the
monolithic Somoza dynasty in Nicaragua had the sole economic power and
owned vast tracts of the best land, the source of wealth in these agrarian
countries. In contrast to this concentrated economic power was the extreme
poverty of the campesinos and the indigenous masses, who had no land or
means of subsistence and were condemned to misery. From these masses the
señores extracted "abundant, obedient, and cheap" labor. During Guatemala's

harvest the poor were rounded up like beasts of burden and obliged to work for nothing to pay the landlords so-called life debts. This condition of slavery was abolished in Guatemala by the governments of Juan José Arévalo and Jacobo Arbenz.[2]

Democracy was only a myth scripted in their constitutions and in the ritual of elections called every four or five years by the military to comply with the law. Such farces, in which the official candidates always "won," complied with the "democratic" duty to allow the populace to express itself by voting.

During the 1950s there was a brief democratic interlude with the governments of Arévalo and Arbenz in Guatemala, Ramón Villeda Morales in Honduras, and José Figueres in Costa Rica. They were liberal, reform-minded, nationalist, and anti-Communist. Inspired by Roosevelt's New Deal and the Mexican Revolution, they made structural changes to correct the profound inequalities, undertook social reforms, and attempted modest agrarian reform.

McCarthyism, rampant in the United States and throughout Latin America, frustrated what could have been important advances in these stratified societies. Accused by Washington of being a Communist, Arbenz was overthrown in a CIA operation. Arévalo did not enjoy a second term as president, despite the fact that his reelection was a sure thing—the military staged a coup before the election in order to prevent the certain outcome. Villeda was also toppled shortly before the election by a right-wing military coup to prevent the victory of the liberal candidate he supported.

Only in democratic Costa Rica were the changes more permanent. Figueres, who governed for two separate terms, expedited laws for social assistance, modernized the educational system, gave women the right to vote, nationalized the commercial banking industry, and dissolved the army, but also made the Communist Party illegal. These were times of economic and social progress for his country. Costa Rica, with neither an army nor a guerrilla movement, was an example of political stability, peace, and democracy in the region.

During the 1960s trade union movements and campesino organizations gained strength in El Salvador, Honduras, and Guatemala, in spite of brutal repression. The Communist Parties—although illegal and persecuted—assisted in these advances. Armed groups with Marxist-Leninist leanings also surfaced. The Cuban Revolution, the radicalization of sectors of the Catholic Church inspired by John XXIII, and the Alliance for Progress were all fundamental factors in the explosion of social and insurgent activity, awakening great expectations of change.[3]

Central America always had insurgencies: rebellions against imperialism, demonstrations against dictatorships, popular struggles for people's rights, campesino and indigenous uprisings demanding land, strikes to demand higher wages and better living conditions (those of the greatest extent and impact were against the United Fruit Company), and armed struggles against repression. And these movements were always put down with extreme force. The military, the oligarchies, the hierarchies within the Catholic Church, and Washington always considered such popular protests Communist, and their obligation was to crush them.

In the 1960s under the leadership of dissident young men and women from Communist parties and left-wing movements, flying nationalist, anti-imperialist, ideological and anti-dictatorship banners, armed movements arose in Nicaragua, El Salvador, and Guatemala. They gained strength in the 1970s. In 1979 the Sandinista revolution triumphed in Nicaragua, and the first guerrilla movements emerged in Honduras.

To counter this explosion of insurgent activity in Latin America, the Kennedy administration initiated a new defense strategy focused on counterinsurgency, doubling military aid to Central America. Throughout the 1960s the number of United States military advisers in El Salvador was so large that Ambassador Murat Williams (1963–1964) asked the state department to recall some of them, since their numbers exceeded that of "the entire Salvadoran Air Force." The state department replied that it looked on this request with sympathy, but that his suggestion "annoyed" the Pentagon.[4]

In 1963 the Pentagon succeeded in creating the Consejo de Defensa Centroamericana (CONDECA: Central American Defense Council) to coordinate its defense policy with the military high commands of these countries.[5] Costa Rica was the only country opposed to its creation. And with the aid of the CIA, the Pentagon, the Green Berets and the state department the governments established a security apparatus in their countries to coordinate intelligence activities in the region. All the Central American countries—including Costa Rica and Panama—joined this intelligence network controlled by the United States.

THE "BANANA REPUBLICS"

Until the 1960s the United Fruit Company—the quintessence of United States imperialism—dominated the region. It was the largest landholder and had a monopoly on bananas, the principal export of Guatemala and Honduras,

Costa Rica's second most important after coffee, and a sizable source of revenue for Nicaragua and Panama. It also had a monopoly on the fruit's transportation. United Fruit owned the Grace Line's White Fleet—the Central American International Railroads was its subsidiary—and controlled practically all Central American ports.[6] It also had controlling interests in the other United States fruit companies operating in Central America.

Given the collaboration, the stupidity, or the venality of the rotating dictators in these countries, United Fruit established dependent economies with semicolonial characteristics. "The Octopus," as the company was known in the region, manipulated governments at will, meddled in their political fights, provided financial assistance to candidates of its choice, and fixed the scales in favor of whoever offered it the most attractive conditions. It was a state within a state. Through pressure, threats, and bribes it obtained concessions and privileges outside the law: tax exemptions, evasion of tariffs and duties, free import and export of earnings, and the payment of a minuscule percentage of its multimillion dollars in profits. Such "services" were repaid with juicy bribes to the countries' leaders, and Washington rewarded their submission by propping up their regimes.

United Fruit was the major source of employment in the region, paying wages two to three times higher than those offered by local companies and providing schools, hospitals, and housing for its employees. No other enterprise offered such conditions. Nevertheless, it was still exploitative: the local workers were granted no vacations and could be fired without reason, compensation, or a right to grievance.

The biggest labor conflicts in Central America were against United Fruit and Standard Fruit, another American transnational. Because of the imperialist nature of the companies, the sometimes massive protests politicized and radicalized the workers. Forces brought to keep public order defended the foreign "boss," and the conflicts ended in bloodbaths. United Fruit engaged paramilitary gangs to terrorize the workers and discourage strikes; labor union leaders were kidnapped and murdered.[7]

As it did with other transnationals, the state department defended the interests of United Fruit as if they constituted a matter of national security. "We do not have friends; we have interests," proclaimed Eisenhower's secretary of state, John Foster Dulles, in reference to General Motors.[8] The case was the same with the banana companies. The destinies of the Banana Republics and their peoples—and even the lives of their rulers—depended on this range of interests. The most dramatic example was the clumsy CIA operation ordered by Dulles in 1954 to overthrow Guatemala's President Arbenz for having expropriated United Fruit's large land holdings.

In Costa Rica, José Figueres, twice elected president, repeatedly denounced abuses by United Fruit but did not attempt to cut off its privileges. Instead, after long negotiations, he succeeded in increasing the percentage the company paid his country. In turn, the company accused him of being a Communist and converting Costa Rica into a paradise for rebels, since he took in the persecuted and the exiled from neighboring dictatorships supported by the United States.

In Cuba, United Fruit (later United Brands and Chiquita Brands) had a monopoly on the sugar industry, the island's principal export, and enjoyed privileges similar to those in Central America. The Revolution put an end to these deals and expropriated all the company's lands.[9]

Cuban experts investigated United Fruit's activities in their country and exposed them as a "case of imperialist domination." They bared the fraudulent means and litigation used to acquire land. United Fruit was the seventh-largest landholder in the country—owning more than 85,000 acres of "continuous and homogeneous" lands—and controlled several municipalities. The company's procedure was a "deliberate policy of armed robbery," with the complicity of the corrupt Cuban government and of magnates who "gave an important part of our country over to the foreigner." The investigators were unable to establish exact figures of the company's profits, since its books were altered to avoid tariffs and duties in both countries.[10]

In spite of its multimillion-dollar business in Central America and its control of the economies of these countries, United Fruit did not offer any advantage to their development. On the contrary, a mid-1960s report by the International Basic Economic Corporation (IBEC)—a Rockefeller family-financial organization—maintained that United Fruit had created a "culture of poverty" throughout Central America and that many workers expressed the "desire for liberty," since they felt that they were at the company's mercy. The report recommended that the company construct "decent" housing.[11]

The fruit giant began to decline in 1958 when the United States Supreme Court ruled that it impeded the free course of business and free competition among fruit companies. By 1970 it was practically bankrupt. Its investments in Central America fell to less than 3 percent of the continent's total.[12] In 1975 Eli M. Black, president of United Brands (the new name of United Fruit after its merger with AMK-John Morrell), jumped out the window from his forty-fourth floor office in a New York luxury building. In the subsequent investigation of the company, serious economic difficulties, enormous debts, muddled bookkeeping, and a mess of bribes to foreign governments came to light.

HONDURAS AND THE "OCTOPUSES"

Of the five Central American countries, Honduras had the lowest per capita income. It was the most barren and backward, with the second highest illiteracy rate (Haiti was first). But it also had the fewest ethnic conflicts since its population was the most homogeneous (90 percent mestizo, 7 percent indigenous, 2 percent black, and 1 percent white). The contrast between wealth and poverty was the narrowest in the region. Wealth, or, to be more accurate, poverty, was distributed equally. "The country is so poor it can't afford an oligarchy," said the Honduran campesina Elvia Alvarado.[13]

Like most other Central American countries, with the exception of Costa Rica, Honduras was under military rule until 1980, when the first civilian president was elected. Its dictatorships, however, were not as brutal as those of its neighbors; it was not until the end of the 1970s that the first armed groups appeared.

Union movements in large and small enterprises and a campesino organization—the first in the region—began to emerge in the 1950s. This phenomenon of labor unity was in large measure due to continuous conflicts with the United Fruit Company.[14] The fruit giant's largest installations in the region were in Honduras, where it committed its greatest abuses and faced its worst labor conflicts. A massive 1954 strike became a milestone in the history of labor struggles in Central America. It broke out on a Sunday when workers refused to load the company's ships unless they were paid double for working on a holiday. The company refused with the support of the Honduran Supreme Court. The strike turned into a massive mobilization of 40,000 workers, joined by Standard Fruit workers, those of many industrial and commercial enterprises, and supported by popular organizations, teachers, and students. The country was paralyzed for seventy days. President General Juan Manuel Gálvez was forced to step down. The strike had profound repercussions not only in Honduras but also in neighboring countries. In 1957 there was another massive strike against the Standard Fruit Company.

The fruit companies and Washington feared that the banana workers' unions would become a political force that might generate a regional movement opposed to their interests. At that moment the CIA was preparing an operation to overthrow the Guatemalan president Jacobo Arbenz for having expropriated United Fruit Company lands.[15]

VILLEDA, A BREATH OF DEMOCRACY

In 1954 Ramón Villeda Morales—liberal, democratic, nationalist, and reformist—won the presidential election in Honduras. However, the assembly argued that he had won by too narrow a margin and instead installed Vice President Julio Lozano Díaz (1954–1956). He was a dictator. Social and labor agitation continued. After a period of coups and countercoups, in 1957 Villeda Morales won again at the polls, and this time he assumed the presidency.

Villeda Morales (1957–1963) was the first president to be elected by popular vote. He respected political pluralism, recognized workers' rights—including the right to strike—approved new labor and social-security laws, and introduced public education; in 1962 he drew up an agrarian reform law to comply with the goals of the Alliance for Progress. In the favorable international economic situation, and helped by Alliance funds, he made great strides forward for the country.

This opening allowed the campesino movements to progress. In the 1960s the movement created the Federación Nacional Campesina de Honduras (FENACH: National Federation of Honduran Peasants), the Asociación Nacional de Campesinos (ANC: National Association of Peasants), and the Asociación Campesina Social Cristiana (ACSC: Social Christian Peasant Association), all with branches in various parts of the country. In their turn the landowners, who felt threatened by the continual land occupations supported by such organizations, created the Federación Nacional de Agricultores y Ganaderos de Honduras (FENAGAH: National Federation of Honduran Farmers and Ranchers).

In Honduras, as in the rest of Central America, the greatest source of conflict was the campesinos' lack of land. A "boom" in the farming and ranching sectors led the landowners to push the campesinos from their fields in order to turn them into pastures for cattle grazing. These actions provoked waves of campesinos to occupy nearby lands, and in turn, their expulsion by the forces of public order. Many campesinos emigrated to the cities. The overcrowding of slums and the enormous increase in unemployment—it rose to 25 percent from 1961 to 1967—sharpened social conflict.

Landholders and the United States opposed Villeda's modest land reforms. The United States Ambassador Charles Burrows asked Villeda not to approve the land reform law until the State Department gave its approval, but Villeda refused. He signed the law in the offices of the Tela Railroad Company union. This gesture was perceived as support for the union movement. Standard Fruit accepted the reform, but United Fruit retaliated. Given the enormous control of the company over the country's economy, and the pressures from Washington, Villeda had no choice but to travel to Miami to meet with its executives. The agreement they reached meant a great step backward for his plans for agrarian reform.[16]

Villeda maintained good relations with Washington without giving in. He remained independent on the sensitive subject of Cuba. Unlike the governments of Nicaragua and Guatemala, he refused to take part in preparations for an invasion, but after the failure of the Bay of Pigs he broke off relations with the island (joining the other Central American nations, who had already done so). Before taking this step, which was unpopular in his country, he organized an anti-Castro demonstration—he wanted it to seem that he was breaking relations in response to popular demand. He spoke out publicly against the Revolution, stating that Central America was "under the gun from a Communist Cuba" and that the Cuban regime was "a cancer" that ought to be eradicated from the hemisphere.[17]

In 1963, his last year in office, the country went through difficult economic times because of the drop in the prices of coffee and cotton on the international market. When Villeda requested economic assistance from Washington, he was refused; nor could he count on the good will of the State Department, its ambassador, Alliance for Progress officials, or the transnational corporations. All opposed his liberalizing prounion policies and his attempt at agrarian reform.

The higher echelons of the military were also opposed to Villeda; some considered him a Communist. But relations were strained not only for political reasons. In a move that deeply disturbed the military, from the onset of his term Villeda formed a civil guard of 2,500 men to guarantee his personal security. Given the military's tradition for staging coups Villeda did not trust them and wanted them far away from the presidency. The last straw was Villeda's support of the Liberal Party candidate, who was presenting an antimilitary speech in his campaign. His term coming to an end, Villeda began to discharge his civil guard, an act that inadvertently facilitated a coup. Colonel Oswaldo López Arellano, commander in chief of the army, toppled Villeda, and within the hour the armed forces appointed him president.

RETREAT

The coup against Villeda Morales worked against President Kennedy's policy of defending democracy. López Arellano justified the coup by accusing Villeda of being a Communist and claiming that he had uncovered a Communist plot and Communist propaganda within the government. Though he promised to hold elections, the United States severed relations. "You'll be back in six months," predicted Honduran friends of United States Ambassador Charles Burrows as he prepared to leave Tegucigalpa.[18]

After Kennedy's death López Arellano sent a message to President Johnson in which he claimed that the military government "which I have the honor of leading" prevented "Castro-type Communism from gaining a foothold in Honduran territory." He further reminded Johnson that the common goal of their two nations was "the defense of liberty and justice as standards of life for peoples and nations."[19] In 1964 Johnson reopened the United States Embassy in Honduras after López Arellano promised to hold elections within a year.[20]

López Arellano (1963–1971) reversed Villeda's social programs, eliminated agrarian reform and work laws that favored the working class, and opened the door to foreign capital. His order to eliminate the civil guard—its members were massacred—initiated a period of brutal repression. He imprisoned hundreds of political and union leaders. Some were murdered, while others were deported.

The military was the only cohesive political force in Honduras, and the armed forces enjoyed complete autonomy. By constitutional order, the president could not be involved in matters of commission and promotion, nor in internal military decisions. López authorized the military to disobey orders it deemed unconstitutional.

FENAGAH asked López to expel the 300,000 Salvadoran campesinos who had immigrated illegally. When, in 1969, a soccer game in Tegucigalpa between El Salvador and Honduras ended in a pitched battle, leaving countless dead and wounded, López saw his chance to force the Salvadoran campesinos out. This event was the prelude to the so-called Soccer War.

The conflict broke out in July. El Salvador invaded Honduras by sea and by air. Its troops committed every kind of abuse, massacring thousands of Honduran campesinos and destroying their villages. More than 100,000 families were left homeless. The victory El Salvador claimed in less than a week was, however, short lived. Honduran ranchers and landholders succeeded in expelling the Salvadorans and reclaiming their lands. The human and economic losses for both countries were immense. Honduras cut off diplomatic and commercial relations with El Salvador and in 1970 pulled out of the Central American Common Market and the Central American Defense Council (CONDECA). Shortly thereafter both institutions disbanded.

At the end of his term López chose the respected judge Ramón Ernesto Cruz as his successor. After winning an election controlled by the army, he governed for only a year. The deportation he ordered of campesinos from lands they occupied legally in the town of Talanquera and the horrible massacre that resulted caused public revulsion. The Supreme Defense Council, the army's highest body, "authorized" López to overthrow Cruz.[21]

During this second term (1972–1975) López governed without a congress and by decree. Aware of the explosive social situation and of growing nationalism—a phenomenon that held true for the whole region—he announced labor reforms, restrictions on foreign mining companies, and the nationalization of a powerful lumber company. After a march by 20,000 campesinos demanding land, he offered agrarian reform.

The economic situation worsened when, in 1974, hurricane Fifi devastated the Caribbean coast and destroyed the richest agricultural areas. The storm killed almost 8,000 people, and 300,000 were left homeless. López requested aid from Washington but was denied. This refusal made him realize that he had to change direction, for his modest agrarian reforms had caused powerful economic sectors, FENAGAH and the transnational fruit companies in particular, to turn against him. López cut back his plans for land redistribution, sent the army to help Standard Fruit take back its land, and eased the terms for foreign investment.

Caught in the web of a bribery scandal concerning United Fruit, López resigned. The company had already distributed $1.25 million—half of the promised $2.5 million—among high-ranking officials including the president (twice the sum Honduran officials requested). This was the "prize" for the enormous reduction in export tariffs on bananas, which deprived Honduras of $7.5 billion.[22] *Time* magazine described the fall of López as a "bloodless coup."[23]

López left the government in the hands of General Juan Alberto Melgar Castro (1975–1978) and the country in an explosive state. In spite of the repressions and the massacres sponsored by landholders and ranchers, extreme poverty drove the campesinos to take over lands. The discovery of the bodies of nine workers on the hacienda belonging to a tycoon unleashed a national backlash. The Church denounced this slaughter, accusing the oligarchy and the transnationals of exploiting and oppressing the workers.

The three years of Melgar's government were filled with repression, violence, rampant official corruption, and drug-trafficking scandals that appeared to involve high-ranking military officers. The competition for power and money within the armed forces led to a coup. Conservative factions placed General Policarpo Paz García (1978–1981) in the presidency. This was a man whose allies were accused of drug trafficking, but once he held the reins of power Paz García prevented an investigation.

In 1979 two guerrilla groups emerged: the Frente Morazán de Liberación de Honduras (FMLH: Morazán Front for the Liberation of Honduras) and the Movimiento Popular de Liberación Cinchonero (Cinchoneros' Popular Liberation Movement), named for national heroes and campesino leaders. The Cinchoneros characterized themselves as "a politico-military organism at the service of the Honduran people."[24] The Morazán Front claimed responsibility for shots fired at the United States Embassy. During the 1980s both groups claimed responsibility for armed attacks on American military personnel.

President Carter was concerned at the possible spread of the armed struggle throughout Central America. The Sandinista triumph in Nicaragua in 1979 had given renewed energy to the Salvadoran guerrillas, and Carter feared that Honduras, subject to brutal military dictatorships, would follow suit. He sent emissaries to convince Paz García to institute democratic reforms and to hold free elections, and he offered to increase economic aid to Honduras. In 1980 Paz García called elections to a constituent assembly. Though there was talk of fraud, doctored documents, irregularities in voter lists and registration, and the exclusion of opposition parties (arousing protests and calls for abstention), the election was ultimately peaceful. The assembly named Paz García provisional president, and he promised to hold an election. In 1980 the rancher Roberto Suázo Córdova, the candidate favored by liberals and the United States, was elected by popular vote, making him the first civilian president after decades of military rule.

EL SALVADOR, CRUCIBLE OF CONFLICT

El Salvador is the region's smallest country, the most densely populated, and the most industrialized, with the highest rate of population growth. Characterized by a history of great social polarization, it has the most advanced union organization, the campesino classes being the first to organize and to lead the struggle for human rights. Unlike its neighbors, El Salvador was never a banana republic nor had it suffered invasions by United States marines. Its principal export was coffee—it was the major producer in the region—an industry solidly in Salvadoran hands.

The country's history is full of internal conflicts, short civil wars, coups d'état, electoral fraud, and confrontations with its neighbors, whose strongmen took sides in Salvadoran politics according to their own interests.

El Salvador also had the region's most egregious gap between rich and poor. The so-called Fourteen Families of the oligarchy owned the most fertile land and controlled industry, banking, and commerce. Their interests were protected by law and by the police force.[25]

The greatest social conflicts were related to land. Their origin lay in the expulsion of the indigenous population from their lands in the latter part of the nineteenth century. These lands were then mainly used for the cultivation of coffee. The periodic indigenous rebellions against this dispossession ended in massacres at the hands of the police.

The extraordinary development of the coffee industry brought great misery to the campesinos. Without land and without any means of subsistence, the farmers were vulnerable to the landholders' exploitation. They provided an abundant work force, were paid subsistence wages, and had work only during harvest time. With all the energies devoted to the cultivation of coffee, the corn and bean crops—the popular nutritional bases—were dramatically diminished, and the people went hungry. Such dire straits prompted campesino revolts and mass emigrations to other countries, especially Honduras.[26]

"EVER SINCE THAT CURSED YEAR . . ."

In December 1931, a campesino revolt in the coffee-growing zones ended in one of the region's most horrendous massacres, marking one of the darkest pages in Salvadoran history. It lasted three months and resulted in the murders of between 10,000 and 30,000 campesino men, women, and children— the number varied depending on the source. Their blood stained the hands of General Maximiliano Hernández, who had taken power in a coup the previous month.

The General, when informed that the young Agustín Farabundo Martí— head of the Communist Party he had helped found in 1925—was leading the campesino struggle, ordered him killed. The army captured him in the capital, in the company of the students Mario Zapata and Alfonso Luna, and shot them down then and there. Their murders marked the onset of what Salvadoran historians called the Massacre of 1932[27] and the beginning of General Hernández's bloody, thirteen-year dictatorship. The oligarchy, the land-owning and coffee-growing bourgeoisie, sectors of the middle class, and Washington, all supported Maximiliano because he had eliminated the insurgents and thousands of campesinos accused of "Communist agitation."[28]

Half a century later President Ronald Reagan's United Nations ambassador, Jeane Kirkpatrick, characterized Maximiliano as a "hero" for being among those "people who made a special contribution to highly valued [public] goods."[29] The support for the massacre by those in power intensified the people's revulsion toward the military and the oligarchy.

"Ever since that cursed year," wrote the poet and revolutionary Roque Dalton, "all of us are different people, and I believe that since then, El Salvador is a different country. El Salvador today is, above all, the result of that barbarity. Our rulers may have changed their style, but the basic mode of thought that still beats us down is that of the slaughterers of 1932."[30] Eventually powerful political groups, sickened by his execution of military officers who had tried to topple Maximiliano, forced his resignation.

The flames of rebellion in El Salvador did not die out with Martí's execution. Though his fight was cut short, it left deep traces among the people, who perceived him as a hero and a martyr for his dream of liberating the campesino and poor classes from exploitation. Both Martí and Augusto Sandino were stellar figures in the Central American liberation movements; they planted the seeds of revolution, which their people took up decades later. In the 1960s, the Salvadoran revolutionaries baptized their movement the Frente Farabundo Martí de Liberación Nacional (FMLN: Farabundo Martí National Liberation Movement), which led the revolutionary war for thirteen years. In 1979, in Nicaragua, the Frente Sandinista de Liberación Nacional (FSLN: Sandinista Front for National Liberation) overthrew the Somoza dynasty.

The military retained power through fraud and coups. In 1960 a group of moderate officers overthrew Colonel José María Lemus (1956–1960) for fear that his brutal repression would result in a revolution as in Cuba. They set up a junta (1960) composed of three civilians and three military officers. Because it was ultranationalist and pro-Castro, Eisenhower refused to recognize it.[31] Three months later a military coup organized "by agents of the oligarchy and of imperialism" overthrew the junta.[32]

The participants in the coup installed a new junta (1960–1961), composed of three civilians and two officers. Kennedy recognized it, but he pressured the junta to enact democratic changes. It called an election, and the sole candidate, Colonel Julio Adalberto Rivera (1962–1967), was elected by fraud. He immediately identified himself with Washington, severed ties with Cuba, opened the doors to foreign investment, and controlled public order with a strong hand.[33]

The United States considered El Salvador the showcase of the Alliance for

Progress. Kennedy sent fifty-five Peace Corps volunteers and increased military and economic aid. El Salvador received the largest amount of United States aid in the region. Although United States penetration in its economy was the least in the region, United States holdings represented 65 percent of all foreign investment in El Salvador.[34] Yet, as in the rest of Latin America, the Alliance failed in El Salvador. Dominant economic and political sectors opposed the agreed-upon reforms—above all agrarian reform—and publicly claimed that the Alliance was "inspired by Communists." To avoid antagonism, the military did not implement the reforms. In the end it was these very sectors that came to benefit from the Alliance, since it allowed them the possibility of new business ventures. The other beneficiaries were the transnational corporations.[35]

Colonel Fidel Sánchez Hernández was elected to the presidency (1967–1972), supported by the military and the oligarchy. He was responsible for the so-called Soccer War or Hundred-Hours War, when Honduras expelled 150,000 Salvadoran campesinos. El Salvador's retaliation overpowered Honduras. Its troops invaded, bombarded Tegucigalpa, massacred thousands of campesinos, and destroyed their villages. Salvadorans fell under the spell of triumphalism and chauvinism.

But with victory came disaster. Honduras—El Salvador's principal market—severed diplomatic and commercial ties and withdrew from the Central American Common Market. El Salvador was the country most affected by this move, since it was the region's major exporter. Furthermore, the return of 150,000 campesinos exacerbated the already explosive social problems. Occupations of land and popular protests increased. The migration of campesinos to the cities made for severe housing problems in the slums and for growing unemployment. The Soccer War resulted in profound enmity between the two neighboring countries, which traditionally had good relations.

Centrist and leftist political parties and movements began to emerge. They were eager to see changes by democratic means and decided to participate in the 1972 elections—a political game usually monopolized by the military—nominating the Christian Democrat José Napoleón Duarte and Guillermo Ungo of the Partido Democrático Revolucionario (PDR: Democratic Revolutionary Party) as candidates for the presidency and vice presidency respectively. They had the backing of the Unión Nacional Opositora (UNO: National Opposition Union), a coalition of the Christian Democrats, of the Union Democrática Nacionalista (UDN: National Democratic Union), the outlawed Communist Party, and the Movimiento Nacional Revolucionario (MNR: National Revolutionary Movement). The official candidate, Colonel

Arturo Armando Molina, had the support of the National Coalition, the military, and the oligarchy.

The campaign was marked by violence, threats, and intimidation directed at Duarte and Ungo; their followers were arrested or murdered. On election day, the national radio reported on the results throughout the day, with Duarte and Ungo leading around the country. At a given moment the broadcast went off the air. When it returned, Colonel Molina was declared the "winner." Although UNO claimed victory, the government alleged that because UNO had not received the required majority, the assembly had "elected" Molina.

With Duarte's support a group of officials dedicated to the constitution attempted a countercoup to put Duarte and Ungo in office. The effort, in which more than 200 died, was thwarted with the help of the Nicaraguan dictator Anastasio Somoza and Colonel Carlos Arana Osorio of Guatemala.[36] Duarte was detained, tortured, and sent abroad—he remained in Venezuela for twelve years.

Colonel Molina (1972–1977) attempted to calm the explosive situation of the campesinos, most of whom had no land to cultivate, with a modest agrarian reform law, but the powerful landholders prevented him from implementing it.[37]

The 1977 elections—supervised by foreign observers—were won by the opposition headed by retired Colonel Ernesto Claramount. But the "victory" of General Carlos Humberto Romero was delivered by armed fraud. Protests led by Claramount were met with gunfire from the police, killing thirty people and leaving hundreds wounded, arrested, and disappeared. Claramount went into exile.

The dictatorship of General Carlos Humberto Romero (1977–1979) launched a reign of terror. He was determined to eliminate the powerful insurgency and ordered the army to "search and destroy" as was done in Vietnam. The failure of his strategy led to massacres of campesinos accused of aiding the guerrillas. Romero brutally persecuted the popular campesino and student movements and organizations, and the parties and movements of the left, and he did not respect the Church. Priests, members of religious orders, and lay people were murdered, arrested, tortured, disappeared, and expelled. Many went into voluntary exile because of death threats.

The 1977 murder of Father Rutilo Grande, a Salvadoran Jesuit, was cause for consternation. In a gesture of protest and grief, the Archbishop of El Salvador, Monsignor Arnulfo Romero (no relation to General Romero) ordered the closing of Catholic schools for three days. He also announced that he would celebrate only one Mass in the cathedral on Sunday and would refrain from participating in official functions until the crime was solved. The oligarchy accused him of sacrilege and of violating canon law. General Romero's "pacification" campaign was an orgy of blood at the hands of the military, of the Organización Democrática Nacionalista (ORDEN: Democratic Nationalist Organization)—a paramilitary organization attached to the presidency—and the Agencia Nacional de Seguridad de El Salvador (ANSESAL: Agency of National Security of El Salvador), a section of army intelligence. Both institutions operated as death squads. General José Alberto Medrano of army intelligence, who was responsible for setting these groups up in 1962, claimed that the organizations were the work of the CIA, the State Department, and the Green Berets. Duarte called Medrano "the father of the death squads and the worst murderer of all," while President Johnson decorated him "in recognition of his exceptional and meritorious service."[38] In 1984 the guerrillas executed him.

The death squads proliferated. The "White Hand" (created by ORDEN), the Secret Anti-Communist Army, the White Warriors, the Revolutionary Anti-Communist Extermination Action, and many others claimed responsibility for most of the political murders and disappearances. According to Amnesty International, the squads' members were "regular army and police agents," on active duty or retired, who obeyed "orders from their superiors." Amnesty International accused the government of using these groups "to shield the government from accountability for torture, disappearances, and extrajudicial executions committed in their name."[39]

Far from slowing down the insurgents, the state of terror stimulated them. The middle months of 1978 saw a violent and growing conflict between the people on one hand and the extreme right and the army on the other. The guerrillas responded to the repression and murder of popular and campesino leaders by assassinating military officers and attacking and kidnapping members of the oligarchy. This violence caused the flight of capital and the withdrawal of investments.[40]

President Carter condemned the excesses of Romero's regime. A February 1979 State Department report on human rights in El Salvador accused the government of torture, murder, disappearances, arbitrary arrests, and illegal searches and raids. It named the national guard, the security forces, and ORDEN as being responsible for most of these crimes.[41]

In April 1979, ORDEN murdered more than fifty members of the Bloque Popular Revolucionario (BPR: Popular Revolutionary Bloc), the most important popular political organization. Between March and April more than 130 political detainees "disappeared." At the beginning of May members of the Bloc protested, occupying the French and Costa Rican Embassies and the cathedral in San Salvador. Twenty (some sources said as many as forty) of the demonstrators were gunned down in front of the cathedral. At a protest organized by the Bloc later that month, fourteen members were killed. In the span of one month, 188 popular leaders were assassinated.[42]

Moderate forces in the oligarchy who supported General Romero asked him to make democratic concessions. Insecurity ran rampant, and many people emigrated. A popular slogan describing the oligarchy emerged: "Patria Libre o Miami" ("Give me liberty or give me Miami"). The situation was explosive. Popular unrest increased with the brutal repression, growing inflation, and high unemployment, exacerbated by the fall of coffee prices on the international market. The unrest was further exacerbated by the failure of the modest agrarian reform and the Alliance for Progress.

Viron Vaky, Assistant Secretary of State for Inter-American Affairs; William Bowdler, director of the Bureau of Intelligence and Research for the State Department; and other high United States officials traveled to El Salvador to convince General Romero to make a gesture toward democracy. CIA agents, diplomats, and United States military officers were pressing the Salvadoran military to stage a coup. (Vaky later claimed that he did not know such a move was being planned). In October of 1979 a group of reformist officers ousted Romero for fear that El Salvador might become another Nicaragua.

ARMED STRUGGLE

The reversal of Duarte and Ungo's victory in the 1972 elections showed the people that democracy was impossible under the military. There were nonstop popular protests, strikes, marches, occupations of public buildings and embassies, and campesino occupations of land. The people opted first for civil disobedience and later for armed struggle.

Campesinos, mass organizations, and labor unions grew stronger. They created the Unión de Trabajadores Campesinos (UTC: Union of Campesino Workers), the Federación Cristiana de Campesinos de El Salvador (FECCAS: Christian Federation of Salvadoran Campesinos), and the Frente de Acción Popular Unido (FAPU: Popular United Action Front), led by ordinary citizens, campesinos, students, and priests.

Armed struggle broke out anew. In 1970 Salvador Cayetano Carpio, a former seminarian and director of the radical wing of the Communist Party and known as the Ho Chi Minh of Central America, formed the Fuerzas Populares de Liberación (FPL: Popular Liberation Forces). Dissidents from the Communist Party and the Christian Democrats, activists from Catholic groups, and members of "The Group"—an organization comprised of revolutionary students—created the Ejército Revolucionario del Pueblo (ERP: People's Revolutionary Army) in 1972. The Fuerzas Armadas de Resistencia Nacional (FARN or RN: Armed Forces of National Resistance), with pro-China leanings, were a result of a split in the ERP after the 1974 "execution" of the poet Roque Dalton by his comrades-in-arms. The same year the Partido Revolucionario de Trabajadores de Centroamérica (PRTC: Central American Revolutionary Workers' Party) allied itself with the Fuerzas Populares de Liberación (FPL: Popular Liberation Forces), which grouped together the greater part of the popular rural, urban, and student organizations. In 1979 the Communist Party created the pro-Cuban Fuerzas Armadas de Liberación (FAL: Armed Liberation Forces). To some degree they all formed part of the "turbulent and prolonged struggle" within the Salvadoran Communist Party, commented one historian.[43]

In October 1980 the five principal groups—FAL, FPL, ERP, RN, and PRTC—formed the Frente Farabundo Martí de Liberación Nacional (FMLN: Farabundo Martí National Liberation Front), to coordinate their political and military actions. From that moment forward the armed struggle became a war of national liberation. Encouraged by the triumph of the Sandinistas in Nicaragua, they engaged in open action.[44]

The insurgency began to consolidate. In January 1980, five aggregate organizations—the BPR, the FAPU, UDN, the Ligas Populares de Febrero 28 (LP-28: February 28 Popular Leagues), and the Movimiento Popular de Liberación (MPL: Popular Liberation Movement) formed the Comité Coordinador Revolucionario de Masas (CRM: Peoples' Revolutionary Coordination Committee). As many as 200,000 workers and campesinos marched through the streets of San Salvador celebrating the formation of the committee. In April thousands attended the creation of the Frente Democrático Revolucionario (FDR: Democratic Revolutionary Front), a broad coalition of the CRM, the Social Democrat and Christian Democrat Parties, 80 percent of the membership of workers' and professional unions, Church people, students, small businessmen, and the National and Catholic universities. It was the broadest political movement in El Salvador's history and the political arm of the insurgency.[45]

THE VOICE OF THE MONSIGNOR

The "reformist" military officers who overthrew General Romero in 1979 formed a civilian-military junta with Colonels Adolfo Majano, a reformist—one of the leaders of the coup—and Jaime Abdul Gutiérrez, a conservative, not a reformist; Guillermo Ungo, the leftist leader of the National Revolutionary Movement (MNR); Román Mayorga, rector of the Catholic University (UCA); and Mario Andino of the middle-class, director of a North American company. The junta was the result of an alliance among conservatives, the Social Democratic and Christian Democratic Parties, and parties of the left.

The junta offered peace and democracy, respect for human rights, the release of political prisoners, and a general amnesty to include exiles. It recognized all political parties and groups and promised agrarian reform. But the people did not want a succession of military officers. They wanted a popular and democratic government. They were mistrustful because the military structure and the high command remained intact. The Communist Party, the Bloc, the ERP, and the FPL made their opposition known to the junta.[46]

Contrary to the junta's announced intentions, within twenty-four hours after they took power the armed forces declared a state of siege, suspended guarantees of individual rights, prohibited gatherings of more than three people, and began a violent persecution directed against popular and leftist leaders. The list of the murdered and the disappeared started to grow. Nothing had changed. The human rights commission of El Salvador denounced these abuses.

The junta quickly issued a decree on agrarian reform and named a commission to investigate the situation of political prisoners and the cases of more than 550 people who were "disappeared" during Romero's dictatorship.[47] And it undertook a cleansing of army and police officers connected to the death squads. It also dissolved ORDEN, which had been responsible for most of these crimes.

The reforms failed to materialize. The police and the army remained intact, the former dictator, General Romero, was not brought to justice (he sought asylum in Guatemala), the brutal repression went on, and the death squads continued to act with impunity.

There was disagreement within the junta. Colonels Jaime Abdul Gutiérrez, a member of the junta; José Guillermo García, minister of defense; and Eugenio Vides Casanova, commander of the national guard, were all responsible for the situation. When Majano, Ungo, and Mayorga, the attorney general, and other high officials protested, Vides Casanova told them, "We will not stop because they are subversives and we have to defend the country. Don't forget that when we want to be free of you, we will do it."[48] In January 1980, Ungo, Mayorga, nine ministers and thirty-seven high government officials resigned in protest against Colonel García's "dictatorship." They demanded his resignation and that of Mario Andino, the oligarchy's representative to the junta. Neither complied.

In May, Majano ordered the arrest of Roberto D'Aubuisson, a photogenic 37-year-old fascist, a former major in army intelligence, and a member of ANS-ESAL, accused of heading the death squads. Although he was caught red-handed in an attempted coup and arrested, an assembly of 700 army officers ordered his release and demanded the ouster of Majano.

With the junta becoming increasingly fascist, Majano was relieved of his duties; a month earlier he had escaped an assassination attempt. Openly accusing the government of supporting the death squads, Majano was arrested. Released a month later, he left the country.

The junta fell apart and reassembled several times as civilian members resigned, always in protest against the defense minister's military dictatorship. Most went into exile. By December 1980, the junta had been reorganized four times. Under pressure from the United States, Duarte was named president of the junta (he joined it during its third restructuring), and President Carter announced that he would resume military aid to El Salvador.

To the Salvadoran people Monsignor Arnulfo Romero, Archbishop of San Salvador, was a hero, a saint, and an inspiration in their struggle. In spite of the leaders' Marxist orientation, the armed groups also saw him in this light—many of them had deep roots in the Christianity of the New Church. Monsignor Romero repeatedly denounced the regime's brutal repression, which did not even respect the Church. After an act of sacrilege in which soldiers, using a tank to break down the church door in San Antonio Abad, murdered the parish priest and four young people and detained thirty-two parishioners, he excommunicated them.

The Monsignor was one of the most powerful voices against United States military aid to El Salvador. In February 1980, when he heard that President Carter aimed to reinstate such aid, he wrote to the President asking him "as a Christian and a defender of human rights" not to do so, since the aid would serve to increase the injustice and repression against the people who were fighting for the recognition of their rights. The junta was not solving the country's problems, he remarked, but returning it to violent repression. The number of dead and wounded was greater than under General Romero's military regime "whose systematic violations of human rights were denounced by the Inter-American Commission on Human Rights."[49]

The civilian-military junta, which was presided over but not led by Duarte, wanted to implement the agrarian reforms supported by Washington with the help of experts from the Agency for International Development (AID), the State Department, and the AFL-CIO American Institute for Free Labor, which was known throughout the continent for its links to the CIA. Carter and Duarte believed that distribution of lands to the campesinos would contribute to peace and create a base of popular support for the government. Duarte also believed that it would diminish the power of the "reactionary" land-owning oligarchy.[50] But achieving peace by giving lands to the campesinos was impossible in the middle of a war in which they were the target of official violence and persecution by the landholders.

Later Carter's former ambassador to El Salvador, Robert White, remembered that the agrarian reform was "rushed through more for its political impact than its social impact." Its actual implementation was a difficult task, since it was opposed by the powerful oligarchy of landholders and agrarian exporters and by a good number of land-owning military officers.[51]

In March 1980, after a big publicity campaign, a three-star colonel announced on television that the government had expropriated 200 haciendas from among the largest in the country as part of the "military's commitment to provide economic and social justice to the people." The following day a state of siege was declared, and troops commanded by army officers began the land distribution. It took the army to carry out this task that affected the most powerful sectors of El Salvador.[52] The agrarian reform had been designed by Roy Posterman, a University of Washington professor who hardly consulted the Salvadoran government, much less the campesinos. Like the agrarian reform he had previously designed for Vietnam, it was intended to prevent victory of the revolutionary forces and change the image of the army.[53]

The reforms in El Salvador were divided into three phases. The first stage was the expropriation of land holdings larger than 500 hectares and their transfer to campesino cooperatives (a plan not much to Washington's liking). The owners would be compensated (the United States appropriated millions of dollars for this purpose). The second, the expropriation of medium-size haciendas, most of which were coffee-growing lands—"the backbone of power for the oligarchy of landholders and agrarian exporters." (Within a year, this reform was suspended for "technical" reasons.) The third phase would consist of issuing deeds to campesinos sharecroppers.[54]

Protected by private armies, the land-holding oligarchy prevented the taking of lands. Undoing with one hand what it did with the other, the army unleashed a campaign of terror against the campesinos to take their lands from them. Some 2,600 were murdered for having done no more than apply for lands, and about 2,000 took refuge in the capital.[55] Government specialists were also murdered. In a letter to Monsignor Romero, the campesinos denounced the murders and abuses of which they were the victims. The reform was a bloodbath, said the Monsignor.[56]

In March 1980, Monsignor Romero was shot to death while he was celebrating Mass. As was his custom, in this, his last sermon, he listed the previous week's crimes by the army and the police. He described them as "terrible and tragic": villages had been bombed, leaving many dead, and soldiers burned and sacked their victims' fields. Romero announced that Amnesty International had found that human rights violations in El Salvador were reaching heights unknown in other parts of the world, and the government responded to such accusations by asserting that the casualties were the results of confrontations between the army and the guerrillas. But the victims, noted the Monsignor, bore the marks of torture. Their corpses had been mutilated and their faces disfigured with acid to prevent identification. His final words were a call to the men in the army and the police, asking them not to kill their brothers. He concluded: "In the name of God, in the name of this suffering people whose cries rise to Heaven more loudly each day, I implore you, I beg you, I order you in the name of God: Stop the repression."[57]

On the day of Monsignor Romero's funeral, the crowds who had come to render him their final respects were fired upon in the Cathedral of San Salvador. Ambassador Robert White accused D'Aubuisson of being the mastermind behind Romero's assassination, which supposedly had been carried out by death squads. The murder was never solved.

THE TRAIL OF VIOLENCE

Of the horrendous crimes committed daily by the forces of order the most atrocious were the massacres of the campesinos along the Honduran border carried out under "Operation Sandwich," in which both the Salvadoran and Honduran armies took part. Both governments denied involvement, or tried to cover it up. Many bodies remained undiscovered for years.

The worst of the massacres took place in March 1989, when 8,000 campesinos were killed as they tried to cross the Lempa River into Honduras.

Bombs were dropped from helicopters while ground troops attacked them with machine guns and mortars. On the Honduran side of the river troops turned the survivors back. A month later, 600 people—the elderly, women, and children—were murdered as they tried to cross the Sumpul River. The Salvadoran army shot at them from helicopters while the Honduran army forced them back into the bloody waters. The president of Honduras, General Paz García, denied the massacre, but a high-ranking military leader admitted that the "incident" occurred, though without the participation of the Honduran Army.[58]

In June 1980 troops occupied the Catholic university UCA in San Salvador and murdered 50 students. In August the army bombed strikers in the streets of the capital, killing 200 workers and wounding hundreds more. In October 3,000 campesinos were massacred in Morazán in a military offensive supposedly against the guerrillas. Some 24,000 succeeded in fleeing to other parts of the countryside, to the cities, or to neighboring countries.

In November six leaders of the FDR were murdered, including its president, Enrique Álvarez, a member of the Salvadoran oligarchy and minister of agriculture under several governments including the junta. These men were dragged out of their office in broad daylight by the Maximiliano Hernández Brigade, a death squad protected by agents of the feared treasury police, termed the Salvadoran Gestapo by the State Department.[59] Their mutilated bodies, which came to light the following day, showed evidence of torture.[60] This crime shocked the whole country and sparked international protest.

A few days later three American nuns and a missionary were murdered after having been kidnapped by members of the army at the San Salvador airport, where they were returning from Nicaragua. A priest informed Ambassador White of the crime, telling him that the bodies were buried in a village 15 miles from the capital. The ambassador ordered the bodies exhumed, and this revealed that the victims had been raped and shot in the head.

Carter suspended military aid to El Salvador. He demanded that the crime be investigated and the guilty punished, sending a government commission to gather information. Two weeks later Jeane Kirkpatrick, who was shortly to become United States Ambassador to the United Nations, declared that the Salvadoran government was not responsible for the deaths since "the nuns were not just nuns. The nuns were political activists."[61]

AT THE STAKE

In 1981 the Salvadoran conflict became a full-out civil war. The FMLN, with the political support of the FDR, widened the struggle. Strikes, demonstrations, protest marches, and peaceful land occupations were more and more frequent, encouraged by the Salvadoran Communist Party and supported by student and political movements and by radical sectors of the Catholic Church. The Christian Grassroots Communities, which worked with the poor in the countryside and with the marginal neighborhoods in the cities, were a powerful voice against social injustice and repression, and they supported and stimulated the insurgent struggle.

In January, a week before Carter left the White House, the FMLN launched what it called the Final Offensive. Carter immediately sent emergency military aid. With the inauguration of Ronald Reagan, the Salvadoran civil war took on a new face. Reagan converted it into an East-West conflict, appropriated the war by militarizing Central America, and unleashed a crusade against international Communism in the region.

SOMOZA'S NICARAGUA

Between 1853 and 1933 United States marines invaded Nicaragua twenty times. In one case, they stayed five years, in another, twenty-one. Before its withdrawal in 1933 the United States organized the Nicaraguan National Guard—a police force—and named Anastasio "Tacho" Somoza García to be its commander-in-chief.

The presence of troops in his country and Washington's interference in its internal affairs were intolerable to a thirty-two-year-old officer, Augusto César Sandino. He decided to resort to arms, and he formed an army made up of workers, most of them from United States companies. He himself worked for a mining company and local campesinos. Only workers and campesinos together, he declared, could fight "to the final consequences."

Sandino wanted social recovery and the expulsion of the invaders. He did not aspire to power. He inflamed the people's nationalism, and soon they saw him as their leader and a hero. With his "Army in Defense of Nicaraguan Sovereignty" he launched the war of liberation. His exploits aroused admiration all throughout Latin America from students, intellectuals, and politicians in solidarity with this struggle against interventionism, imperialism, and Uncle Sam's big stick. Venezuelan, Mexican, Colombian, and Peruvian revolutionaries joined his small army.

When Juan B. Sacasa was voted into office (1933–1936), in elections supervised by the marines, Washington pulled out its troops. Sandino believed that Nicaragua had freed itself from the Yankee occupation. He accepted the truce offered by Sacasa and successfully negotiated peace. But in February 1934, as he was leaving a dinner at the President's house, Sandino was ambushed. As he and his brother Socrates, as well as two senior officers of his army, were riding in a car, they were stopped by the national guard, taken to a nearby town, and assassinated. "Tacho" Somoza García, commander of the guard, had ordered them killed. Sacasa tried to punish the killers, but his son-in-law, Somoza, stopped him.[62]

Somoza had his eye on the presidency. Sacasa knew that the National Guard was a threat to his government—Sandino had asked him to disband it. In a poignant letter to Secretary of State Cordell Hull, cosigned by the former presidents Emiliano Chamorro and Adolfo Díaz, Sacasa expressed his fear that the guard could "eventually" become "a threat to peace and order." He asked for protection from this institution created by the United States. Hull replied that since the marines had pulled out, the "special relations" between their countries were at an end.[63]

On March 31, 1937, civil revolt broke out; it lasted for eight days before being crushed by the National Guard. Somoza executed a coup and ousted Sacasa, beginning his nineteen-year dictatorship. He made his oldest son, Luis, president of the congress and named his other son, Anastasio, known as "Tachito," commander of the National Gard. Thus the security of the state and of his person (for him they were one in the same) remained under family control.

"Tacho" took 15 percent of the best lands for himself, thus becoming the most powerful rancher and industrial magnate in the country. He owned the most lucrative businesses, and his riches accumulated at the expense of the national treasury. He built schools, hospitals, roads, and a hydroelectric plant, modernized ports and agriculture, and extended the cattle industry. The best roads, however, led to his haciendas, all acts of modernization improved his crops, the cattle were fattened on his land, and foreign trade was waged with his products. The brutal and corrupt National Guard, commanded by his son, maintained internal order. The prisons remained full of opposition figures and suspects—the most bothersome were shot "while attempting to flee."

Somoza relied on support from the United States. In January 1939 President Franklin D. Roosevelt invited him to Washington. Dressed in full regalia, Roosevelt met him at the train station and led him into the city with an imposing military parade and air force display. The procession moved through the streets of Washington to the White House, with Somoza and Roosevelt riding side by side in an open car. Roosevelt's reply to the criticism of that splendid display for a dictator was, "Somoza may be a son of a bitch, but he's our son of a bitch."[64] He was, in fact, the most servile of the heads of state in the hemisphere. In return for this submissiveness, Washington remained silent about the scandalous corruption and brutality of his regime.

The U.S. ambassadors gave Somoza unconditional support. Thomas Whelan (1951–1961) went even further by publicly supporting the National Guard in the murder of four students in the city of León for leading a demonstration against Somoza. Whelan felt justified because the students were "Communists." He also demanded that the students at the University of León be expelled for having criticized the United States. The students burned a United States flag and an effigy of Whelan. The ambassador panicked, for it was the first anti-Yankee demonstration in Nicaragua.[65]

In preparation for another one of his "reelections" Somoza went to León to proclaim his candidacy at the Casa del Obrero (House of the Worker). En route he was brought to a halt by a young man who aimed a small revolver at him and emptied it at point blank range. The assassin, Rigoberto López Pérez, a twenty-three-year-old poet, was killed on the spot by Somoza's bodyguards. Near death, Somoza was transported by the United States to its hospital in the Panama Canal Zone. Eisenhower sent his own personal physicians. Somoza died nine days after the attack, on September 21, 1956. "His constant demonstration of friendship for the United States will never be forgotten," John Foster Dulles wrote to Somoza's widow.[66]

The funeral was conducted with great pomp, military salutes, ringing oratory, and High Masses. Meanwhile Somoza's security forces were torturing innocent people presumed to have opposed Somoza, alleging their culpability in his assassination. Some were tortured in the gardens of the presidential residence, to the delight of his family.

The line of succession began. Somoza's oldest son Luis, thirty-five, was chosen to succeed him, "elected" with 89 percent of the vote. "Tachito" remained in charge of the National Guard. Luis cultivated good relations with the United States, breaking off relations with Cuba and expelling its diplomats. Such measures provoked wild demonstrations of solidarity with the Revolution, protesting against Luis's submissiveness to the United States and his collaboration with Washington in preparing the invasion of Cuba. The country remained under martial law until the end of his term.

Luis had no desire to be reelected. He set up a fake election, and René Schick was elected (1963–1966). Pedro Joaquín Chamorro, editor-in-chief and owner of the daily *La Prensa* and in constant opposition to the dictatorship, denounced this huge scam. Chamorro went into exile on various occasions because of persecution by the regime—Somoza had not dared to silence him, since he was admired both in Nicaragua and abroad.

Schick was a puppet who took care of minor matters. The important decisions were made by the Somozas. In 1966 Schick died of natural causes. The campaign to elect his successor was violent and bloody. Tachito emerged the winner and governed for thirteen years. He was one of the most corrupt and rapacious of dictators in all of Latin America. In the gardens of his residence he kept cages for his lions, panthers, jaguars, and other animals, as well as select political prisoners. It was there that Chamorro was imprisoned after the assassination of Somoza, having been accused of being part of the conspiracy.

United States military aid was unwavering and substantial. It accounted for 13 percent of Nicaragua's defense budget, and a contingent of twenty-five military advisers was assigned to the country. The number of Nicaraguan officers trained at the United States' School of the Americas in Panama, was the highest of all Latin American countries.[67] The State Department considered Nicaragua the most stable and calm country in the region. Nonetheless, opposition to the dictatorship mounted.

Tachito's decline began after a massive earthquake hit the country in December 1972. It was so intense that many believed the end of the world was coming. It left between 8,000 and 10,000 dead, 20,000 injured, 51,000 unemployed, and more than 100,000 homeless amid the ruins. Half of Managua was destroyed, along with four hospitals, 210,000 square miles of public buildings, 250,000 square miles in the commercial zone, and 95 percent of small factories. The loss was estimated at $1.2 billion.

The people and the National Guard sacked businesses and private properties. Somoza declared a state of emergency, suspended constitutional guarantees, and created the National Emergency Committee, appointing himself its chairman. The committee was to receive the incoming funds from governments, foreign businesses, and individuals to aid those who had suffered damage and for the reconstruction of Managua.

The family's looting of these funds began immediately. One of Somoza's sons sold food and clothing, earmarked for relief, on the black market, and he allowed members of the National Guard to share in the loot. Somoza, along with his family and friends, bought public lands cheaply, and then sold them for huge sums to the government[68] for the construction of public housing—which was never built.

Somoza did not make public the amount he received in foreign aid—it came to tens of millions of dollars in goods and cash—nor did he explain what he did with the millions in loans and credits that he obtained at low interest from AID, the World Bank, the Inter-American Development Bank (IDB) and the International Monetary Fund (IMF). His greed and his insensitivity to the country's tragedy scandalized sectors of the oligarchy and the Church and disgusted the people. The number of disaffected people in sectors that had previously supported the regime grew. Henry Ruiz, one of the commanders of the FSLN, noted that these people realized that something new was happening. They sought the support of the lower middle class, whose members were now opposed to Somoza.[69]

THE SANDINISTAS

The armed struggle against Somoza began in 1958. Ramón Raudales, Chale Haslam, and other veterans of Sandino's army once more resorted to armed struggle to combat the dictatorship. Between 1960 and 1962 some twenty anti-Somoza, nationalist, anti-imperialist, and revolutionary organizations emerged, some of them identified with the Cuban Revolution. The proliferation of such movements showed that the youth and the general population were determined to overthrow the dictator. Outside Nicaragua exiles formed other armed groups. Pedro Joaquín Chamorro led one such group in Costa Rica, with the help of Jose Figueres and the National Liberation Party. Edén Pastora and Harold Martínez created others. After the triumph, Martínez was discovered to be one of Somoza's agents.[70]

The FSLN was the most important of these groups. Formed in 1961 by Carlos Fonseca Amador, Tomás Borge, and Daniel Ortega, the FSLN led the armed struggle until its triumph.

Fonseca, the leader of the rebellion, launched his fight at the University of León, where he was studying law. The revolutionary vanguard was located in León. His life was one continuous passage back and forth between armed struggle and prison. He was captured, imprisoned, freed, deported; then he returned to take up the clandestine struggle until his next capture. During one of his periods in Nicaragua, he created the Movement for a New Nicaragua (MNN). Once he was deported to Guatemala on a Nicaraguan Air Force plane, and there he was confined to the Petén rain forest. There, he met Luis Turcios Lima, a young Guatemalan officer serving in the area. Later Turcios became the head of the first Guatemalan guerrillas, the Fuerzas Armadas Rebeldes (FAR: Rebel Armed Forces).

Set out in a document published in 1969, inspired in its essence by Fonseca,

the goals of the FSLN were to take power by armed force, destroy the dictatorship's bureaucratic and military apparatus, and install a revolutionary government "based on an alliance of workers and campesinos and supported by
all anti-imperialist forces in the country." It proclaimed the intentions of
nationalizing the mining and lumber industries and of reclaiming riches
"usurped" by Yankee monopolies, the properties, factories, sugar refineries,
transportation systems, and other possessions "usurped" by the Somoza family and other "enemies of the people," such as politicians, military officers, and
other accomplices in the corrupt administration. The banking industry would
be nationalized, and "usurious loans imposed on the country by Yankee
monopolies" would not be recognized. Capitalist agricultural industries, large
land holdings, and "parasitic" tenancy of the land by exploiters would be expropriated; the document further declared its solidarity and active support of the
struggle against imperialism, colonialism, and neocolonialism by the peoples
of the third world. Its slogan was *Patria Libre o Morir* (Free Homeland or
Death).[71] Such goals, similar to those of the Cuban Revolution, made
Washington and the Nicaraguan and Latin American right wing tremble.

The fight against the dictatorship was long and unequal. The FSLN grew
amid terror, murder, torture, the disappearance of opposition figures, and the
massacres of campesinos. Somoza bombed cities and towns in his persecution
of the guerrillas, and the National Guard murdered campesinos and ransacked and destroyed their fields, crops, and animals.

The first major blow against Somoza by the FSLN came in December 1974.
A commando led by Borge broke into an exclusive post-Christmas dinner party
in honor of the United States ambassador, Turner B. Shelton. The guests
included government ministers and personalities, among them Somoza's
brother-in-law and ambassador to the White House and the United Nations,
Guillermo Sevilla Sacasa. When the rebels arrived, Ambassador Shelton had
already left, but they killed the host, Doctor José María Castillo, and
announced that they would continue to kill hostages unless the government
freed fourteen Sandinista prisoners—among them Daniel Ortega—paid them
$1 million, and published the FSLN communiqué. Somoza complied, and a
government aircraft took the rebels to Cuba.

In 1977 the FSLN launched several offensives against the National Guard.
The insurrection became widespread in 1978 after the assassination of Pedro
Joaquín Chamorro—a crime that infuriated the people. In August a com-
mando led by Edén Pastora, Commander Zero, occupied the National Palace.
A total of sixty-seven deputies and more than 1,500 others ranging from con-

gressional employees to ordinary citizens were inside the building. The rebels held the deputies "most hated by the people" and one member of Somoza's family as hostages. They announced that they would be killed unless fifty-eight revolutionary prisoners of the regime were freed. Borge was one of them. After two days the prisoners were freed. Somoza paid $500,000, and published an FSLN communiqué. When the rebels were escorted by bus to the airport, the people lined the streets to cheer them on. It was a spectacular blow.

The FSLN continued attacking the National Guard, occupying towns, haranguing the populace, and gaining ground. In September 1978, they used the underground radio station Radio Sandino to call for an insurrection. Though the Sandinistas had insufficient weapons and combatants and were lacking in military preparation, the FSLN had the support of the people and succeeded in controlling parts of Masaya, León, Estelí, and Chinandega for several hours.[72]

Though this offensive had not been decisive, nor had it been a real threat to the regime, it did reveal the government's weak spots. The FSLN continued to grow in power and militancy.[73] Somoza responded with extreme violence. He ordered the bombing of cities taken by the guerrillas and caused innumerable deaths and enormous destruction.

Catholic priests and members of religious orders, followers of liberation theology, joined the Sandinista fight in defense of social justice and the rights of the poor and against the dictatorship. After the triumph, prominent priests became part of the government to help with the reconstruction of Nicaragua and the construction of a just and egalitarian society. Miguel D'Escoto, a member of the Maryknoll Order, was named chancellor. Fernando Cardenal, a Jesuit, was appointed minister of education; as such he headed the literacy campaign. His brother Ernesto, an acclaimed poet and founder of a contemplative community on the small island of Solentiname in Lake Nicaragua, became the minister of culture.

THE TRIUMPH

After the September 1978 FSLN offensive, when the Sandinastas took Masaya, León, Chinandega, and Estelí, President Carter feared that the rebel triumph would later support guerrilla movements in El Salvador and Guatemala and that the influence and involvement of Cuba would expand dramatically in Central America. He sent the career diplomat William Bowdler to Managua to negotiate with Somoza for a peaceful solution and a transition to democracy. The only way out was for Somoza to resign.[74] Bowdler returned empty-handed. Somoza refused to leave, and the opposition would accept nothing less.

Carter opposed intervention both for and against Somoza, though Venezuela's president Carlos Andrés Pérez—called the godfather of the Sandinista revolution—and other Latin American heads of state asked him to force Somoza's resignation. Carter tried several formulas. He initiated an OAS mediation commission, on which Bowdler sat, to negotiate between Somoza and the opposition (not including the FSLN). The resolution hinged on Somoza's resignation. Again Somoza refused, but he proposed calling a plebiscite supervised by the OAS, so that the people could decide whether he should resign. If he won, he would reorganize the government, and if he lost he promised to resign and let the Frente Amplio de Oposición (FAO: Broad-Based Opposition Front)—an amorphous political movement composed of anti-Somoza moderates, businessmen, professionals, and party heads—take over. The opposition had no faith in Somoza's honesty or the possibility of a clean plebiscite. It imposed conditions that Somoza found unacceptable.[75]

In May the rebel leadership, exiled in Costa Rica, named a reconstruction junta that would become the government after Somoza's fall. It was composed of Violeta Barrios de Chamorro (Pedro Joaquín Chamorro's widow), Alfonso Robelo, Sergio Ramírez, Moisés Hassan, and Daniel Ortega. They represented the five current political orientations. Carter sent a new ambassador, Lawrence Pezzullo, to block a Sandinista victory by insisting on Somoza's resignation and by helping to compose a national reconciliation government with members of the National Liberal Party (Somoza's party), the FAO, and the FSLN, but not the most radicals. He suggested Adolfo Calero, Alfonso Robelo (later members of the "contra" directorate), Archbishop Obando y Bravo, and Edén Pastora. This government would then hold elections with the help of the OAS. The United States wanted to keep the National Guard under new leadership. Somoza said he would accept resignation in an orderly transition under the supervision of the OAS.

With the triumph of the FSLN imminent (it came the following month), and with the rebels supported by several Latin American governments, United States Secretary of State Cyrus Vance proposed at a special session of the OAS a national reconstruction government with broad support from different social sectors, the suspension of military aid, a cease-fire, and that the OAS send a peace-keeping force to Nicaragua.

This plan provoked a strong reaction. Jorge Castañeda, chancellor of Mexico, said it was not the business of the OAS, or anyone else, to tell the

Nicaraguans how they should constitute their government when the dictatorship fell. In the name of the "provisional government" of Nicaragua (the Panamanian delegation ceded him its place at the podium), Miguel D'Escoto denounced the proposal as an attempt to violate the rights of Nicaraguans, who were on the verge of overthrowing Somoza's dictatorship. Vance's proposal did not go to a vote.

Two days later, an OAS resolution condemned the "inhuman conduct" of Somoza's "dictatorial regime," demanded his "immediate and definitive replacement" and the installation of a democratic government that would include representatives of the major opposition groups and reflect the free will of the people. It was adopted by a vote of 17 (including the United States), 2 against (Nicaragua and Paraguay), and 4 abstentions (the dictatorships of Chile, El Salvador, Guatemala, and Honduras).[76]

Pezzullo continued negotiating a transition of power and formulas for preserving the National Guard. Somoza, in turn, continued bombing the people. In a cable to the State Department, Pezzullo asked that it not pressure Somoza to suspend the bombing, since it was the only effective measure against the guerrillas, who must be kept from victory at all costs.[77]

On July 13 the National Reconstruction junta sent a communiqué from Costa Rica to the Secretary General of the OAS, Alejandro Orfila, asking for an immediate end to the "genocidal government," Somoza's resignation before the Nicaraguan congress, and the appointment by congress of a provisional president who would hand over power to the junta.[78] On July 16, Somoza presented his resignation in a terse letter. He wrote, "I have fought against Communism, and when the truth comes out, history will justify me."[79] He advised Francisco Urcuyo, on whom the presidency fell as the senior member of congress, not to hand over power.

Hounded by the growing insurrection, internationally isolated, and under pressure from the United States, which withdrew its support, on July 17 "Tachito" left for Miami in the company of his mistress, Dinorah Sampson, with "coffins and coffers," as described by Salman Rushdie in *The Jaguar Smile*. In these, he carried the remains of his assassinated father, "Tacho I," and his brother, Luis—as well as the cash of the national treasury. He left behind only $3.5 million. The country was in ruins, with farms devastated, towns destroyed, and a foreign debt of $1.6 billion. Casualties totaled 40,000, leaving tens of thousands of widows and orphans.

Somoza's fortune amounted to nearly $1 billion. The family owned 10,000 square miles of land, and he owned all the factories and every industry in the country. He also controlled rail and shipping lines, the fishing industry, the gold mines, the lumber companies, and the largest brewery in Nicaragua. He had investments in casinos and houses of prostitution, had a hand in the drug trade, and owned property outside the country, mainly in the United States.[80]

Urcuyo did not hand over the power. He announced that he would remain in office until May 1981, the end of Somoza's term. He praised the National Guard, asked all irregular forces to surrender their arms, and began making nominations. He promoted Lieutenant Colonel Federico Mejía González to general, and named him head of the National Guard (the higher echelon of the staff officers having fled to Miami with Somoza, while others fled to Honduras and Guatemala), and he called on the troops to "redouble [their] efforts in the present struggle."[81]

The rebel junta moved to León, declared it the "provisional capital," and demanded the unconditional surrender of the National Guard. Urcuyo "governed" for forty-three hours. After a night of chaos, he fled with his family to Guatemala in an airplane sent for him by General Lucas García. The National Guard surrendered.

On July 19, 1979, the rebels entered Managua accompanied by the large crowds, the cheers of the people, and a rain of flowers. It was the Day of National Joy.

President Carter chose to back the Sandinista government. He sent emergency food aid—$39 million worth—and saw to it that Congress approved $75 million for the reconstruction of the country. He believed that it was important to maintain good relations with the new Nicaragua in order to prevent an opening for the other side, as had happened in Cuba. He understood that the people's resentment of the United States was due to its long history of interventions and military occupations, and to its unqualified support for the Somoza dynasty. He declared that the change happening in Nicaragua was inevitable, and that insurgency and instability in Central America were the results of inequality, underdevelopment, and repression. He did not lay the responsibility for the Sandinista triumph at Cuba's doorstep or on the Soviet Union, as the Republicans had. Later Reagan would accuse Carter of "losing" Nicaragua.[82]

GUATEMALA AND ITS VIOLENCE

Guatemala was another banana republic until the United Fruit Company began to fall apart. During the regime of Manuel Estrada Cabrera (1898–1920),

an ignorant, coarse, depraved, and thieving dictator, the transnational company started taking over the country. United Fruit established a banana
monopoly, became the major landowner, monopolized the communications
and rail systems, and took possession of the ports. The country benefited little since its venal rulers granted the company tax exemptions and other privileges under the table in exchange for juicy bribes. Twenty years later General
Jorge Ubico (1931–1944), another dictator, allowed the company to continue
its march to the Pacific. He exorbitantly extended its lands, broadened its pub-
lic-service concessions, canceled its debts, and exempted it from tax payments— all of this largesse came free of charge.

THE BIG FARCE

The United Fruit empire in Guatemala continued smoothly until the presidency of Jacobo Arbenz (1952–1954). He deepened the reforms—the so-called
revolution—of his predecessor, President Arévalo, applied the agrarian reform
law, and began expropriating major underused land holdings, among them
270,000 hectares belonging to United Fruit (it owned 550,000) that lay fal-
low. This measure unleashed the fury of the Empire. Secretary of State John
Foster Dulles demanded they be returned and forbade the company from
accepting the monetary compensation it was offered (United Fruit assessed its
lands at sixteen times the offered price).

In the midst of the McCarthy fever gripping the United States, Dulles
turned this conflict into a Cold War issue and Arbenz into its first victim. The
president of United Fruit backed Dulles. And the company's public relations
head, Spruille Braden, launched a shocking campaign in the press, asking for
United States intervention to oppose Communist infiltration in Latin America,
particularly in Guatemala. (Braden had been an undersecretary of state and
ambassador to Colombia, Cuba, and Argentina and was well known for his long
and unfortunate interventionist history in these countries.)

At the Tenth Inter-American Conference requested by Dulles and held in
Caracas in 1954, he easily persuaded the meeting to adopt a declaration condemning international communism and advocating hemispheric solidarity and
mutual defense against "Communist aggression." The chancellor of Guatemala,
Guillermo Toriello, warned that on "the pretext of combating Communism,
fundamental principles of democracy can be contravened, violations of human
rights justified, and the principle of nonintervention infringed upon." The declaration, he argued, was "the internationalization of McCarthyism." The

majority—all dictatorships—supported it; Argentina (under Perón) voted against it, and Mexico abstained. Costa Rica did not attend the meeting, since José Figueres refused to participate in this "assembly of dictators in a country governed by the most brutal and corrupt of them all, General Pérez Jiménez."[83]

At the United Nations Security Council, Guatemala denounced the "conspiracy threatening its country" as plotted by foreign governments. The United States, supported by Colombia and Brazil, maintained that the matter should first be handled by the OAS. The United States dragged out the discussion until the CIA's "Operation Success" against Arbenz was completed. When the OAS again took up the debate, Arbenz had already fallen.

"Operation Success" was supposedly an invasion by Guatemalan "rebels" coming from Honduras to "liberate" the country from the "Communist" government of Arbenz. In reality it was plotted by John Foster Dulles and his brother Allan, director of the CIA, with the cooperation of the faithful dictators—Trujillo, Somoza, and Pérez Jiménez—and United Fruit, without whom it would have been impossible, according to one CIA agent.[84]

This alleged invasion was cleverly managed by the CIA through an underground radio station. "Now [is] the time for the final big lie," said the CIA head of publicity while signaling for the operation to begin. The "Liberation Army," 200 Guatemalan and Central American mercenaries under the command of Colonel Carlos Castillo Armas, an obscure military officer and permanent fan of coups,[85] entered the capital carrying an image of the Christ of Esquipulas. The CIA's underground radio station reported on the advance, announcing that the rebels, heavily armed, were heading for the government palace. Night flights of unregistered aircraft, piloted by American "volunteers," dropped flyers urging the people to rebel. Burdened by this psychological warfare and unable to stop the supposed invasion since his comrades-in-arms had abandoned him (Ambassador John Puerifoy had convinced them to desert), Arbenz resigned.

The accusation that Arbenz was a Communist and the staged "invasion" paid for by the CIA were both outright fabrications. The finishing touch was the exaggeration of his fall: Dulles let it be known that it was "a victory against international Communism," and Eisenhower congratulated the CIA for the "cleanness" of the operation and for having aborted a "Soviet beachhead in our hemisphere."[86] Few doubted that Arbenz's fall was the work of the CIA. The governments did not object—the majority were dictatorships allied with Washington, and the rest feared reprisals. This sordid imperialistic act against a small country violated international law. It frustrated the giving of land to hungry peasants and set a precedent for the so-called inviolability of United States interests. According to Guatemalan historians, this was the beginning of a forty-year period of political violence in their country.

Colonel Carlos Castillo Armas, the new president (1954–1957), under the banner of McCarthyism and at the service of the "master" who had put him in power, set off a bloody anti-Communist campaign in accordance with a plan previously agreed upon with the CIA in Tegucigalpa, Honduras. This campaign was backed by all the sectors of power in Guatemala, including the hierarchy of the Catholic Church.

Castillo Armas returned confiscated lands to the United Fruit Company and other previous owners, removed the campesinos from their own lands as well as from those received through agrarian reform, and massacred them. The United States played an active part in this process. Dulles personally conducted a "diplomatic crusade with the stridency of a Torquemada."[87] The United States Embassy drew up lists of Communists the government was to eliminate, with instructions to treat them roughly.[88] In 1957 Castillo Armas was assassinated inside the Presidential Palace in a conspiracy that was never explained. Eisenhower declared it "a great loss to Guatemala and the world," sending his son to attend the funeral.[89]

After a period of chaos, a provisional government, coups, and countercoups, the annulment of the 1957 elections for fraud, and new elections in which no one won the necessary majority, the Guatemalan National Congress named General Miguel Ydígoras Fuentes to the presidency in January 1958.

Ydígoras gave the United States his invaluable aid for the invasion of Cuba without consulting with the army high command. He permitted the installation of clandestine military bases on inland haciendas to train anti-Castro mercenary forces. In return, he asked for a share of the Cuban sugar quota cut by the United States and the forgiveness of a $1.8 million debt contracted by Castillo Armas with the CIA for the plot against Arbenz. Washington accepted the terms.[90]

When the *New York Times* exposed the existence of these bases and United States plans to invade Cuba—an embarrassing moment for the Eisenhower administration and Ydígoras—Guatemalan military officers protested. Such foreign military enclaves in their country were an affront. Popular and student sectors also staged large protest demonstrations of support for Cuba and against the government. Other protests followed when relations with the island were severed in April 1960. Ydígoras repressed them with extreme violence.

In October, in the United Nations Security Council, Cuba denounced the United States' plans to invade its country and accused the governments of Guatemala and Nicaragua, and United Fruit, of collaborating with them. Cuba's Chancellor Roa denounced the clandestine bases in Guatemala where Yankee advisers were training the anti-Castro mercenary forces. Both governments denied their existence.

THE FIRST GUERRILLAS

In July 1960 there was a military uprising in Guatemala. Another occurred on November 13, in which a third of the army tried to occupy the military bases at Zacapa and Puerto Barrios on the eastern coast, to create a revolutionary focal point and take up the armed struggle against the dictatorship.

Ydígoras filled an airplane with anti-Castro Cuban mercenaries, intending to combat the rebels, but United States Ambassador John Muccio dissuaded him. The rebellion was put down within seventy-two hours. Its failure was partly due to disloyalty, since only forty-five out of 100 rebels participated in the revolt.[91]

The United States increased military aid to Guatemala and sent in advisers from the Special Forces—the Green Berets—to support the fight against the guerrillas. Four days later Eisenhower sent air and naval units to patrol the coasts of Nicaragua and Guatemala. Cuba protested this military deployment in the UN Security Council, denouncing it as a flagrant violation of the principles of nonintervention and free self-determination, its true purpose being to sustain the dictatorial regimes of Guatemala and Nicaragua.

The Kennedy administration's strategy of counterinsurgency was tried out principally in Guatemala. In 1962 the United States installed a secret training base for the army in Guatemala, and for the first time set into motion the civil-military actions of this strategy. This was the so-called "soft war," the precursor of the "low-intensity conflict" strategy, put in place after the United States' defeat in Vietnam.[92]

By 1962 the whole country opposed Ydígoras. There was criticism of his incompetence, brutal repression, and the corruption of his government. Even the Catholic Church hierarchy, usually so silent in the face of repression, political crimes, and social inequities, started to question him in pastoral letters signed by the bishops. A series of violent demonstrations against his government—which lasted nearly a month—and coup attempts caused his downfall. A few days before the March 1963 elections, Defense Minister Colonel

Enrique Peralta Azurdía ousted him. Kennedy immediately recognized Peralta.

After the military uprising on November 13, 1960, the first Guatemalan guerrilla movement emerged, headed by Lieutenants Marco Aurelio Yon Sosa, a twenty-two-year-old mestizo of Chinese ancestry, and nineteen-year-old Luis Turcios Lima. Both received military training from the United States and had participated in the uprising. When it failed, they took refuge in the mountains near the Sierra de las Minas in the Izabal region. Colonel Sessan Pereira, who led the revolt, fled to Mexico.

In 1962 Yon Sosa and Turcios Lima created the Movimiento Revolucionario 13 de Noviembre (MR-13: Revolutionary Movement of November 13) with campesinos, workers, students, and members of the Guatemalan Workers' Party (the Communist party). Students operated in the cities as urban cells.

Their nationalist and reformist motivation soon took on a radical and socialist orientation, like the Cuban Revolution. Their priority was to transfer lands to campesinos and to the indigenous population. In 1962 they successfully attacked army posts and police stations. After four years Yon Sosa and Turcios parted ways, following different ideologies and strategic concepts. Yon Sosa remained at the head of MR-13, and Turcios formed the Fuerzas Armadas Revolucionarias (FAR: Revolutionary Armed Forces). MR-13 operated in Izabal Province, where there were large United Fruit plantations, and FAR in the Sierra de las Minas, which covered Zacapa Province. In both the majority of the population was ladinos (whites and mestizos). Their differences neither broke up their friendship nor disrupted the coordination of their struggles.

Yon Sosa was pro-Castro and preferred the focus strategy. He decided to indoctrinate his troops politically first before going into action. But the rebels were less interested in doctrine than in fighting the dictatorship, and the MR-13 quickly lost strength. For Turcios, on the other hand, the armed struggle came first. The FAR, also proponents of the focus strategy who believed in establishing small nuclei of activity from which to expand the struggle, attracted student and popular sectors and included almost the entire country, particularly the ladino areas. They struck rapidly and effectively, liberating regions, occupying towns, haranguing the people about the goals of the struggle, attacking military and police barracks to "capture" weapons, assaulting banks to obtain funds, and kidnapping officers, politicians, and members of the oligarchy for ransom and to obtain concessions from the government. The FAR established an urban network active in sabotage and terrorism.

Yon Sosa's relations with the PGT (the Communist Party) were not good. The PGT did not trust him: He was not a member of the party, and he was critical of Moscow's policy of peaceful coexistence, the line followed by the orthodox Communist parties.[93] At the Tricontinental Conference in Havana in 1966, which brought together representatives of Communist parties, the left, and liberation movements from Africa, Asia, and Latin America, Fidel Castro strongly criticized the Trotskyite tendency of M-13, an accusation to which some objected. In 1968 the United States Congress investigated M-13 to determine its relations with Cuba, but it concluded that there was no connection aside from the circumstance that both followed the Cuban battle strategy.[94]

In the mid-1960s the guerrillas controlled various areas, some only an hour from the capital. Their activities were not reported in the international news since the more audacious actions in El Salvador and Nicaragua overshadowed them. After the Tricontinental Conference in Havana, the M-13 fought harder, and sectors of M-13 and FAR joined together. The PGT helped FAR organize their forces and gave them political direction. In 1968 FAR broke with the PGT, causing division within the guerrillas and the Party, giving way to a new group, the Fuerzas Armadas Rebeldes (Armed Rebel Forces).

The armed movements grew weaker and broke up into factions as the result of internal conflicts and power struggles (some were leaning on the political direction of the PGT), and the Trotskyite tendency of the M-13, objected to by some.[95] At the end of the 1960s, after the virtual extinction of M-13, the guerrillas realized that one of their errors was in overlooking indigenous zones, missing the opportunity to raise the consciousness of their population and involve them in the struggle.

VIOLENCE AND "PACIFICATION"

Colonel Enrique Peralta Azurdía's government (1963–1966) heralded another time of terror. One of Peralta's first acts in office was to call for the assassination of eight political and union leaders in Puerto Barrios, which was controlled by United Fruit. Some were crushed alive by trucks loaded with stones.

Peralta was faced with an explosive social situation: 87 percent of the population lived in extreme poverty, and unemployment and underemployment reached 70 percent. As many as ninety percent of the campesinos and indigenous people either had no land at all or had too little to ensure their subsistence. The guerrilla groups continued to strike. The United States pressured Peralta to accept advisers from its Special Forces and an increase in military aid. Peralta did not yield. He understood that the Pentagon wanted to use Guatemala as a laboratory to experiment with counterinsurgency—the guerrillas were under the direction of former military officers, and Guatemala's potential for revolution was the most ominous in all of Central America.

Peralta had the support of his army for his brutal campaign of "pacification." Raids, murders, tortures, and disappearances were the order of the day. During his time in office death squads connected with the military and security forces—paid by transnational enterprises such as United Fruit Company—set out to "clean out undesirables." In August 1966, a memorandum from the United States Embassy recommended that the government create such groups for "antiterrorist" operations.[96] The ambassador further suggested that "certain tasks" of repression be undertaken by civilians, because the people's disgust with the army benefited the insurgent movements.[97]

Under Peralta, there was a proliferation of kidnappings and murders at the hands of these clandestine groups, the guerrillas, and common criminals. The country was sinking into an orgy of blood. It was "a civil war on an underground level," out of the government's control, according to the Guatemalan author Juan Mestre.[98]

Washington saw that the only way out was by constitutional means. Peralta agreed to hold elections. On the eve of the election twenty-eight revolutionary leaders were arrested and disappeared, but the elections were more or less clean. Professor Julio César Méndez Montenegro, an opposition candidate, moderate reformer, head of the center-leftist Partido Revolucionario Ortodoxo (PRO: Orthodox Revolutionary Party), and dean of the faculty of law at the University of San Carlos, became the president-elect. The other candidates were military officers. Méndez was the first civilian in fifteen years to be elected president by popular vote. But before he could take office, the military officers presented their demands, among them a free hand in the counterinsurgency struggle.

Méndez promised a Third Revolutionary Government (the first and second were Arévalo's and Arbenz's, respectively) and the PGT supported him. Turcios Lima, on the other hand, declared the elections a "trap," calling the voters "accomplices of imperialism." Méndez announced that his first aim was to achieve peace through negotiations with the guerrillas, and he offered them generous terms to surrender their weapons. Turcios declared that he would not stop fighting as long as there was social injustice, but he offered a truce if the army would suspend hostilities. Before Méndez could respond, the army declared that these conditions were unacceptable. On October 20, 1966—just a few days later—Turcios was killed in an automobile accident near the capital. The unexplained death prompted many versions of the incident, leaving many questions unanswered. César Montes, a twenty-one-year-old student of economics, took over command of FAR.[99]

United States military aid began to arrive: weapons, bombers, napalm bombs, radar, technologically sophisticated apparatus, and approximately a thousand Green Berets. Though United States officials denied that they had sent such a large number of military advisers, the number was confirmed by various sources, including officers of the Guatemalan police.[100]

After the death of Turcios the army, with the participation of the Green Berets, launched a brutal "pacification" campaign to "dry up the ocean where the guerrilla fishes." The guerrilla movements Edgar Ibarra and Alejandro León, fronts of the M-13, were disbanded. The civilian population was decimated, with close to 8,000 campesinos and indigenous people massacred in the combat zones. Captured guerrilla leaders were murdered, among them Yon Sosa and the guerrilla poet Otto René Castillo, who was captured in March 1967, tortured for four days, and burned alive. But the guerrillas continued to deal crushing blows to the army.

The Méndez government—at the mercy of the military—saw the birth of the paramilitary groups Mano Blanca (White Hand), Movimiento Anticomunista Nacionalista Organizado (MANO: Nationalist Anti-Communist Organized Movement), Nueva Organización Anticomunista (NOA: New Anti-Communist Organization), Comité de Represión Antiguerrilla (CRAG: Anti-Guerrilla Repression Committee), La Rosa Púrpura (The Purple Rose), Frente de Resistencia Nacional (National Resistence Front), Rayo (Lightning), and Comité Anticomunista de Guatemala (CADEG: Anti-Communist Committee of Guatemala). Their members were both active and retired military and police officers. They all announced their existence, statutes, and objectives in the newspapers, claimed responsibility for their criminal acts, and issued lists of people threatened with death, complete with photographs, which they posted in public places. Some of those who had been "already executed" showed signs of torture. People were kidnapped in broad daylight and in official vehicles by uniformed agents who acted "with the impunity and calm of those who know they are protected," commented Mestre. People knew where the torture centers were, and they knew the names of the torturers. They saw the kidnappings and knew that all of this was the work of the security forces.[101]

The victims of these groups were well-known liberals, high government officials, outstanding Communist leaders, former officials holding high positions in the governments of Arévalo and Arbenz, the rector of the university, the deans of economy, law, and medicine, numerous professors, heads of student associations, ambassadors, government ministers, reporters, lawyers, economists, union and popular leaders, and hundreds of campesinos and indigenous people. Almost all were assassinated. After a raid on the offices of the outlawed PGT (Communist Party), where a secret meeting was being held, the twenty-eight people arrested were disappeared, among them Víctor Manuel Gutiérrez, a former member of congress from Arbenz's party. Rumor has it that he was thrown alive from an airplane over the Pacific Ocean.[102] The violence went to an extreme surpassed only by Colombia, where the victims numbered 300,000, according to Mestre.

The fierce brutality of the Guatemalan oppression was unparalleled in the continent. In 1967 Rogelia Cruz, "Miss Guatemala" and the fiancée of a member of the guerrillas, was assassinated. She was brutally raped and tortured, and her murderers skinned her and cut off her breasts. This crime shook up the country and became an international scandal. To avenge the savage murder, the guerrillas shot down the military and naval attachés to the United States Embassy in broad daylight on the streets of the capital, accusing the embassy of having encouraged this act of violence. Hours later the principal leaders of a number of death squads met their deaths during a pitched battle between the forces of the state and guerrilla fighters. Both sides suffered tremendous losses, among them a man named Alejo, a landowner who looked for Communists even among the gringos of the Alliance for Progress.

Under pressure from the military, Méndez authorized Colonel Carlos Arana Osorio to pacify the Zacapa region, the guerrilla zone of which he was in command. The result was a blood bath. Arana Osorio deployed incendiary bombs against the campesino and indigenous communities, causing enormous destruction and countless deaths. From then on he was known as the "Butcher of Zacapa." A United States military attaché, Colonel John Webber, advised Arana, and hundreds of Green Berets took part in his pacification campaigns.[103] Between 1967 and 1970 more than 10,000 Guatemalans were assassinated for political reasons.

The guerrillas killed twenty-eight American soldiers. In January 1968 they executed Colonel Webber and his deputy, Ernest A. Munro. In August, they assassinated United States Ambassador John Gordon Mein, whose body was riddled with bullets; this killing took place in plain sight, at the heart of the capital. In 1970 they kidnapped the West German ambassador and assassinated him when the government refused to release political prisoners.[104]

The kidnapping of the Archbishop of Guatemala, Monsignor Mario Casariego, alerted Washington to the seriousness of the situation. It indicated that the clandestine death squads were out of the control of the government and even the military. The government set its machinery in motion to find the Archbishop. They found him, only to discover that his captors were members of the upper middle class. Some of them were imprisoned, while others succeeded in fleeing the country. In the course of this operation the government dismantled some of the ultra-right underground organizations; among their members were landowners, members of the Movimiento Nacional de Liberación (National Liberation Movement) founded by Castillo Armas, and high-ranking officers of the army and the police, all of whom had been trained by foreign specialists. After the Archbishop's kidnapping Colonel Arana went into exile in Honduras.[105]

The Archbishop's kidnappers had tried to make their act seem to be a guerrilla operation. They also planned to burn down churches. Their reasons for the kidnapping were to punish the Archbishop for his affirmation that the origin of the violence lay in the "tremendously unjust and unbalanced" social and economic situation, and his insistence on the need for "a change in our corrupt structures which is felt in every corner of our country."[106]

Kidnappings became so frequent that they lost their ability to shock. The guerrillas kidnapped and executed military officers, police officers, members of the security forces, landowners, oligarchs, and other "exploiters of the people." They sent out bulletins with their own lists of people threatened with death, which included the names of directors of ultra-right-wing organizations. They "brought to justice" several members of the Movimiento de Liberación Nacional. The death squads responded by murdering members of insurgents' families and leaders of popular and leftist organizations.

Despite the virtual extinction of the guerrillas and the loss of much of their popular support, the survivors formed the core of the armed movements of the 1970s. Analysts claimed that in Guatemala the guerrillas had the greatest popular support and were closest to victory after the Cuban and Sandinista revolutions.

In 1968, at a particularly low point for the guerrilla movement, a new front arose near the border with Mexico. The government, Guatemalan society, the Catholic Church hierarchy and Washington were astounded to learn that Maryknoll priests and nuns supported this front, and that an "appreciable number" of sons and daughters of the best families were guerrillas.[107]

In 1970 Arana Osorio—the Butcher of Zacapa—was elected president with the backing of the military and the oligarchy. They held him up as a hero because of the success of his "pacification" efforts. But 50 percent of the people stayed away from the polls. Touting his slogan of "Law and Order," Arana promised to wipe out the guerrillas even if he had to turn Guatemala into a cemetery, and he proceeded to act accordingly. A thousand alleged leftists and a score of Social Christian and Christian Democratic politicians were assassinated within two weeks. The army occupied entire towns, executed popular leaders, campesinos, and indigenous people, and established "free fire zones" where it dropped incendiary bombs.[108] Between 3,000 and 15,000 people were killed in the first three months of Arana's presidency (records of casualties differ, depending on the source). Corpses were mutilated to hide their identities.[109] Members of grassroots Christian communities were murdered, and others went into exile because of death threats.

In 1972 the Ejército Guatemalteco de los Pobres (EGP: Guatemalan Army of the Poor) emerged on the Mexican border, and the armed struggle intensified and spread to several provinces. Until the beginning of the 1980s it was the strongest movement in the country, with broad popular support.

General Efraín Ríos Montt was the actual winner of the openly corrupt 1974 elections, but the High Command "elected" General Eugenio Kjell Laugerud. Ríos Montt protested, but later accepted the post of military attaché in Guatemala's embassy in Spain.

Laugerud (1974–1978) continued the violence; secret prisons, torture chambers, and clandestine cemeteries proliferated. The president of the committee of Relatives of the Disappeared, Eduardo Guerra, denounced the "disappearance" of more than 50,000 people by the forces of order and paramilitary organizations. Shortly thereafter, Guerra was assassinated.

In February 1976 Guatemala suffered a large-scale earthquake. Parts of Guatemala City were destroyed, 25,000 people died, and 70,000 were wounded. More than a million—20 percent of the population—were left homeless.[110] Laugerud declared martial law, ordered his troops to fire on looters, and took the opportunity to "clean out" leftists. It was not known how many were killed in his political "cleansing."

The earthquake lent a crucial stimulus to the struggle of the insurgents. It also gave the lower classes, those most immediately affected, a stronger impulse in their struggle for survival. New popular organizations were created on a national level. The labor movement, which was practically extinct after the coup against Arbenz (1954), succeeded in rebuilding. After an aggressive strike by workers for the Coca-Cola company, supported by workers throughout the country and the solidarity of international labor, the movement created the Comité Nacional de Unidad Sindical (CNUS: National Labor Unity Committee), which included the most important unions. From then on, the

CNUS organized endless strikes and protests, the largest since 1954, with the support of the PGT and sectors of the Christian Democratic Party.

In 1978 elections were held amid military, paramilitary, and guerrilla violence. Since no candidate received the required majority, the congress elected General Romeo Lucas García (1978–1982). His government was yet another bloodbath. Two months after he took office, the army murdered more than a hundred indigenous people, wounding upward of 300. This massacre, which occurred in broad daylight in the Panzós region of Alta Verapaz, was related to the strategic value of this area to the development plans of military officers, government officials, and the United States oil and mining industries. The government intended to put fear into these communities, which were becoming increasingly politicized, conscious of their rights, and determined to fight for them. More than 80,000 people marched on the capital in a show of protest. In the year following the slaughter the tragedy was commemorated by more than 100,000 demonstrators.[111] In 1978, after the Panzós massacre, ladinos and indigenous people created the Comitè de Unión Campesina (CUC: Campesino Union Committee), the most broadly based organization in the country, allied with the EGP.[112]

The government initiated a campaign to wipe out the popular organizations and their leaders. In 1979–1980 more than 400 students, university professors, and political leaders from the center and the left were murdered. The following year 120 members of the Christian Democratic Party were killed, and 1,500 indigenous people died in an extensive military operation in Chimaltenango.

After the assassination of two political leaders, aspirants to the presidency, the Frente Democrático Contra la Represión (FDCR: Democratic Front Against Repression) was formed with seventy union, campesino, student, professional, media, and people's organizations, the FUR and PSD parties, and the support of progressive groups in the Catholic Church. This organization was the first broad front of opposition against the dictatorship.[113] The CNUS and CUC played an important part in the creation of this front.[114]

The triumph of the Sandinista revolution in Nicaragua in 1979 and the advances of the FMLN in El Salvador brought hope and encouragement to the Guatemalan armed struggle, with the ever-growing participation of indigenous people, the principal victims of the violence. New political-military movements arose, and the FAR was restructured. In September 1979 the Organización Revolucionaria del Pueblo en Armas (ORPA: Armed People's Revolutionary Organization)—90 percent of its members were indigenous—led by Rodrigo Asturias, son of the winner of the Nobel Prize for Literature,

Miguel Angel Asturias, announced its existence with an armed attack. The EGP and ORPA increased their contacts with Havana. There was a flow of arms, and militants were trained on the island. Both groups broadened their bases with indigenous support (60 percent of the population). In October 1980 they announced the formation of a "unified vanguard," the Unidad Revolucionaria Nacional Guatemalteca (URNG: National Guatemalan Revolutionary Unit) to lead the people to "the final victory." The guerrillas controlled several regions of the country.

Of all the atrocities committed by the Lucas García regime, the one that caused the greatest international scandal occurred on January 31, 1980: a flamethrower attack on the Spanish Embassy. A delegation of campesinos and indigenous people from the Quiché region protesting the repression and the disappearance of its leaders were inside the building. Thirty-nine campesinos and indigenous people were burned alive, among them the father of Nobel Peace Prize winner Rigoberta Menchú. The ambassador miraculously escaped.

The Church was also persecuted. Lucas García ordered the closings of churches, convents, and seminaries. Six priests and more than a dozen lay people and members of religious orders, some American, were assassinated between 1970 and the early 1980s. More than twenty people, among them both laypersons and priests, including Protestant pastors, were forced to flee the country.[115] In August 1980 several priests and members of religious orders formed the Guatemalan Church in Exile to aid the refugees and support their struggle.[116]

The brutal history of violence continued until the signing of peace accords between the civilian government of Álvaro Arzú and the URNG in December 1996.

THE PARTY'S OVER

When Jimmy Carter left the White House in January 1981, Central America had radically changed. In Nicaragua the Sandinista revolution had triumphed; the FMLN was gaining strength in El Salvador's civil war. The armed struggle in Guatemala was widening under the impact of an unprecedented state of terror. And in Honduras the guerrillas were on the rise.

After the FMLN's "final offensive" in January 1981, El Salvador became front-page international news, and "war correspondents" from the United States, Europe, and other parts of the world settled into San Salvador's Hotel Camino Real. Many believed that they were witnessing the emergence of another successful revolution.

CHAPTER V

WITH WEAPONS IN HAND

REVOLUTIONS IN THE CONTINENT

The 1960s was a decade filled with hope. Most Latin American nations returned to democracy after longer or shorter periods of corrupt and brutal military dictatorships. Civilians—some well known throughout Latin America—were elected to presidencies. The caudillos (dictators) were consigned to the dustbin of history, no longer able to depend on the support of the United States, since John F. Kennedy was vehemently opposed to dictatorships and de facto governments.

The breeze of revolution blew through Latin America. The powerful messages of nationalism, anti-imperialism, and social justice that Fidel Castro and Che Guevara sent out awakened a desire for change. Armed struggle was the answer to the inequalities, social injustices, and the ever-widening gap between rich and poor that prevailed in these archaic societies. The avenues for popular participation remained closed, and social demands were met with violent repression by the police. Armed groups with Marxist leanings emerged, eager to emulate Cuba's heros. *La Guerra de guerillas* (Guerrilla Warfare), a handbook for armed struggle by Che Guevara, and Regis Debray's *¿La Revolución en la revolución?* (Revolution in the Revolution) became bedside reading for the leftist movements in Latin America, and Havana became a haven for the politically persecuted and for revolutionaries.

The United States felt threatened by the Cuban Revolution. All of the large United States–owned landholdings and businesses had been expropriated, and the United States feared that other countries might take similar action.

Nationalist and anti-imperialist sentiments—a new phenomenon in Latin America—stretched from Mexico to Patagonia.

The Cuban Revolution was not the only source for the emergence of rebellion. Following the Second Vatican Council, the new views of the Catholic Church on the needs of the poor and on social justice provided the ethical and moral basis for the people's struggle for their rights. The political debate acquired a whole new dimension. Progressive sectors of the Catholic Church, student movements, people's movements, and left-wing politicians and intellectuals defended the poor and the exploited masses and supported their struggle for justice.

The main objective of the United States defense strategy against the revolutionary explosion was to combat the armed movements, a task entrusted to the military. The battle was directed not only at armed groups but also at popular protests. Criollo McCarthyism—in dictatorships and democracies alike—labeled them as Communists or Communist sympathizers and fought them with equal violence. The alliance of political and economic power sectors with the military, supported by national hierarchies of the Catholic Church, fiercely defended the establishment and its privileges. The result was a growing and dangerous social polarization.

The frontline fighters in the armed insurgency were the students. Most of them came from dissident sectors of Communist youth movements, which had broken from the orthodox party hierarchies opposed to armed struggle. In most countries the guerrilla groups were rural and composed of campesinos. Only in Argentina, Uruguay, and Brazil were the guerrillas urban and led by university students and professionals, members of the middle and working classes.

CHE

Che Guevara's arrival in Bolivia in 1967 encouraged the armed groups of Latin America. They believed that his presence signified the beginning of a Latin American revolution. His message to the Tricontinental Conference in Havana called them to create "two, three, many Vietnams." His dream was to turn the Andes into a new Sierra Maestra.

Che believed that the Bolivian Communist Party and other leftist forces would support him and that fighters from all over the continent would join the Ejército de Liberación Nacional (ELN: National Liberation Army) he commanded. The armed struggle in Bolivia "will be a school" in which many would learn combat, he declared.[1] He chose Bolivia as the place to start the continental revolution because the country was politically unstable and had powerful campesino and union movements. It was also a moment of strong student and popular protests against the brutal and corrupt dictatorship of General René Barrientos. Che was convinced that this explosive situation would be a veritable petri dish for the cultivation of Latin American revolutionary struggle on the mainland. From Bolivia it could be spread to other countries.

While such was Che's dream, the reality was something else entirely. The Bolivian Communist Party did not support him. Its secretary, Mario Monje, wanted to be the one to lead the political-military struggle in his country. Che did not accept his leadership, calling him a traitor. Fidel knew that the party was divided, and he invited its leaders to Havana to urge "unity" and support for Che. But he failed.

Che kept a diary in which he documented the daily development of his action. His entries included critical analyses and recriminations, lists of difficulties and adverse situations. He found the terrain rough and unhealthy. He was asthmatic and did not have his medication with him. He wrote that the scarcity of food was discouraging the rebels. He further mentioned the poor discipline and low morale among his ranks. He noted the numerical superiority of the Bolivian army, but he also noted its incompetence. From the outset the ELN was able to defeat the army with ease, costing them many casualties. In a battle in March 1967 many Bolivian soldiers were killed, and the ELN took prisoners and captured 200 weapons. At that point in time no one yet knew of Che's presence in Bolivia.

Instead of support, Che encountered fear and mistrust among the campesinos and failed to incorporate them into the guerrilla forces. Month after month he took note of this failure and commented that to convince them "will be a long and patient task." These oppressed, poor, and illiterate masses wanted only to survive and for the government and the guerrillas to let them work in peace. Hostilities and denunciations from the peasants came later, when the army paid them to be informants.[2]

In April the Barrientos government discovered Che's presence in Bolivia. Quickly it began to strengthen the army, using training by Green Berets and help from the CIA.[3]

Che's dream ended on October 7. He was wounded and captured during an army ambush arranged with the aid of informers. Between 1,500 and 2,000 soldiers and Green Berets, CIA agents, and Cuban veterans of the Bay of Pigs were part of the operation. He was later killed in captivity on General Barrientos's express orders; a drunken officer dealt him the final blow.

"His death is a tremendous blow to the continental revolution, since it deprives it of the most capable of its leaders," said Castro, who nevertheless maintained that Che's death would not be the end of his theories and strategies. He remarked that Che "is an example and a model for our people." Later the Italian journalist Gianni Miná asked Castro whether Che's fight was a mistake. Castro replied that it was not, explaining that it had been Che's dream since their first meeting in Mexico in 1953 to start a revolution in Latin America and in his homeland, Argentina. Their agreement had been that Che could leave after the triumph of the Cuban Revolution. Che chose his own field of operations, and he organized it "down to the last detail." Castro supported Che, he added, because "his decision was the correct one." Miná asked if Cuba could have done anything to assist Che in "this final stage of his epic struggle." Fidel replied that this would have been impossible since the laws of guerrilla warfare were different and depended entirely upon what the guerrillas were doing.[4]

Che's diary fell into the hands of Barrientos, who sent photocopies to the Pentagon and to the CIA. He wanted to sell the rights for $300,000, but his minister of the interior, Antonio Arguedas, secretly sent another photocopy to the Cuban government. When Cuba had established its authenticity, it published the diary with an introduction by Castro. Arguedas was forced to flee the country.

Barrientos declared that Che was buried in a secret location in the Andes. His intention was to keep Che's grave from becoming the site of a pilgrimage for millions of his followers. He was also determined to cover up any evidence of the cowardly assassination.

MILITARISM RISING

On July 14, 1961, the *New York Times* noted that Kennedy's military strategy had radically changed the concept of defense in the hemisphere.[5] The defense and the weapons provided by the United States to the Latin American countries were now used to fight the guerrillas. Kennedy's secretary of defense, Robert McNamara, maintained before the U.S. Congress that the insurgencies were "inspired by outside agitators."[6] This strategy strengthened the national armies and Kennedy's new policies concerning the military establishments. According to an article by Edwin Martin, Undersecretary of State for Inter-American affairs, published in the New York *Herald Tribune*, it not only assigned the army control of public order but also gave the military a role in the planning of national development. This policy bolstered the military, creating an imbalance between armies and civilian powers to the detriment of democracy.[7] The negative effect was immediately apparent: constitutional governments began to fall to military coups hoisting anti-Communist flags. Kennedy's defense strategy and the National Security Doctrine—the work of "theoretician" Brazilian generals— assigned to the army the task of liquidating subversion and participating as "agents of change" in plans of national development. A fundamental—and new—component of this strategy and this doctrine was civilian-military projects, such as the construction of roads, schools, and sanitation facilities. Their goal was to remove the guerrillas' social base and break popular resistance to the army, whose image was one of violence. It turned out to be successful.

In 1961 the United States spent $21 million on military aid to Latin America. Thousands of officers received instruction at military centers in the United States and at its bases in the Panama Canal Zone, which the Pentagon upgraded to increase their capacity for that purpose. The CIA and the FBI trained these officers in antisubversive techniques, including ways to "interrogate" prisoners, which were undetectable torture practices. After the military coup against João Goulart (in 1964, during Johnson's presidency) Brazil became a center for experimentation with sophisticated torture techniques taught by American agents. These methods were later applied in other countries.[8]

Officers in Latin American police and security forces received training in counterinsurgency techniques at the Inter-American Police Academy (IPA) in Panama, created in 1962. The first year more than 600 officials from 15 countries passed through this center. That same year the Pentagon created the Inter-American Defense College at Fort McNair in Washington, a superacademy on economic, social, and military policy for high-ranking officers and carefully chosen high-echelon government officials. It also created a mobile unit of the Green Berets to reinforce its foreign military missions, which operated in all Latin American countries except Mexico, Haiti, and Cuba, and it began to recruit Latino soldiers[9] so as to be able to send camouflaged troops to Latin American countries in conflict.[10]

The era of neofascist dictatorships of the National Security doctrine and the so-called dirty wars began after the military coup in Brazil. Most of the armed forces of Latin America adopted this doctrine.

ARGENTINA: OPEN FIRE

In 1961 the candidate of the Radical Party Arturo Frondizi was elected president of Argentina by an overwhelming majority. Peronists—still banned—gave him their decisive support, as did the Communists. He was the first civilian president after sixteen years of military dictatorships.

Frondizi, a leftist intellectual, nationalist, and anti-imperialist, disconcerted the country when he announced in his inauguration address that he would grant amnesty to military officers. They would not be tried for the political crimes they had committed against the people during their dictatorships. This decision was part of a secret agreement made with the generals, which included keeping the proscription of Peronism and wiping out its trade-union and leftist movements. He made another agreement with Juan Domingo Perón, to the exact opposite effect: Frondizi was to make concessions to the union bureaucracy and to Peronista policies, follow the economic model of the last stage of Perón's government (populist, with an emphasis on development and ample foreign investment), and prepare conditions for the legalization of Perón's party.

But the greatest conflict was in the area of economics. The military looked for neoliberal policies, but such policies would have come at a high social cost. If Frondizi were to adopt them, the masses would turn against him. The policies desired by the Peronistas—more in accord with those Frondizi himself espoused and that had carried him to the presidency—put him at odds with the powerful oligarchy and the military.

When the economic situation began to deteriorate rapidly and labor agitation grew, stimulated by the Peronist union movement—the people had had enough of inflation and high taxes—Frondizi moved to the right. He named a neoliberal and free-trade advocate, Alvaro Alsogaray, to be his minister of finance. The military, economic sectors, and investors applauded this appointment. Turning his back on his anti-imperialist rhetoric, Frondizi gave in to the demands of the IMF and the World Bank, opened the doors to foreign investment, paid large sums to foreign and national companies expropriated by Perón, increased contracts with American oil companies by a billion dollars—he granted them large tax concessions—and gave the oligarchical elite lucrative contracts. He was also generous to the Church.

Frondizi's foreign policy was at once progressive, third world, and independent. He sought closer relations with Janio Quadros, the president of Brazil. He received Che Guevara in the Casa Rosada upon Guevara's return from Punta del Este, where he had headed the Cuban delegation to the Inter-American Conference which adopted the Alliance for Progress. At the Eighth Consultative Meeting of the OAS, Argentina abstained from the vote to expel Cuba, and Frondizi refused to sever relations with the revolutionary government in spite of pressures from Washington and the Argentine military.

Frondizi's domestic policies were repressive. Even though the Peronist movement had put him in office, he did not lift the ban on the party. He outlawed the Communist Party, despite its support for him, and he put down union and left wing movements. In 1961 he issued the Law in Defense of Democracy, retroactive by three to five years, which mandated prison for "all members and sympathizers of movements or parties that are Communist or might be favorable toward Communism in the future."[11] He kept the country under the Plan de Conmoción Interna del Estado (CONITES, Plan for Internal Disturbances in the State), an Argentine version of a state of siege, and abolished civil liberties one by one. He allowed arbitrary arrests, torture, raids and confiscations by the police, and he dissolved a commission named by the congress of Argentina to investigate such abuses. He harshly controlled the press; several newspapers and magazines were seized, and more than thirty were forbidden to publish. And he did nothing to end the activities of Nazi and other anti-Semitic groups.

The internal situation began to make complications for Frondizi. The Peronists, who were persecuted and turned into enemies, accused him of treason. The military's opposition grew—Frondizi had never been a favorite of the military, since they did not agree with his foreign policy that favored Cuba. They made demands on him and tried to overthrow him. By March of 1962, there had been thirty-five coups attempted, but Frondizi could not risk arresting the conspirators.[12]

Frondizi decided to make some concession to the Peronists and their movement. He granted amnesty to some, returned confiscated properties to others, and allowed Peronists to participate in the provincial elections of 1962. But when their Peronist candidates won in some important provinces—among them Buenos Aires and Tucumán—he banned them. The military criticized this measure, declaring that he was destroying the basis of legitimacy of his government. They overthrew him, arrested him, and imprisoned him on the island of San Martín García in the Plata River. No one protested.

Because of the profound divisions and conflicts within the armed forces, the military did not seize power. To comply with the constitution, the military leaders placed José María Guido, president of the senate, in the presidency. He was a mere puppet, who only signed the military's decrees. He lasted one year.

Doctor Arturo Illía won the 1963 elections. His opponent was the former president General Pedro Eugenio Aramburu, the candidate of the military. An honest democrat, Illía rejected the meddling of the military in politics and of foreign agencies in the internal affairs of the country. At the beginning of his term there was peace and a stop to the fearful spectacles of military tanks driven by opposing gangs—the Colorados ("Reds") of the right and the "legalist" Azules ("Blues")—settling their disputes in the streets.

As promised, Illía broke with the World Bank and the IMF and canceled contracts with foreign oil companies, most of them owned by the United States. These measures proved disastrous for the country's economy. In 1965, when President Lyndon Johnson invaded the Dominican Republic, Illía refused to send troops as a part of the Inter-American Force approved by the OAS, in spite of pressure from the military and from Washington.

Illía's politics were nationalist and with a social context, but he was forced to deal with more than a hundred union strikes, protests from entrepreneurs, and efforts to overthrow him instigated by the media, as well as opposition from the military sector, Peronist factions (Peronism began to splinter at this point), unions, and businessmen. They all accused him of misgoverning, inefficiency, paralysis, or moving too slowly.

The planned coup against Illía in 1966 was well known and eagerly awaited by hundreds of politicians and union officials, who had been either consulted or notified by the military. Illía refused to renounce his office, and the army literally threw him out into the street, hustling him out of Casa Rosada without the slightest show of respect.[13] The brief democratic spring came to an end.

Illía's fall was a relief to the Argentines because the country could finally emerge from the morass. They did not foresee that Argentina was on the verge of a long period of military dictatorships marked by violence and repression, nor did they predict that not one shred of their democracy would survive.

ONGANÍA'S "TYRANNY LITE"

Although General Juan Carlos Onganía was a "legalist" and opposed to the coup—he believed in working within the constitution—when he was placed in the presidency (1966–1970) by the military, he decided he wanted to hold on to power. Naming his government's program "Revolution Argentina" and declaring that it would be the responsibility of the military high command, he immediately staged a "military takeover" of civilian institutions. He closed parliament, dissolved the supreme court, imposed tough censorship on the press, dictated anti-Communist laws (in accord with the Pentagon), intervened in university affairs and repressed students, dissolved political parties, and prohibited all political activity.[14] Someone observed that it was the "institutionalization of illegality."

Both a Catholic of the pre–Vatican Council variety with Falangist ideas[15] (like those prevailing in Franco's Spain) and an anti-Communist obsessed with counterinsurgency, Onganía surrounded himself with military officers, oligarchs, and fascist politicians. He imposed on the government and on the society a spirit and climate of medieval piety and morality, which resulted in measures that reached the height of the ridiculous, as the Argentine journalist Mark Kaplan wrote.[16]

Onganía's "Dictablanda" ("Tyranny Lite")—as the public christened it—brought with it the political and ideological radicalization of students, workers, and sectors of the Church, and the first armed groups emerged. They were reacting to the people's discontent with the economic crisis and the subsequent growing unemployment and repression of the working class and students. This new movement from the left was willing to counter official violence with violence.

In 1969 a widespread work stoppage promoted by students and automobile workers broke out in Córdoba. The protestors marched through the center of the city burning cars and buses, the populace joining them along the way. Their battle against the police lasted almost forty-eight hours. Once the police had been routed, the army intervened. This "cordobazo" was a milestone in the history of Argentine insurrections. For the first time armed groups, flying their banners, took part in similar uprisings in Rosario, Tucumán, and other cities. The government brought in army units from Buenos Aires to put them down. These clashes left many people dead, hundreds wounded, and thousands arrested.[17] Onganía saw these violent uprisings, strikes, and mass protests in several provinces as the work of dangerous extremist groups, inspired by international Communism. General Alejandro Lanusse knew that the "cordobazo" was not coming from subversive movements alone, but was a sign of a spontaneous expression of disgust with a government that had counted on broad support from political, popular, and Church sectors. Rumors of a coup began to circulate.[18]

After massive popular mobilizations, strikes, occupations of factories, the general work stoppage called by a confederation of unions, the kidnapping and "ajusticiamiento" (execution by a court of revolutionary justice) of General Aramburu by the Montoneros, and Onganía's announcement that he would impose the death penalty for terrorist actions, Lanusse toppled him.

THE MONTONEROS, THE ERP, AND THE CHURCH

"In no other Latin American country except Cuba have the structures of state and society been so shaken by the guerrillas as in Argentina," wrote the German sociologist Peter Waldmann. He was surprised that until 1982, there had been no study of these insurgent movements or their activities.[19]

The Argentine guerrillas appeared in June 1966, under Onganía's military government, when the junta of military commanders announced the Statute of Argentine Revolution—a series of arrangements that abolished civilian authorities. The Peronist youth movement chose armed struggle as the only way to combat the dictatorship. The armed group, Fuerzas Armadas Peronistas (FAP: Peronist Armed Forces) established a "cell" in Tucumán, composed of thirteen men and one woman. Almost immediately, the army found them out, arrested them, took them to Buenos Aires, and tortured them.

After the "cordobazo," other armed groups arose. The youth of the Communist Party and the Partido Revolucionario de Trabajadores (PRT: Revolutionary Workers' Party) created the Trotskyist Ejército Revolucionario del Pueblo (ERP: Revolutionary People's Army). This was one of the most important groups, and the only one to establish an active rural "cell" in the mountains of Tucumán.

Like those in the rest of Latin America, the Argentine armed movements were inspired by the Cuban Revolution. They admired Castro, and were inspired by Che's presence in Bolivia. To them his death was a tremendous blow. The FAR intended to become part of a broad Latin American revolutionary movement, as an Argentine appendage to the ELN led by Che, and to return under his orders.

"Later came a period of ebb tide, bitterness, and defeat," commented one rebel leader, "and later still came the luminous glimmer of the 'cordobazo,' which marks a cycle of redefinition through which we completely revise our strategy and tactics and change our organizing methods." He related that members of the FAR received military training in Cuba, where it was offered with the greatest generosity.[20]

Of the five armed groups, four were Peronist: Fuerzas Armadas de Liberación (FAL), Fuerzas Armadas Revolucionarias (FAR), Fuerzas Armadas Peronistas (FAP), and the Montoneros (who joined the Peronist movement in 1970). After carrying out spectacular actions, these groups either joined together or disappeared. The Montoneros, the ERP, and the FAL remained the most important guerrilla groups, with the greatest impact in Latin

America. During the 1970s they were at their military and political apogee, and Argentina was on the brink of civil war.[21]

The Montoneros and the ERP battled the police forces and defeated them in humiliating ways, leaving many dead and wounded in their wake. They attacked military and police barracks—some in the center of Buenos Aires— and kidnapped prominent citizens (such as business leaders, politicians, and military officers) for ransom and to issue demands to the government. "Under revolutionary justice" they shot down and executed military and police officers. They placed bombs at the homes of military officers, blew up places that "symbolized" the government and the aristocracy, and denounced the corruption that reigned in the seats of power—both economic and political— and the regime's brutal repression.

The Montoneros came from right-wing nationalist sectors and from Catholic youth associations (some priests were militants and others sympathized). Their members were intellectuals, professionals, university students, and the children of middle- and upper-class families. They ranged in age from twenty to thirty, with some even younger. The majority were workers, and close to half were women. Because the women took part in almost all operations, the press drew attention to their brutality and cold-bloodedness. In 1967 an eighteen-year-old woman carried out one of their most audacious coups, against the Buenos Aires chief of police.[22]

The Montoneros had plenty of financial resources, radio transmitters, printing presses (to publish pamphlets, to falsify official documents, and to counterfeit money), scores of provisions, fleets of vehicles, hospitals, firing ranges, parade and training grounds, and even weapons factories.[23] Their entry into the Peronist movement brought them more popular support and encouraged greater militancy.

The most daring coup, for which the Montoneros took credit, involved the kidnapping of the former President General Pedro Eugenio Aramburu and his execution in May 1970, a deed that profoundly shook the nation. The sense of alarm grew exponentially when the police stormed a luxury mansion in an exclusive residential neighborhood and, after a violent exchange of gunfire, arrested several young people (among them a married woman) who turned out to be the children of the leading Catholic families of Córdoba.

A communiqué declared that Aramburu had been subjected to the people's revolutionary justice. He had been judged "a traitor to the nation and the people, for the assassination of twenty-seven civilians, for putting eight Peronist military officers to death by firing squad, for profaning Evita's remains, for annulling the social advances of the Justicialist Revolution, for the repression of the Peronist people, and for intending, once again, to seat himself on the throne of power to sneer at the people and continue selling out the nation. In accordance with this judgment we detained him and executed him."[24] Perón, from his exile in Spain, proclaimed his solidarity with the rebels. He called them patriots and justified their action as a response to official violence. The youth movement and the Peronist armed groups supported Perón and prepared for his triumphal return. The support he gave them from exile changed as his return to Buenos Aires approached, however, he began to distance himself from them.

On the day of Perón's return to Argentina the Peronist youth movement— the Vanguardia—welcomed him with a massive demonstration, a show of its enormous mobilizing capacity. But instead of pleasing Perón, this reception worried and annoyed him. He wanted the fighting to stop, but the movement would not obey his request. He turned the Vanguardia into enemies and subsequently persecuted them. Perón surrounded himself with right-wing Peronists and marginalized the youth movement, creating an abyss between them.

In 1967 a group of young priests created the movement called Priests Movement for the Third World and joined the Peronists, attracted by the social content of the Justicialist Party. The group determined that the Church could not remain neutral in the conflict between the Peronists and the anti-Peronists, since it was essentially a confrontation between the dispossessed and the powerful classes. Within a year, they had 400 members.[25] At the beginning of 1969 the second national conference of this clerical movement brought together priests from all over the country, and the conference concluded that a revolutionary process was afoot. Many sectors believed that all peaceful avenues had been exhausted. "That inescapably calls for our firm adherence to the revolutionary process for radical and urgent structural change," stated one of the group's documents, which additionally declared their rejection of the capitalist system.[26]

After Aramburu was executed—an act that implicated young men and women of Argentine high society—a journalist interviewed Father Hernán Benítez to get his opinion on this "jungle law" assassination. Asked if his preaching on violence was in part responsible for this assassination, the priest answered, "We are all responsible." The young people the police identified as the assassins, he noted, were of the upper middle-class, "Catholics who regularly attend Mass and take communion." They grew up hearing that Peronism was a plague and reacted violently against the social stratum in which they lived because of "the conviction that only violence will erase social injustices, for like it or not the privileged have never given up even one of their privileges," he added.[27] The Priests for the Third World were a militant force against the dictatorship. In speeches, open letters. and manifestos the organization protested against social injustices and political repression, and its members took part in strikes and student demonstrations. The doors of members' churches were open to student meetings. Publicly the clergy criticized the Church hierarchy for not observing the resolutions of the Consejo Episcopal Latinoamericano (CELAM).[28] A smaller number of priests participated in the armed struggle. The regime considered such activities subversive.[29]

The military, the Vatican (after John XXIII), and the powerful and reactionary hierarchy of the Argentine Church—blind and mute to their grave violations of human rights—supported the military regimes and identified with the interests of the oligarchies. All these found the Priests for the Third World to be a threat, accusing them of being Communists. The Archbishop of Buenos Aires prohibited any member of the group from any involvement in politics and from continuing activities and preaching that touched on social issues. Refusing to follow his orders, the group broke with the Church hierarchy, thus undermining its authority.

BRAZIL AND ITS MILITARY "GORILLAS"

Although Janio Quadros won Brazil's 1961 presidential elections by the largest margin ever, his term was stormy and fleeting; he governed only eleven months. His domestic policy was a disappointment—he did not make good on his campaign promise to implement plans for social reforms and economic development. What mattered were his foreign policies: third world, leftist, and independent. He unexpectedly visited Cuba before his inauguration, a move that disconcerted and alarmed many at home and abroad.

United States relations with Quadros were highly complex. President Kennedy was concerned with and irritated by Quadros's leftist tendencies and his early courting of Communist nations, especially Cuba. Brazil was the Latin American power with the greatest military, political, economic, and demographic significance, and Quadros's friendship with Cuba was potentially disastrous.

Quadros, unfazed by Washington's reservations about his relations with the Soviet bloc, pointed to the United States and its relations with the Soviet Union and its satellites. His policy, he declared, was to broaden foreign markets, and he feted leading Communists without worrying about Washington's reaction. He decorated the first Soviet cosmonaut, Yuri Gagarin, and a high-level dignitary from the Kremlin. He also honored Che Guevara when he arrived in Brazil upon his return from the Inter-American Conference in Punta del Este. This homage to the "heroic warrior" was the last straw for powerful sectors of the right and the military. They believed that Quadros's policy of independence and opening to the Communist world was influenced by Havana.

In the midst of a severe economic crisis; opposition from the military, politicians and from the dominant classes who accused him of being a Communist (he was actually a conservative); and accusations from governor of Guanabara, Carlos Lacerda—who claimed that Quadros intended to shut down the congress and become a dictator—Quadros abruptly resigned. It was not known or understood why he took such drastic action, though some people attributed it to his lively and unpredictable character. Congress accepted his resignation; the people remained unmoved.

The military wanted to take measures to prevent Vice President Joao Goulart, whom they considered a Communist, from stepping into the presidency. At that moment he was on an official visit to the People's Republic of China. But Goulart, political heir to Getulio Vargas, was supported by powerful popular, union, and student movements, liberal groups, and sectors of the military, particularly lower-ranking officers. The military command feared that a coup could provoke a civil war. To prevent the coup, Leonel Brizola—Goulart's brother-in-law and governor of Rio Grande do Sul—and Mauro Borges—governor of Goias—organized an uprising with popular brigades and the support of their respective military and police garrisons.[30]

The military, the Brazilian oligarchy, and Washington were convinced that Goulart would lead Brazil toward a Cuban-style revolution. Before he assumed the presidency (1961–1964), the military imposed a constitutional reform measure that established parliamentary rule and restricted presidential power. Goulart accepted the measure and submitted to parliamentary control. But in 1963, with the support of the people, he called a plebiscite, which abolished the constitutional reform, and thus he reassumed full power.

With the nation's profound economic crisis—it had the highest inflation rate in its history—Goulart was put in the difficult position of either satisfying the working class (the source of his greatest support) or mollifying the middle class and Washington. He chose a policy of stabilization and development, which satisfied no one. The workers were upset that their wages were being frozen and their demands ignored. The dominant classes were angry with him for his inability to control the continuous strikes and protests by popular sectors, students, and campesinos—who entered the political fray for the first time—and the land "occupations" by residents of the favelas (slums). Furthermore, Goulart had to deal with uprisings and protests by the military and by police officers. In the midst of this confusing situation Goulart delivered an incendiary speech announcing his plans to expropriate landholdings. The big landowners and the military were furious, and the people did not give him the support he was seeking.

Ousting Goulart was no easy matter, however. Powerful popular support was solidly behind him. The middle class and the landowners undertook a campaign to marshal their forces in order to prepare a climate favorable to the coup, organizing demonstrations that were clearly fascist in several cities. The March With God, For the Family, and For Democracy in Sao Paulo were attended by more than half a million people, most of whom were of the middle class.[31]

In the early morning of April 1, 1964, the military staged a coup that overthrew Goulart. They justified it as a "preventive counterrevolution" to deter the "communization" of Brazil. Goulart did not resist. His passivity neutralized the fighting spirit of the people, the union movement, and the nationalist sectors of the military, his main supporters. The streets of Sao Paulo and Río de Janeiro were deserted. The discouraged masses made a few weak attempts at protest, which were put down by the new regime using extreme brutality. Later Goulart explained that he had not wanted to call on the people to fight. He was anxious to avoid a civil war.

The United States helped to prepare for the coup. Ambassador Lincoln Gordon and the military adviser General Vernon Walters (later an assistant director of the CIA) conspired shamelessly. Before the coup, American warships arrived off the coast of Río de Janeiro at Gordon's "urgent" request.[32] "Enough of the middlemen! Gordon for President!" was scrawled on the walls of the capital.

Goulart had not yet left for exile when President Lyndon Johnson's congratulatory message to the plotters arrived. In a speech at the Brazilian War College, Gordon called the coup a "defense of democracy," comparable to the Marshall Plan, the Berlin airlift, the defeat of the Communists in Korea, and the withdrawal of the missiles from Cuba. He considered it one of the most important moments of change in world history in the second half of the twentieth century.[33]

With Goulart's departure Brazilian democracy died. The military no longer respected constitutional order. The long period of the neofascist National Security doctrine dictatorships began, launching a twenty-one-year-long era of brutal repression.[34] The National Security doctrine, which was pressed into service after Goulart's ouster, was the work of a select group of War College officers headed by General Acervo Golbery do Couto e Silva. From the time of its founding in 1949 the college maintained close contact with the Pentagon through a member of its military mission in Brazil.[35]

The doctrine was the guideline of the military regimes. It was the essence of anti-Communism, inspired by McCarthyite doctrines. The concepts of "internal security," "subversion," "the enemy within," and "threats to the state"—all included in the doctrine—were derived from United States laws. Several of do Couto e Silva's "theories" were simply copied from Pentagon manuals.[36] According to the doctrine, security and development, the management of the state, plans for national development, congress, and the judiciary were all the responsibility of the military, not of civilian society. It granted the security apparatus the job of identifying and imposing sanctions on any activity that affected the safety of the state. Communism and socialist ideologies were proscribed. Do Couto e Silva believed in "ideological borders" and envisioned a world divided into two antagonistic sides: the democratic and Christian West and the Communist and atheist East. The United States, the leader of the Western world, was to coordinate hemispheric actions, which included fighting Communism and socialist ideologies. Brazil was set to be the leader on the continent of Latin America.[37]

Marshal Humberto Castelo Branco was the first president (1964–1967) under the National Security dictatorships. He was one of the most repressive in Latin America's history. His relations with Washington attained unheard-of proportions. Hundreds of advisers and technicians from the United States were placed in key positions within his public administration as well as in the military and security institutions. The number of officials in the United States embassy in Río was larger than that of any other United States Embassy, except those in Indochina and India.[38]

Castelo Branco severed relations with Cuba, the country he considered to be the gravest threat to the hemisphere. He sent a general and a military police officer to the Dominican Republic to direct the Inter-American Force created by the OAS after Johnson's invasion of that country. He also threw the doors wide open to foreign capital—mainly American—which he provided with important resources from his country.

The dictatorship of Castelo Branco was one of the most repressive in Latin America's history. With the executive decree, Inquiritos Policial Militar (IPM: Military-Police) and the "Operation Clean Up" —both meant to rid the country of communists—thousands of people were detained, and thousands more had their homes ransacked by the police.

Castelo Branco suspended congress for two years and abolished the political rights of 441 prominent Brazilians including Kubitschek, Quadros, and Goulart.[39] The purges in all federal structures, ministries, the judiciary, the armed forces, and the police were broad and immediate. Left-wing politicians, union and political leaders, students, priests, and the simply suspicious were arrested. Political parties, along with popular, worker, campesino, and student organizations, were dissolved, the unions were controlled, and the press was censored. Works of art, music, plays, and movies that he considered subversive were also banned.[40]

From the very first day of Castelo Branco's mandate, prisons and detentions centers (stadiums and warships were used) were filled with political prisoners to be tried by military tribunals and sentenced for "crimes against the security of the State." In the first month alone, at least 50,000 people were arrested. [41] The extended use of torture on detainees stunned and alarmed Brazilians and created a scandal abroad. It was the beginning of the dirty war.

A week after the coup he undertook his "legitimization." He decreed the first Institutional Act, legalizing every one of the National Security doctrine's postulates: the military takeover of the state, congress, and the judiciary. The generals began to expedite the passage of constitutional amendments, legislative and institutional acts, laws, decrees, and resolutions—promulgated as events dictated—in order to structure the security policies of the state, reinforce military institutions, broaden presidential powers, and severely restrict civil liberties.

General Arthur da Costa e Silva (1967–1969), who succeeded Castelo Branco, decreed Institutional Act Number 5, the most unconstitutional, antidemocratic, arbitrary, and repressive decree in Brazil's history. It gave the president absolute power and authorized the government to dissolve congress, suspend and disqualify its deputies, and confiscate their property. Members of the security services could not be tried, giving them complete immunity from any crimes. In cases of crimes against national security, the decree suppressed the right of habeas corpus, and raised the penalties for political crimes, which included any activities that annoyed the government. Da Costa e Silva rigorously enforced this law.

But just when corruption scandals linked to his government were starting to come to light, da Costa e Silva died from a cerebral hemorrhage; some people argued that the exposure of the corruption caused his death. According to the constitution, the vice president (who happened to be a civilian) was to succeed him. The military ignored the law, however, and instead installed General Emilio Garrastazú Médici in the presidency.

The Brazilian military dictatorships were neither as firmly placed nor as politically stable as they appeared, since broad sectors of society were in opposition to them. They sustained themselves with brutal repression. The fight against subversion, mass organizations, unions, and movements and parties of the left made for a bloody manhunt. The victims were political militants, popular leaders, professors, journalists, intellectuals, students, priests and nuns.[42] Not even the military was exempt from repression. Nearly 10 percent of the officer corps was purged for ideological reasons.[43]

Added to this macabre picture were the summary executions and many forms of torture used by the military in their detention centers during interrogations. They were characterized more by their brutality than their "refinement," according to the testimony of one woman victim. Political detainees "disappeared" from prisons that had been converted into torture chambers.[44] Since the civilian justice system was not allowed to try military officers or their security forces—that was the job of military tribunals—they had total impunity.

The military and police institutions were the most repressive organizations within the wide net cast by the state. Their invisible components were the official paramilitary groups that operated as "special security forces" (death squads), whose members were former police officers, and the ultraright terrorist organizations: Comando Caza Comunistas (CCC: Communist-Hunting Commandos) and the Milicia Anti-Comunista (MAC: Anti-Communist Militia).

Each branch of the armed forces had a detention center that was converted into a torture chamber. The most sinister was the Centro de Informaciones de la Marina (CENIMAR: Navy Information Center). The Departamento de Orden Político y Social (DOPS: Department of Political and Social Order), Operación Bandeirante (OBAN) in Sao Paolo, and the Centro de Operaciones de Defensa Interna (CODI: Internal Defense Operations Center) in Río de Janeiro had their own torture centers too.

The brutal acts of repression provoked protests from international human-rights organizations, the legal community, the United Nations, the OAS, and the Brazilian Catholic Church. The government denied their denunciations of the assassinations, tortures, and disappearances and accused these organizations of meddling in governmental affairs. Officially the government declared that "no one is tortured in Brazil."

THE INSURGENCY

"The military took power violently, and they themselves paved the way for subversion," noted Carlos Mariguela, a Brazilian Communist Party leader who served as the top director of the armed struggle against the fascist dictatorships. In 1967 he created the Alianza de Liberación Nacional (ALN: National Liberation Alliance), one of the most powerful armed groups.

The guerrilla struggle arose in response to Castelo Branco's reign of terror. During this period an impressive number of revolutionary organizations grew out of the splinters of Communist and leftist parties. In the course of the struggle they either united or subdivided—mobility within the insurgent movements was characteristic of the Brazilian armed struggle. The workers' movement (POLOP) gave birth to the Comando de Liberación Nacional (COLINA: National Liberation Commando) and the Vanguardia Popular Revolucionaria (VPR: People's Revolutionary Vanguard), which later merged to form the Vanguardia Armada Revolucionaria (VAR: Armed Revolutionary Vanguard) and Ala Roja (Red Wing). These groups were composed primarily of members from the middle class—students, professionals, and former military officers.[45]

The armed struggle expanded in the major cities with terrorist actions, sabotage, bombings, kidnappings, the capture of arms, and attacks on government institutions and American businesses. September 1969 brought the most daring and spectacular blow. A joint commando of the ALN and the MR-8 kidnapped United States Ambassador Charles Elbrick. A female guerrilla seduced embassy guards and some of the Ambassador's bodyguards in order to learn his routes and itineraries. The guerrillas demanded freedom for fifteen political prisoners and their safe conduct from the country on a special flight to be arranged by the government.[46]

This kidnapping—the first kidnapping of an ambassador in Brazil—caused great consternation in and humiliation for the government and for Washington. The junta, in transition after the death of da Costa e Silva and under pressure from the United States State Department to save the ambassador's life, immediately agreed to the guerrillas' demands. The prisoners were freed and taken to Mexico, and the government published the rebel manifesto against the dictatorship in the major newspapers and broadcast it on the radio.

Subsequent kidnappings of the Japanese consul general and the Swiss and German ambassadors did not achieve the desired results. On those occasions the government did not agree to all of the kidnappers' demands, but the diplomats were nevertheless freed.[47]

After three years the armed struggle began to hit rock bottom. The state's repressive apparatus captured important guerrilla leaders, among them Mariguela, by means of information obtained by torture. Their capture was a severe blow to the guerrillas.

Though the Brazilian guerrilla groups sometimes coordinated their operations in spite of their ideological differences, they did not succeed in mounting as extensive and crucial an action as the Tupamaros in Uruguay or the Montoneros and the ERP in Argentina. Their tendency to organize into cells kept them separated, and internal conflicts, disagreements about strategy, and rivalries among the leadership weakened them. None of the groups bothered to involve the workers or the campesinos, though they counted on their support. They came to regret it.

The guerrillas recognized the reasons for their failures: some actions were launched without the necessary preparation; they underestimated the risk posed by the political and military inexperience of many of their militants, most of them young; and worse yet, they misjudged the great power of the government's repressive apparatus. There were two decisive reasons for their failure, noted the journalist Marcio Moreira Alves. First were the difficulties they encountered in working underground. They were an urban guerrilla group composed mainly of people from the middle classes who could not hide in the favelas, so they were easily detected by the police. The guerrillas were forced to set up their centers for operations in "enemy territory," in neighborhoods and buildings of the big cities, where the police were able to set up a network of informers with the help of doormen and neighbors. There were continuous denunciations. The second factor working against them was torture. Because of the inadequate political training of some of the militants, and the fact that the guerrillas did not establish strict "compartmentalization," some of them talked. The capture and torture of a student involved in the assault on a bank resulted in the loss of more than fifty operations centers in apartments, the destruction of the work of the Brazilian Communist Revolutionary Party in Río, and the arrest of its entire leadership. The torture of two Dominican priests led to Mariguela's death. Other information obtained through torture resulted in the capture and assassination of important political leaders and hundreds of revolutionaries.[48]

The CIA was behind the antisubversive operations. Under the military dictatorships the political, economic, and security presence and influence of the United States was open and overwhelming. "The government has sold our country to the United States. CIA spies operate here with facilities equal to those in their own country, directing Brazilian police searches for Brazilian patriots and supervising the government's repression of the people," Mariguela wrote.[49] In 1970 the number of murdered political prisoners rose. There were indications that from 1971 on the military made the systematic "elimination" of prisoners a policy, Moreira Alves commented. This policy was responsible for the deaths of Joaquim Cámara Ferreira, Mariguela's successor in the ALN directorate; Devanir José de Carvalho, leader of the Tiradentes Revolutionary Movement; and Eduardo Leite, a commander of the VPR, among many others.

THE LIBERATION CHURCH

The generals needed the support of the Catholic Church, not only because of the enormous influence it exercised over the people—the majority of whom were Catholic—but also for its favorable image within and outside the country. Few governments were able to resist a Church set against them. For General do Couto e Silva, the Church was the symbol of Western culture, a bulwark against Communism. And religion was a powerful weapon to control the masses.

The military regime's brutal repression and grave human-rights violations, however, roused the bishops to protest. Dom Helder Camara, named Archbishop of Olinda and Recife shortly after the coup against Goulart, emerged as the principal voice of the Church against repression and for social justice. He was the first to publicly criticize Castelo Branco. In July 1966, Dom Helder Camara led a group of fifteen bishops from the states of Pernambuco, Paraíba, Rio Grande do Norte, and Alagoas—the poorest regions in northeastern Brazil—in support of the manifesto of three Catholic activist groups, which protested the exploitation of workers and official repression. Castelo Branco traveled to Recife to pacify the bishop, but Dom Helder refused to receive him. The Church and the State were on different paths.[50]

The Brazilian Church was one of the first to follow the direction given to the Catholic Church by Pope John XXIII and the Second Vatican Council in favor of the poor and of social justice—the pastoral and theological renewal that spawned liberation theology. But the Vatican and its dignitaries in Latin America accused the liberation theologians of being under the influence of Marxist theories. Pope Paul VI declared that Communist subversion sometimes hid "under the robes of priests." His successor, John Paul II, who was even more conservative, punished the Brazilian Franciscan Leonardo Boff, one of the most distinguished liberation theologians, and imposed on him "a period of penitential silence." The liberation theologians did not deny that their social analysis was based on Marxist concepts, but they maintained this basis did not mean that they adopted Marxism as such.

Ordered by Cardinal Paulo Evaristo Arns, the Archdiocese of San Paolo undertook a secret investigation that lasted several years to document repression in Brazil during twenty-one years of military dictatorships. Though the military was still in power at the time, the report was published in 1985 under the title *Brasil: Nunca Mais* (Torture in Brazil). It documented cases of assassination, torture, and disappearance, described the methods and implements used by the torturers, identified 242 underground torture centers, and provided the names of 444 torturers.[51] The book revealed that members of the Church were also victims of the repression. Between 1964 and 1978, 488 priests and members of religious orders were imprisoned, 31 were tortured, 5 were murdered, 11 disappeared, and 28 were expelled from the country.[52]

The dirty war held on to its impunity—before they handed over the government, the military passed a general amnesty protecting themselves from being brought up on charges that would force an accounting of their crimes before the civil courts. They extended this amnesty to political prisoners, guerrillas, and the insurgents. In silence and oblivion they closed this dark chapter of their history.

URUGUAY: A MOCK DEMOCRACY

Uruguay, a small and orderly country with a population of 2.5 million—known as the Switzerland of South America—was an oasis of peace and democracy. The Blanco and Colorado Parties alternately succeeded each other in free and fair election processes. The Socialist and Communist Parties were neither repressed nor illegal except during the brief dictatorship (1933–1935) of Gabriel Terra, who outlawed them all. The Uruguayan legislature was one of the most advanced and progressive in Latin America. The professional army, subject to civilian oversight, respected the constitution and did not intervene in politics, nor did the Church interfere in affairs of the state. Nationalist, consistent, and vigorous economic policies, with healthy regulation of foreign capital, kept Uruguay less vulnerable to external pressures than the rest of the continent.[53]

This economic prosperity and political stability came to an abrupt end in 1960 during one of the worst crises in the history of Uruguay. The economy stagnated, and Uruguay's image as a democratic nation began to falter as repression started to creep in with a gradual increase in militarism. Uruguay began to resemble the rest of Latin America.

The country suffered inflation, recession, and the precipitous fall of the peso in 1963. Lacking reserves, the government sought foreign credits and opened the country to foreign investments, which came to control the banks and important areas of production, affecting whole sectors of the economy. Protests against this difficult economic situation by the working classes, public functionaries, and students were supressed by the impositions of martial law.[54] This internal agitation led to the emergence of the Movimiento de Liberación Nacional Tupamaros (Tupamaro National Liberation Movement), which evolved into one of the most important guerrilla movements on the southern continent.

In 1966 General Óscar Gestido of the Colorado Party won the election by a narrow margin. Constitutional reform restored one-man rule, the government having been administered until that point by a governing council in which the parties had been equitably represented.[55]

The powerful union movement—banking, industrial, and commercial employees were unionized—was controlled by the Communist Party and had the capability of paralyzing the country. The strikes by the unions and public employees to protest the slashing of wages, high unemployment, and the housing shortage were massive and ongoing, as were student protests against repression. These demonstrations were put down by force. For the first time ever one of the most egalitarian societies in Latin America was confronted by virulent class conflicts because employers refused to talk with the workers and to address their justified demands.

Uruguay was drawn into the orbit of the IMF and agreed to its demands. Foreign capital and American transnational companies invested in key industrial and financial sectors. Foreign debt skyrocketed. This surrender to foreign capital and the consequent loss of autonomy was harmful to many economic sectors. Only the agricultural exporters and financiers, tied to foreign capital and the monopolies, were satisfied.

The sudden death of President Gestido in 1967 (he had been in office only a few months) brought Vice President Jorge Pacheco Areco to the presidency (1967–1971). He was a corpulent former journalist and boxing fan and, like his predecessor, a member of the Colorado Party. Pacheco Areco increased the dependence on foreign capital, increasing the friction between the economic and political sectors who gained from it and those who stood to lose.[56]

Responding to the general discontent, popular protests, the radicalization of the lower middle class sectors and prestigious intellectuals (who were favorably inclined toward the popular struggles and guerrilla activity), Pacheco Areco declared a "permanent state of siege." He proceeded to lead the country into a de facto dictatorship, which the people called a constitutional dictatorship.[57]

Pacheco next strengthened presidential power. His congress did not object. Invoking martial law, he banned leftist parties, alleging that "they intend to destroy the present regime by means of armed struggle." He closed newspapers, imposed press censorship, and prohibited union activities and student movements, which he severely repressed. The strikes and popular and student demonstrations ended in violent confrontations with the police at the price of deaths, wounds, and arrests (those who were detained were also tortured), and hundreds of job losses. He ordered the occupation of university campuses without regard for their autonomy, and he intervened in their curricula, expelling professors for ideological reasons. The Tupamaros held that the president was exercising an unnecessary repression, with the sole aim of maintaining a "bourgeois democracy that was a mockery."

The government's abandonment of constitutional and democratic principles was received with a surprising degree of apathy by the political community. When a deputy tried to bring a legal action against Pacheco for the arbitrariness and illegality of his procedures, he found no support in the congress.[58]

Amid the turmoil, corruption flourished in the government and among small financial groups, which tried to enrich themselves through frenetic and deceitful speculations and monetary conversions (they exchanged large sums of Uruguayan pesos in Argentina and Brazil for pesos and cruzeiros). Prominent figures were involved in monetary devaluations caused by these groups and denounced as fraudulent by the director of the Bank of the Republic.

The rapid enrichment of these groups contrasted sharply with the increasing impoverishment of the middle and lower classes. In June 1968 real wages were down by 47 percent, compared to the 1961–1966 norms. In 1964 the Uruguayan peso had an exchange rate of 16 to one United States dollar; in 1968 it had fallen to 250 to 1. The cost of living jumped 100 percent in June 1970, and six months later to 118 percent. From 1967 to 1968 overall production was only 0.3 percent, lower than Haiti's—the lowest in the southern hemisphere.[59]

The general discontent could be measured by the enthusiastic way the people supported the actions of the Tupamaros, which shook the power structure while the police forces had not been able to touch them. In 1969 the government passed a law forbidding the press to report on the guerrillas. The media were not allowed to mention the name Tupamaros or use seven synonyms for guerrilla. The papers avoided this decree by using such terms as "the unname-ables," "the seditionists," "conspirators" or "those who take the name of the Inca Tupac Amarú."[60]

Uruguay's friendly relations with its powerful neighbors, Argentina and Brazil, were nerve-racking and almost a matter of survival. The colossuses to the south, under military dictatorships—also confronted with powerful insur-gent movements—kept their eyes on developments in Uruguay, ready to inter-vene. They believed that a Tupamaro victory was possible. Brazil's concern for Uruguay was reflected in the sheer profusion of news coverage.[61]

When the Tupamaros kidnapped the Brazilian consul, Aloysio Dias Gomides, and the American agent Dan Mitrione in Montevideo, Brazil mobi-lized troops on the Uruguayan border. The troop presence alarmed the Uruguayan people; Pacheco Areco energetically protested this "intervention," but the Uruguayan press reported that Pacheco had asked the Brazilian pres-ident, General Garrastazú Médici, for aid in the form of troops to fight the guerrillas.[62] The governments of Argentina, Brazil, and Uruguay knew that the guerrillas were making a mockery of their security systems and offering one another aid across the borders. Military sources maintained that the Tupamaros brought together the principal leaders of South America's armed movements in Montevideo in a "coordination" meeting between the Montoneros and the Tupamaros, who became co-conspirators in Aramburu's kidnapping and assassination.[63]

The collaboration between the Argentinian, Brazilian, and Uruguayan secu-rity services to capture activists and opposition figures who had taken refuge in other countries was undeniable. In 1967 a Brazilian student arrested in Uruguay tried to commit suicide by slashing his wrists to keep the Uruguayan police from handing him over to the Brazilian Political Police (DOPS). There were frequent denunciations of foreign agents for having participated in interrogations and tor-ture sessions of political prisoners; the prisoners, who were blindfolded, recog-nized them by their accents.

CHE SHOWED US THE WAY

One day in 1965 the Uruguayan populace was surprised and the security forces intrigued when they saw the word "Tupamaros" scrawled on the walls of Montevideo. Shortly thereafter they learned from terrorist actions, propa-ganda, and denunciations in public places that the Tupamaros were a guer-rilla group. Their official name, the Movimiento de Liberación Nacional

Tupamaros led by Raúl Sendic—he had a long political history of organizing workers and peasants—became a new phenomenon in Uruguay.

The Tupamaros had been preparing for battle for more than a year. Their militants, both men and women, were students and professionals from the middle class and the landholding community. Some of them were the sons and daughters of powerful families, and most were Catholic. As they grew, so did the militancy of the lower classes. Their center of operations was in Montevideo.

At first they were more or less inconspicuous, since the country's attention was focused on the presidential election. The country was experiencing social and union agitation because of the economic crisis, which led many to favor the guerrilla struggle. The Tupamaros consolidated the movement, armed their fighters, and began to assault banks, steal weapons, and engage in armed confrontations with the police. At the beginning of 1968 the movement launched its first large-scale offensives.

In August of that year the kidnapping of Dr. Ulyses Pereyra Reverbel, the president of the Union de Trabajadores Estatales (UTE: State Workers' Union) and the Bankers' Association, brought the Tupamaros more prestige. In a communiqué they denounced the corruption of bankers and financiers, the "fascist" repression of the unions, students, and sections of the populace, and the politics of "surrender" to United States capital. They warned that "nothing will go unpunished." The people's justice would act "in ways that are fitting and suitable." According to them, Pereyra was detained as "an appropriate representative of the regime." They indicated that Pereyra had never been called to account for the murder of a young newspaper vendor whom he had ordered killed for selling the daily that had accused him of being gay. Because of Pereyra's connections with the government, he was released from captivity after a short time. But before the guerrillas released him, they had to ascertain whether the state's forces respected the integrity of the Tupamaros under arrest. The police could not find where they were keeping Pereyra. The Tupamaros would let him go when they saw fit.[64]

The Tupamaros, protected by the silent but unwavering sympathies of many Uruguayans, moved quickly and quietly, mocking the police blockades. They applied their own brand of justice: trying and executing both officers who were torturers and corrupt bureaucrats; they also carried out raids on banks and financial institutions in order to "withdraw" funds, and they obtained documents that they then provided to the press. They raided the Casino San Rafael in Punta del Este for 55 million pesos, and took 6 million from the Monty Financial Company, publishing its books to expose crooked and fraudulent operations involving prominent members of the financial sector and the government. The courts were forced to act and to confirm the truth behind the Tupamaros's accusations. The minister of finance subsequently resigned. The attack on the French-Italian Bank and the demonstration of its fraudulent dealings irreparably damaged its reputation, almost putting it out of business. The Tupamaros made the Uruguayan banking system tremble.[65] By 1970 official estimates had the Tupamaros with close to 3,000 activists and 4,000 sympathizers and a solid infrastructure, which could not be easily dismantled.[66]

The most daring of their actions took place in July 1970 with the simultaneous kidnapping of United States Security agent Dan Mitrione, Brazilian Consul Dias Gomide (founder of the ultraright movement Tradition, Family, and Property), two senior officials from the United States Embassy (one escaped, the other was released), and Claude Fly, an officer of a United States corporation rumored to be a CIA agent. The kidnappings had a serious impact at home and abroad. A communiqué of the Tupamaros accused Mitrione of being "a United States spy placed by the Uruguayan government at the heart of the state security apparatus" who had admitted being "a technical consultant" to the Montevideo police. They published photocopies of his identity papers, including his FBI credentials. They alleged that he was an "agent of imperialist repression" disguised as an AID adviser, whose function was to teach methods of terror and torture, something he also did in Brazil. Mitrione's theory on torture, they said, dictated that "a police officer is not much good if he kills, because he loses his informer."[67]

The Tupamaros demanded the release of 50 guerrilla fighters followed by all political prisoners—more than 300, among them 30 women—who were to be flown to Algeria, Mexico, or Peru. But the capture of Raúl Sendic, head of the Tupamaros, along with other leaders changed the rules of the game. The government refused to exchange Mitrione for the political prisoners, in the belief that the Tupamaros were powerless without Sendic.[68]

Washington refused to negotiate. Like Pacheco Areco, the United States believed that the movement had been decapitated and that the Uruguayan government would launch an offensive to dispatch it altogether. The government's refusal to negotiate led to the execution of Mitrione. His corpse was found on the morning of August 10, with four bullet wounds from guns of different calibers. This incident was told by Costa Gavras, in the movie *State of Siege* (1980). The government decreed a period of national mourning and continued the "raking" operation, this time with the assistance of a hundred Brazilian policemen.[69] The Tupamaros released the other hostages.

The Cuban Revolution was the primary inspiration for the Tupamaros, since it was the first socialist revolution carried out by non-Communists. They deeply admired Che Guevara, as they did the Colombian priest Camilo Torres Restrepo for his Christian conception of revolutionary struggle, declared "Urbano," a Tupamaro leader who was interviewed by the Cuban press agency *Prensa Latina* in the 1970s "somewhere in Montevideo infested with bayonets." He added that "the trail Che blazed is revolutionary consciousness," which authentic revolutionaries would follow. He spoke of taking power with the people to achieve a socialist revolution. The Tupamaros were nationalists and anti-imperialists, but their fight "to the death" was against government corruption, powerful national and foreign economic sectors, and "the class enemy in the bourgeois apparatus and its agents."[70] Their objective was to improve the lot of the dispossessed and to free Uruguay from dependence on foreign powers.[71] Their hard, daring, and successful fight spanned six years. Many of the Tupamaros were murdered, brutally tortured, or disappeared. But "the dead you have killed are in good health," assured Urbano.[72]

Pacheco Areco gave full discretionary powers to the armed forces to combat the subversion, and these acted with furious violence, shooting to kill. For the first time in Uruguay there were systematic tortures, disappearances, and shooting of students. But in four years, the government did not succeed in defeating the activists. The failure was due to incompetence, to the guerrillas' skill, and to the protection provided the guerrillas by broad sectors of the populace, making their capture immensely difficult. "We probably all know someone who is a Tupamaro, but what happens is we don't know that he is one. What counts in the long run is the people's support, these normal, peaceful people above suspicion. They are the stream where the Movimiento de Liberación Nacional (MLN: National Liberation Movement) fish swim," observed an Uruguayan intelligence officer.[73]

The green light Pacheco Areco gave the military paved the way for a coup. The military did not hold positions in his government, but it was the power behind the throne. Juan María Bordaberry, his successor—also a tool of the military—authorized the most brutal repression to liquidate the guerrilla movement. The dirty war spread and became more intense, and he allowed the military to govern. Later the military removed him.

COLOMBIA: DEMOCRACY AND VIOLENCE

Colombia entered the 1960s under the government (1958–1962) of Alberto Lleras Camargo, the head of the Liberal Party and the first president of the National Front, of which he was the architect. This alliance between the two traditional parties—the Liberals and the Conservatives—sought to end the violence against the Liberal Party unleashed in 1948 by the conservative hegemonic dictatorships and continued by the military rule of General Gustavo Rojas Pinilla. The death toll of that period, known as the Violence, was close to 300,000, most of them campesinos. A consequence of this violence was the emergence of armed groups whose purpose was to defend their lives and their families.

The National Front, approved by a huge majority in a national plebiscite, succeeded in establishing political peace between the parties, but not in ending the violence in the countryside. The most important guerrilla groups laid down their weapons by accepting the "general and unconditional" amnesty decreed by General Rojas Pinilla in 1953. But the government did not keep its promise to grant them lands and respect their lives, and the army kept killing them. Many of them returned to the mountains to continue the struggle. Rojas Pinilla's amnesty was extended to the army and the police, the perpetrators of the violence, whose crimes would remain unpunished. This situation created enormous mistrust and resentment, not only among their victims, but throughout the country.

Lleras Camargo's main intent was to bring peace by political and social measures. "Amnesty and Rehabilitation" became the prevailing slogan of his government. He used this theme to attract those who continued the armed struggle. In 1959 he offered a second amnesty and set in motion programs of social assistance, community development, and communal action. The amnesty was to be extended only to those people who were seeking peace and rehabilitation as verified by the authorities. Individual prosecutions remained open and could be brought back to court in the event that the person returned to violence. It was not an amnesty that pardoned and forgot, like Rojas Pinilla's, but one of liberty and watchful assistance.[74]

However, the negative legacy of Rojas Pinilla's amnesty was still fresh in people's minds and caused Lleras's offer to fail. The memories of the murders of guerrillas amnestied by Rojas also lingered undiminished, among them the assassination of Guadalupe Salcedo, the most distinguished figure among the liberal guerrillas from the Llanos region. His corpse was riddled with bullets, the result of a police ambush in the capital. At the end of the legal term of

Lleras's amnesty in 1959 the violence grew more acute in a vicious cycle of harassment and military abuses against the civilian population and confrontations between guerrillas and the army. In January 1960, in different parts of the country, the army baldly assassinated three popular guerrillas who had been amnestied. And in 1963, after an intense shootout between the army and his band, the famous guerrilla Chispas, from Tolima, who had also been granted amnesty by Lleras, was killed. Continuous harassment by the army, which accused him of numerous crimes and called him the country's "number one bandit," had forced Chispas to renew his struggle and caused the government to place a juicy reward on his head.

In the end, many refused the amnesty offered by Lleras, since they found his guarantees "insufficient, suspicious, and deceptive." Several of those who accepted the amnesty returned to the mountains after the army continued to harass them. Others took up the struggle again because they could not adapt well to civilian life. Some turned to vandalism and common crime.[75]

The government's inability to stop the violence—an impossible task in such a short time—served as the central argument in the political debate against Lleras. The conservatives accused him of tolerating what they called "independent republics," five zones controlled by the Communist guerrilla movement which, they argued, were breaking up the national sovereignty. Rojas Pinilla was also unable to recapture those zones. In 1965 the Communist guerrillas became the Fuerzas Armadas Revolucionarias de Colombia (FARC: Colombian Armed Revolutionary Forces), which, in a span of forty years, would spread to nearly fifty guerrilla fronts around the country.

Frustrated by the continuing violence, political sectors demanded that the army get rid of the guerrillas, who were by then referred to as "bandits." Many, nevertheless, were alarmed by the brutality of the army, which was engaged in a sort of "punitive war" against the people accused by the army of being guerrilla supporters. The army was killing campesinos, raping their women, burning their huts and crops, and stealing and killing their animals. The violence had reached new levels.

The narrow range of democracy of the National Front—its bipartisan hegemony and alternation in power prevented participation by the other political parties—was the source of growing popular discontent and student rebellion. The people sought new paths. Workers' unions emerged: the Confederación Socialista General de Trabajadores (CSGT: General Federation of Socialist Workers), which was stimulated by the Colombian Communist Party, and the Confederación General de Trabajadores (CGT: General

Federation of Workers), which was promoted by the Christian Democrats whose goal was to break the monopoly held by the official trade union confederations, the Confederación de Trabajadores de Colombia (CTC: Federation of Colombian Workers), and the Union de Trabajadores de Colombia (UTC: Union of Colombian Workers).

New parties also formed: the Movimiento Revolucionario Liberal (MRL: Liberal Revolutionary Movement), a dissident faction of the Liberal Party led by Alfonso López Michelsen; the Frente Unido (United Front), created by the young priest Camilo Torres Restrepo; the Alianza Popular (ANAPO: Popular Alliance), created by Rojas Pinilla; and the Movimiento Obrero Estudiantil Campesino (MOEC: Workers', Students', and Campesinos' Movement), a political-military movement of non-Communist students.

The MRL, which opposed the alternation of power in the National Front, was the most significant new development in the political scene traditionally dominated by the Liberal and Conservative parties. The MRL represented the major defection, politically and numerically, within the Liberal Party. Initially called Movimiento de Recuperación Nacional (National Recuperation Movement), it later changed the term "recuperation" to "revolutionary," which was then fashionable in Latin America. By February 1960 the group's proposals had become more radical. Its members spoke of nationalizing natural resources, genuine agrarian reform, and support for the Cuban Revolution. Young liberal politicians and leaders joined the MRL. They were eventually joined by the popular and guerrilla movements, which were attracted to its political positions.

Within the MRL two factions emerged. The more flexible one, led by López Michelsen, sought to replace the liberal leadership monopolized by the so-called traditional bosses with new people who could count on popular support to achieve revolutionary reforms within the constitutional framework. The other faction, the hard-liners, consisted of the youth movement Juventud Movimiento Revolucionario Liberal (JMRL, Youth Revolutionary Liberal Movement), supported by the Communist Party and popular sectors who wanted revolutionary change and "People Power."[76] The MRL penetrated rural zones with a campesino membership campaign that offered to protect the insurgents under its banners. Surprising numbers of campesinos and armed groups supported the MRL as a tactical ally in electoral campaigns. The MRL made electoral alliances with the Communist Party (illegal from 1949 to 1969), though this was not to López's liking, since he was not eager to get mixed up with Communists or to take extreme positions.[77]

To the United States State Department, "Alfonsito" López's "capricious" left-ist ideas were a threat and implied Communist participation in the activities of the MRL. The United States feared that López would divide the Liberal Party and "set in motion a popular movement that will ultimately be taken over by the Communists." Roy Rubottom, assistant secretary of state for Inter-American affairs, made a marginal note on a confidential document from the embassy in Bogotá that "[Lopez] should be discredited." Around the same time, Julio César Turbay Ayala, Lleras Camargo's chancellor, offered Washington his cooperation in dealing with "the problem of Communism" in Latin America.[78]

The Cuban Revolution, the revolutionary events in the People's Republic of China, the Vietnam War, the independence of Algeria, and the new direc-tion of the Catholic Church under John XXIII, all became incentives for the drastic reevaluation and change in the ideas and goals of the Colombian armed struggle. The partisan armed movements of the 1950s were events of the past.

The 1960s brought the rise of several armed groups whose struggle was both military and political. In 1960 there was the Movimiento Obrero, Estudiantil, Campesino (MOEC: Workers, Student, and Campesino Movement), and from an internal schism in MOEC arose the Fuerzas Armadas de Liberación (FAL: Armed Liberation Forces).[79] In 1961 came the pioneer group, the Ejército Revolucionario de Colombia (ERC: Colombian Revolutionary Army). In 1962 there was the Ejército de Liberación Nacional (ELN: National Liberation Army), a pro-Castro group created by university students. In 1965 came the Fuerzas Armadas Revolucionarias de Colombia (FARC: Colombian Armed Revolutionary Forces), the oldest campesino Communist guerrilla movement in Colombia, originally organized in the 1950s against the political violence. In 1964 the Ejército Popular de Liberación (EPL: People's Liberation Army) was born out of a division within the Communist Party. Some of these groups tried to involve remnants of the guerrilla movements of the 1950s, with neg-ative results; their goals were different.

The enrollment of the priest Camilo Torres into the ELN in October 1965 surprised and alarmed both Colombian society and the Church. A man of cul-ture, educated in the Catholic University of Lovaina, and a member of a prominent family, he was the first priest to take up arms against the establish-ment. His drastic step grew out of his frustration with his inability to convince the backward-looking and reactionary hierarchy of the Colombian Catholic Church that the people were suffering great injustices, misery, and poverty, that there had to be change and that the Church had a responsibility to bring it about. The Church sanctioned him, and he submitted to the restrictions it imposed. But he was convinced that his duty as a Christian was not to turn his back on social problems and conflicts, as the high officials of the Church did. He recognized that solutions to social conflicts were impossible to attain in Colombia through the limitations of legal avenues. He joined the ELN because its members shared in his goals. He was killed by the army. News of his death had a tremendous impact nationally and throughout Latin America. Camilo became a major figure in the calendar of Latin American revolutionary saints.

In Colombia "many priests, nuns, and laypeople were sympathizers and involved in the work, a proselytism directed to the ELN, although they were not organically part of it," attested two ELN activists, Rafael and Felipe. "Camilo is our *Comandante* because of what he did, not only as a priest, but also as a revolutionary. His investigations, his studies, his leadership of the United Front, his life in struggle go far beyond the priesthood."[80]

Members of the armed movements and the JMRL received military instruction in Cuba. By the 1960s the Colombian guerrilla movement was in full swing.

COLOMBIA AND CUBA

No country in Latin America was more determined to oppose the Cuban Revolution than Colombia under the government of Lleras Camargo. But he did so without making public pronouncements. Privately, he commented to John M. Cabot, the United States ambassador, that Fidel's triumph was as if the bandit known as Mariachi had become the president of Colombia. He added that it would be a long time before Cuba recovered from the effects of the Revolution, believing, as Washington did, that the current regime was a transitional phenomenon.[81]

Lleras Camargo enjoyed great prestige in the upper echelons of Latin American society and was highly appreciated in Washington. He was the architect of the Organization of American States (OAS) and served as its first secretary general. Washington always consulted him because of his knowledge of the problems of Latin America.

The paranoia inspired by revolutionary Cuba convinced governments throughout Latin America that the succession of small unsuccessful attempts to "invade" Panama and Caribbean countries, which had their starting point on the island, were evidence of Cuba's intention to "export" its revolution and destabilize other nations. The Cuban government denied all responsibility for such incidents. After investigating the "invasion" of Panama, the OAS exonerated Cuba of having instigated it.

Fulgencio Lequerica, the Colombian ambassador in Havana, told his government that "the movement of arms in the Caribbean is undeniable." A Cuban warship had confiscated a large number of weapons from the schooner *Nautilus*, which was sailing toward an unknown destination. And Central American exiles in Cuba continued their nebulous preparations to invade their respective countries. Lequerica asked the chancellor to send him a couple of detectives to serve as his "eyes and ears" and to mingle with the people in places his position did not allow him to frequent and where the Colombian community in Cuba had no access. This community "is no good to me," he claimed, since it consisted of a bunch of nuns and delinquents.[82] The Colombian press reported that Samuel Moreno Díaz, Rojas Pinilla's son-in-law, was planning an invasion of Colombia in cooperation with Che, and that he intended to bring 400 Cubans to reinforce the Colombian guerrillas.

Washington consulted with Lleras Camargo about convening the Consultative Organ of the OAS to study the situation in the Caribbean—and Cuba's alleged "exportation" of its revolution—and about Colombia's hosting the meeting. Lleras agreed to the conference but suggested that it meet in Washington. Ultimately it was convened in Santiago, Chile, in 1959. Turbay Ayala, the chancellor of Colombia, was chosen to chair this Fifth Consultive Meeting. Washington failed to win a condemnation of Cuba.

Lleras's government collaborated with Washington in setting the agenda for the Seventh Meeting of the Consultative Organ, in San José, Costa Rica, in 1960. Again Cuba was the focus for having accepted the Soviet military aid offered by Khrushchev. Oddly, the word "Cuba" never appeared on any document from this meeting. Once again Cuba was not accused.

Fidel responded to the San José Declaration with the First Declaration of Havana, in which he condemned the "miserable submission of traitor governments" and imperialism. Lleras felt that Fidel was offending the government and cut off relations with Cuba (shortly before President Kennedy arrived in Colombia for an official visit). When Turbay Ayala explained to his congress the reasons for the break—it was immensely unpopular among the people—he noted that many countries had "beat Colombia to the punch." These nations were the Central American and Caribbean dictatorships and Peru, whose president, Manuel Prado y Ugarteche, was a member of the Peruvian ultraright.

After Fidel's 1961 declaration on the socialist nature of the Revolution and after the Bay of Pigs fiasco, Kennedy was even more determined to put an end to the Revolution and Fidel. He gave the green light to the CIA's Operation

Mongoose and mobilized his diplomatic corps to organize Cuba's expulsion from the OAS and to apply sanctions.

Once again Colombia led the political moves against Cuba and proposed at the OAS that the Consultative Organ be convened under Article 6 of the Río Treaty. The article referred to military aggression, which did not apply in this case. Nevertheless, the majority supported the petition. Chancellor Turbay traveled from capital to capital seeking support. The agenda for this meeting was set in an exchange of visits between State Department officials and the Colombian chancellery. By an irony of fate Turbay's tour was interrupted when his plane was hijacked and forced to land in Havana. Fidel went to meet with him at the airport. At that moment Che was with the Cuban delegation at the Inter-American Conference in Punta del Este, Uruguay. When he learned of Turbay's forced arrival in Havana, he burst out laughing.

At the Eighth Consultative Meeting in Punta del Este, Uruguay, in February 1962 Cuba was expelled from the OAS. The six most influential Latin American nations abstained. In Colombia—as in the rest of Latin America—the measures taken against Cuba were met with violent protests, demonstrations and the stoning of the United States Embassy and the burning of its flag.

VALENCIA'S "PACIFICATION" POLICY

When Guillermo León Valencia—the second National Front president (1962–1966)—was elected, the guerrilla movement in Colombia was on fire, and the United States policy of counterinsurgency was in full swing throughout Latin America. Valencia and the military were determined to get rid of the *bandoleros*—armed groups left over from the violence of the 1950s—and the guerrilla movement that had been ignited by the heat of the Cuban Revolution.

No Colombian government fought the insurgency harder than Valencia's. He opened the door to intervention by the Green Berets; in 1962 a mission arrived in the country to train and advise the army.[83] The army undertook a "pacification" campaign with "search and destroy" missions, and from that point on civilian-military actions were put into practice. Both methods were new to Colombia. The Pentagon also initiated the LASO Plan (Latin American Security Operation), a brainchild of the Pentagon that combined the concepts of national security and development and involved the army in internal security and national-development plans.

General Alberto Ruiz Novoa, the minister of war and veteran of the Korean War (Colombia was the only Latin American country that sent troops), was an asset to the Pentagon. He put into effect his own "LAZO" Plan—a faithful copy of the Pentagon's plan—and indoctrinated the armed forces with anti-Communist ideology. Many had already been indoctrinated at American military bases in the United States and Panama.[84] In 1962 his army mounted the so-called Campesino Defenses in the conflict zones; they became a new factor in the violence.

In 1965 General Ruiz Novoa mounted an extensive operation—it was not the first—against Marquetalia, a zone controlled by the Communist guerrilla movement led by Manuel Marulanda, known as "Tirofijo" ("Deadeye"). To prepare the people psychologically and break down the campesinos' resistance to the army before the attack, Ruiz Novoa organized civilian-military actions—the construction of roads, schools, and health centers and the supply of medicine, clothing, and food. The army demanded that the town be evacuated, but many of its inhabitants stayed. Then came the attack in which 1,500 soldiers of the Batallion Colombia (Colombia Brigade) took part. Because they were Korean War veterans and had already experienced a real war against the "Communist enemy," they employed the same tactics in Marquetalia. They strafed the town with helicopters and fighter-bombers and launched 5-ton bombs to annihilate the guerrillas. The action was a prolonged war of skirmishes, ambushes, and firefights in which both sides inflicted casualties. The army, with its 15,000 men, took the town.

The army turned the military "takeover" of Marquetalia into a memorable event. It celebrated with an open-air Mass in the mountains attended by the military high command, cabinet ministers, and high-ranking government officials. And in an equally solemn ceremony in the capital, the army symbolically presented a "Marquetalia free of *bandoleros*" to President Valencia. Nevertheless, the army had not fulfilled its primary objective of destroying the guerrillas and capturing "Tirofijo," on whose head a 50,000-peso reward had been placed. The guerrillas took to the mountains, and the Communists retained military and political control of the zone, resisting the army's relentless aggression.

After the Marquetalia experience, the Communist guerrillas organized themselves as a military group, which was the origin of the Fuerzas Armadas Revolucionarias de Colombia (FARC: Revolutionary Armed Forces of Colombia), which was established in 1965. The zone continued to be surrounded by the army, and Tirofijo still kept to the mountains, and, moving along secret paths cleared by the Indians, he came and went unseen.

On several occasions the army announced that it had "eliminated the guerrillas," but after every blow the guerrillas seemed to come back stronger. In spite of the military operations with assistance from the Green Berets and the many casualties, the army failed to defeat them.

THE END OF THE 1960s

By the end of the decade and over the course of three shared governments alternating the presidency between the two parties, the National Front had consolidated political peace and erased the political and ideological barriers between liberals and conservatives. Their common struggle targeted subversion and the guerrillas. The conflict between the Liberal Party and the MRL also disappeared when López Michelsen, its leader, accepted the post of minister of foreign relations in the government of Lleras Restrepo. The MRL lost activists and political importance, and the opposition weakened. The movements and parties of the left splintered and turned themselves against one another, and thus were never able to transcend a minimal level importance in the political arena. The MOEC fell apart under hard blows. The FAL and the ERC (Ejercito Revolucionario de Colombia) disappeared, and the ANAPO, a centrist populist party created by Rojas Pinilla, failed to attract the masses. But the Communist Party retained control of the Sumapaz and Viotá zones and the southern part of Tolima.

The FARC broadened its fronts, and the pro-Castro ELN and the EPL consolidated their forces, but they had no meaningful military or political strength, nor were they a threat to the government. The counterinsurgency stagnated. Twenty years later a retired general maintained that, "neither can the army defeat the guerrillas, nor can the guerrillas defeat the government."[85]

In 1970 the ANAPO candidate, Rojas Pinilla, came close to winning the presidency but he was defeated by the conservative candidate, Misael Pastrana Borrero, by a ridiculously narrow margin. According to members of ANAPO—and many prominent voices—the government robbed Rojas Pinilla of his victory by means of an electoral fraud. As a reaction to this event, in 1973 young members of ANAPO created the armed April 19 Movement (M-19), the first urban guerrilla movement in Colombia. From the beginning it aroused great interest and sympathy among the people in intellectual and leftist circles.

PERU: DECLINE OF THE OLIGARCHY

When Manuel Prado y Ugarteche took office early in the 1960s, Peru was in the midst of a severe economic crisis and extreme political and social unrest—

General Manuel Odría was forced to call for elections and to retire in response to popular pressure. The nation was at the boiling point. The people had fought for twenty years for a political opening and the democratization of the country.[86] The rightist military dictatorships had ended, and the country was undergoing a transformation. Students, the people, and an impoverished lower middle class were becoming radicalized, and a powerful people's, union, student, and campesino movement, which demanded change, was gaining strength. Strikes over wages and salaries were constant, and the conflicts over land in the sierra reached unprecedented heights. The most serious occurred in 1959 and 1960 in Casa Grande and Paramonga, two large sugar refineries, on land owned by the American Copper Corporation and by the Torreblanca hacienda. These conflicts ended in combat with the police,[87] with the government supporting the owners and the foreign company.

Prado came to power through an alliance with Haya de la Torre, head of the Alianza Popular Revolucionaria Americana (APRA), the most important political party and the one most deeply rooted in the masses. This alliance, which was called "*Convivencia*" (coexistence), was mutually beneficial. Haya de la Torre wanted to become legitimate and forge paths to power. The APRA wanted stability after shifting back and forth between a legal and an illegal status decreed by various military and oligarchic governments that persecuted it, fearing APRA's popular strength. It was a constant, often bloody struggle.[88] Prado and his supporters in the oligarchy believed that they needed APRA at their side. Haya de la Torre agreed to abandon his radical positions in exchange for government programs and measures that assured a just income distribution and wider social benefits for the general masses.[89]

Haya de la Torre was a nationalist rather than a Communist. His political life was a prolonged series of ups and downs; he was always either on the verge of being elected president or in prison or exile. The military prevented his election victory by engaging in electoral fraud. APRA members rejected the alliance with Prado and the oligarchy. Student and middle-class sectors resigned from the party and created APRA Rebelde, and later the Movimiento de Izquierda Revolucionaria (MIR: Movement of the Revolutionary Left), an armed group. Other sectors joined the Acción Popular (Popular Action), the party of Fernando Belaúnde Terry, the Christian Democrats, the Social Progressive Movement, and the resurgent Communist Party. Although APRA lost strength and Haya de la Torre lost prestige, it continued to be the major political force in the country.[90]

For the first time the campesino, popular, and marginalized masses entered the political arena under the banners of nationalism, antioligarchy, and social reform. They asked for agrarian reform, housing, employment, fair wages, education, and health care—all basic needs—and their just demands were supported by military circles, students, and the Church.

Sectors of the oligarchy were also in the process of change. "The presence of shantytowns in the capital are a source of worry to the upper and middle classes. They saw that this poverty—contrasting sharply with the luxuries of Lima—as a latent threat, and the programs for social assistance were insufficient to close this breach."[91] For the first time, the major daily newspapers—owned by members of the oligarchy—dealt with social themes and recommended changes.

Government measures in favor of the United States transnational International Petroleum Company (IPC) and the rise in gasoline prices caused a bitter political debate in the chamber of representatives against the IPC, for the nationalization of oil, and in defense of national sovereignty. Popular and student demonstrations sporting anti-imperialist slogans demanded the same, as did sectors of the military and the Church. This topic was the central one of the decade.

In 1962 the APRA candidate Raúl Haya de la Torre, won the presidential election by 14,000 votes. Belaúnde Terry, his opponent, the oligarchy, and the military alleged that his victory was fraudulent. Within a week, just before Prado left the presidency, the military staged a coup.

A military junta (1962–1963) took power, announcing that it would restore order to the political and social unrest convulsing the country and find solutions to the problems derived from an unjust society, since repression could not solve the people's problems. The junta did, in fact, initiate important social measures, passing an agrarian reform law, legalizing campesino land takeovers, and recognizing their de facto control of the lands they occupied. But it insisted that the land must be paid for, a demand they never met. Nevertheless, the junta suppressed the campesinos of the sierra to maintain law and order.[92] After a short time it called for elections as promised. The junta stepped down with a glowing reputation for having realized important reforms, and having kept its promise to relinquish power.[93]

Fernando Belaúnde Terry defeated Haya de la Torre and served as president (1963–1968). He offered reformist measures, brought new people into the government, and promised a solution to the problems with IPC within ninety days. The nationalization of oil had been one of the central themes of his campaign.

The people saw in Belaúnde a promise of renewal and change. In the first ninety days he presented an executive order on agrarian reform, but congress—controlled by a majority alliance between the APRA and the Unión Nacional Odrista (UNO: Odrista National Union) founded by the former dictator, Manuel Odría—modified it so as not to affect the interests of powerful national and foreign landowners. Their properties remained intact. The reforms were applied only in the conflict zones in the sierra. Campesinos and indigenous people awaited Belaúnde's fulfillment of his pledge to solve the land problem. The government sent commissions of experts in agrarian reform, cooperatives, and state loans and social investigators to the sierra with the mission of attending to the people's demands. The problem was not resolved.

In mid-1963, in all the departments of the sierra—with the exception of Puno—there was a wave of violent land occupations under the slogan "Land or Death," in which approximately 300,000 campesinos, collective farmers, sharecroppers, and workers participated. The activists were put down harshly in actions that sometimes ended in bloodbaths. The campesino movement gained strength with the support of students, retired military men, and lawyers who helped to create collective and union organizations.[94]

Belaúnde's government lost support and prestige in broad segments of the population for failing to implement the president's campaign promises. The people responded with violence to an unforeseen 44 percent currency devaluation and to his failure to resolve the IPC problem. Armed groups, such as MIR and ELN, formed during Belaúnde's government and became active in the sierra. Belaúnde swore he would eliminate them.

It became public knowledge that Belaúnde held secret negotiations and reached an agreement with IPC. The IPC was to hand over oil wells in exchange for the cancellation of a debt of about $200 million (some claimed that the sum was $600 million) and the promise that IPC would modernize and expand its installations. The government granted it a concession of a million hectares for new oil exploration. Its monopoly on gasoline would continue for forty years.

Political leaders confirmed that these agreements were damaging to the national interest and that Belaúnde had hidden important elements from them. His party, Popular Action, withdrew its support; APRA washed its hands of him, and the influential daily *El Comercio* attacked the President and asked that the army take the situation in hand.[95]

The government collapsed in a profound crisis of legitimacy, caught up in this scandal and in another involving widespread smuggling, in which members of congress, high officials, and members of the armed forces were implicated. It was high-level corruption. Belaúnde's deception of the country and the behavior of the congressional majority, who for petty political reasons blocked important social reforms and mismanaged public funds, were too much for many, especially for the military. They shared an antioligarchy sentiment, which was catching hold of the country and assuming enough power to effect changes. On October 3, 1968, General Juan Velasco Alvarado overthrew Belaúnde and deported him to Buenos Aires.

THE INSURGENCY OF THE 1960s

Peru's economic and social situation was the culture medium for the insurgency and the revolutionary armed struggle. The society was semifeudal and the majority—illiterate campesinos and indigenous people descended from the Inca—were stuck in miserable poverty, completely abandoned, and exploited like beasts of burden by bosses and landowners. On the other side of the social scale was the dwindling class of would-be aristocrats and antidemocrats—owners of extensive lands, in control of the principal economic sectors and the major newspapers, whose enormous influence played an important role in the country's destiny.

With the support of students, sectors of the middle class, and the lower middle class, the campesinos and the workers continued to organize unions. Hugo Blanco, a "disciplined Trotskyite," emerged as the main figure of the campesino and indigenous movement in the sierra where he had gone to further the movement. With the help of Cuzco lawyers, these activists began to ally themselves with the Federación de Trabajadores del Cuzco (Workers Federation of Cuzco), controlled by the Communist Party.[96]

Blanco wanted the Movimiento Sindical Campesino (Campesino Union Movement) to become a democratic force that could confront the power of the *patrones* (masters) and *gamonales* (bosses). He did not intend to encourage a revolutionary struggle for power (or so he claimed from prison in 1964) because he considered it to be premature. His goal was to resolve the land issue, to defend the campesinos and indigenous people in their occupation of lands, and to protect them from the army, the bosses, and the landowners. Alarmed by the campesino uprisings and the land occupations, the landowners, the bosses, and the Lima press—the mouthpiece of the oligarchy—asked the government to impede their further organization. The press began to sound the alarm about Hugo Blanco's work in the sierra.[97]

In 1963 under Belaúnde, Blanco and most of the campesino and indigenous leadership were arrested in a large-scale offensive against the campesino movement. Nevertheless the struggle continued. Populist trends gained strength and won a political position.[98] The response to these conflicts, which more than once arose within the transnational corporations, was violent repression resulting in many dead and wounded.

In spite of the repression, student, popular, intellectual, and leftist forces—more radicalized every day—continued to fight for political and democratic openings. The Chinese-Soviet ideological contest of the time produced the well-known political-ideological controversies and the splintering of the parties on the left. These schisms gave rise to armed groups. From the APRA came the Comité de Defensa de los Principios Apristas y de la Democracia Interna (The Committee for the Defense of APRA Principles and Internal Democracy), the APRA Rebelde (Rebel APRA), and later the Movimiento de Izquierda Revolucionaria (MIR) and the Vanguardia Revolucionaria (Revolutionary Vanguard). And from the Communist Party came the Frente de Izquierda Revolucionario (FIR, Left Revolutionary Front) and the Ejército de Liberación Nacional (ELN, National Liberation Army).

The pro-Castro ELN was composed of students, intellectuals, politicians, Communist workers, and some campesinos, organized in "cells." Its political focus was a popular government, the expulsion of foreign monopolies, an agrarian revolution, national sovereignty, and good relations with all other nations. The ELN was "infiltrated" and was subject to desertions and denunciations. From its ranks came the army's best informers and the guerrillas' worst enemies.[99] In 1965 the army provoked a confrontation with the ELN that proved disastrous for the guerrillas.

The MIR was always in crisis, with internal polemics, struggles, and fights and with ill-conceived strategies, according to Héctor Béjar, one of its activists. Although its numbers were too few, it attempted to create three fronts in order to force the army to disperse. But the army's superior numbers—it had 50,000 men—allowed it to wage the war on several fronts at once, soundly defeating the guerrillas. In spite of conceptual, political, and strategic discrepancies between the ELN and the FIR, both made a vain effort to unite and coordinate their actions. Without realizing it, both fought more or less simultaneously against the same target. The MIR and Blanco were also unable to overcome their differences.

A negative factor in the Peruvian insurrection was the behavior of the "new left." Public infighting, the lack of coherent ideological and political proposals, the failure to study the complexities of Peruvian realities caused it to fall apart, wrote Béjar. [100] Discord and disunity also existed in the campesino organizations, making them more vulnerable to the army's depredations.

Politically the situation on the left was no better. In 1961 there was a call to unity. Juan Pablo Chang and an unaffiliated group created the Asociación para la Unificación de la Izquierda Revolucionaria (APUIR: Association for the Unification of the Revolutionary Left), with the goal of forming the Partido Único de la Revolución (The Only Revolutionary Party) with the organizations and parties of the left. It was to offer strong support to the campesino struggle and to Hugo Blanco, who continued without political support in the sierra. The parties ignored the call. The few who did support Blanco failed to give him what he most needed: money, men, and weapons.

In seven months of intense combat the army scattered the armed movements, destroyed their fronts, and imprisoned their most important leaders. Many guerrillas, disillusioned with the left, went over to the enemy side, making the army's job that much easier.[101]

THE LATIN "NASSERITES"

In 1968 General Juan Velasco Alvarado and a group of officers secretly prepared for a coup against Belaúnde. When Velasco Alvarado took power (1968–1975), he negotiated with the high command. He announced that the "revolutionary government" would be a coalition of the armed forces, led by a revolutionary junta made up of the oldest and highest-ranking generals. He chose his cabinet from the high military hierarchy.[102]

The military officers of the revolutionary government were progressive, nationalist, anti-imperialist, and antioligarchy. They were called "Nasserites" because of this tendency, so different from the continent's military dictatorships. Though not repressive, the government did keep order by force. It did not include popular sectors in the government, but it did provide them with political participation through cooperatives and communal and union organizations. It gave land to campesinos and rural workers for use in association. The political parties continued to function, but they carried little weight with the government. The government did not touch the press though it nationalized it in 1974.[103] The government ended the long period of alliance between the military and the oligarchy, which lacked political strength for the first time. The lower and middle classes were the new forces entering the political scene. It was a revolutionary event, since it generated a class change, wrote the historian Pease García. [104]

The "Nasserites" were also a new kind of military class, different from the one that had ruled the country's destiny for the previous twenty years. They began to modernize, purging ranks that were not in line with their principles and educating themselves at the Centro de Altos Estudios Militares (CAEM: Center for Higher Military Studies), established in 1956. There the officers received a scientific education and studied national problems. The Center's goal was to form cadres to execute the plans for national development and foreign policy in order to modernize the country and strengthen Peru in the international arena.[105]

Most members of the officer corps were of the middle class and well aware of the inequality in Peruvian society. They knew the extent of the people's poverty and the government's abandonment of popular and campesino masses. They understood that it was this situation that caused the general malaise throughout the nation, as well as the insurgency. They understood that repression was a dangerous path to take.[106]

Their diagnosis of the country's situation was pessimistic: Peruvian underdevelopment was more acute than that in neighboring countries. Real power was in the hands of landowners, agricultural exporters, bankers, and foreign corporations—for the most part owned by the United States—whose interests were generally not those of Peru. The nation had to plan a new course of development.[107]

In 1969 the powerful press underwent its first frontal assault from the government when the latter tried to control it. The editorial directors of the leading papers accused Velasco of being a Communist and of attacking private property, and then strongly criticized his agrarian reform. Five years later Velasco nationalized the press.

The government monopolized the management of the economy, the huge agroindustrial concerns, foreign commerce, and the banking industry. In 1969 it passed the Agrarian Reform Law to give land to campesinos and indigenous people and to broaden the production of foodstuffs to stop the currency drain. It expropriated large national and foreign-owned estates and "Peruvianized" private enterprises with the Industrial Reform Law, converting them into "mixed" enterprises, implementing a system of workers' comanagement based on the Yugoslavian model.

The nation applauded the expropriation by armed force—it took six days—of the IPC petroleum complex, as well as the nationalization of industrial plants, sugar refineries, chemical plants, paper plants (owned by W. R. Grace) and the United States-owned Cerro de Pasco Corporation, with its great reserves of copper, tin, gold, and silver.[108] Such support lent the government substantive legitimacy and allowed it to advance its programs for changing the economic structure to centralize its management. The intellectual and political lower middle class supported the government, and some of its members held important positions.

These policies invited the United States' displeasure. The government was concerned that the United States would apply sanctions, as it had done with Cuba. But Washington, in turn, worried that similar treatment would lead to the "Cubanization" of Peru and proceeded with caution. Nixon sent a representative to deal with the question of the IPC, without success. But when the Peruvian navy captured American fishing boats in its territorial waters, Nixon cut off military aid and suspended the sale of arms to Peru. In reprisal the Peruvian government expelled the United States military mission and denied entry to the Rockefeller Commission, which was on a Latin American tour on Nixon's behalf.[109]

Velasco Alvarado's foreign policy was pro-third world, independent, and open. He tightened relations with Communist countries. In 1971 he restored relations with Cuba and led a regional movement to persuade the OAS to lift the sanctions imposed on Cuba in 1964. In 1974 Peru joined the Nonaligned Movement.

In 1975 a worldwide recession caused the price of Peru's export products to fall, reducing its exports and throwing the nation into a grave economic crisis. Its foreign debt, the fiscal deficit, and inflation skyrocketed. Contradicting his third world rhetoric, Velasco submitted to the requirements of the International Monetary Fund.

This crisis triggered popular mobilizations, union protests, and strikes, which the government declared illegal. A police strike left Lima without police control, resulting in the looting of many stores and commercial centers. The strike was harshly put down. Border conflicts with Ecuador and Chile in July and August 1975 added to the tension.

Unhappy with the situation, the military forced Velasco to resign. On August 29 he left the Presidential Palace alone, with no announcement to the people of Lima.[110] He left behind a new Peru, having turned the country upside down; he had favored the masses and reduced the power of the oligarchy. But the grave economic, social, and political difficulties that affected the entire country opened the floodgates to the opposition from the left as much as from the right. No one was happy. His successor, General Francisco Morales Bermúdez (1975–1980), buried the Nasserite revolution, and the country returned to its old ways. The change of president marked the end of an extraordinary experience, managed by progressive military officers with a social conscience, which aroused great hopes among the Peruvian masses and was widely admired beyond the nation's borders.

VENEZUELA: THE BIRTH OF DEMOCRACY

Rómulo Betancourt, the leader of the Acción Democrática (AD, Democratic Action)—a party of the masses—was elected president of Venezuela (1959–1964), with the massive support of the people. He was a liberal figure of continentwide stature and was considered one of the wisest and most brilliant politicians of his time. He was the first civilian president after a long period of bloody, brutal, and corrupt military dictatorships. His arrival marked the birth of democracy.

Betancourt had to contend not only with the surge of a powerful guerrilla movement in the cities and the mountains, but also intense social unrest, a serious economic crisis, military uprisings, and attempted coups by rightist military officers "nostalgic for dictatorship."

There had been bitterness among the leftist movements, marginalized in spite of the fact that the patriotic junta, promoted by the Communist Party, led to the fall of Pérez Jiménez's dictatorship. This junta was made up of Betancourt's party, Alianza Democrática (AD: Democratic Alliance), the Comité de Organización Politico-Electoral Independiente (COPEI: Committee of the Independent Politico-Electoral Organization), and the Unión Republicana Democrática (URD: Democratic Republican Union).

Amid the euphoria at the tyrant's fall, the Communists ordered the popular forces to postpone their social struggles until constitutionality was restored and a president was elected by popular vote. They were so "dazzled by the triumph of democracy" that they did not negotiate for their representation in the government, according to one former activist. "We did not see that the usual political birds of prey were looking for the seats of power," he said. With a certain bitterness Pompeyo Márquez, one of the five leaders of the insurrection, recalled, "While we were running through the stadiums shouting 'hurrahs' for liberty, the dominant sectors were running to Miraflores (the presidential palace) to take over the government."[III] The courageous "days of popular struggle" during January 1958, when the people, led by the Communists, took to the streets to confront the police and the army, were a thing of the past. In the end they were left empty-handed.

Betancourt, an anti-Communist to the core, also excluded them. Even from exile before the fall of Pérez Jiménez he warned that he would have nothing to do with the Communists. They were not part of his government coalition—called "Fixed Point"—in which only the AD, URD, and COPEI were represented.[112]

Social violence and repression began in the early months of his government. The country was suffering a recession, fiscal crisis, depleted reserves, a fall in oil prices, a budget deficit, and high unemployment. Betancourt responded to the economic crisis with drastic and profoundly unpopular emergency measures. He reduced salaries (a first for Venezuela), laid off thousands of public employees, raised taxes, and eliminated the Emergency Plan that had been developed by the civilian-military junta (the first government following the dictatorship) to help the unemployed.

A demonstration by unemployed workers in the Plaza de la Concordia in Caracas in August 1959 to protest Betancourt's laws was dispersed with police gunfire, leaving four dead and several wounded. The violent repression against the lower classes and the unemployed, Betancourt's alliance with the oligarchy, his invitation to foreign capital, his anti-Communist and anti-Cuban policies, and his hostility toward the left radicalized the lower classes and unemployed, generating a strong movement in opposition to the government.

In April 1960 an important sector of the AD youth withdrew to found the Marxist-Leninist Movimiento de Izquierda Revolucionaria (MIR: Movement of the Revolutionary Left). In July, Jóvito Villalba—the head of the URD—resigned from the Fixed Point coalition because he disagreed with Betancourt's internal and foreign policies and supported the Cuban Revolution.[113]

A military uprising was staged in April 1960 amid this highly charged atmosphere. It was led by General J. M. Castro León, the minister of defense under the previous government. Though it was put down, four days later there was an assassination attempt on Betancourt. An OAS commission determined that the attempt was the work of the Dominican dictator Generalissimo Rafael Leonides Trujillo. In November there was a gigantic progovernment demonstration by campesinos and workers. But the clashes between the government and the people continued. The student demonstrations at universities and secondary schools were met with violent police confrontations, leaving many wounded and dead. The MIR newspaper demanded a change of government. Betancourt in turn ordered the arrest of journalists and deputies allied with MIR because he believed that they were instigating a coup.

In January 1961 the economic situation began to improve with a rise in oil prices—Venezuela's principal export—in foreign markets. But the political situation grew more complex with more military uprisings. In February rightwing officers tried to take over the military college and the barracks of the presidential guard, and in June a takeover was tried at the Pedro María Freites barracks. Both actions failed.

In January 1962 there were massive popular protests, among them one by transportation workers, which reached unprecedented proportions. In June and July there were new military uprisings, this time by progressive officers, in La Guaira, Carúpano and Puerto Cabello. Though they failed, they did succeed in causing a great stir among the people and deep concerns for the government. After these failed attempts a contingent of ranking officers created the Fuerzas Armadas de Liberación Nacional (FALN: Armed Forces of National Liberation) and began the armed struggle. Young people of the left, the Communist Party, the MIR, and the URD went into the mountains.

Analysts defined Betancourt's government as constitutional but antidemocratic. His extreme anti-Communism led him to undertake severe repression of the guerrillas, Communists, and lower-class sectors. The violence in Venezuela in the 1960s coincided ("not by chance, I imagine," the former *comandante*, Alfredo Maneiro, conjectured) with a decade of violence throughout Latin America. The detonator of this explosion was the Cuban Revolution.[114]

The situation in the country improved during the final years of Betancourt's government. The economy was slowly improving, and support for the government grew with the passage of the Agrarian Reform Law and the distribution of lands in the conflict zones, with the resulting jolt to industry, and new oil policies. Betancourt promised greater participation by the state, changed the rules on concessions to foreign companies, and created the Venezuelan Petroleum Corporation to manage this primary sector of its economy.[115] But Betancourt's repression of the left and his anti-Cuban politics elicited explosive protests from the people and discomfort among the military. The demonstrations in defense of the Cuban Revolution, which brought together the masses, students, and intellectuals, were violently suppressed. "Only Betancourt and the police are against the feelings of the people," commented Luben Petkoff, one of the most distinguished former guerrilla leaders[116]

Betancourt's foreign policy was firm, consistent, and upright. He is remembered as one of the most fervent defenders of democracy, tenacious in his opposition to the dictators Trujillo and Somoza and de facto governments. He insisted that the OAS take measures to defend democratic principles and expel the dictatorships for going against the Inter-American system. In a letter to President Kennedy in July 1963 he declared that he was "burdened by worry before the somber panorama taking shape in Latin America," and he reminded Kennedy of his words in defense of democratic values.

Betancourt severed diplomatic relations with the dictatorships of Trujillo in the Dominican Republic, Colonel López Arellano in Honduras, and Francois Duvalier in Haiti. After the military coup against Peruvian President Manuel Prado y Ugarteche, Betancourt requested a meeting of the OAS's Consultative Organ to condemn this deed, and when the Brazilian military toppled Joao Goulart, he asked Latin American governments to refuse to recognize the new government.

The OAS confirmed that the assassination attempt in 1960 was indeed the work of Trujillo. Venezuela succeeded in getting the Organization to impose sanctions on the dictator and in persuading the member governments to cut off diplomatic relations.

Betancourt was also a determined opponent of the Cuban Revolution and one of Fidel's biggest critics. He granted no credit to Cuba for the purchase of oil, and he supported the United States' policies against Cuba in the United Nations and the OAS. At the OAS he accused Cuba of trying to sabotage the Maracaibo oil fields and of "interference in the internal affairs of Venezuela." The army captured a shipload of weapons that came from Cuba and discovered the presence of Cuban military personnel among the Venezuelan guerrillas. Though Betancourt had already left office by 1964, the OAS imposed economic and diplomatic sanctions on Cuba for these actions. Mexico, Chile, Uruguay, and Bolivia voted against them. Secretary of State Dean Rusk accused Cuba of trying to destroy Venezuela's democracy.[117]

It turned out that Fidel did lend economic support, weapons, "advisers," and training to the Venezuelan guerrillas to help them overthrow Betancourt. At some point there was talk that Che would get involved in the Venezuelan armed struggle, but the Venezuelan Communist Party opposed this plan. "It would have enormously aggravated the Venezuelan revolutionary process and confirmed Betancourt's accusation that Castro communism was driving our insurgent movement," Luben Petkoff, the former guerrilla leader, commented later. Pompeyo Márquez agreed. "It would have completely distorted the national content of our struggle."[118]

Betancourt often denounced the exploitation of Venezuelan oil resources by United States transnational corporations and enacted measures to change the terms of concession to these companies and raised their taxes. The corporations took steps in reprisal. By means of market manipulations, which Betancourt had condemned, they lowered the price of crude oil. In 1960 at Venezuela's initiative, the Organization of Petroleum Exporting Countries (OPEC) was created to unite the oil-producing countries (Venezuela and the Arab nations, that is) and to control the price of oil on the world market. From this position of strength they could negotiate with the capitalist oil-consuming powers.

Betancourt was repressive and rode roughshod over civil rights on the one hand but guaranteed democracy on the other. The most powerful sector of the country supported him. He was the first Venezuelan president to complete his term and hand over the reins of power to a successor, Raúl Leoni, who was elected with 90 percent of the vote.

THE *COMANDANTES*

Universities and the youth movements of the Communist and leftist parties were the main support of the Venezuelan armed insurrection of the 1960s, the so-called decade of violence. Groups of professors and young people from the middle class banded together and went into the mountains, where they created "focos" and filled out their ranks with campesinos. These armed groups were part of the Latin American revolutionary explosion.

Not everyone who went to the mountains stayed there. Life in the open air was filled with danger and called for physical and mental toughness, especially from those who were accustomed to the comforts of the city. Some felt demoralized and wanted out. As the number of defections grew, the *comandantes* had to call a halt to that trend. From that point forward, whoever wanted to leave would be considered a deserter, and "whoever asks out will be shot." Some were.[119] The Venezuelan "firing squad executions" scandalized public opinion within the country and abroad and created profound discontent among the leftist movements and the guerrillas.

Most of the guerrillas were campesinos. Elegido Sibada, "Magoya," a former *comandante*, commented that the majority of them were illiterate and lacked any military training or ideological position. Some did not even know that the Communist Party existed, and they learned to read from Marxist literature. They joined the guerrillas because they wanted to fight, to be the army of the people. These were mountain people who feared the city, which they saw as "a graveyard for the revolutionaries," noted Sibada. Campesinos were also caught in the crossfire between the army and the guerrillas. The army tortured them, raped their wives and daughters, robbed them, and killed them. The army then went to supposed guerrilla zones and bombed them from planes and helicopters. The troops fought them with "funnel" and "search and destroy" operations. "Many troops and murderous soldiers came to the sierra and obliged us to withdraw but we learned to outwit them," remembered Sibada. He stated that the guerrillas also harassed the campesinos. "We went through whole rural villages and told them, if you go around talking nonsense, we will shoot you. We set up focos and began to spoil everything."[120]

There were deep conflicts within the leftist parties. Some sectors of the youth movement did not agree with the old leadership of the Communist Party, and controversies arose between the "civilians," accused of wanting to sabotage the armed struggle, and the "militarists," accused of wanting to take over the leadership of the Party. Both sides acted in isolation. Their armed movements included the MIR, Marxist-Leninists, the Frente de Liberación Nacional (FLN: National Liberation Front), and the Unidades de Tácticas de Combate (Tactical Combat Units)—urban cells of the Communist Party.

The Venezuelan guerrilla struggle was unlike Cuba's. These activists gained no ground. Instead they lost in the political and military arenas. "We were on the bleak high plateau, Fabricio Ojeda, Luben Petkoff, Lunar Márquez, and others. We were celebrating the anniversary of the Cuban Revolution, and we said to ourselves: Fidel arrived at Columbia Camp in a tank after two years, and we, after three, are sitting up here on this rock with our dicks in our hands," commented a former *comandante,* "Pablo."[121]

It was frustrating to compare the Cuban triumph with their own struggle because "all that national unity policy in the name of constitutionality, of which the Communist Party had been the leader, seemed to make no sense. [Here] the mountains had given birth to a mouse," said Alfredo Maneiro.[122]

Why did the guerrillas fail? The former *comandantes* recalled an insurrection plagued by mistakes and internal conflicts. They blamed the "focos'" strategy, naïveté, adventurism, lack of planning, and haste. They also pointed to the political ambiguities of the Communist Party, the political and ideological conflicts at the heart of the leftist parties, the lack of unity among the leadership, directives given too late or outside the political context, the desire to copy foreign paradigms, and the attempt to imitate the Cuban example.[123]

They recognized that they had also made a grave error in judgment when they assumed that people would support a fight against the regular army, the bulwark of a popularly elected president with the support of the establishment. The people did not give that support, primarily because they did not understand the movement. The parties and the guerrilla movements had not done political work among the masses. The Communist Party did not explain to them why they were fighting a constitutional government after having fought for thirty years against dictatorships that violated that constitutionality. The *comandantes* had imposed directives without listening to the people, dedicated themselves to the armed struggle, and grown increasingly isolated.

Several former *comandantes* declared that in 1962 Betancourt was on the point of falling because of the extreme weakness of his government. That he did not, however, was due to the guerrillas' mistakes. Had the military uprisings that occurred that year in La Guaira, Carúpano, and Puerto Cabello been conceived within a plan for general insurrection, with other simultaneous actions and consistent leftist ideologies, he would have fallen.

Politically the insurgency's mistakes and failures were serious. After a vigorous campaign to persuade people not to vote in the elections, there was a 90 percent turnout. When the guerrillas attacked a train carrying families and children at El Encanto, leaving several people wounded and dead, the country turned against them. The government ordered that the perpetrators be tried in a military court and arbitrarily punished the elected representatives from the Communist Party and the MIR, accusing them of having instigated the attack. They were imprisoned and their parties were outlawed. The court of justice approved these measures.

Another serious misjudgment was the so-called Caracas Plan, conceived to strike an overwhelming blow to the government through confrontations with the police forces. A shipment of arms for the guerrillas was to arrive from Cuba. When the arms reached the coast near Falcón, so did the army. Years later, viewing these events in retrospect, several former *comandantes* expressed relief that these weapons had been seized. The seizure prevented an incalculable massacre of people of the left. From one mistake to another, from one failure to the next, the insurgent movement faltered. The Caracas Plan was the final blow.

The Communist Party lost strength in the union movements, in the guild organizations, among the campesino forces, and in the student, professional, and technical sectors. And it lost the majorities in the congress it had succeeded in wresting from the government.

Was this armed struggle justified? In testimony by the participants in the decade of violence, contained in a collection of books published by the Central University of Venezuela, many former *comandantes* expressed frustration at having lost the "revolutionary moment" because of the failures and the errors that had been committed. The movement did not achieve political importance, nor did it compensate for the enormous sacrifices and efforts made, they insisted. For Petkoff, the revolution was necessary, however. In all revolutionary processes, he remarked, the road to victory is strewn with defeats and failures without which it would be impossible to advance. Pedro Ortega, former guerrilla, considered it to have been a backward movement in the Venezuelan revolution, since it fractured the left, which was then unable to reunite in time to put up a single viable candidate. Pompeyo Márquez believed that his own greatest mistake was in contributing to the insurrection line. He felt that he had been correct in promoting a "process of reflection not limited to a simple change of tactics or a mere operational change" but "as a path of intellectual, theoretical, and political inquiry" in an effort to form a fundamental ideology for a revolutionary future. For Maneiro, the time of the violence was canceled out, the task at hand being not to "blow on the coals but to gather the wood for the fire that is coming."[124]

The Venezuelan guerrillas received underground aid from Cuba, the Soviet Union, China, Algeria, Albania, and Italy. These allies provided funds, weapons, training, and some "advisers" (among them, Arnaldo Ochoa Sánchez, who became a star among the Cuban high military command and led his troops in Angola. He was later executed for his involvement in a serious narcotics-trafficking scandal). It was a war funded by many outside as well as homegrown resources, according to former *comandante* Luis Correa. But there was corruption and embezzlement in this clandestine traffic of arms and funds for the armed struggle. Some of those sent abroad on "purchasing missions" remained in Europe, living "like Pashas." The Communist Party used these funds to sustain its bureaucracy and not for the armed struggle for which they were earmarked.[125]

In 1966 Petkoff received direct assistance from Fidel, who sent fifteen men rather than the hundred Petkoff had requested. "If they kill you," Fidel noted, "a hundred Cubans will be stranded in unknown territory, empty-handed and alone. They will be seen as intruders."[126] The Cubans arrived on July 24, on the birthday of the Liberator, Simón Bolívar, after whom the operation was named. The men brought with them tremendous experience and arms. Little by little Petkoff's group was joined by other guerrilla detachments. "We were seventy-some," remembered Sibada, "a well-armed bunch, all veterans; this was a column made to strike, to take large towns, but nothing was done. We arrived at the rural villages, and there was eating and dancing and screwing around. We only mounted three or four operations to satisfy the people's anxiety."[127]

At first Cuba gave unrestricted aid to the Venezuelan guerrillas, while the Venezuelan Communist Party fed them a pack of lies so they would not suspend that aid, remembered *Comandante* Luis Correa. They told Fidel that they already had a mountain army and that the armed struggle was going well, and they showed him maps of "liberated zones." They told similar lies to the Communist Parties of Korea, China, and Vietnam.[128] Quarrels erupted between the Cubans and the Venezuelan Communist Party when the latter proposed a policy of "withdrawal." *Comandante* Douglas Bravo promised that he would keep on fighting, and the Cubans supported him. At one point his column had the best arms, the best men, and the best Cuban advisers. Later on the Cubans became disillusioned with Bravo.

Fidel lined up against the Venezuelan Communist Party. Given his moral stature, his attacks were shattering, since his criticisms made them look like cowards, according to one former *comandante*. Cuba severely criticized the withdrawal, for it represented a serious setback in its revolutionary plans for Latin America. Che was already in Bolivia, ready to put a match to the fuse of a continent wide revolution.[129]

Had the Cuban leadership betrayed them, as some *comandantes* maintained? The lies by the Venezuelans hurt the Cubans, although some held that Cuba provided aid because the most important thing at the moment was to encourage revolutionary fervor, however incipient it may have been. Cuba's change of policy with respect to the Venezuelan guerrillas, they said, must be seen in the international context, bearing in mind Cuba's growing dependence on Moscow, Khrushchev's policy of peaceful coexistence with the West, and the Soviet Communist Party's opposition to armed struggle. Moscow did not agree with Cuba's assistance to Latin American insurgent movements. The help Fidel provided Douglas Bravo and Petkoff was the last "small effort" he made to see if the lies were true. He stopped only "when he c[ould] no longer do it."[130]

LEONI'S "PACIFICATION"

When Raúl Leoni assumed the presidency (1964–1969), the insurrection movement was all but wiped out and there was a sense of peace. The Venezuelan Communist Party decreed a "unilateral truce" so that the president could develop the plans for peace offered in his campaign. Later, it proposed a "democratic peace," a policy approved by the party plenum in spite of its internal discrepancies. Finally, it decreed the "withdrawal."

Leoni's "pacification" policy was one of extreme repression and offered amnesty to former activists. The police raided universities and detained hundreds of students and leftist party activists. Some were assassinated or disappeared, their corpses found horrifically tortured.[131] Under this policy of extermination the insurgent movements started to wither away.

After Leoni, the head of COPEI Rafael Caldera, was elected to office. The road was paved for a succession of constitutional presidents elected by popular vote. Coups and militarism became things of the past. From this point forward, the candidates from the social and political elite of the two biggest parties, COPEI and Acción Democrática, succeeded one another without incident.

Betancourt, Leoni, and Caldera, democrats of principle and ideas, did not seem to have moral or ethical scruples about violating human rights and negating constitutional guarantees. They justified their actions by claiming that their priority was to defend democratic institutions against the Communist threat. All sectors of power supported them. The former guerrillas entered the national political arena without obstacles or threats on their lives, thus enjoying the privileges of a country with a democratic vocation, open to the play of politics and to change.

THE PARTY'S OVER

In Latin America the 1960s went from revolutionary turbulence to the virtual elimination of armed insurgencies. Only the Montoneros and the ERP in Argentina and the Tupamaros in Uruguay continued their activities at full throttle. The motivations, objectives, processes, and boom times of the armed struggles and the reasons for their dissolution were similar, though their effectiveness and impact were not. Some produced widespread internal shocks and tremors but constituted no real threat to their governments. Contrary to Cuba's situation, where the armed struggle went up against a corrupt and bloody dictatorship, and the Southern Cone, where the insurgents fought the neofascist dictatorships, revolutionaries in Colombia, Peru, and Venezuela were fighting against constitutional governments of the so-called democratic renaissance.

The end of the decade was a celebration for the counterinsurgency, which served the United States defense strategy and the National Security doctrine. Washington continued to support the dictatorships, and Nixon arrived in the White House with his eye fixed on Chile, where the Socialist Salvador Allende governed. Later came his decisive and extensive clandestine intervention.

CHAPTER VI

WHAT ABOUT CUBA?

THE 1960s AND 1970s: CUBA IN THE INTERNATIONAL ARENA

Fidel wanted to unite the revolutionaries of the third world in opposition to imperialism, and to encourage and, ultimately, lead revolution throughout Latin America. In January 1966 he convened the First Tricontinental Conference, with more than 500 representatives from the National Liberation movements of Africa and Asia and the guerrilla movements of Latin America. The Organización de Solidaridad con los Pueblos de África, Asia y América Latina (OSPAAAL: Organization in Solidarity with the Peoples of Africa, Asia and Latin America) and the Organización de Solidaridad con América Latina (LASO: Latin American Solidarity Organization) were both born out of the conference and set up their headquarters in Havana.

The Tricontinental Conference reaffirmed the "unconditional assistance" to revolutionary and liberation movements and encouragement of their struggle in the third world. From Bolivia, Che relayed a message to the Conference, affirming that "true liberation of the people [is] by way of armed struggle, for the most part," and that in Latin America, "almost inevitably," it would be a socialist revolution.[1] The salient aspect about the conference was not its anti-Yankee rhetoric but the anti-Soviet tone, as the United States writer Carla Ann Robbins noted. According to her, Fidel was using this forum to affirm his commitment to the revolutionary armed struggle, which the Kremlin opposed—it went against Khrushchev's policy of peaceful coexistence with the West.[2] This situation caused friction between Cuba and the Soviet Union and controversy between Cuba and Latin America's Communist parties. The divergence between young Communists and the leadership of their parties, who followed the orthodox Moscow line, caused them to split. From these schisms emerged pro-Castro armed groups.

The resolutions and recommendations approved by the Tricontinental Conference raised a dust storm of criticism and denunciations against Cuba in the United States and in Latin American governments. In a letter to the President of the United Nations Security Council, eighteen Latin American ambassadors—Mexico did not sign—denounced the objectives of the Conference, stating that it "encouraged and triggered" violent change in their governments and institutions and an attempt against their sovereignty and political stability; it violated international law and the United Nations Charter.

In a letter to the United Nations Secretary General, Fidel accused the signers of the letter of "cynicism," and of being "accomplices in the subordination, domination, and exploitation of their own countries by North American imperialism," which "reserves for itself the right" to a military occupation of the Dominican Republic (Johnson invaded that nation in 1965). He attacked this interventionist policy, which was "clearly expressed" in a resolution recently approved by the United States House of Representatives. He added that while in Havana, the revolutionaries from the three continents had decided to intensify the struggle and support the people who were fighting for their independence. A resolution adopted by the OAS—again without Mexico's support—"emphatically" condemned the Tricontinental Conference's policies of intervention and aggression and asked that a special commission investigate the Conference and inform the OAS's council.³ Such a vigorous condemnation sharply contrasted with its silence regarding United States aggression against Cuba.

The following year Fidel called the first conference of OLAS (Organization of Latin American Solidarity). In the opening speech he declared "war to the death" by the people against the monopolistic interests of the United States and the oligarchies of Latin America that dedicated themselves to furthering those interests. He declared that the conditions were ripe to begin and escalate a revolutionary war in which the people's army would be victorious.

THE DISTANT ALLY

Severing its dependence on the United States left a void in Cuba that was quickly filled by the Soviet Union and the socialist nations. Their relations—politically, economically, scientifically, culturally, and militarily—grew closer every day. Some analysts maintained that the United States policies of aggression against Cuba threw Fidel and the Revolution into the arms of the Soviet Union and Communism. Others claimed that Fidel had already established himself as a Communist and identified with the Soviet model and policies of anti-imperialism and confrontation with the United States. But at the triumph of the Revolution, Fidel was not a Communist. His adherence to Marxism-Leninism came later.

Relations with the Soviet Union—vital to the further growth of the Revolution—did not change the independent line of Fidel's foreign policies. Cuba was not an unconditional ally, nor did it serve as a satellite. During the open and sharp controversy between the Soviet Union and the People's Republic of China, Fidel remained neutral, establishing diplomatic relations with China (which he announced in his First Havana Declaration in 1960). Although Khrushchev called Cuba's policies of support of guerrilla and national liberation movements in the third world "adventurist" and "putchist," he nevertheless appreciated Fidel's independence, political clarity, and extraordinary negotiating abilities, which showed him to be a useful ally, according to Tad Szulc in his book on Fidel. Still, such independence had its consequences. The Soviet Union took measures in reprisal; it delayed sending oil and signing the commercial-exchange agreements, both of which were vitally important to the Cuban government.[4]

The first public break between Havana and Moscow occurred during the crisis over the Soviet missiles in Cuba in October 1962. Fidel expressed his anger to Khrushchev for having made the agreement with Kennedy to withdraw the missiles behind his back—the Cuban leadership learned of the deal from international cables. He told Khrushchev that Kennedy's promise not to invade Cuba was not enough; Khrushchev should first have demanded an end to both the embargo and the aggressions, and the return of the Guantanamo base, which the United States held against the wishes of the Cuban people.

In Che's last public speech, on February 1965 at a seminar of the Afro-Asian Solidarity Organization in Algiers, he accused the Soviet Union of being to some degree "an accomplice of imperialist exploitation," and denounced the "immoral character" of its treatment of the recently independent African nations. In particular, he pointed out the excessive requisites the Soviet Union set before the African nations in their "mutually beneficial" commercial agreements. Next to Fidel, Che was the most vigorous voice of the revolutionary government.[5] In March, Fidel also criticized the Soviets for not aiding North Vietnam—a victim of United States aggression— more effectively and for not reacting with greater force to the United States bombings that had begun a month earlier.

In a communiqué that appeared in the May 1967 issue of *Granma Semanal*, the Cuban Communist Party criticized the Soviet Union's policy of peaceful coexistence, since it failed to guarantee national integrity, sovereignty, and independence. The article asked what sort of coexistence the United States was practicing in Vietnam. In his letter to the Tricontinental Conference, Che noted that Vietnam stood alone. "It is not a question of wishing good luck to a country under attack," he noted, "but of making its fate your own, standing by it in death or victory." Che alleged that the Soviet Union was as responsible as the United States for Vietnam's fate by refusing to defend it.[6] The Soviet Union, however, did not become involved in the conflict to avoid a confrontation with the United States.

On the Cuban calendar, 1967 was marked as the Year of Heroic Vietnam. To Fidel, Cuba and Vietnam had much in common. Both were small countries fighting against United States imperialism and both were dangerously isolated—thousands of miles from their allies in the socialist bloc. After the way the Soviets had handled the missile crisis, Fidel feared that the Soviet Union would not protect Cuba. In several speeches he tried to pressure the Soviet Union into giving crucial support to Vietnam. It would mean survival for both countries.

Moscow was not indifferent to Cuba's criticism, and relations between the countries became more complex. The Soviet Union's costly "fraternal solidarity" brought with it political commitments for Cuba—it was to support the Soviet Union at crucial moments. Cuba was trying to figure out how to do so without giving up its own principles of defense and respect for national sovereignty, independence, and nonintervention. Its trial by fire came in August 1968, when Soviet tanks and 600,000 Warsaw Pact soldiers invaded Prague. This "fraternal aid" to Czechoslovakia in defense of socialism, as Leonid Brezhnev termed it, violently thwarted the Czech national uprising, the so-called Prague Spring. It marked the beginning of the Brezhnev doctrine of limited sovereignty, which he imposed on the nations of the Soviet bloc. It was as controversial and interventionist as the United States' Monroe Doctrine is to Latin America.

The Soviet intervention was condemned not only by the European countries but also by the rest of the Western world. Three days later, in a televised address, Fidel laid out his government's position. "It was a superb intellectual challenge for Fidel," wrote Tad Szulc, "and he handled it superbly." He termed

it a "flagrant" and "illegal" violation of Czech borders but, presented with the
fait accompli, he said: "We accept the bitter necessity that required the dispatch
of these forces to Czechoslovakia, we do not condemn the socialist countries
that took this decision." But, he added, "as revolutionaries we have the right
to demand that a consistent position be adopted toward all the questions
affecting the revolutionary movements in the world." And he asked, "[W]ill
Warsaw Pact divisions be sent to Cuba if Yankee imperialists attack our country?" In this fashion, continued Szulc, Castro demonstrated his solidarity with
the intervention in defense of socialism and put the Soviet Union in a position
of having to defend Cuba militarily in case of an attack by the United States.[7]
Friends and partisans of the Cuban Revolution, intellectuals, Communist parties, socialists, and movements of the European and worldwide left condemned
Cuba's support of the invasion. They did not forgive Cuba for espousing independence and respect for national sovereignty while turning its back on a small
country knocked down by a superpower.

In 1968 and 1969 Cuba's foreign policy changed. Its independent line was
swallowed by unavoidable commitments with its principal ally. Though the
Cuban leadership managed this situation with undeniable skill, it appeared
to the world that Cuba was sinking into the Soviet orbit as the most peculiar
and erratic of its allies. Always direct and stubborn, Fidel was an enigma to
the Kremlin, or so claimed Anatoly Dobrinin, the Soviet ambassador in
Washington from the Kennedy to the Reagan administrations. It was a long
period of intense Cold War.[8]

On repeated occasions Fidel pointed out with gratitude the fundamental
contribution of the Soviet Union and the socialist countries to the development of the economic, industrial, technical, and scientific sectors of his country; the Revolution, he declared, would not have survived without it. In
January 1969, at the tenth anniversary celebration of the triumph of the
Revolution, while acknowledging the importance of foreign aid, Fidel also
referred to the differences between Cuba and the Soviet Union. "At times and
on certain questions we have had different criteria, and we have expressed them
with all honesty, but at the same time this very honesty obliges us to proclaim
that their assistance was decisive for this country during difficult times." He
noted the provision of foodstuffs when production was low, free military aid
when threats were great, and specialized personnel when Cuba lacked
technicians.[9]

For the Soviet Union, the alliance with Cuba was convenient: it provided
an enclave 90 miles from the United States coast. Cuba also brought the

Soviet Union closer to Latin America. Its generous support of Cuba drew sympathy from progressive sectors in Latin America; it suggested to them that they could receive this support as well in case of need.

THE REVOLUTION AND THE PRIESTS

Controversy with the Cuban Church hierarchy came immediately after the triumph of the Revolution. Cardinal Manuel Arteaga and some of the bishops had had excellent relations with Batista. In turn, Batista and his second wife, Marta Fernández, were generous contributors to the Church. The hierarchy never said a word against the regime's brutality, in spite of the fact that priests and members of religious orders were arrested and tortured. This changed when Batista began to lose his footing. Although the majority of laymen and priests were opposed to the dictatorship, they also opposed the rebels' armed struggle. A small number did support it, and some of them went to the Sierra Maestra. After the triumph, Fidel gratefully acknowledged the aid of Catholics toward the "cause of liberty." Many priests jubilantly saluted the victory of the Revolution. The Auxiliary Bishop of Havana and the director of the most important Catholic magazine defended revolutionary justice when Cuba was attacked in the world press for the executions of Batista's men after having been judged by the people.

In an interview with the Brazilian priest Frei Betto in the 1980s, Fidel explained that the Agrarian Reform Law and the Urban Reform Law were at the heart of the tension with the Church—they went against the interests of the privileged classes with which the Church identified. In Cuba, Fidel remarked, the Church was an institution of and for the upper classes. A large number of the priests were foreigners, most of them Spaniards "infused" with reactionary ideas of the right—even of Franco's fascism. The Church did not have a single chapel or priest in the countryside, nor did the Church preach there, though 70 percent of the population was campesino. Neither was Catholic education for the people; the private schools, run by religious orders, were meant for the children of the oligarchy and the middle class. Fidel maintained that it was not the Revolution that had emptied the churches but the people, who were as alienated from the Church as it was from the people.

A quarter of the Cuban population is black and keeps alive its African traditions, and it was difficult for the Church to evangelize them. Fidel claimed that the conflicts with Catholic institutions had less to do with belief than with politics, because of the Church's counterrevolutionary activities. Priests, mainly

Spaniards, openly conspired, and the government decided to suspend permission for permanent residence to foreign priests and order some of them out of the country. Some 70 percent of the priesthood left during the first years of the Revolution. When the private schools became centers of conspiracy, they were nationalized. For many years relations between the government and the Catholic Church were distant, but there was no official religious persecution, and the government did not close the churches or prohibit the practice of Catholicism. Nevertheless, belief contradicted the Marxist-Leninist tenets of the Revolution: whoever wanted to climb the bureaucratic ladder did well to abstain from practicing his belief in public or making it known.

CUBA IN THE 1970s

The 1970s marked the stage of socialist "institutionalization" of the Cuban state, the "democratization" of its political system within a framework of "democratic centralism," and the restructuring of the mechanisms of the state and the Communist Party (CPC)—the backbone of the Revolution. During these years Cuba solidified its leadership in the third world and its role in the international arena.

In 1970 the CPC leadership reorganized, restructured, and strengthened the party to concern itself with plans for national development and its functions within the state. It enlarged the secretariat, created regional departments (including one for the Americas), and increased the number of members of the central committee. In five years the Party doubled its active membership. In June and July 1974 it tested popular power in elections to the municipal assembly for Matanzas Province. For the first time the vote was direct and secret. In 1975 the First Congress of the CPC met; this was an event of extraordinary importance for the country, and in February 1976 the Cuban people approved the new National Constitution in a popular referendum—the text had been discussed for a year in peoples' organizations throughout the country. December 1976 brought the first series of meetings of the Asamblea Nacional del Poder Popular (ANPP: National Assembly of People's Power), the "supreme organ of state power" and the expression of the "sovereign will of all working people" (Article 57 of the new constitution). At this session the highest governing body, the State Council, was elected. Fidel was reelected president with Raúl Castro as first vice president. The State Council designated the Council of Ministers, the People's Supreme Court, and the attorneys general and approved a new political-administrative division—fourteen provinces instead of eight—and reduced the number of townships.

In 1977, the "Year of Institutionalization," all these newly approved measures were put into effect. Elections were held throughout the country, and for the first time the people elected their representatives to the municipal, provincial, and national assemblies. Fidel confirmed that this was the most important step in the whole process.[10]

But the decade opened with the failure of the "ten-million-ton sugar harvest," a plan Castro had launched the previous year called the Year of Heroic Effort. In May he announced that the goal had not been met (the 8 million tons produced was still a record). For an entire year more than half a million technicians, workers, students, and teachers left their offices and workplaces to cut cane. Volunteer brigades from abroad came to Cuba to help. Fidel and the top leadership set the example, machete in hand, under the hot sun. The grave economic situation the country was experiencing because of errors, failures, low production (because of absenteeism and administrative slovenliness), enormous losses in the fishing and farming industries caused by hurricane Inez in 1967, a severe drought, and the international economic picture, all made it critical for Cuba to reach the goal set for the sugar harvest. But the price of sugar fell in foreign markets. Short on cash, Cuba was forced to reduce the importation of essential goods from the capitalist world, unobtainable from the socialist countries. Fidel spoke of "the agony of the country."

On July 26, 1970, for the seventeenth anniversary of the attack on the Moncada Barracks, a profoundly depressed Fidel delivered a speech in which he declared that the leadership, not the people, had lost the battle over sugar. He recognized that the "heroic effort" had caused imbalances in the economy; other industries had been abandoned, resulting in lower production in important sectors. He announced that the difficulties would increase in the coming years. And then he spoke of stepping down. The people's morale plummeted, while social problems and the incidence of delinquency rose.

In 1975, during his Report to the First Congress of the CPC, Fidel noted important economic advances in the five-year plan in different branches of industry and production and in the most important sectors of health and education. "Today we may proclaim with pride," he said, "that we are a country without unemployment, without racial discrimination, without hunger or beggars, without prostitution, without drugs, without illiteracy, without barefoot children who cannot go to school, without slums of the indigent, and without sick people abandoned to their fate. Our public education and health systems are models of social success which are the cause of much admiration throughout the world." The situation marked a sharp contrast with the prevailing conditions in Latin America.[11]

IN THE INTERNATIONAL ARENA

Cuban foreign policy was based on "proletarian internationalism," "fraternal friendship" with the Soviet Union and the socialist countries, and the advance of socialism in the world, as laid out in the preamble to the new constitution. Cuba was in solidarity with the socialist, progressive, and anti-imperialist governments of the third world and all liberation movements. It provided them with technical assistance, military aid, and political support. In the 1970s Cuba established diplomatic relations with more African countries and with the Palestine Liberation Organization. During the mid-1970s it had programs of cooperation with 37 countries of Africa, Asia, and Latin America. Cuba sent thousands of advisers, especially to Africa, to assist in basic areas of development, and thousands of young people from these countries received free education in Cuba.

Cuba's foreign policy was one that indulged in long projections. Jorge Domínguez, a Cuban professor at Harvard University, considered it to be the policy of a great power in spite of Cuba's small size.[12] Its influence extended to several continents, transcended its reduced continental orbit, and was not confined to relations with the Soviet bloc, although tit was vital to Cuba's development and defense. In 1972 Cuba joined the Council of Mutual Economic Assistance (COMECON), the economic organ of the Soviet bloc, and developed its economy as an integral part of this market. It exported tropical products to these countries. Trade with them rose to 85 percent of total exports. In 1976 Cuba signed a new five-year pact with the Soviet Union, which doubled the economic and technical aid Cuba received.

Cuban policy toward Latin America changed direction during the 1970s. It abandoned support for insurgent movements and sought to move closer to the governments. "We are in this hemisphere, on this side of the Atlantic. We are Latin Americans. We believe that one day we will be politically and economically integrated with the rest of the peoples of Latin America," Fidel proclaimed in a 1972 speech.[13]

With the election of the former president of Ecuador Galo Plaza as secretary general of the OAS in 1970, a movement favorable to Cuba began with the adoption of so-called ideological pluralism in Latin America. In 1971 Peru (under Velasco Alvarado) proposed lifting the sanctions but could not prevail, since Washington controlled a majority. The following year the OAS approved a resolution calling for the reexamination of the embargo and diplomatic relations with Cuba by 14 votes in favor, 8 abstentions (including the United States), and none against. In 1974 Colombia (under López Michelsen) requested a meeting of the consultative body to study the lifting of the embargo. This also failed to obtain the needed majority.[14] Only in 1975 were the sanctions lifted by a vote of 16 for (including the United States under Gerald Ford), 3 against (Chile, Paraguay, and Uruguay, all under military dictatorships), and 2 abstentions (Nicaragua and Brazil, also under dictatorships).[15] Washington warned that its policies toward Cuba depended on a "change of attitude on Castro's part," essentially in his foreign policies.[16] The United States would not "tolerate" the Cuban presence in Africa. Although several countries were in favor of Cuba's rejoining the OAS, Cuba was not interested because the United States controlled the organization. Cuba wanted a regional organization that excluded the United States.

In 1970 Cuba's isolation from the continent began to evaporate when Chile (under Salvador Allende) and Peru (under Velasco Alvarado) reestablished relations. In 1974 and 1975 they were followed by Argentina (under Juan Domingo Perón), Venezuela (under Carlos Andrés Pérez), Colombia (under Alfonso López Michelsen), and Panama (under General Omar Torrijos). Barbados, Trinidad and Tobago, Guyana, and Jamaica—former British colonies that had gained their independence during the 1960s—opened embassies in Havana. In 1975 the ad hoc Latin American group in the United Nations invited Cuba to rejoin. And in 1979 Cuba acquired new allies with the victories of Maurice Bishop in Grenada and the Sandinista revolution in Nicaragua.

The economic embargo also began to crack. In 1970 President Eduardo Frei of Chile signed a commercial treaty with Cuba for $11 million. In 1973 Héctor Cámpora, president of Argentina, granted Cuba credits amounting to $1.2 billion, and the following year Argentine businessmen signed commercial pacts with Cuba for $100 million dollars. In 1975 Mexican President Luis Echevarría granted it credits of $20 million for the purchase of machinery, equipment, and other Mexican products, and shortly thereafter Mexico signed agreements of cooperation worth some $1.2 billion in the areas of industry, agriculture, and tourism.[17]

The embargo from Western Europe also crumbled. In 1971 Great Britain sent a commercial mission to Cuba and Spain signed a four-year commercial pact; in 1972 the foreign ministers of the European Economic Community (EEC) agreed to extend commercial preferences to countries of the third world, including Cuba. Between 1971 and 1975 Cuban imports from these countries accounted for 49 percent of its total trade. The commercial agreements, bank credits, and loans with the Western powers were possible because Cuba boasted a solid credit rating. It was not a risk.[18] In January 1975, the Federal Republic of Germany established diplomatic relations with Cuba.

By the mid-1970s Cuba's prestige in the third world was at its peak, principally because of the crucial role Cuban troops—with Soviet support—played in the triumphs of Angola and Ethiopia against their aggressors. With the support of most of the Nonaligned nations—they represented two-thirds of the United Nations membership—Cuba became the host of the Sixth Summit, and Fidel became president of the movement for three crucial years.

TOGETHER IN AFRICA

For the Cuban leader, Africa was the continent with the greatest possibilities for the spread of socialism. Cuba's aid to progressive countries and liberation movements was broad and generous. In 1960 it sent arms and a medical team to the Algerian National Liberation Movement, led by Ahmed Ben Bella. Once Algeria was independent of France, Cuba installed a guerrilla training camp and sent a battalion to aid it in its territorial war against Morocco. Cuba also built military training camps in Ghana and Guinea. It maintained a kind of praetorian guard of 500 men in Guinea to defend President Sekou Touré, who was threatened by internal instability promoted by the opposition.

Fidel and Che made long trips to Africa. Che visited eight countries in 1965 on a three-month mission. He aimed to further their political, economic, and military union and strengthen their struggle against colonialism and imperialism. After this trip, when he made contact with Agostino Neto, the leader of the Movimento Popular de Libertação de Angola (MPLA: People's Movement for the Liberation of Angola) in exile in Brazzaville in the Congo, Cuba began sending him arms and advisers. It did the same for FRELIMO, a liberation movement in Mozambique. Che became involved with the Congolese guerrillas in their fight against President Moise Tshombe. Cuba sent 200 soldiers and weapons. They pulled out when the guerrillas asked them to, so that the guerrillas could sign an armistice with the new government.

In 1972 Fidel made a long official tour (it lasted 63 days) to six African countries, South Yemen, countries of Eastern Europe, and Moscow. In Africa he was received with massive popular demonstrations and expressions of personal admiration and solidarity with the Revolution on the part of the leaders. In some countries there were ribbon-cutting ceremonies for projects realized with Cuban assistance and named for Fidel. The joint communiqués were emotional revolutionary and anti-imperialist declarations condemning United States policies concerning Cuba and Vietnam and the racist regimes of Rhodesia (Namibia) and South Africa, with its policy of apartheid. They also supported the reunification of Korea and the struggle of the Palestinian people and condemned Israel's occupation of Arab lands; they also expressed support for President Salvador Allende of Chile, the nationalist policies of the Peruvian military government, and the struggle of the Panamanian people to regain the Panama Canal.[19]

Although Havana and Moscow's positions in the international arena were not identical, both found areas of mutual interest and benefit in Africa. Their plans were compatible, if not complementary. Cuba was not a Soviet pawn as Washington claimed. On the contrary, it was Cuba that was able to bring the Soviet Union into the Angolan war and later into Ethiopia's war against Somalia. Without Soviet help, it would have been impossible to realize such ambitious military operations. Cuba opened the way for the Soviet Union, whose indirect aid of arms and advisers was well received and served to improve the Soviet image in Africa.

Cuba's military aid to the MPLA, the first Angolan independence movement, began in 1965 after Che's visit to Africa. Cuba sent twelve military advisers to the Congo, where MPLA leader Agostino Neto sought asylum. When South African troops invaded Angola in October 1975, Neto asked for urgent assistance from Cuba and the Soviet Union. The next day Cuba launched Operation Carlota, and the Soviet Union began sending arms and advisers. A battalion of 18,000 Cuban soldiers arrived secretly by air and sea. At this point the South African troops were 15 miles from Luanda,[20] and the United States was already giving arms and instructors to the Frente Nacional de Libertação de Angola (FNLA: Angolan National Liberation Front) led by Holden Roberto, and to the União Nacional para Independência Total de Angola (UNITA: National Union for the Total Independence of Angola), headed by Jonas Savimbi. Aid from the superpowers and Cuba internationalized the Angolan conflict, making it an occasion for confrontation in the context of the Cold War.

On November 11, 1975, Portugal pulled out, and Neto declared the independence of the Angolan People's Republic. More than thirty countries recognized the new nation. The United States Congress prohibited further aid to the FNLA and UNITA, which were on the verge of disintegrating.

The following month 36,000 Cuban soldiers and the Angolan army carried the fight on four fronts and forced the South African troops to leave the country. In March 1976 the last of the troops left. Angola's triumph, with Cuba's crucial help, and the rout of racist South Africa were applauded in Africa. It was an "African Girón," remarked Fidel, referring to Cuba's victory over the United States at the Bay of Pigs.[21]

Fidel went to Conakry at the invitation of Sekou Touré to celebrate this victory in the company of Agostino Neto and Luis Cabral, President of Guinea-Bissau. At a massive demonstration these leaders expressed their gratitude to Fidel for Cuba's international aid to the African countries.[22] In June 1976 the United States vetoed Angola's admission to the United Nations.

Angola's war against South Africa and UNITA (supported by South Africa and the United States) continued, lasting a total of twelve years. Cuba maintained an average of 40,000 combat soldiers there, and the Soviet Union continued to send arms and military advisers. This was a coordinated Cuban and Soviet operation in Angola, but it was the Cubans who served as the leaders. In 1976, while referring to the presence of Cuban soldiers in Angola and explaining Cuba's solidarity with Africa at the CPC's First Congress in 1975, Fidel proclaimed, "We are an Afro-Latin nation."

South Africa's aggression against Angola was repeatedly condemned by the United Nations Security Council, which often called for South Africa to pull out its forces. The government in Pretoria ignored these requests. South Africa's brutal bombing caused enormous destruction and numerous deaths among the civilian population. Cubans also died.

The war ended in March 1988. After three months of fierce combat in Cuito Cuanavale, the Cuban and Angolan troops defeated the South Africans and forced their withdrawal. It was a triumph for the Cuban troops, since they were the ones who had led the fighting from the beginning of the war. Afterward came the difficult process of peace negotiations between Angola and South Africa and for the independence of Namibia, with the intervention of the United States and Cuba. These negotiations began in May. By August two tripartite accords—one on the withdrawal of South African and Cuban troops from Angola, and the other on the independence of Namibia—were concluded. They were signed at the United Nations in December. In January 1989 Cuba began to withdraw its troops amid warm demonstrations of affection and gratitude from the Angolan people.

Cuba risked the prestige of the Revolution on this war, Fidel remarked, since defeat would have carried an enormous political cost within and outside the country. For an entire year the Cuban leader dedicated himself to leading the fight from afar until the defeat of South Africa was assured—the only way of achieving peace.[23] But peace did not come. UNITA kept fighting. In 1990 Angola's President Eduardo Dos Santos accused the United States of continuing its support for UNITA. The last Cuban soldiers left in May 1991, a week before Dos Santos and Savimbi signed a peace agreement.[24]

In 1977 Cuba involved its troops in another African conflict. Lieutenant Colonel Mengitsu Haile Mariam, the Ethiopian head of state, asked its help when Somalia invaded the Ogaden province. This was another joint operation between Cuba and the Soviet Union. President Carter warned Cuba that this intervention was an obstacle to the "normalization" of their relations. The same month, the United States and Cuba agreed to open "interest section" offices in Washington and Havana. Fidel asked "by what right" Carter issued such a warning when United States troops were stationed at Guantanamo. It would be "ridiculous," he declared, for Cuba to demand the withdrawal of United States troops from the Philippines, Turkey, Greece, South Korea, or any other country as a precondition for improving relations.[25]

In February 1978, 20,000 Cuban soldiers arrived in Ethiopia along with Soviet weapons and military advisers. A month later Cuban and Ethiopian troops led by a Soviet general forced the Somali troops out of Ogaden. Carter accused Cuba of being a "Soviet pawn in Africa."

Cuba's intervention in Ethiopia's conflict with Somalia—both were members of the nonaligned bloc—caused further problems. Somalia severed relations with Cuba, and Marshal Tito of Yugoslavia, a pillar of the Nonaligned Movement, accused Cuba of aiding Soviet expansionism in Africa. Tito had been a severe critic of Cuba's alliance with the Soviet Union and Fidel's efforts to persuade the nonaligned nations to accept the Soviet bloc as their "natural ally," since such a change would nullify the movement's neutrality in regard to the two blocs. This was one of the reasons Yugoslavia cited in opposing the Sixth Nonaligned Summit Meeting held in Havana. Such critiques weakened Cuba on the eve of this summit, so vital to its aspirations to leadership of the third world.

The United States Congress and government rained criticisms on Cuba, and Carter again warned that Cuba's military presence in Africa was an obstacle to the normalization of relations. Zbigniew Brzezinski, the National Security Adviser and an opponent of easing tensions with Cuba, counseled Carter to harden his stance. Brzezinski saw the situation in the context of the East-West conflict and détente with the Soviet Union. He held that Cuba "threatens vital

United States interests" in Africa, and he did not exclude the possibility of United States military intervention on the island. He did not hesitate to distort and manipulate CIA reports to show that Cuba was increasing the number of its troops in Angola and Ethiopia. Secretary of State Cyrus Vance did not agree with Brzezinski; he thought it was dangerous to convert the question of Ethiopia into a confrontation between the superpowers. He declared that the United States could not force the withdrawal from Africa of Soviets and Cubans, who, furthermore, did not constitute a danger to United States interests on that continent or anywhere else in the third world.[26] Other than issuing strong declarations condemning Cuba, Carter did not modify his policies.

THE UNITED STATES AND CUBA

Richard Nixon continued the policy of aggression toward Cuba, seeking to isolate it politically and diplomatically. He continued the economic embargo and the CIA's covert operations—to which he seemed addicted—including its attempts to assassinate Fidel (in 1971 there was an attempt on his life while on a visit to Chile).

Despite these tactics and Nixon's aggressive anti-Cuban rhetoric, there was a relative easing of tensions during his administration. The priorities of his foreign policy were the great powers, the Soviet Union and the People's Republic of China, and the Vietnam War—he knew that the United States was losing the war and that it was immensely unpopular. In February 1970, in a speech to Congress laying out his foreign policy, Nixon did not mention Cuba; it was a secondary problem compared with the growing nationalism in Latin America. Chile and Peru were expropriating powerful United States corporations. Nixon did not impose sanctions on Peru for fear that it would follow the same path as Cuba. Henry Kissinger, who was the Nixon administration's leading voice on foreign policy, recommended keeping a low profile when it came to Latin America. It was pragmatic advice for a United States that was becoming more isolated every day.

In September 1970 a U-2 spy plane discovered that Cuba was building a submarine base in Cienfuegos Bay. But Nixon was not interested in unleashing anti-Cuban "hysteria" during a congressional election campaign, which was more important to him and the Republican Party; he minimized the discovery. In January 1971, in a televised interview, he said that this base did not represent a threat to United States security, since the Soviet Union reiterated that there would be no "offensive" missiles in Cuba. Nevertheless, he asked the Pentagon to study plans to mine the port and blockade Cuba.[27] In February 1973 the United States and Cuba signed an agreement on airplane hijackings, and Washington authorized congressional visits to Havana. In 1974, under pressure from within the United States and the governments of Latin America, the Nixon administration allowed American subsidiaries to do business with the island.

Drowning in the huge Watergate scandal, Nixon resigned, and Gerald Ford assumed the presidency (1974–1977). Ford tried to reduce tensions with Cuba through a covert dialogue. In November 1974 William Rogers (Nixon's former secretary of state) and Undersecretary of State Lawrence Eagleburger initiated a series of "exploratory" meetings to clarify the main points of controversy and to seek solutions. The conversations continued through 1975.[28]

At the First Congress of the Cuban Communist Party in December 1975 Fidel noted that during the 1960s Cuba had approximately 300,000 men in uniform for its defense. But in the past few years, "in the midst of a relative climate of peace" Cuba had been able to concentrate on problems of economic development and to reduce its defenses by more than 150,000.[29]

Some members of Congress supported the idea of moving closer to Cuba. The policies of hostility undermined United States prestige among its allies and especially in Latin America. Some felt that the economic embargo was a failure. In March 1975 Senator Edward Kennedy presented a proposal to lift it. Anti-Castroites in Florida called this resolution a "despicable act" and announced that they would respond with violence if it was approved.[30]

When Cuba sent troops to Angola in October 1975 at the request of the MPLA to resist the invasion by South Africa, Washington ended the covert dialogues with Cuba and increased its aid to the FNLA and UNITA to prevent a victory by the MPLA. After Angola became independent, the United States continued supporting the FNLA and UNITA in their attempts to bring about a change of government in Luanda.

A major conflict erupted in October 1976, when a Cubana Airlines plane leaving from Barbados exploded. Seventy-three people died, among them the young members of the Cuban fencing team, which was returning to the island loaded with medals. Fidel accused the CIA (of which George H. W. Bush was the director) of this sabotage, broke off the airline-hijacking agreement with the United States, and announced that Cuba would not sign another until this terrorist campaign ended "once and for all." Kissinger and other high officials denied that the CIA was implicated in this act.[31] In November 1975, the

United States Senate Intelligence Committee published a 347-page report on CIA involvement in the assassinations or attempts on the lives of foreign leaders, which revealed that between 1960 and 1965 there were some eight or more attempts to assassinate Fidel and other Cuban leaders. In February 1976, Ford signed an executive order prohibiting intervention by the CIA or any other United States intelligence agents to make attempts on the lives of foreign leaders.[32]

Carter (1977–1981) wanted a foreign policy of peace, nonintervention, and relaxation of the Cold War. This was a period of relative easing of political tensions with Cuba, supported by some groups in Congress. In 1977 several members of Congress traveled to Havana to talk with Fidel; and on their return they proposed that the embargo be lifted. In April, Undersecretary of State Terence Todman traveled to Cuba to sign an agreement on fishing and territorial waters and to establish diplomatic contacts between the two countries. In September the "interests section" offices were opened in Washington and Havana, in the Swiss and Czech Embassies respectively.

Secretary of State Cyrus Vance told the Senate Foreign Relations Committee that he believed it necessary to remove the obstacles to normalization of relations. Carter made such normalization conditional on an improvement in the human-rights situation (the release of political prisoners), the withdrawal of troops from Angola, suspension of Cuba interference in the internal affairs of the hemisphere, and compensation for United States citizens whose property was confiscated by the Cuban government. Fidel replied that he would agree to the repayments "when and if the United States agree[d] to compensate Cuba for the damage caused by the embargo."[33]

Carter did not renew the ban on United States citizens traveling to Cuba as was required every six months. He lifted the prohibition on using dollars in Cuba, suspended the spy flights (though satellite surveillance was continued), and allowed charter flights between Miami and Havana. In 1979 he authorized Cubans resident in the United States to travel to Cuba. This was the "family reunion" plan promoted by powerful Cuban exiles in the United States and agreed upon with the Cuban government.

In Cuba, Carter's policy in defense of human rights focused on the release of political prisoners. In 1978 and 1979 Cuba freed around 4,000, leaving 250 imprisoned. The United States Interests Office served as a channel for obtaining these prisoners' freedom as well as the freedom of United States citizens being held in Cuba.

In May 1978 Washington accused Cuba of having encouraged Katangans exiled in Angola to invade Shaba (Katanga), a Zaire province of the Congo immensely rich in minerals. Chancellor Isidoro Malmierca of Cuba emphatically denied the truth of this accusation. Although Brzezinski and CIA Director Admiral Stansfield Turner claimed that the evidence against Cuba was "overwhelming," a Senate committee investigation concluded that the CIA evidence was "not convincing." Publicly Castro claimed that he himself had warned the United States about a possible uprising in Katanga. Carter acknowledged that this statement was true, but he argued that Castro should have given the warning "long before" he did.[34] But the two governments kept up their dialogue during 1978 in spite of these tensions. Their representatives met in Washington, New York, Atlanta, and Mexico City. The conversations centered on the subject of political prisoners in Cuba. They would remain limited to this topic until Cuba pulled its troops out of Africa. In June the Senate approved a resolution that demanded the severance of "all" ties with Cuba— meaning the withdrawal of the United States "interest office" in Havana. The State Department opposed this resolution since it would adversely affect the United States interests.[35]

In mid-August 1979 Brzezinski made public a CIA report on the "discovery" of a "Soviet combat brigade" in Cuba. Carter made a public accusation in September, coinciding with the Sixth Summit of the Nonaligned Nations in Havana and ordered the U-2 flights over Cuba to resume. This Soviet Brigade had been in Cuba since 1962, when the Soviet Union installed the missiles on the island, and many United States officials were aware of its presence. They also knew that these were not combat soldiers and did not threaten United States security. This alarm set off by Brzezinski was repudiated in Congress. The Democratic majority leader, Senator Robert C. Byrd, called it a "pseudo-crisis." In Havana delegates to the summit laughed at Carter.

WITH THE NONALIGNED NATIONS

At the Third Summit of the Nonaligned Movement in 1970 in Lusaka, Zambia, Cuba—a founding member since the organization's inception in 1961—began airing the thesis that the socialist countries were the "natural allies" of the nonaligned nations and the most solid bulwark against imperialism. The majority opposed this concept.

At the Fifth Summit in Algiers in 1973—the "summit of summits"—for the first time equal attention was paid to both political and economic issues, and oil became a tool for exerting political pressure. The oil-producing Arab countries decreed an embargo of crude oil against the countries that supported Israel against the Palestinian people. The restriction on oil, on which the Western powers depended, the steep rise in its price, and the announcement by the Arab oil powers that they would withdraw their funds from Western banks created a panic. The "United Nations of the Poor"—as the nonaligned nations were disparagingly called—now emerged as a sixth power center in a multipolar world. Washington and the rest of the Western powers, which opposed the Nonaligned Movement, had a change of attitude after this summit.

At the summit, Castro continued to promote closer ties between the non-aligned nations and the Soviet bloc. In his speech he pointed out that the world was divided "between capitalist and socialist countries, imperialist countries and the neocolonized, colonialists and colonized countries, reactionary and progressive countries; between governments that support imperialism, colonialism, neocolonialism and racism" and those that stood against all these. On the theory of two imperialist nations, each led by one of the superpowers, he asked rhetorically, where were the Soviet monopolies, its multinationals, its industries, mines or oil wells in the underdeveloped world? Where were the workers exploited by Soviet capital in these countries? He reminded his audience that the weapons Cuba used to defend itself from the United States at the Bay of Pigs, as well as those sent to Arab, African, and Asian countries for use in their struggle against imperialism, came from the socialist countries, principally the Soviet Union. He warned that the confrontation with the socialist camp that was developing within the movement only favored United States "imperialist interests."[36] Yugoslavia, India, and Algeria—all founding members—and Tanzania strongly opposed these positions.

The Cuban government undertook intense diplomatic activity on the three continents to make Havana the seat of the Sixth Summit. For an entire year Cuban and Yugoslavian delegates traveled back and forth between Belgrade and Havana to clarify controversial points of and preserve the unity of the Movement. The point of greatest conflict was Cuba's alliance with the Soviet Union. Tito feared that Castro would steer the Movement in the direction of the Soviet bloc.

In September 1979 the Sixth Summit was held in Havana. There was broad Latin American and Caribbean participation: Argentina, Cuba, Panama, Peru, Guyana, and Jamaica were members; Bolivia, Nicaragua, Grenada, and Surinam joined the Movement, while Brazil, Colombia, Costa Rica, Venezuela, Dominica, and Saint Lucie attended as observers. A total of ninety-five countries attended.

Washington, aware that the proposed Final Declaration, prepared by Cuba as the host country, contained severe criticism of the United States, quickly attempted to modify the accusations by circulating a text of its own to its allies and friends. A nation friendly to Cuba provided Castro with the United States modified text. In his opening speech Castro denounced these maneuvers.

Many countries presented amendments to the Summit. India and Yugoslavia—founding members and guardians of the group's principles— wanted to reaffirm the Movement's position with regard to the two blocs as far as pacts and military alliances were concerned. They would not allow concessions to the Soviet bloc. Their amendment remained in the final text. Cuba's proposed declaration was gradually modified and deradicalized in the meetings of the commissions, where decisions were made by consensus. The Latin Americans succeeded in suppressing a paragraph that called for the dissolution of the Río Treaty, CONDECA (the Central American Defense Council), and the Inter-American Defense Board. They were forced to eliminate the paragraph, since they could not hope to undo commitments and dependencies to the United States superpower with a stroke of the pen without suffering grave consequences.

In October 1979 Castro, as president of the Movement, went to New York to present the results of the Sixth Summit before the United Nations General Assembly. When he entered the hall packed with delegates, its galleries filled with journalists and the general public, he received a tribute never before given a government representative in the world organization's history. He was greeted with a long standing ovation. His speech was interrupted several times by applause, and when he concluded, there was another long standing ovation.

"I have not come," he said, "to speak of Cuba. I come not to expound before the heart of this Assembly a denunciation of the aggression of which our small country has been the victim for twenty years. Neither do I come to wound with unnecessary adjectives our powerful neighbor in its own house." His speech was, in fact, not directed at the United States, but his denunciations of the injustices, the inequalities, the oppression, the exploitation, and the anxious situation of the developing countries constituted an implicit criticism. Armed with statistics, Castro noted the levels of the "insupportable" foreign debt and the multimillion-dollar military outlays, which ought to have been used for development. He reiterated his call for an easing of tensions, demanded an end to the exploitation of poor countries by rich ones, and related peace to development. In conclusion, he said, "Let us say farewell to arms, and let us devote ourselves like civilized nations to the most demanding problems of our times. This is our most sacred responsibility and duty. This is, moreover, the indispensable premise of human survival."[37]

When the Soviets invaded Afghanistan, Cuba did not condemn them. Its ambassador to the United Nations, Raúl Roa Kourí, interpreted the invasion as another confrontation between imperialism and the socialists. This position lost him credibility, and not only among the nonaligned nations. Most of the delegates criticized him harshly. Cuba was once again called Moscow's "pawn" by the United States government.

MARIEL

The end of the 1970s was extremely difficult for Cuba, both at home and abroad. The economic situation was critical, and Castro asked for sacrifices from the people. He declared that Cuba needed to focus its efforts on industrialization. In December, at a closed session of the National Assembly of the People's Power (ANPP)—its deliberations were leaked and published in the United States press—Castro enumerated the grave difficulties: the sharp drop in sugar prices on foreign markets, the decrease in imports from capitalist countries because of the shortage of foreign exchange, the fact that the socialist countries sent products that were not essential or even needed. He said it was impossible to predict what would happen in the next five years. He noted the serious agrarian problems caused by sugar-cane plagues (they affected one-third of production), tobacco blights (they destroyed 90 percent of production), and African swine fever (all pigs had to be slaughtered). All these catastrophes were under control, but Castro said that they came "strangely" simultaneously and accused the United States of introducing them.[38] This was biological warfare.

Discontent was mounting as a result of the economic crisis. In addition, there were tensions caused by the hundreds of former political prisoners who had been promised but had yet to receive immigration visas from the United States. This delay was intentional to elicit an internal malaise, alleged Castro. The "family reunion" plan was also creating pressure, because not everyone agreed with it, some for reasons of morality and revolutionary ideals. They did not accept that those whom they had always fought—whom they called "worms" for having abandoned the country and "betrayed" the Revolution and who allowed themselves to be used in terrorist actions against Cuba in collaboration with the "enemy"—should be welcomed on the island. Others objected because they thought it unfair that those with family in the United States should have the privilege of receiving goods the population as a whole lacked. In effect, thousands of exiles arrived laden with presents for their relatives, and this situation caused animosity and unease. The black market began with this shower of gifts. The government established limits and opened a store for imported products—at exorbitant prices—so that the "community" could buy them in Cuba. It was a way of obtaining foreign currency.

In 1979 graffiti and flyers against the government started to appear in the streets. In the National Assembly in December, Castro warned that, "we will smash" the growing extremism. The atmosphere heated up, with a growing numbers of Cubans leaving for Florida in stolen boats. Their flight was encouraged by a radio campaign from anti-Castro Cubans living in Miami. When the refugees arrived, they were welcomed like heroes, and the media provided wide coverage of their statements, all opposing the Revolution. This outlook was a condition imposed on them. They were shown off as disaffected "dissidents" who had fled the "Cuban hell."

With the appointment of Ramiro Valdés as minister of the interior—a hero of *Granma* and one of the regime's hard-liners—the persecution of the "antisocials," the black market, and petty crime began. The police searched and arrested campesinos who sold their products "on the open market." These measures led to greater malaise and discontent among the people.

The Cuban government was infuriated by Cubans who forced their way into foreign diplomatic quarters in Havana seeking sanctuary, since such behavior created friction with the respective governments. In September 1977 one group managed to get into the Venezuelan Embassy. Under pressure from the government of Carlos Andrés Pérez, who was in turn pressured by the influential Cuban community resident in his country, Cuba authorized the group's departure but did not give them safe conduct, since they were not politically persecuted, as they themselves had stated. Cuba conceded because it did not want problems with Venezuela, an important country, or with Carlos Andrés, whom it appreciated and respected. Neither did it want to create a conflict at the time when relations with the United States were strained because of the presence of Cuban troops in Africa and when some of the nonaligned nations were annoyed with Cuba because of the break in relations with Somalia.[39]

The departure for Venezuela of the Cuban refugee group in a Venezuelan airplane prompted renewed refuge in the embassy. On one occasion the military police fired to prevent the entrance of yet another group. There were no casualties, but the Venezuelan government protested that such "vigilance" restricted its rights and asked that the guard be removed.

At the end of 1979 a military police officer gained asylum in the Peruvian

Embassy. According to the inter-American asylum law—signed by both governments—Peru was to surrender him to the Cuban authorities. It did not. The Cuban government warned that it would not allow him to leave the country. In April 1980 a group of twenty-seven men, women, and children forced its way into the embassy, killing one of the police officers on guard. This act angered the Cuban government. The Peruvian ambassador, Edgardo de Habich, kicked the refugees out and published a note in *Granma* warning that no more refugees would be allowed to enter, since such an act constituted an infringement on his country's diplomatic headquarters. Because of the bitter attacks on the Peruvian ambassador by the influential Cuban community in Caracas, the Peruvian government asked him to return the Cubans to the embassy and to grant them "political asylum." He did so, thus bringing to forty the number of Cuban refugees in the Venezuelan and Peruvian embassies.

In an angry speech Fidel accused the Latin American governments of "fraud and cowardice," of having "sold out" to the United States by participating in the economic boycott and the diplomatic boycott of Cuba. He denounced Venezuela and Peru for harboring "common criminals, hooligans and antisocial elements" in their embassies and said that he would withdraw the guards that were protecting the Peruvian embassy. Less than seventy-two hours later the embassy was invaded by 10,800 men, women, and children, and they kept on coming. The embassy, the grounds, and even the roof were packed with Cubans. The stench was nauseating. Two days later the government announced that all who wanted to leave Cuba could do so, except for those who had entered embassies by force. On April 18, 1980, an editorial in the daily *Granma* reported that the government would not attempt to stop those who wanted to leave for Florida by boat. Castro declared that he had repeatedly warned the United States—both publicly and through diplomatic channels—about the possible consequences of its policy of encouraging people to leave the island illegally and then denying entry visas to those who sought them by legal means. "Caimarioca can open up again," he added. He was referring to the exodus of thousands of Cubans from that port, which the Cuban government had permitted in October 1965.

After the announcement in the *Granma*, boats from Florida began to arrive at the Port of Mariel to pick up emigres' relatives. In one week, more than 6,000 boats and thirty-two aircraft arrived. At a mass rally in Havana on May Day, Castro declared that they would not be met with gunfire because they did not come to make war. They would be treated cordially. The United States opened the door, and now it would see whether it could be closed, he remarked. "They are doing us a great clean-up service," he added.[40]

The Cuban authorities collaborated with the United States visitors. Officials from INTUR (the Cuban tourism institute) looked after them—they bought rum and cigars—and vessels of the Cuban Coast Guard escorted them in international waters until they could make out the coast of Florida.

Although President Carter said that he would welcome the Cubans— known as Marielitos—with "open arms and heart," he knew that he was looking at a possible invasion of refugees. He announced military maneuvers— Solid Shield 80—to begin on May 8 with a naval and aerial landing at the Guantanamo base. The Cuban government mobilized the army in the Oriente provinces and announced its own military maneuvers—Girón 19—to begin one day earlier.

On April 19, the anniversary of the victory at Playa Girón, the "March of the Fighting People" took place on Havana's Fifth Avenue. More than a million people participated, carrying signs and chanting slogans of support for the Revolution and Fidel, and against the United States, and shouting to the refugees in the Peruvian Embassy for them to leave the country. On May 1, another million Cubans, also in a militant mood, gathered in the Plaza de la Revolución. The people were ready to go to war. That day Castro announced the creation of the Milicias de Tropas Territoriales (MTT: Territorial Troop Militias). They would be "the people armed." By the end of the year, there were a million young people, male and female, with weapons sent by the Soviet Union, trained and ready for combat. That same day the news from Washington reported that the United States was suspending the Guantanamo landings. Myles Frechette (later a controversial ambassador to Colombia), head of the Office of Cuban Affairs at the State Department, confirmed that the maneuvers had been "completely" canceled.[41] Cuba canceled its own plans.

Some 129,000 Cubans arrived in Florida in the Mariel exodus. Of these, 20,000 were confined in refugee camps, and around 2,000 were sent to federal correctional facilities. Thousands of criminals and the mentally ill arrived in the so-called Freedom Flotilla. The United States accused Cuba of having taken these people out of the prisons and mental hospitals and forcing the captains of the vessels to take them to the United States. The Cuban government denied this allegation. In an editorial *Granma* insisted that the "anti-social element" was leaving of its own volition.[42]

Any sympathy that the American people might have had for the "Marielitos" changed as their arrival became a chaotic invasion, which created enormous problems for the Florida authorities, the refugees, and even for their relatives. Carter tried to negotiate repatriation of the anti-socials and the sick with Cuba, in exchange for the normalization of visa distribution. The Cuban government said it would study it case by case and accept only those who wanted to come back voluntarily. But no one did.

The conclusion of this episode, which originated in the erroneous and arrogant policies of the United States in encouraging refugees in an effort to cripple the Revolution, was a severe blow for the Carter administration and United States esteem. According to opinion polls, 62 percent of Americans were convinced that Fidel made a fool of their great nation.

THE PARTY'S OVER

The Mariel exodus could have alarmed the Cuban government because of its size; it served, however, as an escape hatch for internal tensions. The swell of illegals had reached Florida because the Miami anti-Castroites encouraged the exodus with their aggressive campaign, and the United States government, pressured by this vociferous community, had to accept the result. The more serious consequences were to Carter's government, because of the internal conflicts between the authorities and the people in Florida. And the most worrisome part was that there was no end in sight for the exodus.

Carter's many international failures had created a national mood of extreme frustration and humiliation. The American hostages remained in the hands of their captors in Iran. Soviet troops were still in Afghanistan, and Moscow had installed a "friendly" government, without the United States being able to exact reprisals. The Mariel invasion, with its numerous and overwhelming problems, was the final blow to Carter's hopes for reelection.

The victory by Ronald Reagan was the "triumph of the right," which would have immediate and grave implications for Latin America. "His election is a threat to the continent, a threat to peace," warned Castro.[43]

CHAPTER VII

THE WARS WITHIN

THE SOUTHERN CONE AND THE NATIONAL SECURITY DOCTRINE

In the Southern Cone the 1970s were years of extreme violence. Argentina, after the "return of Peronism" governments, and Brazil were both under neofascist National Security doctrine dictatorships. Chile and Uruguay, paradigms of democracy, fell under military rule. The decade was characterized by what the military called "internal wars" of several countries against powerful guerrilla movements and "dirty wars" against their own people. Thousands of men, women, and children were killed, tortured, and disappeared. These conflicts continued into the next decade. Never before had Latin America seen such brutal, widespread, and profound violations of human rights.

By the end of the 1980s the armed movements had been virtually eliminated, and the military regimes, decadent, without prestige, and under pressure from a growing internal and international opposition—called elections in which democratic presidents were elected. When these took office they granted broad amnesties to the military and security forces, for the sake of internal peace, which was threatened by the military's "unrest." These laws, dubbed end-points by the people, exonerated the military and security forces from being brought up before civilian tribunals to account for their crimes. Once this dangerous precedent was established, legitimizing impunity and violating the universal principle of equality before the law, the new governments set out on the difficult road toward reconstructing democracy. The military officers could rest easy: nothing had happened.

ARGENTINA: DICTATORSHIP AND INSURGENCY

Argentina entered the 1970s under General Juan Carlos Onganía's (1966–1970) *dictablanda* (light dictatorship). Unbeknownst to him, 1970 would be his last year in power. After the "Cordobazo" the year before in Cordoba Province— an explosive protest demonstration organized by students and workers at an automobile plant and supported by sectors of the middle and lower classes— the insurrection spread like wildfire to the Tucumán and Rosario provinces, where armed groups arose and guerrilla flags flew for the first time. These protests were not organized by Communists and extremists, as Onganía claimed, but were expressions of the popular rejection of his government and the armed forces. Several generals understood as much and were concerned.

In March 1970, the armed group Frente Argentino de Liberación (FAL: Argentine Liberation Front) kidnapped the Paraguayan consul (they released him later), and in June, the Montoneros abducted and executed the former president, General Pedro Aramburu. This event was too much for the high command, and General Alejandro Lanusse overthrew Onganía. No one protested; to the people, this was just another of many military switches.

Lanusse did not take over the government. He chose General Roberto M. Levingston (1970–1971), a former intelligence officer and Argentina's representative to the Inter-American Defense Board in Washington. Lanusse expected Levingston to be his puppet, but Levingston had his own plans for the government and gave free rein to the military to combat the insurgency.

The Montoneros, the FAL—both Peronist—and the Ejército Revolucionario del Pueblo (ERP: People's Revolutionary Army)—Trotskyist—escalated their activities. There was a string of detentions, kidnappings, murders, and disappearances of popular leaders, leftist military officers, and people suspected of belonging to or supporting the guerrillas. Covert paramilitary groups took responsibility for most of these crimes. Civil unrest reached the point of paranoia. Anyone could be arrested on mere suspicion, and everyone suspected everyone else. Those arrested were judged in the Federal Penal Chamber—a mechanism created by the military—which was a kind of inquisition court.

In February 1971 a strike by 2,500 workers at the FIAT-Concord plant in Córdoba to protest the firing of two coworkers led to a chain reaction: The workers took over the factory and took hostages. More people were fired, and Levingston demanded that they vacate the factory and release the hostages, or he would use force. The strike continued with the support of unions in other plants, students, popular sectors, and politicians. Bernardo Bas, the governor of Córdoba, refused to obey the order to suppress the strike and resigned. The Confederación General de Trabajadores (CGT: General Federation of Workers) in Córdoba decreed a work stoppage and called for a demonstration, in which ERP flags were raised. The mass of demonstrators marched down the Avenida de Colón, attacked the exclusive Jockey Club and government buildings with firecrackers, and in front of the Encausados Prison, where Peronists and Montoneros were held, yelled angry protests against the dictatorship. From inside, the prisoners joined in.

The new governor, Camilo Uriburu, labeled the protest as coming from a "sinister anti-Argentina organization in which nestles a poisonous serpent whose head may it please God to give me the honor of cutting off with a single blow." The people threw up some 200 barricades and declared certain areas to be liberated territories, where they would not allow the police to enter. A hundred men from the antiguerrilla brigade (the federal police), sent from Buenos Aires, reoccupied these "territories" little by little. Uriburu resigned.[1] To the government's humiliation, the workers were reinstated.

The "viborazo" or "uprising of vipers" sounded the alarm against Levingston and the armed forces. The entire country wanted these people out of the government. In December broad political sectors—Peronists, radicals, conservatives, socialists, and opposition movements—had already published the communiqué "The Hour of the People," asking for free elections and a civilian government. In March 1971 Lanusse overthrew Levingston, and this time he took over as president of a junta of commanders.

Lanusse's Great National Agreement, the government program to save the country, asked that all democratic forces combat subversion, and he offered to hold elections and step down in favor of a civilian government. He chose his cabinet from Agreement figures who favored dialogue, lifted the restrictions on political parties and unions, and began a secret dialogue with the Peronists. Lanusse knew that it was impossible to proceed without Perón. He believed that the Caudillo was behind the social unrest, manipulating the powerful Peronist political, armed, and union forces from his exile in Madrid.

The masses of union members, youth movements, and guerrilla movements—most of them Peronists—opposed the Great Agreement. They said the elections were a trap to put the brakes on popular struggles, and that the military would annul them if the results went against them. The Montoneros and the FAP (Fuerzas Armadas Peronistas, Peronist Armed Forces) announced that they would continue to fight. They wanted Perón back. Though Lanusse spoke of national reconciliation, he started a "dirty war."

It began with a wave of kidnappings, assassinations, and disappearances of Peronist leaders, union leaders, and leftist activists, but social protest, union belligerence, and guerrilla activity did not let up. Between March and July 1971 the newspapers reported 316 terrorist acts by the ERP (which was responsible for most of them) and the Montoneros, with takeovers of military and police barracks, the capture of weapons and equipment, assaults on banks, sabotage of military installations, government institutions, and "symbols" of the aristocracy with bombs and explosives, and kidnappings and assassinations of prominent citizens and military officers. The ERP, the FAP, and the Montoneros freed their comrades from several of the country's prisons in daring joint operations. In Córdoba they rescued Mario Santucho, Enrique Gorriarán, Jorge Ulla, and Humberto Toschi—the top leadership of the ERP—who had been captured only a few days earlier. Six guards died in this operation. (The same day in Uruguay the Tupamaros took the Punta Carretas Prison and rescued 106 guerrillas without firing a single shot.)[2]

In March 1972, the ERP machine gunned down a military commander and a storekeeper; the "Descamisados" ("Shirtless Ones"), a new guerrilla group, blew up the San Jorge Military Riding Club—a symbol of the military aristocracy—the Montoneros attacked the headquarters of the New Force Party; another commando killed Roberto Mario Uzal, the New Force leader, and came away with 402 million pesos—a record sum—in an attack on the National Bank.

The ERP kidnapped the general director of the FIAT-Concord plant, Oberdan Sallustro. In exchange for his release the guerrillas demanded the release of workers and leaders of the powerful SITRAC-SITRAM unions, safe passage to Algeria for fifty guerrilla prisoners, and a million pesos to "indemnify" the people. But the government, in an impressive operation, found the place where the hostage was being held. Heavy gunfire ensued. The guerrilla commando succeeded in escaping, but not until Sallustro, whom they deemed an "exploiter of the people," had been executed. On the same day a joint ERP and FAR commando killed General Juan Carlos Sánchez, Commander of the Army Second Corps, in the city of Rosario. Lanusse wanted Perón to condemn these crimes, but the Caudillo kept silent. Later he explained, "I made no statement because I believe the people's violence is in response to the government's."[3] In April 1972, in Mendoza Province, a massive demonstration broke out in protest against the drastic rise in electricity rates imposed by the governor. The CGT declared a work stoppage, and other unions joined in. A confrontation with the police outside the Government House resulted in scores of wounded, hundreds being arrested, and one death. The mutineers burned vehicles, put up barricades, and forced the police to retreat. The government declared Mendoza an emergency zone, ousted the civilian governor and installed a military officer in his place. The "Mendozazo" proved more violent than the "Cordobazo" and the "Viborazo." Lanusse ordered the suspension of the controversial rate increases. The people won this battle.

One of the most sinister episodes of Lanusse's regime was the Trelew Massacre of August 1972. The ERP, the FAP, and the Montoneros rescued their top leaders from the Rawson Prison in an extensive joint operation. More than 100 of them reached the airport, hijacked an Austral Airlines plane, flew to Chile, and requested asylum from Allende's government. Shortly after the first group, another group of nineteen arrived at the airport but did not succeed in boarding an aircraft. Pursued by troops, they blockaded themselves and offered to make a deal. They demanded that their physical safety be respected and asked for medical examinations so that they could leave evidence of their good state of health, and be returned to Rawson Prison. The army confined them at the Admiral Zar de Trelew air and naval base in Patagonia and massacred them in an alleged attempted escape. "We heard our comrades' moans and death rattles, even streams of curses and insults, and isolated shots began to ring out. I realized that they were finishing them off," remembered one of them. Ana María Villareal, the wife of the ERP's top leader Mario Santucho, was one of the victims; Santucho managed to escape to Chile. This massacre provoked a nationwide revolt against Lanusse and raised the guerrillas' spirits. They chanted the slogan, "They will see, they will see, when we avenge the dead of Trelew." Shortly thereafter, the ERP assassinated Rear Admiral (ret.) E. R. Berisso.[4]

PERÓN MATERIALIZES

The post-Perón governments, including Arturo Frondizi's, tried to finish off Peronism. They outlawed it, destroyed its unions, and persecuted its militants and drove them out of public administration. Nonetheless, Peronism continued to be the most important political force in the country, and it grew with the addition of new and younger followers. Most of the guerrilla movements—FAP, FAR, FAL, Descamisados and Montoneros—were Peronist. The Priests of the third world movement also followed, attracted by the social orientation of Justicialism. Everything converged toward Peronism, a binding force against the dictatorship. Perón was the magnet for this immense and heterogeneous force, which was increasingly confused, contradictory, and militant.

Powerful economic and financial sectors, the oligarchy—which supported the Great National Agreement—and large foreign corporations were in favor of reaching an accord with Perón, since he was the only one capable of controlling this loose "riffraff" and building a dike against the danger that was falling upon them. Perón's earlier bitter enemies no longer feared him, since Perón did not threaten their society, system, or interests.

In 1971, using intermediaries, Lanusse opened secret negotiations with Perón behind the backs of his colleagues in the junta. The following year, in an interview with the Italian magazine *L'Espresso,* Perón exposed him. He told of Lanusse's proposals, negotiations, challenges, insults, and the offer—which looked like a bribe—of $4 million and retroactive payments if he would renounce his candidacy. Lanusse not only looked ridiculous but he faced serious problems with the rest of the junta.

Perón did not want an agreement. He named Héctor Cámpora—a Peronist dentist with no political background—to the post of secretary general of the Justicialist movement, and Rodolfo Galimberti as secretary general of the Peronist Youth movement, the representative of youth to the High Justicialist Council. Galimberti's appointment was a gesture of support for the "special formations" of Peronism, as he called the guerrilla movements.

Lanusse got even. He created legal impediments to Perón's candidacy in a decree that dictated that only those who had been residents of Argentina for at least six months could be candidates. Perón refused to return from Spain and announced that he would continue to run. Lanusse challenged Perón. Cámpora went to Madrid and returned with the good news that Perón was coming back. The Peronists prepared "Operation Return" for his triumphant reentry into the country.

Perón wanted to return as a "messenger of peace," the "unifier of the Argentine people," the "servant of the motherland." He was intent on showing that his return to politics was a sacrifice. At the beginning of 1972, in a widely published interview, he accused the government of serving the oligarchy and of having turned Argentina into a "satellite of Yankee imperialism." The magazine *Primera Plana* commented that Perón's declarations were "tinged with guerrilla ideas."[5]

Galimberti united the seven regional organizations of the Peronist Youth movement to broaden their political activities and support the guerrilla struggle. This alliance opened the gates to political prominence for the Montoneros. The goal of the Peronist Youth was Perón's return to Argentina and to power. Their fervent support became more militant by the day. In

October, Perón announced his return and sent a document with the "minimum bases for an agreement on national reconstruction." Some sectors of the Peronist Youth did not approve of the memorandum, since this disposition to dialogue aided the shaky dictatorship. The ERP accused Perón of "negotiating with the blood of the fallen, the sufferings of the prisoners, the misery of the people, and the ruin of the country." The Montoneros did not question Peron's act; they claimed that it was part of the strategy of revolutionary war.

With the youths' support and the military regime seeking to reach an understanding with him and Peronism, Perón once again felt strong and needed. From exile he could take a hard position against the dictatorship, radicalize his discourse, and, "like God the Father," bless the armed groups, the union struggles, and the "revolutionary war." He justified the "execution" of oppressors, as in the case of Aramburu. He showed his satisfaction with the Peronist Youth and spoke of the need for a generational change, since without it Peronism would "become stale and die." He praised this "marvelous youth" that shouldered the direct struggle against the dictatorship. But as the day of his return grew near, his position and his discourse changed. He declared, "I have neither hate nor rancor. This is not the time for revenge. I come to bring peace to the spirit." Such words contrasted with the aggressive mood of the Peronist Youth. Perón distanced himself from the revolutionary struggle—a prelude to times of torment.

The Peronist movement prepared for the triumphal return of the Caudillo and actively promoted Cámpora's candidacy, but the power was for Perón. Galimberti called on the people to go to the Ezeiza airport on November 17 to give him an overwhelming welcome. The impressive security operation the government mounted to prevent access to Ezeiza—35,000 soldiers and heavy artillery—and the torrential rains on that day did not deter the crowds.

Perón's presence in Buenos Aires monopolized national attention. He continued to be the most important political figure of the last thirty years of Argentine history. His residence became the center of political activity, and bigwigs, friends, and old rivals made their way to it. Everyone in the political arena attended a meeting he called in a Buenos Aires restaurant to discuss the country's future. For the Peronists, these were fiesta days. The masses were with Perón, and the most powerful respected and feared him.

Whether he liked it or not, Perón had to deal with the explosive Peronist Youth. The Revolutionary Tendency—the vanguard of the movement, led by the FAR and the Montoneros—was determined to broaden the war, form a

Peronist army, achieve the triumph of Argentine national socialism, and take power. The Peronist Youth knew that they had politically defeated the dictatorship and made possible the return of Perón to Argentina and Peronism to the political arena. They wanted a new country, and not merely the personal vindication of the old Caudillo.

In January 1973 the presidential campaign began. Since Perón's candidacy was made impossible by Lanusse's "legal coup," Cámpora served as the Peronist candidate. To insure his triumph he formed the Frente Justicialista de Liberación (FREJULI: Justicialist Liberation Front), which other groups joined. It was a bitter campaign.

Cámpora's progressively radicalized programs and the proguerrilla slant of the Peronist Youth movement alarmed the military. In February it published a five-point document as the basis for the military's relations with the new government. The program ruled out "indiscriminate amnesties." FREJULI rejected it, but Lanusse could no longer drag out the electoral process, even though it would be an unconditional surrender.

The Peronist Youth enthusiastically supported "Uncle," as they called Cámpora, who was elected on March 11 with 49.59 percent of the vote. He did not win the 50 percent required by Lanusse, which would have meant a second round of voting. But the government preferred to recognize his victory; not to do so would have been a costly error.

The country hoped that guerrilla activity would cease with the triumph of Peronism and the retreat of the military to its barracks. It was not to be. For the Revolutionary Tendency and the ERP the war was not over. Two weeks after Cámpora's election the ERP seized the Atucha nuclear plant; five days later it planted a bomb at the Naval Command; a week later it kidnapped Rear Admiral Francisco A. Alemán, and the following day it assassinated Colonel Héctor Iribarren. Cámpora was in Rome with Perón when Iribarren was assassinated. He returned immediately for fear of the military reaction. Upon his arrival he repudiated these guerrilla actions and asked the guerrillas for a truce so that his government could fulfill its goals. He needed peace, and the people expected it from a Justicialist government. The ERP responded in the negative, declaring that the real interests of the working class and the people demanded that the fight be redoubled and its fronts widened in order to give the "enemy" no time to prepare a counteroffensive. On the eve of Cámpora's inauguration the FAR and the Montoneros, in a joint communiqué, announced that they would continue the war until they could assume power, since Peronism had won a battle but not the war. They would continue to fight against imperialism, the monopolies, the oligarchy, the "gorillas" (military thugs), the rest of the proimperialist military lobby, the "traitors" of FREJULI, and those it called "enemies of the people."[6]

Perón became enraged when Galimberti proposed the creation of popular militias. He called him to Madrid, and in the presence of a group of distinguished rightist Peronists, he dismissed him from office. This was a rude and unexpected blow to the guerrillas and the vanguard of youth, a veiled threat to the left wing of Peronism. Perón began to surround himself with the most select, notable, and reactionary elements of Peronism.

Cámpora's inauguration day, May 25, became a revolutionary celebration. Masses of young people, union members, and students concentrated in the Plaza de Mayo wearing red and black armbands, carrying signs, and chanting slogans against the military, the dictatorship, imperialism, and the oligarchy and for solid loyalty to the Caudillo and the guerrilla movement. The traditional military parade did not take place, since the military wanted to avoid a confrontation.

In his inaugural address before the legislative assembly, Cámpora praised the Peronist Youth movement. "This is a marvelous youth movement," he declared, "which knew how to answer violence with violence and to oppose the blind and sickly passion of a delirious oligarchy with decision and courage. How can this victory not belong also to these youths?"

On that day the Peronist Youth confronted the police and pressured it to withdraw. They prevented William Rogers, the United States Secretary of State and Nixon's representative, from arriving at the Casa Rosada after the ceremony at the congress. Surrounding his vehicle, they forced him to retreat amid shouts of anti-Yankee and anti-imperialist slogans. Meanwhile Presidents Oswaldo Dorticós of Cuba and Salvador Allende of Chile were given ovations. And Cámpora, in an act of surpassing deference, asked Dorticós and Allende to sign the act of transfer of power.

The Peronist Youth forced their way into the Casa Rosada, and the leaders of the regional organizations appeared on the balcony at Cámpora's side as he greeted the people. When a helicopter took off from the terrace of the Casa Rosada carrying the members of the military junta, the crowds bade them farewell, shouting, "They're leaving, they're leaving, and they're never coming back."

The events overwhelmed Cámpora. At midnight of his first day as president he was forced to pardon all the political prisoners because a mob of 40,000 people outside the Villa Devoto Prison demanded it. The pardon was legalized the following day by the senate and the house by means of amnesty laws adopted unanimously in the midst of ovations and grandiose speeches.

Cámpora repealed all the repressive laws and regulations imposed by the military and dissolved the Federal Penal Chamber, a monument to military arbitrariness. But the peace he so ardently sought escaped him. The popular struggles continued; the guerrillas granted no truce, and the University of Buenos Aires continued to be the hotbed of insurrection.

"Cámpora in the government and Perón in power" became the slogan of the Peronist Youth and a reality recognized by all. Perón governed from exile. The mixed cabinet—Peronists of the right, the center, and the left—was his doing. The Peronist Youth movement was represented by the ministers of foreign affairs and the interior, the unions by the labor ministry—the minister was an important director of the CGT—and the key ministries of finance and social welfare were put in the hands of his closest followers: José Ber Gelbard and José López Rega, both of the extreme right.

The "triumphant" Peronist Youth movement occupied the governors' seats in Buenos Aires, Santa Cruz, Mendoza, Salta, and Córdoba, the most important provinces. Nonetheless, the division of power saw the advance of Peronism of the right, promoted by Perón himself.

In effect, the figure with the highest profile in Cámpora's heterogeneous cabinet was the sinister López Rega, who passed from being a corporal in the federal police to Perón's private secretary, his confidant, and the confidant of his third wife, María Estella Martínez. "The Witch Doctor," as he was called because of his affinity for esoterica, was named minister of social welfare. He called it the ministry of the people. He was the superminister of the three Peronist governments, responsible for social policies. Ever since the glorious years of Eva Perón, this was the most powerful political weapon of Justicialism. The three governments assigned him plentiful resources, with which López Rega sustained the Triple A—a death squad—and clandestine groups of the extreme right. Abductions, disappearances, and assassinations of politicians, workers, students, and popular and leftist leaders began to proliferate. These underground groups claimed responsibility.

The great and dangerous contradiction within Peronism came to the surface in Cámpora's government, as did tensions between Perón and the Peronist Youth and guerrilla movements, and within the union movement, where a war to the death was beginning to unfold. On one side were those faithful to Perón, politically and militarily supported by the Montoneros, and on the other, the Vandorists, led by Augusto Vandor, head of the metallurgical union, the most powerful in the CGT. He was promoting "Peronism without Perón."

Overtaken by this violence from the left and the right, Cámpora lost authority, prestige, and something more valuable: Perón's political support. From exile Perón saw that his Social Pact project was in danger, and he decided to return. His triumphant return to Buenos Aires on June 20, 1973, turned into a great tragedy. A multitude of more than two million Peronists marched to the Ezeiza airport to welcome him. At the head of the march were the Montoneros, chanting slogans of support for Perón and Evita and the socialist homeland.

This large welcome for the Caudillo showed the extraordinary power of the Peronist Youth movements and the Montoneros to call out their supporters—the Revolutionary Tendency—and their strength among the people. But the Peronist right decided to confront their power. A pitched battle ensued between armed union members and the Montoneros. Hundreds of people were killed. Many were certain that López Rega had tutored the rightist forces who caused this tragedy. Perón's airplane had to land at a military air base.[7]

The errors of the Peronist left "led it defenseless to the June 20 march," wrote the Argentine journalist Horacio Verbitsky. That march marked the beginning of the battle with their internal enemies concerning loyalty to Perón, "whose ideas they did not know in depth," and without taking into account that their enemies' positions were just as Peronist as their own. They had become accustomed to "interpreting reality in terms of military strategy, without foreseeing that arms would be taken up to slow its impetuous march. It was at once arrogant and ingenuous," he added.[8]

Far from being pleased with his overwhelming welcome, Perón perceived it as a danger. He was afraid that the Montoneros would compete with him for the leadership. The following day in an energetic speech, he indicated the direction his policies would take: "We are Justicialists; we are who the twenty truths of Peronism say we are. Those who ingenuously think that they can take over our movement or take the power the people have won are mistaken." The "marvelous youth" did not sense that the Caudillo was beginning to see them as a potential enemy, and that he would use his own overt and covert powers to destroy them. The Ezeiza tragedy was the beginning of a new wave of violence, bloodier than ever, between the militant and revolutionary left and the fascistic right and ultraright of Peronism, sponsored by López Rega. Some believed that it marked the beginning of the end of the "Montonero phenomenon" and the start of a war to exterminate the entire left.

Cámpora served as president for forty-nine days. With no support from

Perón and suspended in political limbo, he "resigned" on July 13; he was actually dismissed. His withdrawal caused profound unease. It signified the rise to power of the most reactionary sectors of Peronism. The drama—directed by Perón to prepare his return to the presidency—was in two acts: Cámpora's resignation and the appointment as provisional president of Raúl Lastiri, López Rega's son-in-law and president of the chamber of deputies. According to the constitution this position should have gone to Alejandro Díaz Bialet, president of the senate, but a few days earlier he was pressured into leaving the country in order to create the "vacuum" and justify Lastiri's appointment. With this shady maneuver the Witch Doctor cemented his own position and the ascension of the Peronist ultraright to the higher realms of power. In his brief passage through the Casa Rosada—prelude to the elections that carried Perón to his third term as president—Cámpora completed the task of "cleansing" the leftist Peronists from the government to open the field for the right that came in with Perón.

Perón would be president again, but it was not known who would serve as his vice president. Many names were considered. No one suspected, however, that the iconic figure for the masses would make the entire country—and the silent Peronists—live under the vice presidency of his third wife, María Estella Martínez, a former nightclub dancer. The people's greatest fear was the strange power López Rega exercised over her. Her appointment left the country stunned.

The Montoneros seemed convinced that the country's movement to the right was the result of the fence López Rega had erected around Perón in order to isolate him. In July they called a demonstration of support for the Caudillo and against López Rega to break through the fence; 80,000 young people participated. They chanted, "If Evita were alive, she'd kill López Rega." Perón's irritation and hostility were no longer hidden. He supported López Rega and named him his representative to the Peronist Youth movement. Now all was clear. The decisions were Perón's and the Peronist ultraright was on the rise because he wanted it to be. The fence did not exist.

Confrontation came almost immediately. In the span of three days, both at the CGT and at a governors conference, Perón sharply criticized the youth movement, declaring that it had chosen a "wrong path" and that it was his duty to distance himself from that movement. He blamed the youth movement for the Ezeiza tragedy.

For the Peronist left, everything from the Ezeiza massacre, Cámpora's dismissal, the rise of the Peronist right wing, María Estella's vice presidency, the growing power of López Rega and José Ignacio Rucci, secretary general of the

CGT—the people closest to Perón—had been a chain of reversals. But Perón's virulent attacks on the Peronist youth were a catastrophe. They expressed their unease and disenchantment in their magazine *Militancia*. Perón had betrayed them and was surrounding himself with right-wingers. They considered his attack unjust, since they had borne the burden of the fight against the military dictatorship. They criticized Perón's Social Pact for favoring the bourgeoisie before the people.

In a daring operation in the center of Buenos Aires in September, the ERP attacked the headquarters of the Military Health Command. Lieutenant Colonel Raúl Duarte Hardoy died in the intense shootout. The rebel commando failed to take the headquarters and was captured. The public was outraged when it learned that the guerrillas who had been given amnesty by Cámpora were now returning to do battle.

Three days after the attack the influential Buenos Aires daily *El Clarín* became a battlefield between Peronist left and right. With *El Clarín's* attorney, Bernardo Sofovich, in the guerrillas' hands, the paper was forced to publish ERP statements attacking the government. The paper's offices were hit with incendiary bombs and explosives, with the damages running to 100 million pesos. The attackers, all union members, were captured. One of them confessed that they had been going to "break up this place that's full of lefties." Perón justified the act. He claimed that it had been provoked by the paper's "bad procedure" for publishing what the guerrillas wanted.

On the eve of the elections that would carry him to the presidency, Perón backed down as a tactical move. He invited Mario Firmenich, Robert Quieto, and Mendizabal—the top leaders of the Montoneros, the FAR, and the Descamisados—and the leaders of the regional Peronist Youth movements, to his residence. He offered to leave the reorganization of the youth movements in their hands. This was not the first time he had met with them, but it was the last time before their relations would hit rock bottom.

ASCENSION, PASSION, AND DEATH OF PERÓN

Juan Domingo Perón and Isabel Martínez, whose real name was Maria Estella, were elected to the presidency and vice presidency of Argentina in September 1973, with 62 percent of the vote. It was Perón's greatest electoral triumph. On October 17, a day long dreamed of by millions of Argentines, the seventy-eight-year-old Perón was inaugurated president for the third time, after eighteen years of exile. Decked out in a military uniform, once again he appeared on the balcony of the Casa Rosada to address the people, this time behind bulletproof glass. In a short and undistinguished speech he laid out his Social Pact plan and announced that the main task of his administration was to integrate the youth into the projects for national reconstruction. While he spoke, the FAR and the Montoneros passed out flyers in the Plaza de Mayo announcing the merger of their movements.

Perón restructured the cabinet but kept López Rega in his post. He initiated his Social Pact and adopted a series of measures to apply his iron fist to the working class: He reformed the law of professional associations and the penal code with measures more repressive than those imposed by the military and repealed by Cámpora, and he imposed sanctions on crimes of terrorism and subversion more severe than Onganía's and also repealed by Cámpora. The penal code did not take into account terrorism by groups of the ultraright.

The right and the death squads unleashed a campaign of threats and assassination attempts against the movements and leaders of the left. Gangs of thugs destroyed the headquarters of the Peronist Youth movements, planted bombs at their journals—*El Descamisado, El Mundo,* and *Militancia*—and members of the youth movements and workers were abducted, assassinated, and disappeared. Responsibility for many of these acts was claimed by the Triple A. The attempt on the life of Hipólito Solari Hirigoyen, a radical senator—claimed by the Triple A—after he had made a forceful allegation against these new laws, struck fear into the hearts of the Peronist Youth leaders, who promptly ratified the new legislation. At the end of 1973 they also voted in favor of the Law of Exclusion, which was even more hurtful to the workers' interests, since it allowed the government to fire, without cause or explanation, anyone it wanted, with only one month's wages as indemnity. This law threw the workers into poverty.

In January 1974 the ERP carried out a daring attack on the most important army regiment at Azul, in Buenos Aires Province, in which Colonel Camilo A. Gay, commander of the regiment, his wife, and a recruit were killed and Lieutenant Colonel Jorge Alberto Ibarzábal was kidnapped. Perón was furious. In military uniform and surrounded by his ministers and the commanders of the three military branches, he appeared on television to deliver one of his most incendiary speeches seeking the support of the people. He announced that he would resign if he did not get it.

Perón's hostility to the Peronist Youth movements heated up the atmosphere. The Montoneros refused to attend a press conference the President called. Early in 1974 Firmenich and Quieto—the top Montonero leaders—and Carlos

Carides of the Juventud Trabajadora Peronista (JTP: Peronist Worker Youth) were arrested and their newspapers closed. General Miguel Ángel Iñiguez, chief of the federal police, resigned and sent out an announcement denouncing the official violence.

Perón was no longer the revolutionary leader of his exile, nor was the Argentina of his third administration the land dreamed of by those who fought the dictatorships and prepared his triumphal return. It was not the homeland in which they so ardently desired to live, under the leadership of the man they respected, defended and—when necessary—excused in a show of blind faith or ingenuous opportunism. The image of the Caudillo crumbled.

For the May Day celebrations Perón wanted an orderly fiesta for the working class, with such innocent amusements as María Estella's crowning of the Queen of Work, a task that would have been performed by Evita in the past. But the Peronist and Montonero Youth movements wanted this day to be one on which the people confronted Perón and he faced the people, to clarify the situation. Some of them were aware that the chasm that separated them was enormous. It was the hour of truth in which all of them—youth, guerrillas, unionists, and Perón—must face a situation that threatened their collapse.

With concerns about this confrontation, Perón ordered security measures to keep this May Day from becoming another Montonero Festival. But the youth managed to break through the police barricades, display their signs, and chant slogans offensive to his ears. Again they showed their strength and militancy, and for the first time they made clear their rejection of his policies. "Friends," Perón raised his voice, "twenty years ago today, on this same balcony and on a day as bright as today I last spoke to the Argentine workers." He recalled the hard times, while the Montoneros interrupted him chanting, "How come, how come, how come, General, that the people's government is full of thugs?" Perón continued and the chants went on until, exasperated and offended, he called them "snotty beardless kids and imbeciles," with pretensions to being better than those who have struggled for twenty years. Again the chants: "How come, how come, General?" Perón continued to explain the bounties of the Social Pact, explaining that it would be the salvation of the republic. He thanked the people for their support and promised better times, while the chants continued. The Montonero columns began to leave the Plaza de Mayo shouting the same slogans. By the time Perón ended his short, spiteful speech, the Plaza de Mayo was almost deserted, according to Óscar Anzorena.[9]

Peronism was menaced by the internal war between irreconcilable factions: on one side those who were blindly loyal to Perón and those who, though loyal, were beginning to question him, and on the other side the Peronist union movements of the left and the right—both armed and determined to annihilate each other. Such divisions and contradictions, and the polarization of their forces, were the result of Perón's ambivalent and contradictory policies. He both strengthened and pitted them against each other. His shifting position on the youth movements, his turn to the right, his abandonment of principles that opposed imperialism and oligarchy and supported "national socialism," which embellished his statements made from exile, were at the heart of this storm. The image of the great revolutionary Caudillo, defender of Evita's descamisados, began to disappear, and another started to emerge, more like that of the "thugs" whom the Peronist youth battled.

On June 29, 1974, Perón signed his final decrees, one accepting Cámpora's resignation from the ambassadorship to Mexico and another provisionally delegating the presidency to María Estella, or Isabelita, as she liked to be called. Two days later, on July 1, Perón died of a heart attack. His death left a power vacuum, profound and widespread grief, and a sense of being abandoned. The people arrived in Buenos Aires from every corner of the country to render the ultimate homage to the man who had been their guide, the most important political figure in the last three decades of their history, who had defended the rights of the people and the working class and created Justicialism and Latin America's first revolution with a social content. The changes in the power structure achieved by Peronism were the most radical until the triumph of the Cuban Revolution. It took power from the oligarchs, but in contrast to the Cuban Revolution, it did not affect their economic interests. It placed the working class in the forefront of its politics. But Perón was a military officer and a right-winger, anti-Communist, anti-Marxist, and populist. He had not threatened the system nor seriously concerned the McCarthyite inquisitors within and outside the country.

Perón wanted to extend Peronism throughout the continent under his leadership. He failed, but several heads of state tried to imitate him, to do what he had done: create union powers controlled by the government and challenge the ruling classes.

Perón's third administration did what it should not have done: to safeguard his Social Pact, he castrated the working class, persecuted the left union movement and the militant and activist youth movements that had carried him to power again, and abandoned the principles that were the rationale for his struggle.

ISABEL ON THE VERGE OF A NERVOUS BREAKDOWN

María Estella Martínez, who preferred to be called Isabel, became the head of Argentina (1974–1976). She occupied this highest position solely by virtue of having been the Caudillo's wife of the moment. In a sense, she recapitulated the history of Evita, the modern Cinderella. Both came from humble families; both had been cabaret artists; both captivated Perón, shared his bed, and arrived at the altar and power on his arm.

Tutored by López Rega, her confidant, Isabel tried to project the image of a second Evita. She tried to copy her oratorical style, to repeat her campaigns of aid to the descamisados, and like her, she dyed her hair blond. But for the Argentine people "there is only one Evita," and they did not allow Isabel to usurp her place. In protest, reported *Time* magazine, they tore up Isabel's posters and cut out her eyes.

The country continued to flounder in violence from both political extremes, and the Social Pact—on which Perón staked his prestige—was shipwrecked. To the popular classes and the Peronist Youth movements Isabel was far from a hope.

Under the tutelage of López Rega, who continued as the head of the ministry of social welfare, Isabel proceeded to rid the government of leftist Peronists. Elected governors were purged from office by decree; leftist unions in Buenos Aires and Córdoba were interfered with; SMATA and Luz y Fuerza (Light and Strength), two important unions, were outlawed, and their leaders were arrested. The newspapers *Noticias, Crónica, La Calle* and the review *Satiricón* were closed, and the police took over the television stations at gunpoint.

Of the Peronist governments, Isabel's was the most repressive—some called her "Bloody Mary." It was a time of terror in which death squads, supported by López Rega, ran wild. The Triple A published lists of those who had received death threats, on which appeared the names of prominent figures (Cámpora among them), other politicians, former ministers, former members of congress, lawyers, artists, actors, singers, university professors, journalists, a bishop, and a general. On one list five names were marked with a small cross. They belonged to those already assassinated, among them Silvio Frondizi, the brother of the former president.

Abductions were carried out in the streets in the middle of the city in broad daylight, in homes, and in workplaces. The kidnappers were officers of the army, police, and security forces dressed in civilian clothes and driving unmarked, unlicensed vehicles. Bodies appeared in barrels in the Plata

River or burned beyond recognition. Alive or dead, some had been thrown out of airplanes over the ocean or the Tucumán jungle. There were many witnesses, but no one admitted to having seen anything, no one knew a thing, no one said a thing, for fear of being the next victim. Some even justified the arrests and disappearances with a "There must be a good reason," or with the well-known "*No te metás*" ("Don't get involved").

Notices from people asking for information on disappeared relatives began appearing in the newspapers. This wave of terror caused an exodus to other countries. But the "hunt" continued abroad, for there was a plan of coordination with the security forces in the neighboring dictatorships.

In August 1974 the ERP staged an assault on an explosives factory, seized abundant weaponry, and kidnapped Major Julio Argentino del Valle Larrabure (he remained in captivity for a year and was later assassinated). The same month, in simultaneous and extremely daring actions, the ERP invaded the barracks in Córdoba and in Catamarca. The attack failed because the army mounted a huge operation and captured sixteen guerrillas, whom it later executed. Others succeeded in fleeing. The ERP accused the army of having shot them even though they had already surrendered, and threatened to avenge their comrades. This vengeance took the form of indiscriminately killing anyone in uniform.

The ERP's crimes resulted in a general disapproval of the guerrillas. Protest grew when Lieutenant Humberto Viola and his three-year-old daughter were killed and another one of his young daughters was severely wounded in an attack at Tucumán. The ERP suspended this absurd punitive war, the victims of which were common soldiers and policemen, people of the class for whom the ERP was supposedly struggling. After the assassination of the much-reviled Chief of Police Alberto Vilar and his wife by a Montonero commando in February 1975, Isabel declared the country under a state of siege. She signed a decree authorizing the army to "neutralize or annihilate" the guerrilla cell (the ERP) in Tucumán. The congress approved a new antisubversive law, more severe than previous ones, and opened the gates to a dirty war.

The armed forces had kept on the margins of the Peronist governments. They did not want to navigate the turbid waters of violence, corruption, and economic chaos under Isabelita. But the broad mandate she gave them to fight subversion was another matter. The three branches unleashed a brutal war against the guerrillas. Each formed its own intelligence network, operational units, and clandestine detention centers, converted into torture chambers—few were left alive. The officers called legal restraints simple formalities.

In October 1975 the Montoneros enacted their own revolutionary code of penal justice, to be applied to its activists. Its penalties included confinement, exile, demotion, expulsion, and execution by firing squad for the crimes of treason, desertion, or informing. "The guerrillas are beginning to resemble the military," commented Jorge Rulli, a former militant in revolutionary Peronism, "some among them are as unscrupulous as the military, as ethically stunted as they are."[10]

There were no brakes on official and paramilitary violence. In April 1975 there was an average of fifty assassinations a week. In successive issues *Time* reported the rise in the numbers of victims—400 in April, 500 in June, 600 in July. The Triple A claimed responsibility for most of these crimes.

Isabel's supporters were reduced to a small group who, rather than serving her, used her to get personal advantages from the government. The country, in the midst of economic chaos, was thrown into turmoil by the violence and corruption scandals in which the President and López Rega were primarily implicated. Congress investigated these scandals with the support of Peronists.

Isabel's administration was incompetent, repressive, violent, and corrupt. It was also erratic and unstable. The unexpected resignations at the top levels and the changes in the cabinet—orchestrated by López Rega in order to install his own people—were continuous, as were the sudden changes of direction in her economic policies. In less than two years, forty ministers and five new teams filed through her government. Labor conflicts, strikes, demonstrations, and national work stoppages—expressions of the explosive social ills—followed the profound deterioration in the economy. Where Perón had seen economic times favorable to commercial exchange, Isabel was hit with the blows of the oil crisis (Argentina was an importer of crude oil), the worldwide recession, and a 25 percent fall in exports of Argentine beef as the result of an epidemic of foot-and-mouth disease.

López Rega—Isabel's confidant and friend, and the most hated and controversial figure in her government—was the first to abandon the sinking ship. Isabel accepted the superminister's resignation. Together with his bodyguard, and with the title of "plenipotentiary" ambassador to Europe, he left for Spain in a presidential plane. The government did not explain the nature of his duties, since it already had a plenipotentiary ambassador in every European capital. Isabel sacked General Leandro Anaya, commander of the army, for refusing to use troops to put down a strike and for denouncing the criminal activities of the Triple A. She named General Numa Laplane as his replacement, but the military demanded Laplane's resignation and forced him from active duty. In his stead they placed General Jorge Videla, a critic of López Rega and the officer most opposed to the idea of the army having any involvement with this government. He demanded an investigation of the Triple A.

Isabel was on the verge of a nervous breakdown and the country was at the edge of the abyss. She asked to take sick leave. In a television broadcast from the Casa Rosada she assured her listeners that this was "only a short good-bye." There were rumors of a coup. Italo Luder, a Peronist and president of the senate, assumed the presidency.

In spite of his interim status, Luder deposed the ministers of defense, the interior, and foreign relations and signed a decree that put the police under the army's control. Luder wanted Isabel to prolong her absence indefinitely and let him govern. She would be the figurehead. To win the military's support, he issued a decree authorizing the armed forces to do away with the guerrillas. Videla undertook a series of "scorched earth" operations. At the Eleventh Conference of American Armies in October 1975, in Montevideo, he declared, "If the Argentine situation demands it, all necessary persons must die to achieve the security of the country."

After her recuperation Isabel returned. Her followers wanted to give her a grand welcome. But the Peronist enthusiasm for her was not enough. Nor was her health; within two weeks she entered a private clinic in Buenos Aires. Again there was talk of a coup. But from her sick-bed she sent a recorded message to the country: "I have not resigned, nor do I intend to resign. I have not asked for a leave of absence, nor shall I." She would continue to fight, she said, since her "mission" was "victory for Argentina against the antinational forces." For this she counted on "the unconditional support" of the armed forces, the Catholic Church, the organized workers' movement, the businessmen's associations, and the political parties—in other words, the entire nation.

But the forces Isabel said she was counting on were moving in another direction. The military high command was preparing a coup and the Church was encouraging it from the pulpit. Monsignor Victorio Bonamín, chaplain of the army, asked in a homily that the military "put itself at the forefront of the whole country toward great future destinies" and gave his blessing to the spilling of blood—it was unavoidable—as a symbol of redemption. Monsignor Adolfo Tortolo, President of the Argentine Episcopal Conference, approved of these words.[11]

But Isabel was determined to govern. They would only remove her dead body from the presidency, she vowed. "I shall fulfill the duties that God and

His inscrutable designs have placed upon me." Two weeks later, on March 24, 1976, General Jorge Videla accused her of administrative corruption, and one of his detachments abducted her. They held her under house arrest. For most of the Argentine public, fed up with the repression, economic chaos, and Isabel's misgovernment, the military coup was a lesser evil.

Isabel's fall closed the cycle of governments of the so-called Return of Peronism. It ended in disgrace. Peronism, the most important political force in Argentina, was smashed, leaderless, in the hands of the most reactionary groups and the most suspect people. With the party in shambles and the country in chaos, no force could threaten Videla. He could do as he pleased.

THE KINGDOM OF THE "DISAPPEARED"

General Jorge Videla (1976–1981), commander-in-chief of the Argentine army, took power with tanks and machine guns. He announced "the end of one historical cycle and the beginning of another." In effect, it was the end of what was left of democracy with all the liberties the word implied, and the beginning of a long period of neofascist military dictatorships based on the National Security doctrine, which unleashed the most widespread and most brutal dirty war.

Videla engaged in an "internal war" against the insurgent movements and the left. He ignored the constitution, closed congress, rid the government of every trace of Peronism, disbanded the unions, and abolished the CGT. Videla prohibited strikes, restricted public liberties, closed newspapers, imprisoned scores of journalists, all while clandestine gangs murdered and disappeared thousands of "internal enemies."

Videla did not respect the Church. The assassination of priests, seminarians, and nuns alarmed the Pope and the Argentine Conference of Bishops. They begged him to do something to stop the rash of crimes against the servants of God and His Church.[12] Countless mutilated corpses appeared on the Uruguayan banks of the Plata River, with their hands tied behind their backs, their fingernails gone. Emilio Mignone, vice minister of education in Lanusse's government, was one of the first people to accuse the dictatorship of serious violations of human rights. In an open letter he denounced the arrest of his daughter Monica by clandestine navy commandos and the abduction of two Catholic priests and fifteen seminarians.

The navy's mechanics' school was the regime's principal torture center. In September officers of this school presented Brigadier General Landaburu with his daughter's corpse; she had been tortured for five months. When she was captured, she was carrying papers recounting the testimony of a young woman who had managed to escape the prison, relating the atrocities committed in this torture center.[13] Arrests were made in widespread operations in which a large number of military, police, and security personnel took part, dressed as civilians. Hoods were put over the victims' heads and they were brutally beaten, and their homes looted and destroyed; these men were thieves as well as murderers. The victims were thrown into vehicles without license plates and driven off to unknown destinations. Others were captured in broad daylight on the streets or at work. All were taken to clandestine detention and torture centers from which thousands did not emerge alive. When the military dictatorships fell, 340 of these centers were discovered.

Videla filled his cabinet with military officers. The lone civilian was the economics minister, José A. Martínez de Hoz (1976–1981), a member of the landholding oligarchy and a well-known figure in the banking industry. In his time he was called the Wizard of Oz for the miracles he performed during the early years of his ministry to save the economy. After his brilliant successes came the recession of 1980, with the crumbling of industry and important banks. After a hasty devaluation of the overvalued peso there was a massive exodus of speculative capital, calculated at $2 billion. The foreign debt stood at more than $8.5 billion in 1980 and more than $25.3 billion in 1981.[14] The unrestrained military budget caused this hefty foreign debt.

Thirty thousand Argentines disappeared under Videla's dictatorship. "We can be certain that the dictatorship produced the greatest tragedy in our history, and the most savage," wrote Ernesto Sábato, president of the Comisión Nacional sobre Desaparecidos (CONADEP: National Commission on the Disappeared), which was created by President Raúl Alfonsín to investigate these crimes. The commission documented 12,000 disappearances of men, women, and children under seven.[15] The torture was so sadistic that it drove some of those who carried it out insane. In September 1976 eight officers of the navy mechanics' school, where the worst crimes were committed, succumbed to mental problems. Their specialties included rape, amputations, vivisections without anesthesia, and skinning prisoners alive. A medical committee verified their serious problems when it discovered that they were also torturing their own families.[16] One case that received worldwide attention was the detention and torture of Jacobo Timerman, editor and owner of the daily *La Opinión*, and the confiscation of his newspaper. Timerman supported Videla but became a victim when the paper began to denounce the disappearances and the tragedy of the Mothers of the Plaza de Mayo. In his best-selling book, *Prisoner With No Name, Cell With No Number,* he compared the Argentine tragedy to the Jewish Holocaust. His case was very controversial. Not everyone believed that his position toward the dictatorships was honorable and courageous. In 1980, at a gathering of Sociedad Interamericana de Prensa (IPS: Inter-American Press Society) in San Diego, California, Máximo Gainza, owner of the Buenos Aires daily *La Prensa,* said that he did not understand why Timerman called the military governments fascist when he had their support. Only Videla's government was fascist, Timerman replied.[17]

The continual denunciations of the brutality of the Argentine regime by national and international human-rights organizations and the foreign press worried Videla, since they damaged the country's image and could hamper the negotiations on the swollen Argentine foreign debt with the European and United States financial centers. The military accused the Montoneros and the ERP of being responsible for the country's "bad press" and of waging an "antipatriotic" campaign against the country.[18]

President Carter and the United States Congress suspended arms sales and military aid as a sanction for the regime's grave human rights violations. The military junta saw this as meddling in the country's internal affairs, and at the first opportunity they returned the blow.

As a matter of fact, when Carter decreed a wheat embargo against the Soviet Union in 1980 in retaliation for its invasion of Afghanistan, Argentina sold its own wheat to the Soviets. The trade was mutually advantageous and paved the way for the two countries to move closer.[19] They exchanged military and commercial missions, and their trade increased. The growing relationship between Argentina and the Soviet Union became a political failure for Carter.

Argentina rejected the OAS's accusations on human-rights violations and threatened to withdraw from the Organization if it continued this campaign. Nevertheless, the general assembly adopted a resolution calling for respect for human rights and repeating the denunciations of the disappearances, the illegal methods used in making arrests, and the lack of information on such arrests.[20] Shortly before the changeover in the Casa Rosada, prominent leaders of organizations in defense of human rights were arrested, and their headquarters and homes were ransacked and razed. Sixty-four relatives of the "disappeared" were also detained.[21]

By 1981, Videla's last year in office, the guerrilla movements had been practically wiped out. Mario Santucho, leader of the ERP, was dead; Mario Firmenich, the Montonero leader, was in exile in Italy; and the guerrillas who were neither exiled nor lying in their graves were rotting in prison. Those seeking refuge in other countries were not safe; they could be captured by Argentine security forces. Through an international network of intelligence services—the Condor Plan—the dictatorships from the Southern Cone, Paraguay, and Bolivia pursued and eliminated their opponents—supposed guerrillas, communists, and leftists. The assassination of Chilean and Uruguayan personalities in Buenos Aires, Washington, and Rome were the handiwork of this network.

Under Videla, Argentina became "the kingdom of the disappeared." Every Thursday the Mothers of the Plaza de Mayo marched in silence outside the Casa Rosada, asking for their children to be returned to them alive. Argentina was also bankrupt: fifty banks had failed; the nation's foreign debt was $25 billion; and the Argentine peso was worthless.[22]

Without fanfare but with an impressive military display before the diplomatic corps and special guests, Videla handed the reins over to General Roberto Viola on March 29, 1981. By decision of the high command the transfer of power occurred without incident. The two men were friends, they had been colleagues since their days at the Military Academy, and they were comrades-in-arms. Military circles considered them moderates. The country was on the verge of economic collapse, with dangerous social problems, but it was again on the way to closer relations with the United States. Ronald Reagan had arrived in the White House two months earlier and was already seeking closer ties with the Argentine "thugs."

Before he took power, Viola went to Washington and spoke privately for an hour with the President, Secretary of State Alexander Haig, and Secretary of Defense Caspar Weinberger. He also met with several congressmen on Capitol Hill. He returned home full of plans and promises. Reagan needed Argentina for his military operations in Central America. Besides, it was a key country in the United States' plans for hemispheric security and the projected South Atlantic Treaty Organization (SATO)—similar to NATO—comprising the countries of the Southern Cone and South Africa.[23]

Reagan asked Congress to lift Carter's embargo on arms sales to Argentina, and he immediately sent military and commercial missions to Buenos Aires. The Argentine military agreed to cooperate in the clandestine CIA operation against Nicaragua. Its task was to train the mercenary Nicaraguan terrorist forces—the Contras—and the Salvadoran army (facing a civil war) in counterinsurgency techniques. The White House assigned $20 million annually to this end.[24]

Though the country was on the verge of bankruptcy, Viola continued to spend exorbitant amounts on weapons. Repression was extremely harsh; there was corruption in the government, and for the first time hungry people were begging in the streets. Consumer prices skyrocketed; the banks refused to lend money for longer than a month; unemployment stood at 12 percent; inflation spun out of control; and the foreign debt reached $30 billion. The unions threatened a general strike, as in the old days.

The military worried that Viola would not be able to control this crisis, and his plans for "openings" and "democratization" and his easy manner with the Peronists bothered his fellow officers. The release of Isabel Martínez de Perón (he allowed her to go into exile in Spain) was the last straw. In June 1982 General Fortunato Leopoldo Galtieri forced Viola to resign, declaring that the country's bad economic situation demanded that such a measure be taken, and put on the presidential sash himself. No one was surprised.

Five weeks before this minicoup Galtieri went to Washington to hold talks with high government officials. It was said that he offered them military bases in Patagonia in exchange for investments in a new natural-gas pipeline and in the oil industry. He offered to continue Argentina's support for the CIA's Central American operations.[25]

Galtieri wanted to be closer to the people and offered popular *asados* (barbecues) in the provinces; the people called his government program The Great National Barbecue. The economic picture worsened. The recession and inflation indexes hit a world record. In a single year the Argentine peso went from 2,000 to 12,000 to the dollar; the budget deficit reached $2.6 billion,[26] and by the middle of 1982 the foreign debt had risen to $35 billion (under Viola it rose $8 billion).[27]

To divert attention from the economic disaster, Galtieri dusted off the conflict with Chile over the Beagle Channel. As this ploy did not succeed in raising nationalist spirits, he revived the conflict with Great Britain over the Malvinas (or Falkland) Islands, to which Argentina claimed sovereignty. He launched a campaign with nationwide repercussions with the slogan, "The Malvinas are Argentina's." The people, led by Nobel Peace Prize-winner Adolfo Pérez Esquivel, chanted a reply: "So are the disappeared."

The generals' secret plan was for a surprise invasion of the islands on a memorable historical date, as a symbolic gesture of Argentine heroism. But the people, already weighed down by the economic situation, protested even more vigorously: housewives against the high cost of living and the rise in taxes, unions against the lamentable state of the economy, and human-rights move-

ments against official violence. One of the largest and angriest protest demonstrations took place on March 23. The people chanted the refrain, "*Se va a
acabar, se va a acabar la dictadura militar*" ("It's going to end. The military
dictatorship is going to end.").[28] Galtieri decided to launch the invasion
immediately.

THE UGLY LITTLE WAR

In 1966 the United Nations General Assembly, with full support from Latin
America, recognized Argentina's sovereignty over the Malvinas Islands, taken
by force by Great Britain in 1833. The British government ignored this
recognition.

Tensions rose in March 1982, when a group of Argentines disembarked on
San Pedro Island in the Georgias del Sur Archipelago to dismantle a whale-
processing factory and to raise their national flag. In response the islanders
attacked the offices of an Argentine airline and raised the British flag. The
British government delivered a complaint to the Argentine government and
asked the support of its allies. Ronald Reagan telephoned Galtieri and warned
that an attack on the islands would have grave consequences: Argentina would
be accused of being the "aggressor," and sanctions would be imposed. He
offered to send Vice President George Bush. Galtieri would not receive him
unless he was prepared to deal with the question of sovereignty. Besides, the
invasion was already under way—a fact of which he did not inform Reagan.

In fact, on April 2 Argentine forces recaptured the Malvinas Islands, overpowered all forty-nine British marines and, together with the governor of the
islands, took them to Montevideo. Argentina made General Mario Menéndez
governor, renamed Port Stanley, the capital, Puerto Argentino, raised its blue
and white flag, and sent military reinforcements, putting them on maximum
alert. No one was going to displace them. The British foreign secretary, Lord
Peter Carrington, pronounced the situation potentially dangerous.

British Prime Minister Margaret Thatcher was not about to tolerate a situation in which a disgraced Latin American dictatorship offended the United
Kingdom, and she prepared to dispatch the British navy to the South Atlantic.
For both countries the conflict became a question of national honor, and life
and death for their battered governments. The Argentine public vigorously supported the invasion. For Thatcher, the invasion brought many problems. It
had surprised British intelligence services—and the Americans as well. When
the Labour Party asked for her resignation, the Iron Lady confronted

Parliament, making it clear that she would not resign. "Now is the time for strength and resolution," she declared firmly. She severed relations with Argentina, froze its assets in Great Britain, prohibited the importation of Argentine products, and succeeded in obtaining the somewhat reluctant support of the European Economic Community. Heads began to roll in London. Burdened with the "humiliation" suffered by the United Kingdom without his having foreseen it, Lord Carrington resigned, and Francis Pym became the new foreign secretary. Defence secretary John Nott also tendered his resignation, but the prime minister did not accept it.

The British government condemned the "flagrant aggression," demanded the immediate withdrawal of the Argentine forces, and set April 5 as the deadline, but it continued to seek a negotiated solution. If this did not succeed, Britain would dispatch a naval war fleet to the Falklands. The United Nations Security Council supported Great Britain: one resolution called for the cessation of hostilities, the unconditional withdrawal of Argentine forces, and the search for a diplomatic solution respecting the islanders' self-determination. Panama, a non-permanent member of the Council, was the only nation to vote against the resolution.

On April 5 the British fleet weighed anchor for the South Atlantic with forty warships, two aircraft carriers, planes, helicopters, a flotilla of light tankers, 25,000 men, and a battalion of Gurkhas, Nepalese mercenaries known for their extreme cruelty. Nott announced the blockade of the islands for 200 miles in all directions. Any Argentine ship that entered this zone would be attacked. That same day, united for victory, members of the Argentine government, opposition figures, Peronists, union leaders, the military, and intellectuals, all traveled to the Malvinas on a charter flight to attend the inauguration of Governor Menéndez.

Caught in a conflict between two allies and two military alliances—NATO and the Río Treaty (The Inter-American Treaty of Reciprocal Assistance)—Reagan spoke of neutrality. His secretary of state, Alexander Haig, made lightning trips between Washington, London, and Buenos Aires in an effort to mediate. He demanded that Argentina comply with the United Nations resolution on withdrawal of its forces and proposed that Argentina, Great Britain, and the United States share the government of the islands. Galtieri did not accept the proposal, since it did not guarantee Argentine sovereignty. "Haig is not a mediator but a British ally," he commented. Failing to reach an agreement, Haig announced that his mission of mediation was over. On April 30 Reagan announced his "unconditional support" for Great Britain, accused

Argentina of "aggression," imposed severe economic and commercial sanctions, and suspended military aid. Argentina accused Reagan of betrayal, causing irreparable damage to hemispheric relations, and dealing a fatal blow to the inter-American system.

Haig's gestures of mediation served as a smoke screen to hide the aid the United States was already sending to Britain, dealing it a winning hand: satellite intelligence, logistical support and tons of weaponry, including 200 Sidewinder missiles whose precision was almost infallible. The transfer was made on the high seas and on Ascension Island, an Anglo-American military fortification in the middle of the Atlantic. News agencies reported that the Soviet Union moved a satellite over the South Atlantic to provide Argentina with intelligence information.

From every corner of the continent came harsh criticism of the United States for turning its back on Latin America and failing to meet its obligations as a member of the Río Treaty. Furthermore, the governments of Brazil, Cuba, Peru, and Venezuela offered Argentina military assistance.

With the British armada advancing toward the South Atlantic, Argentina requested an urgent meeting of the OAS Consultative Body under the Río Treaty, which called for collective action when one of its members was attacked. A week later—the war was already under way—OAS approved a resolution condemning Great Britain for the "unjust and disproportionate armed attack" and asked the United States to lift the economic and military sanctions it had imposed on Argentina. The resolution was approved by a vote of 17 in favor, 0 against and 4 abstentions: the United States, Chile, Colombia, and Trinidad and Tobago. In a virulent speech the Argentine chancellor, Nicanor Costa Méndez's, accused the United States of giving "illegal and repugnant" aid to Great Britain. He was fervently applauded. And in May, in the midst of the war, the Coordination Office of the Nonaligned Nations in Havana, with Chancellor Costa Méndez' participation, gave Argentina its full support. Javier Pérez de Cuéllar, the United Nations Secretary General, proposed an interim government by several countries under the United Nations flag.

Colombia was the only Latin American country that did not stand by Argentina. When the latter called for the meeting of the Consultative Body of the OAS, invoking the Río Treaty, to raise the issue of British aggression, Colombia abstained. Ambassador Carlos Bernal stated that his government had doubts about the application of the treaty in this case, since the United Nations was already dealing with the issue. He added that the OAS must not ignore the United Nations request for the withdrawal of Argentine troops, nor act on the issue, since this would create a "serious precedent" that could weaken the United Nations and result in a serious crisis. He appeared to ignore the fact that the two organizations repeatedly acted simultaneously on matters that threatened peace. Colombia also abstained from the resolution condemning Great Britain, alleging that it was rejecting the use of force. Colombia was criticized for breaking continent-wide unity. In Argentina, Colombia earned the title of the Cain of the Americas, and it was the subject of protests outside its embassy in Buenos Aires and a boycott of its products. In Colombia the government's position was met with feelings of frustration and shame. The former Chancellor, Alfredo Vásquez Carrizosa, declared that denying Argentina's rights was a "terrible precedent," and he referred to two contradictory letters from President Turbay Ayala to Galtieri. In one Turbay expressed full support—he did not criticize the use of force—and in the other he said, without mentioning the invasion, that he could not support the steps that Galtieri had taken.[29] Isolated but powerful Colombian voices supported the government's position, and Turbay received congratulatory messages from President Reagan and Mrs. Thatcher.

The Colombian position was political, not juridical, as the government claimed, since there was no legal basis for denying Argentina its right to call a meeting of the Consultative Body under the provisions of the Río Treaty whenever it was in danger. To do so was to prejudge the content of its complaint. A Peruvian, Bustamante y Rivero, who was the former president of the International Court of Justice, upheld Argentina's right of recourse to the Río Treaty.

On April 23, 1982, the British fleet undertook the so-called reconquest of the Falkland Islands. Troops landed on Georgia del Sur, and again the British flag was raised. This first stage of the war was received with jubilant, almost delirious, approval by the British government and people, and "Maggie" obtained a stunning victory in the English and Scots municipal elections.[30] Buenos Aires was furious. Thousands of people congregated outside the Casa Rosada shouting slogans against Great Britain and Galtieri's dictatorship. In Caracas demonstrators burned British and United States flags.

Manipulation of public opinion was easy for the Argentine dictatorship. It kept patriotic fervor high by means of public statements. It reported that its military forces were advancing from one victory to the next. Some newspapers, under bold headlines, announced that Argentina was winning the war.[31] In May 1982, in the midst of the war and the patriotic and triumphant euphoria, Galtieri organized a rock festival, which some 60,000 young people attended. When the Patagonian singer León Gieco began his famous song "Underground," with the lines, "All I ask of God is that war is not indifferent to me," the festival turned into a revolt against the dictatorship. The young people asked for peace, and thousands confronted the police and infuriated the military by chanting, "It's going to end. The military dictatorship is going to end!"[32]

Pope John Paul II had wanted to mediate avoidance of the war. Before it started, he asked both governments to suspend hostilities, but Mrs. Thatcher replied that she would proceed, since she could not allow aggression to triumph, international law must be defended, and the freedom of the Falkland inhabitants must be respected.[33] The Pope traveled to London in June—it was one of the most controversial of his pilgrimages—to build bridges to the Anglican Church. The Vatican explained that this trip had been scheduled before the conflict erupted. The Pope did not want his presence in London to be seen as supporting Great Britain. From there he announced a trip to Buenos Aires. During the thirty short hours he remained on Argentine territory there was violent combat in the southern waters, during which ships were sunk, planes were shot down, and close to a thousand were left dead. When he boarded his plane to return to Rome, the British troops were advancing on Port Stanley. Two days later Argentina surrendered.

The nationwide astonishment rose to a climax when Galtieri announced the defeat. More than 11,000 soldiers, many of them adolescents, surrendered. It was a stunning and ignominious defeat.[34] In a brief and sober ceremony in Port Stanley, General Menéndez signed the Act of Surrender, in which he crossed out the word "unconditional" as written by the British. Thousands were taken prisoner of war, and several officers were taken to London to be interrogated. The humiliation could not have been deeper.

In Buenos Aires there were violent riots, and the people confronted the police. Scores were wounded on both sides. Galtieri was prevented from speaking from the Casa Rosada balcony by the whistles and jeers from the multitude. He spoke on television instead. "There will be no final peace if Britain keeps the islands," he said. In the protest demonstrations there were more chants against the United States for its "betrayal" than there were against Great Britain, the aggressor.

The masses demanded an immediate trial of the junta members. They should answer for the defeat and the thousands who had died in the war. Costa Méndez resigned. Raúl Alfonsín, the leader of the Unión Cívica Radical (UCR: Radical Civil Union), the party that was second only to

Peronism, asked for the immediate resignation of the military junta "so that we can begin to take the road to democracy."

Great Britain suffered many losses. The Argentine air force sunk its navy's most modern warship, a troop transport, a destroyer, and two modern frigates, damaged one destroyer, wrecked another, and shot down five jets. Argentina lost half of its planes and a large number of irreplaceable pilots. The British navy sank the Argentine ship *General Beltrano*, its only cruiser, with 1,042 men on board. Argentina claimed to have rescued nearly 800. Argentina accused Great Britain of attacking the ship outside the 200-mile exclusion zone, and the act was condemned throughout Latin America. The loss of so many lives in this absurd war profoundly shook the world. Great Britain claimed that it had been a war of legitimate defense. The Argentine navy hugged the coasts in fear of British nuclear submarines. Some 2,000 young Argentines died. The cost of the war was estimated at more than $2 billion. The Argentine military lost its most precious remaining quality: military prestige. The diplomatic suit that Argentina was winning in the United Nations was gone.

In mid-July, under strict security measures, the last 593 soldiers captured by Britain arrived in Buenos Aires. The military authorities prevented the media from getting close to them. The resentment of these young people, victims of dictatorship and war, was profound. They arrived not as heroes but as renegades. Some of them tried to commit suicide. This alienated youth was the greatest price of the war, irresponsibly undertaken by the dictatorship for dubious political gains.

EPILOGUE TO A HORROR STORY

The Malvinas/Falklands war, the "ugly little war," the "ridiculous war" as the American press dubbed it, the "absurd and sloppy war" as the Nobel Prize–winning Colombian writer Gabriel García Marquez called it, was something more than the story of a humiliating military and political defeat for Argentina. It was more than a British victory. It was a game of power, a story of changing and unthinkable alliances, of Western loyalties and hemispheric disloyalties. It was evidence of a world irremediably divided between North and South, the scene of nonexistent third-world solidarity, of fragile European unity, of Latin American incapacity to unite in political struggle and to respond immediately and adequately to the arbitrary impositions of the great powers. It was furthermore a display of American arrogance toward the southern continent and one more occasion when the United Nations—where great-power interests were paramount—demonstrated its incapacity to avoid conflict and prevent war. It was also one more piece of evidence that the voice of the OAS was no more than a leaf in the wind.

This absurd and sloppy war, in which more than 2,000 Argentines and hundreds of British died, which ruined Argentina and strangled Britain's economy, this unholy war with which a disgraced dictatorship attempted to wipe out its record of ineptitude, corruption, and violence, was, for the "Masters of War," a platform for their war games. The South Atlantic had served as a laboratory for sophisticated weaponry—not yet traded on the arms markets—and the first war "of microchips and computers, faster than the human brain," wrote *Time*.[35]

The war became merely a sad chapter in Argentina's history. High British and United States officials who played an important part in the conflict confirmed that United States aid to Britain was so broad that to have divulged it would have been shattering, since it would have shown the weakness of Britain's defense. The lion rampant, the emblem of the United Kingdom, had no teeth. Without United States help, Great Britain would have been defeated, affirmed United States Secretary of the Navy John Lehmann. And a curious detail: the Pentagon provided Britain with an "extremely useful little book," confessed a high British official, with its evaluation of Argentine military tactics—particularly its submarines—obtained in joint military maneuvers. The Argentine military never imagined that the Pentagon would give it to its "enemies" to use against Argentina.[36]

Had Reagan irreparably damaged United States relations with the Latin America, as many claimed? "We should not take this lightly, but in six months it will be forgotten," remarked a high United States official.[37] Reagan wrote personal letters to several Latin American presidents. He declared that "although I understand the frustrations of the Argentines, the United States had to support the principle of avoiding force in resolving disputes."[38] Some might have been surprised or perhaps indignant at his cynicism. Contrary to world opinion, his love of force was exposed in his unholy wars in Central America.

This war was also the beginning of the end for the National Security Doctrine military regimes in Argentina, the single favorable result. The people were indignant at having been deceived. They were humiliated by the defeat, they grieved for the sacrifice of thousands of their youth in the Malvinas, and they were furious at the prolongation of the military's dirty war in which tens of thousands of Argentines were killed or disappeared. They resolved to

put an end to the military presence in the Casa Rosada. They demanded justice, wanting those responsible for both tragedies to be brought before civilian courts. Three days after the surrender Galtieri was forced to resign, and
the commanders of the three service branches were relieved of their duties.

The government of the retired General Reynaldo Bignone, who replaced
Galtieri, was transitional. Suits and ties began to appear in the Casa Rosada
and at the highest levels of government. Bignone's cabinet was composed of
nine civilians and one military officer: the minister of the interior. During the
year and a half that he occupied the presidential seat (June 1982 to December
1983), Bignone paved the way for a return to democracy, as the people
demanded.

The past began to be stripped of its cover. Soon denunciations for murders
and disappearances started to shower the armed forces, the security services,
and the police as the perpetrators of these crimes. The remains of the disappeared began to appear, buried as N.N. (No Name) in mass graves. The government assured everyone that these were the corpses of "beggars and the
indigent." It could not explain why there were bullets from coup de graces in
their skulls and traces of torture on their bodies. The hard-liners in the armed
forces were not in agreement with Bignone's opening actions, nor with the surrender of power. They wanted to impose conditions before the election to
assure their "constitutional presence" in the civilian government and to bury
the investigations and trials coming their way under a law of amnesty. Rumors
of a coup were rife. The "dirty war" continued. Ultraright underground
groups, connected to sectors of the military, carried out terrorist acts, sabotage, abductions, and assassinations of politicians and popular and leftist leaders, and even military officers who favored Bignone. These acts created a
tension that could spoil the election and the transition to democracy.

A month before the vote the military junta decreed the law of amnesty,
which it called an act of national pacification. After almost a decade of the dirty
war the military wanted to make clear that what had happened was an "internal war" against subversion. The armed forces, "in fulfilling their duty," prevented
the destruction of the republic and its institutions. With this law these men placed
themselves beyond the reach of the courts, the investigations of human-rights
abuses, verdicts on the responsibility for the Malvinas War, corruption probes,
and explanations of the enormous national debt, which reached $43 billion as
a result of multimillion-dollar weapons purchases.

The amnesty law was met with national revulsion. Large protest marches,
led by Nobel Prize-winner Pérez Esquivel and the Mothers and Grandmothers

of the Plaza de Mayo, showed the military leaders that they would not allow such a law. The two presidential candidates, Raúl Alfonsín, of the UCR, and Italo Lúder, a Peronist of the right, promised to repeal it. But so great was the fear that the military might not hand over power, or would postpone the election, that when the two most powerful union groups called for a general strike a few days before the elections, the daily *La Nación* termed it "a collective suicide." They should not tempt the men in uniform.

ALFONSÍN AND THE MILITARY CASTE

Raúl Alfonsín, leader of the Unión Cívica Radical (UCR), a center-left party, was elected president of Argentina with 52 percent of the vote. It was the first electoral defeat for Peronism. "We have won, but we have defeated no one. This is a victory for Argentina," Alfonsín announced to the enthusiastic crowd. He entered the Casa Rosada through the front door, with immense popular support based on his charisma and honesty, his honest and courageous stance toward the military, and his promises to see justice done and bring the officers before civilian courts.

The country was on the verge of bankruptcy, and the people were traumatized and demoralized by the political violence and the humiliating defeat in the Malvinas. Economic indexes were catastrophic: recession, an annual inflation rate of 1,000 percent (1982), 15 percent unemployment, a foreign debt of $43 billion—the third largest in the world—and a lack of foreign currency. There was panic because of successive bankruptcies of banks, financial institutions, and industrial enterprises. The deterioration of living conditions reached intolerable levels. The Argentine peso was in a vertiginous free fall; salaries and wages were insufficient to cover the necessities of life for most people; there was a lack of housing and uncontrolled increases in rents. Some 500,000 people were forced to abandon their homes and take refuge in boarding houses, often "filthy and decrepit."[39]

Alfonsín was facing the monumental task of leading the country out of bankruptcy and bringing the untouchable military class to justice. The people demanded as much. Relatives of the victims published lists of thousands of the "disappeared" and asked for justice. Mass graves and corpses were discovered in the mountains of Tucumán. Even soldiers and officers, veterans of the Malvinas War, denounced strategic and political errors committed by Galtieri and his advisers, incompetence and corruption in the army ranks, and acts of cowardice by their superiors. Confronting the military caste, forcing it to give in, and bringing it to court was not an easy job, nor without danger for the fragile democracy. The powerful military class considered itself an aristocracy by social origin, the excellence of its professional education in the Prussian tradition, and the hegemony it had held for more than half a century. No president came to power without the previous approval of the military.[40] Argentine history was plagued with military presidents. They considered it their duty and right to exercise power.

One of Alfonsín's most serious mistakes was delaying in taking on the military immediately, while it was weakened and while he enjoyed broad national support. It was a case of now or never. He should have dismantled the repressive apparatus and the intelligence units—the detention and torture centers—of the three branches, restructured the military institutions and cleaned out their ranks. which were rife with criminals and potential coup leaders. By leaving them intact he exposed his government and the country to grave dangers.

Within three days of assuming power, Alfonsín authorized the trials of the nine commanders of the military juntas, the former generals Videla, Viola, Galtieri, and Bignone, and the former admiral Emilio Massera, but he assigned this task to the Supreme Council of the Armed Forces, the military's highest court. There was harsh criticism of this measure. No one believed in the efficacy and impartiality of military justice. To correct this impression, Alfonsín introduced reforms to the code of military justice that gave to the civilian courts power to act in cases of "undue delay" by the military tribunal and to the civilians the right to appeal its sentences. Congress approved these reforms, but most of the political sectors, organizations, and human-rights groups criticized them because the military could obstruct justice.

Alfonsín named a Comisión Nacional de Personas Desaparecidas (CONADEP) and appointed the writer Ernesto Sábato to head it. Its function was to shed light on the crimes committed against civilians by the military dictatorships during the seven years of the "internal war," but it was not authorized to denounce them before the courts of justice.

The military demanded total amnesty from the government. They would not accept being brought before civilian courts, since their fight against subversion, according to Videla, had been a just and necessary war won by the military. He considered the prosecutions an injustice against the armed forces and "a blot on the honor of the military." Displaying a disrespectful and threatening manner toward the government and justice, the high command promoted officers who were accused of serious human-rights violations.[41]

The Supreme Council of the Armed Forces put the trials of the military officers and more than 2,000 lawsuits brought by relatives of the disappeared in abeyance for three and a half years. It did absolve the controversial naval Captain Alfredo Astiz, accused of twenty murders, among them two French nuns and a Swedish-Argentine teenage girl. Alfonsín demanded Astiz's resignation, but the high command did not obey the order and promoted him instead.

Faced with the military tribunal's inaction, in 1985 the federal appeals court in Buenos Aires initiated proceedings against the former commanders Videla and Viola, and the former admiral Massera. The trials lasted five months. Some thousand witnesses were heard. Crowds gathered outside the courthouse shouted slogans against the military and demanded that the defendants be found guilty.[42] The Court convicted Videla and Massera to life in prison for murder, torture, illegal arrests and theft, and Viola to seventeen years for the same crimes. Other high military officers were given lesser sentences. The court absolved Galtieri, the former Admiral Jorge Anaya and other officers responsible for the defeat in the Malvinas.[43] The Court also convicted Generals Menéndez, commander of the Argentine forces in the Malvinas, and Carlos Suárez Masón. Masón fled to the United States with false papers, but he was captured and extradited to Argentina in 1987 and sentenced to twenty-five years in prison for murder, abduction, arbitrary arrests, and torture and for the disappearance of 171 Uruguayan citizens (thirty-five of whom were students). The former General Ramón J. Camps, a former chief of police of Buenos Aires Province—considered one of the most sadistic executors of the repression—was also convicted. He was sentenced to twenty-five years for numerous murders, tortures, and disappearances, among them that of a group of high-school students. This horrendous crime was recalled in the Argentine film *La noche de los lápices* (Night of the Pencils), directed by Héctor Olivera (1986). The Supreme Court ratified all the sentences.

With contempt for the courts and as a challenge to the government's authority, former generals and admirals indicted by the tribunals refused to appear before the courts. The court ordered the arrest of twelve high navy officers, among them four retired admirals and the naval officer Alfredo Astiz.[44]

Alfonsín's popularity declined because of his weakness regarding the military and the way he managed the serious economic crisis. His Austral Plan— a change in the currency—to combat the hyperinflation was met with violent strikes in which store windows were smashed and businesses were looted. The strikes were suppressed by the police, resulting in several deaths and many wounded. He was also criticized by opposition parties regarding the convictions of the officers. Some pointed out the slow pace of justice—in three years only ten had been sentenced—and others thought that they should not have been tried at all, since such procedures served only to increase the nervousness in the barracks and rail the calm of the citizenry. These people wanted peace with the military at any cost, including their exoneration. In fact, the more the cases moved forward and the civilian courts convicted the officers, the more uneasiness grew in the military ranks and nervousness among the people, since they knew the military had a propensity for coups.

The entire country suffered anxiety at the growing military "unease." Amid this great tension, Alfonsín ordered that the court cases be speeded up and presented congress with a bill—a slanted amnesty—that he called "national reconciliation" but the people dubbed Full Stop. It fixed a term of sixty days in which to summon officers accused of human-rights violations; once this deadline was passed, no court, civilian or military, could subpoena any member of the armed forces or police, no matter the seriousness of his crime, nor appeal the sentences. The Full Stop law was the subject of a bitter national debate, rancorous confrontations in the congress, and violent popular protests including battles with the police, with the result that countless people were wounded and arrested. Political and popular sectors, human-rights movements, the Mothers of the Plaza de Mayo, and relatives of the dirty war's victims impugned the law as unconstitutional, since it violated the principle of equality before the law, and they accused the government of covering up genocide. Nevertheless, the chamber of deputies and the senate approved it by large majorities, the president signed it, and the supreme court of justice declared it constitutional. It took effect on February 24, 1987.

A storm of criticism of the government, congress, and the courts came from all sides. A group of relatives of those killed by guerrillas objected to the fact that the government was making no moves to bring back into the country the "terrorists that were freewheeling abroad." The rightist Peronists supported the government. They retorted that this law was "the point of departure to pacify the country."[45]

Reeling from these criticisms, Alfonsín maintained that history would remember him more for this law, meant to bring about a reconciliation between civilians and the armed forces, than for the trials of the former commanders of the military junta. He believed that the raw nerves of the uniformed services would be soothed when they realized that this law benefited them. Such a realization did not occur, nor was there a decrease in anxiety among those in uniform. They demanded total amnesty to restore the stained honor of the armed forces.

A MILITARY HEART ATTACK

With the Full Stop Law Alfonsín gave militarism mouth-to-mouth resuscitation. From this point onward he was faced with serious military uprisings. They began on April 15, 1987, with a rebellion by the commander and the military regiment in the province of Córdoba in support of Army Major Ernesto Barreiro, who was accused of serious human-rights violations. He was discharged for refusing to appear before a civilian court. The police tried to arrest him, but were unsuccessful owing to the intervention of his fellow officers. Barreiro fled. The regimental commander was accused of sedition and relieved of his duties. The mutineers surrendered.

On Holy Friday, two days after this surrender, some 200 officers under the command of Lieutenant Colonel Aldo Rico mutinied at the Campo de Mayo, 15 miles from Buenos Aires, in support of Barreiro. They appeared in combat uniform, with bulletproof vests, heavily armed and with black camouflage on their faces. They demanded total amnesty for the officers involved in the revolt and the suspension of all trials of military officers.

Alfonsín refused, declaring a state of siege. His motto was "Democracy or Dictatorship." The Plaza de Mayo filled with people cheering the President and democracy and booing the military. When the President appeared before congress with his account of the facts and declared that democracy was not negotiable, the chamber shook with applause.

Half a million people with banners and signs in the Plaza de Mayo shouted to the mutineers, "Don't you dare, don't you dare! If you dare, we'll burn down your barracks." Thousands of unarmed demonstrators attempted to gain entry to the barracks. The police tried to hold them back, but they broke through the barricades and reached the entrance, demanding, "The firing squad for the traitors of the Motherland."

The enormous and spontaneous demonstration of support for the government and for democracy, rejection of the mutineers, and the backing of Latin American, European, and United States heads of state showed that everyone within the country and abroad supported the President. On Easter Sunday, Alfonsín flew by helicopter to the Campo de Mayo to talk with the mutineers. An hour later he announced their unconditional surrender. "As the law requires, they will be arrested and brought to justice," he proclaimed.[46]

But the President's victory had a hidden aspect. His order to put down the Campo de Mayo rebellion had been boycotted by the commander-in-chief of the chiefs of staff, General Ríos Ereñú. To carry out the order Ríos Ereñú called in an army corps—between 1,000 and 2,000 men—quartered more than 217 miles from Buenos Aires. The convoy advanced slowly. "No commanding officer will willingly suppress his comrades by force of arms," said one of the *carapintadas* (painted faces, worn as camouflage) in the Campo de Mayo. Ríos Ereñú acknowledged the order but did not carry it out.[47]

Presidents José Sarney of Brazil and Julio María Sanguinetti of Uruguay maintained permanent connections with Alfonsín. They feared the effect "by example" of the uprisings in their own countries. Analyzing the situations of each country, and assessing support for or disagreements with Alfonsín's management of the military problem revived the debates in Uruguay and Brazil on the thorny topic of the military and justice, with ensuing national alarm.

Front-page news presented Alfonsín as the winner, democracy strengthened, the mutineers under control. Aldo Rico and the other rebels were arrested and given discharges. A Buenos Aires newspaper trumpeted, "Everything Under Control." Still, the epilogue to this story was not so brilliant. Democracy stood on the shifting sands of the Full Stop Amnesty Law. The military's passive disobedience of the President's orders was a pathetic demonstration of the civilian government's haplessness when confronted with military power.

The uprisings and chronic military anxiety led Alfonsín to make more concessions. He presented to his congress a rider to the Full Stop Law that legitimized the concept of "due obedience" in the cases against the officers. Those who committed human-rights violations in carrying out the orders of their superiors under "pressure" or "irresistible coercion" were exonerated of guilt. Some 400 of the accused officers benefited. Thievery—there was a great deal of theft at high levels—would be punished, since the "orders" were to kill and torture but not to rob the property of others.

In May 1987, the Law of Due Obedience was adopted by wide majorities in the chamber of deputies and the senate, and the supreme court of justice declared it constitutional. Only one judge dissented.[48]

This law divided Argentina. Politicians, intellectuals, judges, representatives of human-rights organizations, and the general population criticized the law, the congress, and the court and again accused the government of propitiating impunity. They pointed out that the law was unjust, arbitrary, unconstitutional, illegal, amoral, and politically misconceived, approved "in a scandalous manner, with pseudo-juridical arguments; 99 percent of those responsible for the crimes committed during the dictatorship can evade justice." The opponents to the law insisted that it converted Argentina into "the first country where torture and murder are legalized."[49]

Alfonsín again believed that with this law he could calm the military's extended "attack of nerves." But the high military command let him know it was not enough. They persisted in their demands for total amnesty, for a political solution to the "political fact" such as the war against subversion, and for moral vindication of the armed forces.[50] Alfonsín's popularity continued to fall. In September 1987 his party suffered a crushing defeat in the elections for governors, deputies, mayors, and council members, and Peronism once again seized the reins of political majority. Peronists returned to the streets to celebrate their victory. It was a vote of no confidence in the President.

The uprisings continued. Former Lieutenant-Colonel Aldo Rico escaped from his place of detention, took refuge in the Monte Caseros garrison in Buenos Aires, and prepared another rebellion with the support of 200 soldiers and officers. They swore to fight "at any cost" to redeem the honor of the Argentine armed forces. Troops surrounded them, and after a short battle and six tense hours they surrendered. Rico was confined to a military prison. Alfonsín could once again boast that democracy had been strengthened and "the house was in order." The people applauded the President once again.

In November more than 200 *carapintada* officers, led by Colonel Mohamed Alí Seineldín—"The Turk"—rebelled in the engineering school at the Campo de Mayo. Seineldín took up the well-known banner of vindication for the armed forces. He demanded total amnesty for officers convicted or accused of human-rights violations and the release of the former commanders who had been members of the juntas. He also demanded salary increases, an increase in the defense budget—which Alfonsín had cut in half—and the removal of General Dante Caridi, commander in chief of the general staff. Again the people crowded the Campo de Mayo in defense of democracy, and again the police tried to break them up by using tear gas.[51]

Alfonsín's order to put down the rebellion—he was in Washington on an official visit—was met with an ambiguity equal to the earlier disobedience. Caridi chose an army corps stationed in Córdoba, 435 miles from Buenos Aires, but its commander refused to take part in an operation against Seineldín. Troops put down the rebellion on Caridi's orders. One person died, five were wounded, and more than a hundred were arrested. As they began to withdraw, the people shouted, "Cowards, cowards! Caridi's just like Seineldín."[52]

On December 1 a squad of fifty-three officers and sailors of the coastal police deserted their garrison in Buenos Aires in support of Rico. Arriving in three trucks and armed with more than 200 rifles, they appeared in the Campo de Mayo among the mutineers led by Seineldín. Also in December, 855 soldiers led by an officer took over the Villa Martinelli base, making the oft-repeated demand for military amnesty. Other garrisons and regiments attempted to rebel but were kept under control. Again democracy emerged strengthened; and again Alfonsín came out with flying colors. He noted that there had been no negotiation, nor had he made concessions to the mutineers. But as before, negotiations were happening under the table. A Buenos Aires newspaper headline read, "There is No Pact, But It Is Being Fulfilled."

The crisis and the deterioration in the military went very deep. The minister of defense (a civilian) assured the country that the military malaise was due to deeper causes, including low salaries, the emotional fallout of the humiliating defeat in the Malvinas, and the national rejection of the repression in their "war" against subversion. All were chronic ailments.

At dawn on January 23, 1989, an armed group of more than sixty-five men and five women attacked the La Tablada regiment in Buenos Aires. Alfonsín ordered the armed forces to stifle it. This time his orders were followed with unusual rapidity and violence. Almost immediately 300 soldiers appeared outside the regimental barracks. The army did not attempt to negotiate, nor did it heed the white flags of the rebels. It leveled everything. The counterattack was massive. It attacked the headquarters with tanks, mortars, long- and medium-range artillery, and firebombs (prohibited under the Vienna Convention). Units of the elite forces were airlifted to the scene.

After thirty hours of fierce combat, the attackers surrendered. Thirty-six people died, among them eight soldiers and one policeman, and sixty-three were wounded. The building was destroyed and in flames. Inside the headquarters there were five burned corpses. The number of arrested guerrillas dropped as the number of the disappeared grew. Executions and tortures were reported. This was the most violent, bloody, confused, and manipulated event of Alfonsín's five years in office.

The armed forces characterized the La Tablada takeover as a widespread international conspiracy of the left and claimed it signaled the resurgence of the guerrillas. It was clear that the assault had not taken the military by surprise. Soldiers' version of the events—confirmed by the Buenos Aires newspaper La Nación—indicated that military and police units had been put on a state of alert, that defenses had been reinforced, and that training exercises to repel "an attack coming from abroad" had been carried out. That day the army arrived at the barracks within minutes of the attack.[53]

The claim that the military had set a trap for the Movimiento Todos por la Patria (MTP: All for the Motherland Movement)—which was responsible for the attack—was confirmed by surviving guerrillas. They testified that they had been infiltrated by military intelligence and that the operation was blown.

The armed forces capitalized on the "successful" capture of La Tablada and the surrender of the subversive group. The President thanked them for their defense of the democratic system. The government appeared to accept the military view of guerrilla resurgence and announced the creation of a national security council, whose function was to deal with situations of public order and subversion. The council was composed of nine members, among them the commanders of the three military branches and some ministers, and presided over by the president.[54]

The MTP was a leftist group organized three years earlier by Jorge Manuel Baños, a respected Buenos Aires lawyer and a former director of an organization in defense of human rights (he died at La Tablada). Enrique Haroldo Gorriarán of the ERP became one of its leaders. Six months after the attack, in a trial plagued by procedural irregularities, all those arrested were found guilty.[55]

CHAOS

By 1988 the Argentine economy was rapidly deteriorating. Economic and social indices were catastrophic: Inflation, unemployment, and the price of basic necessities were spiraling upward. The drop in real wages for the working class threw many Argentines into absolute poverty. The astronomical foreign debt exceeded $60 billion (the third largest on the southern continent), and defaulted interest payments (more than $2 billion) caused the government to have serious quarrels with the international banking industry.

The Austral Plan and the Spring Plan—which decreed drastic currency adjustments—with which Alfonsín attempted to mitigate the crisis, caused a wave of work stoppages and labor protests. A general strike called by the CGT in September 1988 became a day of violence and looting without precedent.

Rumors of a coup persisted in this tense situation, and the President admitted that such a possibility existed. His relations with the military had been as explosive as a minefield. The military command continued the "battle of the

Generals" to make the government—already exhausted—vindicate them publicly.[56] The protests by human rights organizations and the Mothers of the Plaza de Mayo also continued accusing Alfonsín of propitiating impunity, with the complicity of the military courts, an impunity which did not allow the trials to proceed, and they protested what they saw as the weakness of the civilian courts. In the five years of democracy—after seven of genocidal dictatorships—only ten officers were found guilty, and those responsible for the uprisings and mutinies, detained in their own institutions, had not been brought to trial.

The people had not forgotten the complicity of the Church with the military dictatorships and with repression. Some priests supported the dictatorships and kept silent on their violence. Others justified the repressive regimes. Some were present and unmoved at the interrogations and assassinations under torture.[57] Eleven years after the military dictatorships ended, when the curia named Father Christian von Wernich priest of the Bragado parish—62 miles from Buenos Aires—the town council declared him persona non grata and asked the bishop to remove him. The bishop refused because von Wernich, he pointed out, had not broken ecclesiastical law. But the people remembered his dark past as the chaplain to the Buenos Aires police (1976–1977) and did not forget his friendship with the former General Ramón Camps, one time chief of police of Buenos Aires Province. (Camps had been sentenced to twenty-five years in prison for numerous homicides, kidnappings, and tortures.) According to the testimony of a former police officer before CONADEP, after watching the torture and murder of two men and a woman, von Wernich said, "What we have done is necessary. It is a patriotic act. God knows that it is for the sake of the country." Relatives of eight of the disappeared also remembered that von Wernich visited them and claimed that he had seen their relatives leave for Uruguay and assured them that they were safe. Because of his involvement in the repressive regime he was subpoenaed to testify at the trials of the military officers.[58]

In December 1988 came the news that von Wernich would celebrate a Mass with Bishop Gillian at the Church of Santa Rosa in Bragado. More than 2,000 people were waiting for him outside the church. When a car carrying a priest pulled up, the crowd pounced on the priest shouting "Assassin, torturer, where is Cecilia?" (A twenty-five-year-old woman of Bragado who was tortured and disappeared). A woman dealt him two blows. As one woman kicked him in the testicles, another shouted, "That's not von Wernich!" Bishop Gillian, who was mistaken for von Wernich, entered the church doubled over in pain, according to the Uruguayan weekly *Brecha*.[59]

In January 1989, during the last year of Alfonsín's administration, a serious energy crisis was brought on by a prolonged drought. The country was half paralyzed. The government had to order the closing of its offices, banks, and many businesses; clinics and hospitals had to cut back their services. Food was rotting in the supermarkets, and industry reported daily losses in the millions. The government lost between $15 million and $42 million a day. The country blamed Alfonsín for not having foreseen this emergency, which had been predicted months earlier by experts. He said he was not the only one responsible, since the crisis was due to a succession of errors going back decades.[60]

The presidential election campaign took place in the midst of this crisis. There was profound national unrest because of the lamentable state of the economy. There were protest demonstrations, marches by housewives banging pots and pans, and supermarket lootings. Four days before the election the economy was pegged to the dollar. Faced with the precipitous fall of the austral (the new monetary unit that replaced the peso) and the minute-to-minute oscillation in the exchange rate, people did all their business with the green dollar bill.

Carlos Saúl Menem—the Peronist candidate for president—threatened to bring Alfonsín before a political court for his "ill-fated" political economy. There was a change in the ministry of finance, and the indices exploded again, without anyone's being able to explain why. Antonio Troccoli, a former minister of the interior, suggested that the only recourse left to the Argentines was prayer.

The general feeling was one of standing at the edge of an abyss. Alfonsín lost control of the economy and the country. The newspapers were more concerned with the price hikes and the ups and downs of the dollar than with the campaign. This disillusionment with Alfonsín worked against Eduardo Angeloz, the URD candidate. On May 14 people came out in droves to vote. Carlos Saúl Menem, Peronist, populist, and demagogue, won 48.7 percent of the vote against Angeloz's 37.3 percent. Peronists in several cities celebrated Menem's victory with an outpouring of joy. The following day the country returned to its harsh reality.

The economic situation deteriorated by the hour. Alfonsín announced a plan for a "war economy," with new taxes, sole control of the exchange rate, and reductions in public spending, but he offered increases in retirement benefits and family aid. While he was proposing these measures, the people in the city of Rosario looted supermarkets. The following day, faced with another wave of looting, which was beginning to spread throughout the country—leaving many dead and hundreds of wounded—Alfonsín decreed a thirty-day state of siege.

It became clear that Alfonsín's resignation was more than a rumor. He announced that he had reached an agreement with Menem for the good of Argentina and that he would resign before completing his term. To get around the legal questions raised by this unusual case, he and Menem agreed that he would renounce the presidency before congress, and that congress would confirm Menem. And that was how it was done.

MENEM: A PARDON AND A FORGETTING

On July 8, 1989, five months before Alfonsín's presidential term was due to end, Menem assumed the presidency of Argentina. He agreed to take the reins of power in a moment of severe crisis because there was no alternative. He took the oath of office before his brother Eduardo, president of the senate.

In his inaugural address Menem announced that the country would experience a difficult, costly, and harsh adjustment. "I can offer the people only sacrifice, work and hope. We have come to say to Argentina, rise and walk. Argentines, on your feet to bring an end to our crisis." In a clear message to the armed forces he assured them that "among all Argentines we will find a definitive and lasting solution to the wounds that have not yet healed. We shall not rouse the ghosts of the struggle; we shall serenade the spirit." He received a lengthy ovation.[61] Afterward, in a brief ceremony at the Casa Rosada, he received the baton and the presidential sash from Alfonsín. The people's fury and frustration poured over Alfonsín. They sent him off with insults, shouting, "Son of a bitch!" He left exhausted, with dark bags under his eyes. In spite of the catastrophic end to his term, he had ensured the survival of the state of law, representative democratic institutions, and civil rights and liberties to the end of his mandate. Many gave him due credit.

In three months Menem pardoned hundreds of officers who had been tried and convicted on charges of human-rights violations, along with 435 *carapintadas*, people responsible for many uprisings during Alfonsín's term, and those guilty of the military defeat in the Malvinas. He also pardoned imprisoned guerrillas. (Mario Firmenich, the top Montonero leader who was serving a thirty-year term, was not included.) The officers were free and exempted from any lawsuits brought against them in the civilian courts. "I know there will be discontent, as there is in all things in life, but I am also convinced that there are millions of Argentines who applaud these measures," Menem remarked.[62]

At the end of December, Menem pardoned Videla, Viola, Massera, Suárez Mason (all former members of the military juntas), and Camps, as well as Firmenich. Opinion polls showed that between 60 and 80 percent were opposed to pardoning these officers, who were responsible for one of the greatest tragedies in Argentine history. The transfer of the officers to the Campo de Mayo—the place where they were to be notified of their release—was carried out in the greatest secrecy and under heavy security. Menem did not want it to become a media spectacle. *Página 12*, a center-left daily, boasted the headline, "Nothing Happened Here."

Other writers might dwell on Menem's economic successes during the early years of his government and what would ensue thereafter. But open wounds remained. In March 1989—the anniversary of Videla's coup—mass demonstrations took place in Buenos Aires, again demanding that the cases of the pardoned officers be reopened, and the Chamber of Deputies repealed the Full Stop laws by a large majority. Time did nothing to ease the heavy consciences of some of the perpetrators. Former officers and priests gradually disclosed hair-raising aspects of the "internal war" against subversion in which they had taken part. The people continued to demand justice, and the Mothers and Grandmothers of the Plaza de Mayo—symbols of the national conscience—continued to march as a demand that their sons, daughters, and grandchildren be returned to them alive.

BRAZIL UNDER ITS "OWN" DOCTRINE

During the first months of the military governments of the so-called revolution—better known as the National Security doctrine dictatorships—the Brazilian press kept count of more than 25,000 arrests and published hundreds of witness accounts of torture cases. These data contrasted with the official statistics, which claimed only 4,700 arrests for political crimes and no deaths in prison ("because there is no torture in Brazil") during thirteen years of dictatorship.[63]

Brazil entered the 1970s under the iron hand of General Emilio Garrastazú Médici (1969–1974)—the third "revolutionary" government—with its international image seriously diminished by the brutal repression of these governments. The military muzzled the press with strict official censorship, preventing it from reporting on matters relating to public order. Serious human rights violations by the military regimes were denounced by human-rights organizations in the country and abroad, as well as by national and foreign jurists, the international press, from the pulpits and the hierarchy of the Brazilian Catholic Church, in pastoral letters, and in public statements. The world was aware of what was happening in Brazil.

The country's negative foreign image worried Médici and other generals, who recognized that the insurgency and social unrest, which continued despite repressive measures, were due to the profound inequalities and injustices in the country's society, and they believed that a change of policies was necessary. To improve Brazil's image, Médici promised to end torture, "decontract" the repression, attempt to stop the activities of the "death squad" (a clandestine organization responsible for many crimes), and narrow the gap between rich and poor through social integration and mass participation in development programs. To counter the accusations that the military had "handed over" Brazil to the United States and the transnational corporations, he quietly adopted a policy of nationalism and greater opening toward Latin America.[64]

Promises were one thing, but reality was another. Médici, a firm believer in the National Security doctrine, issued executive decrees and introduced constitutional amendments to legitimize the concentration of power in the executive branch and reduce that of the courts and the congress. He dealt with questions of national security by means of "secret or confidential decrees." But the military's lax interpretation of the concept "threat to security" covered everything that displeased them at any level.

The repression of Médici's regime was more brutal than that of his predecessors. Cases of torture in the detention centers rose at alarming rates. He also reinstated the death penalty (suspended since 1822) and established a policy of banishment for those deemed "undesirable and harmful" to national security. In the first three months of his government there were more than 600 cases of torture, among them fifty-two police and military officers accused of subversion who were tortured by their colleagues. Cardinal Paul Arns, Archbishop of São Paulo, asked his priests to pray for them.

The Church hierarchy was the main voice of denunciations of official repression. Cardinal Arns and Dom Helder Camara, Archbishop of Olinda and Recife—Brazil's impoverished northeast—and other bishops never ceased to condemn the regime's brutality, from which members of the Church were not exempt. Some of the priests and lay persons working with the Christian grassroots communities among the poor were arrested and tortured.[65] The Brazilian bar association published the results of an investigation into the activities of the death squad—which included among its members active and retired police officers, some of the highest rank—and revealed the names of sixty police and military torturers, the methods they used, and the deaths under torture in the prisons. This information was obtained from a document, signed by thirty-five political prisoners, in which they recounted the tortures they suffered in the detention centers.

Although the Brazilian guerrilla groups had neither the size nor the impact of the Tupamaros in Uruguay or the Montoneros and the ERP in Argentina, they became a huge problem for the military, and at times they shook the regime with the international repercussions their attacks caused. Médici had to deal with the abduction in 1969 of United States Ambassador Charles Elbrick by a commando from two guerrilla groups (a woman guerrilla had seduced his guards in order to procure information on his comings and goings). This event caught Médici off guard. He had just assumed the presidency, because the former president, Arturo da Costa e Silva, was forced to resign after suffering a cerebral hemorrhage. To prevent harm coming to the ambassador, the military bowed to the guerrillas' demands. In March 1970 guerrillas kidnapped the Japanese consul in São Paulo and the West German ambassador—they were outraged by his arrogance—and later the Swiss ambassador. The diplomats were freed after a few days, since the government kept its promise to free the imprisoned guerrillas, transfer them to other countries (Mexico, Algeria, and Chile), and publish their communiqués. The Swiss ambassador was held for forty days because the negotiations with the government on the list of prisoners—there were seventy—took longer. Such blows humiliated the regime and called international attention to the brutal repression used by the Brazilian military dictatorships.

Médici aspired to turn Brazil into a world power and a leader in Latin America. Washington had the same desires. "As Brazil goes, so goes South America," said President Nixon, encouraging Médici on his official visit to Washington in 1971. Brazil was a paradise to its investors and the multinationals and was the United States' principal ally in Latin America.

With these dreams of grandeur and "in connection with the triumphant extravagance of his government," Médici undertook the construction of a gigantic bridge between Río de Janeiro and Niteroi; of the trans-Amazon superhighway; and of soccer stadiums in several cities, since soccer was the favorite sport of the Brazilian people.[66]

The construction of the superhighway through the jungle, important as it was, resulted in enormous tragedies. It meant the violent confiscation of the lands of indigenous people and settlers and massacres when they tried to resist, and the cutting down of the rain forest caused irreparable ecological damage. In April 1972, when construction began, a new armed group—the Fuerzas Guerrilleras de Araguaía (The Guerrilla Forces of Araguaía)—took up the defense of indigenous peoples and campesinos to prevent them from losing their lands.[67]

Médici also aspired to turn Brazil into a nuclear power. He refused to sign the Tlatelolco Treaty banning nuclear proliferation in Latin America; in 1975 he signed an agreement on nuclear cooperation and technical assistance with West Germany and another with Israel for the exploitation of Brazil's uranium reserves. Brazil developed its military industries and became an arms exporter.

The so-called Brazilian miracle aroused international admiration. It fostered growth that put the country in eighth place in world industrial development, by means of a high foreign debt and the opening of the country to foreign investors. It attracted such investment with broad fiscal incentives, ten-year tax exemptions, free exportation of profits, and the "climate of political tranquillity" it offered. Much of the multimillion-dollar foreign investment came from the United States. There was an influx of its multinationals, which made inroads into key sectors of Brazil's economy. In five years economic growth reached the record annual figure of 11.4 percent.[68]

The "miracle's" cost was the dependency that the multimillion-dollar investments imposed on the government, since it was obliged to consult with the multinational corporations and their governments about its own economic policies.[69] Such policies led to an excessive concentration of wealth—the greatest in Brazil's history—that benefited powerful wealthy minorities, such as bankers, landholders, and national and foreign businessmen, and widened the gap between rich and poor. In 1974, Médici's last year in office, the "miracle" stopped being miraculous. The growth index fell to 4 percent, and the following year to 3 percent. An economic recession began, inflation reached 100 percent, and the foreign debt came in at $21 billion, an unpayable sum.

Impoverishment hit not only the lower classes but also the middle classes and business sectors. A growing mass movement protested the critical economic situation and the brutal repression. Continuous strikes, work stoppages, land takeovers, and student and popular demonstrations demanded justice, the restoration of democracy, and an end to repressive measures and the suppression of the Institutional Acts. The violent opposition was not against Médici alone but also against the military dictatorships.

THE BIRTH OF DEMOCRATIZATION

When General Ernesto Geisel (1974–1979)—the fourth National Security doctrine president—assumed power, all that remained of the insurgent groups were the Fuerzas Guerrilleras de Araguaía. They were in the forests defending indigenous peoples and campesinos against the despoiling of their lands and the army's brutal repression.

The military governments sustained themselves by terror. As social tensions grew and deepened, they passed laws and issued decrees and institutional acts to solidify their power and legalize the repression. But this thicket of new laws, adopted in the heat of action, led to contradictions within the military establishment. Not all officers were in agreement with these policies. One of the detractors was Geisel.

Geisel knew the world was aware that the price of internal "order" had been paid with brutal repression. He could no longer speak of the economic "miracle," which had ceased to exist, having been artificially sustained by an astronomical foreign debt. In his inaugural address he spoke of the gradual "redemocratization" of the country, of a more open and secure society, letting up on press censorship, and involving civilian society in plans for development. The foreign press reported his speech in the optimistic opinion that it signaled a promise of change. Geisel understood that retreat was necessary but that he must do so without creating conflict in the armed forces.[70] He opted for the policy of "decompression." He lessened press censorship and police repression and opened the political arena to the Partido Movimiento Democrático Brasileño (MDB: Brazilian Democratic Movement Party), the only legal opposition party. The MDB was not a threat to the military, since the government controlled the majority in congress through the Alianza Nacional Renovadora Party (ARENA, National Alliance for Renewal), which it created.

But in November 1974, in elections to the parliament and provincial assemblies (the first direct legislative elections under the military regimes), the MDB almost doubled its representation in the senate and the chamber of deputies and defeated ARENA in the provincial assemblies of São Paulo, Río de Janeiro, and Río Grande do Sul, which were the most important ones. The government was alarmed by these results, since the MDB could win in the election of governors, which was scheduled for the following year.[71]

Geisel found that sectors of the military opposed his open policies and boycotted his plans to lessen the repression; his main objective was to improve Brazil's international image. The army command did not allow him to control the security apparatus, which continued acting on its own, and its actions continued to be denounced in the foreign press. The arrest and torture of a former United States Methodist missionary, an occasional correspondent for *Time* and the Associated Press, were a great scandal because of Washington's vigorous protest. Such acts worried Geisel because they damaged his government's image.

Cardinal Arns, Archbishop of São Paulo, a harsh critic of the military, gave Geisel a list of twenty-two "disappeared" persons—twenty-one of whom had been taken under his government—and asked that he investigate them. Geisel promised to do so, but he could not fulfill his promise since he could not control the security services.[72]

The murder of the journalist Vladimir Herzog in the São Paulo military prison in October 1975 caused a great national and international scandal. The official version was that Herzog had committed suicide. No one believed that story. Cardinal Arns rejected the idea of suicide from the pulpit of the Cathedral[73] and later officiated at a "dramatic ecumenical funeral"—Herzog was Jewish—in the Cathedral.

The military commission named by the government to investigate Herzog's death "confirmed" the suicide version, and the investigation was suspended. The "suicides" in the detention centers usually happened in the São Paulo and Río de Janeiro barracks. Whenever an officer was found responsible for such a death, he was relieved of his duties at worst.[74]

In 1976 a wave of repressive measures was unleashed against servants of the Church. In July Father Rodolfo Lunkenbein, a German missionary working with indigenous people in the Amazon, was murdered. In October the police killed Father Joao Bosco Penido Brunier for having protested the torture of a woman. In September Dom Adriano Hypolito, Bishop of Nova Iguazú, was kidnapped, beaten, and left naked on a highway.

In spite of his declared intentions to abolish the repression, Geisel made use of the Institutional Act #5 (AI-5), a monument to military arbitrariness, when it suited him. In 1977, empowered by this act, he closed the congress when the MDB refused to approve a judicial reform proposed by the government. The MDB held that it made no sense to approve the measure until the government abolished AI-5 and the National Security law.[75]

Still, Geisel's "decompression" policies opened the door to popular and student demonstrations, supported by vast sectors of the people and the Catholic Church hierarchy, protesting the repressive measures and demanding the restoration of democracy. For the first time under the military regimes, the media also denounced official violence and pointed to the army's repressive apparatus as responsible for this violence. In May 1978, in a public declaration, the National Law School asked for a return to the state of law, a new constitution, amnesty, and the complete revision of labor legislation.

Day by day the government felt stronger pressure from the people and the growing demand that it permit a return to democracy and suppress the repressive laws, especially AI-5, since they impeded the democratization of the country.

The weight of the opposition MDB party was strong enough for the congress to approve a constitutional amendment to abolish AI-5, reestablish habeas corpus for political detainees, cease media censorship, do away with the death penalty and life sentences, and restore the powers of the judiciary. The president could no longer order congress closed as before, or deprive members of congress of their mandate or the citizens their political rights. Certain articles of this amendment, however, gave new, extensive powers to the executive branch. The Lawyers' College and the opposition said that they were "the resurrection of AI-5."

Geisel reestablished political rights for 120 persons—most of them in exile—but he excluded eight prominent political figures, among them Leonel Brizola, governor of Río Grande do Sul, and Luis Carlos Prestes, the former secretary general of the Communist Party, both in exile.[76]

Geisel chose General Joao Baptista Figueiredo, the ARENA (official party) candidate, to succeed him in the presidency. It was not a direct election: Figueiredo was elected in the electoral college 355 to 266. It continued to be the job of the electoral college, imposed by the military after the coup against Goulart in 1964, to control the election of presidents.

Figueiredo was the fifth and last president (1979–1985) of the so-called revolution. He promised to continue Geisel's policies of political opening and gradual democratization. He granted amnesty for "political crimes," approved by the congress in August 1979—it did not include terrorist acts or armed resistance against the government—and restored the political rights suppressed by the Institutional Acts. Many exiles returned to the country, among them Leonel Brizola, Luis Carlos Prestes, and Mario Moreira Alves, a journalist and member of congress. Communists and Trotskyists also returned. Brazil showed a democratic face for the first time in many years. Figueiredo's popularity was enormous, both at home and abroad.[77]

Figueiredo assumed office in the midst of a massive strike by 160,000 workers in the metallurgical industry in São Paulo, supported by workers from other industries and vast numbers of the population. Social unrest, which increased under Geisel's government, gained strength with the support of the Church, led by Cardinal Arns. Between January and October of 1979 there were 400 work stoppages in Río de Janeiro, Sao Paulo, Belo Horizonte, and Río Grande do Sul by workers in the transportation, steel, education, sanitation, construction, stevedore, trucking, banking, and telecommunications industries and by public officials. Business leaders opted to solve the labor conflicts in direct negotiations with the workers, since they understood that repression, which had been used, was not adequate. Such a policy favored the workers.

The economy was in a spiral of deterioration because of the oil crisis, the effects of a worldwide recession, and the cost of the "boom" connected with the "miracle," based on the crushing foreign debt. The economic indices were catastrophic: the fiscal deficit, inflation, unemployment, and the cost of living were at their worst in many years. There was flight of capital; the country's reserves dwindled to $2.9 billion, and foreign investment fell from $10.1 billion in 1978 to $6.5 billion in 1979.[78] The greatest cost of the "miracle" was the miserable poverty of the lowest classes. The minister of planning announced that the "miracle" was dead. But the economic elite, who had lived through eleven years when industry and business flourished and the powerful classes pulled down large profits, did not want to hear bad news. The minister was made to resign. Figueiredo named Delfim Neto, the architect of the "miracle," in his place; he was welcomed with unbridled enthusiasm by this elite.

Figueiredo enjoyed a degree of popularity not given to his predecessors. Civil advances continued under Figueiredo. In 1982, in the first direct gubernatorial elections under the military regime, the opposition candidates won once again, with 59 percent of the vote. They won nine states, including São Paulo, Río, Minas Gerais, and Paraná. Leonel Brizola was elected governor of Río. Nevertheless, the MDB remained the minority party in congress and in the electoral college, which was responsible for electing the president. A presidential election was slated for 1984.

The economic situation continued to be difficult in the extreme. In January 1983 Figueiredo signed an agreement with the IMF and obtained an enormous loan. Reputable economists were alarmed and questioned the deal. The conditions the IMF imposed on Brazil—austerity and a drastic reduction in the swollen inflation rate and the public deficit—were not realistic. The economists insisted Figueiredo had committed the country to the impossible. In September, Figueiredo signed another, less stringent agreement. An official of the IMF declared that the Fund had adjusted to the country's reality. In 1984 Brazil registered the fourth year of reduction in per capita income.[79]

When corruption scandals and embezzlement of huge sums involving people in the upper levels of government made the front pages of the newspapers, the government was struck a severe blow. The accusations were leveled not only at Figueiredo but at the armed forces and the military dictatorship as well.[80] Figueiredo called for presidential elections. On January 15, 1985, the electoral college chose the opposition candidates Tancredo Neves and José Sarney by 400 out of 606 votes. The official candidate, Paulo Maluf, received 100 votes.

Neves promised to redemocratize the country, achieve economic growth by controlling inflation, and stop the "bleeding of foreign debt interest payments" with the "philosophy" of negotiation. He offered to convene a constitutional convention in 1987 to set the rules of the game for the new republic and remove the "authoritarian rubble" without revenge. He promised to promote social justice. He declared that the social debt was at least as explosive as the foreign debt—the world's largest—and needed to be dealt with immediately.

Neves died before his inauguration, and the people wept "as if they had lost a savior." José Sarney, his running mate, stepped into the presidency by constitutional mandate. The people did not believe in him, since he was "one of the most conspicuous civilian servants" of the military. "He directed the parliamentary battle that defeated the constitutional amendment reestablishing direct elections . . . an action responsible for the people's bitterness."[81] They accepted him because it was the law.

BRAZILIAN SUB-IMPERIALISM

Brazil was Latin America's great power. It was the largest and richest country, and it exercised undeniable leadership. Its foreign policy had been an example of balance, independence, and pragmatism, directed toward the economic and commercial good of the country. The same policy was followed by the military. Though Médici, without taking positions on principle, supported Portugal's policy against liberation movements in its overseas provinces; Brazil was the first to recognize the MPLA's victory in Angola; it maintained a strong and fruitful commercial exchange with South Africa—a quarter of its trade was with Africa—but condemned apartheid.[82]

With its neighbors it maintained a policy of imperialism, intervention through investments by the private sector—especially in the banking industry—plans for the exploitation of their riches in the construction of large-scale engineering projects, and it pushed campesino emigration toward the frontier districts, employing the theory of "living borders" as a means of transgressing geo-political boundaries; but covertly the ploy also affected the country's internal affairs. In 1971 Brazil collaborated in the preparation of General Hugo Bánzer's coup in Bolivia against General Juan José Torres, who was considered a leftist. This coup was a military conspiracy by Brazil, Argentina, Bolívía, and the United States.[83] Brazil's intervention was so open that it moved President Allende to exclaim, "Chile now has a border with Brazil."

Relations with the United States fluctuated. In 1964 the United States Embassy conspired with the coup leaders to overthrow Joao Goulart. Later under military dictatorships there was an invasion of American advisers in Brazil—part of United States aid—who were placed in key positions in the administration, the armed forces, the police, and the security forces. American counterinsurgency policy and the National Security doctrine were identical.

To the United States, Brazil was the Latin American superpower and its most important ally in the continent. Nixon's secretary of state, Henry Kissinger, went on a lightning tour through several countries in Latin America in February 1976, and he told Geisel that Brazil was the "great power . . . called to join the club of rich nations." He signed an agreement with Geisel that covered questions of economics, politics, security, education, law, culture, and technology. They also spoke about the South Atlantic Treaty Organization (SATO), which was opposed by some segments of the Brazilian military. In spite of all these measures, Nixon froze aid to Brazil when the military passed the Institutional Act #5 (AI-5), which granted absolute power to the military regimes.

With the arrival of Jimmy Carter in the White House in 1977, relations worsened because of his defense of human rights, which these regimes seriously violated. He talked of cutting off aid to Brazil. Geisel considered this threat an interference in Brazil's internal affairs and broke off the bilateral military accord (MAP). United States military and economic aid was suspended. To the opposition, on the other hand, Carter was a beacon of hope.

Brazil sought closer cooperation with Europe and Japan, developed its own military industry—it became an arms exporter—and undertook nuclear programs in partnership with West Germany (Washington tried to hamper them) and Israel to exploit its uranium reserves. With the arrival of Ronald Reagan, relations once again turned excellent. Both spiritedly waved their anti-Communist and counterinsurgent banners. They were birds of a feather.

URUGUAY AND ITS "INTERNAL WAR"

In 1970, the last year of Jorge Pacheco Areco's administration, Uruguay was afflicted with a severe crisis: economic disintegration, social agitation, union struggles, and growing guerrilla activity. The Tupamaros held the government in check.

The country was suffering the effects of ten years of economic recession. Inflation, the fiscal deficit, and foreign debt were on the rise, currency was losing value at an accelerating rate (from 6 pesos to the dollar in 1959, it dropped to 400 in 1970).[84] There was flight of capital and a high unemployment rate. The salaried, lower and middle classes, the most strongly affected, protested with strikes, work stoppages, and large demonstrations. Pacheco ruled with a heavy hand. The country continued under the Security Measures (MPS) he had imposed in 1968 to meet the challenge of guerrilla activity and the social and student unrest. The majorities in the National (White) and Colorado (Red) parties approved the repressive measures the government asked for, even though they curtailed civil liberties: they limited freedom of the press and of association, barred the holding of meetings, and prohibited union activities. The exemplary Uruguayan democratic tradition disappeared. Without direct opposition, since the parties were in shambles and leaderless, and with the support of powerful political and economic sectors, Pacheco slowly strengthened a de facto dictatorship. The common terms were that he was imposing a "constitutional dictatorship" or a "fake" democracy.

In Montevideo—the main scene of violence—there was an atmosphere of anxiety and insecurity, since the repressive measures were not against subversion alone, but also against popular, union, and leftist movements and organizations. The union movement, the Confederación Nacional de Trabajadores (CNT: National Workers' Federation)—made up of most of the country's unions—and the Tupamaros, who enjoyed enormous sympathy among students and in segments of the political, professional, intellectual, and leftist movement sectors, opposed the repression. They were the stream where the guerrilla fish swam.

The Tupamaros' daring blows against the financial, industrial, and banking industries elicited tremendous enthusiasm among the popular majorities, since they exposed the corruption of the government and of powerful economic sectors. In their assaults on these institutions the Tupamaros appropriated millions in money as well as documents, which they released to the press. Fraud and the names of persons involved in these crimes came to light. Such scandals shook the banking system. The Tupamaros became "one of the central vectors of the political landscape" in Uruguay.[85]

The government did not succeed in putting an end to labor agitation, or in putting down the growing guerrilla activities. In April 1970 the Tupamaros executed Police Inspector Héctor Morán Charquero, whom they accused of instituting torture. In July they kidnapped the British Ambassador and three diplomats, and in August the Tupamaros abducted and executed Dan Mitrione, an American security agent who was advising the Uruguayan police. This last action was traumatic for Pacheco, since the United States did not want him to negotiate with the guerrillas. When Mitrione's corpse appeared—with bullet wounds of various calibers—Pacheco decreed a "state of exception." In daring operations in September 1971, the guerrillas freed their companions from three prisons, and in another action they freed 100 guerrillas from the Punta Carreras prison without firing a single shot. In April 1972—their d-day—they executed four people they accused of being members of the death squad. This was their response to the assassination of three guerrillas by paramilitary groups. The appearance of these ultraright groups—a new phenomenon in Uruguay—marked the beginning of the dirty war against the left.[86]

Uruguayan society was alarmed by this violence, and the majority in the congress approved the government's repressive measures. Between September 1972 and March 1973 it agreed on three occasions to retain the MPS security measures to fight subversion.[87]

In order to participate in the impending presidential elections, political segments created the Frente Amplio (Broad Front). It included the Communist Party (illegal but tolerated), movements and parties of the left, the Christian Democrats, factions of the Colorado and Blanco (National) Parties, independent sectors, and retired military officers. The Front was supported by the powerful CNT and the Tupamaros. Its candidate was Liber Seregni, a prestigious retired general. The Blanco Party's candidate was Wilson Ferreira Aldunate. The official candidate, supported by Pacheco, was Juan María Bordaberry.

Two months before the elections Pacheco gave carte blanche to the armed forces to fight the guerrillas. The MPS and the "State of Exception" gave legal sanctions to unleash brutal repression against subversive activities, popular and union organizations and their leaders, politicians of the left, and the Front. More than 300 attempts were made on its members' lives, among them Seregni. Clandestine paramilitary groups of the ultraright took part in this violence.

As in the rest of Latin America, the Uruguayan military and security forces received training and were aided by advisers from the United States. This had been Mitrione's mission.[88]

WHERE THE GENERAL RULES, BORDABERRY DOES NOT

In October 1971, amid a climate of violence, the presidential elections were held—the most turbulent in Uruguayan history, according to many observers. José María Bordaberry, the official candidate, was elected by a margin of 100,000 votes over Ferreira Aldunate, the Blanco (National) Party candidate, who claimed that Bordaberry had won a "pyrrhic, dirty, and fraudulent victory." Though McCarthyite attacks (another new phenomenon to Uruguay) were in abundance during the campaign against Seregni, the candidate of the Broad Front, he registered 20 percent of the vote nationally and 30 percent in Montevideo (which had the highest turnout). In spite of this advance for the opposition, official power was not weakened.[89] Bordaberry's victory strengthened the ultraright. A member of the landholding oligarchy, a pre-Vatican Council Catholic, and a man with fascist tendencies (he professed to admire the Brazilian dictatorship as a "political model"), he began his presidential term of six years (1971–1977) as a continuation of Pacheco's regime.

Extreme guerrilla activity, the popular mobilization promoted by the Broad Front, and the campaign of union agitation launched by the CNT—work stoppages, protests, and strikes—to demand agrarian reform, an increase in salaries, and price controls, all gave the military and Bordaberry reason to increase the repression. Within a week of taking office Bordaberry sent to the senate a proposal for a Law on State Security and Public Order—more severe than the MPS and with greater resources for the military—which was immediately passed. This law paved the way for the military to move into power.

After a national work stoppage of heretofore unseen proportions and four guerrilla operations in April 1972, in which the Tupamaros executed members of the regime they accused of belonging to the death squad, the army initiated a wave of raids and arrests. It persuaded congress to enact, immediately, a law declaring the country to be in "a state of internal warfare," though such a concept did not exist in the Uruguayan constitution.[90] The deputies from the Broad Front were the only ones to vote against it. The government suspended guarantees of individual freedoms and expedited a decree making political crimes and subversive actions "acts of war," which would be tried in military courts.

Under the "state of internal warfare" the armed forces drowned the country in blood. The war was carried out indiscriminately against the left. The army leveled its party and union headquarters, systematically arrested hundreds of people, used torture during interrogations, and killed or disappeared activists and supposed guerrillas. Nine members of the Communist Party were killed in their offices, and Tupamaros were massacred where they were found. In November, according to military sources, sixty-two guerrillas were killed and 2,873 were captured. Eighteen soldiers also died in these confrontations.

The government was in the hands of the military, and Bordaberry became increasingly unpopular and isolated. Many called for his resignation.[91]

The traditional parties, who approved Pacheco and Bordaberry's antidemocratic and fascistic measures, were now alarmed by the limitless repression exercised by the military. Bordaberry gave them a free hand to "control public order," a function not contemplated in the constitution. The traditional parties were alarmed by this increase in militarism, but they lacked the power to stop it. The political class, increasingly marginalized, saw that the military was invading its territory. The threat was real. Some attempted to retake power with a timid antimilitarist campaign. Still, when Bordaberry needed the politicians' backing to parry the public show of contempt by the army and the air force, they would not give it. After the military refused to follow Bordaberry's order to oust the recently named minister of defense, they called for the President's resignation and a national inquiry.

Without an opposition, the way was opened for the military to intervene in the management of the state. They dealt the first blow. In February 1973 they signed the Boisso Lanza Pact with Bordaberry (named after the military base where they met), which allowed them to take control of parts of the administration. They created the Consejo de Seguridad Nacional (COSENA: National Security Council), composed of the president; the ministers of defense, foreign relations, economy, and planning; and the commanders of the three branches of the military. This pact reduced the President's formal powers—very little real power remained to him—but Bordaberry did not protest, the parliament and the political parties remained silent, and the left showed a "relative passivity and neutrality."[92]

With extraconstitutional powers and a free rein, the military dealt the second blow. At dawn on June 27, 1973, they placed Montevideo under military rule, and a 7:00 AM radio broadcast announced an executive order closing the congress. The announcement declared that it would be replaced by a council of state and that the constitution would be reformed and approved by a national plebiscite. The same night Bordaberry took responsibility, in a broadcast on all the communications media, for this unique coup, which established an equally unique civilian-military dictatorship: Bordaberry would continue as the constitutional president, but the armed forces held the power. He had become a puppet. The people said, "Where the General rules, Bordaberry does not."[93]

This second blow caused protest from the parties and the Broad Front. The CNT called a strike, which was joined by segments of the people and of the left. It lasted fifteen days and paralyzed the country. Seregni called on Bordaberry to resign.[94] The opposition had no success, and the country returned to routine under the consolidated "civilian"-military dictatorship. The political class and the opportunistic and "pragmatic" middle class began to empower themselves through compliance with the regime.[95] In July Seregni was arrested; he remained imprisoned for more than ten years.

The military began to destroy democratic institutions. They closed the congress for refusing to expel Enrique Erro, a senator from the Broad Front, whom they called a traitor. They outlawed the CNT, prohibited political activity by the parties, shut down independent newspapers, imposed censorship on the rest, intervened in the university, and declared the opposition a danger to state security. The prisons proved to be too small. They set up concentration camps and detention centers, including railway cars and abandoned boats. "A new prison opens every month. This is what the economists call a development plan," wrote historian and writer Eduardo Galeano.[96]

In Uruguay, as in Argentina and Brazil, "suicides" and "death while attempting to escape" became routine in the prisons. And the disappearances, arbitrary arrests, and denunciations of torture in the detention centers mounted. As in Argentina, raids were carried out with beatings, looting, and property destruction, and the perpetrators did not bother to erase the traces they left. There was no danger to them, for no one investigated these crimes.

Bordaberry, still occupying the seat of the presidency, sought closer friendships with the neighboring military dictatorships. In April 1976 he presented the Great Cross of Protectors of Free Peoples (a medal he created) to the Chilean dictator Augusto Pinochet, on whose shoulders rested the assassination and disappearance of thousands of Chileans, and Alfredo Stroessner, who suffocated Paraguay with his dictatorship for twenty years. He visited the Bolivian dictator Hugo Bánzer, who came to power in one of the bloodiest coups in his country's rocky history, and invited Ernesto Geisel, the Brazilian "thug," to Montevideo. This high-level social life was all he had left.

More than a hundred Uruguayans living in exile in Argentina, Chile, and Brazil were assassinated, abducted, or disappeared in operations coordinated among their security forces. Also in 1976, Héctor Gutiérrez Ruíz, President of the Uruguayan chamber of deputies, and Zelmar Michelini, a longtime senator, were assassinated in Buenos Aires within two hours of each other. The same day in the same city the Uruguayan doctor Manuel Liberoff "disappeared." The Argentine minister of defense claimed that these assassinations were "an Uruguayan operation" but that he was still not certain whether they were "official or not."[97]

The upheavals in Uruguay went beyond mere bloodshed. The civilian-military government became deeply immersed in a sort of cultural revolution. They burned thousands of books, prohibited certain songs (including three of Gardel's tangos), closed plays, decreed prison terms of one to six years for those who sang the national anthem in public ceremonies with a blatant emphasis on the phrase "Tremble, tyrants," and for anyone who disparaged the armed forces. The university was under military control and it remained closed for several months; the military imprisoned professors and deans and closed the faculties of the social sciences and economics for being "subversive" as well as the institutes for scientific and economic research. No meeting could be held, not even a birthday party, without a permit from the police.[98]

By 1976, the country was bankrupt. The foreign debt stood at $1 billion. The deficit, inflation, and unemployment were growing at an accelerated rate. The economy became denationalized, since important sectors passed into the hands of foreign capital and the multinational corporations. Beef—the main export—was controlled by United States and British capital, wool by the Dutch, leather and oils by the Belgians.

Uruguay became one huge prison. There were more than 8,000 political prisoners, and about 800,000 Uruguayans chose exile. With a population of 2.8 million, Uruguay set the record in Latin America for the per capita repression and exodus of its citizens. The country was emptying. The graffiti on a wall at the Carrasco International Airport in Montevideo read, "The last one to leave, turn off the light."[99] Someone else, who believed in the struggle, had written, "Comrade, don't go."

By 1976 the Tupamaros had been virtually disbanded by the brutal repression. Many died, others were rotting in prison, and still others were in exile. But sabotage against the government and the army and citizen resistance continued. There were more than fifty strikes in spite of the prohibition. The civilian-military dictatorship began to hit bottom. Its only support came from the far right and from members of the oligarchy connected to foreign and agro-export capital. No one could tolerate Bordaberry any longer, much less the military.

In 1976 Bordaberry was constrained by constitutional mandate to call elections. But they could not be held, because the military would not allow them. Before they could prohibit them, Bordaberry proscribed them absolutely. In June the military took control of the government but kept Bordaberry in the presidency. Weighed down by the military's misdeeds, which he endured in silence, and having been the butt of the people's jokes because of his ludicrous but harmful role, he finally resigned.

The council of state named Dr. Alberto Demichelli president by decree. On the day of his inauguration he signed Institutional Acts 1 and 2, suspending the elections that were to be held in November and creating the Council of the Nation as the highest government service. In September, when he refused to sign Institutional Act 4, which prohibited all political activity, the military ousted him and named Dr. Aparicio Méndez in his place. The military kept changing presidents in what seemed to be a political version of musical chairs.

Nothing remained of the state of law. The military assured its complete autonomy with an intricate tangle of laws and institutional acts. It had already removed the disaffected and the skeptics from its ranks. The international community, alarmed by what was happening in Uruguay, denounced the regime's brutality and demanded a return to democracy. International pressure and accusations of human-rights violations forced the military to take steps to improve its image. It decreed Institutional Act 5, which recognized human and individual rights.[100] This inadequate gesture fooled no one.

In May 1980 Méndez sent the proposal for the new constitution—written by the military—to the council of state. It was to be ratified by a national plebiscite. One article designated the national security council—controlled by the military—as part of the executive branch. Thus the participation of the armed forces in the government was assured. The presidential elections were scheduled for November 1981, with only one candidate and no participation by the left. In the 1986 elections two candidates would be allowed to run. The military mounted a great campaign seeking popular support for the new constitution, and only in the last few weeks did it allow limited propaganda from those who opposed it. The plebiscite—limited to a yes or no vote—was held in November, resulting in 58 percent against, and 42 percent in favor.[101]

This defeat at the voting booth weakened the military and stimulated popular protest against the dictatorship. The people and civilian movements

demanded a return to democracy. But the military was not inclined to negotiate. Instead, it imposed conditions and maintained its autonomy in the new
government.

The Blanco (national) and Colorado Parties did not accept the military's ulti-
matums or the changes the military wanted to impose on the constitution.
Dialogue was suspended. Repression and press censorship continued. In May
1984 a coalition of parties—Colorado, Blanco, Broad Front, and Civic Union—
published a statement demanding elections without restrictions or exclusion
of the parties of the left; the coalition further asked that any constitutional
reform be submitted to a plebiscite.

Ferreira Aldunate returned from exile, and the military imprisoned him.
The Blanco Party announced that it would not continue negotiating until
he was freed. In August they arrived at an agreement known as the Naval Club
Pact. The details were kept secret by both parties to the negotiations. It was
supposed that the parties guaranteed that they would not put military officers on trial and that they could leave their posts "with clean hands."[102]

Presidential elections were held in November. The candidacies of Ferreira
Aldunate—still in prison—and Seregni had been proscribed, as had participation by the Communist and leftist parties. Five thousand people were
refused the vote because of so-called political unfitness, as determined by the
military. Julio María Sanguinetti, the Colorado Party candidate, was elected
president. Although he was in the military's good graces, and the elections had
been far from democratic, his was a civil victory.

A "PROTECTED" DEMOCRACY?

Julio María Sanguinetti (1985–1990) was the first civilian president after twelve
years of military dictatorship. He took office in March. He wanted national
peace and a policy of "reparations for damages." He immediately restored to
their positions thousands of civil servants who had been dismissed by the military for political reasons, approved a law to release all political prisoners who
had been in prison for at least eleven years, and offered to revise the sentences
of those who were convicted of "blood crimes" and to count the years they
served in prison as double. Raúl Sendic, the top Tupamaro leader, who had
spent thirteen years in prison, was released.[103]

Sanguinetti faced an inevitable and dangerous situation with the military
establishment. The mass of people demanded that he try those responsible for
the dirty war. On this view, military officers who had committed serious vio-

lations against human rights ought to pay for their crimes. For an entire year this was the gist of the public debate. Because Sanguinetti knew that the opposition was weak and that the parties were splintered, he dropped the bomb: he proposed an amnesty conducive to "national coexistence."

Broad popular sectors, human-rights movements, relatives of the victims, the Broad Front, and the Tupamaros—legalized as a political party—protested. The atmosphere heated up when the military warned that it would not appear in court. The Blanco and Colorado Parties and the Broad Front suggested other forms of amnesty, but Sanguinetti presented congress with a proposal for a law titled Expiration of State Punishment, which was a renunciation by the state of the right to convict and penalize members of the armed forces, the security services, and the police indicted for political crimes. Astutely, he called it the National Conciliation Law; the people spoke of it as the Law of Impunity, or Full Stop. It was passed on December 22, 1986, by two thirds of the parliament. The Broad Front and one part of the Blanco Party voted against it.

A national movement led by Matilde Rodríguez Larreta (the widow of Héctor Gutiérrez Ruiz, the former president of the chamber of deputies, kidnapped and assassinated in Buenos Aires in 1978) and supported by the Broad Front, parts of the Blanco Party, and the Tupamaros, undertook a campaign to annul the Full Stop law in a plebiscite. Its slogans were "Equality for all before the law" and "Search for truth." Some parts of the military supported it because they wanted to cleanse their ranks and improve the bad image of the military institution.

The debate and propaganda for and against the amnesty lasted three years. On April 16, 1989, people voted yes or no in a referendum. The results were 52.62 percent in favor of keeping the amnesty and 40.1 percent against. The rest of the ballots were left blank or voided. In Montevideo, home to most of the population, the no vote won with 54 percent. There were no celebrations for the victory. A Montevideo newspaper headline read, "They Won But They Did Not Persuade." Those responsible for the dirty war could rest easy, as could the government.

On November 26, 1989, the Uruguayan people, who were paralyzed by apathy, went to the polls to elect a new president. The opposition candidate, Luis de Lacalle of the Blanco Party (of the center-right) won with 39 percent of the vote. The Colorado Party candidate, Jorge Battle, received 28 percent, and Liber Seregni of the Broad Front had 13 percent. De Lacalle was inaugurated in 1990, and Uruguay continued its journey along familiar democratic roads.

CHILE: THE MILITARY TAKEOVER

Because of its strong democratic tradition, Chile did not experience the political and social violence that plagued the rest of Latin America during the 1960s and early 1970s. It was a veritable paradise of tolerance. The Socialist and Communist Parties were able to carry on their recruiting activities and encountered no obstacles in putting their candidates up for election. Those persecuted by the dictatorships found refuge there. But the anti-Communist hysteria unleashed by Washington in response to the Cuban Revolution reached as far as these southern climes. The Kennedy administration feared victory by the Socialist candidate Salvador Allende in the presidential elections to be held in September 1964. The Chilean right and the United States transnational corporations with branches in the country shared this fear, and they fed on each other. A plot against Allende, sponsored by the Christian Democratic Party, was set into motion. Its candidate, Eduardo Frei, launched a tough and well-financed campaign ($2.6 million, half from the CIA) portraying Allende as a danger to Chile and all of Latin America. His government, it warned, would be Cuban-style, and Communism and subversion would spread throughout the continent in a domino effect.

In 1963 the CIA began to offer money to political leaders, democratic forces, parties from the center and the right, newspapers and journalists, and individuals it considered "useful" to the cause, according to William Colby, chief of operations in the CIA (Nixon named him director in 1973).[104] The Pulitzer Prize–winning American journalist Thomas Powers wrote that Chile received more aid per capita from the United States during these years than any other country except Vietnam, but that these sums, generously distributed by the CIA, seldom achieved the desired results. He commented that some political "beneficiaries" of the CIA thought of that agency as their private bank.[105]

Kennedy wanted to strengthen Chile and show it off as a model of democratic development as opposed to the Cuban Communist model. He stimulated investment by tycoons—Rockefeller's family among them—and gave the CIA the green light to block Allende's candidacy. The CIA orchestrated an impressive campaign against Cuba, Communism, and Allende and his Socialist Workers' Party, describing it as Stalinist and supported by Soviet funds. In 1964 posters began to appear in Santiago showing Soviet tanks in the streets of Budapest and executions by Cuban "firing squads." The idea was to terrorize the Chilean people. If they elected Allende, the same thing would happen to them. Frei won the elections with a comfortable margin, and the CIA got what it wanted: the electorate was polarized to Frei's benefit, and the movements of the left were split.[106]

In 1965 a scandal broke out when Alvaro Bunster, secretary general of the University of Chile, denounced a Pentagon plan to carry out a socioscientific investigation in Chile, funded with millions of dollars and camouflaged by a contract between the University of Chile and American University in Washington. Named the Camelot Project, its goal was to measure the potential for subversion in Latin America and design counterinsurgent policies for the continent. Chilean media and columnists condemned this plan as undue intervention in their country's internal affairs. The international community of sociologists called it a classic case of intervention and espionage with clear political objectives.[107] The uproar in Chile forced the Pentagon to cancel the plan. It had not consulted with the department of state or informed the ambassador.[108]

When Richard Nixon arrived in the White House in January 1969, the Latin American situation had grown much more explosive and complex than during his 1958 "good will" visit, when he was welcomed in Caracas and Lima with stones and rotten eggs. In the 1970s most of the continent was under military dictatorships and engaged in wars against Marxist-Leninist armed movements—the most powerful were those in the Southern Cone. In Panama and Peru, Generals Torrijos and Velasco Alvarado, both with leftist and anti-American leanings, caused him problems. Panama sought support in the United Nations and the OAS to take over the canal and reestablish sovereignty over the Zone. The Peruvian generals were nationalizing the transnational companies in their country, and in democratic Chile the congress was debating "Chileanizing" the copper industry—Chile's principal product—which was in the hands of the American multinationals Anaconda Copper and Kennecott. Frei announced that he was prepared to carry out the promised nationalization gradually.[109] Cuba was another problem. In spite of United States attempts to isolate the island, several countries reestablished relations during the 1970s and reopened their embassies in Havana. Still, Cuba did not cause him to lose sleep, since his priorities in foreign policy were the great powers of the Soviet Union and the People's Republic of China.

Nixon's policies toward Latin America, on the advice of Secretary of State Henry Kissinger, were to keep a low profile. It was not a region of primary importance. Nixon's experiences on the continent had not been pleasant, and as Kissinger explained to Chilean embassy officials in Washington in 1969, "I am not interested in, nor do I know anything about, the southern portion of the world, from the Pyrenees on down."[110]

In spite of their supposed lack of interest, Nixon and Kissinger kept their eyes on Chile. They wanted to prevent Allende from winning, and their intervention was thorough. The United States could not stand by and watch as this country "[went] Communist because of the irresponsibility of its own people," remarked Kissinger. He saw Allende as a threat to the continent and claimed that Chile was more dangerous than Cuba, since it had a greater capacity to undermine other nations and support insurgency, and that Communist ideology would get timely Soviet support.[111]

In 1969 rumors of a coup—a phenomenon unknown in Chile—began to circulate. Brigadier General Roberto Viaux, the commander of a tiny regiment in Tacna, led an uprising. According to secret ITT documents published by Jack Anderson in the *Washington Post* in 1972, Viaux prepared a "preventive" coup to stop Allende's candidacy, with the direct advice of the CIA.[112] The *tacnazo* was brought under control, but it showed that there were divisions within the armed forces and politicization of some sectors, another phenomenon unknown in Chile.[113]

In January 1970 the presidential campaign began in an atmosphere of unrest and political and social aggressiveness. Viaux continued to make statements hinting at a coup. He accused Frei of "dysgoverning" and the congress of "anarchy" and demanded a strong leader and political, economic, and social reforms. General René Schneider, commander-in-chief of the army, condemned the coup attempts. "Our doctrine and our mission," he remarked, "is to support and respect the constitution."[114] Allende of the MIR and Jorge Alessandri of the Christian Democrats were the principal candidates.

A conspiracy orchestrated by the transnational ITT and the CIA was mounted against Allende's candidacy. The conspirators tried to foment a coup by bribing military officers. The United States ambassador, Edward Korry, was authorized to contact them. Washington in turn took measures to stifle the Chilean economy. After the coup they were preparing, Frei would go into exile and return after six months, when everything would have returned to normal, and again announce his candidacy for the presidency and be supported by "all democratic forces."[115]

In May 1970 two rightist military groups, one led by Viaux (from retirement) and the other by General Camilo Valenzuela, decided to kidnap General Schneider, the greatest obstacle in their plans for a coup. They made the attempt on October 22. Schneider resisted and was severely wounded.

Three days later he died in the hospital. Five of the attackers, young rightists from prominent families, fled the country. Frei decreed a state of emergency.[116]

The CIA had contacts with both the conspiratorial groups, according to Colby, a former director of the CIA. It had supplied them with weapons, but it had not taken part in the action.[117] Frei named General Carlos Pratts commander-in-chief of the army to replace Schneider.

At a large public rally in September, Allende referred to the plots being hatched to destabilize the country. He spoke of bribes given to members of the armed forces, and mentioned the intention to create economic chaos. He announced that the people would oppose the plans with a national strike.[118]

ALLENDE

Salvador Allende won the elections of September 4, 1970, with 36 percent of the vote (39,000 more votes than Alessandri), but he did not win the necessary majority. The congress would have to choose which of the two would be president. Political maneuvers to prevent the congress from confirming Allende began at once. The CIA, the United States embassy, United States transnationals (especially ITT), and Chilean politicians and economic sectors took part, announcing that a military coup would be supported by Washington.[119] Jorge Edwards of the Chilean oligarchy, the director and owner of the influential daily *El Mercurio*, went to Washington to arrange for United States intervention.[120]

On November 4, in an atmosphere of extreme tension, the congress confirmed Allende and he became president (1970–1973). But before confirming him, it imposed on him the Statute of Constitutional Guarantees—a demand by the Christian Democrats—to keep him from "communizing" Chile. At a rally the following day in Santiago's National Stadium, Allende spoke of a socialist road to development for Chile, of ending its dependency and of initiating relations with the People's Republic of China and reestablishing them with Cuba.

Allende cautiously but firmly began to expropriate powerful national and foreign monopolies and large estates and to buy shares in the principal banks, two of them United States institutions. The congress unanimously approved the nationalization of copper production. The United States responded with measures intended to destroy the Chilean economy. It suspended aid from the Export-Import Bank and AID and closed off credits from the IMF, the World

Bank, and the Inter-American Development Bank, all institutions controlled by Washington. These measures resulted in the flight of national and foreign capital. Allende spoke of a "secret blockade" against his government.[121]

Allende invited Fidel Castro to visit Chile. He arrived in November 1971 and stayed nearly a month. His presence infuriated the Chilean right and the military. They accused him of interfering in the nation's internal affairs. In his speeches Fidel characterized the opposition as fascist and the program of workers' self-management proposed by the Christian Democrats as "criminal demagoguery." He declared that Chile and Cuba were moving toward socialism along different roads, but that their aims were the same.[122]

The economic policies of Allende's socialist government met with great success in the first year. they lowered the inflation rate, reduced unemployment, raised wages, froze the price of basic necessities, and increased production. But soon they began to deteriorate: inflation rose, the price of copper on foreign markets fell, and imports and reserves dropped. Chile successfully renegotiated part of its foreign debt and found new markets for its copper, but the situation quickly worsened.

Sabotage, food hoarding (to produce scarcity), monetary speculation, black-market dollars occurred, and there was a succession of work stoppages by truckers, engineers, doctors, and lawyers, all instigated by the CIA. The masses were opposed to these stoppages. To meet this crisis, Allende appointed high-ranking military officers to his cabinet. Sectors of the Chilean right and the United States pressured the military to stage a coup. In November the plot began to brew.

The thousand days of Allende's government were in constant conflict with the principal political and economic sectors, the military, the transnationals, and Washington. He was forced deal with strikes by different sectors and had to dodge opposition in the congress. To seek solutions, he held conversations with the political parties and made more than ten changes in his cabinet. In one of the last he named as ministers the commanders of the three military branches and the police. He called it the National Security Cabinet. There was a wave of repression, which he was powerless to stop. Under the Weapons Control Law the army leveled factories and workers' homes and repressed the left.

Even though Kissinger said that after Allende's election Chile was not a major preoccupation of the United States, it was to the extent that Nixon— personally—authorized the CIA to blockade Allende's government. He was convinced that Chile was going down the Cuban road and that the Revolution would spread to the rest of the continent. The United States Congress and the transnationals thought likewise.

The Pentagon maintained contact with the Chilean military and continued to provide it with weapons, and the CIA kept on fomenting a coup. It distributed some $6 million among the opposition parties, newspapers, radio stations, unions, and professional associations, and it supported the strikers. Without CIA funds, there would not have been so many strikes, nor would they have lasted so long. The anti-Communist ideological component proved extremely effective in polarizing political forces and splintering the leftist movements.

The coup began to gain strength on August 20, 1973, with a crisis within the armed forces. General César Ruiz, commander of the air force and minister of public works and transportation—whose responsibility it was to put an end to a prolonged truckers' strike—resigned from his ministry, and Allende asked for his resignation as commander. When he refused, General Pratts, the minister of defense, threatened to take control of the air force. Hundreds of officers' wives protested in solidarity with General Ruiz in front of Pratts's residence and delivered a letter to his wife calling for his resignation. The police came in to break up the demonstration, spraying tear gas at the people. Pratts asked for a declaration of support from the generals. They refused to give it to him. Furious, he resigned from the ministry of defense and command of the army. Allende named General Augusto Pinochet in his place. Pinochet was surprised because he was not—as he himself said—among the generals with whom the president was friendly.[123]

The offensive against the president continued until September 11, 1973, the day of the coup. The opposition in congress attempted to impeach him. One deputy accused him of dictatorial actions and demanded that the military ministers put an end to all the de facto situations that violated the constitution. A broad majority (81 to 41) supported Allende.

Allende continued to talk with the Christian Democrats and proposed that a plebiscite decide whether he should remain president or resign. Meanwhile the truckers' strike continued, the military demanded changes in the cabinet, there were street demonstrations for and against the president, and the economic crisis grew more severe. The Christian Democratic Party demanded that the congress and the president resign and that new elections be held. It was very late for Allende to negotiate a democratic and constitutional solution. In the midst of this crisis the Chilean and United States navies held joint military maneuvers, titled UNITAS, off Chile's coast. This action was an act of harassment against the government.

On September 11 at 6:00 AM Allende was informed that the naval forces had taken Valparaíso. At 8:30 AM Radio Agricultura, an anti-Allende station, announced that the coup had begun. At 9:00 AM Allende briefly appeared on the balcony of La Moneda Palace, and half an hour later he delivered his dramatic last message over the radio. He said that he refused to resign and that he would repay the Chilean people's loyalty with his life, so that it would serve as a lesson in "this ignominious history to those who resort to force instead of to reason."[124] The Palace was surrounded by tanks. At 11:55 AM the air force bombed it. La Moneda was in flames. At 1:30 PM the Palace personnel left. A doctor reported that he had seen Allende shoot himself with a machine gun he was holding between his knees. He was buried in his family's mausoleum in Viña del Mar.

AND PINOCHET

On September 11, 1973, Chilean democracy succumbed in a military coup led by General Augusto Pinochet. It was a tragedy for its people and for Latin America because Chile had been a paradigm of civility and democracy.

After the air force bombed La Moneda, the military took over the city like an army of occupation. Pinochet came to power stained with the blood of the people. With Pinochet began one of the most brutal repressions the continent had ever witnessed. The jails filled with political prisoners, and the streets were strewn with the dead. Amnesty International estimated that no fewer than 45,000 people were arrested in the first few days, and thousands were killed by the army. Some people succeeded in taking refuge in embassies. Approximately 800 political refugees requested protection from the United Nations and the Chilean Church, and many were expelled from the country.

After two weeks the military decreed a state of war. Under the code of military justice in time of war, it abrogated civil liberties and gave the police a free hand to detain, interrogate, judge, and execute "Allendists" and leftists, and it instituted torture—prohibited by Chilean law—and extra-judicial executions.

Pro-Allende media outlets were closed, and their directors were assassinated or forced into exile. The parties of the Popular Unity—Allende's governing coalition—were outlawed and their members were arrested. The Central Única de Trabajadores (CUT: the Only Workers' Central) was declared illegal, and the rights to strike and associate were cancelled. From this point on "political crimes" were the concern of military tribunals. Confessions obtained under torture were admissible evidence. International human-rights organizations, national and foreign journalists, the Chilean Catholic Church, lawyers, diplomats, and victims' relatives began to investigate, document, and denounce the regime's human-rights violations. Consternation over what was happening in Chile spread throughout the world. Within a month delegations from the International Human Rights Federation and the International Movement of Catholic Jurists arrived, followed a few weeks later by a delegation from Amnesty International. Each reported the tragedy the Chilean people were suffering under military repression. The Santiago stadium was turned into a concentration and death camp. Thousands of people were executed there, among them the famous singer and guitarist Victor Jara, whose corpse was found riddled with bullets, mutilated, and with his hands amputated. This crime was a turning point for the world.

Henceforward the national and international clamor against the butchery grew. Chilean Cardinal Raúl Silva Henríquez became the strongest voice of protest against the repression. Catholic Church documents revealed the existence of seventeen detention centers where death by torture was daily fare. The Inter-American Commission on Human Rights of the OAS also reported on the physical and psychological torture of prisoners. The sadism of the executors of the repression and the tortures alarmed the world.

At the end of 1973 the junta created the Directorio Nacional de Inteligencia (DINA: National Intelligence Directorate) under Pinochet's direct control, with hundreds of agents from the three military branches and the police, as well as civilians contracted by the government. The Directorio installed clandestine detention centers and had a fleet of unregistered vehicles. DINA was the backbone of the military regime's repressive forces.[125]

Two months after Pinochet's coup, DINA's head, Colonel Manuel Contreras, along with the heads of security services of Argentina, Brazil, Uruguay, Paraguay, and Bolivia set up "Operation Condor," a network of intelligence to operate around the world, centralized in DINA. Teams of agents cooperated in conspiracy plots to capture, interrogate, torture, and murder their political opponents. The Chilean General Pratts and his wife were assassinated in Buenos Aires, as was Bernado Leighton in Rome, Orlando Letelier in Washington, D.C. Former president of Bolivia, General Juan Jose Torres, and two congressmen from Uruguay were murdered in Buenos Aires.

Pinochet grasped permanent power, as he stated in the "Declaration of Principles of the Chilean Government," published in March 1974. He set no limit to his term, because his job, he claimed, was to achieve the moral, institutional, and material reconstruction of the country, a task that demanded profound and prolonged action. Changing the Chilean mentality was an imperative, he assured his audience. He declared that elections would be held at an opportune time and that the armed forces would not be idle when it came to choosing the next government. There would be a new constitution to safeguard national security and guarantee the armed forces' participation in government.[126]

Pinochet promulgated the so-called Governing Junta Statute. The government was to remain in the hands of the armed forces, and the power in the hands of the president of the junta. According to this statute, the order of things might be changed only if the commander in chief of the army—Pinochet— ceased to be President of the junta by reason of "death, resignation, or total incapacity." In other words, Pinochet, who was now the Supreme Chief of the Nation, would not be able to be removed from office. The cabinet was composed of generals.[127]

Six months after this statute was decreed, Pinochet introduced a tremendously significant change by a new decree: he would no longer be supreme leader of the nation but president of the republic, with full powers, and the junta would remain under his control. He began to distance himself from the other members of the junta so that there would be no doubt, within the government or outside it, that his was the sole power.

The matter of anti-Communist ideology—the apparent motive for the coup—was defined in the document "National Objective of the Chilean Government," based on national security and neoliberal economics. Presidential messages, legal dispositions, and Institutional Acts 2, 3, and 4 indicated that the government's theme was counterinsurgency. It characterized Marxism as the "enemy" and a "perverse doctrine in the service of Soviet imperialism." The government's job was to abolish it.[128] The junta's economic policy, neoliberal and monetarist, was managed by a team called the Chicago Boys. In the first year it reduced the annual rate of inflation from 600 percent to 350 percent. People in Chile and abroad spoke of the Chilean miracle. But at the end of 1974 the prices of basic necessities rose, inflation set in, and the country was in an economic crisis. In April the Chicago Boys took over the ministries of finance and economics and the presidency of the central bank.

In 1975 production dropped 13 percent, and the recession was catastrophic. Hundreds of industries were paralyzed; public investment decreased by 50 percent; annual inflation stood at 343 percent, and unemployment rose to 20 percent. But in 1977, the boom times of the "Chilean miracle" began. The annual growth rate was 9.9 percent, a rate that continued in 1978 and 1979. The

Chicago Boys promised a growth rate similar to that of European countries and the Asian tigers of Taiwan, Singapore, and South Korea. The world was astonished by this "miracle." And many, in Chile and abroad, felt that the brutal repression was justified, since it brought progress. But the Washington, D.C., assassination of Orlando Letelier, Allende's former chancellor, and his assistant, Ronni Moffit, a young American woman, catapulted them back to reality: Pinochet's regime was one of the continent's most brutal. Letelier's assassination elicited international disapproval. The FBI and other American agencies pointed at DINA, its director general, Manuel Contreras Sepúlveda, and other military officers as the perpetrators of this crime. Washington demanded the extradition of Contreras, but the Chilean government and court of justice refused.

With the arrival of Jimmy Carter in the White House in January 1977, Chile's relations with the United States became more complicated for Pinochet. Carter pressured the junta to stop violating human and political rights, imposed sanctions, and tightened them when Chile refused to extradite Contreras.

In a speech in Chacarillas in July 1977 Pinochet spoke of "democratization" for the first time and proposed a three-stage program: the armed forces would gradually leave the government, though they would not relinquish power. The process would conclude in 1991 with "total democracy."[129] In August, motivated by Undersecretary of State for Latin American Affairs Terence Todman's visit to Chile, the junta dissolved DINA and created the Centro Nacional de Informaciones (CNI: National Information Center) in its place. It was the same animal with a new name. Its purpose was to relieve international pressure and ingratiate Chile with Washington.

Pinochet continued investing himself with new titles and functions and exalting his own authority. Now, in addition to president, he was generalissimo of the armed forces and the forces of order. The Chilean regime's criminal record did not diminish the enthusiasm of national and foreign economic sectors for the "miracle." Many Chileans reclaimed their properties—expropriated by Allende—and benefited from the government's economic policies. The transnationals returned. But the "miracle" had a hidden face: it produced an accelerated concentration of wealth, and the economic opening and low tariffs caused imports to rise disproportionately and weakened national industries. Many small and medium-size businesses went bankrupt. The cuts in government spending raised unemployment among professionals and white-collar workers, while the salaries of the military rose generously. Foreign bank loans to the private sector for investment in industry were used to purchase shares, business ventures with the state, and weak businesses. The economic empires did not help investment, particularly low during these years.[130] A high percentage of the loans made to the government by international and private banks went toward the purchase of arms. With these policies, the rich (5 percent of the population) grew richer and the poor grew poorer. Infant mortality increased dramatically.[131] By the end of 1980 the Chilean foreign debt stood at $1.82 billion (in 1977 it was at $481 million). But Chile showed off its prosperity. The peso had been revalued. The upper and middle classes traveled the world. The markets were filled with foreign luxury goods, and the relations of the government and the private sector with international financial institutions and foreign investors were excellent.

"GOD PLACED ME IN POWER"

Buoyed by the economy, Pinochet called a national plebiscite to approve the new constitution, the text of which had been written by a commission appointed by the junta, with no participation by independent jurists. Authoritarian and antidemocratic, it included acts and decrees by the junta that curtailed civil liberties, all previously approved by congress and the military junta.

The plebiscite—with the vote limited to yes or no—was held on September 11, 1980, the seventh anniversary of the coup. It was held under a state of emergency decreed a month earlier, with all political parties proscribed, without electoral lists, on transparent paper that allowed officials to monitor the voting, and the entire process supervised only by government functionaries.[132] According to official data the result was 67 percent in favor of the new constitution and 30 percent opposed to it. The new constitution "institutionalized" the prolongation of Pinochet's term to 1989 (eight more years) and left open the possibility of his reelection. It created the National Security Council, the government's highest agency, in which the three branches of the military were represented by their commanders and the officers had the right of veto.

The plebiscite was denounced as a fraud in Chile and abroad. The process had been totally controlled by the government, with no supervision by the opposition, and it was not the free expression of the people's will because Chile was not a free country. Pinochet's voracious appetite for power imposed a new constitutional order that gave him absolute power.

But not all was euphoria for the junta, since the miracle was beginning to fade. Its prosperity did not reflect economic recovery; investments had not been in productive sectors, and many industries were crumbling. There was an economic recession and a profound crisis in the banking and financial systems. Foreign debt was enormous, and the debt accumulated by the private sector and the financial conglomerates (more than $4 billion), granted without government guarantees, could not be paid off.

The crisis grew more severe, and in November 1981 the government was forced to take control of four banks and four financial institutions that were on the verge of bankruptcy. It took over seventeen more between 1981 and 1983 to keep the banking system from collapsing and pulling the rest of the economy down with it. The Chicago Boys' neoliberal economic policy ended in yet another economy controlled by the state.[133] The industrial situation was just as dramatic: collapses, suspension of loan payments, and massive layoffs. The economic crisis had given birth to a greater political and social crisis. During the first half of 1983, unemployment (including subsidized employment) rose to 34 percent, and 50 percent among the poorest sectors. The lower classes were reduced to abject poverty.[134] The situation led to protests by upper- and middle-class housewives. They took to the streets, beating on empty pans.

The people and the weakened unions began to confront the dictatorship in demonstrations and strikes, and the political parties formed moderate opposition movements. The Christian Democratic Party, the most active during the dictatorship's hardest years, formed the Alianza Democrática (AD: Democratic Alliance) with five other parties from the right, the center, and the left. The Communist Party, which was excluded from this Alliance, created the Movimiento Democrático Popular (MDP: Popular Democratic Movement) with the MIR, the part of the Socialist party led by the former Allende minister Clodomiro Almeyda, and with other leftist parties and movements. Some of these favored armed struggle against the dictatorship.

Pinochet named Sergio Onofre Jarpa of the extreme right as his minister of the interior. He was the first civilian to hold this post under the dictatorship. Pinochet persuaded him to start negotiating with the democratic opposition.[135]

A civilian protest movement began in May, 1983 with a "march of the pots and pans" and continued in June with a demonstration called by the copper workers' union to protest the arrest of its leader, Rodolfo Seguel. Another strike followed in July, after the arrest of Gabriel Valdés, the minister of foreign affairs under Frei. All these protests were quashed by the police, leaving many dead and wounded and hundreds arrested. The government decreed a curfew.

During another protest in August, Pinochet announced that 18,000 soldiers would occupy the capital with orders to proceed "harshly." The repression was widespread. According to official documents, twenty-nine were killed and a hundred arrested in clashes with the police. According to the left, the dead numbered eighty.

The demonstrations continued sporadically and with increasingly less participation from the middle and upper classes. On the other hand, there were more and more student and lower-class demonstrators. In November 1984 the government declared a state of siege, and under the pretext of the curfew, troops raided homes in the working-class quarters in the middle of the night. They went from house to house arresting all the men older than fifteen. The people were terrorized, and the protests failed.

With Santiago's Archbishop Monsignor Juan Francisco Fresno as mediator, Jarpa began negotiations with the AD that proved futile and were discontinued. Pinochet declared that while the conversations might lead to agreements, he would never make concessions.[136]

In another protest in March 1984, the first armed movement against the dictatorship, the Frente Popular Manuel Rodríguez (FPMR: Manuel Rodríguez Popular Front) planted bombs in the subway, attacked trains and buses, and assassinated soldiers and policemen. It claimed responsibility for the 1986 kidnapping of Colonel Mario Kaeberie and the 1987 kidnapping of Lieutenant Colonel Carlos Carreño. It destroyed high-voltage electrical towers, which left vast regions of the country without power. The government maintained that this guerrilla movement was the "armed branch" of the Communist Party.

From the streets, scenes that showed the brutality against the Chilean people by the forces of order were broadcast to the world by foreign television news programs. Such acts of official brutality resulted in international protest against the Chilean regime. The most monstrous crime was the burning of two young protesters arrested by military patrols in Santiago in July 1986. They were doused with paraffin and set afire. The young man died, and the young woman's face was disfigured. Of the twenty-five military personnel indicted for this crime, only one lieutenant was convicted of "quasi-homicide" and released on bail. The protest demonstration in response was put down with the regime's accustomed brutality.

In August 1986 the government declared that it had found a powerful arsenal on Chile's north coast, and claimed that it had been brought in with Cuban and Soviet aid. It showed 3,000 "captured" weapons. Many doubted the truth of this claim. But the government covered itself with the declaration by United

States State Department spokesman Bruce Ammerman, who claimed that the weapons were destined for the FPMR and that "evidence" implicating foreign terrorist groups had been found. Relations between the Pinochet and Reagan governments remained excellent.

The following month, in September 1986, there was an attempt on Pinochet's life. He was not injured, but several of his bodyguards were killed. This was the first attempt on the life of a president in Chile's history. The government declared a state of siege and responded with an unprecedented wave of repression. Clandestine paramilitary groups brutally assassinated four activists whom they had dragged out of their homes. The weapons incident and the attempt on his life made Pinochet strengthen himself within the armed forces and with his followers from conservative sectors and the moderate opposition of the AD parties. A few days later, on September 11—the thirteenth anniversary of the coup—there was a massive demonstration in support of Pinochet. Opposition sectors claimed that it was organized by the government to launch Pinochet's presidential candidacy. The same two incidents also allowed Pinochet to increase the repression, claiming threats to internal stability. On September 21 he announced a new antiterrorist law, harsher than the previous laws. In October he reiterated his refusal to negotiate with the opposition.

Needing to sweeten his image before the plebiscite on his presidential candidacy, in his end-of-the-year message Pinochet announced that he would lift the state of siege, which had lasted two years, and would allow some exiles to return. In January 1987 he approved legislation on political parties and their future organization (Marxist parties were prohibited), and in February he opened election offices.

In April of the same year Pope John Paul II visited Chile, the only Latin American country still under military rule. The Catholic Church was not only the regime's toughest critic, but also a major support of the people's struggle against Pinochet. The Vicariate of Solidarity, created by Cardinal Raúl Silva Henríquez to support the people in the fight against the repression, published a bulletin that constantly denounced the regime's serious human-rights violations. Relations between the Church and the government were tense. Pinochet recommended to the bishops that they would be better off sticking to praying.

The political connotations of the Pope's visit was feared equally by the Church, the people, and the regime. His words would be scrutinized. But the Pope, a careful orator, supported the Church's struggle. In his homilies he called for coexistence and an end to the violence, and he condemned physical and moral torture. He visited the National Stadium—after the coup it had become a place of detention, death, and torture—where 90,000 young people awaited him. He kissed the ground and remembered the stadium as a place of "sufferings." Among the crowds, guarded by large police detachments, there were violent confrontations, resulting in dead and wounded spectators. When the Pope left Chile, the opposition gained strength and demanded a return to democracy by way of free elections.

The government fixed the date for the plebiscite. It would take place on October 5, 1988. "God placed me in power," declared Pinochet. The opposition formed the Comando Nacional del No (National Commando for a No Vote). Its demonstrations were met with police bullets, and hundreds of people were wounded and arrested. When the junta announced that its candidate was Pinochet, there were massive protest marches and confrontations between the Yes and No partisans and between the No's and the police. Thousands were arrested, and the number of casualties grew. That night Pinochet appeared on television smiling, and dressed in civilian clothes, to ask the people's support for a new democracy and to ask them to pardon him for any errors he might have committed.[137]

The country's future was at stake in the plebiscite, and the results surprised many. Opinion polls showed the No vote rising, but there were fears of fraud in Pinochet's favor. The votes came in at 54.68 percent No and 43.04 percent Yes. Although Pinochet was defeated, it was not the end of the dictatorship. The election of a new president would take place in December 1989, and the transfer of power in the following March. Pinochet remained in power for another year and a half in accordance with the constitution approved by a fraudulent plebiscite. During this difficult time the opposition achieved some constitutional reforms in tough negotiations with the government, including that a civilian be appointed to the national security council (the highest governing body), on which the military held a veto. The reforms were approved by 85.7 percent of the vote in a plebiscite. The Communist Party pointed out that the new government remained under the aegis of "military superpowers." The opposition trusted that the new congress would reform the Chilean magna carta to restore true democracy.

THE ROAD TO DEMOCRACY

On December 14, 1989, Christian Democrat Patricio Aylwin, the candidate of a coalition of seventeen parties, was elected President with 55.2 percent of the vote. Hernán Buchi, the official candidate, got 29.4 percent. The new parliament was also elected. Aylwin took office in March 1990, declaring, "Chile will not have a democracy overseen by the military" since, he explained, the armed forces were under civilian control. Nevertheless Pinochet, commander of the armed forces, was a member of the national security council, with a lifetime seat in parliament, and could not be forced to retire from either of these posts by constitutional mandate.

The people demanded that military officers be tried for human-rights violations. They also called for the new government to annul the amnesty law decreed by the junta in 1978, which covered the worst period of the repression, and the new law—passed two days before the elections—that prevented the new parliament from investigating the government functionaries who served during Pinochet's regime. This was the most hotly debated topic of the new democracy. Aylwin asked Pinochet to remain at the margins of political activity and to renounce the command of the army, but he refused.

Pressured by public demand, Aylwin named the Truth and Reconciliation Commission in March to investigate human-rights violations committed during the seventeen years of military dictatorship. In spite of the verdict by the supreme court in October 1990, upholding the 1978 amnesty law, Aylwin reiterated his readiness to clear up such acts.

Forced to put up with Pinochet's arrogance, which was supported by the military establishment and by powerful sectors on the right—they organized a demonstration backing the general—and powerless to stop the repression and the abuses of the police and the military, Aylwin publicly recognized that "There will be justice as long as democratic stability is not put at risk, and that the correlation of forces now is not favorable to justice."[138]

Aylwin applauded the people's decision to transfer Allende's remains from the Santa Ana cemetery to Santiago. It was an "act of reparation," stated the President. The ceremony was held on September 4, 1990. About 9 feet away from his grave the cornerstone was laid for a new mausoleum to honor those who had died or were disappeared under the dictatorship. On September 11—the anniversary of the coup—there was a demonstration by Pinochet's followers outside his residence to "thank" him for his government.

The Truth and Reconciliation Commission presented its findings to the President in February 1991—2,000 pages in six volumes. In March, Aylwin made them public. The press called them horrifying. They documented 2,279 murders—most of them summary executions—and 965 disappearances, deaths by torture at the hands of the state security services. It also brought to light terrorist attempts by DINA (created and dissolved by Pinochet) and implicated it in the assassinations of General Carlos Pratts and his wife in Buenos Aires and Allende's former chancellor, Orlando Letelier, in Washington. To Pinochet such acts were part of the "internal war" he waged against subversion.

Aylwin announced he would not annul the amnesty law but that keeping it would not be an obstacle to carrying on legal investigations and determining responsibility, especially in cases of disappearances. He begged forgiveness from the relatives of the victims in the name of the entire country, since by "action or omission," the whole of society was responsible. He offered them moral and material reparations and announced the creation of an organization that would continue searching for the disappeared and maintain archives on human-rights violations. Aylwin asked the people and the armed forces to transcend this tragic past.

THE PARTY'S OVER

At the end of the 1980s, in the countries of the Southern Cone—free of dictatorships and insurgent movements, which had been virtually eliminated— the governments set out on the difficult road of consolidating democracy. Though they left their military establishments intact—no one dared to touch them—the military was a threat no longer. Only Pinochet, arrogant, cynical, and pigheaded, continued grasping the props of power he himself had written into the national constitution to perpetuate himself in the Chilean political landscape. His presence in the parliament as senator for life and by constitutional provision—the last expression of his dictatorial will—was an affront to the Chilean people and government and a warping of its democracy. When he appeared in parliament, the popular and democratic sector protest, demanding that congress revoke this "right" he had acquired fraudulently, failed. Pinochet would remain a part of the Chilean political scene, perhaps until his last breath.

With the exception of Chile, the military dictatorships had left their countries in ruins, with runaway inflation, economic recessions, and huge foreign debts caused mainly by the multimillion-dollar purchases of weapons, which were used to kill their own people. This was another matter no civil government dared to investigate. The new democracies' priority was to solve the economic problems they inherited. They all opted for neoliberal economic policies, which accentuated the gap between rich and poor. Amid this landscape of great problems and hopes the colossi of the Southern Cone began this new phase of their history.

CHAPTER VIII

REAGAN'S WARS

THE ANTI-COMMUNIST CRUSADE IN CENTRAL AMERICA

When Ronald Reagan burst onto the scene as a viable presidential candidate with an avalanche of conservative and anti-Communist ideology and bellicose anti-Soviet rhetoric worthy of the McCarthy era, both United States and the world were given a preview of the stormy days ahead. The "detente" of the 1970s became history. Reagan's aims were militaristic, and his first priority was to increase the United States' power in relation to the Soviet Union, which he held responsible for international terrorism and "Communist expansion" in Latin America by way of Cuba and Nicaragua.

Reagan's proposals at the Republican Convention and those in the Santa Fe Committee report—prepared for his campaign by conservatives of the New Right and civilians connected with the military-industrial complex—signaled a change of direction in United States foreign policies. The Santa Fe Committee demanded that "war, not peace" be the norm of United States relations with Latin America. It also recommended strengthening the hemispheric security apparatus under the Río Treaty (Inter-American Mutual Defense Treaty)—a regional military pact for collective action in cases of attack on one of its members—and revitalizing the military ties among their armies. It saw the Central American crises as part of a "Communist conspiracy"—its four-stage plan culminated in total war—to "subvert the capitalist order, transform the world," and destabilize and overthrow governments. Such a process, it stated, had already taken place in Nicaragua, and would "probably" occur next in El Salvador.[1]

Reagan, the most conservative, most anti-Communist, and the oldest head of state to occupy the White House (he turned seventy-two weeks after his inauguration), signaled a radical change on the United States political scene and in the mentality of the American people. He arrived in Washington flanked by powerful multimillionaire friends from California, industry magnates who left big business to become part of his cabinet, and the intimate circle of presidential advisers: the "troika" of the White House. With Ron and Nancy came the glitz and glamour of Hollywood, the opulence of the upper-middle class without the pretensions to Mayflower ancestry of the sophisticated Kennedy clan. Washington was the new scene for Reagan, and he took center stage.

Reagan—the "Great Communicator"—charmed the public and the scornful press and kept them captivated throughout his two terms in office. Also called the Teflon president, his frequent waffling, vagueness, and exaggerations inspired satire, but his grave mistakes, cynicism, and violations of the country's laws were ultimately forgiven. He emerged unscathed from one of the greatest scandals in United States political history: the Iran-Contra Affair. The people felt safe and satisfied. Ronald Reagan was a good guy.

Reagan's strong ideological motives meant the return to an intensified Cold War, the East-West conflict, and the confrontation with the Soviet Union, which he dubbed the Evil Empire. His worldview was simplistic, dogmatic, black and white: the good capitalists versus the bad Communists; the United States and the Free World (a concept he dusted off and revived) versus the Soviet Union and international Communism.

The appointment of General Alexander Haig, former supreme commander of NATO, to the post of secretary of state surprised and alarmed both friends and enemies. Handing the portfolio for foreign policy to a general of his caliber indicated that military matters, possibly even war, would be at the forefront of international relations. Haig, a "politicized" soldier, was the major supporter of the anti-Communist crusade taken up by the new presidency.

With Reagan in the White House, the chests of Latin America's right-wingers and military officers swelled with joy. They identified with him. The Guatemalan ultraright celebrated with fireworks, with a mariachi serenade at the United States Embassy, and with cheerful parties in their homes.[2] The Salvadoran oligarchs showed their pleasure by firing their pistols into the air.[3] With his election, coincidence or not, military and paramilitary violence in Central America began to escalate.

"INVENTING" A POLICY

General Haig stated that human rights were no longer foreign-policy prior-ities, as they had been for Jimmy Carter. The priority of the Reagan admin-istration was to be a war against international terrorism, for which he blamed the Soviet Union. His list of terrorist countries included Libya, Iran, North Korea, Cuba, and Nicaragua. He announced that the United States would show its resolve to "roll back" Soviet and Cuban expansionism in Central America, "draw[ing] the line" in El Salvador, which was facing an armed con-flict led by a Marxist-Leninist guerrilla movement. The solution to this con-flict, he maintained, would be "drastic and military," and he saw a quick and easy victory. "This is a war you can win, Mr. President!" he told Reagan.4

Haig announced that he would reestablish good relations with the anti-Communist governments—the genocidal military dictatorships of the Southern Cone and Central America—and step up the harassment of Cuba and Nicaragua.5 His priority was Cuba, for him the source of hemispheric sub-version and Communist conspiracy. He would impose a naval blockade on that island to cut off the flow of arms that, he held, flowed from Cuba to the Salvadoran guerrillas.

Testifying before the Foreign Relations Committee of the House of Representatives in March 1981, he exposed an aggressive Soviet plan to "take over" Central America (similar to the one laid out in the Santa Fe Committee report), and asked for $6.5 billion to put the brakes on Soviet "adventurism" in "strategic sectors vital to the United States' interests." He did not mention Latin America.6

Emissaries from Reagan began trotting about throughout the globe tout-ing his anti-Communist message. Thomas Enders, Undersecretary of State for Inter-American Affairs, went to Colombia and Venezuela. Upon arriving at the Bogotá airport in June 1981, he told reporters that the purpose of his visit was to coordinate a policy against the Cuban regime, which he called a dan-ger to the hemisphere. He claimed that Cuba had Soviet arms and equip-ment—36 MIG airplanes—and a "broad and coordinated plan" for intervention in the area in collaboration with Nicaragua and Grenada. He added that "his country w[ould] not refuse the request to purchase arms, which Venezuela has already made, to make a stand against this threat." Arms sales were an important objective of his mission.7 To President Julio César Turbay Ayala he insisted on the necessity of coordinated action in seeking a military solution to the Caribbean problem. The United States wanted to create an inter-American naval force to stop arms traffic in the region.8

The Reagan-Haig policies concerning Central America went only one way: militarily. There was immediately opposition from parts of Congress, influential newspapers, and public opinion to the military assistance and the dispatch of military advisers—Green Berets—being sent to El Salvador. They saw Vietnam written all over the move. At once groups and movements arose in support of the struggles of the Salvadoran people, their fervor reminiscent of the antiwar movements that emerged in the 1960s. Just two months after Reagan's inauguration opinion polls showed that 60 percent of the people were opposed to military aid to El Salvador and only 2 percent approved.[9]

Within the higher levels of government there was concern about this internal opposition, which was expanding throughout the country—there were demonstrations in various cities—and about the isolation the country was beginning to feel from the rest of the continent. The majority of the governments were in favor of negotiated solutions to these conflicts. Uncomfortable with this militaristic image of its policies and the wide criticism they elicited, as counterbalance the administration proposed a plan for economic aid. In July 1981 Haig convened a meeting of the chancellors of Canada, Mexico, and Venezuela in Nassau in the Bahamas, to study the "Caribbean situation" and present a program of economic aid for the region. (Colombia protested that it was not invited.) At this meeting Haig established the basic principles of the Caribbean Basin Initiative (CBI), introducing it as a mini-Marshall Plan" that Reagan would launch the following February. Aside from the United States, contributors included Mexico, Venezuela, Canada, and also Colombia, and the beneficiary countries would be all except Cuba, Grenada, and Nicaragua. The Initiative, more modest than the Alliance for Progress in both funds and objectives, would provide tax-free access to United States markets for nontraditional products from these countries. The $350 million he offered to underwrite the program's initiation was a modest sum. In the final analysis this plan would particularly benefit multinational corporations and United States investors and increase the dependence of the beneficiary nations on American markets.[10]

In the White House political kitchen, with its many chefs, there were some who opposed Haig's militaristic plans. The differences within the inner circle of the administration were plain to see in November in successive interviews with Secretary of Defense Caspar Weinberger, Attorney General Edwin Meese—the most important member of the troika—and Haig by the television networks CBS, NBC, and ABC. Meese and Weinberger categorically ruled out military intervention in Cuba and Nicaragua, which Haig espoused. Weinberger and the joint chiefs did not believe a military "victory" was possible or that Congress and public opinion would accept a military option.[11]

In spite of their characteristic arrogance and obstinacy, Reagan and Haig knew that they had to convince the public, and above all Congress, that military aid to Central America was necessary to fight Communism and for the security of the United States. They exaggerated the facts, distorted the truth, spread false reports, and told outright lies to justify the growing United States military presence in El Salvador and Honduras, thus providing a rationale for the more extreme measures they considered taking in the near future.

LIGHTING THE WICK

In the narrow view of foreign policy taken by the Reagan administration, the Central American crises were part of the East-West conflict. The triumph of the Sandinista revolution in Nicaragua and the guerrilla struggle in El Salvador were perceived as an expansion of international Communism. Reagan made this region the principal, if not the only, focus of his inter-American policies during his eight years in office. A few days before Reagan's inauguration the Salvadoran guerrillas, the Farabundo Martí National Liberation Front (FMLN), launched its "final offensive." Carter sent emergency military aid and Green Berets. A week after he took office, Reagan increased this aid substantially. Thus began the United States immersion in and eventual takeover of the Salvadoran civil war.

Under a banner of anti-Communism, Reagan's objectives were the miltary defeat of the Salvadoran guerrillas and the overthrow of the Sandinista government in Nicaragua. Keeping Congress in the dark, the CIA started a clandestine operation organizing Nicaraguan counterrevolutionaries into a paramilitary force. Reagan kept up this "secret war" throughout his eight years as president. Honduras—which shared common borders with Nicaragua, Guatemala, and El Salvador, all three of them countries with internal conflicts—became the springboard for regional military operations. Although Reagan did not discount the possibility of direct military intervention in those countries, his strategy was that of "low-intensity conflict," giving multi-million dollar military aid and sending Green Berets without involving his regular troops.

Throughout the Reagan years military maneuvers in the Caribbean and along Honduras's border with Nicaragua followed one upon the other almost without interruption. The volume and extent of these maneuvers were unprecedented. They were threatening displays of force that included hundreds of fighter planes, warships, frigates, gigantic aircraft carriers, and thousands of troops simulating invasions and ground operations, some at Guantánamo.[12]

The governments of the hemisphere, frightened by such shows of force—they saw them as a prelude to military intervention in Cuba, Nicaragua, or El Salvador—opposed this aggressive militarist policy as dangerous. They felt it solved none of the conflicts, which arose from poverty, inequalities, grave endemic and unresolved social and economic problems, and the people's frustrations with decades of injustices, criminal disregard, violence, and brutal repression. In 1983, following President of Colombia Belisario Betancur's quick and successful tour to Mexico, Venezuela, and Panama—its objective was to forge a negotiated peace and put an end to United States military intervention in the region—Contadora was founded. From the outset the Reagan administration boycotted all their efforts.

For Central America the eight years of Reagan's presidency resulted in the period of the greatest violence, the most severe tensions, the worst dangers, the most extreme social polarization, and the most extensive and brutal violations of human rights ever recorded. These conflicts claimed 75,000 lives in El Salvador—the great majority civilians—and in Nicaragua more than 30,000 civilians and fighters from both sides in Nicaragua. These wars left both countries bankrupt.

COSTA RICA IN THE GAME

Reagan pulled neutral Costa Rica into these Central American conflicts. President Luis Alberto Monge (1982–1986) secretly permitted the militarization of the police force in exchange for aid—a total of more than $6.2 million—to his country's battered economy. Advisers from United States, Israel, and other countries trained four police battalions in counterinsurgency techniques (Costa Rica's army had been disbanded forty years earlier). Now, it had 10,000 armed men and many more in civilian militias. It was an army camouflaged as civilian police.[13]

Costa Rica's sacrosanct neutrality disappeared. Monge allowed Nicaraguan rebel Edén Pastora, formerly the Sandinista revolution's "Commander Zero," to set up camp for a band of Contras on the border with Nicaragua. He also did not object to the CIA's operations, nor to United States Ambassador Lewis Tambs's clandestine activities in support of the war against Nicaragua. He allowed the CIA to build a secret airstrip in Santa Helena, which was used (though no one would admit it) for undercover flights to bring in arms and supplies for the Contras. The base was run by Richard Secord, a former United States Air Force general who had gained a great deal of experience in paramilitary and intelligence operations in the United States' wars in Southeast Asia.

With the election of Óscar Arias in 1986, such arrangements became impossible. Arias wanted to broker a peace deal for the region, and within days of his election, he informed Ambassador Tambs that he intended to close the landing strip at Santa Helena. Tambs assured him that the flights would be suspended. Not so. When Arias found out that they had continued, he was furious and immediately called a press conference to announce the closing of the base. According to Tambs's notes, made public much later, Assistant Secretary of State for Inter-American Affairs Elliot Abrams and Lieutenant Colonel Oliver North (later both were implicated in the Iran-Contra scandal) telephoned Tambs with a message to deliver to Arias: If he closed the base, the United States would cut off economic aid to his country, and he would never set foot in the White House. They needed to keep the clandestine and illegal operations in Central America from coming to light. Arias canceled the press conference, but the question of the landing strip was discussed in the Costa Rican media. William Casey, director of the CIA, flew to San José, but Arias refused to receive him and passed him on to the chancellor.[14]

Meanwhile Costa Rican police began to arrest and disarm people suspected of belonging to the Contras. The ministry of health closed a clinic near San José that attended to wounded Contras, and the immigration authorities refused entry into Costa Rica to Adolfo Calero and other members of the Contra political leadership. Arias suggested to Reagan that instead of supporting a war, he should support the economic development of the region.

THE OCCUPATION OF HONDURAS

The militarization of Honduras, the region's poorest country, began immediately. When Roberto Suázo Córdova donned the presidential sash in 1982 as the first civilian head of state not chosen by the military (after decades of military dictators), he found that Colonel Gustavo Álvarez—the Honduran strongman and chief of the previous regime's security forces—had already made a pact with the Pentagon and the CIA. Honduras would serve as the base for military operations against Nicaragua and in support of the antiguerrilla struggle in El Salvador. Before his inauguration Suázo Córdova was informed by Álvarez that matters of internal public order and foreign relations would be the domain of the armed forces and that he must not interfere in military affairs.[15] Suázo had no choice but to accept this condition. Under pressure from the State Department, he was forced to raise Álvarez to the rank of general and appoint him minister of defense. Suázo Córdova was in the hands of the military and Washington.

Honduras and the United States proceeded to amend the Mutual Assistance Program (MAP), established in 1954 to legalize the United States military occupation. (In 1988 it was again amended to expand its range even further.) The United States began the construction of nineteen bases and landing strips and started opening access roads to the Nicaraguan border. At these bases the United States installed 15,000 soldiers from its Rapid Response Force and Green Berets as well as from the Nicaraguan Democratic Forces (FDN, as the CIA dubbed the Nicaraguan contras). Palmerola, about 40 miles from Tecucigalpa, in the middle of the country, became the most important United States base in the region—even more important than its bases in Panama. There the United States trained the Honduran and Salvadoran armies and the Contra forces and carried out constant maneuvers. On the Gulf of Fonseca—its shores were shared by Honduras, Nicaragua, and El Salvador—the United States built an air and naval base, and on Tiger Island (in the Gulf) and on the Sierra del Mole the United States set up radar stations.[16] It also took over Honduran ports to deepen them for the berthing of warships. Although the treaties recognized that the bases belonged to Honduras, they remained under United States control and outside of the Honduran government's peripheral vision for an indefinite period of time.

Honduras had turned into "an enormous aircraft carrier," reported *Time.* Military aircraft entered and left without Honduran government clearance. Travelers arriving at Toncontín International Airport at Comayagüela, near the capital, could see American troop transports and military helicopters on the runways, and young men with crew-cuts in fatigues everywhere. The gringos nicknamed Honduras "our little whore in Central America."[17]

Honduras was effectively occupied by United States military forces and contras, imposed by the United States, whose bases were foreign territory outside Honduran control. The training of Salvadoran troops at Palmerola, also imposed by the United States, was an affront to the Honduran people, considering the rout Honduras had suffered in the so-called Soccer War with El Salvador in July 1969.

During Reagan's terms in office, military and economic aid to Honduras was the second-highest in Latin America.[18] Nevertheless, a substantial part of that economic aid had to be turned over to the CIA to support FDN operations. This was the way Washington avoided supervision by Congress, which expressly forbade such aid.

The Honduran government collaborated in all the Reagan administration's illegal activities in support of the secret war in Nicaragua. It aided the clandestine network set up by Lieutenant Colonel Oliver North to arm the FDN by providing counterfeit import licenses. The Honduran army participated in joint military maneuvers with the United States on Honduran territory (operations used by the Pentagon—behind Congress's back—to build a military infrastructure for the Contras, to arm them) and gave the Contras logistic support by covering their retreat from Nicaragua.

At the time the CIA's most important station was in Tegucigalpa. It was the command center for the biggest United States paramilitary operation since Vietnam. Its chiefs were the "commanders in the shadow" of the FDN. By 1983, the operation included more than 150 agents and former agents, former Green Berets, personnel reassigned from the Pentagon, Cuban veterans of the Bay of Pigs, and foreigners under contract. In a country of three million inhabitants, the American military presence and the swarm of secret agents was overwhelming.

The CIA installed its high security headquarters in a rented house near the Toncontín airport and filled it with powerful and sophisticated communication devices, linked by satellite with its central directorate in Langley, Virginia. From this headquarters and with the collaboration of Argentine advisers, it ran the war against Nicaragua.[19]

Reagan's ambassador to Honduras, John Negroponte, was a man with long experience in intelligence and clandestine activities in Southeast Asia. The importance Reagan had assigned to the war against Nicaragua was demonstrated in this appointment. The Tegucigalpa embassy moved from category four— the lowest rung in the State Department's classification system—to category two. It was staffed by 147 diplomats (including some CIA agents) and 97 military personnel. It was the third-largest staff in Latin America, behind only Mexico and Brazil.[20] Relations between Minister of Defense General Álvarez and the ambassador—the Hondurans had dubbed him Master—were excellent, since they "shared power." "They discuss what needs to be done, and then Álvarez does what Negroponte tells him to do," stated a Honduran official.[21]

Suázo's foreign policies (cued from Washington) and the overwhelming United States and Contra military presence created a profound malaise among the Honduran people and their military. Both popular and student protests erupted against the government—a new phenomenon—for having "sold out" Honduras to the United States and for collaborating in the war against Nicaragua. Suázo suffered bitter criticism from the media.

In 1979, Honduras saw its first guerrilla movements, the Cinchonero Movement for National Liberation and the Lorenzo Zelaya Popular Revolutionary Forces. Both claimed responsibility for bank robberies, kidnappings, and assassinations. In 1981, they hijacked an airplane, exploded a bomb in congress, fired on the U.S. Embassy, and assassinated two American officers. The following year, they occupied the San Pedro Sula Chamber of Commerce and held 105 hostages.[22]

Honduras was beginning to resemble its neighbors. It became a cauldron of military, paramilitary, and guerrilla violence, while the people fell victim to a dirty war launched by Álvarez. There were also countless murders, kidnappings, rapes, and robberies by the Contra forces. Crime, prostitution, and venereal diseases rose at an alarming rate, and the first of many cases of AIDS were documented.

THE DIRTY WAR

General Álvarez, the minister of defense, unleashed his own dirty war. With his support, death squads were organized, and the bodies of political, union, and student leaders began to appear, tortured to death. The list of the disappeared grew and clandestine cemeteries cropped up. This bloodshed was an unprecedented chapter in Honduran history.

Álvarez created Battalion 316, a secret unit of army intelligence that operated as a death squad. In order not to involve the army in this war, he recruited gunmen from Tegucigalpa's Central Penitentiary; later he ordered these men killed so that their activities would remain secret. He followed the Argentine advisers' counsel to use the Contras for tasks of "social cleansing."[23]

This dirty war provoked protests, denunciations, and a growing feeling of unease among the military sectors. In 1984, Álvarez was detained in the San Pedro Sula airport, on orders from the high command. He was handcuffed, put on a plane, and sent into exile. A group of colonels began investigating the 247 political assassinations and disappearances from the four years of Álvarez's anti-Communist crusade and brought to light the contra involvement. Ricardo Lau ("El Chino"), a former colonel in Somoza's secret police who was head of the FDN's counterintelligence unit and had his own death squad, appeared to be implicated in numerous cases of disappearances. When he was questioned, he admitted to having done a few "little jobs" for the Honduran armed forces. He was invited to leave the country.[24]

NICARAGUA AND THE "SECRET" WAR

The Sandinistas knew that with Reagan in the White House there would be no peace. Aggression came at once. He cut off economic aid to Nicaragua, authorized the CIA to create a paramilitary force with Nicaraguan counter-revolutionaries, and launched a campaign to disparage the Sandinista revolution. He painted it as a military threat to the region and to United States security, and he developed an active diplomatic offensive to isolate Nicaragua.

The CIA found fertile ground to form the counterrevolutionary paramilitary force. Former Somoza guards were already receiving military instruction in clandestine camps in Florida and in Argentine military centers. The CIA task was to unite the forces. High officials of the former National Guard who had fled with Somoza were in Miami. Others were in neighboring countries (3,000 in Honduras), and hundreds remained in Nicaraguan jails.[25]

A former colonel, Enrique Bermúdez, once Somoza's military attaché in Washington (and on the CIA's payroll since 1980), and a group of Somoza's guards hidden on a Guatemalan hacienda formed the September 15 Legion and proclaimed themselves the Army of the Nicaraguan National Guard. They included a contingent of Somoza's personal bodyguards who arrived in Guatemala after an Argentine rebel commando "executed" him in Paraguay, destroying his car with a bazooka on September 17, 1980. Bermúdez supported the Legion with funds from Somoza's cousin Luis Pallais Debayle and from payments made to him by Mario Sandoval (godfather of the Guatemalan death squads) for "special operations" (robbery, extortion, abductions, torture, and assassinations),[26] and funds received from the Argentine army in exchange for his help in hunting down Argentine refugees in Nicaragua.[27]

Other figures among these forces included Luis Fley (with the intentionally misspelled nom de guerre "Jhonson"), who deserted the Sandinista ranks and joined the Contras in 1981, and Pablo Emilio Salazar (*Comandante Bravo*), exiled to Honduras and considered by the Sandinistas to be the most ferocious of Somoza's former officers. He led a counterrevolutionary group. Tomás Borge, Nicaragua's minister of the interior, persuaded one of Bravo's former girlfriends to travel to Honduras to kill Bravo. His disfigured corpse was found four days later. "The head of a counterrevolutionary sector has been cut off. The enemies of our people will fall one by one," Borge commented coldly in a radio talk when the remains were discovered.[28]

Bermúdez united small groups of former guards camped out in Honduras, Guatemala, and Florida. Within a month he had 600 men in arms. General Vernon Walters, Reagan's ambassador-at-large, demanded that those forces be kept under the command of the former guards for their military training. He was not concerned about their bad image within Nicaragua and abroad because of the innumerable and horrendous crimes they had committed under Somoza's dictatorship. Some of the "rebels" agreed to remain under their command because without United States aid they could never succeed. The Legion formally joined with these counterrevolutionary forces to form the main nucleus.[29]

They were also volunteers, like Jhonson, who joined out of conviction and others who had become disillusioned with the Sandinistas when they confiscated their lands, closed their small businesses, or met with hostility and were called counterrevolutionaries for refusing to collaborate or refusing to work on the state cooperatives. There were also those who served by necessity: exiles dying of hunger, adventurers, and unemployed Hondurans. The CIA also recruited mercenaries in Latin America.

Another counterrevolutionary was Edén Pasotra (*Comandante Zero*), who deserted from the Sandinista ranks because of the government's leftist tendencies. He formed a group that included Miskitu indigenous volunteers and installed himself in Costa Rica on the Nicaraguan border. Teadman Fagoth created MISURA and Brooklyn Rivera, MISURASATA.[30]

The CIA baptized the contra forces "Fuerza Democrática Nicaragüense" (FDN: Nicaraguan Democratic Forces) and named Bermúdez Comandante. He was a lusterless officer with no military experience at all, but the CIA wanted him to be a figurehead, to pay and organize the forces, recruit, and obey orders.[31]

Washington's secret aid to the FDN came to light on December 23, 1982, when the *New York Times* and other papers reported the existence of clandestine camps in Florida where former Nicaraguan guards were being trained by Green Berets and Cuban Bay of Pigs veterans. The media also revealed that a force of Nicaraguan counterrevolutionaries was being formed in Honduras. In Florida a "rebel" noted that, "under the Carter and Nixon administrations these activities were a crime," but that under Reagan nobody interfered with them. Undersecretary of State for Inter-American Affairs Enders excused such activities claiming they were not breaking any laws or preparing any particular invasion.

Day by day the Reagan administration's support of these paramilitary forces became more evident and more worrisome for Congress. The House Foreign Relations Committee wanted Haig to testify about whether the government was aiding or supporting the Nicaraguan exiles in an attempt to overthrow the Sandinista government, and further if he was considering imposing a naval blockade on Nicaragua, since such acts would violate United States neutrality laws. Haig limited himself to repeating his accusations against the Sandinista government, which he called totalitarian, and said that a naval blockade would be "a sensible measure" against such a government. "Based on your response," said Representative Michael Barnes, "if I were a Nicaraguan I would begin building a bomb shelter this afternoon."[32]

PREPARING FOR THE WAR

Reagan immediately sent General Walters to Argentina and asked Congress to lift the arms embargo Carter had imposed on that country. Reagan needed the collaboration of Argentine military officers—masters of "dirty war"—for his Central American operations, to train the Nicaraguan "rebel" forces. This was an easy task given that they were already training the armies and security forces of El Salvador, Honduras, and Guatemala and advising their intelligence services. Besides, they had been giving military instruction to Somoza's former guards at their military centers since 1980.[33]

At the end of 1981 the governments of the United States, Honduras, and Argentina came to an unwritten "tripartite" agreement to develop the war against Nicaragua and define their tasks. The United States would finance arms purchases and direct operations, and Argentine military officers would train the contras and the Salvadoran army and would serve as intermediaries for the military and economic assistance, which the Reagan administration could not send directly, since it had been prohibited by Congress. Honduras would be the base of operations.[34]

With funds from the CIA, the Argentines rented the hacienda La Quinta (the property of a French national), located seven miles from the Toncontín International Airport, and installed their secret base. The Argentines—"authoritarian" and "distant," commented a contra—warned them that they were there to learn how to make war and should not concern themselves with who their teachers were. These men were not allowed to have contact with anyone but their own commandos and were not allowed off the base. In December 1981, after several weeks of training, the first "combat unit" was ready. These men were issued blue uniforms, explosives, and detonators and taken to the border. They left La Quinta at night and hid in Honduran military trucks.[35] In spite of the secrecy and the precautions they took, by the end of 1981 reporters were beginning to verify the mysterious truck movements and the uniformed men leaving this tumbledown hacienda.

The Argentine advisers were the CIA's right hand, since they trained the FDN and planned and directed its operations. In 1982 Argentina reduced its collaboration because of Reagan's "betrayal" in the Malvinas War and ended it altogether when Raúl Alfonsín was elected president in October 1983. At that point the CIA took over direction of the operation, and Bermúdez emerged as the "true Comandante." This move was a disaster, since the war was leaderless.

When the Argentines left, the gringos built their barracks at La Quinta far from the contras and kept the groups separated from each other. Compartmentalization was the catch-phrase. The contras commented that the gringos were friendlier than the Argentines, though they wouldn't let them leave the base either. The food was better as well. On the weekends most of the gringos—never dressed in military uniforms—went to Tegucigalpa to get drunk. One of them stayed at the base, as a kind of babysitter, explained one contra. Confined to their base, they remained ignorant of the fact that the FDN was only one of four armies patronized by the CIA. They did not know that there were two groups of Miskitu Indians, another led by Edén Pastora in Costa Rica, and a fifth, a smaller and more lethal elite group of sabotage technicians, composed of mercenaries from Colombia, Ecuador, Honduras, and other Latin American countries, which was under direct CIA control.[36]

The CIA placed great hopes in Edén Pastora, the flamboyant Commander Zero, who resigned from his post as vice minister of defense, escaped to Panama in 1982, went to Costa Rica, and installed a group of counterrevolutionaries on the Nicaraguan border. For a year the CIA gave him $150,000 a month to support the group. When the agency proposed that he open a southern front and join the FDN, and he refused, they cut off his support. Pastora declared that he would never join the "fascist" and "genocidal" former Somoza guards on orders from the CIA and Washington. "Before I'll work with them," he said, "the CIA will have to kill me."[37]

In May 1984, during a press conference with several foreign journalists at La Penca, Costa Rica—a small hunting lodge on the San Juan River—an attempt was made on Pastora's life. Some of those present were killed and others were gravely wounded—Pastora was seriously wounded. Many saw the long arm of the CIA behind this assassination attempt. Tired and frustrated with the lack of support for his movement, Pastora announced in 1986 that he was leaving the guerrilla movement. "There is no reason," he announced, "for another Nicaraguan to die, since there is no possibility of a military victory." The government of Óscar Arias had already told him that he was no longer welcome in its country.[38]

The CIA and Bermúdez lost a valuable ally when General Álvarez was arrested and sent to another country by his comrades-in-arms. The Honduran military officers distanced themselves but agreed to cooperate. Henceforth, they stated, the operations would be "entirely the responsibility of the United States."[39]

In December 1981, the FDN launched its first operation against Nicaragua—"Red Christmas"—with the objective of establishing a "liberated zone" and installing a "provisional government" to which the United States would give military aid. It was meant to signal the beginning of the collapse of Sandinismo. While they did not succeed, they did manage to kill sixty campesinos and torture and assassinate seven Sandinista soldiers.[40]

The Sandinistas moved 8,500 Miskitu and Sumus Indians from the Río Coco region on the Honduran border, an area repeatedly attacked by the contras, to a camp 50 miles away. The militarization of this zone, with the burning of crops and houses, caused the exodus of 10,000 Miskitus to Honduras, a move that was harshly criticized both within and outside Nicaragua. The Catholic Church hierarchy sent a strongly worded statement condemning it as a violation of human rights. Washington accused Nicaragua of genocide. Ambassador Jeane Kirkpatrick did likewise in the United Nations, and Haig exhibited photographs of soldiers burning the corpses of Miskitus. Two days later, the French weekly *Le Figaro*, from which the photos were taken, explained that the photos showed the Red Cross burning the corpses of people assassinated by Somoza's National Guard in 1978. Americas Watch countered accusations by MISURA leader Fagoth, who was brought to Washington by a United States ultraright organization to present his accusations to Congress and officials at the State Department. Fagoth accused the Sandinista government of murdering 300 indigenous people and disappearing thousands. Some time later the Sandinistas recognized the terrible abuses committed during this relocation. In 1986, they announced that they would compensate the families of the dead and disappeared.[41]

From December 1981 to June 1982 the contra operations were brutal. The contras ambushed military patrols, attacked towns, destroyed government installations and agricultural cooperatives, assassinated officials and Cuban advisers, and killed and abducted some 600 campesinos to force them to join their ranks.

The CIA became involved. In March 1982 the simultaneous demolition of two main bridges over the Río Negro, near the towns of Somolillo in Chinandega and Ocotal in Nueva Segovia in Nicaragua's north, indicated to the Sandinistas that the United States was becoming directly involved in this "war." They accused the CIA of sabotage. The White House refused to confirm or deny the accusation, but two months later, in testimony before the House Intelligence Committee, the CIA admitted that one of its specialized demolition teams had destroyed the bridges. The Committee did not object to this confirmation, commented the *Washington Post*, because these bridges were supposedly used for the illegal shipment of arms to the Salvadoran guerrillas.[42]

Since Nicaragua was a victim of outside aggression, the Sandinista government declared a state of emergency, put the army on total alert, imposed press censorship, limited civil rights, prohibited strikes and free transit in the war zones, and increased its vigilance over dissidents.[43] Daniel Ortega called an urgent meeting of the United Nations Security Council to denounce the aggression, but at the same time he expressed his willingness to negotiate with the United States to improve their relations.

Though Washington was not interested in such a discussion, it did not want to appear to be opposed to negotiating. In August, Enders went to Managua with a plan for a feasible arrangement with Nicaragua. He asked the Nicaraguans to suspend their aid to the Salvadoran guerrillas, stop arming themselves, reduce the number of soldiers from 23,000 to 15,000, and substantially decrease military relations with Cuba and the Soviet Union. In exchange Enders gave assurances that the United States would not isolate Nicaragua economically or diplomatically, would renew aid, and would not support the Nicaraguan counterrevolutionaries.[44]

The Sandinistas called the plan an ultimatum, since it was not negotiable. Arturo Cruz, Nicaragua's ambassador to Washington, commented that they seemed like the "conditions of a victorious power." The Sandinistas denied that they were sending arms to El Salvador. They claimed that the weapons circulating in the region belonged to private individuals. They offered to help stop the flow if the United States would reveal what they knew about this matter. They did not accept Enders's plan. "It's a question of principles," said Comandante

Bayardo Arce to *New York Times* correspondent Stephen Kinzer. They could not make a deal with a man like Reagan.[45] Enders returned empty-handed.

Neither the CIA nor the Argentines were satisfied with the FDN's performance. Despite the training it received, the supply of arms, and the careful strategies, its military activity amounted to nothing. The groups did not succeed in staying in Nicaragua nor taking a piece of territory as a "liberated zone," their mentors' primary objective. Its activities were reduced to short incursions in zones close to the border, assassinations, torture, abduction and mutilation of campesinos, rapes and kidnappings of young women and girls, and silent retreats to their bases in Honduras.[46]

If the results of this "war" were poor, the State Department did no better. In March 1982, the lack of foundation for its accusations was exposed. Haig wanted to show that Cuba and Nicaragua were involved with the Salvadoran guerrillas and to demonstrate the dangerous connections of Central American subversion by means of testimony from a Nicaraguan guerrilla, Orlando Tardencillas, who joined the Salvadoran guerrillas and had been captured the previous year in El Salvador. They pulled him out of a prison in San Salvador, in violation of international legal practice, and took him to Washington to present him on television. He was supposed to say that he had been given military training in Cuba and Ethiopia, and that he was sent to El Salvador by the Sandinista government. Instead he revealed on camera that he was "physically and psychologically tortured before being brought to the United States, that United States Embassy officials in El Salvador told him what to say, and gave him the option "to come or face death." He testified that the accusations about his training in Cuba and Ethiopia were false, that the Nicaraguan government had nothing to do with his decision to join the Salvadoran guerrillas, and that he had not seen a single Cuban or Nicaraguan involved with the Salvadoran guerrillas. Tardencillas returned to Nicaragua a hero. "It was a disaster. I don't know whether I should laugh or cry," said a high United States official.[47]

The CIA urgently needed a quick and spectacular contra victory. It prepared a large military offensive to "take" the city of Jalapa in Nueva Segovia Province in northern Nicaragua, declare it a "liberated zone," and install a provisional government, which the United States would immediately support. According to the CIA, Jalapa was an easy target, since it was near the border and abutted on three sides by Honduras. At the end of 1982, a thousand contras, trained and armed with light artillery and mortars, attacked Jalapa, but the Sandinista defenses prevented them from occupying it. Nevertheless they caused substantial destruction to Jalapa and neighboring towns. Pedro Javier Núñez, known as "El Muerto" ("The Dead Man"), who was captured in this operation, confirmed that the objective was to install a provisional government. Four other attempts to take Jalapa between March and June 1983 also failed.[48]

By the end of 1982, the FDN gangs were attacking almost daily. They burned and destroyed government installations, but their main activity continued to be brutal attacks on the civilian population. Father James Feltz, a Protestant pastor in Bocana de Paiwas in the Matagalpa region, was a witness to several of these attacks. He said that when he saw them crossing the Río Grande and invading the area it was "like death descending." He compared them to Attila's hordes.[49]

The Sandinistas infiltrated their agents among the campesinos captured in the contra raids. From information provided by one of these in 1982, led by Francisco Baldivia ("Dimas Tigrillo"), a rebel campesino, they located the Wina base in northern Nicaragua. Hundreds of soldiers, their advance covered by helicopters, surrounded and destroyed it, killing scores of contras.[50]

THE "RESURRECTION"

The image of the FDN, whom Reagan dubbed "freedom fighters" and compared to the Founding Fathers, was lamentable. They were nothing more than gangs of terrorists and assassins dominated by Somoza's former guards, who made up 99 percent of the command and directorate. Their atrocities were common knowledge, as was the fact that the CIA had resurrected Somoza's national guard.[51] This image urgently needed to be changed. At the end of 1982 it hastily created the Political Directorate of the FDN to serve as a decorous civilian cover, uncontaminated by connection to Somoza. It was formed by Adolfo Calero, a political conservative and a former director of Coca-Cola in Nicaragua; Alfonso Robelo, a former member of the Sandinista junta and president of the Movimiento Democrático Nicaragüense (MDN: Nicaraguan Democratic Movement, a faction of the ARDE movement created by Pastora); Edgar Chamorro, the FDN spokesman, a former Jesuit who took off his priestly robes in 1969; Alfonso Callejas, the former vice president of Nicaragua until his break with Somoza in 1972; Lucía Salazar, the widow of assassinated anti-Sandinista conspirator Jorge Salazar; Indalecio Rodríguez, a doctor and former dean of the university; and the former Colonel Enrique Bermúdez (the only one tainted by Somozismo), Commander of the FDN. Calero accepted the presidency of the directorate and the post of commander-in-chief of the FDN and moved to Miami.

Arturo Cruz called the members of this Directorate, who were generously paid by the CIA and installed in luxurious offices and residences in exclusive neighborhoods of Miami, the "Key Biscayne Mafia." In March 1985, after being recruited by North, Cruz joined this mafia[52] and began publicly supporting United States aid to the FDN, defending the "rebels," justifying their atrocities—he blamed Sandinista negligence—and lobbying Congress to renew military aid to the group. At a certain point he admitted to having secretly received money from an organization connected with the CIA.[53] He resigned in 1987.

In the middle of 1983, the CIA discovered that the FDN had its own courts, its own prisons, its own torture chambers and clandestine cemeteries where it buried those it executed. Other corpses were thrown in the river or buried inside Nicaragua so as to leave no traces. Women prisoners were raped daily. Such a display of brutality terrorized even the contras.[54]

In three years of "war" the CIA was never concerned with these crimes—not because it was unaware of them, since the agency had been monitoring the FDN's activities since the previous year. One of its agents, a "Major Ricardo" of Colombian extraction, went every day from camp to camp, refuge to refuge, commander to commander, asking questions and taking notes on what he saw and heard, to report to his superiors. The CIA also paid informants in the FDN ranks. It had them in every base and unit. One of them was Ernesto Ortega, a former Lieutenant in Somoza's guard and Bermúdez's personal secretary.[55]

The CIA was shocked, not by the crimes, but by the thievery and embezzlement it discovered. At least half of what it paid Bermúdez for the support and salaries of these forces went into his pockets and those of the group personnel closest to him. The forces went hungry, and their commanders went unpaid. The agency also discovered that they were selling weapons to the Salvadoran guerrillas. But what bothered it most was the evidence that in the past three years Bermúdez and the commanders installed in Tegucigalpa were increasingly less concerned with the "war." They passed the nights in bars, or playing roulette in the Hotel Maya casino, surrounded by whores, while the "secret war" became big news in the United States and Congress began to consider "cutting off funds for CIA operations in Central America," wrote American journalist Sam Dillon.[56]

A great many commanders signed petitions to have the CIA expel Bermúdez, FDN chief of counterinsurgency Ricardo Lau, and the whole command structure, not only for stealing their paychecks but because they remained ensconced in Tegucigalpa, 186 miles from the "theater of opera-tions."[57] Bermúdez began to bribe his accusers and Lau—an assassin—to alert them that he was not responsible for their lives and to circulate lists of those he was going to execute. Some of the signers went into hiding. The executions of prisoners, contras, and even commanders—alleged Sandinista "infiltra-tors"—created a whirlwind of terror and mistrust among the ranks.[58]

The CIA expelled the members of the command but did not touch Bermúdez. Removing him would have meant leaking the corruption scandal, which would devastate the FDN and, even more, the CIA. It dressed him up with the title Commander General of the Strategic Forces of the FDN and agreed that he should name new aides and move to Las Vegas, close to the Nicaraguan border.[59] They turned a new leaf.

OF "WAR" AND PEACE

At President Reagan's request Congress approved a multimillion dollar fund for military aid to El Salvador and other grants equally generous to stop the supposed flow of arms to the Caribbean. Congress did not know that the pay-ments meant to stop this flow went instead to support the war against Nicaragua. CIA Director William Casey, who was responsible for informing the Intelligence Committees about operations in Central America, gave false information, assuring the committee that these payments were used only for the purposes Congress had intended.

In his turn Haig continued denouncing Nicaragua. He claimed that the "unusual" buildup of its military power with Soviet weapons threatened the security of its neighbors and the United States' Enders did the same, claim-ing that Cuba was becoming a base for military operations in the Caribbean.

Nicaraguan Minister of Defense Humberto Ortega responded that Nicaragua did not have to account to anyone for the weapons it acquired, and "much less to those who are carrying on a campaign against us." In his turn he denounced Washington's plans for invading his country with the Nicaraguan mercenaries it was training in clandestine camps in Florida.

Haig continued his attacks at the OAS General Assembly at Santa Lucía in December 1981. He alleged that Nicaragua's policies were militaristic and interventionist and warned that the United States would not allow Central America to become a "platform for terror and war." Nevertheless he expressed his government's willingness to improve relations. "We do not close the doors," he said. From Managua, Daniel Ortega responded that the door he left open was "so low that in order to pass through it, we would have to do so on our knees."[60]

In January 1982, at Suázo Córdova's inauguration as president of Honduras, attended by several Latin American presidents, Enders pulled a proposal out of his hat for creating a Central American Democratic Community. This would not include Guatemala, since General Efraín Ríos Montt's genocidal regime would have given a bad name to this institution, created during a time of crisis "in defense of democratic values." The presidents of Colombia and Venezuela, Turbay Ayala and Herrera Campins signed on. Enders announced that the United States would also be part of this "community." It was a mechanism conceived to oppose Nicaragua.

Mexican President José López Portillo proposed a peace plan at a COPPAL (Conference of Latin American Political Parties) meeting in Managua in February 1982, and offered himself as a mediator among the parties to resolve what he called the three cruxes of the crisis: the conflict in El Salvador, the tensions between the United States and Nicaragua, and relations between Washington and Havana. He proposed various nonaggression pacts, the demilitarization of Nicaragua, the removal of United States forces in the area, demobilization of the FDN, and the suspension of training of exiles in the United States. Nicaragua immediately supported Mexico's proposal.[61] The day López Portillo arrived in Managua, a bomb exploded at the international airport. Four baggage handlers were killed and three were seriously wounded.[62]

López Portillo's visit to Nicaragua and his peace proposal were a serious problem for Washington. Haig gave the cold shoulder to his proposal. He found it insufficient since it did not guarantee that Cuba and Nicaragua would suspend their subversive activities. A few days later, at a special session of the OAS, Reagan presented his Caribbean Basin Initiative and ignored Mexico's proposal. He also ignored a petition by 100 members of Congress, who urged him to accept Mexico's mediation.[63]

Shortly thereafter, Mexican Chancellor Jorge Casteñeda had a long conversation with Haig in New York, which both characterized as positive.[64] Afterward he traveled to Havana and interviewed Fidel Castro. In a letter to López Portillo, Castro expressed his willingness to cooperate but stated that the United States must first promise not to attack its neighbors and put an end to its continual threats, suspend aid to the "genocidal governments" of Central America and its subversive activities in the region.

The new ambassador to Nicaragua, Anthony Quainton—a former Director of the State Department Office for Combating Terrorism—arrived in Managua with an eight-point plan, which was essentially the Enders proposal rejected by the Sandinistas with one addition: Nicaragua was to democratize its policies and hold elections.[65]

Nicaragua responded with a thirteen-point plan and repeated its willingness to negotiate with Washington. It asked that representatives to such talks be high level, meet in Mexico, with Mexican mediators present. The United States replied that the representatives would have ambassadorial status, without Mexican mediators.[66]

Honduras and Nicaragua were nearly at war over the terrorist activities of the contras, who were operating from Honduras. Everything pointed to Washington involvement, with the intention of provoking a conflict so that it could later intervene. Presidents Herrera Campins and López Portillo offered to mediate, and Honduran President Suázo Córdova accepted at once. Without responding to the presidents, Reagan rushed to organize what he termed a Forum for Peace and Democracy in Costa Rica, from which Nicaragua was excluded. Mexico and Venezuela sent their regrets. The meeting was a farce.

In mid-1982 the *Miami Herald* and *Newsweek* revealed that the contra war was a CIA operation and that Reagan was breaking the law. He was using funds meant to stem the arms flow to back the war against Nicaragua. To this point he had presented no evidence that any arms had been captured or even that the "arms flow" existed. Deane Hinton, the former Ambassador in El Salvador, assured the Senate Foreign Relations Committee that "not even a pistol" had been seized. Honduran Army Captain González, commander of the fleet of speedboats called Piranhas, whose job was to stop such trafficking in the Gulf of Fonseca, said that for an entire year he had not seen so much as a single weapon.[67] To keep this diversion of funds from continuing, the House unanimously passed the Boland Amendment in December—introduced by Representative Edward "Tip" Boland—prohibiting the CIA, the Defense Department, and any other department or intelligence agency from using fiscal 1983–1984 funds directly or indirectly for operations whose goal it was to overthrow the Nicaraguan government or foment war between Nicaragua and Honduras. These funds could only be used to stem the flow of arms to the Salvadoran guerrillas. According to analysts, the terms of this amendment were ambiguous enough to give the CIA grounds to continue its operations against Nicaragua. Reagan signed the bill into law and proceeded to ignore it.

That same month Reagan undertook a five-day trip to Brazil, Colombia, Costa Rica, and Honduras, with the intention of persuading their governments to support his policies in Central America, which most of Latin America opposed. Reagan arrived surrounded by a swarm of secret agents, who were reinforced in every country by troops, police, and security agents. The streets through which his bulletproof limousine (sent from Washington) passed were secured by cordons of heavily armed policemen. Reagan did not see the angry demonstrations caused by his presence.[68]

Washington announced that the visit was at the invitation of the governments. However, at a banquet in Reagan's honor Colombian President Belisario Betancur stated that the invitation had been made at Washington's suggestion. He then criticized Reagan's Central America policies and those against Nicaragua and Cuba and deplored that Cuba was still being excluded from the OAS.[69]

In San José, Costa Rica, Reagan spoke with President Monge and Salvadoran President Alvaro Magaña, and in Honduras with Suázo Córdova. He flew to San Pedro de Sula on the Guatemalan border to talk to General Ríos Montt, whom he gave, in his own words, "a pat on the ass." From Managua, Daniel Ortega said, "Reagan's embrace comes full of blood, death, and tragedy."[70]

The press commented on Reagan's embarrassing mistakes during his tour. At the banquet given in his honor in Brazil, he toasted Brazilian President General Joao Figueiredo as "the President of Bolivia." He corrected himself. "That's the next country I will visit"; his next stop was Colombia. Returning to Washington, he said that he "learned a lot" about Latin America and that he was surprised to see that they were individual countries. When the *Washington Post* mocked his ignorance, he said privately that what he had meant to say was that it was not a single entity, as many perceived it to be.[71]

CONTADORA: SOUNDING THE ALARM

Latin America could not stand aside while Reagan lighted a match and torched the region. Colombian President Betancur went to Venezuela, Panama, and Mexico and agreed with their presidents in a quick and successful move to seek a negotiated solution to the explosive situation. In January 1983, the chancellors of these four countries met on the Panamanian island of Contadora, and penned a declaration that expressed (without mentioning the United States) their "profound concern" about "direct or indirect foreign interference in Central American conflicts," and that such conflicts were being viewed as part of the East-West confrontation. It urged the conflicting nations to establish a dialogue to reduce tensions, for "all States to refrain from using threats or force in international relations" or engage in any action that might worsen the situation and cause the conflict to spread throughout the region.[72] This was Latin America's first alert concerning the serious regional crisis and the United States policies in the region.

Between April and May of the same year the Contadora and Central American chancellors agreed on the form for initiating the peace process and agenda for the negotiations. Their greatest concern was the tension between Honduras and Nicaragua, which were on the brink of war.[73] That July, in Cancún, Mexico, the presidents in the Contadora Group issued another declaration in which they expressed their "deep concern" about the rapid deterioration of the situation in Central America. They urged its people to sign agreements to suspend hostilities, freeze the level of armaments, eliminate foreign advisers, and prohibit foreign military bases. Nicaragua supported the declaration and announced that it would participate in multilateral negotiations.

On July 19, the fourth anniversary of the triumph of the Sandinista revolution, Daniel Ortega expressed his support of Contadora and presented a six-point peace proposal on security concerns. He proposed a nonaggression treaty with Honduras, an end to arms shipments to El Salvador, suspension of military aid to any forces opposed to any Central American government, guarantees of respect for free self-determination and nonintervention, suspension of economic discrimination and hostilities toward any of its countries, prohibition of foreign military bases in Central America, and the suspension of maneuvers with foreign forces.[74]

The United States and its allies in Central America, though they acknowledged the importance of the Cancún Declaration, declared that the proposal omitted many important matters, among them democratization and verification—these were United States priorities. In a letter to the Contadora chancellors, Secretary of State George Shultz claimed that "only by assuring free and open participation in the democratic process can the people of Central America achieve reconciliation within their societies."[75]

At a fourth meeting in Panama in September 1983, the chancellors approved the document of objectives, known as the 21 Points of Contadora, and announced that they had negotiated with Central American chancellors to arrive at agreements and establish mechanisms tending to formalize and develop these objectives. Again, without naming the United States specifically, they criticized its policies and sought to put an end to its war against Nicaragua and the United States military presence in Central America. The United States had to pull out its forces thirty days after the agreement was signed.

In October Nicaragua proposed—in the framework of Contadora—four nonaggression treaties with Honduras and the United States and one on the Salvadoran conflict. The United States rejected this proposal.

In the upper echelons in Washington there was considerable alarm over the growing Latin American opposition to its Central American policies, over the exclusion of the United States from regional negotiation forums, and Contadora's enormous support in Congress. Its boycott of Contadora was more unpopular at home and abroad with each passing day, and its militaristic policies more harshly criticized. In March 1983 Reagan named former Republican Senator Richard Stone as his envoy to Central America to seek solutions with the governments there. (Stone performed his futile mission until February 1984). In July Reagan set up a bipartisan commission, comprised of six Republicans and six Democrats and led by Henry Kissinger, to visit those countries including Nicaragua, and develop a long-term policy for the region. Both were measures that served no purpose other than window dressing.

The Kissinger Commission made two brief visits to Central America (accompanied by Oliver North). It arrived in Managua on October 15 and stayed less than a day. It met with Daniel Ortega and other members of the government, but it spent most of its time interviewing opposition leaders. Nora Astorga, vice minister of foreign affairs and Nicaragua's ambassador to the United Nations, said that Kissinger arrived with preconceived ideas and wanted nothing more than to confirm them. She commented that during the interview with Ortega, she heard someone whisper in Kissinger's ear, "Let's not listen to this son of a bitch any longer."[76]

In January 1984, the commission published its findings in a 132-page document, in which it proposed increasing military aid to El Salvador only on the condition that the human-rights situation improve (a demand by San Antonio's Mayor Henry Cisneros, one of the commission members), aid for the war against Nicaragua (Cisneros had reservations), and an economic aid program of $8 billion over five years (this was unrealistic, given the enormous economic difficulties of the United States). The commission offered no solution to the conflict to Congress, which was deeply divided over the issue of aid to the FDN.

THE "FIGHTERS" ON THE ATTACK

In 1983 the war against Nicaragua began to spread and become bloodier. Raymond Doty, CIA station chief in Tegucigalpa (1982–1985), a former army sergeant and a veteran of the war in Laos, pushed the contras to plunge further into Nicaragua and remain in "combat" longer. The group, led by the wild Luis Moreno Payán—"Mike Lima"— a former second lieutenant in Somoza's guardia, advanced 60, 80, possibly even 100 miles into Nicaraguan territory, leaving in its wake death and destruction. Its theater of operations covered broad campesino areas.

FDN spokesman Edgar Chamorro claimed that the "rebel" forces—4,000 armed men—were ready to confront the Sandinistas. He claimed that the CIA had transformed them into a well-organized, well-armed, and well-trained combat force "capable of inflicting great damage on Nicaragua."[77] The CIA formed the Special Operations Commando, an elite sabotage unit, with twelve of its best men (among them Jhonson), and placed it in the Las Vegas region close to the Nicaraguan border. This was the headquarters of the FDN's Strategic Command under Bermúdez. In Las Vegas the CIA created its own unit.[78]

In spite of so much preparation, the Special Operations Commando went from failure to failure. Some of its operations, planned by the Argentines, were led by Jhonson. He failed twice to destroy twelve new Soviet tanks stationed at the La Laguna military base 12 miles from Chinandega. He also botched three attempts to blow up the Pasa Caballos Bridge, the longest on the Pacific Coast and of special strategic importance because it was heavily protected by the Sandinistas. (A CIA sabotage team also failed to destroy it.) Between March and June 1983 he again failed in four new attempts to take Jalapa, and five Miskitu columns comprised of 125 men each, which attempted to take Puerto Cabezas on the Atlantic Coast, were dispersed by the Sandinistas. The objective of most of these operations was still to "liberate" a piece of territory in order to install a "provisional government."

In September 1983, Operation Marathon, a plan for simultaneous attacks on towns close to the border, began with attacks on Ocotal and Somoto in the north. In October, Mike Lima, a man obsessed with raping and killing campesinas, according to one of his men, attacked other northern Nicaraguan towns, causing enormous destruction and death.[79] His offensive against the town of Pantasma, 80 miles from Managua, was one of the most devastating and bloody of this dirty war. His men destroyed a substantial part of the town, robbed the bank, rounded up the terrified people, and stabbed several persons in public. Ten officials from the ministry of education, armed with rifles and among them three female teachers, put up the fiercest resistance. When the contras demanded their surrender, they responded, "Eat shit, Guardia pigs! We are Sandinistas!" Some thirty-five contras surrounded the building where they were, lobbed grenades into it, and set it on fire. The people heard the teachers' screams, trapped in the flames while the building collapsed. Approximately fifty died in the Pantasma attack, with material losses calculated at 34 million córdobas (roughly $2 million). The Sandinista government called this attack a "massacre" and an "atrocity" and cited it as an example of contra savagery.[80]

When he returned to Honduras, Mike Lima's comrades welcomed him as a hero. The CIA sent a helicopter to bring him to Tegucigalpa, so that Doty and other agents could congratulate him. For the CIA and the FDN it was a brilliant coup—one of their few successes—and a "great victory." From his behind-the-lines war in Miami, Adolfo Calero promised, "There will be more Pantasmas!"[81]

Lacking the funds denied by Congress, the White House sought to fund the FDN with aid from friendly governments and the United States private sector. It encouraged the formation of foundations and pseudoprivate humanitarian organizations to collect donations. Contributors to the "noble cause" of supporting the Nicaraguan people in their struggle for the "liberation" of their homeland included nongovernmental organizations, friendly governments, princes and sheiks—owners of Middle Eastern oil wealth—and a handful of "altruistic" potentates and millionaires' widows who opened their pocketbooks to the "rebels" so that they could kill Communists "down there."

At this moment of need Secretary of Defense Caspar Weinberger offered the President "broad" and secret Pentagon support for CIA operations in Central America. He would give them arms and military personnel. He proceeded to send military teams and weapons destined for the FDN, including three Cessna aircraft modified to carry rockets, helicopters, and personnel from Pentagon intelligence divisions. This personnel took part in terrorist operations, in sabotage by dynamite, in rocket attacks on Nicaragua's ports, in blowing up its only oil pipeline at Puerto Sandino, and in the destruction of several bridges. They also participated in the contras' military activities.[82]

In April 1983, Reagan asked for a joint session of Congress to explain his Central American policies. In the speech, described by *The Nation* magazine as "ferocious, distorted and inflammatory," full of "false historical analogies" and "willful fabrications of fact,"[83] Reagan presented this crisis as a problem of vital national interest. He declared that the geographic proximity of the region directly affected the security and well-being of the people of the United States. Congress was not convinced by his rhetoric and his alarm at the "Red Menace." The House and the Senate decided to send their own missions to Central America. Upon their return, both commissions concluded that Reagan was in violation, at least in "spirit," of the Boland Amendment. In May the House Intelligence Committee cut off funding for CIA operations in the region, since the money was not being used to intercept weapons, as the administration claimed, but to attempt an overthrow of the Sandinista government. The same month CIA Director Casey and Enders assured the Intelligence Committees of both houses that the FDN had "good possibilities" for overthrowing the government, which they predicted would fall by the end of the year. "They told us," commented one representative, "that if we cut aid we w[ould] be responsible for aborting a great opportunity to roll back Communist advances in Central America."[84]

In June the press revealed that the United States administration wanted public opinion to see the Nicaraguan question as an international matter by provoking a crisis similar to that of the Soviet missiles in Cuba in 1962. Official sources did in fact claim that the Sandinistas intended to receive Cuban troops and install a Soviet nuclear base in their country. If that happened, wrote the *Miami Herald*, the "Soviet or Cuban" military installations would be bombed, and if Nicaragua acquired MIG aircraft, a naval blockade—possibly including Cuba—would be imposed and United States combat forces and military aircraft would be based in Honduras. Tomás Borge strongly denied these tall tales.[85]

Soon after Contadora presented its first peace proposal in July 1983, the United States dispatched fleets of warships to the Caribbean and Pacific and announced joint maneuvers with Honduras—Big Pine II—in Honduran territory.[86]

Intelligence reports began to be leaked to the press, indicating large FDN advances and predicting its "victory" within six months. There was haste and worry at high levels in Washington. A National Security Council document from July 1983 noted that the Pentagon saw the Central American situation as reaching a "critical point," but that it was still possible to achieve its objectives without the direct involvement of United States troops, provided effective action was taken.

Also in July, the *New York Times*, in an article headlined, "Reagan Plans to Increase Military Activity in Central America," reported that naval and aerial maneuvers starting in August would serve to augment the United States military presence in the region and to prepare for a blockade of Nicaragua. The maneuvers lasted six months. A spy ship equipped with combat helicopters and a force of Latin American mercenaries (UCLA) was anchored off Nicaragua's coast. From this "mothership" the CIA began to sabotage industrial and commercial enterprises along the coasts.[87]

After the United States invasion of Grenada in October 1983 Nicaragua feared that it was the next target. It mobilized the army, the reserves, the popular militias, and the Sandinista defense committees and prepared shelters and emergency medical assistance and evacuation systems throughout the country. The message to Washington was that an invasion of Nicaragua would be much more costly than that of Grenada. At the same time it made motions to lower tensions with Washington: press censorship strictures were loosened, the Salvadoran insurgents were asked to move their offices to another country, and Cuba was asked to remove its technicians and teachers (some 2,000 left). In December it freed the Miskitu prisoners, decreed an amnesty for the insurgents in the north of Zelaya Province, and announced that it would allow exiles and contras (excluding Somoza's guards) to return. It said that if they returned, they could participate in the distribution of agrarian reform lands, and that those who lost their lands would have them returned with compensation. By mid-December more than a hundred had returned.

Nicaragua again presented peace proposals. Chancellor D'Escoto proposed four treaties within the Contadora framework, but Undersecretary of State for Inter-American Affairs Langhorne Motley (Enders had been replaced for being too "soft") rejected them. This new refusal by Washington to negotiate with the Sandinistas troubled Democratic members of Congress. Representative Michael Barnes stated that the administration's claims that the covert operations against Nicaragua were intended to force the Sandinistas to come to the negotiating table were untrue, since Nicaragua had tried from the outset to initiate such a dialogue, and it was the United States that refused to negotiate. He added that it became clear that the real purpose of these operations was to overthrow the Nicaragua revolution, a move that Congress had forbidden.

The invasion of Grenada, perceived by the United States public as a "victory," gave Washington a new impetus for its conceit that it could push a military solution on Nicaragua. The Central American military saw an invasion and the Sandinistas' collapse as imminent. On the advice of the southern command they revived CONDECA, a regional agreement among their armies, since Washington needed to unite these armies for an eventual intervention. In secret meetings in Tegucigalpa on October 22 and 23, 1983, United States high command and the southern command studied the possibility of a joint military action to "pacify Nicaragua" and discussed supporting a "provisional government," to be installed by the "rebels" in some part of the country. General Álvarez, the Honduran minister of defense, asserted that he intended to celebrate his birthday on December 12 in Managua.[88]

The House of Representatives also saw that Nicaragua might be Reagan's next target. On November 17, three weeks after the invasion of Grenada, it approved a resolution supporting Contadora. Its message was that it would not allow Grenada to be repeated in Central America. The solution must be a negotiated one.

THE CONTRAS' TERRORISM

Reagan's "secret war" against Nicaragua became an international grab bag. Criminals, terrorists, mercenaries, paramilitaries, soldiers of fortune, unemployed people of various nationalities, former Green Berets, Cuban veterans of the Bay of Pigs, retired military officers, former CIA agents, Argentine thugs, and Israeli advisers (some 30 in 1983) participated in one way or another.

In August 1984, Dana Parker and Jim Powell, American mercenaries, Vietnam War veterans, members of the ultraright paramilitary organization Civilian Military Assistance (CMA, founded by members of the Ku Klux Klan and the John Birch Society), arrived at the Las Vegas base, brought in by Adolfo Calero's brother Mario to serve as trainers. Within a month Bermúdez authorized them to carry out an attack on the Apalí military base ten miles from the Honduran border, one of the CIA's targets. They filled three small Cessna aircraft and one helicopter of the FDN "Air Force"—donated by the Pentagon—with rockets, machine guns, and enough ammunition to "kill Communists from the air," as they put it. The Cessnas, piloted by Nicaraguans, bombed the base and killed one woman who worked in the kitchen and three children. Not one soldier was wounded. The Sandinistas shot the helicopter down and Powell, Parker, and Marco Pozo, a Nicaraguan, died. The Sandinistas published documents and maps found in the rubble to show that Uncle Sam was deeply entrenched in this "war."[89]

This incident shocked the United States. Everyone was enraged: Congress was angry at the CIA, which it held responsible for ordering the attack; the CIA was angry at Bermúdez for authorizing it without its permission; and Bermúdez, shaking with fear, was angry at the "idiot gringos" who had convinced him to go ahead with the attack.[90]

Another great scandal began to develop when Adolfo Calero, the FDN's highest political leader, helped Frank Wohl—a twenty-one-year-old American obsessed with ultra rightwing causes who was "in love" with this war—connect with the "right guys" in Honduras. He arrived in the middle of 1984, presented himself to Bermúdez's command as an independent photographer, and

Bermúdez authorized him to go to the Las Vegas base. There he was given the distinctive FDN blue uniform, and adopted the pseudonym Rata Asesina (Assassin Rat). He came to know Benito Centeno "Mack," a former Somoza guard at whose base, La Lodosa, there occurred crimes that alarmed even the FDN Comandantes. But Mack was surrounded by a handful of assassins, his old colleagues, and was on good terms with Bermúdez, the Argentines, and the CIA agents, a trio that lacked respect for human rights. No one reproached him.

Wohl and Mack became friends, and Mack invited him to La Lodosa. Wohl spent three months with Mack's men and made incursions into Nicaragua with them. He returned to the United States from this first trip full of fervor for the contras and the war. But after his second trip, he came back disillusioned. The comandantes did no fighting. They remained in Honduras, "saving their skins," and the patrols returned claiming to have destroyed targets they had not even attacked. Wohl had thirty rolls of film and a series of thirty-two color slides. He showed them to a friend, who was horrified. The slides showed the murder of a man, from the moment he dug his own grave until an indigenous youth plunged a large knife in his heart.[91] *Newsweek* magazine published four photos from the series in April 1985, with the caption "Execution in the Jungle." This revelation led to a huge scandal. Calero, the CIA, and Oliver North objected, not to the horrible crime but to its publication. They began making high-level declarations asserting that the photos were "faked," "a trick," a piece of Sandinista propaganda. Jhonson knew this crime was the work of Mack's men. The CIA demanded that Bermúdez investigate the matter. Mack suffered no repercussions, nor was his name mentioned in connection with the crime.[92] The House of Representatives rejected (by a vote of 248 to 180) the additional aid for the FDN requested by the administration. Washington, Calero, and the contras attributed this setback to the photographs.

In March 1985, major United States media publicized the report, entitled "ContraTerror in Nicaragua," of the investigation commission led by Reed Brody, a former assistant district attorney of New York. It collected testimony from thousands of victims and eyewitnesses to contra acts from the beginning of their operations in December 1981 through January 1985. The report also included cases investigated, documented, and published by organizations in defense of human rights, and those cited in the Sandinista government report to the International Court of Justice, based on a list prepared by the Nicaraguan Catholic Church hierarchy.[93]

The Brody Report was a thorn in the side of the Reagan administration, since it exposed the "rebels'" crimes, which could potentially undermine

Reagan's campaign to obtain funds from Congress. In a speech at one of the foundations that collected money for the FDN, Reagan stated that the "so-called 'independent investigation' . . . ignored Communist brutality, the murder of the Indians and the arrest, torture, and murder of political dissidents." He claimed that Brody had been "shepherded through Nicaragua by Sandinista operatives."[94] In his *New York Times* column Anthony Lewis accused Reagan of using "Orwellian language" and "McCarthyite tactics" in his accusations against Brody.[95]

The FDN's image was one of incompetence and brutality, Bermúdez and the command were seen as inefficient and corrupt, and the political directorate— presided over by Adolfo Calero—was deemed useless and corrupt. Calero placed relatives and friends in the most lucrative positions. Besides, the operation's economic situation was critical, which was due to wastefulness or theft, as Oliver North warned Calero and Bermúdez at a meeting in Miami.[96] The bitter reality for the Washington hawks was that "their war" had been a costly failure, and the opportunistic and corrupt "freedom fighters" were plumping up their nests at Washington's expense.

TERRORISM USA

Irritated by the FDN's lack of military skill, the CIA decided to take the action against Nicaragua more directly into its own hands, though it would make it appear to be the work of the contras. The Sandinista government exposed an assassination plot against Chancellor Miguel D'Escoto. A Nicaraguan woman double agent, recruited by the CIA at the Nicaraguan embassy in Tegucigalpa, provided the information and evidence. Nicaragua expelled three American diplomats implicated in the attempt. In reprisal, the United States closed its six consulates in Nicaragua and expelled twenty-one Nicaraguan consular officials from the United States[97]

In December 1982, Tomás Borge, the minister of the interior, denounced a CIA sabotage plan and showed the press the plastic explosives, camouflaged as flashlights and lunch boxes, that were to be placed in movie theaters, supermarkets, and public transportation on Christmas Eve. The code name for this operation was Bitter Christmas.[98]

The CIA launched a series of terrorist actions from the "mothership" off Nicaragua's coast. In September 1983, the agency attacked Puerto Sandino with rockets. The following month, frogmen blew up the underwater oil pipeline in the same port—the only one in the country. In October there was an attack on Puerto Corinto, Nicaragua's largest port, with mortars, rockets and grenades, blowing up five large oil and gasoline storage tanks. More than a hundred people were wounded, and the fierce fire, which could not be brought under control for two days, forced the evacuation of 23,000 people.[99]

At dawn on September 8, two small planes flew over Nicaraguan territory and bombed a residential neighborhood in Managua near Chancellor D'Escoto's residence, the international airport, and a nearby military base. One plane was shot down and crashed into the control tower. Part of the passenger terminal was destroyed, but no one was hurt. The two pilots died. Although Edén Pastora's organization, ARDE, claimed responsibility for this act of sabotage, captured documents showed that the Cessna aircraft was registered to a company in Virginia, where the CIA had its headquarters.[100]

The most serious sabotage, however, was the mining of the ports at Corinto, Puerto Sandino, and El Bluff in January 1984. It had national and international repercussions. Faced with a flood of criticism and protests by France and Great Britain and by the governments whose ships had been sunk or damaged, Congress panicked. "[It is] an act violating international law. It is an act of war. For the life of me, I don't see how we are going to explain it," wrote angered Republican Senator Barry Goldwater, chairman of the Senate Intelligence Committee, to CIA Director William Casey.[101] The Nicaragua daily *Barricada Internacional* reported that the mines damaged the ships of nine nations, sank seven Nicaraguan fishing boats, and killed seven Nicaraguan fishermen. In March one of the mines blew a hole in a Soviet tanker and wounded several of its crew. The *Wall Street Journal* pointed out that responsibility for such acts fell on the United States since the mining was the work of the CIA.

Nonetheless the CIA attempted to hide its hand in the scandal. FDN spokesman Edgar Chamorro claimed that early on the morning of January 5, 1984, a CIA agent awakened him to give him a press communiqué written in "excellent Spanish," which he was to read immediately over the "rebel" radio station before the Sandinistas aired the news. It claimed that the FDN had placed mines at several Nicaraguan ports. This was not the first time the CIA tried to give the contras credit for operations they knew nothing about, Chamorro commented. He added that when the incident involving the Soviet tanker occurred, the same agent urged him to deny any FDN responsibility for the action.[102]

Unable to deny its responsibility for the mining of the ports, the Reagan administration went on the attack. High officials declared that this was an act of "self-defense" justified by international law, since Nicaraguan support for the Salvadoran guerrillas was an "act of aggression" to which it was responding. Reagan cynically claimed that the mines were "home-made" and could not sink ships. "I think that there was much ado about nothing," he added.[103]

In April the Sandinista government denounced this and other acts of aggression by the United States and the contras against its country at the International Court of Justice in The Hague. Nicaragua won the suit. Unanimously the court ordered the United States to immediately suspend any attempt to blockade or mine Nicaraguan ports and to respect its sovereignty, which was not to be endangered by "any military or paramilitary" action—the American judge abstained from this part of the decision. Reagan warned that the United States would not recognize the jurisdiction of the court in relation to Central America for a period of two years.

In October another major scandal erupted when the media reported the existence of a manual on terrorism produced by the CIA for the FDN's use. The manual—similar to one used for troops in Vietnam—recommended selective terrorism: assassination of government officials, state security officers, heads of the Sandinista Defense Committees (CDS), et cetera. This "et cetera," commented one analyst, was an implicit authorization to extend terrorism to other categories. The manual recommended kidnapping public figures and civilians, since there would always be a way to "rationalize" such actions; carrying out public "executions"; and "if possible," contracting professional criminals and unemployed people to do "selected jobs." It also recommended creating "martyrs" by provoking firefights with the authorities.[104]

Edgar Chamorro helped translate the manual into Spanish, leaving out all the passages that recommended contracting criminals and creating martyrs because they were immoral and dangerous. "I was not interested in becoming a martyr of the CIA," he said. The complete manual, edited and translated by a "soldier of fortune," was already circulating among the contras. Reagan did not deny the existence of the manual, but he claimed that it was merely a draft.[105]

Under the Reagan administration the United States was the paradigm of a terrorist state, ironically, the very thing Reagan claimed to be fighting.

THE "CIRCUS OWNER"

As Nicaragua prepared to hold the first elections after the revolution, Reagan launched a campaign to depict the proceedings in advance as a "Soviet-style farce." His Managua embassy pressured and bribed the opposition parties and politicians not to participate. After a visit from the United States ambassador, the Liberal Independent Party's candidate, Virgilio Godoy, announced that he and his party were withdrawing from the race. He was said to have been bribed with $300,000.[106]

On November 5, 1984, two days before Reagan's reelection, Nicaragua held its own elections under international supervision. Daniel Ortega and Sergio Ramírez were elected president and vice president respectively, with 63 percent of the vote, and the Sandinista Front won 61 of the 96 seats in the new legislative assembly. Nicaragua legitimized its revolution in spite of Washington's attempts to scuttle the elections.

Though most of the international observers verified that the elections had been free and fair, Washington maintained that they were fraudulent. "The most fraudulent part of the Nicaraguan elections," wrote *New York Times* editor John Oakes, "is the part the Reagan administration played in it," since its "United States Embassy officials in Managua had admitted to pressuring opposition politicians to withdraw from the ballot in order to isolate the Sandinistas and to discredit the regime."[107]

On November 6, 1984, as millions of Americans were following developments in the election within their own nation, CBS reported that official sources claimed a Soviet cargo ship was headed for Nicaragua with MIG-21 fighter planes. Washington warned Moscow that it would not tolerate their delivery and would take appropriate military measures—selective bombings—to destroy the planes and their installations in Nicaragua.[108] Three months before this pseudoscandal, Daniel Ortega told reporters that Nicaragua was not expecting any MIGs from the Soviet Union and that he had been unable to purchase combat aircraft from any other country.[109]

Simultaneously with this barrage of intimidation from high officials, the Pentagon increased the military harassment of Nicaragua with joint maneuvers in Honduras, while a warship searched the Pacific near Puerto Corinto, where Soviet ships were anchored. For an entire week the people were terrorized by a supersonic "Blackbird" SR-71—the United States Air Force's most sophisticated plane—as it made daily flights over Managua. In the meantime the Pentagon announced that units of the 82nd Airborne Division and logistical elements from the 18th Airborne—at that moment engaged in combat exercises at Fort Bragg, Georgia—"would spearhead any United States invasion."[110]

So many shows of force concerned Nicaragua as well as Congress and United States public opinion, since it was feared that preparations for an invasion of Nicaragua were afoot. High officials denied that such a plan existed, but the *New York Times* recalled November 8, that they had issued the same denial before the invasion of Grenada.

The Sandinista government prepared for the worst. It mobilized the armed forces, the reserves, and the militias, and surrounded Managua with tanks and anti-aircraft defenses. After the Grenada invasion, Nicaragua could be next.

The United States shows of force and threats to Nicaragua alarmed Latin America. The Contadora group continued its efforts to negotiate peace in Central America, with the support of most of its governments, Congress, the most influential media, and parts of United States public opinion. Reagan cared about none of these. His hawks continued to systematically boycott any peace agreement. Daniel Ortega noted that for the negotiations to work, they would have to be held directly with the "circus owner," since no peace was possible unless the United States formally agreed to abide by the pact.

It was clear that the Reagan administration was not disposed to negotiate. It wanted only a military solution. The bilateral negotiations it held with Nicaragua at Manzanillo, Mexico, began in June 1984 and went on for eight rounds, achieving nothing. They were a guise to soothe public opinion and Congress during the presidential election (Reagan's reelection was assured). The conditions laid down by Harry Schlaudeman, the United States negotiator, were so extreme that they could not be taken seriously. His instructions were to talk without coming to an agreement.[111] In fact, the United States withdrew abruptly after Reagan's reelection, but not without first accusing Nicaragua of using the negotiations to undermine Contadora.[112]

Two months before Reagan's reelection, the Contadora Group presented a twenty-one-point peace treaty. El Salvador, Honduras, and Costa Rica, the Tegucigalpa Group allied with the United States, all expressed their agreement (the Guatemalan military regime remained on the sidelines), and Secretary of State Shultz called it "an important step forward," since it contained positive elements.[113] But when Nicaragua announced that it would sign the pact without modifications, the United States and its Central American allies began to express objections. Nicaragua "caught us off base," stated one American official. No one believed that the Nicaraguans would sign, because of the enormous demands the treaty would make on them.

The treaty was the fruit of eighteen months of intense and difficult labor, obstructed by Washington. The administration went on supporting the contras; the CIA persisted in its terrorist attacks, and the Pentagon continued to hold joint military maneuvers with Honduras. The chancellors of Colombia and Mexico protested. They wanted the treaty signed before the United States elections because they feared that, with Reagan's reelection, the war would be go on for another four years.

Washington claimed that the text of the treaty was unsatisfactory, partial, and unclear regarding matters of security and verification, that it included Nicaragua's primary objectives—cessation of United States support for the FDN and the suspension of United States military presence in the region—and offered only vague promises of "democratization" and "verification," which were its main concerns. Washington objected to cutting off military aid to Honduras and El Salvador—as suggested in the treaty—while Nicaragua would not reduce its military forces.[114] Its Central American allies presented the same objections.

Mexican Chancellor Bernado Sepúlveda expressed his irritation. He claimed that Washington clearly intended to block the treaty, and he pointed out that from the start it had been accepted as a "final" document by everyone, including the American officials.

The House of Representatives rejected a new Reagan request for $21 million to support the FDN. Support for Contadora was widespread. Washington was criticized at home and abroad for trying to obstruct it.

The three countries of the Tegucigalpa Group presented their proposal for amendments that eliminated everything unacceptable to Washington. They proposed that verification be carried out by the Central American chancellors and that there be a parity of military potential in the armed forces among these countries.[115]

Nicaragua was opposed. It did not accept, among other things, military parity, since it was the only Latin American country under United States military attack. It insisted that the United States sign an additional protocol promising to comply with the agreements and suspending its aid to the contras.[116]

The Tegucigalpa Group's subjection to Washington was made explicit in a National Security Council document celebrating the "success": "We have trumped the latest Nicaraguan/Mexican efforts to rush signature of an unsatisfactory Contadora agreement." The paper also noted that after intense consultations, the Central Americans presented a modification that "reflects many of our concerns and shifts the focus of Contadora to a document broadly consistent with U.S. interests."[117]

In July 1985, during the inauguration of Alan García as president of Peru, the Argentine, Brazilian, Uruguayan, and Peruvian leaders (all from democratic governments) created the Contadora Support Group. This unexpected measure was applauded by Latin America and sectors of the United States Congress, as well as influential newspapers. It was an important support for Contadora and a rejection of Reagan's policies.

Its creation was enormously irritating to the Reagan administration. Before the meeting of chancellors from the Contadora Group scheduled for September 1985, the administration geared up to attempt a boycott. It sent Schlaudeman, its Manzanillo negotiator, to these countries to try to convince them to persuade the Sandinistas to negotiate with the contras. Elliot Abrams ordered the Central American embassies to develop "active diplomacy" to oppose any move by Contadora that went against United States interests. Shultz explained the interests of his country to the Tegucigalpa Group and indicated the importance of internal reconciliation in Nicaragua. He wanted to make the Sandinistas negotiate with the contras. Mexican newspapers reported that Washington sent a mission to several countries to make them desist from signing the Contadora treaty.[118]

In September the Contadora Group presented a revision of the peace treaty, with greater emphasis on verification and execution of the treaty and including the Tegucigalpa Group's amendments. The Sandinista government announced that it would not sign, since the treaty was now "totally" favorable to United States interests, nor would it sign any other agreement until the United States committed to abide by it and suspend aid to the contras.[119] Nevertheless Nicaragua did accept 100 of the 117 points in the revised draft; the 17 it did not accept referred to matters of security. The modified treaty omitted the prohibition on military maneuvers, guarantees of security for Nicaragua from United States aggression, and its proposal for a "reasonable balance" of military forces in the region. Nicaragua asked that these points be reinserted. This was not done. It then suggested that negotiations be suspended for five months, until after presidential elections in Costa Rica, Guatemala, and Honduras. At that point the common perception was that Contadora was not dead exactly, but that it was terminally ill.[120]

On his way to the OAS assembly in Cartagena, Colombia, in December, Shultz said he would not cut aid to the FDN and that he would maintain his policies against Nicaragua, which he called a "cancer" on Central America.[121]

THE SANDINISTAS ON THE ATTACK

In 1984 and 1985 Nicaragua strengthened its military potential with modern and sophisticated Soviet arms whose total cost, according to Washington data, was $550 million. It had an army of 60,000 troops, 150,000 armed and trained young men and women in the popular militias, new military installations near the Honduran border, and a battalion 1,000 strong across from the Contra base at Las Vegas, Honduras.[122]

The Sandinistas went on the attack in the "enemy" camp. Hostilities along the border increased in frequency and intensity. Its armed forces were superior in number, weaponry, and motivation. They attacked the FDN's Las Vegas base with modern projectiles. In one attack the Sandinista troops, supported by helicopters, launched rockets at the contra bases, killing four contras and one Honduran corporal and wounding several Honduran soldiers. The Honduran population evacuated the area.[123]

The number of dead and wounded and the destruction of their camps terrified the contras. A mortar smashed one of Mike Lima's legs—one of the most brutal contras and the most appreciated by the CIA. Another tore up star commander "Tigrillo's" knee, and after an attack on Mack's camp at La Lodosa, he moved to a zone far from the border.[124]

The number of wounded outstripped the capacities of the CIA hospital in a mansion 12 miles from Tegucigalpa (with only fifty beds); it had to set up field hospitals at its base at El Aguacate. The constant traffic of wounded to this base—they were moved in helicopters—showed the intensity of this war. Honduran newspapers gave full reports on the attacks and the movement of the wounded. The Honduran government became alarmed, and the military protested.[125]

The Honduran military were fed up with the Sandinista attacks—which put their security at risk, and caused deaths and injuries in the population—and more than fed up with the contras. They ordered Bermúdez to abandon Las Vegas and send planes to cover his retreat to Yamales several miles to the north, beyond the range of Sandinista rockets.[126]

The contras' military defeats and failures infuriated their mentors. Their poor image kept Congress from supporting Reagan. At a meeting in Miami in the summer of 1985 Oliver North, who was in charge of these operations, demanded that Bermúdez attack the principal Nicaraguan cities. When he returned, Bermúdez ordered an offensive against La Trinidad, a town of 8,000 near the Panamerican Highway 77 miles from Managua, and the destruction of several bridges. He sent a commando of 2,000 men. The contras entered La Trinidad, but they were met with Sandinista fire, covered by fighter planes and helicopters. There were more than 100 contra casualties. The strafing and the casualties terrorized the contras. They did not leave

Honduras again during 1985, and thousands who found themselves inside Nicaragua, dying of hunger and without provisions, turned back.

Minister of the Interior Borge set up an intelligence network to detect the counterrevolutionary cells inside the country and the individuals who supported them. There were mass arrests, mobilizations of the people in the most exposed zones, and resettlement of hundreds of campesinos to zones far from the borders. These measures were deemed draconian. There were also bombings of suspected nests of counterrevolutionaries.[127]

The soldiers committed excesses against supposed collaborators; there were even cases of torture and murder. A Protestant pastor denounced these abuses. The government arrested the soldiers and the police responsible for these acts and publicized their sentences to show that justice had been served in Nicaragua.

The government managed its security policies roughly but tried to win over the campesinos by paying higher prices for their products and distributing lands to individuals and families, recognizing that it was in error to distribute them only to government-controlled cooperatives. These measures improved relations with the campesinos[128] and stimulated the return of exiles to Nicaragua.

THE CHURCH ON THE ATTACK

Another battle for the Sandinistas was waged with the Catholic Church. Archbishop Miguel Obando y Bravo, a harsh critic of the revolution, opposed representatives of the Church who collaborated with it, and he urged the prominent priests who occupied high positions in the government to resign. They were Ernesto Cardenal, the minister of culture; his brother, Fernando Cardenal, a Jesuit and the minister of education; and minister of foreign relations, Miguel D'Escoto of the Maryknoll order. Other priests held high positions in the administration, and many more supported and cooperated with the government's social programs.

The religious factor played a determining role in Nicaragua as in no other revolutionary process in the continent. Tomás Borge, one of the founders of the FSLN (he was now serving as the revolution's minister of the interior) sought the support of progressive priests in the fight against Somoza's dictatorship. The first to join him was Ernesto Cardenal. The FSLN established an alliance between revolutionaries and Christians. The contradictions that might have existed could be overcome, since the fight was against dictatorship and for the rights of the people, noted Borge. Priests and nuns, followers of liberation theology, mobilized the masses and later became involved in help-ing the people construct the "New Nicaragua."

As the revolution grew more radical, Archbishop Obando y Bravo sharp-ened his critique of the Sandinistas and the so-called Church of the Poor because, so he claimed, it created a parallel hierarchy. Relations were tense, with highs and lows. The minister-priests had to deal with the Archbishop's pres-sures and respectfully resist those from high Vatican circles, since both were asking them to resign.

The United States poured forth millions of dollars, not only into terrorist activities, but also to strengthen the internal opposition. Political leaders, conservative parties, private organizations, and the Church hierarchy received funds through AID. It gave $493,000 in start-up money to the Archdiocesan Social Promotion Commission created by the Archbishop.[129]

Archbishop Obando y Bravo actively worked to take away the government's popular base, through pastoral letters and critiques widely broadcast by the press and from the pulpit. He removed progressive priests and replaced them with conservative ones. His position was in accord with that of Pope John Paul II's. In 1981 the Conference of Nicaraguan Bishops issued an ultimatum to the min-ister-priests: they must resign and return to their pastoral mission; not to do so would be seen as open defiance of the authority of the Church, and they would be sanctioned under Church law. The Christian Grassroots Communities organized protests against the ultimatum. And the Sandinista government sent a delegate to Rome to negotiate the "delicate" situation with the Vatican. The priests did not resign. They responded, "We declare our unbreakable com-mitment to the Revolution in loyalty to our people, which is the same as say-ing in loyalty to the will of God."[130]

The government considered Archbishop Obando y Bravo's attacks, and especially those of Monsignor Pablo Antonio Vega (nostalgic for dictatorship), as the Church meddling in politics, straying far from its pastoral mission. A month after the publication of the pastoral letter, the government rescinded permission for the Church to air Masses and the Archbishop's sermons on tel-evision—a long-standing tradition—and suspended Radio Catolica's license. When the broadcasts were again allowed to air, the station was warned that it could not broadcast news.

The Church hierarchy supported Reagan's policies. Monsignor Vega was one of the first to defend the contras publicly and to lobby for United States aid. But those who spoke in favor of the contras mentioned nothing about their crimes or the CIA's terrorist actions, which were doing enormous damage to their country. The Church remained silent when United States backing of the war against Nicaragua came to light, but loudly condemned the government's call to patriotic military service in July 1983, which was necessary because the country was at war. In a widely published declaration, it announced that no one was obliged to register, because the army represented the FSLN and not the country.[131] The government called the declaration "treasonous."

Pope John Paul II's visit to Nicaragua in 1983 was plagued by tensions, misunderstandings, and tendentious and distorted reporting. For some it spelled disaster. Daniel Ortega's welcoming speech at the airport, which the United States press characterized as a "tirade"—quoted several times a 1921 letter from a bishop to a cardinal denouncing the occupation of Nicaragua by United States marines. The Pope was not interested. What he cared about was Church "unity." He was concerned with the dissention and with the collaboration of prominent priests and nuns with the revolution. He wanted the Nicaraguan Church unified under the Archbishop's leadership (he ordained him a Cardinal in 1985). The people, victims of United States aggression and crimes committed by the contras, were not interested in what the Pope had to say.

Crowds followed the Pope as he moved through Managua and León. The middle classes wanted to spin this popular enthusiasm for the Holy Father's presence as support for the hierarchy of the Nicaraguan Catholic Church. The people were waiting for words of support from the Pope, of recognition for the achievements of the revolution. They hoped that he would condemn the war or at least offer words of solace. But the Pope spoke only of Church unity. As he was delivering his homily during the Mass he celebrated in Managua—the day before, the funerals of seventeen young men and women killed by the contras had been held in the same place—the people interrupted him with chants of "We want peace." Mothers and widows held up photographs of their slain children and husbands. The Pope became exasperated, demanding "Silence!" The Holy Father's public recrimination of Ernesto Cardenal, who was profoundly respected by the people and was a hero of the revolution, offended many people. They did not accept the Pope's opposition to the collaboration of priests and nuns with the revolution and his wish to force them to retire from the government. "The Pope has undone in one day what they had built in four years," they declared.[132]

In February 1986 Cardinal Obando y Bravo traveled to Washington to express his support for Reagan's offensive in order to obtain $100 million for the FDN, and Bishop Vega openly agreed with United States policies directed against his country. Chancellor D'Escoto, clearly offended, told the Cardinal in a speech that his hands were "stained with blood" and that he was betraying the people.[133]

In July 1986 the government expelled several priests and nuns who sympathized with the contras and did not allow Bishop Vega to return to Nicaragua after a highly publicized visit to the United States where he had expressed his support for the "rebels"—not the first time he had done so. Coinciding with the congressional debates on this topic, every time he went to Washington he backed Reagan's requests.[134]

RAISING THE TONE

Strengthened by his electoral triumph, Reagan took up his war against Nicaragua with even greater determination. He would do anything to win it. In his second term Nicaragua was the central focus of his foreign policy to which he dedicated much time and many important speeches, commented Robert Pastor, a National Security Council member under the Carter administration.[135] In his State of the Union message in January 1985 he portrayed contra aid as a messianic national policy, an anti-Communist crusade, a moral imperative for the United States. Supporting the contras, he said, was "self-defense" since the Nicaraguan struggle was bound up with United States security.

Determination and exasperation fueled the Great Communicator's tone. With ever greater rage he lined up his artillery to "remove" the Sandinista government. He called Nicaragua a "totalitarian Communist state." After yet another incendiary speech, a reporter asked Reagan if his intention was to overthrow the Sandinistas. He responded, "No. Not if the present government turns around and, well, says 'Uncle' and tells them [the contras], 'Come on' and 'we'll work things out and they set their goals."[136] In other words, capitulation: either they would negotiate or the war would continue.

Reagan and his hawks were convinced that they could win this "war" with more weapons and many more millions of dollars. North assured National Security Adviser John Poindexter that with adequate support, the FDN would be in Managua by the end of the year.[137]

Washington now insisted on the "democratization" of Nicaragua and demanded that the Sandinistas hold direct talks with the "rebels." But that "democratization" had another reading: the United States needed to get the mercenary forces off its hands. The solution was to force the Sandinistas to absorb them. It became obvious that they were not going to win the war, and sustaining them was becoming harder, less popular, and more expensive by the day. High officials feared that this war would end with a humiliating defeat, that it would be Reagan's Vietnam or Bay of Pigs.

Washington also had a serious problem with the Honduran government, which wanted the contras out of its country. Honduras feared that the lack of funds—Congress continued to vote against contra aid—would leave the contras stranded and adrift. Counting contras, their families, and refugees, some 56,000 Nicaraguans occupied twenty towns and 280 square miles of Honduran territory, which they dubbed the New Nicaragua. They called the town of Capire "Little Managua."[138]

In March 1985 in San José, Costa Rica, Calero, Robelo, Alfonso Callejas, and Arturo Cruz—the FDN Directorate—met to sign the Document of the Nicaraguan Resistance concerning a national dialogue, at a meeting with Pedro Joaquín Chamorro Jr., MISURA leader Steadman Fagoth, and other contras. The text was written in Miami with the help of North and other United States officials. It called for "National reconciliation, authentic political pluralism, and a mixed economy in Nicaragua." Edén Pastora and Alfredo Cesar refused to sign it.[139]

To solidify the San José Declaration, Washington proposed that Congress grant "humanitarian" aid to the FDN for a period of sixty days after a cease-fire, at the end of which time, if the Nicaraguan government had not reached a peace agreement with the "rebels," the funds would revert to military aid. Speaker of the House Tip O'Neill called this suggestion a "dirty trick," and Colombian President Betancur maintained that "this is no peace proposal, but a preparation for war."[140]

Reagan turned Daniel Ortega's trip to Moscow at the end of April 1985 into a security matter. He declared a "national emergency," claimed that Nicaragua was "an unusual and extraordinary threat to the national and foreign policy of the United States," and decreed an economic embargo.[141] Reagan received broad support from Congress, and the House approved $27 million in "humanitarian" aid for the "rebel" forces. There were protests against the embargo in several United States cities, and some 2,000 demonstrators were arrested. Opposition to intervention in Central America was growing in the colleges and universities.

The government's strong campaign to demonize Ortega's visit to Moscow—it used it as evidence of strengthening ties between Nicaragua and the Soviet Union—weakened the hand of the Democrats who opposed aid to the FDN. One of them declared that this trip was a "stupidity," since Ortega was making it at the time Congress was debating aid. Several Democrats no longer opposed giving it.[142] Spokesmen for the Sandinista government declared that Ortega's trip was an "important business mission" to several Eastern European countries and seven in Western Europe, since Nicaragua needed economic aid and was low on oil. They also indicated that a vote in the United States Congress was not a reason to call off a trip vital to the needs of the country.

Military intervention in Nicaragua was the topic of the day among the Washington press corps, according to the *New York Times* in June 1985. In two long articles it referred to progress in the military preparations, and noted that the "apparent consensus" in the administration and in Congress was that the United States could "easily and rapidly overthrow the Sandinistas." The Joint Chiefs urged caution—it would take 125,000 soldiers, and casualties could run around three or four thousand in the first few days—and expressed their doubts that public opinion would support "such an effort."

Reagan asked Congress for $100 million in military aid to the FDN after a fiery speech in March 1986, which the *Los Angeles Times* described as "full of lies, falsehoods, distortions, misinformation and deception" about Nicaragua. Anthony Lewis, in his *New York Times* column, characterized it as a "flagrant distortion of the facts." Congress turned him down.

Five days later there was another incursion into Honduras by Sandinista soldiers in pursuit of contras—it was not the first—and Reagan turned it into an "invasion." He forced President José Azcona Hoyos to ask "in writing" for military aid and immediately sent him $20 million. American helicopters stationed in Honduras transported Honduran troops to the border. By the time they got there, the Sandinistas were back in Nicaragua.

Congress discovered the farce in the "invasion" from declarations by high officials in the Honduran government. Chancellor López Contreras claimed that the incident was "in no way a threat" to his country, and another official stated that the United States was trying to use it to obtain aid from Congress and bring about a confrontation with Nicaragua. Such declarations irritated Washington enormously.[143]

But the hundred-million-dollar offensive was not dead. Reagan did not give up. In June he persuaded Congress to approve it, 221 to 209. The American writer Cynthia Arnson pointed out that after the defeat he had suffered with the Boland Amendment, this was a great victory for Reagan: he achieved bipartisan support for aid to the "rebels."[144] And Holly Sklar, another American writer, wrote, "The 100 million was a *de facto* pardon for administration deceit, contra atrocities, terrorist manuals, the mining of harbors, sabotage of the Contadora treaty, and widespread lawlessness [of Reagan's government] condemned by the World Court."145

Reagan gained this "victory" through what reporters called his propaganda ministry. This was a steamroller composed of the departments of state and defense, the NSC, and pro-Reagan and pro-contra organizations, in which McCarthyite ideology played a principal role. The strong ideological component, characteristic of his administration, limited free expression, the Democratic opposition, and debate and controversy over his policies, according to analysts' observations.146

In the summer of 1986 Reagan and his hawks were delighted with their hundred-million-dollar victory, the CIA was pleased with the rain of dollars that allowed it to intensify the "war," and the "rebels" were breathing easy. It was a great relief for the Honduran government as well; this was the opportunity for the contras to take their "war" into Nicaragua. For others it was an invitation to profit. Honduran officials set up an arms "supermarket" to sell weapons to the CIA. But the CIA suspected that this million-dollar investment might have come from drug traffic and abstained from buying.

The euphoria came crashing down in October, when a Sandinista rocket shot down over Nicaraguan territory a decrepit C-123 cargo plane carrying ten thousand pounds of munitions and supplies for the contras. Eugene Hasenfus, the man responsible for dropping the bundles, saved himself by parachuting, only to be captured. The crew, three United States citizens, perished.

Hasenfus, a Vietnam veteran, started to talk. Before television cameras he stated that he was under a CIA contract to transport arms for the "rebels." Captured documents brought to light for the first time the extent of the agency's network to arm the FDN, and the names of the members of this network managed by Oliver North.147 Reagan and other high officials denied any connection of this flight with the government. Hasenfus was sentenced to thirty years, the maximum for terrorism. On Christmas Eve Daniel Ortega released him, stating, "This is a very concrete peace message."148

The Senate Justice Committee asked Attorney General Edwin Meese to name a special prosecutor to investigate possible illegalities connected with this incident. This was the beginning of the great scandal known as Irangate or Iran-Contra. It exploded a month later, when a Lebanese magazine reported the exchange of weapons for hostages between the United States and the Iranian governments. The story began to unravel, obstructed all the more by White House machinations.

THE "WAR'S" DEATH RATTLE

The effect of the $100 million flood of aid to the contras was seen in 1987. By the middle of that year some 10,000 contras were inside Nicaragua: ambushing convoys, blowing up electric towers, burning agricultural cooperatives, and killing scores of campesinos. Half the Nicaraguan Air Force's helicopters had been shot down, and several Soviet radar posts destroyed.[149]

In May the Sandinistas attacked the new FDN commando base at San Andrés. According to Daniel Ortega, this was the largest military operation yet. After several days of fierce attacks with rockets and mortars, covered by the air force, they forced the contras to retreat. Bermúdez moved his headquarters to El Aguacate.[150]

At the end of December the FDN engaged the Sandinistas in combat for the first time in six years of "war." They attacked Nicaragua's major mining center. This operation had been managed long-distance by the CIA and the Green Berets without the participation of the FDN Command. The instructions were given by their agents. The messages about combat developments were received by their agents, and the euphoria over the destruction the attack was causing belonged to the gringos. Green Beret Don Johnson gave the orders; "Sign this, Colonel," he told Bermúdez. And Bermúdez signed orders about which he knew nothing and on which he had never been consulted.[151]

Some of the contra leaders, surprised at the commotion inside the CIA complex at El Aguacate, got closer and saw agents coordinating on maps the movements of the "rebel" forces inside Nicaragua. Victor Sánchez of the FDN's strategic command remarked: "This is a gringo party in their own house, where they are playing with little tin soldiers. Whose war is this?" he asked. Bermúdez, profoundly demoralized, was taken to the San Andrés base. Foreign journalists were also taken there so that they could interview the FDN "Commander in Chief" about this "victory." The reporters noted that he struck them as distracted and that his answers were vague. The second day Bermúdez told them that he had given the troops the "order to retreat." Photographs taken at this meeting showed him pointing out on maps the movements of the troops he knew nothing about.[152] Johnson continued to order attacks to impress Congress with the FDN's "victories." They went unnoticed, since the whole country was immersed in the televised Iran-Contra hearings, which implicated the President, the Vice President, and the highest officials of his administration.

In 1987 the CIA discovered a widespread Sandinista espionage network. It had agents in every FDN unit, including the El Aguacate headquarters. The agency found that numerous "accidents" occurring between 1983 and 1986 were Sandinista sabotage. Among these were the downing of cargo planes, and the continual capture of arms and provisions airdropped for the "rebels." According to a report in the *Los Angeles Times*, one United States officer complained that they were dealing with a "sabotage operations system functioning since 1983, extremely sophisticated and very well done, and this has been going on for a long time."[153]

The war ruined Nicaragua's economy; 50 percent of the national budget went toward defense. The country was staying afloat only by new issues of money that was nothing but paper. Inflation was on the rise, prices were spinning out of control, and industry was collapsing. Children were begging in the streets, hospitals had no anesthetics and pharmacies had no aspirin, stores were empty, and the people's desperation was growing, reported one correspondent.

The government understood that this situation could not continue, and that the hemorrhage of the war should be stopped. In November 1987 it announced that it was ready to hold negotiations with the contras.

THE CALVARY OF PEACE

In three years of difficult negotiations and the presentation of three proposals for Central American peace treaties with revisions, modifications, and more modifications, the efforts of Contadora and its Support Group were frustrated by the Reagan administration's systematic obstruction, backed by his obsequious Central American "allies." The situation changed in 1986 when Óscar Arias was elected president of Costa Rica and Vinicio Cerezo of Guatemala. For the first time Central America had civilian presidents elected by popular vote, and all wanted peace. At Cerezo's inauguration he proposed to his colleagues attending the ceremony the creation of a Central American parliament and invited them to a summit in the city of Esquipulas to study the proposal. The new heads of state supported Contadora, but they saw that a joint effort would be needed to achieve peace in the region. At Esquipulas in May 1986 they created the parliament and opened the road to their own peace process.

After a new incursion by Sandinista troops into Honduras in December 1986, the United States resumed the attack. General John Galvin, head of Southern Command, arrived in the country to supervise the operation. Again United

States helicopters ferried Honduran troops to the border in violation of congressional prohibitions. Honduran aircraft attacked a base in Nicaragua, killing seven Sandinista soldiers and wounding twelve people, including two children.

The chancellors of Contadora and the Support Group, meeting in Río de Janeiro, referred to this incident in a joint statement as an "exacerbation of policies and interventionist actions by countries outside the Central American area, in clear violation of international law." They announced that they were going to Central America with the secretaries general of the United Nations and the OAS, Javier Pérez de Cuéllar and Joao Baena Soarez. Both offered the assistance of their respective organizations to achieve a peaceful solution to the conflicts. The United States tried to stop them. Nevertheless, in January 1987 they went, but without success, because the Central American governments continued to finger Nicaragua as the "problem."

In February, Óscar Arias brought together the Central American presidents in San José, but without inviting Daniel Ortega. His peace plan proposed an immediate cease-fire, negotiations with the unarmed opposition, an end to foreign support for the insurgents and sixty-day amnesties and set a schedule for regional "democratization." All present supported it but announced that they would not sign it until Nicaragua agreed to it. They scheduled the next meeting for three months later, this time with Ortega. In their communiqué, "A Time for Peace," they recommended national reconciliation, the democratization of Nicaragua and "an end to the dictatorships that continue to exist in the region."[154] Ortega announced that he would attend the next summit, in Guatemala.

The Contadora and Support Group chancellors showed support for the Arias Plan because it complemented their peace efforts. The United States set its boycott in motion, this time through President Azconaof Honduras. In July, at a meeting in Tegucigalpa to study the Arias Plan, Azcona surprised them with a peace proposal—written in English and Spanish—that, Arias stated, was in fact the United States objection to his plan. Azcona's proposal fell on deaf ears.[155]

In August, on the eve of the Esquipulas "summit," House Speaker Jim Wright presented the Reagan-Wright peace plan. It proposed an immediate cease-fire, before the withdrawal of military aid to the FDN, the continuation of "humanitarian" aid, and an immediate end to Soviet aid to Nicaragua, and it required Nicaragua to end the state of emergency and declare a general amnesty. In an addendum the White House noted that the plan called for a "gradual" reduction in aid to the FDN "as the resistance forces are integrated into Nicaraguan society," and that Nicaragua must hold elections "well in advance of the scheduled 1990" date. If the Sandinistas did not comply, the United States was free to renew military assistance. This plan was criticized by legislators on both sides, since they thought it went too far. They objected that the Sandinistas would not accept it and that Reagan could then renew aid to the contras. "If the White House had thought the plan was acceptable [to the Sandinistas], they would have changed it," said one United States official.[156]

That same month in Guatemala, the Central American presidents signed the "Agreement for Peace in Central America," known as Esquipulas II, with the Arias Plan as its basis. They agreed to take simultaneous steps toward national reconciliation through negotiations with internal opposition groups that laid down their arms and accepted the amnesty. Within ten days each country was to name a national reconciliation commission. They were to ensure citizen participation and provide guarantees in democratic processes. They must decree an immediate cease-fire and hold general elections in accordance with their constitutions. The agreement also forbade the use of their territories to attack another country. An international verification commission, composed of the foreign ministers of Central America and Contadora and the secretaries general of the United Nations and the OAS, would insure that the treaty was fulfilled. It was to go into effect in the five countries ninety days after signing.

The Esquipulas II treaty was received with enormous enthusiasm and hope throughout the Americas, and by Congress and public opinion in the United States. Salvadoran President Duarte called it a "second declaration of Independence for Central America." Ten days after it was signed, Nicaragua created the national reconciliation commission—the first country to do so—and named Cardinal Obando y Bravo, a severe critic of the revolution, to head it. It pardoned prisoners and took other measures to reduce internal tensions. It rescinded the law to expropriate the property of those who abandoned the country, lifted censorship of the daily *La Prensa*, and created a peace commission, with Red Cross and Church cooperation, to monitor the amnesty. The United States State Department called these measures "cosmetic."[157]

The Esquipulas II accord did not mean a second independence for Central America, or even peace. Though it included the United States demands, Reagan persisted in sending aid to the FDN. In the United Nations General Assembly, Reagan insulted Daniel Ortega. He turned to him and said, "Neither we nor the world community will accept the false democratization of your country, designed to mask the perpetuation of your dictatorship." The following day Daniel Ortega criticized the United States for violating the Central American peace accords and for attacking his country in an effort to overthrow the government. The United States delegation left the hall. Ortega continued, "Some people's ears hurt when they hear the truth. . . . They undertook to attack us; they've killed our people, but now they are annoyed when they are told the truth." He asked the United States to agree to an unconditional bilateral dialogue and to sign agreements guaranteeing their mutual security, making possible the normalization of their relations. He said that he had listened to Reagan when he spoke in the Assembly, that he hoped he would not reject his proposal, and that before consulting with people who put "hot ideas" like military options and invasion in his head, he would remember that Rambo existed only in the movies.[158]

A month later at the OAS, Reagan declaimed, "I make a solemn vow: as long as there is breath in this body I will speak and I will work, I will struggle and I will fight for the cause of the Nicaraguan freedom fighters."[159]

In November the Nicaraguan government announced its willingness to begin negotiations with the contras and presented a cease-fire plan. In December, in the midst of a contra attack on the mining complex—one of their biggest offensives against Nicaragua—FDN and Sandinista representatives began talking through mediators staying in different hotels in Santo Domingo, the Dominican Republic. The talks failed because of the excessive demands by the FDN spokesmen: control of more than half of all Nicaraguan territory, surrender of weapons not after the cease-fire but when the country was completely "democratized," abolition of collective farms, and the release of all political prisoners. Through the "rebel" chiefs, the United States was trying to force the Sandinistas to surrender. In January 1988 in San José, Costa Rica, negotiations began—this time face to face—but again without results.[160]

THE COLLAPSE OF "HIS WAR"

In February 1988, deeply involved in the Iran-Contra scandal, Reagan asked Congress for another $36 million in military aid for the FDN, and the House again denied it. The margin was narrow (219 to 211) but wide enough to bury the request once and for all.

This failure was the final blow to Reagan's war against Nicaragua and to the morale of the contras. The Sandinistas seized this moment of the "enemy's" demoralization and weakness and sent six battalions of 4,500 men against the

San Andrés base that month. Bermúdez sent 1,500 men to defend it, and flew to Tegucigalpa. It was a duel to the death, with scores of casualties on both sides. The contras abandoned the base. The CIA and United States officials, terrified and frenetic, begged Washington for reinforcements. Some 3,200 soldiers arrived at the Palmerola base. This military deployment provoked protest demonstrations in several United States cities, in which hundreds of the protesters were arrested.[161]

There was a mass retreat of "fighters" returning to their bases in Honduras. Hundreds of civilians—new recruits—went with them. Bermúdez had given the order to return to Honduras. He meant to unite the "rebel" forces, force the United States to renew military aid, and continue the "war."

Four days after the rout at San Andrés, Calero, Alfredo César, and Arístides Sánchez—the contra political leadership—agreed to renew peace negotiations. They met at Sapoá, a small Nicaraguan town near the Costa Rican border. This discussion between enemies attracted hundreds of journalists and foreign activists. Though the Nicaraguan people wanted peace, many were against negotiating agreements with representatives of the old Somoza guard. When Calero and the other FDN delegates arrived from Costa Rica, they were met with shouts, and there was an exchange of insults.

The negotiations concluded at midnight of the third day, and the negotiators prepared to sign the accord that decreed a total suspension of hostilities for sixty days, during which time they were to arrive at an agreement to end the war.

The Sandinista government, exhausted by this war, made great concessions. It agreed to grant a general amnesty to those indicted for violating the national security laws and former Somoza guards for crimes committed before July 19, 1979, the date of the Sandinista triumph. It also agreed to release political prisoners in stages, and guaranteed that exiles could return and participate in political, economic and social life under the same conditions as everyone else under the laws of the republic. The contras agreed to settle in zones to be determined by special commissions. There was no language on the surrender of weapons. The verification commission led by Cardinal Obando y Bravo and Baena Soares was to verify that everyone complied with the accord.

Calero, César, Sánchez, and the other FDN leaders struck up the national anthem by the side of Daniel Ortega, Sergio Ramírez, and other Sandinista leaders. In an emotional ceremony Baena Soares read the text of the agreement. The Sapoá accords were the first step in the difficult process of "national reconciliation" and the beginning of the end of eight years of fratricidal war that caused more than 30,000 deaths and ruined the country.[162]

But peace was impossible as long as Reagan occupied the White House. His boycott was underway before the Sapoá accords were signed. Bermúdez tried to sabotage them with "tirades" against Calero over Costa Rican radio stations. He questioned Calero's authority as a negotiator and announced that "his men" would "never" lay down their arms until "the final victory." He became enraged when the agreement was signed. In Miami, Nicaraguan and Cuban exiles—the Cuban exiles were the main lobbyists for the contras—orchestrated bitter campaigns against the Sapoá accords. They accused Calero and the other negotiators on Latin radio and television stations of having "sold out" the "rebels." In their turn, twelve of the thirty-two "rebel" commanders and more than a hundred contras accused Bermúdez of "servility" toward the gringos, and of corruption and inefficiency.[163]

In April 1988 Calero and César went to Managua to continue the negotiations. The Sandinistas raised the question of disarming of the contras, implicit in the Sapoá accords. Calero and César refused. They also demanded a new constitution, an end to military recruitment, and the release of all political prisoners. Three months after the signing of the Sapoá Accords, the talks broke off.[164]

The Esquipulas II accords fared no better. A year after they were signed, Reagan and his "allies" from the Tegucigalpa Group brought the agreement to the brink of collapse. With his country occupied, Azcona could not fulfill the promise to make the United States withdraw its troops and advisers from Honduras, suspend its aid to the contras, and move them out of his country.

After an anti-Sandinista demonstration in July 1988 the government arrested thirty-eight of its leaders, closed the daily La Prensa and the Catholic radio station for "distorting" the facts, and confiscated the largest private sugar refinery. A few days later, Chancellor D'Escoto expelled United States Ambassador Richard Melton and seven embassy officers for meddling in Nicaragua's internal affairs. He held them responsible for the disturbances. "This is a tough move," said Melton. "It is nothing compared to the systematic policy of murder and terror that Mr. Reagan's government has carried out against Nicaragua," responded D'Escoto. Washington expelled Nicaragua's ambassador, Carlos Tunnermann.[165]

Toward the end of Reagan's administration, Congress occasionally approved "humanitarian" aid items for the FDN. Thus the stubborn old leader could fulfill his solemn promise to aid the "freedom fighters," if not to his last breath, at least to the end of his term.

EL SALVADOR'S WAY OF THE CROSS

When Reagan arrived in the White House in January 1981, El Salvador was at war. Nine days earlier, in the midst of an unprecedented state of terror and under the army's "total offensive," the FMLN guerrilla movement (a unified front of five main armed groups) launched what it called its Final Offensive. The goal was to overthrow the civilian-military junta presided over by José Napoleón Duarte, to present an accomplished and irreversible fact to the new United States president, who touted his rabid anti-Communism and aggressive rhetoric against the Soviet Union, Cuba, and Nicaragua throughout the world.

In support of the FMLN's "offensive," the Frente Democrático Revolucionario (FDR: Democratic Revolutionary Front), the insurgency's political arm and the main opposition force, called a general strike. Within five days half of the country's businesses shut their doors, and some 20,000 government employees did not come to work. The FDR, formed the year before as a broad people's front in defense of its struggle for liberation, bound together revolutionary and popular organizations, leftist parties, union locals, and democratic figures opposed to the regime.

The offensive did not achieve its goal, nor was it a threat to the regime. The people did not support it in the hoped-for way. The strike fell short, and it was clear that the FMLN lacked sufficient military training to carry out a wide-ranging military operation. It was an army in formation. Duarte, the United States Embassy, Washington, and the foreign press deemed it a failure. Some believed this was the end of the guerrillas. Reagan scoffed at the "solitary guerrillas," and Ambassador Robert White commented, "They gave a war, but nobody came."[166]

In fact, the guerrillas did not show up in the capital. Later they recognized that this was one of their most crucial mistakes. But the offensive was not the complete failure ripe for ridicule by its "enemies." The FMLN took several cities, carried out massive attacks against the garrisons in most cities and towns, succeeded in forcing the army to withdraw from large rural areas, attacked air force installations, and destroyed important parts of its equipment. In Santa Ana, the second-largest city in the country, the garrison revolted, its commander was executed, and a company went over to the rebels after first blowing up the munitions dump.[167] But their most important achievement was the coordination of their actions in almost two-thirds of the country.

After the final offensive, United States military aid began to pour into El

Salvador. During the week of his inauguration Reagan sent $25 million worth of "emergency" aid in weapons of all kinds, attack helicopters, and fifty-six Green Berets. (Carter had sent $5 million in lethal aid, weapons, helicopters, and nineteen Green Berets.) The Salvadoran insurgency saw a radical change in the situation as a result of United States intervention. The government and the ultraright saw it coming, too. "With Reagan we will eliminate the wicked and the subversive from Central America," read the message left by a death squad on a mutilated corpse abandoned on a San Salvador street the day after his election.[168]

The United States began to take over this civil war and turn it into an East-West conflict. Alexander Haig announced that the solutions would be "drastic and military," and that the United States would demonstrate its determination to fight Communist subversion in El Salvador, which was "supported by the Soviet Union, Cuba, and Nicaragua." He believed that the victory would be "easy and quick."[169]

In February, with great fanfare and "great concern," the State Department presented to the Latin American and Caribbean ambassadors a white paper on "Communist Interference in El Salvador," allegedly based on nineteen documents seized from the Communist Party and the guerrillas. The State Department insisted that they contained "indisputable" evidence that the political direction, organization, and provisioning of the Salvadoran insurgency was coordinated and strongly influenced by Cuba, with the active support of the Soviet Union, East Germany, Vietnam, and other Communist states. It also stated that the Soviet Union was sending tons of arms to El Salvador by way of Cuba and Nicaragua. It claimed that the Salvadoran insurrection had progressively changed into a classic case of indirect armed aggression by the Communist powers by way of Cuba.[170] The implicit message was to uphold the United States' "right" to act in "legitimate defense," since its security and that of Latin America were threatened.

The claims and conclusions of the white paper, unsupported by concrete evidence, led Robert G. Kaiser of the *Washington Post* and Jonathan Kwitny of the *Wall Street Journal* to study the documents. In June, the *Post* concluded that the papers did not support the State Department's denunciations. The *Journal* reported that the only "Soviet aid to the rebels" it could find was a plane ticket from Moscow to Vietnam for a Salvadoran guerrilla. Jon Glassman, the author of the white paper, admitted in an interview with the *Post*, that parts of the document were misleading, others "excessively embellished" or contained "errors" and that some of its conclusions were based on "suppositions." Nevertheless, he defended the truthfulness of his sources.[171]

In *Newsweek* an article entitled "El Salvador: Tearing Apart a White Paper" noted that the *Journal* and the *Post* showed, contrary to what the State Department alleged about a flood of weapons from Communist countries to the Salvadoran rebels, that according to one of the "captured" documents, the guerrillas had only 626 weapons for more than 9,000 fighters.[172] The State Department insisted that the charges of errors in the report did not invalidate its basic conclusions. Haig repeated his accusation, that the Soviet Union was sending "tons" of weapons to the Salvadoran guerrillas through Cuba and Nicaragua and that he would "go to the source"—Cuba—to prevent the flow of arms from continuing.[173]

In his testimony before a congressional committee, Carter's former ambassador to El Salvador, Robert White, criticized the Reagan administration for focusing the Salvadoran conflict as "Communist aggression," while omitting the fact that the cause of the conflict was social injustice, not the interference of foreign Communism. He asked Congress not to increase military aid to this country, since its security forces were the "biggest murderers" of the people. He challenged Congress not to approve it. Did they want to be associated with these mass murders? Reagan kept on sending arms and advisers and announced that he would increase military aid.[174]

New York Times Central America correspondent James LeMoyne reported on the causes of the insurgency. El Salvador was at war, he wrote, because "it is one of the sickest societies in Latin America." Its archaic structure was dominated by an urban elite and a military caste that "essentially rule, but do not effectively govern" and that the campesino majority and the inhabitants of the slums, illiterate, ill, and frustrated, were violently repressed. He noted that the country had no just legal system and that the rebels had "ample cause to lead a revolution."[175]

United Nations Ambassador Jeane Kirkpatrick held a contrary view. The violence, she said, was not caused by social injustice, which "has existed for decades" and the people were used to it, but the "introduction of arms from the outside."[176]

Reagan's militaristic policies alarmed the archbishop of San Salvador, Arturo Rivera y Damas. He went to Washington to lobby for a negotiated solution to the Salvadoran conflict, but all his pleading fell on deaf ears. Upon his return he noted that Reagan's policies were a "serious danger" for his country and for the region. In April, during his homily at a Mass in the cathedral, he "intensely" regretted foreign intervention in the internal affairs of his country. This conflict, he said, would be resolved not by military but by political, humanitarian, and civilized means. He asked the United States and the socialist countries to suspend arms shipments and the junta to recognize the FDR and to free political prisoners.[177]

Haig gave assurance that no troops would be sent because such a course was not "necessary." In fact, his strategy in El Salvador was "low intensity conflict:" the United States could make war without sending in troops. But the huge and growing military aid package required a multimillion-dollar appropriation, and Congress was reluctant to grant it, principally because El Salvador was one of the worst human-rights violators in the world. A few days after Reagan's inauguration, the director of the Agrarian Reform Institute—a Salvadoran—and two United States technical advisers were assassinated in the Sheraton Hotel in San Salvador. A month earlier (during the end of the Carter years) four American nuns were killed. These crimes moved and angered Congress and the American people. In February, Reagan called off the investigation of the murder of the nuns—attributed to the army—since he did not want to trouble the Salvadoran high command.

The debate in the United States on El Salvador focused on the serious police and military human-rights violations. In several cities, groups, movements, and organizations emerged, composed of students, professors, intellectuals, professionals, and clerics who supported the struggle of the Salvadoran people and opposed the militarization of Central America and the aggression against Nicaragua. They were opposed for political anti-imperialist reasons, moral reasons, and out of fear that Reagan would repeat the tragedy of Vietnam in El Salvador. The Catholic and Protestant Churches, opposed to a military solution in El Salvador and to the aggression against Nicaragua, created a sanctuary for refugees from these countries who entered the United States illegally, fleeing from the wars.

The government could have measured the unpopularity of its policies by the intense activity in such groups, protesting and supporting the struggle of the Salvadoran people. Large demonstrations were held in major cities—New York, Chicago, Washington, and Los Angeles—whose fervor was comparable to that of the antiwar demonstrations of the 1960s. Most of these marches were organized by the Committee in Solidarity with the People of El Salvador (CISPES), the most extensive and active of the groups. CISPES had chapters throughout the country. The White House received considerable correspondence from all over the country protesting Reagan's Central America policies.

To counter this growing opposition, the White House and the State

Department rolled out a national campaign to "sell" their policies. They claimed that the opposition was supported from abroad. The FBI maintained surveillance on the activist groups and their leaders, especially CISPES and the Church organizations, which helped Central American refugees. This illegal espionage—clandestine break-ins and searches of their headquarters and harassment—lasted five years. It was suspended in the middle of the 1980s when the *New York Times* and the *Washington Post* denounced it.

Petitions for a negotiated peace arrived on Reagan's desk from all parts of the world. In March 1981, at the United Nations, the Mexican chancellor, Jorge Castañeda, offered his government's good offices. In July the recently elected French President François Mitterand expressed his support for the struggle of the Salvadoran people. Pope John Paul II, supported by the five Salvadoran bishops, urged negotiations between the government and the guerrillas. Public opinion and the media throughout the Americas and Europe criticized the militaristic United States policies in Central America. And in a communiqué the Socialist International expressed its "deep preoccupation" with Washington's conversion of the Salvadoran people's liberation struggle into an East-West conflict.

In March 1981 Prime Minister Pierre Trudeau of Canada invited Reagan for an official visit. He was met by noisy demonstrations and signs protesting his intervention in El Salvador.[178] Haig was barraged by catcalls at the universities, where he went to explain the government's policies. But the hardest blow was a joint French and Mexican declaration published in August. It stated that "only the Salvadoran people," without foreign intervention, could find a "just and lasting" solution to the country's "profound crisis." It also recognized the alliance between the FMLN and the FDR as a "representative political force" with the right to participate in peace negotiations.[179] This statement legitimized the insurgency as a belligerent party.

In a swift and effective diplomatic move, Washington succeeded in persuading ten Latin American governments, including ones who supported a negotiated solution, to condemn the French-Mexican declaration, calling it interventionist. And at the OAS General Assembly in Castries, St. Lucia, in December 1981, Haig managed a formal condemnation and the adoption of a resolution, proposed by the Salvadoran chancellor, supporting the Salvadoran elections and "suggesting" that the governments accept Duarte's invitation and send observers. Mexico, Nicaragua, and Grenada voted against the resolution. Panama, Trinidad and Tobago, Suriname, and St. Lucia abstained.[180]

In October 1981 Nicaraguan President Daniel Ortega presented an FDR-

FMLN proposal to the United Nations General Assembly to initiate a "direct and unconditional" dialogue with the Salvadoran government to achieve peace.

The heavy pressures the White House put on Congress—ignoring the savagery taking place in El Salvador—forced the Senate Foreign Relations Committee to demand that Reagan "certify" improvements in the human rights picture in that country every six months before the committee would recommend military aid.

Because the Reagan administration needed to improve the much-questioned militaristic image of its Salvadoran policies, it announced its support for agrarian reforms and the elections of a new constitutional assembly to draft and approve a new constitution, elect a provisional government, and set the date for a presidential election. It stated that the guerrillas could take part if they laid down their arms and that they could consider sharing power only as a result of voting. But to speak of "free" elections in a country at war, where respect for life did not exist, and the granting of lands to campesinos who had been expelled from them by the large landholders and massacred by the army, was either naïve or mistaken.

The debate on the Salvadoran conflict—war, elections, and peace formulas—developed not in El Salvador but in Washington, in the administration, Congress, and the media. That country's destiny was decided in the White House. The war was in the hands of the Pentagon, the CIA, the State Department, and the National Security Council. According to the "National Plan for El Salvador," written by the Southern Command, it developed by combining military strategy and plans for economic development. Duarte was a Washington subject, who was not allowed to negotiate for peace with the guerrillas despite his wishes. The Salvadoran military brass and oligarchy supported Washington's policies.

The violence and repression under the civilian-military junta were worse than they had been under General Humberto Romero's dictatorship, which was condemned by the world community for serious human-rights violations. The new wave of brutal repression was the work of Colonel Jaime Abdúl Gutiérrez, a member of the junta; General José Guillermo García, the minister of defense; and Colonel Carlos Eugenio Vides Casanova, commander of the national guard. The military officers went against what was agreed upon with the civilian members of the junta. This "dictatorship" caused a slew of civilian resignations from the government. During its third restructuring in March 1980, under pressure from Carter, Duarte was named a member of the junta and later president of the fourth junta.

The violence continued in the midst of endemic impunity for its perpetrators. Crimes against the civilian population by the forces of order went unin-
vestigated. The government denied them or covered them up. If some officer
became too visible through denunciations in the foreign press, he was transferred or sent abroad on a diplomatic mission.

In testimony before the United States House of Representatives' Foreign
Relations Committee in March, the principal adviser to the Agrarian Reform
Institute, León Gómez (who abandoned the country after the assassination
of his colleagues at the Sheraton Hotel), severely criticized Washington's support for the junta. He stated that the army was the "fundamental problem"
in El Salvador, since it controlled the security forces and the death squads.
He noted that the massacres traumatized the people. "One is very cautious
about rising up against the government when one has seen bodies of people sawed in half, bodies placed alive in battery acid or bodies with every
bone broken."[181]

The Salvadoran reality was one of horror. A United States journalist who
arrived in the country in mid-1981 stated that when he went out in the morning to cover his first story, he saw the corpses of the people who had been assassinated the night before strewn on the streets of San Salvador. He noted that
they were the poor, leftists, servants of the Church, intellectuals, or people who
had the misfortune of having been caught out in the streets after curfew. He
saw them with their thumbs wrenched off, chests caved in, faces mutilated,
and throats so deeply cut that when the bodies were moved, the heads hung
by no more than a few strands of muscle. "Anyone can kill," he wrote, "but
this is truly the work of monsters. I force myself to look at and listen (and smell)
every atrocity."[182]

Several of the horrendous massacres of campesinos covered up by the government came to light later through denunciations in the foreign press. The
massacres on the Honduran border became known as Operation Sandwich
because both armed forces collaborated. In one such operation in March 1981
thousands of refugees were mowed down trying to cross the Lempa River into
Honduras. The army bombed them from helicopters while soldiers gunned
them down with machine guns and mortars. In April, there was another,
known as the "massacre at Monte Carmelo," a suburb of San Salvador.
Uniformed personnel murdered twenty people, mostly workers and students,
whom they dragged out of their homes by force.

In October, there was another massacre in an army "security" operation at
the Lempa River: 147 campesinos were assassinated.[183] One of the worst—

reported and denounced by United States journalists—occurred in December 1981 at El Mozote and in nine neighboring communities, in a region close to the Honduran border. Eyewitnesses reported that it was a "deliberate and systematic" massacre of the entire town by several army battalions. Some 600 to 1,000 campesinos—men, women, and children (around 300)—were slain. The government and the army denied that it ever happened. It was also denied by the United States Embassy, the State Department, and Undersecretary of State Thomas Enders before a congressional commission, which subpoenaed them to explain what had happened.

A report by the San Salvador Archbishopric's Office of Judicial Assistance, created and directed by Monsignor Arturo Rivera y Damas (named archbishop after the murder of Monsignor Romero), certified that in 1980 and 1981 there had been 21,000 "political" assassinations of civilians at the hands of the government forces.[184] This was but one part of the Salvadoran people's tragedy.

THE PEOPLE'S WAR

In spite of massive United States military aid, the Salvadoran army did not have the ability to defeat the guerrillas, according to a Pentagon document leaked to the press in February 1981. Defense Secretary Weinberger declared that this was "one man's basically inaccurate view of the El Salvadoran army." At that point the FMLN had eight military fronts and controlled an extensive strip of land near the Honduran border and areas around the four great volcanoes. The army showed signs of demoralization because of continuous high casualties inflicted by the guerrillas. A map published by *Newsweek* in March showed FMLN offensives throughout the country.[185] Most of the attacks were on economic targets. The FMLN blew up bridges and electrical networks, set fire to factories and export warehouses, buses, trucks, and transportation facilities and blockaded highways to stop commercial transport.[186]

What angered the government, the armed forces, and Washington most were the guerrilla attacks on military objectives. In January 1982, in an attack on the Ilopango air base—the country's most important base, used by the United States to support its operations against Nicaragua—half the air force was destroyed. According to official sources, the guerrillas, attacking at dawn with mortars, dynamite, and machine guns, destroyed six airplanes, as well as six of the fourteen Huey helicopters supplied by the United States and seriously damaged eleven other planes. According to the guerrillas, they destroyed twenty planes. Nine people died. Ilopango was turned into an inferno, *Time* reported.[187] After the demolition by dynamite of the Puente de Oro bridge over the Lempa River a year earlier (it was the country's most important bridge because it united east and west), the attack on the Ilopango base was the most devastating blow of the war.[188] It was also the most destructive of the armed forces' image and unity, since base personnel helped the guerrillas.

The day after the Ilopango attack, the FMLN opened a series of offensives and ambushes against the army in Usulután Department, in which there were 34 casualties. The army responded by bombing the countryside and mounting raids in the cities. At Nueva Trinidad it assassinated 150 civilians and killed 32 more in San Antonio Abad, a San Salvador neighborhood. Students and workers comprised most of the dead, and many of the women were raped before they were killed.[189]

In January 1982 Reagan presented Congress with his first certification of the human-rights situation in El Salvador, which stated that the situation had "improved." It claimed the number of dead was down, that the six soldiers responsible for the murder of the four nuns had been arrested and sentenced, and that agrarian reform and the "democratic process"—preparations for the election of the constitutional assembly—were progressing. He recognized, however, that the problems were far from resolved.[190]

The same week, in a 297-page joint report, Americas Watch and the ACLU denounced the continuing political assassinations—some 200 a week—and the tortures and disappearances at the hands of Salvadoran security forces. A month earlier the horrendous El Mozote massacre had occurred. Washington blamed the guerrillas for these political crimes.

Amnesty International, the World Council of Churches, the Russell Tribunal, the El Salvador Archdiocese's Office of Judicial Assistance, journalists, and independent observers unanimously rejected Reagan's certification, and members of Congress introduced a resolution to declare it null and void. It did not pass.

The devastating guerrilla attack on the Ilopango base gave Reagan room to breathe. This guerrilla advance placed Congress in a great dilemma: if it denied military aid to El Salvador based on the human-rights situation, it could be guilty of allowing the army to be defeated. It approved $66 million in emergency military aid—half of what Reagan requested.[191] The possibility of a military victory, such as the one dreamed up by the ardent Mr. Haig, grew more unachievable every day. Duarte publicly admitted that the war was being lost.

After Reagan's certification, the FMLN sent him a letter to remind him that the Salvadoran people had been under military rule for the past fifty years, and that their fight was against the dictatorship—supported by the United States—which was responsible for the murder of 30,000 Salvadorans and the murder of four American nuns in the past two years. It pointed out that his interpretation of the Salvadoran conflict as a confrontation with the Soviet Union was "totally divorced from reality" and that the soon-to-be-held elections for the constitutional assembly were a "farce," since there could be no guarantees of a democratic process in the middle of indiscriminate repression. It "respectfully" asked him to change his policies.[192]

THE ADVENT OF "DEMOCRACY"

In the midst of military, paramilitary, and guerrilla violence and common crimes, preparations continued for the election for the constitutional assembly. Reagan saw a need to demonstrate democratic progress in El Salvador in order to break down congressional resistance to military aid. Defense Minister General García guaranteed that the election would be held, even if it took place "in the midst of bullets," and that the armed forces would respect the results "whatever they are."[193]

During this preelection period the human-rights situation was crucial for Duarte and Washington. They had to demonstrate a climate of peace and show that there would be guarantees that in fact did not exist. Thus the report of the murder in Chalatenango of four journalists—a Dutch television crew—eleven days before the election threw both governments into a panic. The minister of defense hastened to assure the press in a plainly worded statement that the "incident" had occurred in a crossfire between army and guerrilla lines. Washington made the same claim, based on an investigation by its embassy in San Salvador. Shortly thereafter anonymous witnesses testified that the journalists had been assassinated by an army patrol.[194]

The election for the constitutional assembly was held on March 28, 1982, with the country at war, after two years under a state of siege without constitutional guarantees, with the opposition press closed or self-censored, and the people traumatized by official and paramilitary violence. There were 200 political murders a week and more than 30,000 deaths. Of the sixty governments who had been invited, only nine sent observers. Few wished to become involved in a process that awakened so much doubt. Few would support this government to please Washington.

The junta set conditions so it could control the election. Votes were stamped on identification cards in indelible ink. The ballots and ballot boxes were transparent and numbered, so that it would be possible to see who voted. "Not voting is treason," warned the minister of defense. Some 700 foreign journalists, most of them from the United States, covered this event, but few knew the complex realities of the country. They reported that the people participated in massive numbers and they published photos showing long lines of campesinos waiting to vote. Their characterization of the election as free, democratic, and legitimate refuted reality. The United States openly intervened in the entire process, with advisers and million-dollar contributions to help Duarte's Christian Democrats. The major opposition force, the FDR, had not participated because there had not been any of the necessary guarantees. The United States press failed to mention these facts. FDR leader Guillermo Ungo spoke from his exile in Mexico, asserting that he had not participated because it would have been "suicide" to do so. When these elections had first been discussed two years earlier, the armed forces published a list of 130 "traitors" whom they considered responsible for subversion and announced that they would be "tirelessly" persecuted. The list included the names of all the FDR leaders.[195]

The massive turnout for the election noted by the foreign press was enthusiastically exploited by Reagan and Duarte. Lines of people waiting for their turn to vote were exactly the image they needed. It was "the triumph of democracy." The turnout exceeded all estimates, said Reagan and Haig. Ambassador Deane Hinton spoke of a defeat for the guerrillas, who asked people to abstain. There was evidently not much popular support for the insurgency, he said.[196]

The Christian Democrats won a majority of 35 percent of the votes and twenty-four of the sixty assembly seats, and the ultrarightist party ARENA, formed by Roberto D'Aubuisson, captured sixteen seats. The results dampened the enthusiasm of Reagan and Duarte for the electoral success, for the assembly was now in the hands of the far right. ARENA allied itself with the Partido de Conciliación Nacional (PCN: National Conciliation Party), party of the military, to achieve a majority. D'Aubuisson—who had been accused of being the head of the death squads and whom former Ambassador Robert White called a "psychopathic killer" and the architect of Monsignor Romero's assassination—was elected assembly president and was in a position to be chosen provisional president of the republic. Reagan sent his Ambassador-at-large, General Vernon Walters, to warn the military and the deputies that if

D'Aubuisson was elected president, the United States would cut all aid to El Salvador.

Agitated and bitter negotiations among deputies, political parties, and the military to choose a provisional president lasted almost a month, under pressure and threats from Ambassador Deane Hinton and Reagan's envoys. Several times the assembly was unable to meet for lack of a quorum. Finally, among shouts and applause on April 29, 1982, Álvaro Magaña, president of the National Mortgage Bank for seventeen years, was elected by a majority of 36 votes with the help of the Christian Democrats and the military. ARENA candidate Hugo Barrera garnered 17 votes.

After three years of a war that was virtually financed by the United States, El Salvador now had a new president, Álvaro Magaña (1982–1984), with a government dominated by the extreme right and the old military command still intact. General García, the minister of defense, and Colonel Vives Casanova, commander of the national guard, who were responsible for the dirty war, remained solidly ensconced in their posts. Members of ARENA were nominated for the four most important ministries; another four were to be filled by nominees "suggested" by the armed forces, and the three positions left for the Christian Democrats had neither political nor social importance.

The new ARENA minister of agriculture did away with agrarian reform. The new 1983 constitution did not mention the subject. On the contrary, it emphasized the obligation of the state to respect and guarantee private property.[197] Charles Percy, chair of the United States Senate's Foreign Relations Committee, warned, "Not one penny will go to the government of El Salvador" if agrarian reform was stopped.[198]

Magaña launched a publicity campaign to "show the world," he declared, that land distribution continued. At a ceremony in the presidential palace, he handed out land titles to campesinos, flanked by high-ranking military officers. "It's pure theater," commented a high Salvadoran official scornfully.[199]

Under Magaña's weak government the war continued with greater intensity. Repression was even more brutal, and the number of political murders kept rising. Of the 30,000 assassinations so far, 700 were Christian Democrats. The death squads continued killing, and Archbishop Rivera y Damas kept denouncing the killings, tortures, and disappearances in his homilies, holding the forces of order responsible. "Obviously they are free to kidnap and murder civilians in broad daylight, with no fear of punishment by the authorities," he said. In August he blamed them for the 270 political murders in the previous two weeks.[200] The same month Magaña named a peace commission to explore the possibilities of negotiating with the guerrillas. The military opposed it.

At the end of June 1982 Reagan presented Congress with his second certification on the human-rights situation in El Salvador, again claiming "progress." Enders defended the report to Congress, maintaining that there were fewer dead, lands were being distributed, the government was in control of the armed forces, and the country held "free democratic" elections. But he recognized that it "has a long way to go to achieve full success." Democratic Representative Gerry Studds accused him of using "ludicrously inadequate" statistics, and with eighty other representatives he introduced a resolution declaring Reagan's certification "null and void." He did not win a majority. The House approved $61 million in military aid.[201]

LOSING THE WAR?

Guerrilla advances and the Salvadoran army's poor performance worried and irritated the State Department and the Pentagon, since the army was heavily supported by the United States They blamed the minister of defense, General García, for his incompetence in not following the instructions of the Green Berets who had planned the operations and directed the counterinsurgent fight (at times participating). Washington decreed: "He must go."[202] In addition, the United States needed to show evidence of progress in human rights. It was made uncomfortable by the fact that the government had not captured those responsible for the assassinations of American citizens, and that Second Lieutenant Rodolfo Isidro López Sibrián, the man accused of masterminding the Sheraton Hotel murders, had been at large for the last year and a half. The courts released him for lack of evidence. Arrest and conviction for these murders was a condition Congress imposed before it would approve military aid to El Salvador.

After the election, the army asked the FMLN to give up its weapons, but the FMLN responded with a series of attacks in Morazán Department. In five days it inflicted 200 casualties on the army and took two cities, which it later abandoned. The army bombed them with recently acquired Dragonfly jets. Later that month the FMLN shot down an army helicopter carrying the vice minister of defense, Colonel Adolfo Castillo, and the Morazán commander (who died in the accident). The guerrillas captured Castillo (whom they freed after two years in exchange for the release of a group of political prisoners).

The FMLN and the FDR launched a double offensive—political and military—to force the government to negotiate peace. The FDR proposed a direct and unconditional negotiation to end the war and reduce tensions in Central America. In the meantime the FMLN was carrying out extensive attacks in the north and east of the country, inflicting 189 casualties on the army and taking 90 "prisoners of war." At a press conference in Mexico, FDR leader Guillermo Ungo and Ana Guadalupe Martínez of the FMLN—both exiled in that country—stated that the government had not responded to their peace proposals. Legislative assembly president D'Aubuisson warned that he would not allow discussions or negotiations with the guerrillas. The State Department dismissed the FDR's proposal as "cosmetic."[203]

The defeats the guerrillas dealt the army accumulated and caused profound malaise and divisions within the armed forces. Some wanted to continue the war; others wanted to arrive at an agreement that would end the conflict. They were irritated by the high command's poor performance. This internal crisis exploded when the minister of defense removed a star commander of the counterinsurgency, Colonel Sigifredo Ochoa, from command of the battalion in Cabañas Department. He was appointed military attaché to Uruguay to get him out of the way, since he had been accused of murdering a sacristan, and he refused to obey the order. Ochoa demanded that the minister resign and accused him of "treason" and prolonging the war without offering other choices. He told Magaña to keep his pants on, and stop letting himself be manipulated by the minister. He warned that he would not give in until General García resigned. The rebel radio station Radio Venceremos reported this as "a fight among the murderers of the fascist high command." The crisis lasted three months. It ended when García, under pressure from the high command, resigned. Vides Casanova, commander of the national guard, was named minister of defense.[204]

In 1983 Reagan's Central America policies sprung a leak. They were failing in Nicaragua and El Salvador, and they were severely criticized at home and abroad by allied and friendly governments. "Reagan's got a war on two fronts, one in Washington and the other in El Salvador, and he's losing on both," commented a congressman.[205]

The insurgents continued their double offensive. The guerrillas kept on attacking the army, causing high casualties and defeats, while the FDR-FMLN continued to insist on negotiation. In March 1983 they presented a new peace proposal: they asked the government for a consensus group to include the guerrillas and their moderate allies, and they demanded that the government dismantle the 10,000-strong security forces, move on economic reforms including agrarian reform, and make agreements with the guerrillas that would provide guarantees for future elections. "We are not so stupid as to participate in the elections and wind up in a cemetery," noted Ungo.[206] In June they proposed another five-point plan. The country must reclaim its sovereignty and carry out a direct and unconditional dialogue with the parties in conflict. The proposal criticized the growing interventionism of the United States, since it prevented the country from achieving peace, justice, and independence. It declared that no accord could succeed without participation by the FDR-FMLN, and asked third parties for their good offices during the peace process.[207]

In March 1983 Reagan defended his Central America policies and showed greater determination to achieve his goals. He insisted that military aid was essential to winning the war against Communist expansion in the region. He took an especially hard line regarding the situation in El Salvador. A victory by the "Communist guerrillas" would lead the country to join forces with Nicaragua and Cuba, and the "domino effect" would extend throughout the region, including Panama and Mexico, he averred.[208]

In April, before a joint session of Congress called by the President (which was unusual) Reagan reiterated that "vital" United States interests were at stake in Central America, and once again he pointed to El Salvador's proximity as a threat to United States security. Only more military aid, he said, would allow this war to be won.[209] The most influential newspapers criticized the speech harshly. Republican papers defended it.[210]

The guerrillas launched a major offensive in the northeast, taking the Panamerican Highway and the town of Santa Rosa de Lima. On Radio Venceremos they announced that this was their answer to "the war declared by Reagan."[211]

For the Reagan administration, its Central America policies had not fulfilled their objectives and the fault lay with the officials who had designed them. The State Department proceeded to remove people from the team. Enders and the ambassador to El Salvador, Deane Hinton, were relieved of their posts. Reagan named former Republican Congressman Richard Stone as his special envoy to Central America, and in June he named a bipartisan commission led by Henry Kissinger to visit these countries—including Nicaragua—and to design a regional policy. At the same time he kept up his military harassment. Stone's conversations with FDR leaders Guillermo Ungo and Rubén Zamora and with FMLN *comandantes* in Costa Rica and Colombia, failed. Stone limited them to their participation in presidential elections after they demobilized.[212]

The Salvadoran government had to either change its strategy or lose the war, concluded John Waghelstein, the director of the Green Berets in El Salvador, in a meeting with President Magaña, his minister of defense, and the United States ambassador. He showed documents that indicated the guerrillas controlled a quarter of the country and an ever increasing number of towns. Besides, they had destroyed the economy. A report from the United States Embassy in San Salvador estimated losses since 1979 at $600 million, and another, from the National University, mentioned 210 acts of sabotage in 11 of the country's 14 provinces. Guerrilla actions had destroyed a third of the electrical power system, 30 percent of public transport, and a tenth of the agricultural sector. Only one main bridge remained standing.[213]

Another of the guerrillas' activities was the trial, by revolutionary courts, and execution of military officers, paramilitary goons, potentates, and politicians. In May 1983, the Fuerzas Populares de Liberación (FPL: Popular Liberation Forces)—the most radical group in the FMLN—assassinated United States First Lieutenant Albert Schaufelberger in front of San Salvador's Catholic University when he was picking up his girlfriend. The guerrillas warned that they would send other advisers back in coffins.

The FMLN continued its offensive. In October and November some 7,000 guerrillas attacked more than 60 towns, and in December they attacked the military base at El Paraíso—the country's largest—and caused 100 casualties. This was a devastating blow. Two days later, they blew up the Cuscatlán Bridge.[214]

Defeats, casualties, and low morale wreaked havoc in the army ranks. Almost half the United States-trained troops quit between September and December. More than 300 soldiers had been killed or seriously wounded in battle, and 450 were "prisoners of war." In November a 135-man battalion surrendered. The guerrillas explained that they would be handed over to the International Red Cross and took their weapons.[215]

Also alarming to Washington was the increase in the number of murders attributed to the death squads, since this showed they were out of the government's control. The State Department compiled lists, one in El Salvador and the other in Miami, of those suspected of belonging to these groups. It published the names of powerful Miami exiles who financed them. Until now Reagan and Magaña had held their tongues about the death squads, though there was clear evidence that they had connections with military officers on active service and D'Aubuisson was their leader. *Newsweek* noted that whenever D'Aubuisson raised his voice against anyone—generally prominent persons—they turned up dead a few days later.[216]

In November 1983, unable to continue to talk about "improvements" in the

Salvadoran human-rights picture, Reagan vetoed the bill that required him to continue certifying human-rights improvements to Congress. That same month, he invaded Grenada.

DUARTE FOR THE PRESIDENCY

In 1984 after fifty years of military dictatorships, El Salvador prepared to elect a civilian president. The country was stuck in a serious political and economic crisis and unprecedented violence by the military, paramilitaries, and guerrillas. The FMLN now controlled a third of the country, and the people's uneasiness was rising.

These elections were crucial to El Salvador because its future, the development of the armed conflict, and the role to be played henceforward by the United States were all at stake. For Reagan, who had one eye on his reelection, they were crucial as well, since congressional support for his controversial military aid to the country and the future of the war depended on the outcome. Of the seven candidates, the two most likely were José Napoleón Duarte of the center-left Christian Democrats and Roberto D'Aubuisson of the extreme right-wing ARENA party. Washington worked feverishly to organize the elections and support Duarte.

The presidential campaign was bitter and steeped in violence. On the eve of the elections, the army—some 30,000 men—and 10,000 guerrillas intensified their offensives. The FMLN declared that it would not interfere with the voting—whoever wanted to vote could do so freely, but it called the elections a "farce" and trumpeted the slogan, "No to the Election Farce, Yes to the People's War." In various places guerrillas blocked roads, confiscated identification cards (which were necessary to vote), ambushed the army causing thirty casualties, shot down a cargo plane, damaged a military highway, and occupied three broadcast stations in the capital. For fifteen minutes they transmitted a statement to alert the people to the electoral "farce," which was not the solution to El Salvador's conflict but a measure needed for Reagan's reelection.[217]

In May the people went to the polls. The AFP, AP, EFE, and Latin-Reuter news agencies reported the chaos and disorganization: voting boxes that arrived late, others that never arrived in guerrilla-controlled zones, shortages of ballots, confusion in the lists that indicated where voters were to go, and extreme security measures deployed at every voting place. The Central Electoral Council published the results a week late: Duarte had won 43.41 percent of the vote and D'Aubuisson

29.76 percent. Since no candidate won the required majority, a runoff vote gave Duarte 53.6 percent. He took office in June.

Duarte's election was praised by the Reagan administration, Congress, and the press as a triumph of democracy. They called Duarte a genuine Democrat, a reformer who wanted peace. In his campaign, Duarte had offered a social pact and promised to end political assassinations, investigate the death squads, and abolish the abuses that had characterized past governments. A few months later, when these promises were a dead letter, he was called the "victim" of the extreme right and of the guerrillas' "intransigence." Nobody mentioned that while he was president of the junta, El Salvador was the worst violator of human rights in the world, with a rate of 1,000 political murders a month by the army and by paramilitary groups.[218]

Duarte went to Washington at Reagan's invitation and was cheered and praised by the government and the media and heard with respect and enthusiasm by House and Senate Foreign Relations Committees. Congress approved a supplementary appropriation of $61 million in military aid and three months later $132 million more, as well as $120 million in economic aid.[219]

On October 15, 1984, at the OAS general assembly, Duarte invited the leaders of the insurgency to a meeting at Las Palmas in Chalatenango. Many were surprised at his proposal to negotiate with the guerrillas, since the military and the right were strongly opposed and Washington even more so. Analysts concluded that Duarte, on a honeymoon with the Reagan administration and the United States Congress, felt strong enough to ignore this powerful and dangerous opposition.

A week before the meeting in Las Palmas, the minister of defense, Vides Casanova (whose appointment Duarte ratified because of military pressure), launched an offensive against the guerrillas, a resounding gesture of his rejection of the talks. Nevertheless, he accompanied Duarte to the meeting in the Las Palmas church. Guillermo Ungo and Rubén Zamora, who were both living in exile in Mexico, and the commanders Eduardo Sancho, also known as Fermán Cienfuegos, Facundo Guardado, and other guerrilla leaders comprised the delegation of insurgents, and Archbishop Rivera y Damas served as mediator. They were not able to arrive at a substantial agreement, but they did agree to name a peace commission, which would include four members from each side, to meet in November.

The military immediately let Duarte know that he must not move too quickly or accept a cease-fire, or he would have problems. Four days later the guerrillas shot down a helicopter, leaving four high-ranking officers dead, including Lieutenant Colonel Domingo Monterrosa, who was commander in the El Mozote zone at the time of the 1981 massacre. Furious, the high command warned Duarte that they would hold veto power over the actions of his government. A group of sixty officers advised him not to accept the insurgents' proposal to share the government and become part of the armed forces and further, not to accept a cease-fire. Duarte did not object to these conditions.[220]

The FDR-FMLN proposal asked for a broadly inclusive transitional government, the integration of rebel troops into the armed forces, and new elections. Duarte would not agree, instead countering with a demand that the rebels lay down their arms, recognize his government's legitimacy, and participate peacefully in the reconstruction of the country. In other words, they should surrender.

Duarte remained under the thumb of the military and Washington, both committed to escalating the war to annihilate the guerrillas. Peace talks threatened their plans. Washington kept sending weapons and helicopters and increased the number of its military personnel in El Salvador. The army continued bombing guerrilla-controlled zones, causing innumerable deaths and colossal destruction. The guerrillas, in turn, continued to attack economic targets and military bases and barracks and ambushing the army, causing even more casualties. They attacked the El Paraíso base and massacred an army patrol. They took over the Cerrón Grande hydroelectric plant—the country's largest—and destroyed part of its equipment.

The State Department continued to reassure Congress that the human-rights situation in El Salvador was improving, but the Salvadoran Human Rights Commission reported that there had been 400 political assassinations, 87 disappearances, two large massacres, and more than a hundred bombings of campesino areas since Duarte had come to power. FDR leader Ungo said in a November interview with the Mexican daily *Uno más Uno* that during the past five months Duarte had ordered 127 bombings, using more than 1,000 bombs in 10 of the country's 14 provinces, and new massacres in Chalatenango, Cabañas, and Cuscatlán. During the same period the FMLN was responsible for 547 military casualties.[221] In November Reagan was reelected.

In March 1985 the guerrillas executed retired General José Alberto Medrano (one of the worst killers according to Duarte), creator of ORDEN, a governmental paramilitary organization that functioned as a death squad, dissolved in 1979. Four days later they shot down Lieutenant Colonel Ricardo Aristídes Cienfuegos inside an exclusive tennis club in San Salvador. In June a group of guerrillas machine-gunned four United States marines—embassy security guards—and two American businessmen in a café in the fashionable Zona Rosa in downtown San Salvador. Seven Salvadorans were also among those killed, and fifteen were wounded. In a statement, the Partido Revolucionario de Trabajo Centroamericano (PRTC: Revolutionary Workers Party of Central America) claimed responsibility and announced that these were only the "first," alleging that the marines were not "innocent" since "no Yankee invader" was free of guilt. The statement "profoundly" regretted the death of the Salvadorans. In the past six months the guerrillas had kidnapped a large number of mayors, bureaucrats, and military officers.[222]

In September 1985 the kidnapping of Inés Duarte Durán, the President's thirty-five-year-old daughter, by an FMLN commando, changed the rules of the game. Duarte bowed to the guerrillas' demands, freeing twenty-two political prisoners and allowing ninety-six wounded guerrillas to be transferred to Cuba. ARENA, the right, and the military all protested that the President's show of weakness affected the army's morale and undermined the government's credibility. Duarte retorted that they were merely singing a "siren's song," since they sent their money out of the country and paid ransoms to free kidnapped family members and that the guerrillas used this money to buy weapons, "kill soldiers," and make the revolution. The guerrillas freed Inés and twenty-eight of the thirty-eight mayors they were holding. Duarte sent his family to Washington.[223]

The concessions Duarte made to the guerrillas complicated his relations with the military, not that they had been easy to begin with. But both knew that Washington would not tolerate a coup.

Politically the government was eroding. The people criticized Duarte for the grave economic crisis and accused him of being Washington's puppet; they also denounced his support for the war against Nicaragua, his collaboration with the boycott of Contadora, and his suspension of the peace talks because of United States and army pressures.

In 1986 national and international human-rights organizations railed against the increase in military and paramilitary violence in El Salvador. Amnesty International pointed out that murders, tortures, and disappearances were now "selective," carried out against those who opposed the government. These crimes were not investigated and their perpetrators were not brought to justice. On the anniversary of the assassination of Monsignor Arnulfo Romero a large demonstration in San Salvador demanded "trials and convictions of his assassins." Six years after the crime these people were still at large.

After the peace talks at Ayagualo were suspended in November 1984, Duarte rejected five different peace proposals offered by the FDR-FMLN, but in June 1985 he announced that he was ready to renew the talks. Two preparatory meetings were held in Mexico and Panama. The third, to be held in Sesori, was canceled by the guerrillas because the army militarized the town before the meeting. Duarte accused the guerrillas of torpedoing the peace talks. In 1986 the army again boycotted attempts to negotiate with the guerrillas.

The opposition to Duarte's government continued to grow, and in January 1987 rumors of a coup circulated. The military openly criticized Duarte. The right was dead set against him—twenty-seven opposition delegates called a "parliamentary strike" because of a tax increase, and a 150,000-strong student demonstration protested "forced recruitment." The guerrillas continued to ambush the army, block transportation routes, and blow up electric transmission towers, which left large areas of the country without light. On January 24 a business strike, a transportation stoppage called by the FMLN, and a road blockage by the guerrillas paralyzed the country. Many called for Duarte to resign. Nonetheless, the military announced that it supported the president's authority.[224]

The signing of the Esquipulas II regional peace treaty by the five Central American presidents in August 1987 opened the gates to a solution for Nicaragua's and El Salvador's internal conflicts. The governments were obliged by the terms of the treaty to take immediate steps toward national coexistence. Duarte presented to the legislative assembly a plan for partial amnesty for people who had been indicted for political or related crimes, but who had not yet been tried, as well as a plan for the repatriation of exiles. In October thousands of refugees returned, under the protection of the Catholic and Protestant Churches and international organizations. Duarte called a third round of negotiations—suspended for three years—but the FDR-FMLN announced that it would not participate, in protest against the murder the previous October of Herbert Ernesto Anaya, Director of the Human Rights Commission of El Salvador.

In November, FDR leaders Guillermo Ungo and Rubén Zamora returned after seven years in exile. They announced that they would continue to support the people's struggle. Duarte dismissed them as terrorists and announced that if they wanted to participate in politics they would have to break their ties to the guerrillas.[225] That same month Duarte presented a "total and absolute" amnesty law to the legislative assembly, which was approved by a wide majority. This law exempted from trial any members of the military, the security services, and the police who were responsible for the assassination and disappearance of tens of thousands of Salvadorans and suspended all trials and investigations of crimes committed before October 22 of that year. More than 400 prisoners convicted of political crimes were released, among them the murderers of the agrarian-reform experts at the Sheraton Hotel. Crimes of kidnapping, extortion, and drug trafficking were excluded. In response to a petition from the Church, Archbishop Romero's killers were not granted amnesty. A report issued by Americas Watch noted that after the amnesty law was passed, there was a marked increase in political crimes.[226]

Duarte could not end the war because the military and Washington would not let him. Neither was he able to improve the difficult economic situation, an effect of the war. The country stayed afloat only with economic aid from the United States. Duarte's emergency measures were rejected by both the left and the right. His promised social pact was not feasible. The country was mired in misery and war. The real weight of this serious economic crisis fell on the poorest classes. Six out of every ten Salvadorans were unemployed, and the prices of consumer products were well out of the reach of most people.

After seven years of war, the society was profoundly polarized. The people were traumatized by the military and paramilitary violence. The country was devastated and in ruins; the dirty war had cost tens of thousands of civilians' lives, with thousands more maimed and tens of thousands widowed and orphaned. A fourth of the population—the vast majority of them campesino—was displaced, in exile in other countries, or with the guerrillas.

During his last year in office Duarte, by now completely discredited, fell seriously ill with liver cancer. In the municipal and legislative assembly elections in March 1988 his Christian Democratic Party suffered a crushing defeat. ARENA, the winning party, was as surprised as anyone. It was handed an absolute majority in the legislative assembly and won 200 of 244 municipalities. Its triumph in presidential elections set for the following year was practically assured.

Throughout the year the bloody fight between the army and the guerrillas continued. Christ turned his back, peace would not come, and cancer was consuming the President. "So, stubborn, proud and alone, as he has always lived, Napoleón awaits death, fighting cancer from the helm of the ship of state," wrote a correspondent for the Spanish daily *El País*. After almost a year of Duarte's battle with cancer, Salvadorans spoke of his survival as a "miracle."

In January 1989, with the country at war, the presidential campaign moved ahead. The FDR-FMLN presented another peace proposal through Archbishop Rivera y Damas that promised that it would respect the election results if the army did not interfere or continue its repressive actions, and would participate in the elections if the government would postpone them until September and insure that the vote would be impartial and clean. It asked for a new electoral council with the participation of the Democratic Convergence—the democratic union created by Ungo and Zamora—a new oversight committee composed of religious, humanitarian, and civil organizations, and the presence of international observers to monitor the elections. The United States would have to remain outside the process. Duarte rejected the proposal, calling it unconstitutional. The military and ARENA rejected it as well.

On January 20, 1989, Republican George Bush was inaugurated as president of the United States. The new administration understood the absurdity of continuing to support the war and recognized a political way out in the FDR-FMLN proposal. The State Department called it "serious," and noted that it contained "positive" elements that deserved further study. This change in Washington's position meant that Duarte and the Salvadoran political parties, including ARENA, would have to change course.

D'Aubuisson proposed a "partial amnesty" to allow the guerrilla leaders to come to San Salvador and meet with the political parties. In February they met at Oaxtepec, Mexico, but the talks came to no agreement. Duarte offered to postpone the elections to April if the guerrillas would declare a unilateral truce until June 10, the day he was to hand over the reins of government to a successor. The FMLN offered a sixty-day truce and proposed a new meeting with the parties in San Salvador. But the political atmosphere was too contaminated to achieve change. The minister of defense, Vides Casanova, who was opposed to negotiations, warned that a coup d'état was possible if the constitution were violated.

The army continued its military operations against the guerrillas, and they, in turn, intensified their own. The central elections council ratified the date for the elections, which would be held on March 19, 1989. This was a dagger in the heart for anyone who had hoped for an accord. The rebel radio station, Radio Venceremos, alerted listeners: "We stand at a historic crossroads: negotiation or the intensification of the war."[227]

The violence continued. There were more political murders, and three journalists were killed, one of whom was Dutch. More dynamite was detonated by the guerrillas, and street disturbances were constant. Duarte militarized the country. The FMLN announced a boycott of the elections, blocked transportation, blew up electric transmission towers, attacked barracks, and threatened with death any officials who took part in this "farce." Throughout the country 136 mayors resigned.

Alfredo Cristiani, the ARENA candidate, captured 53.81 percent of the votes cast, Fidel Chávez Mena, the Christian Democrat, 35.59 percent, and Guillermo Ungo of the Democratic Convergence, a pathetic 3.2 percent. The abstention of 50 percent of the voters was the highest in El Salvador's history. Chávez Mena and Ungo attributed their defeat to FMLN's boycott. Spokespeople for the guerrillas claimed that the large-scale abstention was evidence of the illegitimacy of a government that did not represent the national majority.

THE COST OF PEACE

With Alfredo Cristiani (1989–1993) as president, power remained in the hands of the most reactionary forces in the country—the oligarchy and the army—represented by ARENA, the party born of the death squads. The defeat of the Christian Democrats and the Democratic Convergence demonstrated that the options for change toward a just society and to achieving peace were no longer possible. The only choice was to keep waging the war.

In his inaugural speech Cristiani proposed renewing the dialogue with the guerrillas. The FMLN opened an intense military offensive in order to come to the table from a position of strength. The army declared itself in a state of "maximum alert" and showed increased determination to annihilate the guerrillas.

The difficult negotiations unfolded over a period of three years, in the midst of extreme violence, without arriving at any substantial agreements. On November 11 the FMLN launched a bold offensive in San Salvador, and the army bombed working-class neighborhoods where 1,500 guerrillas had barricaded themselves. The FMLN took the Sheraton Hotel, where four Green Berets and OAS Secretary General Joao Baena Soárez were lodged. Bush sent a commando from the Delta Force. The evacuation of the Green Berets without incident prevented them from moving into action. Hours earlier Baena Soárez had left with the guerrillas' help. The combat lasted for five days, leaving 1,000 civilians and fighters dead in its wake, mostly as a result of the bombing.

Five days later, on the campus of the Catholic University (UCA), six Jesuits, including the rector, Father Ignacio Ellacuría, their housekeeper, and her daughter, were assassinated. This incident moved the world. The government tried to blame the FMLN, but it was almost immediately clear that the murder was the work of the army. Washington demanded that the crime be cleared up, and Congress made further aid contingent on the investigation and punishment of the perpetrators. A commission of twenty United States representatives proceeded to investigate it.

The peace accords between Cristiani's government and the FMLN that put an end to twelve years of war were signed at a dramatic United Nations session in New York early in the morning of January 1, 1992, just hours before the end of Secretary General Javier Pérez de Cuéllar's term in office. Immense joy broke out throughout El Salvador and the world. Nevertheless there were still key issues to be resolved, and these would depend on the political will of both sides. The government had to reduce the armed forces from 56,000 to 20,000, purge their ranks, bring to justice the members of the police forces responsible for serious human-rights violations—the officer class was firmly opposed to this—and the FMLN had to agree to demobilize its forces. The definitive cease-fire was set for February 10, 1992.

The United States Truth Commission—part of these accords—published its report in March 1993. Its job had been to investigate "the most serious political crimes" committed during the twelve years of war. The report received support from all over the world. President Bill Clinton praised it, and the *New York Times* commented that "the White House stopped short of drawing the conclusion that the Reagan and Bush administrations, which strongly supported the Salvadoran military in its war with leftist guerrillas, bore some responsibility" for the "gross human rights abuses."[228]

The commission certified that 85 percent of the crimes were committed by the army, the security forces, and the death squads. It accused high-ranking officers, based on "sufficient evidence," of being the architects of the Jesuits' murder. It mentioned former ministers of defense René Emilio Ponce and Vides Casanova and air force commander Juan Rafael Bustillo. It also accused other officers of having issued the order to kill the four North American nuns, the four Dutch journalists, and Monsignor Romero. It indicated that D'Aubuisson was behind his murder.

At a press conference held the day after the report was made public, Cristiani urged the legislative assembly to pass a law of "total and general amnesty," which, he assured everyone, was essential to consummate the national reconciliation and "leave the past behind." The assembly, controlled by ARENA, did just that. "This inappropriate haste to shield the guilty," wrote the *New York Times*, "is an affront to the peace process promoted by the UN, to international human rights laws, and to the memory of the victims in El Salvador."[229]

The amnesty went into effect at the end of March, and confessed and convicted military criminals began coming out of the jails. Guerrillas responsible for killing United States citizens did not benefit from this amnesty. This was a discriminatory measure without legal basis. The truth commission's accusations were no more than simple testimonies for the history books, since the commission had no power to bring the perpetrators of the crimes to justice.

THE INVASION OF GRENADA

Another of Reagan's wars was the invasion of Grenada on October 25, 1983. The invasion was announced in advance. Maurice Bishop, the prime minister, saw it coming many times, and many times he denounced before the world the peril hanging over the tiny island. The American press dismissed Bishop's fears as paranoia. When the invasion came, he was already dead.

In March 1979 Bishop, the leader of the New Jewel Movement, overthrew the repressive and corrupt regime of Eric Gairy. Thousands of Grenadians poured into the streets to welcome the new government. The working classes and the mass organizations supported it.[230] Within a month Bishop established diplomatic relations with Cuba, and Washington subsequently became alarmed.

Grenada was another revolution that began to have an impact on its neighbors. In the Caribbean island of Dominica, a broad-based popular movement overthrew the dictatorial regime of Patrick John; in Santa Lucía the leftist Labor Party won at the polls and defeated the rightist regime of more than fifteen years; and a popular coalition, MAN-MER won a victory in the Netherlands Antilles.

These changes upset Washington, since they complicated the United States presence in the Caribbean, where Cuba extended its influence. The prime minister of Jamaica, Michael Manley, Forbes Burnham of Guyana, and Eric Williams of Trinidad and Tobago—all progressive, nonaligned leaders—maintained close relations with Havana.

Castro celebrated Bishop's victory and immediately began to send him aid. Neither Bishop's government's leftist leanings nor his courtship of Cuba and the Soviet Union pleased Washington and Great Britain (Grenada was a member of the British Commonwealth and had a governor representing the Queen). The Carter administration warned that such policies would bring the withdrawal of United States aid and sought to isolate Bishop. It pressured the members of the Caribbean Community (CARICOM) to disavow the New

Jewel government and offered an economic development plan for the region, with loans from the IMF and the World Bank, for which only "friendly" nations qualified. Carter's intervention was indirect and failed.

Bishop established the People's Revolutionary Government. "With the working people," he said, "we will build and advance toward socialism and arrive at the final victory." The country was in ruins, with corruption running rampant, an unemployment rate reaching 50 percent, and no social services. Bishop dismantled the army, created a new one as well as a militia, sought popular participation through mass organizations, broadened health and education services (he made secondary education free), promoted the unionization of the working class (it rose to 80 percent), and introduced social legislation to bring gender equality in the workplace. Economic growth in 1982 was 5.5 percent, compared with the 1.1 percent of neighboring islands, and the private sector increased by 10 percent.[231]

The people loved Bishop, supported his policies, and applauded his honest position in the face of imperialism and Reagan's accusations against the country. Other political and economic sectors did not agree with his government's socialist orientation and put up resistance. But they were an unthreatening minority.

Reagan was not eager to allow Bishop's revolution to progress. During his presidential campaign he was already calling him a Communist—a most serious condemnation coming from his lips—and Grenada a "threat" to United States security. His alarm was an extremely ridiculous position, from a representative of the world's superpower. Grenada was a tiny Caribbean island of 110,000 inhabitants, 215 square miles in size, with an economy based on the export of nutmeg, and it had no army or navy. This threat was also taken up by the report of the Santa Fe Committee written by a group of Republicans for Reagan's campaign. They claimed that Grenada was part of a "Communist conspiracy" led by the Soviet Union, like Cuba and Nicaragua, constituting a direct threat to United States security.

Reagan's heaviest attack was waged on the international airport being built with Cuban assistance. He declared that it would be a Soviet and Cuban military base. Bishop assured him that it was being built to stimulate tourism, not terrorism, and that it would not be used by the Soviet Union or Cuba.

Bishop tried to maintain normal relations with the United States but was met with hostile treatment. The State Department did not accept the credentials of the Grenadian ambassador nominated by Bishop and accredited its own ambassador to Grenada but stationed him in Barbados. Reagan ignored two letters from Bishop, in which Bishop set forth his government's good intentions toward the United States. In the second letter, dated August 1981, he mentioned the hostile policies of Reagan's government toward his country and the gestures of United States envoys to the European Economic Community in trying to dissuade these countries from aiding Grenada with the construction of the airport. He also referred to the training of Grenadian mercenaries in Miami who were being prepared to invade his country, the United States blocking of Grenada's loan requests to the World Bank and the IMF, and the condition set forth that both exclude Grenada, the country to which the United States attached its grants to the Caribbean Development Bank.[232]

In 1981 the extensive United States military maneuvers in the Caribbean, Ocean Venture 81, and the simulated invasion and rescue of supposedly kidnapped Americans on the island of Vieques in Puerto Rico carried the code name Amber Ambarines in a clear allusion to Grenada and the Grenadines. Bishop understood the message and launched a campaign in the United Nations, the OAS, the Non-Aligned Movement, and with friendly governments and political parties throughout the world, to denounce the United States threat of an invasion of his country.

In March 1983 the Pentagon published aerial photographs that showed military installations in Grenada and claimed that they were "Soviet-type" and that they contained anti-aircraft emplacements.[233] That same month, during a televised speech, Reagan showed "secret" photographs to claim, once again, that the airport was a danger to United States security because of Grenada's obvious militarization by the Soviet Union and Cuba. During an official visit to Barbados, Reagan alerted Prime Minister Tom Adams and Jamaican Prime Minister Edward Seaga to the "propagation of the Communist virus" in the region, "from Grenada." The two heads of state shared his concerns.

Bishop called Reagan's accusations that he was militarizing the country, building a naval base, an air base, munitions depots, barracks, and a military training camp on the island, a pack of lies.[234] In a radio broadcast he warned his "brothers and sisters" about an imminent invasion by "counterrevolutionary gangs organized, financed, trained, and directed by North American imperialism."[235]

In April 1983 the Grenadian delegation to the United Nations rejected Reagan's accusations and ridiculed the photographic display it created to demonize the airport. It asserted that the United States was the first country Grenada had asked for assistance in building the airport, but that Grenada was rebuffed. Reagan became "the laughing-stock of the world," according to the daily *Granma*, referring to his campaign against Grenada.[236]

In June, Bishop went to Washington uninvited and spoke with members of Congress, journalists, intellectuals, and Grenadians residing in the United States. He was seeking their support and help in convincing Washington to suspend its hostility. In a speech at New York's Hunter College he spoke about his country's situation, the social and economic advances his government had made. He mentioned the difficulties he was having and the Reagan administration's hostility in spite of the efforts he was making to improve relations. He mentioned a secret Defense Department report that maintained that the revolution in Grenada was "worse" for the United States than the Cuban or Nicaraguan revolutions because the people there spoke English and could communicate directly with the United States. Grenada's population was 95 percent black, and its leaders could set "a dangerous example for the 30 million American blacks." This aspect, Bishop argued, was doubtless one of the most sensitive in the document.[237]

General Hudson Austin led a coup d'état on October 19, 1983, and Bishop, three members of his cabinet, and two labor leaders were assassinated. Seventeen people died in the riots the coup unleashed. Bishop's assassination and the takeover of the island by a Marxist group—supposedly more radical—was the pretext Reagan needed to justify invading Grenada. He availed himself of the tired old excuse that he was "saving the lives of American citizens" and reestablishing internal order. As many as 600 young United States citizens were studying tropical medicine at a United States school.

The Pentagon diverted a fleet to Grenada carrying 1,900 marines intended for Lebanon, where a car bomb had just exploded at a United States barracks, killing 237 marines. A United States military transport and a helicopter, both loaded with soldiers, landed in Barbados, followed by a DC-9 with more soldiers. The orders were to ready for a possible evacuation of American residents of Grenada.

THE OFFICIAL STORY

The official story about the invasion of Grenada—code named Urgent Fury—was that it was multinational, as major United States newspapers headlined it. The Pentagon reported that at dawn on October 25, 2,000 marines and assault troops landed at Saint George, the capital of Grenada (a town of 4,800 inhabitants), and that later 200 soldiers from six Caribbean countries joined them. The invasion began with the landing of 400 soldiers by helicopters from the warship *U.S.S. Guam*, anchored to the east of the island. They attacked the Pearls airport, and hundreds of rangers—an elite American force—parachuted onto Point Salinas where the controversial international airport was being built. According to a statement from the Pentagon, the rangers were met with anti-aircraft fire from the barracks where the Cuban engineers were lodged. The first reports mentioned that two United States soldiers died, twenty-three were wounded, and "most objectives" were "taken" within twelve hours. The Pentagon prevented any journalists from getting onto the island for a period of five days (this was the first time such a prohibition had been issued) and later shepherded a small group of them to restricted locations.

Time reported that the invading troops found 600 well-armed and trained Cubans. Secretary of State George Shultz stated at a press conference that the Cubans were "resisting and firing" and "of course, this obliges the United States to respond." Some 1,200 soldiers and between 2,000 and 5,000 Grenadian militia members faced the rangers.[238] On the third day, according to the Pentagon, its troops numbered 5,000 paratroopers, 500 marines and 500 rangers. Later reports mentioned a combined force of 12,000. On October 25 they began the evacuation of the 500 or 1,000 United States students and teachers.

Shortly after the start of the invasion Reagan spoke to the nation to declare that he had received "an urgent, formal request" from the five member nations of the Organization of Eastern Caribbean States "to assist in a joint effort to restore order and democracy on the island," and that he "acceded" to the request to join the multinational forces. The "overriding importance" of the effort, he claimed, was to protect human lives, "forestall further chaos," and establish law and order where "a brutal group of leftist thugs violently seized power, killing the Prime Minister" and members of his cabinet. He asked that this "collective action" not be misinterpreted, since it had been "forced on us by events that have no precedent in the eastern Caribbean."[239]

The Cuban government accused the United States by noting that "the invasion begun this morning was prepared and rehearsed for over two years on the Puerto Rican island of Vieques" and that the invasion was "not improvised," taking advantage of the situation created by Bishop's death. "What is going on here is a premeditated aggression by Washington," accused *Granma*.[240]

The resistance of Cuban platoons and armed workers came to an end on October 26, the news agencies reported. "They immolated themselves for the Motherland," commented Castro, who gave the order not to surrender. On that day new United States military reinforcements arrived. Secretary of Defense Caspar Weinberger reported the deaths of six soldiers, eight "lost," and thirty-three wounded. He claimed that they had encountered "much more resistance than expected."[241]

The "victory" over Grenada caused enormous cheer in the United States, and Reagan's popularity surged. An opinion poll indicated a 71 percent approval rate for the invasion. Reagan spoke of it in superlatives, calling it a major foreign-policy success, and the marines "heroes of freedom" for "defeating some 750 Cubans and their Grenadian allies." "It was a great victory not only politically but strategically," he added. A high official crowed that now the world would know that the United States was "no paper tiger." The Pentagon spoke of a military victory with few casualties (nineteen died in accidents); twenty-four Cubans and forty-four Grenadians died in combat or from the bombing, according to United States media.

Five years later when the truth emerged, *New York Times* correspondent Joseph Threaster wrote that the invasion was not a "glorious demonstration for the military." The operation was plagued by errors (it destroyed a hospital for mental patients, for example) and full of improvisations. The commandos from the various forces could not communicate because their radios were not compatible, and they only had tourist maps.[242]

The broad support for Reagan's "warring action" in Grenada was surprising, wrote the United States journalist Steven Volk, but it was explained by the public's need for a "victory" to get out from under the humiliations of Vietnam, Iran, and the most recent tragedy of the death of 237 marines in Lebanon two days before the invasion. "While the Reagan administration was preparing the Grenadian dish for public consumption, the nation's electronic and print media were setting the table," wrote Volk. The media transmitted only the official message: It was not a matter of the United States invading Grenada, but of a United States confrontation with Cuba and the Soviet Union. That was the way the *Washington Post* and the *New York Times* reported it.[243]

INTERNATIONAL DISGUST

The invasion of Grenada left the world community indignant, stupefied, and disgusted. Governments, institutions, organizations, churches, prominent personalities, and parliaments of many countries condemned the United States government. Even Reagan's loyal ally, British Prime Minister Margaret Thatcher, complained that the United States had the nerve to invade an island of the British Commonwealth and violate its sovereignty without informing Her Majesty. Reagan was surprised and hurt by Maggie's criticism. He did not expect it after the generous and wide-ranging help he had given Great Britain, assuring its victory in the Falkland/Malvinas Islands war.

Castro called it a "Pyrrhic victory and a disastrous moral defeat." For Latin America it was the renaissance of the worst moments of the Monroe Doctrine and the Big Stick.

Reagan associated the invasion of Grenada with the terrorist attack in Lebanon. He stated that Moscow had not only aided and abetted the violence in both countries, but that it had provided assistance through a network of terrorists and agents. Conversely, many compared the invasion with the Soviet Union's invasion of Afghanistan. This point of view hurt Reagan; his "invitation" from the tiny Caribbean countries was just as equivocal as Brezhnev's from the Afghan government.

To demonstrate the legitimacy of the "multinational" intervention in Grenada, Dominica's prime minister, Maria Eugenia Charles, requested an extraordinary session of the OAS's Permanent Council, but only as a form of "protocol" and without debates. She wanted to avoid the avalanche of criticism that opposed the invasion. The majority was able to express its revulsion and point to the flagrant United States violation of the principles of free self-determination and non-intervention, and of the OAS charter. There was no resolution. In the United Nations Security Council, during a meeting requested by Nicaragua, the terms of the resolution condemning the invasion were toned down so that the United States would not veto it, but it vetoed it anyway. This was the only vote against it. Eleven nations voted in favor of it, and Great Britain, Togo, and Zaire abstained. Shortly thereafter the General Assembly adopted a resolution condemning the invasion by a vote of 108 in favor, 9 against (the United States and the Caribbean countries that participated), and 27 abstentions. Most of the 63 speakers condemned the United States for violating international law and "clear principles on which are based the relations of a civilized world." Reagan commented that this news did not "spoil" his breakfast.

Reagan was not troubled by the fact that the United States was isolated in the United Nations, that his administration had lost credibility in the world community, that there was general condemnation, or that not one of his NATO allies had voted in his favor. Neither did he care about the barrage of internal criticism from the press. With this unprecedented action he had kept the public in the dark and enabled the Pentagon to manipulate it. This episode was a display of arrogance such as the world had never before seen.

FIVE YEARS LATER

Five years after the invasion—or the rescue operation as the Grenadians called it— Grenada began to bloom. It had a new democracy "with all its frailties." Under Prime Minister Herbert Blaize, elected in 1984 (in an election plotted and arranged by the United States), new businesses grew, agroindustry prospered, the big international airport at Point Salinas (constructed in large part by Cubans and completed with United States, British, and Canadian help) was operational, and the hotels, which had remained vacant for four years, were beginning to welcome a few tourists, mostly British.

But not everything was coming up roses. Economic difficulties were on the rise, and United States aid—never enough, though it tried to repair the damage it caused with the bombing—diminished. Unemployment hovered between 20 percent and 30 percent, health and education services deteriorated with the departure of the Cuban teachers and doctors, and the United States troops initiated the flowering of prostitution and venereal diseases. The international airport attracted drug traffic. Growing drug use forced Blaize to mount a campaign against it. "We are seeing crimes here we've never seen before," commented one Grenadian.[244]

Five years after his assassination the much-loved Maurice Bishop remained in the memories of most of these people, who pined for the social laws of his revolution, dismantled in the short period of semicolonialism imposed by the invaders. At the beginning of December 1988 fourteen people implicated in Bishop's murder went to the gallows, among them Hudson Austin, commander of the extinct Revolutionary Armed Forces, who had taken over the government, and the vice prime minister, Bernard Courd, the brains of the coup, and his wife, a major leader of the New Jewel Movement.[245]

THE PARTY'S OVER

In January 1989 the Reagan era ended. In his farewell address he assured the country he was leaving it "more prosperous, more secure, and happier." The reality was somewhat different. He left it with the highest budgetary and commercial debts in its history; in fact, he left it the biggest debtor in the world. His economic policies strengthened the rich and impoverished the poor—the majority—whose social welfare programs he had slashed. Small enterprises and businesses were going under. During his administration the number of homeless had grown to massive proportions, with many people wandering the streets of New York and Washington, sleeping in cardboard boxes on the streets or underground in subway tunnels.

The most militaristic of United States presidents had led the country into miserable failures in Nicaragua and El Salvador, two small, poor countries. When he left the White House, in spite of the massive amounts of hugely expensive military aid he had given El Salvador to defeat the guerrillas, the latter continued to wage the war, until the government was forced to seek a negotiated peace. Reagan's "secret war" with the contra mercenary gangs was revealed to be a costly fiasco; the Sandinistas he had wanted to overthrow continued to govern. The two sides arrived at peace accords only after he left the presidency.

The Iran-Contra investigations continued. This episode, according to the final report of the congressional commission that investigated it, had been one of fraud, contempt of law, and the President's persistent lack of honor. But no one challenged him in Congress. No one contradicted his distortions and his outright lies, and almost all tolerated the "I do not recall" with which he dodged his responsibility for this huge scandal, the most serious abuse of power by any United States head of state. He lied to Congress, the public and his allies, contradicted his own foreign policy (he secretly broke the arms embargo on Iran, which he had forced his allies to join), did business with terrorists, and violated the United States neutrality act. But he walked away unscathed, and nobody went to jail. North considered a run for president, and Bush, in one of his last acts before being defeated by Clinton, pardoned the main figures in the Iran-Contra scandal, among them, Weinberger, Abrams, Alan Fiers, and Robert McFarlane. The *New York Times* headlined an editorial, "Bush's Unpardonable Act." The editorial noted that with this pardon Bush was pardoning himself as well as closing this shameful episode of American history. It was the bloodiest and most painful period of the superpower's relationship with the small Central American countries.

CHAPTER IX

PANAMA: "DEAD MAN WALKING . . ."

AUTOPSY OF THE INVASION

The "lost decade" for Latin America—the 1980s—ended with the brutal United States invasion of Panama at dawn while its people slept on December 20, 1989. In a massive air, sea, and land operation, somewhere between 22,000 and 27,000 soldiers—varying numbers were cited—occupied the small country of only two million inhabitants. This was the "theater of war saturation" of the rapid deployment strategy. The United States' declared objective was to capture General Manuel Antonio Noriega, accused of drug trafficking, to bring him before a court of justice, and to "restore" Panamanian democracy.

The undeclared objective, however, had to do with the status of the Canal Treaties, which forced the United States to dismantle its military bases and leave the country before the year 2000, which it was loathe to do. It needed to place a government in power that it could manipulate to change the treaties. In the midst of the bombardments, the destruction, the massacres, the panic, and the humiliation of the Panamanian people, a most unusual ceremony took place at the American military base of Fort Clayton: the chief of the United States Southern Command installed Guillermo Endara as the new president of the republic.

Operation Just Cause (the code name given the invasion by the Pentagon) was the most extensive military action undertaken by the United States since the Vietnam War. The United States justified it as an act of "legitimate defense." The superpower's attack on a small third world country called forth feelings of indignation and consternation. Once again the world could see that no matter who was in the White House, respect for the principles of international law was nothing more than rhetoric.

In contrast to the relaxation of world tensions promoted by the Soviet leader Mikhail Gorbachev, which Ronald Reagan joined with one foot in the stirrup and one eye on history, this act of war cast the new, post-Cold War reality into relief. The Soviet Union, without its Eastern European allies and in the process of internal disintegration, was no longer the superpower confronting the United States in the international arena. The United States had the world firmly in hand and made all the rules.

A PACT WITH THE DEVIL

Ever since Theodore Roosevelt's unforgettable "I took Panama" in 1902—its secession from Colombia provoked by the United States—Panama had been subject to United States dominance. Roosevelt built the canal between the two oceans, and in the treaties he signed with the recently installed Panamanian government, the United States acquired perpetual dominion over a strip of land 10 miles wide and stretching across the country, and the "right" to intervene in Panama's internal affairs. These rights were included in its first constitution. The imperial eagle extended its sheltering wings—and its claws—over the new republic, which it converted into a quasi-colony.

The Colombian historian Eduardo Lemaitre called the invasion a disaster and described Panama's tragic reality: "The Panamanians have to believe that, from the moment they separated from Colombia under the protection of the North American shield, to create what they believed would be an absolutely sovereign nation, they sold their country's soul to the Devil. For it is materially impossible that a people can enjoy such prerogatives of independence and sovereignty when its territory is divided in two by a zone where a gigantic power has so many and such vital interests."[1]

Panama paid for its independence with part of its territory and compromised its sovereignty and its identity as a nation. With this foreign enclave in the middle of its territory and subject to constant United States interference, the Panamanian people grew under the syndrome of United States domination, with the complex of their own powerlessness, governed by a white minority—90 percent of the populace is black, mulatto, or mestizo—subjected to the military, tied to foreign capital, and allied unconditionally with Washington. General and President Omar Torrijos (1968–1978) changed these rules, but only for a short time.

United States interference, electoral fraud, and changes in government at the whim of "strongmen," always "legitimized" by the legislative assembly and recognized by Washington, were constant in Panama's political history. The invasion was a part of this history.

THE "STRONGMEN"

Torrijos was not the first Panamanian strongman, and his government was not a military dictatorship as the United States claimed. The first was Antonio Remón Cantera, the police commander who, in 1948, grasped the baton of political power as a result of unusual electoral developments. He was the first to run the country from the barracks, presiding over the president. In 1952, he was elected president. After his death, there occurred a succession of strongmen—Torrijos was one of them—who made and unmade presidents. This continued until General Manuel Antonio Noriega.

Upon Torrijos's death, Noriega (then chief of army intelligence) assumed command of the national guard in a Machiavellian move plotted with the military command. Like the others, he began to manipulate the presidents from the barracks. Noriega had Washington's support. He had been on the CIA's payroll for three decades as an informant. He also provided information to the Pentagon and the National Security Council. During the 1970s Noriega was the principal asset of the new and dominant CIA station in Panama City.

Panama was the United States' political and military spy center for the entire continent. The Canal Zone held fourteen United States naval and air bases and the School of the Americas—though in the 1980s President Jorge Illueca evicted it from Panama—where military and police officers from all over Latin America received military training on counterinsurgency techniques and anti-Communist ideological indoctrination. Noriega received instruction at this school.

Washington had long known that Noriega was giving intelligence information on the United States to the Cuban government, but his services to the CIA and other intelligence organizations were more important. In April 1976 Carter's CIA director, Stansfield Turner, discovered that Noriega had infiltrated its networks and promptly took him off the payroll. The southern command's "singing sergeant"—supposedly a Puerto Rican—sold Noriega the transcription of telephone conversations of members of the government, the army, and Panamanian politicians intercepted by United States intelligence services. This business continued and spread wide. Two or three

American soldiers sold him classified material with the complete plan for United States "electronic surveillance" of the entire southern continent, as well as the National Security Agency's secret technical manuals with the list of intercepted telephone numbers in all its countries. The CIA did not punish the "canaries" in exchange for their collaboration in assessing the extent of the damage.[2]

REAGAN: WEEDING OUT NORIEGA

According to some, relations between the United States and Noriega began to deteriorate in September 1985, when he removed President Nicolás Arditto Barletta, a former high World Bank official, and installed in his place Vice President Eric Arturo Delvalle. He ousted Barletta for having named a commission to investigate the assassination of Hugo Spadafora, of which Noriega was accused of being the architect. Spadafora, the former vice minister of health, a former fighter in the Sandinista guerrillas, and a former contra under the command of Eden Pastora, was a prominent figure of the opposition and one of the first to accuse Noriega of drug trafficking. His body turned up, headless and brutally tortured, at the Costa Rican border.

Noriega's version of the events was different. He insisted that relations had begun to go downhill after National Security Adviser Admiral John Poindexter came to Panama in December 1985 to ask Noriega to have the Panamanian defense forces take part in an invasion of Nicaragua and he declined. He explained that Poindexter had threatened him and warned him he "had better think of the consequences." According to Noriega, this was why the United States launched a campaign to discredit him. Noriega's version was confirmed by the *Miami Herald*. Citing official American sources, the newspaper reported that Poindexter and Noriega had spoken about the Nicaraguan situation, with Poindexter asking for Panama's support for the contras, and that Noriega had refused. Ambassador Everett Briggs, who was present at the meeting, claimed that this topic had not been touched upon. He further explained that in the "long and painful" meeting Poindexter had humiliated Noriega in front of his subordinates by mentioning the existing suspicions about his relations with drug traffic, arms dealing, and the laundering of dollars in Panama.

The *New York Times* and the NBC television network reported these stories to coincide with Noriega's visit to the United States in June 1986, claiming that he had developed these illicit activities while he was chief of army intelligence—

a post he held for thirteen years—and that he continued them as commander-in-chief of the defense forces. They also mentioned the suspicions against him regarding the assassination of Spadafora and the intelligence information he passed to the Cuban government. In July the United States House of Representatives made the same accusations.

The *New York Times* commented that the State Department "was surprised" at these accusations and ordered an investigation. The Washington Office on Latin America (WOLA) maintained that this information had been fed to the media by Elliot Abrams, a high State Department official, with Poindexter's authorization.[3] This relentless press harassment precipitated Noriega's return to Panama. He immediately met with his advisers in the presidential palace and jokingly dismissed the importance of the accusations: "These are matters of gringos and wannabe gringos [gringueros]" who were plotting against me," he declared.[4] In a letter to United Nations Secretary General Javier Pérez de Cuéllar, President Eric Arturo Delvalle accused the United States of this "orchestrated campaign" to pressure and discredit Panamanian authorities, in which the United States Congress and press took part in order to destabilize Panama. He averred that the accusations were "calumnies, of anonymous origin, based on supposed secret sources and on the claims of functionaries who have asked not to be identified." He pointed out that the moment chosen for these accusations happened to coincide with the campaign by some Americans to prevent the fulfillment of the Panama Canal Treaties' terms.[5]

Opinion within the Reagan administration was divided. The White House, the State Department (encouraged by Elliot Abrams), and Congress wanted to destroy Noriega, but CIA Director William Casey, the Pentagon, and Vice President (and former CIA director) George Bush believed that Noriega was extremely useful and praised his intelligence work highly. They did not want to create a conflict in the midst of the extensive clandestine operation (managed by Lieutenant Colonel Oliver North) to sustain Reagan's "secret war" against Nicaragua behind the backs of Congress and United States public opinion. The CIA gave Noriega $11 million to buy arms for the contras. He did not want this transaction to be known and warned that he would suspend the operation immediately if it became public. The Iran-Contra investigation documented that Noriega offered Poindexter and North a deal: he would have the Sandinista leaders assassinated if Washington would "clean up" his image and lift the embargo on arms for the Panamanian defense forces. The United States did not accept because the law prohibited any United States government involvement in assassinations.[6]

The United States Drug Enforcement Agency (DEA) knew about Noriega's connections with drug traffic but needed his collaboration to control the flow of drugs in Panama, the main transit point for drugs en route to the United States and a center for money laundering, as well as for arms dealers. In letters to Noriega, the DEA wrote that his cooperation was effective and valuable. The American journalist Alexander Cockburn pointed out this double standard: while the DEA was praising Noriega, White House assistant Norman Bailey claimed that he had a "21-cannon barrage of evidence" that Noriega was a drug trafficker.[7] "The Panamanians knew that we knew," claimed a former member of the Senate Intelligence Committee, and according to the American journalist Seymour Hersh, the public was convinced that Washington contributed to the creation of "one of the biggest thugs of recent times."[8]

THE CRISIS BEGINS

In the middle of 1987 Panama was an oasis of peace and prosperity in comparison with the convulsive situation of its Central American neighbors. President Delvalle was the visible figurehead of the government, while the supposedly invisible head of government was Noriega, the commander of the defense forces. The calm began to turn stormy in June when retired Colonel Roberto Díaz Herrera, a first cousin to Torrijos, accused Noriega of corruption on a grand scale, electoral fraud in 1984, and complicity in the assassination of Spadafora and the death of General Torrijos. These accusations, coming from the man who until three days earlier had been second in command in the army, led to the most serious political crisis in Panama's history. Díaz Herrera returned with interest the blow Noriega gave that forced him to retire from the army and prevented his rise to the top of the command of the defense forces, as had been agreed and for which post he had been in line. In August Díaz Herrera was arrested, and in depositions to the attorney general he retracted his words. He stated that he lacked proof, especially about the drug trafficking.[9]

The day after Díaz Herrera's accusations, the people took to the streets to demand Noriega's resignation, the dismissal of the military officers accused of corruption, an investigation of the denunciations made against them, and a return to democracy. The mob blocked the main roads with barricades and burning tires and provoked confrontations with the police. The city was paralyzed.

The opposition formed the Civic Crusade, with more than forty business committees and associations, professional people, and students. It was supported by the Catholic Church hierarchy. This was a middle- and upper-class movement—no sectors of the lower classes were represented—known on the streets as *rabiblancos* ("white-asses"). The Crusade called for civil disobedience, and thousands of people took to the streets blowing whistles, banging on pots and pans, and blowing their automobile horns to demand Noriega's resignation. Schools, banks, and businesses shut their doors.

After three days of protests, with scores of wounded and arrested, the government decreed a state of emergency and suspended constitutional guarantees—freedom of expression, movement, and assembly; habeas corpus; and the inviolability of the home—and imposed press censorship. Delvalle held Díaz Herrera and "external forces" responsible for the disturbances. On the other side of the barricade, the southern command put its 10,000 soldiers on a "state of alert."[10]

In June the United States Senate adopted (by an overwhelming majority of 86 to 2) a resolution strongly criticizing the Panamanian government and the country's defense forces. It asked that Noriega and other officials accused of drug trafficking be ordered to resign or retire until the results of the investigations were known and called on the government to restore constitutional guarantees and hold "free and fair" elections.[11]

President Delvalle called this resolution an "inconceivable, intolerable, and unacceptable intervention" into Panama's internal affairs. The high military command issued a virulent statement against the United States, stating that its Senate had become a "center of political conspiracies against Panama." The Panamanian chancellor sent a note of protest to Washington and recalled Panama's ambassador. The legislative assembly found the resolution "offensive," declared United States Ambassador Arthur Davis persona non grata, and demanded his immediate recall.[12]

More than 15,000 people protested outside the United States Embassy, shouting anti-Yankee slogans: "Those brutes in the Senate think we are their cattle!," "Southern Command out!," "Yankee, go home!," "Davis out!," "Davis or Noriega!" Stones and pots of red paint were thrown at the diplomatic headquarters.[13] Washington closed its consulate in Panama, cut military and economic aid (some $14 million), and suspended the sugar quota. It also presented a protest "in the most energetic terms" to the government because of the attack on its embassy in which, so it said, the government participated in violation of its international obligations to protect diplomatic missions. It demanded that Panama pay the cost of the damage to the embassy.

Panama took its complaint to the OAS, accusing the United States Senate of meddling in its internal affairs and requesting strict compliance with the Canal Treaties. The resolution was adopted by 17 votes to 1 (the United States); 8 abstentions (Costa Rica, Honduras, Haiti, and the small islands of the eastern Caribbean); four countries were absent, and Paraguay did not participate.

The protests against Noriega and Delvalle continued for more than a month. Thousands of people dressed in white—a symbol of the opposition—and waving handkerchiefs took to the streets to demand free elections and Noriega's resignation. The crowds were violently broken up by the special antiriot forces—the so-called Dobermans—with more than a score wounded and hundreds arrested. Noriega's followers organized demonstrations of support, and anti-Yankee demonstrators threw stones at American businesses and banks. The office of the daily *La Prensa*, which accused Noriega of "state terrorism," was burned. Entrepreneurs and businessmen organized shutdowns to protest the destruction of their businesses and shops. Some banks closed their doors in fear of vandalism. The university called off classes after the Dobermans shot at students and wounded forty. Businesses and luxury boutiques were looted, and some were destroyed. Looting and armed robberies extended to private residences as well.

The city was militarized, and the government prohibited public demonstrations. Three days later, however, thousands of people dressed in white took the streets again. About 150 demonstrators were wounded, and 300 were arrested, in battles with the Dobermans. The opposition protested this official violence. Delvalle ordered a general amnesty for those arrested in the disturbances against the government.[14]

On July 31, at a ceremony on the anniversary of Torrijos's death attended by Delvalle, Noriega, the high military command, and more than 100,000 people, the military officers called for the people to unite for peace and expressed their vigorous condemnation of foreign interference in their internal affairs.[15]

On the eve of a planned antigovernment demonstration on August 5, six well-known businessmen, leaders of the opposition, were arrested. The government claimed that a raid of the chamber of commerce, headquarters of the Civic Crusade (which by this point boasted a membership of more than a hundred political, business, and professional organizations), had turned up a plan to overthrow Delvalle, to dissolve the legislative assembly, and to hand power to a civilian junta.[16] They were released two days later.

In November 1987 Delvalle announced to Washington that Panama would not participate in joint military maneuvers planned for January and ordered officials of the United States Agency for International Development (AID) out of the country. The legislative assembly approved the government's decision to suspend the visas of United States military personnel.[17]

Rumors ran rife through Panama. There was talk of Noriega's possible resignation, of conspiracies and coups against him being forged in Washington and Panama, and of secret negotiations by Noriega with United States emissaries to find an honorable way for him to step down. In October *Newsweek* reported that José Blandón, Panama's consul general in New York and a confidant of Noriega's, delivered a plan to "restore complete democracy in Panama" to Elliot Abrams, assistant secretary of state for Latin American affairs.[18] He let him know that Noriega agreed. The plan foresaw Noriega's retirement from the command of the defense forces in April 1988 and new elections in 1989. As a quid pro quo it asked immunity for Noriega from the cases brought against him in Panamanian courts and those in United States courts and an explicit guarantee by Reagan that these court cases would not continue. Noriega asked Blandón in a cable dated in December 1987, and quoted by *Newsweek*, not to "lose strict control of the document and the discussion" since he did not want to appear like "the Japanese surrendering on the decks of the Missouri."[19] He made it clear that he did not want to leave Panama, but if he must, he retained the right to return whenever he wanted. He said that he would only leave his country in a coffin. At the end of January 1988 Noriega rejected the plan and fired Blandón.[20] It was said he did so because he knew that Blandón was consulting with Delvalle behind his back.

Washington believed that the deterioration of the economic situation and the slowly but surely growing discontent in Panama would lead the defense forces to topple Noriega. Abrams claimed that the General was "hanging on by his fingernails." Several times he mentioned a date for his fall. But Noriega did not fall, and the crisis intensified.

AN ORGY OF "VENDETTAS"

The accusations by federal courts in Tampa and Miami that Noriega was involved in drug trafficking were based on testimony by convicted drug traffickers, United States citizen Michael Kalish and Panamanian Floyd Carlton Cáceres. The Justice Department offered to reduce their sentences and other privileges in exchange for their collaboration—in other words, if they would finger Noriega. This system of "buying witnesses" is an operating procedure in the United States justice system. Still, the Justice Department was worried by the scant credibility of such testimonies.

In February 1988 the parade of Noriega's enemies and former friends began, accusing him before the courts, at Congressional investigation committees, and in the press. It was a vendetta party by people who had some reason to bear a grudge against him, among them General Díaz Herrera—over the cause of his disgrace—and Colonel Rubén Darío Paredes—whom Noriega had advised to give up his command and launch a campaign for the presidency. According to one reporter, for Paredes to do this was like jumping from an airplane without a parachute. Paredes accused Noriega of having killed Paredes's son.

Another of his accusers was Blandón, the former consul in New York, whom Noriega had demoted. Stripped of diplomatic immunity, he implicated Noriega before a Miami grand jury and a Senate subcommittee of having connections with the narcos, receiving million-dollar bribes, allowing the laundering of dollars, and having ordered Spadafora's murder. He described Noriega as a "businessman" who would as soon sell weapons to the Sandinistas as to the contras or the Salvadoran guerrillas. He alleged that money drove Noriega's relations with the CIA and the Cuban government. Blandón became a key player for Washington, since he also implicated Fidel Castro in drug dealing. Blandón and his family were placed in the federal witness protection program.[21]

Blandón claimed that Noriega had conspired with Lieutenant Colonel Oliver North (the major figure in the Iran-Contra scandal) but spoiled a plot of North's to send weapons to the Salvadoran guerrillas, which North wanted to use to accuse the Sandinista government of arming the FMLN. Noriega helped to dispatch the shipment—it came from the German Democratic Republic—but later had it intercepted, and the operation subsequently went awry.[22]

Blandón claimed that in 1984 he had accompanied Noriega to Havana and had been present at a meeting with Castro. He showed photographs and averred that he had seventy-five hours of taped conversations. According to him, this meeting had been intended to resolve a dispute between Noriega and the Medellín cartel since Noriega had ordered one of the cartel's cocaine laboratories in Panama's Darien Province to be destroyed. He swore Fidel mediated the dispute.[23] He also claimed that Bush had called Noriega at the start of the Grenada invasion to ask him to warn Castro not to intervene. Bush denied this.

Blandón's torrent of accusations, none accompanied by evidence, moved Democratic Senator John Kerry, the chairman of the Senate Investigations Subcommittee, to beg him to restrain himself.[24] In his book on Noriega, *New York Times* journalist John Dinges wrote that after many months of investigation and interviewing the swarm of people involved in the Noriega case, he had come to the conclusion that many of the accusations were impossible to confirm and others were unlikely or clearly false. He pointed out inconsistencies, confusion of dates and facts, data that did not agree with the testimony, and the fact that almost the entire legal case against Noriega was based on the testimony of convicted drug-traffickers. Dinges quoted Captain Felipe Camargo, a former member of the Panamanian defense forces (arrested after the invasion) who was present at the meeting in Havana and who swore Blandón's version of the events was a "distortion" of the facts.[25]

Ramón Milián Rodríguez, a virulently anti-Communist Cuban-American (implicated in the Iran-Contra scandal), the brains behind the dollar-laundering network and other criminal subtleties in the field of drug-traffic, was among Noriega's victims. He was a convicted criminal (he was paying with a forty-five-year prison sentence for money laundering and extortion), and became another of Noriega's accusers. Before the Senate subcommittee he claimed that in 1979 Noriega agreed to launder money in Panama and that four years later he abruptly broke the agreement and reported Milián to United States authorities. Milián had been arrested. "Now I am returning the blow, and if you want to call this a personal vendetta, fine with me." He testified that he had helped set up a $4.6 million commission from the Medellín cartel for Noriega to allow the shipment to the United States of 4,000 pounds of cocaine and a million pounds of marijuana.[26] The investigator preparing the case against Noriega for the Miami district attorney rejected Milián's accusations as "totally lacking in credibility."[27]

Floyd Carlton Cáceres, the Panamanian who had once served as Noriega's private pilot, came to the committee with his face covered by a black hood. He declared before the Senate subcommittee that the Medellín cartel had offered Noriega $30,000 to allow it to land its planes in Panama, at which the General laughed and asked if they thought he was a beggar. He says that in this way Noriega received $100,000 for the first flight and $150,000 and $200,000 for later ones.[28]

Noriega's firm demand to Reagan's emissaries—they wanted him to resign and leave Panama—was for the United States to drop the cases against him and grant him immunity from prosecution. The reply of high White House,

State Department, Justice Department, and DEA officials remained the same: "Not possible." "No way." "Can't be done."

While the United States administration, Congress, and media furthered this intense moralistic campaign against Noriega the drug trafficker and the Justice Department rounded up and tampered with witnesses, accusations about drug traffic in Central America implicating the CIA and the DEA came to light in the hearings of the Senate committee investigation of the Iran-Contra scandal (which erupted in 1986). Several sources corroborated them. The American pilot Gary Betzner and Colombian immigrant Jorge Morales—both serving time for drug trafficking in a federal prison in Miami—testified in separate interrogations that they had carried contraband cocaine with the help of these agencies. They declared that CIA planes carried weapons to the contras and returned to the United States loaded with cocaine. Both agencies denied such accusations.[29]

Members of this congressional committee also confirmed that the network supplying the contras with arms introduced drugs into the United States with the aid of United States intelligence services and Central American countries.[30] Milián, in turn, maintained that the money from drug sales was used to support the contras. He admitted that he laundered money and facilitated the transfer of funds.[31] And in October 1988 *Newsweek* reported that the contras bought weapons with the profits from the sale of cocaine they had brought into the United States with the help of the CIA and the DEA. The *New York Times* revealed that a DEA affiliate in Guatemala had confirmed the existence of such a connection, and the *Washington Post* reported that Jorge Ochoa, one of the principal Colombian drug "lords," was involved in supplying arms to the contras and transporting cocaine from Central America to the United States. That same month, news agencies reported that federal agents were investigating forty United States banks supposedly implicated in money laundering operations.[32]

THE ITINERARY OF A FIASCO

"We're destroying Panama to free the Panamanians from Noriega," a high State Department official commented sarcastically.[33] The measures Reagan took to bring him down shook the Panamanian banking sector—one of Latin America's most important—but not the General. The climate of instability and mistrust accelerated capital flight and depositors' withdrawals. The 120 banks—most of them American (only fourteen were Panamanian)—lacked currency.

On several occasions they closed their doors to prevent withdrawals. In March 1988, the Panamanian foreign debt was $2 billion, and debt service went up to $82 million.[34] This disruption of the economy affected mainly the poor and salaried workers. The fiscal crisis and the government's lack of currency prevented the payment of wages owed to 140,000 public servants and 15,000 members of the defense forces.[35] The government had no recourse to the issuance of currency—an option open to all other countries—since its currency was the dollar, issued by the United States Federal Reserve.

The Panamanians were desperate because of the difficult economic situation and the fear of United States military intervention. They saw its invasion of Grenada, its threats against Nicaragua, and its frequent maneuvers in the Caribbean as a prelude to its intervention in Panama. Anti-Yankee sentiment was evident not only among the people, but also in important sectors of Panamanian commerce, since they were suffering from economic sanctions imposed by the United States in an effort to topple Noriega. This militaristic display and the threat of an invasion of Panama alarmed the rest of the southern continent as well.

Also in 1988, former Presidents Alfonso López of Colombia, Carlos Andrés Pérez of Venezuela, and Daniel Odúber of Costa Rica (it was with their help that Torrijos had achieved the new Canal Treaties in 1977) went to Panama to try to convince Noriega to resign. They warned him that remaining in power would not benefit him, Panama, or Latin America. Venezuela and Spain offered him asylum. They told him that military intervention by the United States would ruin the agreements on the Canal and become a threat to all their countries. Noriega agreed to resign in a few months and to speak with the opposition to fix a date for elections. They left Panama convinced they had won Noriega over.

Four days later Delvalle went to Miami for a meeting with Elliot Abrams. Who called whom? From this meeting emerged the decision to remove Noriega from office. Jorge Eduardo Ritter, a former Panamanian chancellor, said that Abrams pressured Delvalle to do it; others said he only agreed to do what he had already decided to do. When he returned to Panama on February 25, Delvalle announced the General's dismissal in a ten-minute television speech, secretly prerecorded.

With the support of the military command, Noriega called an urgent meeting of the legislative assembly. In the early morning, also in ten minutes, the assembly dismissed Delvalle and the vice president and named the minister of education Manuel Solis Palma "provisional" president, all with a unanimous vote by the thirty-eight legislators present (the assembly total was sixty-seven).[36]

After this bombshell Delvalle remained isolated—the night before, he had taken his family to the United States ambassador's residence—having no contact with the outside world, since his phone lines were cut. The following day he disappeared. It was said he was in "some secure place" in Panama or "hiding" at a United States military base under the protection of the southern command.[37]

Reagan was surprised by the Panamanian people's disinterested reaction to Delvalle's dismissal. He had been hoping for a massive popular protest leading to Noriega's fall. He did not seem to understand that for Panamanians— and for the opposition—Delvalle was no more than Noriega's puppet and the product of fraud and that the repeated changes at Las Garzas Palace (the presidential palace) engineered by strongmen did not exactly make them lose sleep. No one, it seemed, was eager to risk anything for politicians. The only support Delvalle could count on was from the United States Embassy. The Río Group, meeting at Cartagena, Colombia decided to suspend Panama (one of its members) and recall their ambassadors for "consultations." Mexico did not join in this gesture.

Reagan, profoundly annoyed, warned that he recognized only Delvalle as the "constitutional" president of Panama. It was "[a] grotesque display of the cynicism with which the American administrations have used Panamanian presidents, attributing to them a nonexistent legitimacy and granting them recognition that is as humiliating as it is laughable," commented former Panamanian Chancellor Ritter.[38] Washington was aware that in the question of legality and illegality, Delvalle and Solis were on an equal footing. Both came to the presidency by the decision of the strongman. Delvalle fell by the will of Noriega, as had Ardito Barletta, whom Delvalle had no problem replacing.

Reagan did not mind that Delvalle's presidency was the result of a fraud, nor that he was deposed in the usual Panamanian manner—a system to which Washington never objected. His interests in Panama were different. Reagan "recognized" Delvalle in order to use him, and Delvalle allowed him to do so. To the world, his "presidency" exercised from hiding somewhere in United States territory might have been grotesque, but for Panama it was ill-fated. The Unites States used it to ruin Panama. On "instructions" from "President" Delvalle, the State Department froze $50 million of the Panamanian government's money on deposit in United States banks. It also suspended payment of $6.5 million it owed Panama under the terms of the Canal Treaties, prohibited United States enterprises in Panama from paying taxes to the Panamanian government, and suspended trade preferences, which affected $96 million worth of trade. Delvalle in his turn "ordered" Panamanian consulates to keep the funds they received from shipping companies that registered their ships in Panama, a business arrangement that brought the country many millions of dollars.[39]

The leaders of the Civic Crusade called a general strike. Some banks, a large part of the commercial sector, restaurants, gas stations, and commercial and professional offices closed their doors. Taxi and bus transportation dropped. Small groups of demonstrators threw up barricades, burned tires, and fought with the police, but the absence of opposition leaders was conspicuous. The Crusade lifted the strike on the fourth day because the chamber of commerce did not want it to interfere with its annual fair.[40] One public employee observed, "They are businessmen and they run the country like a business, from Monday to Friday, and on the weekend they go to the beach. You can't make a revolution that way."[41]

The social and economic situation was critical. Strikes and protest demonstrations demanding the payment of wages became an everyday occurrence. The government handed out checks it could not cover and bonuses no one wanted. Food and basic necessities were becoming scarce. There were strikes by some 140,000 public employees, chain stores, gas stations, doctors, and teachers and marches by 60,000 retired people. Commerce and industry were paralyzed by a strike of stevedors in Balboa. They were demanding complete payment of their wages in cash. "This is not political," claimed a striker. "Noriega's not the object. It's a question of workers' rights, of feeding our children. No pay, no work. Simple as that." The army broke up the strike.[42]

On March 16 there was an attempted coup against Noriega by a small group of officers led by Leonidas Macías, chief of the national police. *Newsweek* called it a comic opera, since the conspirators trapped themselves when they closed a door by accident, and were arrested. A few minutes later Noriega appeared on the steps of army headquarters, smiling and sarcastically answering reporters' questions.

With the exchange of fire inside the barracks, the news of the attempted coup spread like wildfire. Some rumored that Noriega had fallen. A violent mob from the popular neighborhoods attacked commercial centers, set fire to warehouses, burned cars, and stoned the police and the army. Telephone and utility-company employees cut services. The army took over these businesses and started them up again.

The antiriot forces moved into action. They broke into the Marriot Hotel, where an opposition press conference was taking place, and arrested twenty of the opposition leaders and twelve journalists, among them five United States nationals. Several were beaten. The government declared a state of siege and closed three newspapers, three radio networks, and a television station, and the army broke up the stevedores' strike, which had spread to other places.[43]

Noriega took advantage of this situation to "clean out" army and police ranks and establish his friends and family in key positions. More than a hundred officers, most from the police and the intelligence services, were arrested and placed under investigation.[44] Panama accused the United States of instigating this coup. The Pentagon declared that it was kept informed but took no part. Abrams, sure of the outcome, announced, as he had on other occasions, that Noriega would fall in a matter of days.[45] In spite of the coup's failure, Washington saw it as a positive sign, since it revealed that the divisions within the defense forces and the police had become sharper. It had faith that the military would topple Noriega.

THE LAST TANGO

Panama was bombarded with threatening news from Washington. Assistant Secretary of State Elliot Abrams announced that the administration was studying new measures to "squeeze" the Panamanian economy, and "if the General remains in power after Easter," it would seek new formulas. One of these, according to a high official, was his "forced extradition," a benign euphemism for the abduction of foreigners from other countries.[46]

Washington was trying to break Noriega and the defense forces' resistance and create confusion and desperation among the people by its military maneuvers in the Caribbean and the "state of alert" activities of the troops of the southern command. The Panamanian government protested the maneuvers by the southern command, since they violated the Canal Treaties, under whose terms Panama was to be notified beforehand, which had not been done. The southern command responded that it was conducting "routine" exercises. The tension continued to rise because of the continual incidents—real and provoked—between the military forces and elements of both countries.

Washington now intended to internationalize the conflict. It presented Panama as a security threat to the United States and Latin America. It maintained that Noriega was stockpiling a large quantity of Soviet weapons from Cuba, as reported by two Panamanian officers in the United States, deserters from the air force. National Security Adviser General Colin Powell said that perhaps Noriega was trying to establish some sort of insurgency for the time when he was no longer in power, but that the most worrisome thing was "the infusion of Soviet and Cuban weapons to destabilize Central America."[47]

At the end of March 1988 the United States Senate unanimously adopted a strong resolution in which it declared that the agitation in Panama "posed an unusual and extraordinary threat to the national security, foreign policy, and economy of the United States" and urged Reagan to increase the economic, political, and diplomatic pressures against Noriega.[48] With such support, Reagan was free to intervene in "legitimate defense."

The State Department asked for an increase in the number of troops in Panama. The Pentagon sent 1,300 marines and twenty-six planes and helicopters. It also ordered the return of the families of its diplomatic personnel to the United States and cut its embassy staff in half. News agencies reported constant meetings at the White House on the Panamanian situation to study possible solutions using force. A State Department official announced that such an offensive was used to pressure the Panamanian government and raise the morale of the Civic Crusade.

Reagan's policies in Panama were a fiasco. In April 1988 the economy began to show favorable signs. The three largest supermarkets and other high-volume sales outlets opened their doors—closed for ten days—and several American corporations, among them Eastern Airlines and Texaco, ignored Reagan's restrictions and paid some $3 million in taxes to the Panamanian government.[49] Vice President Bush, who had just declared his presidential candidacy, made an unexpected charge. He claimed that the millions of dollars going into Panamanian banks were sent by Libyan President Muammar El-Qaddafi. Reporters asked where Bush got his information. White House spokesman Marlin Fitzwater claimed that it was from intelligence sources he could not reveal and that it was a sign of "the White House's conclusion on Libya's relations with Noriega"—in other words, the relations of a terrorist with a drug trafficker. The United States Embassy in Panama denied any information on the subject. When Qaddafi heard Bush's remarks, he declared that he supported his candidacy because "no president could be as demented as Reagan."[50]

The president of Mexico, Miguel de la Madrid, remarked that "no country could claim a monopoly on truth in politics, nor could democracy be imposed from abroad." Carlos Andrés Pérez, the former Venezuelan president who was running again for office, agreed that United States meddling complicated the situation and "it had unfortunately turned Noriega into an anti-imperialist and nationalist leader, and a defender of Latin American sovereignty." At a meeting of the Sistema Económico Latinoamericano (SELAL: Latin-American Economic System) in Caracas in April, a unanimous vote (including the representative from the Chilean military dictatorship) called the United States policies against Panama coercive, and SELAL showed its willingness to provide economic aid to counteract their effects.[51] No United States head of state had ever managed to create a greater continent-wide consensus against his policies than Reagan.

For Reagan the ridicule to which Noriega had submitted him was humiliating. His demands and the failures of his emissaries had been too public. Each time he offered more, without ever succeeding. First he set a date for Noriega's resignation; later he promised not to seek his extradition if he went to another country; then he said that he could stay in Panama if he resigned. Each emissary was given the same reply by Noriega: the United States should drop the cases against him. Their response was again the same: No way.

In the election year and in the final months of his term, Reagan could not permit a failure in Panama. He was already loaded down with the enormous Iran-Contra scandal and the failure of his policies in Central America. He was subject to bitter attacks from the Democratic candidates Michael Dukakis and the Reverend Jesse Jackson and from members of his own party who were afraid that they would lose the election. Washington offered Noriega another deal: it would stop court cases against him if he left Panama.

When the press revealed that Reagan was disposed to negotiate the question of immunity with Noriega, the Justice Department and the DEA protested, and the administration retracted its offer.[52] In May, to prevent the negotiations entirely, the Senate adopted a resolution by a crushing majority prohibiting any negotiations that implied the cessation of the cases against Noriega.[53]

A summit meeting between Reagan and Gorbachev was planned for the same month in Moscow, and Reagan, president of the world's superpower, could not arrive carrying this load of failures. Without allowing the congressional resolution and the opposition of the Justice Department and the DEA to stand in his way, he opted to negotiate with Noriega and offered to drop the court cases against him if he resigned and left Panama. Secretary of State Shultz again sent the high State Department official Michael Kozak to Panama with this message (he had gone there on secret missions previously). Kozak even proposed to Noriega the possibility of returning to Panama to celebrate Christmas with his family. In the meantime the United

States kept military harassment and psychological warfare at a fever pitch.

Reagan and Shultz were convinced that this mission would be a success. Noriega could not refuse because he would be getting what he had always wanted. His withdrawal from Panama was the solution to the crisis. Shultz, who was supposed to accompany the President to Moscow, postponed his departure, hoping to bring good news. Abrams once again announced the "imminent" fall of the General. Kozak did his job and made the generous offer; but again, Noriega did not accept.

Profoundly depressed, Shultz informed the nation of this new failure. It meant the collapse of negotiations with Noriega. Reagan received the news in Helsinki, Finland, on his way to Moscow. There, a journalist asked him if he thought the United States looked like "an idiot" in the face of Panama. "I don't think so," answered the President. But everyone else did, including many inside his own administration, noted *Time*, referring to this brief exchange.[54]

The politics of force espoused by the State Department was not shared by those in charge of defense. The Pentagon publicly stated that confrontation would not succeed. It counseled "measured and adequate" steps to achieve the government's objectives. Anonymous sources in the Pentagon leaked what they themselves called an "idiotic" State Department plan to kidnap Noriega. Abrams declared that such comments were "irresponsible and dangerous."[55]

The public quarrels between the departments of state and defense on the Panama issue revealed that the government was entangled in a round of blind man's bluff. It was not the first time such a situation had happened, but it was the first time they aired their differences in public. The situation turned "sinister," commented a high State Department official. Noriega was not toppling, and the possibilities for ousting him were running out.

There was fear in Panama and throughout the continent of United States military intervention because of Noriega's blind intransigence in refusing to retire. On three occasions in 1988 and 1989 López Michelsen and Carlos Andrés Pérez attempted to convince him that this game against the great power was dangerous and that the only way out was for him to resign. Their intention, commented López in an interview in the Colombian magazine *Semana* in 1991, was to maintain the neutrality of the Canal, insure that the United States complied strictly with the Torrijos-Carter Treaties, and avoid a United States military intervention. "What happened later we had foreseen," he added.

Nine members of the Panamanian conference of bishops also asked Noriega to resign "to avoid more suffering among the people," and Archbishop Marcos

Gregorio McGrath offered to mediate. Costa Rican President Óscar Arias and Spain's Prime Minister Felipe González asked the Archbishop to accompany them to convince Noriega of the danger that was hanging over Panama. To their surprise the Archbishop told them that he had consulted the leaders of the opposition and they told him that the State Department had asked them not to get involved.[56]

The Civic Crusade was Washington's tool. The CIA funded it, and the State Department gave it political "orientation" to prevent it from reaching an agreement with Noriega. The Crusade called for a national work stoppage. Some 75 percent of commerce and industry shut its doors, and the streets were empty. The people reappeared on August 10 to receive the body of Arnulfo Arias—three times president and three times deposed—who had died in Miami. Arias had been a harsh critic of Noriega. A hundred thousand people went to the airport, and the funeral became a loud protest against Noriega: "Arnulfo presidente, Noriega delincuente" ("Arnulfo president, Noriega criminal") shouted the people.

The incidents and friction between United States uniformed and civilian personnel and Panamanians were becoming ever more frequent and intense. Washington charged that its military personnel and their dependents were subject to kidnapping, rape, beatings, and extortion by Panamanians and warned that it would do whatever was necessary to protect them. The Panamanian government accused the United States of meddling in its internal affairs, violations of its air space and territory, and endangering the lives of its citizens with low-level flights by airplanes and helicopters over its military installations. La Estrella and Crítica, two Panamanian newspapers, listed more than seventy United States violations of the Canal Treaties.[57]

In September 1988 the United States Embassy circulated a document communicating its government's decision not to comply with the Canal Treaties as long as "a process of democratization" in Panama had not been certified—in other words, a change of government and Noriega's departure.[58]

Not even a miracle could save Reagan from his failure in Panama before he left the White House, but he needed to show that he was still working to bring Noriega down. The media reported his constant meetings with Secretaries of State and Defense George Shultz and Frank Carlucci and with National Security Adviser Colin Powell, to analyze the Panamanian situation. They announced new measures and new dispatches of troops, weapons, and war materials to the southern command. Government spokespeople talked of the possibility of an invasion and the abduction of Noriega. The government did not know what to do in this conflict.

In January 1989 Reagan left the White House, and Noriega remained in place. He had succeeded in getting rid of Delvalle without any protest; two attempted coups against him had failed, and he had "cleaned out" the colonels and generals without creating conflicts within the defense forces. Now it was Bush's turn to get around this crisis without having any better options to resolve it.

MR. BUSH GOES TO WAR

To many, George Bush's administration would be the "four more years" that Reagan wanted to govern but the Constitution wouldn't allow. His feeble political character grew in the shadow of the most popular United States head of state since Franklin D. Roosevelt. Bush's candidacy held sway in the Republican Party not because he was the best candidate but because Reagan supported it. Bush was Reagan's heir apparent.

There were few opportunities for negotiation in the Panama crisis after Noriega's rejection of the biggest concession the United States could offer him: forgetting about the court cases against him if he left the country. This had been a humiliating process for the great power, and the possible threat of force became more apparent.

Bush did not openly tackle the Panama question. It was a delicate affair that could have put him in embarrassing situations. Noriega had been a long-time CIA informant, and Bush—according to former CIA Director Stansfield Turner—put him on his payroll during his term as CIA Director (1976–1977). During the presidential campaign journalists inquired about his relations with Noriega while he had been CIA Director and Reagan's drug czar. Bush, a paradigm of ambiguity, did not answer.

The Panama crisis was a heavy load for the new head of state. A month after his inauguration he approved a CIA plan to oust Noriega. Bush personally pressured Congress to approve $10 million to start the operation. The money was intended to support the Panamanian opposition and encourage a coup. Rumors ran rife of plans for United States or Panamanian commandos to kidnap Noriega.[59] This information, published by the magazine *U.S. News and World Report*, was not denied by the administration.[60]

Panama's economic situation improved in spite of the sanctions imposed by Washington. Commerce functioned on a barter system and discounts initiated by business leaders, and money returned to the bank vaults. According to *Newsweek*, official sources in Washington confirmed that this recovery was due to an infusion of $20 million in credits from the President of Libya and from West German and Asian banks. These sources neglected to mention the $565 million Washington deposited in the same banks to pay its military personnel in Panama and the Canal Commission.[61]

But the real source of the Panamanian banks' recovery, the one everyone suspected without being able to prove, was the money laundering from narcotics operations. With these funds, it was claimed that in January 1989 Noriega founded the Banco Institucional Patria (Institutional Bank of the Homeland), a private entity belonging to the Fondo de Beneficencia de las Fuerzas Armadas (Defense Forces Welfare Fund), which he controlled as president of the junta. Its headquarters were near the general headquarters of the defense forces, where he had his command post.[62]

THE BULL'S EYE: NORIEGA

Panama prepared to hold elections in May 1989, and the campaign grew heated. The Civic Crusade leaders, Guillermo Endara (who had been secretary to three-time president Arnulfo Arias); Ricardo Arias Calderón, head of the Christian Democratic Party, the major electoral force in Panama; and Guillermo Ford of the Molinera Party all had presidential aspirations. Although their guns were turned primarily on Noriega and Carlos Duque, a businessman and the official candidate and leader of the Democratic Revolutionary Party founded by Torrijos, they still attacked one another.

The battle among the opposition candidates worried Washington. Its ambassador was given the job of convincing them to come together to support Endara as their presidential candidate. Arias and Ford were to be vice presidents. They agreed to this arrangement.

The sector supporting the government comprised the Coalición de Liberación Nacional (Colina: National Liberation Coalition) with the Democratic Revolutionary Party and seven small parties. Duque was its presidential candidate, and Ramón Sieiro, Noriega's brother-in-law, and Aquilino Boyd, Torrijos's former chancellor, ran for the vice presidential posts. Colina counted on the government's political machinery, the support of the defense forces—even though they were not all of one mind—and a favorable press. The government had shut down the opposition press, *El Siglo*, *La Prensa*, and *Extra*, and the television and radio stations that were opposed to Colina. It could also count on the dignity battalions, a civilian armed front, and shock troops, created by Noriega for defense against United States aggression.

For the first time, Panamanian society was divided, with its political forces polarized not by internal problems but by the conflict between Noriega and the United States. The opposition's priority was to normalize relations with Washington and persuade it to suspend the sanctions and end the isolation it imposed on Panama. Not for a moment did it question Washington's aggressive and provocative acts nor its violation of the Canal Treaties. Its attacks were on Noriega as the cause of the crisis.

Duque's banners were nationalist and anti-imperialist. For Colina the important issue was Panama's future, threatened by the United States, the defense of its sovereignty, and the fulfillment of the Canal Treaties to insure that the United States military enclave in its country be dismantled. Its slogans emphasized that the choice was between being a free and sovereign nation or being a United States colony if it voted for Endara, whom Colina accused of having "sold out" to Washington. The people welcomed Duque's opposition to United States intervention and his defe nse of the Canal Treaties, but his prestige was diminished for being Noriega's candidate. Simplistically, national and international public opinion saw that support for Duque was to defend Noriega, and to defend Noriega was to be a drug trafficker.

Washington's strategy was to delegitimize the government and discredit the election before the people of Panama and in international public opinion, to convince them that Noriega was setting up a "massive fraud" in Duque's favor. This was a psychological campaign run by United States experts. President Bush and Secretary of State James Baker warned that they would not recognize any president who kept Noriega in a position of power.

Bush continued the strong economic sanctions, since they were legal—according to Washington, they were in response to the requests of the "constitutional president" Eric Arturo Delvalle. Bush ratcheted up military harassment with a gradual increase in the number of troops at the United States bases in Panama and with more frequent and threatening maneuvers in the Caribbean. Although his spokesmen stressed that military action was a "last resort," the danger of an intervention was more evident every day. Many people in Panama and the United States wanted just that in order to be free of Noriega.

Washington's candidate, Endara, was not in favor of such intervention and stated publicly that he preferred to "swallow" a few more years of Noriega, "we can get rid of him, even though it may cost us blood." He noted that United States officials had assured him that military intervention was "absolutely inconceivable."[63]

The refusal by opposition leaders to negotiate with the government, and Noriega's refusal to abandon power, closed off the possibility for a political solution and opened the doors to United States intervention. This fear existed in Panama and abroad. Several former heads of state in Latin America continued to try to convince Noriega of the necessity for his resignation and the danger of such an intervention. His confrontation with the United States was absurd. Spain and Venezuela repeated their offers of asylum.

"Governing" from United States territory, Delvalle also offered to talk with Noriega, but Noriega refused the offer. Delvalle had no credibility with the Panamanian government or with the opposition. To the government and to the people, he was no more than Washington's "puppet."

The greater the United States interference, the stiffer were the controls Noriega established to counter it. In April, a month before the elections, he suspended tourist cards for United States citizens, a device in force for more than fifty years. They would now have to apply for visas at Panamanian consulates. Nevertheless, this restriction was easy to circumvent because entering Panama from United States military bases with or without a visa was simply a matter of a short walk.

That same month Panamanian intelligence services dismantled a clandestine radio and television network set up by the CIA with sophisticated equipment. Its agent, Kurt Muse, who was arrested in this operation, revealed that the operation was meant to destabilize the country, create chaos, and stimulate popular insurgency against Noriega. It was to begin in the first week of May, and the videos were already set.[64] (Muse was freed by the invading troops in an operation at the prison that killed the Panamanian guards and in which many criminals escaped.)[65]

Newsweek reported that Noriega's aptitude in manipulating "psychological warfare" techniques was admired by sectors of the United States military. It was claimed that he had learned them in the military's own training centers and that now he was using them against the United States. Noriega's reaction to the increasing military harassment was at once defensive and provocative, but "just short of a major provocation." This approach prevented his moves from becoming major incidents. "He keeps us off balance, chasing our tails, distracted," a military spokesperson said.[66]

In April 1989 the Panamanian government requested an urgent meeting of the United Nations Security Council to denounce aggressive United States harassment, its "flagrant intervention" in Panamanian internal affairs, and the latent threat of a military action against its country. This intervention, said

Panamanian Chancellor Ritter, was to establish a government subject to Washington, renegotiate the Canal Treaties, and maintain its military presence in Panama after the year 2000.

The United States representative to the United Nations, Thomas Pickering, denied these accusations. He stated that there was no pressure or meddling; Panama's crisis was the result not of a conspiracy by his government, as the Panamanian chancellor claimed, but of Noriega's policies. He reiterated that Panama must hold "free and impartial" elections and that his government possessed information that allowed it to predict that the elections would not be "clean."[67]

According to opinion polls, 80 percent of Panamanians opposed Noriega. Nevertheless, Washington and the Panamanian opposition feared that whatever the election results, Noriega would refuse to step down. Knowing the pool of Panamanian generals, Washington also recognized that whoever replaced him would be much worse.

In the midst of one of the worst crises in its history and an atmosphere vitiated by open United States interference and military harassment—it became more intense, abusive, and threatening every day—as well as subjected to severe economic sanctions, Panama prepared to hold the most important presidential election in its history. The race had less to do with a contest for the presidency than with a conflict between the United States and Noriega in which the sovereignty and independence of Panama and the future of the Canal Treaties were at stake.

The government established a series of controls to insure that the process would not get out of its hands. Magistrate Yolanda Pulice de Rodríguez, a solid ally of Noriega's, was the president of the electoral tribunal, which was certifying the voter returns. The former Colonel Díaz Herrera had accused her of electoral fraud in 1984, a tactic he claimed was planned in her home.

A few days before the elections hundreds of foreign reporters arrived. The government imposed strict controls on their registration, places of residence, and journalistic activities. It prohibited press conferences not approved by the chancellery and the broadcast of "news, interviews, and reporting on the electoral contest" that did not come from the electoral press center. It also "strictly" prohibited them from carrying the press card issued, in an abuse of power, by the southern command.[68]

Panama was also overrun with invited and uninvited observers, among them former United States presidents Jimmy Carter and Gerald Ford, who led an international group of 200. Others were sent by Bush without consulting the

Panamanian government. United States representatives Robert Graham (Democrat) and Connie Mack (Republican), and Miami Mayor Xavier Suárez arrived without invitation or visa. They traveled in a military airplane that landed at Howard Air Force Base in the old Canal Zone. They entered Panama without incident

The foreign press and the Panamanian opposition accused the government of manipulating voter registration. They claimed that names of opposition voters disappeared while names of dead or fictitious voters were inscribed in their place and that there had been changes in the locations of the voting booths to make access more difficult for the opposition. The government sector denounced United States interference and its measures to strangle the economy in violation of international law and the Canal Treaties, and it accused the opposition of having "sold out" to the United States by accepting the "donation" of $10 million to buy votes. In relation to Panama's small population, this was a fabulous sum.

The day for Panama to hold the most controversial, dangerous (for its own future), and corrupt elections in its history arrived on May 7. "Life is normal. The cities are plastered with posters. Everyone is out in the streets. There is no militarization. Businesses are open. Restaurants are full of people. Parties are at their headquarters attending to last-minute details," wrote a Colombian correspondent.[69] A high turnout was expected, and a winning margin of 50,000 to 100,000 votes. Univisión, one of the Spanish-language television networks that airs in the United States, predicted that 63 percent would vote for the opposition and 24 percent for the government candidate.

The voter turnout was massive, but no one could declare as a certainty that these elections had been free and clean. Voters were overwhelmed by an avalanche of pressure from both the United States and the Panamanian governments—the latter, it was said, was pressuring public employees to vote for Duque. The following day, before there had been any official communication concerning the results, Panamanian Archbishop Marcos Gregorio McGrath announced to the foreign press that the opposition had won, with 74.2 percent of the vote to the government's 24.9 percent. He stated that he had these figures from a sampling carried out by the Church at 115 polling places (there were 4,255 in all). These results became tantamount to "revealed truth." Carter quoted them in claiming that Endara had won by a 3-to-1 margin, and the United States observers who had entered Panama illegally confirmed upon their return to Miami that "the Panamanian Church and former President Carter claimed" that Endara had won.

"Noriega has stolen the elections." Carter's pronouncement, issued after he had been prevented from verifying the recount being carried out by the national scrutiny committee, resonated throughout the world. Well-known United States and European election observers endorsed the thesis Bush had advanced months earlier, that there had been massive electoral fraud in Panama. The members of Congress who had gone to Panama demanded the use of force against Noriega and the abrogation of the Canal Treaties if fraud was proven, which they took as a given.[70]

Three days after the election ended, there were still no official reports on the results. Solis Palma and Noriega remained silent. But the international news agencies—AP, AFP, EFE, Ansa, and Reuter—broadcast to the world that the "fraud of the century" had been committed in Panama and denounced serious irregularities perpetrated by the government and the defense forces, which pressured and threatened the people to make them vote for Duque. Members of the military, with their special identity cards, could vote several times in different places. Electoral certificates were stolen and ballot boxes burned at gunpoint. The media pointed to members of the defense forces and the dignity battalions as the "presumed" authors of such acts. But many Panamanians were implicated.

On May 10 the national scrutiny committee released partial data. According to fifteen certificates examined out of a total of forty, the majority had the official government candidate Carlos Duque winning 105,522 votes to 51,844.

The city was under military control, but some 5,000 people took to the streets to protest outside the building that housed the electoral tribunal. Within a few hours there were 80,000, said one correspondent. They were shouting slogans against the government and Noriega: "*Esta vaina se acabó porque Endara ya ganó*" ("This stuff is over because Endara's won"), "*Ni un día más*" ("Not another day"), "*Endara presidente, abajo Noriega*" ("Endara's the president, down with Noriega"), "*Vamos a hacer chicha de piña*" ("We are going to mash pineapples into liquor"), a reference to Noriega, who was known as "Carepiña" ("Pineapple face") because of the acne scars on his face.

The antiriot forces and the dignity battalions quelled the demonstrations with extreme violence. Endara received a head wound from a steel rod and was taken to a hospital; Ford was brutally beaten with sticks and sequestered in a hospital as a detainee (one of his bodyguards died). The image of his bloodied body facing a man attacking him with a steel rod was broadcast all over the world. Arias was mildly wounded. Several people in the scuffles were shot to death, among them Endara's bodyguard. Some hundred people were arrested and accused of attacking the nation's security.[71]

The night of May 10, after the day of violence that had resulted in five deaths and twenty-three wounded men, Yolanda Pulice read a statement over the radio and television (transmitted every fifteen minutes) announcing that the elections had been voided "at all levels"—the presidency, parliament, and municipalities. She said that in the midst of the fiscal and economic crisis and the foreign media campaign about fraud, numerous irregularities had been committed, among them the purchase of votes, the disappearance of ballots, and the lack of certificates. She denounced "the evident intention of those who have come in the capacity of observers" to further "the thesis of electoral fraud, proclaimed to the world by United States authorities since long before the election," and the "obstructionist actions of many foreigners called here by national and foreign political forces without benefit of an invitation. The proclamation of any candidate [as winner]" under such conditions "is absolutely impossible." This decision, she said, was made after long meetings at the republic's presidential offices, with the participation of Solís Palma, his cabinet of ministers, General Noriega, and most of the high command. She made no mention of dates or plans for new elections.[72]

For several analysts, among them former Chancellor Ritter, the evidence of an "overwhelming" defeat of its official candidates determined this drastic decision by the government.[73] Others spoke of the opposition's "smashing" victory.

The annulment of the elections roused the ire of Washington hawks to dangerous levels. Congress and public opinion pressured Bush to order a military action. The White House announced that the President, together with his advisers, was studying all possible options—both economic and military—with the goal of preparing a plot against Noriega. He was consulting with several governments of the region in order to take collective actions and force the General out.

The next day Bush summoned his ambassador and ordered the Pentagon to send 2,000 more soldiers and station the aircraft carrier USS America off the Panamanian coast to protect United States citizens from the violence that broke out after the elections had been annulled. He asked United States nationals to return home and United States businesses to move to other countries. "We will not be intimidated by the bullying tactics, brutal though they may be, of the dictator Noriega," declared Bush at a White House press conference.[74]

Washington spokesmen insisted that military action would be the last resort. But to Panamanians it was clear that the intervention was already underway. Ritter remarked that Panama was not threatened by an invasion, since it was already an occupied country and always had been. In order to take this extreme step, Bush was relying on support by the United States public and the Panamanian opposition—which included the most important economic sectors and the oligarchy—backed by the Catholic Church hierarchy. Bush spoke daily with Archbishop McGrath, who informed him about what was happening in Panama.[75] "Many people, nationalists and patriots" were asking the United States to liberate them from Noriega, claimed the Panamanian sociologist Raúl Leis.[76] But no one believed that the intervention would be so massive an act of war, with the bombing of the civilian population and the occupation of their country.

As the "constitutional" president, Delvalle held a press conference at Washington's National Press Club to inform the press and the people of "his" government's policies in the face of this crisis. He declared that it "will not discount any option," including the military one for removing Noriega. He explained that he had discussed such measures with Bush, whom he had also asked to formally recognize Endara and the "winning slate" in the May elections.[77]

The annulment of the elections and the unbridled violence of the antiriot brigades and the dignity battalions—they had wounded all three opposition candidates—caused a worldwide revolt against Noriega. Presidents Alan García of Peru, Carlos Salinas de Gortari of Mexico, and Carlos Andrés Pérez of Venezuela expressed strong condemnations. García warned that he would "denounce and reject" any manipulation of the Panama election results and "any pressure or intervention from outside Latin America." Bush applauded the Peruvian president's declaration insofar as it condemned fraud, but he ignored his rejection of outside interference.

The Río Group (from which Panama had been suspended), in a joint statement dated May 10, expressed its "profound consternation" about the events in Panama, since they could "still further alienate" the government from the Latin American democratic community. But it stated that it was refraining from "pronouncing judgment on the causal factors and the specific matters that determined, on the occasion of the election, the political crisis in Panama," because of its "absolute observance of the nonintervention principle." The statement reiterated the need for "complete compliance" with the Canal Treaties.[78] Once again Latin America tried to stem the United States military's lack of control by clinging to the defense—rhetorical and utopian—of the principles of nonintervention and free self-determination.

In spite of the serious crisis, a few days later Panama returned to normal life within the context of abnormality. The streets, which had been semi-deserted, again filled with people, and the country returned to its routines. The markets, banks, and offices gradually resumed their activities; the supposed "winning candidates are recovering from their bruises," and the Panamanians amused themselves by watching the arrival of United States military aircraft with new units of soldiers without much excitement, wrote one Colombian correspondent.[79] Panamanians explained this lack of reaction in the face of grave crisis as evidence of their pacifist nature.

The Alianza Democrática de la Oposición Civilista (ADOC: Democratic Alliance of the Civilian Opposition), a political coalition, called for an open-ended general strike to begin on May 17, a date that coincided with the OAS chancellors' meeting in Washington to deal with the Panamanian crisis. The strike call failed. The opposition blamed the languid response on the government's repression.

THE OAS IN ITS LABYRINTH

Two days after the annulment of the elections Venezuela requested a meeting of the OAS Consultative Organ to take up the Panama crisis. Carlos Andrés Pérez noted that very serious matters were at stake, such as the future of the Canal. The entire membership, including the United States and Panama, supported him, but Brazil, Chile, and Mexico expressed reservations about the OAS's competence to deal with the internal affairs of its member states, as in the case of the Panamanian elections. To circumvent this difficulty, the matter under discussion was given an international flavor: the Twenty-first Consultative Organ meeting would study "the Panamanian crisis in its international context." The meeting took place in Washington and began on May 17, 1989.

Many feared this would be a tortuous meeting because of the conflicting interests between the United States and the rest of the continent. The crisis superseded Panama's internal situation because of the open military and political intervention of the United States and the threat of an invasion, which everyone dreaded. The chancellors' goal was to try to prevent this invasion, but no government was eager for a confrontation with the Master of the North over Panama.

The Mexican government questioned Noriega's moral position in a statement but declared it "inadmissible" that the OAS should be turned into "the court of last resort for the electoral processes of Latin American countries."

Presidents Julio María Sanguinetti of Uruguay and Carlos Andrés Pérez of Venezuela expounded another thesis: Sanguinetti maintained that the principle of nonintervention "has its limits," and Pérez held that nonintervention was "at times" a form of intervention. In other words, the OAS had to act.[80]

The meeting began several hours late, amid tension and expectation. The debates were held behind closed doors. There was only one public session. The Hall of the Americas was packed with delegates and journalists. Within it were present the leaders of the Panamanian opposition brought in by the State Department.[81] The importance the United States put on this meeting could be seen in the size and caliber of its delegation. It was said to be "overwhelming." Headed by Secretary of State James Baker, it was filled with State Department heavyweights and the government's principal experts on Latin America.[82]

Bush actively consulted with some presidents to coordinate a diplomatic offensive and joint actions "in support of Panamanian democracy" and to force Noriega to resign. With an avalanche of pressures on the presidents, delegations, and chancelleries of the member states, Washington sought to have the OAS approve concrete actions and drastic sanctions against Noriega, such as expelling Panama from the OAS, collectively breaking off diplomatic relations (a measure supported by the United States and chancellors Rodrigo Madrigal of Costa Rica and Ricardo Acevedo of El Salvador), economic and commercial blockades, and the recognition of the "victory" of Endara in the May elections (the United States had already done so). It did not succeed in any of these.

The Panamanian chancellor laid out United States aggression against his country in terms of the violation of principles of international law and the Canal Treaties and denounced the economic sanctions as violations of the OAS and UN Charters. He demanded that all this activity cease and warned of the dire consequences of a military intervention in Panama to all of Latin America.

Colombian Chancellor Julio Londoño, who was chairing the meeting, rejected intervention in all its forms in his opening remarks: "We cannot accept that any country should attempt to constitute itself as the supreme arbiter of situations in another state, nor that it should be the supreme authority in deciding when an electoral process—abnormal as it might have been—shall be supported, and when a series of coercive and discriminatory measures of an economic character should be applied." The threat and use of force, he maintained, served only to unite the enemies of liberty and democracy. He rejected the annulment of the elections but held that this crisis must be resolved by the Panamanian people alone.[83]

Venezuela, which appeared to have adopted a tough position opposing Noriega, circulated a draft of a resolution characterized as "soft" and "extremely diplomatic," since it merely "urged" the member states to make gestures "within their powers" to find the solution to the Panamanian problem, within "scrupulous" respect for the principle of nonintervention. It asked them to abstain from any action that might be "contrary to these principles or incompatible with a peaceful and long-term solution of the problem."[84]

The seriousness of the internal situation in Panama and the disparities among the delegations' criteria led the chancellors to work out consensus solutions in advance. The formula—proposed by eleven chancellors—was the creation of a commission composed of Ecuador, Guatemala, and Trinidad and Tobago and attended by the Secretary General of the OAS. It was to go to Panama to seek a national agreement and formulas that would assure "within the mechanisms of democracy and in the shortest possible time, the transfer of power with full respect for the sovereign will of the Panamanian people." It further reiterated the defense of the nonintervention principle and the validity of the Canal Treaties.[85]

After an agitated closed-door debate, the United States succeeded in including a condemnation of Noriega in the resolution, though the majority opposed it, but the United States did not succeed in winning the strong condemnation it wanted. The one agreed upon read, "The serious events initiated by General Manuel Antonio Noriega in the crisis and in Panama's electoral process could cause an intensification of violence, with the consequent risks for international peace and security."[86]

Baker let it be known that the resolution adopted by the meeting did not meet the minimum demands of his government. Bush applauded the condemnation of Noriega and the demand for a "transfer of power" in Panama.[87] The government of Panama found the resolution acceptable, since it succeeded in neutralizing the United States attempts at manipulation. The Democratic Revolutionary Party (the party in power) stated that the OAS was short on "ethics and respect for international law" for attacking General Noriega "in gross and contemptuous" terms. Finally, the Panamanian opposition noted that the condemnation of Noriega corresponded "substantially to the expectations of the Panamanian people" but energetically objected to the OAS failure to recognize its "victory" in the May elections.[88] Londoño, the chair of the meeting, commented that the results were positive, since they had avoided a stormy session and since a formula acceptable to the majority had been adopted.

Between May 23 and August 1 the commission appointed by the OAS and headed by the chancellor of Ecuador, Diego Cordovez, a skilled diplomat and United Nations negotiator for the withdrawal of Soviet troops from Afghanistan, made four visits to Panama. The commmission warned in advance that it did not intend to intervene but rather to build a bridge between the sides to try to find a solution to the crisis. Nonetheless, it always came up against the inflexible position of Endara, Arias, and Ford, who refused to negotiate with the government, insisting that their electoral "victory" be recognized and that Noriega leave office. Noriega responded that he would talk to no one, for his was a matter to be solved by the government and the opposition, and the military should stay out of it. The government warned that the question of Noriega's resignation was not on the table and that the primary issue was the cessation of aggressions and sanctions against Panama by the United States.

Cordovez always concluded his reports by noting that nothing could be achieved because both parties were inflexible. The commission's term was extended twice by the chancellors, despite opposition by the United States, the Central American and Caribbean states, and the Panamanian opposition. The majority understood that failing to arrive at an agreement was opening the door to United States intervention.

Faced with the impossibility of achieving a resolution reconciling the different positions, the chancellors decided that the final document would be the declaration by the chairman of the meeting, Londoño Paredes. It was unanimously approved, with no objections and in absolute silence. The declaration extended the commission's mandate to August 23 (Solís Palma's term ended on September 1). It asked the Panamanian authorities to bring about the change of government "by democratic means and in conformity with current internal Panamanian procedures" and hold new elections "as soon as possible," and it outlined the topics they themselves proposed as the basis for dialogue.[89]

The "unanimity" on the content of the declaration was only superficial. The United States let it be known that it was not satisfied. Others found its language imprecise, since it mentioned the transfer of power without including a formula acceptable to all parties, asked the government to hold elections "soon" without specifying whether this date should be before or after September 1, and did not mention Noriega, who could well remain exactly where he was.

To Assistant Secretary of State Lawrence Eagleburger, the United States representative to the OAS, "transfer of power" meant that "General Noriega must go." This result would mark the end of the crisis, and the Panamanian people would resume control of their own future. To Panamanian Chancellor

Ritter, it meant finding a replacement for Solís Palma. To the opposition, "transfer of power" through "free elections" meant leaving its electoral "victory" out of account. Arias said the declaration was "ambiguous and contradictory," since the question was not whether or not there were elections but whether or not Noriega would go. Again he criticized the extension of the commission's term, since this extension meant prolonging "the suffering, repression, and impoverishment" of the Panamanian people.[90]

Londoño maintained that it was impossible to reconstruct the elections because of the loss of the ballot boxes and numerous ballots. He declared that "although most Latin American countries, among them Colombia, express their disagreement with Panama's electoral process, no nation has recognized or is inclined to recognize that Endara won the elections and that therefore he should assume power."[91]

Noriega let it be known that if no agreement was reached by September 1 (the date set by the constitution for the change of government), a military junta would be formed. During the May-to-August deliberations of the OAS commission, Solís Palma proposed to the opposition on several occasions that they form a national-unity government together to save the country, but the opposition always refused, insisting instead on its demands: recognition of its electoral "victory" and Noriega's ouster.

In early August the opposition suggested that the government hold a plebiscite so that the people could express their opinions of the formulas proposed in the OAS dialogue. The government issued a statement rejecting this proposal because the Panamanian constitution neither contemplated nor regulated this sort of consultation.[92]

Cordovez insisted that it was still possible to arrive at a negotiated solution and that limiting the term of his mission served no purpose. Londoño again proposed extending his mandate to deal with the request by Panamanian political forces. Again the United States and the Panamanian opposition were against it, and again the commission's term was extended.

At the end of August, near the time when the Consultative Meeting would receive the fourth report from the commission (Solís's term would end the following week), the government once more proposed forming a "national union" government to take office on September 1 and holding elections in one year's time. The opposition rejected the idea. Noriega commented that they were "useful fools" programmed to say no to everything, since they had been offered a half-share in the government, and with the great economic resources and support of the United States behind them, they could have had it all.[93]

Faced with the impossibility of finding a solution after four months of fruitless efforts, the chancellors held an informal meeting to hear new ideas. After twelve hours of anxious deliberations on five projected resolutions, they were deadlocked. The way out of this impasse was once again to approve another of Londoño's declarations, in which he thanked the commission for its efforts, expressed "profound concern" at the parties' failure to arrive at a solution to the crisis, reiterated that such a solution was "uniquely and exclusively" the business of Panamanians, and exhorted the parties to make "new and urgent" efforts to arrive at an agreement before September 1.[94]

They never arrived at an agreement. Those who had this possibility within their power and who were conscious of the great danger hanging over Panama did nothing to avert the enormous tragedy.

THE "RAMBOS"

All measures the United States government took to remove Noriega—for this was what its policies in Panama came down to—had been a failure. In spite of the general condemnation of the "fraud of the century" and the annulment of the elections, the United States had not been given the support it needed to apply the drastic sanctions it wanted to impose. After this failure it intensified its harassment with military maneuvers in the Caribbean and at its bases in Panama, ever more in violation of Panama's sovereignty. Scores of combat aircraft, armored vehicles, helicopter gunships and naval units, and thousands of marines, rangers and elite rapid-deployment troops took part in the maneuvers. The southern command continued, over Panamanian government complaints, to assert that these exercises were "routine."

The departure of United States citizens from Panama, ordered by President Bush, continued. Panama City emptied. Thousands of luxury apartments stood empty, thousands of Panamanians became unemployed, and commerce lost the important business of the gringos. On the deadline set by Bush, July 1, the last of them left. This was a great blow to the already beaten economy and to the people's morale—they saw in this exodus the prelude to United States intervention.[95]

The month of August saw a series of provocations by the United States troops and confrontations between uniformed services of both countries. United States officers arrested twenty-nine Panamanians, among them nine soldiers, one of whom was Noriega's brother-in-law Manuel Sieiro; two days later the Panamanian defense forces arrested two United States military police officers. The southern command mobilized its forces and blockaded the Panamanian military center Fort Amador for more than three hours.[96] But both sides decided to exchange their prisoners in order to ease tensions.

On August 11, in "Operation Alicia," a thousand United States soldiers landed on one of the Panamanian islands outside Panama City where Noriega had an office known as the bunker. The southern command claimed that this operation was only to reaffirm United States rights as stated in the Torrijos-Carter Treaties, which included freedom of transit in Panama. The command remarked that the operation was being mounted on President Bush's orders.[97]

A few days earlier Bush had mentioned the possibility of trying to "capture" Noriega, but White House spokesman Marlin Fitzwater clarified that what the President had said had nothing to do with this operation, which was only for training purposes. Panama responded with a military operation it dubbed *Zape al Invasor* ("Invader, Scram").

The Panamanian government was reaching the limit of its resistance. The following day it called for an urgent meeting of the United Nations Security Council to denounce United States acts of aggression. Chancellor Ritter declared that the United States had turned Panama "almost into a theater of war" and asked the Secretary General to send an "observation mission," proposed urgent measures to reduce tensions, and presented in a closed session a videotape to demonstrate how United States military forces—both air and land—moved into Panamanian territory and acted like an "army of occupation," violating the Canal Treaties and "humiliating" the Panamanian people.[98]

The United States delegate, Herbert Okun, denied all these charges. He replied that the increase in the number and strength of military forces was a "direct response to the hostile actions" of General Noriega's regime and "in the exercise of their rights according to the Torrijos-Carter Treaties." The session closed without addressing Panama's request, making any decision, or setting a date for another meeting.[99] This is the way the Security Council functioned under United States domination.

Three days did not go by before the southern command carried out lightning helicopter landings on the United States Embassy grounds and at the ambassador's residence in Panama City; Black Hawk helicopter gunships took part while others hovered over the city.[100] This was a rehearsal for a defense and rescue mission, it was explained.

This aggressive military activity reached "intolerable extremes" with "unforeseeable" consequences, declared Chancellor Ritter. In this situation the government, the defense forces, and the officialist parties proposed that the opposition cosign a document asking the United States to cease its provocative military actions. The opposition declined to sign without explanation.[101]

Three days later, United States troops occupied Panamanian court buildings for three hours. That same day forty Panamanian women protested outside of Fort Clayton, a United States military base in a suburb of Panama City. Some tried to assault a soldier, but a Panamanian officer restrained them.[102]

The danger of United States military intervention in Panama worried Latin America, though some heads of state still believed that the United States would not go to extremes. High-ranking Panamanian officials maintained that it would be a serious error for the United States to invade, since the political and economic cost would be too high.[103] Colombian Chancellor Julio Londoño signaled that such an act would change the context of inter-American relations and open "an abyss that cannot be closed even in thirty years."[104]

In August, in a strangely worded editorial in *Granma*, the Cuban government denounced the provocative United States military maneuvers in the area of the Canal and its environs, which it called "virtual intervention," creating a "psychological tension raised to extremes." The editorial indicated that this "brutal pressure" was increased by the "overwhelming press campaign, the economic and financial blockade, and the disturbing declarations by United States military and political leaders that call for the ouster by force of the government of the Isthmus." It claimed that United States efforts to force Noriega to resign also tried to keep the Torrijos-Carter agreements of 1977 from being fulfilled, and it asked Latin American nations to use their influence to prevent any intervention.[105] The Cold War had not ended in the Caribbean, warned Castro.

In the United States powerful voices opposed intervention in Panama. Jimmy Carter rejected it completely, and in both civilian and military circles some counseled against it because of the political cost and because success was uncertain. *Newsweek* cited a Pentagon source who stated that "a massive invasion" would serve to unseat Noriega but would constitute a bloodbath—many United States soldiers would return in body bags, the political cost would be "terrible," and it would "trigger nationalist resentments," which would only help Noriega. "Killing Panamanians," he added, "would unite the entire hemisphere against us."[106]

ATTEMPTS AT "DAMAGE CONTROL"

Having failed to persuade Endara, Arias, and Ford to compromise and to name a provisional government, on August 31, 1989 (just as a "constitutional power vacuum" was about to be produced), the government council named fifty year-old Francisco Rodríguez, comptroller general of the nation, as president and Carlos Ozores, a former vice president of the republic, as his vice president. Former Chancellor Ritter explained that these men had been agreed upon with Noriega and officers of the high command the previous night. The council announced the composition of the provisional government and promised that elections would be held when "adequate conditions" existed—in other words, when United States aggression ended and the Panamanian funds illegally held by the United States government were unfrozen. The council fixed a date six months later to evaluate the situation and, if conditions allowed, when elections would be held.[107]

That same day, at a press conference at the White House, Bush expressed frustration about the failure of the efforts made by the United States government to remove Noriega and called the appointment of Rodríguez a joke on the Panamanian people. He announced that he would recognize no government installed by Noriega, that he would summon his ambassador and maintain the economic sanctions in order to deprive this "illegal regime" of funds. He was taking such measures, Bush claimed, in "support of self-determination and democracy" in Panama and to "confront the threat presented by General Noriega's support of drug trafficking and other forms of subversion."[108] A press release issued in Washington stated that Delvalle, "respecting the limits of his constitutional mandate," was closing the Panamanian Embassy in Washington and delivering it to the United States "for safekeeping," along with $300 million in Panamanian assets.[109]

The opposition launched a campaign called Not One More Cent for the Dictatorship exhorting the public to pay neither taxes nor services, or buy lottery tickets from the national lottery. Endara declared that he was on a hunger strike. He announced that he would follow in Gandhi's footsteps until the Panamanian people supported the campaign and would take only water, the pills prescribed for him by doctors, and the "sacred host" if a priest would give it to him.[110] Ricardo Arias and eight opposition leaders were arrested in the interior of the country when they promoted this campaign. They were released the following day.

On October 3, 200 young officers, led by Major Moisés Giroldi Vega attempted to depose Noriega. This was the second coup attempt in eighteen months. They broadcast a statement on the radio to announce Noriega's overthrow and the "retirement" of the entire military high command. They warned that theirs was strictly a military movement. They asked for the support of the defense forces and asked any forces loyal to Noriega to stay away from the central headquarters, the target of the coup. They retained control of the headquarters and held Noriega and several members of the general staff for six hours, but by noon they were surrounded by government troops. After a brief exchange of fire, the uprising was smothered. The coup was not supported by the military forces, the police, or even the United States. According to military sources, Noriega directed the effective countercoup.[111] That same night, accompanied by several generals, Noriega appeared on television to announce that the coup had failed, and he accused the United States of having sponsored it.

Panama remained calm, though normal activity was reduced. Some civilians paraded in the streets with banners, shouting slogans against Noriega and for the rebels. Sources in the opposition announced that Endara and Arias were in "safe places" but did not indicate whether they were in Panama or at United States bases.

The following day the defense forces announced that ten officers who had participated in the coup had died in combat, among them Major Giroldi; 21 officers and five civilians were wounded; and 180 troops and 100 members of the dignity battalions were under arrest. Witnesses claimed that the dead numbered around 25 and the wounded closer to 100, and victims' relatives denied the official version and claimed that the officers had been executed. A European diplomat told the *New York Times* that Noriega, "in a temper tantrum," had ordered the execution.[112] The spokesman of the defense force denied that there had been any firing-squad activity.

White House spokesman Fitzwater, Secretary of Defense Richard Cheney, and Pentagon sources declared that they were informed of the coup attempt in advance but that the United States did not take part because it did not trust the coup. Rebellion leader Giroldi was a well-known Torrijos man, and the coup could have been a trap of Noriega's to catch them with their hands in the cookie jar and expose them to the world. The opposition also believed that the coup was Noriega's doing, since Giroldi had helped squelch the coup attempt against Noriega in March 1988.[113]

The United States did not become involved but asked the conspirators to hand Noriega over if they captured him, but they refused. Cheney authorized his capture but "without the use of force." The orders to proceed, from General Colin Powell, head of the Joint Chiefs of Staff, to southern command chief General Maxwell Thurman, arrived after the coup had already failed.[114]

This failure led to bitter criticism of Bush. Democratic and Republican members of Congress lamented that he had not intervened, since he had the

12,000 trained and "highly motivated" men in Panama, and they called it a mistake to "lose" this opportunity. One called the failure a "great reverse for [United States] foreign policy."[115]

The Panamanian opposition also bemoaned the lack of United States support for the coup conspirators. Juan Sosa, a former Panamanian ambassador to Washington, believed that such assistance might have encouraged other garrisons to join the rebels.[116] A *New York Times* editorial, opposing this interventionist wave, maintained that those who criticized Bush for not openly supporting this insurrection were mistaken.[117]

The attempt at and failure of the coup changed the terms of the contest between the United States and Noriega and radicalized it. Bush felt the weight of internal criticism, which called him an indecisive wimp, but established that the majority in public-opinion polls was in favor of the use of force against Noriega. Convinced that the coup had been instigated by the United States, Noriega announced an "iron hand" policy against the opposition and emergency measures to confront the "state of war" that Panama was experiencing because of United States aggression.

Noriega knew that time was not on his side, that military action was underway, and that he was its announced objective. With phrases spoken here and there, he let Bush know he was inclined to negotiate new terms to modify the Canal Treaties. Rodríguez introduced the idea in the United Nations General Assembly. Bush did not take the hint. The intervention had been decided on and was already underway.[118]

Noriega tried to save his skin and impede the plans for his abduction with legal sophistries. In 1988, in absolute secrecy, the Panamanian attorney general had carried out an investigation of the charges of drug trafficking and money laundering made by United States courts against Noriega and other officers, and following a constitutional mandate, he transferred this investigation to the supreme court of justice. The court, likewise in the most absolute secrecy, determined that there was no basis that would allow these accusations to be verified, closed the case for lack of proof, and stopped prosecution of the accused. United States courts could no longer try him, since no one could be tried twice for the same crime. This judicial farce was discovered by accident after the invasion. A Panamanian lawyer succeeded in entering the bombed-out supreme court building, which was guarded by marines. Among the rubble she discovered the records of this "case."[119]

In October, twelve days after the coup attempt, the council of state revived the national assembly of representatives of municipalities (created by Torrijos) and "chose" its 510 representatives (they were supposed to be elected), and the assembly elected Noriega "Leader of the National Liberation Process" and "Coordinator of Plans and Programs of the Popular Power Parliament." In December, five days before the invasion, it named him head of government by acclamation, granted him extraordinary powers to confront the "state of war" the country was experiencing as the result of United States aggression, and declared that the "integrity of the nation" was "seriously threatened" and that it would be necessary "to organize the war against the aggressor" under a single command. Noriega believed that with this mandate the United States would not dare to abduct him. Such an act would be an unprecedented violation of international law.[120]

Bush, Cheney, and White House press secretary Marlin Fitzwater called the assembly's declaration on "organizing the war against the aggressor" a sufficient "declaration of war" against the United States to justify its intervention as an act of "legitimate self-defense."[121]

"JUST CAUSE"

For Bush, the straw that broke the camel's back was the death of a United States official, Robert Paz Fisher (whose father was Colombian) the night of December 16 in a shoot-out near the central headquarters of the defense forces, where Noriega had his office. Bush called it an assassination. The following day the *New York Times* reported the incident on the front page under the headline, "President Calls Death in Panama a Great Outrage." The Panamanian government's version was that American soldiers, traveling at great speed near the headquarters in an automobile that did not stop at the checkpoints, fired on and wounded a girl, an adult civilian, and a soldier, all Panamanians. The southern command said that the four officers were not on duty, were dressed in civilian clothes and were unarmed, and were set upon by Panamanian military personnel, who killed one of them. Immediately both sides put their troops on "combat alert" and mobilized soldiers to reinforce their respective defenses.[122] *Newsweek* commented that these officers were possibly on an intelligence mission in preparation for the military intervention, since in the "weeks preceding the invasion, officers posing as tourists visited the places they would later attack."[123]

The military operation was set in motion, and Panama's defenselessness against the Empire was absolute. Of the 16,000 troops in its defense forces, including the police and women, it could count on only 5,000 poorly equipped men. The United States had 10,000 troops in Panama who could be immediately reinforced from their bases in the United States, from Palmerola in Honduras, Guantanamo in Cuba, and bases in Puerto Rico.

The United States unleashed its hordes on Panama. At midnight on December 20, in the midst of the Christmas season, it launched Operation Just Cause. Bombardment of the capital began at midnight. Planes and helicopters flew over the city, and the sky filled with paratroopers. By land, sea, and air between 20,000 and 27,000 marines, rangers, and elite army troops, as well as the air force and the navy, occupied this small country. It was a joint operation by paratroops, infantry, and navy units. The troops had their faces darkened and their helmets covered with camouflage cloths. Many were Hispanic, some Panamanian. More than half of them had been airlifted during the night and early morning from bases in Los Angeles, Nevada, North Carolina, and Washington, D.C. The transport aircraft were landing every ten minutes.

The people woke up to the explosion of bombs. "I thought it was thunder," wrote Panamanian sociologist Raúl Leis. Later he saw that the state television announced the Yankee invasion, and that southern command's Channel 8, which operated from one of its bases, ordered its troops on maximum alert, "Echo Code." The seismograph at the Institute of Earth Sciences at the University of Panama registered the bombs exploding, one every two minutes, a total of 422, some of them tremendously destructive. The city looked like a "little Hiroshima," commented Leis.[124]

The operation used fighter planes, B-52 bombers, supersecret Stealth F-117 A bombers—their first time in action—AC-130 helicopters armed with rockets, Apache AH-64 helicopters equipped with night-vision capability, scores of tanks, heavy artillery, Humvee high-mobility jeeps, and battleships. All this military paraphernalia was launched to knock out 5,000 Panamanian soldiers. Not everyone was in the barracks on this night.

At 1:00 AM the National Radio put out its first alert: "The Yankee invasion has begun!" and "The imperialist invasion has started!" It broadcast the alert on the bombing by planes and helicopters of the central headquarters where Noriega had his offices, located in the poor Chorrillo quarter. The national television made incessant urgent calls on the people to take up arms in defense of their sovereignty and on the civilian militias to report: "Alert, Alert, Dignity Battalions, Codepadi [a code word] Urgent, Urgent. Key Cutarra [another code word], Weapons on Your Shoulders. Urgent, Urgent."

Panamanian television was occupied a little later, and the image and message changed. The seal of the United States defense department appeared on the screen, and a Pentagon spokesman asked the Panamanian people "not to allow themselves to be manipulated by the dictator Noriega and his gang of criminals." It called on Panamanians to unite to "reestablish order and the democratic process" and offered them protection: "We are with you." And warned: "Whoever takes up arms in an attack on the property or lives of Americans or Panamanians will lose the protection granted by the Geneva Treaty" and would have to face the United States armed forces. It announced that when the conflict ended, such people would be prosecuted for "their crimes." That is to say that the defense of their country was a crime. So that the citizenry would not heed this message, National Radio warned that the state television station had been taken over by the United States occupation forces and demanded that the United States cease this "cruel operation" in which many Panamanians had already died. Shortly thereafter the radio station was bombed and destroyed and went off the air.[125]

The attack on the central headquarters in Chorrillo lasted four hours. It was a ferocious onslaught by air and land. By morning the neighborhood was in flames and the headquarters in ruins. A resident claimed to have counted nearly eighty tanks. The invading troops approached the headquarters only after it was destroyed. Many men, women, and children were killed in the attack on this densely populated poor neighborhood, and thousands of homes of the poor were destroyed.

In the afternoon San Miguelito, another poor neighborhood on the outskirts of the city where the inhabitants lived in overcrowded conditions, was bombed in order to destroy the *Tinajitas* military barracks and to put an end to the "cells of resistance." The hill where the neighborhood was situated was virtually leveled. The attack continued. Through loudspeakers mounted on armored cars cruising the streets, the Yankees warned the residents to abandon the neighborhoods, which would be bombed.

That night Noriega sent a message over the Nicaraguan radio station Radio Sandino. "We are in the trenches," he announced, "and we will continue to resist. We ask the world, we ask other countries to help us with everything, with men, dignity, power. . . . Our motto is victory or death, not one step backward." No one knew where he was. Some believed that he was in the jungle, others thought he was in Costa Rica or had sought asylum in the Cuban or Nicaraguan embassies.

Reports coming out of Panama delivered the news of "ferocious bombings." Within a few hours military headquarters were destroyed, airports rendered useless, and supposed pockets of resistance bombed. Also under attack were civilian targets, apartment houses, the offices of political organizations, and newspapers that opposed the gringo policies.[126] Armored helicopters flew over the city at low altitudes in every direction. There were fires everywhere; hundreds of corpses lay in the streets, some of them burned or flattened by the tanks. The wounded got no help. The hospitals began laying out hundreds of cadavers on their floors. Terrified people were fleeing the brutally bombed-out poorer quarters of the city.

In spite of the iron control the United States troops imposed on the press, news agencies transmitted scenes of violence by the marines against the Panamanian people. Images of United States soldiers triumphantly patrolling the city, their faces camouflaged in paint, were seen around the world. They showed rows of blindfolded Panamanians with their hands tied behind their backs, face down on the pavement with rifle barrels at their necks; people in the streets, hands raised, being searched by marines; concentration camps with thousands of prisoners; refugee camps in schools and churches for the thousands who had been made homeless. Such scenes revolted and horrified the world.

They also transmitted scenes of Panamanians applauding and cheering the invaders. Someone commented that the soldiers seemed very nervous. This euphoria was an expression of the relief the people felt at Noriega's departure, which would mean the end of the penury they had had to endure because of him. Many did not understand such a warm welcome for the invaders in the midst of the great tragedy; hundreds, perhaps thousands, of corpses lay in the streets, in the destroyed homes and buildings, in the hospitals and in the morgues—their compatriots, victims of the invading forces.

During Operation Clean-up, the invading troops arrested thousands of Panamanians in the streets and in their homes. Maps in hand, they searched them out one by one. They confiscated weapons, raided and semidestroyed the homes of politicians, military officers, and people close to Noriega, among them the home of Carlos Duque, the former candidate for president. The raids were followed by looting. The troops confiscated some 15,000 boxes of government documents for study by the intelligence services.[127] Another operation had them decommissioning weapons and collecting corpses, $150 was paid for each weapon and $6 for each body.[128] Noriega's houses and offices were raided, and the news agencies reported the contents of the captured official and private documents and correspondence.

At a press conference southern command chief General Thurman stated that his troops found 50 kilos of cocaine—others claimed 110 or 150—in a house frequented by Noriega, with a street value of an estimated $1.25 million. The white powder turned out to be flour for tamales. A news agency reported that a "long list" of State Department officials supposedly bribed by Noriega had been found at Fort Amador.[129] Washington remained silent on the subject.

Bush had to prove his just cause to national and international public opinion. He assured everyone that this had been a "surgical" strike, a "clean" operation with a minimum loss of American lives and that it had achieved his objectives. But where was Noriega?

At 1:00 AM on the day of the invasion, at a press conference with scores of United States and foreign journalists, White House spokesman Marlin Fitzwater made the first official announcement of the invasion, explaining that the sole objective was to capture Noriega. From this point on, the news emanating from the White House, the Pentagon, and the State Department were triumphant. Everything seemed to be under control. But in evident desperation eighteen hours after the operation had begun—though he insisted on the success of the operation that had "decapitated the dictatorship"—Bush offered a reward of a million dollars to anyone who gave information leading to Noriega's capture.

The Cuban and Nicaraguan embassies were surrounded by troops and armored vehicles, since it was assumed that Noriega, his family, military officers, and members of the government might have taken asylum there. Cuban and Nicaraguan diplomats were insulted. Cuban Ambassador Lázaro Mora was detained for an hour and a half. The Nicaraguan ambassador's residence was raided and searched for weapons. In response to the raid—Ortega called it an "act of insolence, in violation of the principles of international law"—Nicaragua expelled twenty United States diplomats and gave them seventy-two hours to leave the country. The United States apologized: it had made a mistake. Its soldiers were not aware of diplomatic immunity. The search lasted more than an hour, and according to Nicaraguan diplomats, the soldiers made off with $2,000 and clothes.

These raids were serious violations of diplomatic immunity, inconceivable under the Vienna Convention. The Peruvian Embassy, where several military officers had sought asylum, was also surrounded, but the Peruvian government refused to hand them over. Peruvian President Alan García was the Latin American head of state who condemned the United States invasion in the harshest terms. Meanwhile the Voice of America, the official United States radio station, broadcast the news that Noriega had asked for military aid from

Cuba and Nicaragua and for political asylum in Cuba. Both governments denied this report.

It was easy for Bush to legitimize the invasion to the main body of public opinion, because it was a popular war. According to an opinion poll by CNN on the day of the invasion, 91 percent of those polled supported it. Majorities in Congress, the major media, and respected columnists applauded it. Television screens showed the taking of Panama as "rapid" and "clean" and with as little loss of American life as Bush claimed.

Before beginning the invasion the Pentagon had airlifted to Panama journalists and camera people from the major United States media who were "covering" the operation. (This was a measure to avoid a repetition of the criticism of the Reagan administration for obstruction of information during the Grenada invasion of 1983). They imagined that they were going as war correspondents to report the invasion, but the Pentagon had other plans. When they arrived in Panama, the southern command kept them on its bases for two days. They were not allowed to watch the attacks or visit the scenes of the "war." They were not allowed to enter Chorrillo, the scene of the heaviest bombing—and the biggest massacre—since access there was blocked by troops.[130]

Several journalists protested. *Newsday* reporter Patrick J. Sloyan wrote that this delay in getting to the scene allowed the Bush administration to manipulate information to give the impression that it was a "flawless feat of arms on an almost bloodless battlefield." And UPI White House correspondent Helen Thomas wrote: "There is a question of a news blackout. Neither Americans, nor anyone else, saw the ravages of the first nights bombing or the dead or the wounded in the first days of the invasion. The United States managed to block such pictures or news reports by inhibiting and frustrating news coverage."[131]

The southern command hid the number of Panamanian casualties. It confiscated the lists of the dead in the hospitals and the morgue. Pentagon sources claimed that 23 United States soldiers died and 265 were wounded, but reporters could not verify these figures, since the Pentagon would not allow them to visit the wounded soldiers in United States hospitals. Sloyan reported the existence of a videotape made by United States officers about the first day of the invasion, which the government would not allow the public to see, and commented that an army officer who saw the tape and still photographs of the invasion noted that the material was "dramatic." Most of the information came from sources in the southern command, the Pentagon, the White House, and the State Department and was published by the media without verification. Endara's government helped with this obstruction. *"De facto* censorship" was imposed on the war correspondents.[132]

Former United States Attorney General Ramsey Clark remarked that there was a "conspiracy of silence" to hide the reality that the invasion was a violation of international and United States laws and that the United States public remained silent during the crisis, enjoyed the demonization of Noriega, and listened in silence to the false reasoning about what would and did occur. "We heard a bunch of lies. We never heard the truth," he declared. Clark went to Panama, witnessed the destruction in Chorrillo, and reported that it was not true that the number of Panamanian dead between the invasion and January 4 was only eighty-four, as the Pentagon claimed. He believed that at least a thousand had died, and perhaps several thousand.[133]

An independent investigation commission, composed of Panamanians, United States citizens from various disciplines, and members of the Church, reported the existence of at least fourteen mass graves where the Panamanian dead were buried. Under public pressure, Endara, his "advisers" from the Pentagon and the State Department, and Attorney General Rogelio Cruz—appointed by the United States—allowed one of these graves to be opened in 1990, in the Jardines de Paz cemetery in Panama City, on the condition that no autopsies be performed. The government reported that it found 124 bodies. Panamanians insisted that there were more mass graves in the old Canal Zone, where "free passage" was carefully controlled, and that it was impossible for Panamanians to investigate, much less exhume.[134]

United States delegates to the United Nations and the OAS maintained that the operation had been discussed in advance with "democratically elected" Panamanian opposition leaders and that they were in agreement. Endara replied that he was only "informed," and that this news had come as a blow to the head.[135]

WE ALL "DEPLORE" IT

The day of the invasion was one of great activity in the international community: announcements, statements, and more or less vigorous protests criticized or regretted the invasion of Panama. At Nicaragua's request the United Nations Security Council and the Permanent Council of the OAS were called into urgent session. Venezuela called for an extraordinary consultative meeting of OAS chancellors. This request was dropped when only five of the thirty-three members responded (the United States, Chile, Honduras, El

Salvador, and Costa Rica). The Río Group issued a strongly worded statement demanding respect for the peoples' self-determination—the basis of international law—and openly condemned the invasion, demanded the immediate withdrawal of United States troops, and stated that Noriega's mistakes were not a proper pretext for the invasion of that country.

At the United Nations, the United States was supported only by its loyal ally Great Britain and by El Salvador, in the throes of a civil war in which the United States was immersed. Canada "lamented" the use of force but found the United States action "comprehensible," and Honduras, which Reagan had converted into an American military bastion, declared that it understood that the United States "found itself in the position of having to" invade. Alan García, the president of Peru, called the invasion "an act of imperialist rape that threatened all of Latin American sovereignty" and whose intentions were to void the Canal Treaties and impose a tame government that would allow the United States to keep its military bases "so it can exercise from them, as in the present case, a permanent threat against the continent." He summoned his ambassador from Washington and requested a postponement of the Andean countries' antidrug summit scheduled for January in Cartagena, Colombia, which Bush was to attend. The Nicaraguan government denounced "this open and straightforward act of aggression against Panama," and Daniel Ortega commented it was not only a flagrant violation of Panama's sovereignty and territorial integrity, "but a threat to the security of all Latin America, Central America, and especially Nicaragua," which had been confronting "the terrorist policies of the United States government" for the past ten years.[136]

Peru's OAS representative called the invasion an "outrageous insult to Latin America" and "an episode that shamefully reflects the region's past." Ecuador's representative called it a flagrant violation of the international rule of law without any justification whatsoever. Uruguay "rejected" United States military measures. Chile condemned this intervention "whatever might have been the reasons the United States used to justify it."[137]

A statement by the Colombian government expressed profound concern at the actions of the United States military forces and characterized the international position of Noriega's "de facto government" as confused, noting that it ignored the people's right to free self-determination and fundamental freedoms, "a deeply disturbing matter in continental circles."

At the United Nations and the OAS there was the problem of the representation of Panama. After heated debates—the one in the UN lasted four hours—both organizations agreed to accredit the representatives of the government in power before the invasion, which was Noriega's. Endara, still in hiding on a United States military base and recognized only by Washington, was unable to win accreditation for his representatives.

In the OAS, Colombia, Venezuela, and the Caribbean and Central American countries (the majority) took a soft line. They accused Noriega of responsibility for the invasion and rejected in the abstract "the use of force in the solution of controversies," expressed their "profound concern," and "deplored" what was happening in Panama without specifying what they meant. The broad majority defended the principle of nonintervention as a foundation stone of international law, without referring to the United States' violation of this principle.

When it came time to edit the proposed resolution, positions were stronger. The text, proposed by Colombia, Mexico, Peru, and Uruguay, "condemned" the United States military intervention in Panama and demanded the immediate withdrawal of the "invading troops." It was modified in order to allow the majority to accept it. Instead of "condemning" the invasion, it "deeply deplored" it; instead of demanding the "immediate withdrawal of the troops," it "urged" the cessation of hostilities, and rather than demanding, it "exhorted" the withdrawal of "the foreign troops utilized in the military operation." It did not mention the United States, and the term "invading troops" disappeared. This text was adopted at 5:00 AM by a vote of 20 in favor, 1 against (the United States) and six abstentions (Venezuela, Costa Rica, Guatemala, El Salvador, Honduras, and Antigua-Barbuda). The United States did not succeed in having Article 21 of the OAS Charter included in the resolution, which obliged member states to avoid the use of force "except in cases of legitimate defense." The United States was supported by Costa Rica, Honduras, Santa Lucía, and Antigua-Barbuda in this proposal. It also wanted to exchange the term "military intervention" for "military action" but received support only from Costa Rica and Honduras.

In the United Nations Security Council, the Algerian delegate declared that this invasion "reflected an abrupt regression with respect to everything that in the course of the last four decades had been defined by the international community as a code of conduct and as rules that were incumbent upon all States, great and small. . . . The action was all the more reprehensible in that it was perpetrated by a state that was a permanent member of the Security Council and thus bore special responsibility as regards international peace and security."[138]

The Cuban government expressed its vigorous condemnation of the "imperialist invasion," and a large demonstration in Havana protested outside the United States Interests Section. In a letter to the Security Council president, Castro wrote, "The President of the United States is attempting to justify the gross violation of international law and the Charter of the United Nations by invoking Article 51 of the Charter, no less, which recognizes that every State has the 'right of self-defense.' Such disdain for the intelligence of member states is on a par with the shamelessness of those who, themselves guilty of the crime of aggression, try to pass themselves off as victims."[139]

The resolution presented to the Security Council by Colombia, Ethiopia, Malaysia, Nepal, Senegal, and Yugoslavia reaffirmed "the sovereign and inalienable right" of Panama to free self-determination "without any form of foreign intervention, interference, subversion, coercion or threat." It "strongly" deplored the armed United States intervention in "flagrant violation of international law and of the independence, sovereignty and territorial integrity of States" and demanded the "immediate cessation of the intervention and the withdrawal from Panama of the armed invasion forces of the United States." Ten countries voted in favor of the resolution. Finland abstained, and the United States, France, Great Britain, and Canada voted against it.[140] This "triple veto," presented by the United States media as a victory for Bush, prevented the adoption of the resolution. A week later the United Nations General Assembly, where the great powers do not have veto power, adopted a similar resolution by a vote of 75 in favor, 20 against, and 40 abstentions. Twenty-four countries did not participate.

Bush and his spokesmen proclaimed that their goals had been the defense of "democracy" and the capture of Noriega. Many doubted that the United States would risk so much for so little. They believed that the real goals were strategic and geopolitical: to preserve United States political and economic hegemony in the hemisphere and to maintain its army, navy, and air force bases in Panama, an important part of its hemispheric defense structure.

Robert Gates, a high CIA officer (Bush appointed him director in 1991) informed the United States Congress that the invasion was not decided on at the last minute, according to the tenor of events. It was ready, carefully calculated, three months earlier. The plan was contained in a document entitled "A Strategy for Latin America in the '90s," known as Santa Fe II, written by Republican Party ideologues in August 1988 to suggest guidelines to the Republican administration for its hemispheric policies. It recommended preserving its military and intelligence interests in Panama, essential to its hemispheric defense strategy, and once the "democratic government" had been installed in Panama, overturning its judicial, economic, and banking structures and reforming its constitution, in order to negotiate with such a government the "adequate" control of the Canal and maintenance of United States military installations, "principally Howard Air Force Base and Rodman Naval Station for the appropriate projection of force throughout all of the Western Hemisphere."[141] All these suggestions were followed.

The United States began going against the treaties before they were even signed, but "the confrontation with Noriega gives it an excuse to deny them completely," maintained Panamanian Chancellor Ritter during the most difficult period of the crisis. "All of us in Panama knew that the United States was preparing various options for the use of force to overthrow Noriega before January 1, 1990." What no one could have foreseen, he added, was an invasion of such proportions.[142]

"The United States defeats itself in an operation like the one in Panama," wrote the Mexican author Carlos Fuentes, "because it demonstrates yet again that it interferes only with nations of less than 5 million inhabitants: Grenada, Libya, Nicaragua, and now Panama. . . . As its enemies become smaller, so too does the United States." Fuentes called the invasion a "disaster," a nineteenth century maneuver, a demonstration of the "arrogant inability" of the United States to accept the way of negotiation.[143]

THE PANAMANIAN "PUPPETS"

On December 20, at 2:00 AM—the invasion having begun two hours earlier—the radio announced the establishment of the new government. From "somewhere" in Panama (another source said from "somewhere" in Costa Rica), Guillermo Endara, Ricardo Arias, and "Billy" Ford assumed the offices of president and the two vice presidents. In spite of the efforts to hide where they were, a witness told the *Miami Herald* that they had been taken to Fort Clayton in the old Canal Zone the night of December 19, hours before the invasion began, and held there in a room from which they were forbidden to leave or to make phone calls.[144]

At that base they took office before General Thurman, chief of the southern command. Bush recognized them immediately, lifted the economic sanctions, and ordered his ambassador, Arthur Davis, who had been away for seven months, back to Panama. That same night Endara addressed the country through a Costa Rican radio station. "I have sworn before God and the nation to carry out my duties as President of the Republic." He justified the invasion, since it was motivated by the "noble propositions" of toppling a dictator and "reestablishing democracy, justice and freedom in Panama." He asked Panamanians not to resist and offered the defense forces "an important role in a democratic Panama, which will be for all."[145]

On December 21—the second day of the invasion—Endara, Arias, and Ford, guarded by United States soldiers, entered the legislative assembly, also under guard by United States troops, to "legitimize" their assumption of office. Endara announced that his government would be called the Democratic Government of National Reconstruction; Arias would be minister of government and justice, Ford would be minister of planning. He also announced that he had asked President Bush for an urgent shipment of food and medicine for those who had lost their homes and were sick and hungry.

Five days later the electoral tribunal issued a decree revoking "in all particulars" its own decree of seven months earlier annulling the elections, and it proclaimed Endara, Arias, and Ford the winners of those very elections. The tribunal explained that it had done a recount of the vote, based on "copies" of the election records "duly worked out" by the metropolitan curia and placed at the tribunal's disposal—the absence of the original records had been "overlooked." It also "validated" the swearing in of the new heads of state (originally performed on a United States military base).[146] These historical documents from before and after the invasion bore the signature of Magistrate Yolanda Pulice, chairwoman of the tribunal. The other signatories joined her in both tasks.

Endara demoted and dismissed Noriega. Without his titles as chief of state and commander of the defense forces, he could be captured as a common criminal by the United States. Endara freed all political prisoners, including seventy-five officers implicated in the coup attempt against Noriega, and decreed a state of siege. Nevertheless, the wave of lootings of businesses, offices, hotels, and homes continued. The poor and the rich, men and women, young and old, all took part. It was a shameful episode, Ritter wrote.[147]

THE TIGER HUNT

Did the military support Noriega? Some officers did so out of conviction, some to save their skins. Many put up no resistance, since the one the United States was looking for was Noriega, and therefore the hunt did not concern them. The generals did not go out to fight. The invading troops did not find them in the barracks, the streets, or in the mountains but at home. Perhaps in bed.

Was there resistance? Was there "ferocious combat," as Pentagon sources claimed? Were there reasons for the southern command chief General Thurman's "surprise" (his word) at the "strength" of the defense forces loyal to Noriega, and the intensity of the battles, "somewhat more serious" than he expected? Or was the truth rather that "they don't fight for long" as Ritter claimed, or that they did not resist at all but "turn tail and run," as a United States soldier claimed?

The roughness of the attack "was to make them understand that resistance was impossible," commented another United States soldier. Americas Watch backed that opinion: "The military might was so great that any resistance would have been suicide."[148] In spite of this crushing imbalance of strength, there was indeed resistance among the people, whose neighborhoods were brutally bombed. On the third day the southern command announced that combat had ceased but that there were still sporadic firefights, particularly in San Miguelito, where civilians and members of the dignity battalions were still fighting. Here was the focal point of the greatest resistance.

That same day the southern command reported a "daring" attack on its headquarters in Quarry Heights, where the fight lasted nearly an hour. On the fourth day it reported that the defense forces had ceased to exist, the barracks in the capital had been abandoned, and those in the country's interior were offering no resistance. Some officers declared themselves in favor of Endara, and others took refuge in the "jungle." The southern command promised that they would be pursued.

The southern command also claimed that Noriega had escaped with a few minutes to spare, that someone had seen him flee in his underwear, with cigarettes still smoldering (he did not smoke) in places where it searched for him. Several times it claimed that his capture was imminent, and an equal number of times it announced his capture.

The troops under Thurman's command undertook a house-to-house search for Noriega among family members, friends, relatives, and colleagues, and they interrogated his mistresses. "They act like Nazis, and look like fools when they don't succeed in catching him," commented Castro. More than 5,000 soldiers and civilians were under arrest in "prisoner of war" camps. Bush announced that he would not withdraw the troops until Noriega was captured. Again he called the operation a success but declared that it was not yet over.[149]

On December 24, the fifth day of the invasion, Noriega turned up safe and sound at the papal diplomatic mission known as the Nunciatura Apostólica. Some said that he had entered at 3:00 PM, others said 4:00. Some said he arrived in a diplomatic car in the company of the Japanese ambassador, others that he walked in on his own two feet, a baseball cap on his head. Some said his arrival at the Nunciatura was negotiated in advance, others that it surprised the Vatican and the Nunciatura alike. But many asked: how was it possible that he could enter the closely guarded mission without being seen by the invaders?

Washington's anxiety, surprise, and displeasure were obvious when Noriega appeared at the mission, and the Vatican spokesman, Joaquín Navarro Valls, announced that the nuncio would not surrender him because there was no legal form to do so. There was no extradition treaty between the Vatican and the United States. With Noriega in their midst, the overwhelming force of United States diplomacy fell upon the representatives of the Vatican. The southern command, without the least respect for the Church, laid out a security ring around the Nunciatura, with 500 soldiers and a score of armored vehicles, and surrounded it with barbed wire. It placed loudspeakers on towers, blasting rock music at top volume day and night. Helicopters flew over the place constantly and landed on the playing field of a neighboring school. Vehicles and people entering and leaving the mission were searched, including the nuncio and his car. Thurman explained that these were "protective" measures to prevent any attack by the dignity battalions. The night after Noriega's appearance General Thurman was seen at the door of the mission talking with the diminutive nuncio, Monsignor Sebastián Laboa, no one knew about what.

Day after day the media reported on Washington's active gestures in Rome and Panama, and on the rising tone of the dialogue. Bush, on vacation in Texas, repeated his decision to bring Noriega before a United States court and commented that the Vatican "complicates matters." On December 30, Valls reported that Noriega had been asked to leave the mission, but that he would not be forced to do so, and he added that the United States had no right to demand that he be surrendered or to interfere with the Nunciatura's work. He called the harassment of his headquarters "unacceptable" and "a very serious matter." He referred to the United States as an "occupying power."[150]

The Panamanian bishops asked the Pope to surrender Noriega to Panamanian justice, but under terms that would guarantee the safety of his person. Endara wanted to avoid such an action, claiming that he could not guarantee due process. He would have to surrender Noriega to the United States, and such an action would arouse a popular reaction against his government. Noriega had a right to be tried in Panama, and Panamanian courts had an obligation to try him. He could not be extradited, since the constitution prohibited such a move. All these points were eventually violated.

On January 2 Giancinto Berlocco, a Vatican expert on Latin American affairs, and United States Assistant Secretary of State Lawrence Eagleburger arrived in Panama. On the following day the Civic Crusade organized a vociferous demonstration outside the mission demanding Noriega's surrender. The southern command warned that if he was not surrendered, it would withdraw its protection from the mission. The mob would be allowed to enter and to capture him. On the night of January 3, at 8:50 PM, Noriega left the Vatican embassy dressed in his military uniform, and General Thurman grabbed him.

Spanish newspapers criticized the Vatican for having forced Noriega to surrender. Noriega was taken to the playing field at the school yard by the mission and placed in a Black Hawk helicopter, which took him to Howard Air Force Base in the old Canal Zone, where he was handed over to General Marc Cisneros and arrested by DEA officers. On the way to Miami, in a United States Air Force C-130, he was placed in handcuffs. The plane arrived at Homestead Air Force Base near Miami at 2:49 AM While the American authorities were taking Noriega to a high-security prison, Bush announced in a televised address to the nation that "all objectives" of the invasion had been accomplished.

THE PARTY'S OVER

For Noriega the surrender was a one-way trip. For Washington it was a "triumph"—now it would be able to modify the Torrijos-Carter Treaties. For the frustrated public opinion in Latin America it marked the end of one of the most grotesque and brutal episodes in United States foreign policy. The United States took its revenge on Noriega: it would make him pay with prison and humiliation for the ridicule to which he had subjected the United States for almost three years, right up to the last minute. He fell into United States hands after two weeks of invasion only because he himself surrendered. Dressed in prison garb and with a criminal's identification tag around his neck, he headlined the news in the world's largest media. This spectacle, wrote the Colombian weekly *Semana*, went beyond the limits of personal humiliation to disgrace a country or an entire continent.

For Endara it was "a night of glory." For Ford it was the "victory of liberty and the consolidation of democracy." And for the Panamanian people it was the end of a crisis that had plunged the country into the greatest tragedy of its history. In a kind of off-kilter carnival, among dances, songs, drunken excess and fireworks, the people and the invading troops celebrated Noriega's capture in one another's arms. Amid this revelry the people turned their backs on their tragedy, forgot their dead, and ignored the loss of their independence, sovereignty, and dignity. Over this brutal attack of a small country by the world's superpower both sides drew a blanket of silence.

To claim that Noriega was the sole cause of the invasion, the collapse of Panamanian institutions, and of its return to semicolonial status was not the whole truth. Equal responsibility must be borne by its "democratic" institutions and the leaders of the Civic Crusade, financed and led by Washington, for declining to come to an agreement that would have permitted a transition to a democratic solution: a government elected by the people. The cost of "their" presidency was the invasion. All were guilty of this tragedy.

On January 12, 1990, while Noriega was being taken to a high-security prison in Miami, the sky over Fort Bragg in North Carolina was suddenly filled with 2,000 paratroopers happily descending from 20 C-130 cargo planes. They were returning from Panama. This impressive spectacle, shown on national and international television, was the triumphant return of the "heroes" (20,000 soldiers were still in Panama). Some commentators crowed that this "triumph" would finally erase the Vietnam syndrome. But, what was the "triumph"? Who was the "enemy"? What were the "battles"? Was this massive surprise attack against a defenseless people a "war"? Did Noriega's capture justify this display of military might, this destruction, and the tragedy wreaked on the Panamanian people?

A month after Noriega's trial began—Bush swore that it would be fair and impartial—Washington had already paid half a million dollars to informants and witnesses to testify against him.[151] Forty-six witnesses testified during the three months it took the prosecution to lay out its case. Most were convicted drug traffickers to whom the department of justice had offered reduced sentences, United States residency, and new personal identities. Some of them were even allowed to keep the fortunes they had made in the drug trade.[152]

People who attended the trial claimed that it was plagued by irregularities, contradictions, and obvious falsehoods. No "overwhelming proof, either written or recorded" was presented to show the connection of Noriega with the traffic in drugs, reported *Newsday*'s correspondent in Miami, Peter Eisner.[153]

But the United States had to win this game, and it did. Noriega was sentenced to forty years in prison.

CHAPTER X

THE HURRICANE OVER CUBA

CUBA, THE UNITED STATES, THE SOVIET UNION, AND THE WORLD

In a speech delivered in Managua in July 1980, on the first anniversary of the Sandinista triumph, Fidel Castro spoke of the threat that would hang over the world if the Republican candidate Ronald Reagan moved into the White House. He called the Republican platform "horrible," "a threat to peace" for intending to resume "big stick" policies toward Latin America, discount the Panama Canal Treaties, support "genocidal" governments, and cut off aid to Nicaragua.[1]

Reagan was elected in November by a wide margin, and the Cuban leader knew that stormy times would accompany him. During his campaign Reagan aired unprecedentedly aggressive anti-Communist, anti-Soviet, and anti-Castro rhetoric. He called Cuba a menace to hemispheric security and claimed that it was part of a network of terrorist states led by the Soviet Union, whose aim was to support subversion in South America, destabilize Central America, and send arms to the Salvadoran guerrillas (their struggle was the major armed conflict of the moment) with the assistance of Nicaragua.

Reagan warned that he "would not tolerate" (the usual United States diplomatic language) Cuban interference in the internal affairs of other countries, and General Alexander Haig, the new secretary of state, announced that he would go to the "source" to stop the flow of arms to Central America. At a White House meeting with Reagan and his advisers, Haig told them: "Give me the word and I'll make that island a fucking parking lot." One of the advisers reported that several of those present went pale, since Haig was proposing to bomb Cuba.[2]

Haig sent Undersecretary of State Lawrence Eagleburger to Europe and the newly appointed Ambassador-at-Large General Vernon Walters to Latin America with "proof" that the Soviet Union, Vietnam, and Ethiopia were sending arms to the Salvadoran guerrillas by way of Cuba and Nicaragua.[3]

On April 21, 1981, on the twentieth anniversary of the Cuban victory at the Bay of Pigs—Playa Girón—Castro refuted these accusations and, in turn, accused Reagan of allowing Nicaraguan mercenaries to train at clandestine camps in the United States to prepare to attack Nicaragua and sabotage its economy, of supporting the "genocidal" governments of El Salvador and Guatemala, and threatening Cuba with a naval blockade. He announced that Cuba was preparing its defenses. In October he stated that the world was undergoing one of the most difficult times, "I don't know whether to say of recent times or of all time."[4] He added that the peace was threatened and that nuclear war would mean the end of humanity.[5]

Leonid Brezhnev, the secretary general of the Communist Party of the Soviet Union (CPSU), denounced this "new campaign of aggression by American imperialism" against Cuba, and warned that the Soviet Union stood by Cuba. *Pravda*, the official newspaper of the CPSU, advised the United States to stop "playing with fire" since it was endangering world peace. Cuba was a part of the socialist alliance, the article added, and acts of aggression against the island were "fraught with dangerous consequences."[6]

Two days after Reagan's election, Cuba created the territorial militia troops, and the Soviet Union sent them weapons. Within a year Cuba trained and armed close to a million youths, men, and women to defend the island. In case of attack, it would be war by "all the people."

DANGEROUS LIAISONS

No United States president dedicated as much rage and rigor to attacking Cuba as Reagan. He launched a virulent and extensive campaign to disparage it in United States and international public opinion and undertook aggressive measures to strangle Cuba's economy. The Treasury and Commerce Departments and the mostly Democratic Congress passed a raft of laws and rules to make the embargo ever more extreme. They closed Cuba off from international sources of finance and from United States and European private banks. These measures overstepped the boundaries of United States jurisdiction, violated international law and the United Nations and OAS charters, and damaged free commerce throughout the world. Federal agencies coordinated their actions to control the embargo, to make sure other governments and international businesses and individuals complied with it, monitored and boycotted Cuban commercial activity, and blocked its businesses. No ship that traded with Cuba was to enter any United States port.[7]

Hundreds of federal agents and diplomats went from country to country, government to government, and one business headquarters to another to prevent commercial accords with Cuba. Threatened with sanctions, reprisals, and blackmail, governments and businesses canceled such agreements or abstained from negotiating and investing in the island.

The aggression covered other areas as well. The Reagan administration expelled Cuban diplomats—causing considerable uproar—and prohibited Cuban newspapers and publications from entering the United States. "Petty in itself," commented the *New York Times* in an editorial, "the restriction carries a worrisome implication that in the guise of national security, the administration was prepared to embargo the import of ideas."[8] Eight months later this measure had to be rescinded because it was unconstitutional. The administration also prohibited United States citizens from traveling to Cuba. Such trips were allowed only with special permission and solely to United States officials, journalists, scientists, and filmmakers for professional reasons, and to the Cuban-American community to visit their relatives. Three months later, the United States decreed that these people could travel to Cuba only if the Cuban government assumed all their transportation and hotel costs. It also reduced the amount of money the Cuban-American community was allowed to send to their families.[9] It systematically denied visas to Cuban intellectuals, scientists, professionals, and artists invited by private universities and institutions or who were invited to attend international events held in the United States.

One problem that riled the United States authorities was the presence of the Cuban criminals and mentally ill who had entered with the Mariel exodus in 1980. Carter did not succeed in repatriating them, and Reagan wanted to solve the problem. Representatives of both governments began secret negotiations and signed an accord in December 1984: Cuba promised to accept the return of 2,746 "Marielitos" confined in federal prisons, and the United States agreed to admit 3,000 Cuban political prisoners and grant 20,000 visas annually to Cubans who sought them (few were provided, very slowly).

When Mexican President López Portillo called an international development conference, an important North-South meeting promoted by former

German Chancellor Willy Brandt and Austrian Chancellor Bruno Kreisky, Reagan called to warn him that he would not attend if Fidel Castro was invited. He also prevented Cuba from participating in the preparatory conference of foreign ministers. His hostility against Cuba was "practically pathological," commented Wayne Smith, former head of the United States interests section in Havana. [10] Cuba protested Mexico's allowing Reagan this "veto."

Two months before the conference was to begin, López Portillo invited Castro. They met in Cozumel. The Mexican government reported on the meeting in a concise statement. It was so secretive that the Cuban people learned of it only when Castro had already returned to Havana.[11]

López Portillo admired Castro and supported Cuba in spite of the pressures from Washington. When Vernon Walters went to Mexico in February 1981 with "proof" of Cuba's involvement in the Central American conflicts, the government received him coldly. Three days later it signed an agreement with Cuba to buy 100,000 tons of sugar, and PEMEX (the Mexican state-run petroleum company) signed another agreement on oil exploration on the island and the modernization of its refineries.[12]

A DIRTY WAR

In mid-1981, Cuba suffered epidemics of hemorrhageous dengue fever (it affected 273,404 people, killing 113, including 81 children) and swine fever (which necessitated killing all the pigs on the island), and blight on tobacco (an important source of revenue), which seriously affected its production. Castro accused the CIA of biological warfare. Around the same time a plague of rats appeared. The government placed advertisements throughout the country requesting that people destroy the rats and their food sources. These ads featured a rat dressed in Uncle Sam's top hat. "They have not accused us of responsibility for this plague, but the message is clear," commented a United States official.[13]

Washington rejected Cuba's accusation of biological warfare as completely unfounded. State Department spokesman Dean Fischer insisted that the Cuban Revolution was a failure and that it was easier for Cuba to blame its own failures on such external forces as the United States than to take responsibility for them. Nonetheless, in 1984 Eduardo Arocena, a Cuban exile in Miami and the head of the anti-Castro terrorist organization Omega 7, testified in a United States suit against him that he took certain "germs" to Cuba in 1980. (Arocena was sentenced in New York and Miami courts to fifty years in prison for murder, attempted murder, sabotage, and perjury.)[14]

Another weapon against Cuba was electronic aggression. Virulent propaganda campaigns against the Revolution and Castro that encouraged the Cuban people to rebel and leave the island were developed by a score of anti-Castro broadcasting stations and the Voice of America, the official United States radio station. In September 1981, high State Department officials announced plans to establish a powerful station, Radio Martí, to broadcast news about Cuba to the Cuban people. This project was funded by the Cuban-American National Foundation (CANF), established earlier that year by Jorge Mas Canosa and other Cuban anti-Castro moguls with Reagan's support. For the *New York Times* this was only "a gimmick, designed mostly for domestic effect,"[15] since Cubans could already listen to United States radio stations. In spite of the fact that this project violated international law and international telecommunications treaties signed by both governments, the House approved a grant of $10 million for its installation (134 representatives voted against it). The Santa Fe Report prepared for Reagan's campaign proposed creating Radio Free Cuba to spread anti-Castro propaganda to the Cuban people, and if this effort failed, the report suggested launching a war of liberation against Castro.

The White House doors were open to Mas Canosa. He had a free hand in designing United States policies against Cuba, and he advised members of Congress, both Republican and Democratic, on the making of laws to extend the embargo and other acts of aggression against Cuba. In exchange, CANF supported their campaigns with funds and votes from the powerful community of anti-Castro Cuban-Americans settled in Florida. This state has the fourth-largest number of electoral votes in the United States.

The Cuban government was furious, calling Radio Martí a new act of aggression by "American imperialism," which violated its sovereignty and offended the Cuban people by using Martí's name, and announced that it would build a powerful station to broadcast information to the people in the United States and to interfere with United States commercial stations. Washington published a menu of the countermeasures it would take if this were to happen. One was "surgical bombing strikes" on Cuban stations. In December, Cuba took the offensive via Radio Havana with English-language broadcasts "of an unusual power," commented officials of the United States Federal Communications Commission.

When Radio Martí went on the air in May 1985, under the management of anti-Castroites, Castro demanded the suspension of its broadcasts, cut off immigration accords with the United States and suspended permission for charter flights between Miami and Havana. The following month the State Department announced that it would stop granting visas to Cubans. More than 1,000 who already had them would not be allowed to enter the United States. Radio Martí continued broadcasting its virulent propaganda, and the Revolution continued on its course.

Reagan announced plans to install TV Martí—also a CANF proposal—and in September 1988, Congress approved a $7.5 million budget line to get the network started. "They will install it only under cannon fire," rowed Castro. "When an adventure like this is started, when an act of aggression against a sovereign country is begun, anything can happen," including an intervention in Cuba, he added. The Cuban people called it a "miserable and cowardly act of aggression," an "electronic Platt Amendment" again meant to "*mediatizar*" (impose limitations on their rights) the country.[16]

President Bush instituted the network in 1989. Its broadcasts began in March; Cuba blocked them, and the programs penetrated only by satellite to the United States Interests Section in Havana. The Cuban people mocked the failure: "They gave birth to a mouse," and "It's the Girón of the air," refer-erring to the United States defeat at the Bay of Pigs.[17]

Top United States officials, starting with the president, participated in the Reagan administration's frenetic anti-Cuban campaign (United States communication monopolies controlled 70 percent of the world's information). Their aim was to show that Cuban military power was a threat to the hemisphere. They claimed that Cuba had 52,000 soldiers in seventeen countries, and that its soldiers were participating in the Central American armed struggles. United Nations Ambassador Jeane Kirkpatrick swore that Cuba had soldiers in Afghanistan.

Castro dismissed these accusations as lies. He denied that he was sending Soviet arms to the Salvadoran guerrillas, since these weapons were for Cuba's own defense and he was not to export them. He also insisted that no Cuban soldiers were in any guerrilla movement. He challenged Haig to prove that Cuba had between 500 and 600 soldiers in Nicaragua, as reported in the *Washington Post*, a news item that had not been denied by the United States government. Haig did not come up with proof. The State Department spokesman accused Cuba's claims of being pure propaganda.

In January 1982 the director of the State Department Office of Cuban Affairs, Myles Frechette, claimed that the Soviet Union had given Cuba $2 billion worth of weaponry and 200 MIG fighter aircraft capable of transporting nuclear weapons.[18]

This campaign was Reagan's way of seeking support in Congress, softening public opinion, and winning backing in Latin America for his anti-Cuban policies. He sent confidential notes to Latin American presidents, and his top officials visited them to alert them to Cuba's military might, offer them military aid, and sell arms for their defense.

TO THE BEAT OF THEIR DRUM

In 1981 a series of diplomatic incidents and accusations by Latin American governments of Cuban intervention in their internal affairs, "coinciding" with Reagan's rise to power, placed Cuba in a state of isolation similar to that during the 1960s. These warlike anti-Cuban policies, issuing from Reagan's campaign, were very welcome in the military dictatorships of the Southern Cone and Central America and in the democracies or quasidemocracies unfriendly to the Revolution and dominated or quasidominated by the military.

The so-called embassy crisis began in February, when a group of Cubans armed with machine guns and grenades entered the Ecuadoran diplomatic headquarters and took the ambassador and his officials hostage. The Cuban chancellery warned that it would not give in to the kidnappers' demands and offered to liberate the Ecuadoran diplomats and return control of the embassy to the Ecuadoran government. Three days later a delegation from that government arrived in Havana and succeeded in winning the hostages' release. Immediately a Cuban commando group raided the embassy, disarmed the attackers, and arrested them. Not a drop of blood was shed. The president of Ecuador, Jaime Roldós, presented his "most vigorous note of protest" against this assault by Cuban forces on his diplomatic headquarters, and "held [the Cuban government] responsible" for those arrested. The Cuban government responded just as vigorously. It claimed that the Ecuadoran government had "absolutely no power" to make such a demand, since the rights of Cuban citizens were the constitutional business of the Cuban government, which it exercised without anyone "needing to remind it."[19] Ecuador summoned back its ambassador but did not break off relations.

The Cuban government accused the Portuguese chargé d'affaires, Julio Francisco de Sales Mascarenhas, of directing the takeover of the Ecuadorian Embassy on orders from the CIA. It declared that it had proof. The chancellery called together the diplomatic corps, and Vice Chancellor Ricardo Alarcón denounced Mascarenhas in front of his colleagues. Before he could be expelled, Portugal called him back and declared the Cuban ambassador in Lisbon persona non grata.

Relations with Venezuela were already tense because the Cuban government had not allowed the Cubans who had broken into its embassy to leave the country, but they reached a breaking point in September 1980 when a Venezuelan military court declared four persons innocent who had been indicted for the sabotage of a Cuban Airlines plane in Barbados in 1976, in which seventy-three people had died, among them young Cubans from a fencing team.. Among them was Orlando Bosch (founder and director of CORU, the United Revolutionary Organization Command, an anti-Castro terrorist organization based in Miami) and Luis Posada Carriles, both Cubans and CIA agents. Castro accused the Venezuelan government of protecting terrorists, and the president of Venezuela, Herrera Campins, charged Castro with being a "dictator . . . incapable of understanding how a government like Venezuela's can respect the courts' autonomy." Cuba withdrew its diplomatic personnel from Caracas.

In 1985, Posada Carriles "escaped" from the maximum-security prison at San Juan de los Moros in Caracas. He walked out the main gate "with the evident support of powerful outside forces" and reappeared in El Salvador involved in CIA activities and the Nicaraguan contras.[20] And Bosch, who was considered a hero by the anti-Castro Cuban-American community for his fight against Communism, was extradited to the United States in February 1988 and confined to a correctional center just outside Miami. The Justice Department freed him "conditionally" in July 1990. His lawyer refused to say what agreement had been reached in exchange for his liberty.

In March Colombia "suspended" diplomatic relations with Cuba after the capture of a commando unit from the guerrilla group M-19 and a "dangerous" shipment of arms in the south of the country. President Turbay explained that he had decided on this action because of the Cuban government's "hostile proceedings." "It has become known," he remarked, "by the confession of one party that the guerrillas were trained in Cuba and that the captured weapons came from the same country."[21]

On the eve of this announcement the army transported a small and select group of Colombian journalists in a military plane to the Tolemaida military base where it was holding the rebel group. It showed them a single blindfolded guerrilla on a stretcher (there were nineteen altogether), who confirmed that they had just arrived from military training in Cuba. This testimony was the basis for the break.

Turbay was given plenty of support from former presidents and the heads of the big political parties, the clergy and the so-called major press. But the rupture was questioned by columnists, left-wing parties and movements, and union and professional organizations. Their reaction was not only one of solidarity with Cuba, but also one of protest at what appeared to be an engineered job by the government and the army, whose relations were particularly close.

The Association of University Professors issued a statement noting that the proof "presented by the Commander of the Third Brigade" to demonstrate a "presumed intervention by the Cuban government in our internal affairs" was insubstantial and proved nothing. It further denounced the Ecuadoran army's surrender to the Colombian army of a group of M-19 guerrillas who managed to escape and had sought asylum, "peacefully," from the Ecuadoran government, citing international treaties, according to reports in the Ecuadoran press. It pointed to this surrender as a violation of the extradition treaties currently in force between the two countries, and commented that such "problems" should be resolved by the chancelleries and "not by the Army Generals in a clear application of the pro-imperialist Viola Plan."[22]

According to a front-page story in the Panamanian daily *La Prensa*, the M-19 weapons had not come from Cuba, as the government claimed, but from Panama. Its correspondent mentioned "mysterious operations of the movement of heavy crates by supposed young M-19 guerrillas" and "mysterious landings by planes from the Pearl Islands' Airlines" with heavy wooden crates that were taken by motorboats to ships anchored in the open sea. He declared that this operation was repeated several times "supervised by a supposed officer from the Panamanian National Guard."[23]

The Cuban government denied having armed the Colombian guerrillas, maintained that it was not responsible for their entering Colombia (it did not mention the matter of their training), and accused the Colombian government of heading up an obscure maneuver "of Yankee imperialism and the rotten Colombian oligarchy" against its country. It claimed that Cuba had abandoned all direct participation in the Latin American guerrilla movements.

There was a wave of support for Turbay and rejection of this Cuban "intervention" by Latin American governments. Two days after the break between the two countries, the Panamanian government announced that it was asking for a hemispheric meeting to examine relations with the Cuban government. It went no further than this announcement. Torrijos and President Royo, friends of Castro's, were in the midst of a serious problem with Colombia because it was evident that Colombian guerrillas were buying arms in Panama. A scandal broke out in Colombia. Misael Pastrana Borrero, a former Colombian president and the leader of the conservative party, demanded a "revision" of relations with Panama for not having prevented these arms sales. The conflict was resolved through diplomatic channels.

In May the Cuban government sent a note to the United Nations secretary general to protest a communication by the Costa Rican government to that organization on the "situation of the political prisoners in Cuba." Cuba stated that this information was based on accusations by a former Cuban prisoner who had served a sentence "for having betrayed the motherland," and accused the Costa Rican government of, among other things, "shamelessly" lending itself to the counterrevolutionary campaign against Cuba, "organized by the imperialist government of the United States."[24] President Rodrigo Carazo closed the Costa Rican consulate in Havana because of the insulting terms of the note.

Changes in Latin America in 1981 meant serious reverses for Cuba. It lost friends. After the tragic death of General Torrijos in a strange airplane accident and the coup against President Royo, who was forced to resign by rightist military officers, Panama aligned itself with Washington and hardened its policies toward Cuba. In Jamaica, Michael Manley, a friend to Castro and Cuba, was defeated by the conservative Edward Seaga, a former senior World Bank official whose campaign was characterized by his anti-Communism and anti-Cuba virulence. Seaga broke off relations with Cuba and ordered Cuban experts out of Jamaica. He was the first head of state in the world to be invited to Washington by President Reagan.

In a declaration published in *Granma* on October 30, the Cuban chancellery claimed that Seaga's decision was in obedience to orders from Washington and that the pretexts he used were "so clumsy" that they warranted no comment. (The reason was Cuba's refusal to return three individuals accused of murder to Jamaica.)

Reagan's policy of turning Latin America against Cuba bore fruit. To the chorus of his attacks and those of the anti-Castro Cubans in Miami were added the voices of high dignitaries denouncing supposed Cuban subversive activities as the cause of the internal malaise in their countries and of the instability of their governments. Analysts saw these denunciations as smoke screens to cover up their internal failures and to please Washington.

REAGAN IN HIS NIGHTMARE

The level of public insults between the Washington and Havana governments arrived at "a most singular point," commented one United States diplomat.

Castro's were excessive. At a meeting of the Inter-Parliamentary Union in Havana in September 1981, he called the Reagan administration fascist and noted that it was "covered with the blood of three continents," a "warmonger and satanic," that it "pushes policies of war" and intervened in the internal affairs of El Salvador, where 20,000 people had been murdered. He also accused it of having approved the Israeli attack on an Iraqi nuclear reactor, the bombardment of Beirut, acts of provocation against Libya (an aerial attack on Libyan aircraft in the Gulf of Sidra), and of backing South Africa's "criminal invasion" of Angola. And he called Reagan's accusations against Cuba "lies, lies, lies."

Castro's burning words inspired a rash of anti-Western resolutions and the condemnation of governments "from Uruguay to Northern Ireland" for human-rights violations, during the conference, reported the UPI press agency. Robert Standford, a United States senator and a participant in this meeting, called Castro's speech an insult to the United States, one that his country would not forget. He noted that this "insulting conference" was making him wonder if the organization was turning into a "forum for propaganda from individuals who do not share the same considerations for truth and decency as those who have actually experienced a true parliamentary tradition." He was interrupted several times by applause.[25] Another newspaper commented that Castro's oratory was the most virulent speech against the United States in many years.

At the beginning of November 1981 the Pentagon called together the chiefs of the military and intelligence services of twenty Latin American and Caribbean nations to study measures to "guarantee the security of the hemisphere against aggression and subversion." At the end of the meeting Pentagon sources declared that the participants had approved several options, some of them collective, and that they hoped for a "hardening of the military line in respect to Cuba and Nicaragua."[26]

Faced with an imminent invasion, Cuba put its military forces on a "state of alert." The daily *Granma* commented in an editorial that the representatives of imperialism were keeping themselves hidden awaiting the propitious moment for aggression, and challenged the United States government to prove its accusations about Cuban support for the Salvadoran guerrilla movement.[27]

Alexander Haig continued to try to set up collective measures against Cuba. In December 1981, at the OAS General Assembly meeting in Castries, Saint Lucia, he exhorted the governments of the hemisphere to take such measures.[28] He proposed the creation of an inter-American naval force under

United States leadership to prevent "Soviet expansionism" in the Caribbean and the arms traffic coming from Cuba to Central America. Washington tried this tactic a number of times in different contexts without receiving much backing. President Turbay Ayala of Colombia proposed the same procedures.

Reagan warned that he would make Cuba pay a very high price for serving as a satellite of the Soviet Union. At a supersecret November meeting between Haig and Cuban Vice President Carlos Rafael Rodríguez in Mexico City—promoted by López Portillo—Haig explained to him in a way that was "very correct and very clear," according to Rodríguez, that his threat to "go to the source" meant that he would go to Cuba with a naval blockade or an invasion.[29] That same month the *New York Times* published a front-page story on the pressures Haig was putting on the Pentagon to study a "series of options" for military action in El Salvador and against Cuba and Nicaragua, to which the Pentagon was opposed.

In his State of the Union address in January 1982 Reagan warned that he would act "firmly" against anyone who exported subversion and terrorism in the Caribbean. In an interview with CBS television, he stated that he did not discount "any" option against Cuba, which must abandon its alliance with the Soviet Union and join the Western Hemisphere. Again he called Castro a puppet of Moscow.[30] Castro responded that if the United States intended to negotiate Cuba's foreign policy, it had better be prepared to negotiate its own role in NATO with Cuba.

In March, Secretary of the Navy John Lehman stated that a naval blockade of Cuba was possible but that it would be "an act of war" that he would not undertake without the support of the United States Congress and people.[31] At the end of the month General Vernon Walters went to Havana to meet with Castro.[32] Wayne Smith, the former United States representative in Havana, commented that this visit was a "pure charade" on the part of the administration to show that it was trying to negotiate but that Cuba would not cooperate.[33] He commented that when he had been head of the United States Interests Section in Havana, he had sent cables to the State Department indicating Cuba's readiness to open discussions and that it had responded that it is was inclined neither to dialogue nor to accept any Cuban "gesture."[34]

In April, Reagan traveled to Jamaica and Barbados to present his Caribbean Basin Initiative to some Caribbean heads of state. In Jamaica he accused Cuba of trying to "undermine democracy throughout the Americas," and in Barbados he declared that Grenada "bears the Soviet and Cuban trademark."[35]

THE "VENDETTA"

Reagan's new weapon against Cuba was human rights. In April 1982 he approved a secret National Security Council plan and immediately began accusing the Cuban government of tortures and disappearances, and claimed that its prisons were full of political prisoners and that it did not respect the fundamental rights of freedom of expression, association, and movement. Leading figures in the United States government took part in this intensive campaign. Year after year the State Department's annual report on the world human-rights situation accused Cuba of violating them. Raúl Roa Kouri, Cuba's vice minister for foreign relations and its ambassador to the United Nations' office in Geneva, called this propaganda against his country a simple vendetta.

Such accusations irritated the Cuban government because they were false. Roa noted that the Revolution's priority was respect for the fundamental rights of the people, which were education, health care—both were free in Cuba—social security, and the right to work. On the subject of "political prisoners," he declared that there were no more than a hundred, since most had been released, and that they were people who had served the Batista dictatorship, sentenced for terrorist actions against the security of the state. He accused Reagan of supporting the military dictatorships in the Southern Cone and Central America and of covering up the crimes committed by the military, the police, and the security forces of these countries—genocide, assassinations, disappearances, torture, and extrajudicial executions—on which he had not commented.

The Reagan administration made use of "testimony" by Cuban exiles, former political prisoners, and deserters in its accusations against Cuba. It went further in the case of Armando Valladares, a former Batista police officer and political prisoner (who was arrested in 1960 for terrorist acts and released by the Revolution in 1982 before the end of his sentence). In 1987 it granted him United States citizenship and named him ambassador and president of the United States delegation to the Human Rights Commission (HRC) in Geneva—a unique and unprecedented case.

Valladares attracted international attention from prison as a poet (two of his books were translated into several languages) and as an "invalid." He claimed to have been paralyzed by mistreatment in prison. French President François Mitterand negotiated his release and received him in France. The Cuban government showed his identification card from Batista's police force and videos of him walking in the prison and descending, on his own, the stairs of the plane that took him to Paris when he was liberated.

Valladares was a virulent spokesman against the Revolution. In newspaper articles and in testimony before congressional subcommittees, he accused Cuba of having about 140,000 political prisoners and common prisoners in jails, prison camps, and concentration camps where, he claimed, people (including children) were executed, tortured, murdered, and mutilated night after night.[36]

The main forum for this "vendetta" against Cuba was the HRC in Geneva. So important was it to Reagan that he sent General Walters to reinforce Valladares's mission. Walters reiterated the accusations of repression, torture and disappearances, and of a political prisoner population in Cuba of more than 15,000.

In February 1987 the United States presented a draft resolution titled "Situation of Human Rights and Fundamental Freedoms in Cuba." It cited reports of the OAS Inter-American Commission on Human Rights (IACHR)— in 1962 Cuba was expelled from the organization—that "carry proof of substantial abuses," noted the "high number of political prisoners," the "extremely large number" of Cubans abandoning the country, the "serious violations" of freedom of expression, association, and personal security. It demanded that Cuba respect these rights and asked the United Nations Human Rights Commission (HRC) to continue to study the subject.[37]

In its turn Cuba also presented a draft resolution in which it accused the United States of violating human rights: racial discrimination against blacks, Hispanics, and Native Americans; aggression, threats, and coercion directed against numerous third world countries; and attempts on the lives of statesmen. It denounced the impunity of the Ku Klux Klan and its actions against blacks and Native Americans with the consent and participation of the police. It demanded suspension of the United States' "covert actions" against sovereign states, respect for the human rights of minorities, and an end to the "degrading situation of the homeless" and racial discrimination. Responding to a petition of the delegate from India, the HRC agreed not to submit either of the drafts to a vote.

The Cuban government asked the HRC to send an observer mission to its country to check out the United States accusations. The mission did go to Cuba, and in February 1989 it presented its report—400 pages—in which, among other things, it noted that it had found no evidence to support the United States accusation of 15,000 political prisoners on the island. That same month the State Department's annual human rights report accused Cuba of being one of the "worst violators" in the world, but added that it had been unable to confirm cases of disappearances or torture. And a report by Americas Watch—a harsh critic of Cuba—maintained that the United States accusations lacked foundation.[38]

Raúl Roa responded to the accusations against his country. He pointed out that for four years, the United States had been maintaining a "huge" propaganda campaign, promoting the creation in Cuba and elsewhere of Cuban pro-human rights groups, sending out publications and endless declarations by officials and members of Congress promoting anti-Cuban motions in the parliaments of other countries, using "small groups of known reactionaries" and "counterrevolutionary and anti-socialist elements in Cuba itself to mount provocations and disturbances." He noted that this psychological warfare had few results and that the report of the HRC mission to Cuba had "categorically" denied Walters's accusations.[39]

Responding to testimony by Cubans gathered by the HRC observer mission on supposed violations of human rights, Roa noted that 65.7 percent of them referred to "entering or leaving" the country. For human rights activists who had suffered harassment—denounced by the United States as the work of the Cuban government—he declared that it was a reaction by the people to "provocative and counterrevolutionary acts." About people who conveyed their intention of leaving the country and were dismissed from their workplaces, he remarked that these were decisions by the managers of the workplaces and not a state policy, and that there were legal avenues for workers to pursue their rights. Regarding the executions by firing squad of counterrevolutionaries—thirteen between 1980 and 1987—he argued that the Cuban Penal Code provided for the death penalty for acts of serious sabotage and terrorism and that the laws of this code, characterized as "draconian," followed "the methods employed by imperialism and its agents" against the Revolution, which "leave no other alternative." He explained that the *plantados* (prisoners who refused to wear uniforms), were sentenced for crimes, for "attempts to assassinate Fidel Castro, for espionage, sabotage, complicity in murder, acts against the integrity and stability of the nation, for the infiltration of enemy agents and weapons, for crimes and abuses against campesinos, for armed assault, for crimes committed while in the service of Batista's tyranny."[40]

Roa criticized the HRC's mission, whose job it was to study the Cuban situation in situ, for having included the testimony of anti-Castroites living outside the island and limiting itself to transmitting them without verifying their truth, and for the lack of a medical evaluation to gauge the allegations of torture and ill treatment mentioned by some of its interviewees. He noted that the political weight that the United States media tried to give to these "small groups" of activists and "dissidents" did not correspond to their scant representation, which was not comparable to the adherence by millions of people to the Revolution and its social, political, economic, and cultural work.

The United States did not succeed in having the HRC condemn Cuba, since Latin America and other third world countries supported Cuba. In spite of this campaign and Washington's pressures, Bolivia, Uruguay, and Brazil reestablished diplomatic relations with Cuba.

THE UNBEARABLE BREVITY OF PERESTROIKA

With the election of Mikhail Gorbachev, fifty-four years old (young for the traditional Soviet gerontocracy) as secretary general of the CPSU in March 1985, a few hours after the death of Konstantin Chernenko, the metamorphosis of the Soviet Union began. Gorbachev introduced the novel policies of perestroika (restructuring) and glasnost (transparency), with which he turned his country and its foreign policy in a new direction. The aim was to reform the calcified Soviet political system, "democratize" society, open channels of popular participation, and relax tensions in relations with the West. The reason was that the Soviet Union had been experiencing a profound economic and political crisis. The general malaise could have led, Gorbachev warned, to something very serious.

Gorbachev aroused admiration throughout the world. He spoke of coexistence and cooperation among all nations beyond ideologies, differing political systems, and obsolete concepts of confrontation and interference in the internal affairs of other countries. He surprised the world with bold measures and proposals for disarmament and the unexpected withdrawal of Soviet forces from Afghanistan, the Soviet Union's Vietnam, which Brezhnev had invaded nine years earlier. Neither victors nor defeated, the Soviets left in disgrace.

Gorbachev proceeded to open discussions with heads of state and governments, political and parliamentary leaders of Europe, Asia, and the Americas. He was received enthusiastically in several capitals. From the ultraconservative Margaret Thatcher, Britain's prime minister, to the Socialist president of France, François Mitterrand, they "fell in love" with Gorbachev. The international press spoke of a "Gorbymania" that was invading the West. More disposed than the

United States to finding a modus vivendi with the Soviets, Europe gave him firm and emotional support.

The capitalist world called perestroika the "second Soviet revolution," this one without bloodshed, as radical as the Bolshevik Revolution but in reverse, and applauded Gorbachev. But at the same time it launched an aggressive campaign to discredit the Communist system, pointing to the Soviet crisis as evidence of its failure. Gorbachev criticized the critics: "There are people in the West who would like to tell us that socialism is in a deep crisis and has brought our society to a dead end. . . . We have only one way out, they say: to adopt capitalist methods. . . . They tell us that nothing will come of Perestroika within the framework of our system. They say we should change this system and borrow from the experience of another socio-political system . . . that if the Soviet Union takes this path and gives up its socialist choice, close links with the West will supposedly become possible. They go so far as to claim that the October 1917 Revolution was a mistake which almost completely cut off our country from world social progress. . . . To put an end to all the rumors and speculations that abound in the West about this, I would like to point out once again that we are conducting all our reforms in accordance with the socialist choice. We are looking within socialism, rather than outside it. . . . Perestroika . . . is fully based on the principle of more socialism and more democracy."[41]

"We began Perestroika in a situation of growing international tension," wrote Gorbachev in *Perestroika: New Thinking for Our Country and the World*.[42] He remarked, "The detente of the 1970s has been cut off. Our calls for peace found no response in the headquarters of Western governments. Soviet foreign policy was slipping. The arms race was spiraling upward. The threat of war was increasing."[43]

The world had, in effect, returned to the tensions of the Cold War with Reagan's aggressive politics of confrontation. But now, swept along by the "Gorbymania" of his allies and Gorbachev's peace offensive, Reagan was forced to deflate his rhetoric and moderate his attacks on the Soviet Union. Gorbachev was pulling him along. The United States lost its position of world leadership.

In 1987 the Soviet policy of closer ties and collaboration with the West began to bear fruit. In December, Reagan and Gorbachev signed a disarmament agreement in Washington for the withdrawal of their medium- and long-range missiles from Europe. The pact was a political triumph for the Soviet Union and the warm acclaim the United States gave him was a personal triumph for Gorbachev. He walked through the streets sharing greetings and smiles. Castro did not hesitate to support Gorbachev's peace policies. He applauded his disarmament proposals and enthusiastically celebrated the accord signed by the two superpowers. *Granma* called it "a historic step without precedent," since for the first time it opened up the possibilities of total disarmament.[44] It was, in fact, the most far-reaching disarmament pact signed during forty years of fruitless negotiations. It also represented a radical change in Reagan's policy toward the Soviet Union.

But the Soviet Union's abandonment of its political and ideological fight with capitalism, and its own interests in conflict with the West, weakened it in the international arena. The new closeness between Gorby and Ron (they were already calling each other by their nicknames) and the éntente cordiale that was beginning to crystallize could lead to a reduction in Soviet support for liberation struggles in the third world and a weakening of its alliance with Cuba. Reagan was pressuring Gorbachev to suspend Soviet aid to Cuba, it was Reagan's condition if he was to "consider" the economic aid Gorbachev was requesting, which the Soviet Union urgently needed. Castro warned the Cuban people who believed that this new closeness between the Soviet Union and the United States would lead Reagan to stop his aggression toward their country that it might have exactly the opposite effect.

Within the Soviet Union, not everyone agreed with Gorbachev's policy of "openness," "democratization" and closer ties with the West. At a CPSU meeting in August 1988 Yegor Ligachev—second-in-command of the Politburo and a Kremlin political adviser—stated, "So much talk about peaceful cooperation with the capitalist countries only confuses the minds of the Soviet people and our foreign friends." He insisted that the priority should continue to be the class struggle against capitalism. Foreign Minister Eduard Shevardnadze opposed him in a speech quoted by the Tass news agency: "The struggle between the two opposing systems is no longer the determining factor of this era," adding that Soviet foreign policy was no longer one of confrontation with the West.[45]

Swimming against the worldwide tide attacking the Communist system and socialism, Castro gave an unequivocal avowal of faith in this doctrine in four speeches in January 1989: "Socialism," he said, "is and will continue to be the only hope, the only road for the oppressed, exploited, and looted peoples. And today, when our enemies want to question it, we must defend it more than ever." He concluded with the slogans: "Socialism or death! Marxism-Leninism or death!" and "Our motherland or death! We will win!" as the people applauded, shouting, "Fidel! Fidel! Fidel!"[46]

THE DISTANT ALLY

The Soviet government invited Castro to Moscow for the celebration of the seventieth anniversary of the October Revolution in November 1987. It was a euphoric occasion. The transformation the Soviet Union was undergoing in its economic structures and in political openness created a favorable climate. The people felt "freer," according to a proud Gorbachev. The great event was celebrated with an imposing military parade. Tens of thousands of soldiers, heavy artillery, tanks, and modern missiles with their launch vehicles proceeded through Red Square, and masses of workers marched to the sound of patriotic music. The feeling was one of celebration and optimism.

One photograph published in the *New York Times* showed Castro in a Russian fur hat and dark glasses, watching the military parade from Lenin's tomb along with the leaders of the Soviet Union and the rest of the Communist world. The *Times* described this event and reported rumors of disagreements between Cuba and the Soviet Union about economic policies.[47]

Although Castro did not join the chorus of praise for the Soviet leader, their relations were excellent, and the cooperation between their two countries increased. Twice they met in the Kremlin. On his return to Havana, Castro commented that this had been his best visit ever to the Soviet Union, reported the *Times* correspondent.[48]

There were, in fact, discrepancies in focus and concept between the two countries' views of perestroika. The way to approach the solution to their grave national problems could not be the same, though the problems might have been similar, noted Castro. The policy of "rectification" Cuba had undertaken long before Compañero Gorbachev began speaking of perestroika was not the same as Perestroika. The latter was not the solution to Cuba's problems in the way that many people outside the island preached it should have been and many at home desired. Castro pointed out that the two countries were different, with their own idiosyncrasies and histories. Cuba's territory was not extensive, it was not a multinational country, it didn't have the large population of the Soviet Union, nor the experience of "historical phenomena" such as Stalinism, abuses of power and authority, or personality cults. Cuba was not in need of Soviet-style reforms.

Castro emphatically rejected the idea of introducing into Cuba the capitalist reforms Washington had been prescribing and the Soviet Union was beginning to apply. He called them "complete garbage." Cuba would "never" adopt the methods, philosophies, or idiosyncrasies of capitalism. Cuba, he declared, was not on the Black Sea but in the Caribbean, 90 miles not from Odessa but from Miami. He made these remarks in a speech on July 26, 1988, as Cuba was preparing to receive thousands of soldiers triumphantly returning from Angola.[49]

"We have made mistakes we must correct, but starting with our own mistakes," said Castro. "We must not correct our mistakes on the basis of other countries' errors." He noted that one error included having "copied" the experience of other socialist countries "who now are saying their experience was not good."[50] Respectful of other countries' sovereignty, Cuba could not criticize Soviet policies since they dealt with the internal affairs of that country, noted Castro. Nevertheless, Fidel could not hide Cuba's disagreement nor its great preoccupation with the internal and external break-ups the Soviet Union had been enduring, with the "reformist wave" spreading through Eastern Europe, the accelerating decline of the Communist Parties, and the growth of multiparty systems in those countries, which Castro termed *multiporquería* (roughly, "multirubbish").

On December 5, 1988, during the celebration of Cuban Armed Forces Day (Gorbachev's official visit was scheduled for that month), Castro expressed his alarm at the "special moment" the international revolutionary process was experiencing. "Several socialist countries," he remarked, "are criticizing what they have been doing for many years, denying what they have been affirming for decades," and he noted that this situation was being exploited by "imperialism" to paint a picture of socialism as "a failure in practice and a system without a future" and "praise to the skies the supposed advantages of its own egotistical and repugnant capitalist system." He sounded a warning about the seriousness of the present moment. "New experiments, new experiences, all kinds of reforms are happening in the socialist camp, especially in the Soviet Union. If they are successful, this will be good for socialism and for the whole world. If they have serious difficulties, the consequences will be especially hard on us."

Diplomats in Havana saw in Castro's words "such shrill notes" that, in their judgment, only an opportune rain—a torrential downpour—kept "the subtle argument elaborated by Fidel against Gorbachev from exploding into a strident public denunciation of the 'sins' of glasnost and perestroika."[51]

In January 1989, a politically strong Cuba celebrated the thirtieth anniversary of its revolution—it had the highest indices for social development in all of Latin America—and was immersed in "rectifying errors and negative tendencies." Without much fanfare, the United States was approaching a transition from Reagan to Bush. Meanwhile in the Soviet Union, perestroika was unraveling and its stunned leaders were seeing that the empire was disintegrating in their hands.

Two years after the introduction of perestroika the internal situation deteriorated at an increasing rate. The decentralization of the economy, which had been intended to increase production and improve the lot of the people, had instead broken the economic structures and affected production, internal distribution, and foreign trade. This situation was also eroding COMECON (Council of Mutual Economic Assistance). Inflation and unemployment spiraled upward, and poverty rose to record levels. For the first time there were beggars in the streets of Moscow and lines of old women selling their belongings or asking for charity.[52]

Glasnost, the other pillar of Gorbachev's strategy, opened the doors to public debate. "It's gone to their heads," commented one leader. The people, stifled under the CPSU dictatorship, the rigidity of the system, and the enormous difficulties of everday life, were euphoric at this opening. For the first time they could denounce the horrors of the Stalin era, question the party and its leadership, criticize the official Marxist-Leninist ideology, and even in some cases, express doubts about the blessings of the October Revolution, which had taken so many lives and caused such great suffering among the people.[53]

The winds of independence began to blow within the Soviet Union. Nationalist movements in the Baltic states, supportive of Gorbachev and perestroika, proclaimed their opposition to the dictatorship of the CPSU and the leadership of Moscow. At the fiftieth anniversary of the annexation pact—signed by Hitler and Stalin in 1939, by which the Baltic States had become part of the Soviet Union—more than two million people formed a human chain across the three republics to express their joint rejection of the pact. The rebellion became widespread. Between January 1987 and the middle of 1988 there were 300 nationalist disturbances (some of them massive) in nine of the fifteen Soviet republics.[54]

The nationalist and independence-seeking "virus," as such movements were called by the CPSU, spread to Georgia, Moldavia, Belarus, and the Muslim republics. At the beginning of 1989 Ukraine, second only to Russia in importance and with the Soviet Union's second-largest nuclear arsenal in its territory, joined the secessionists. What was happening was catastrophic. The CPSU lost strength, prestige, and credibility. It could no longer contain the nationalist protests that were breaking out everywhere.

The tumultuous elections for the new congress in March 1989 reflected the loss of faith in its institutions and leaders. This was the first time the Soviet people could elect their representatives, and the defeat of the Communist candidates and the victory of the independents demonstrated the profound changes at work in the society.

The malaise spread throughout the immense nation, while the basic structures of the country fell apart. In March 1990 the Soviet parliament approved by a wide majority Gorbachev's proposal to strengthen his presidency and put an end to the political monopoly of the CPSU. This act marked the end of seventy years of party dictatorship.

Gorbachev's prestige plummeted. Many believed that the people were suffering the worst situation in their history. Disorganization and chaos were the rule. Some at the top criticized Gorbachev's indecision and lack of leadership. He was unable to please the opposing forces, all of which were pressuring him equally.

The Soviet empire was disintegrating. The strategy of perestroika and glasnost created a deep anxiety among Eastern Europe's leaders. The Soviet "democratization" and its "hands-off" policy about the internal affairs of other countries, including its own member states—another radical change in Gorbachev's foreign policy—stimulated open debate against its institutions. Popular nationalist movements arose, opposed to the "dictatorship" of the Communist Party and its dependence on Moscow. The "liberalization" of its institutions had not served to advance socialism, as Gorbachev preached, but was instead destroying it. The Communist parties either transformed themselves or disappeared at the sound of perestroika and the chants of "Long live Gorbachev!"

In mid-1989 the Eastern European Communist regimes were falling, and the Berlin Wall was torn down without Gorbachev's raising a hand to defend them. With a greater or lesser degree of trauma the regimes were moving from socialism to capitalism, from the dictatorship of the proletariat and the Communist Party to the chaos of multiparty systems and the transition to democracy. The Warsaw Pact, the Eastern military alliance, and COMECON (the Soviet bloc economic integration organization, of which Cuba was a member), disintegrated. It was the end of more than forty years of Communist rule in Eastern Europe and the end of its relations with Cuba—a devastating blow to Havana.

"They fell apart like a house of cards," commented Castro in a speech on December 8, 1989. "In those countries nobody is talking of the fight against imperialism any more, nor of the principles of internationalism. These ideas are practically erased from their political dictionary; on the other hand, the capitalist vocabulary is gaining unique power in these societies." He affirmed that capitalism would "never" be the tool to pull socialism out of its difficulties. And he added: "If destiny casts us in the role of one of the last defenders of socialism, we shall know how to defend it to the last drop of our blood!" He concluded with the slogan, "Socialism or Death, Our Motherland or Death, We will overcome!" among shouts of support for Fidel and the Revolution.[55]

RECTIFICATION IS NOT PERESTROIKA

With the extraordinary changes happening in the socialist world, and with Gorbachev anointed by the powerful in the capitalist world as the architect of the new climate of world understanding, Washington opened an extensive and aggressive campaign demanding the "democratization" of Cuba. Castro denounced it as "imperialist propaganda" meant to destabilize his country and encourage internal subversion. Reagan—and later Bush—and his spokesmen, great and small European and American figures—the "democrats" of the world—used the media in developed and underdeveloped countries and "Radio Martí" to demand that Cuba take the path of "openness," political pluralism, and "democratization," that it hold "free" elections and make room for opposition movements. The United States media devoted many feature stories to these small groups of activists and "dissidents" who arose on the island, encouraged by Washington and the anti-Castroites in Miami.

The process of rectification of errors and negative tendencies—as Cuba dubbed its own perestroika—began before the world had ever heard of perestroika. In a speech on April 19, 1985—the twenty-fifth anniversary of the proclamation of the socialist nature of the Revolution—Castro explained the need to attack corruption and administrative deterioration, and seek solutions to the difficult economic situation the country was going through.[56] Castro recognized that many economic difficulties followed from errors in economic planning and management. There was frequent theft in businesses, and the loss of large sums of money through carelessness, poor management, and disorder, lack of discipline, and absenteeism. He accused party and government officials of using their posts to obtain personal privilege, teachers of not teaching, students of cheating on their exams. "Things are not working well, and conscience is not working well," he remarked. He added that this was no "cultural revolution" but a permanent and lifelong struggle to fight such tendencies.

He noted that corruption was the worst because it could "put [the people's] revolutionary conscience to sleep."[57]

After a year of wide-ranging national debate, the proposed solutions were analyzed in a deferred session of the third congress of the Cuban Communist Party. The rectification process sought to "perfect" economic mechanisms, and the political and institutional system and to strengthen the "democratization" of its society. Economic incentives were suppressed, and emphasis was placed on moral aspects, labor discipline (similar to that of the early years), and "slowing the invading wave of capitalism." The free campesino markets, created in 1984 to improve the distribution of foodstuffs among the populace, were suspended. Castro declared that they should never have been created, calling them an error since the campesinos stopped selling their products to the state and began selling them *por la libre* (on their own), charging higher prices, enriching themselves excessively, and halting the cooperative movement essential to the nation's economy.[58] In 1990 more than 500 people were arrested, including government officials. Castro called them "magnates of crime." *Granma* observed, "There is not, nor will there be, impunity."[59]

The Cuban and the Soviet processes moved in opposite directions. While the Soviet Union was decentralizing its economy, reducing the power of its Communist Party, and giving free rein to political pluralism, Cuba was strengthening the leadership of the Cuban Communist Party as the country's sole party that guided the development of the country and kept its economy centralized. Castro asked the people to defend socialism now more than ever "against the attacks of the enemy" and give greater support to the Communist Party. "Whoever destroys our faith in the Party is undermining the foundations of our confidence, the foundations of our strength," he added.[60] He noted that in Cuba, there was only one party "in the same way as Lenin needed only one party."[61] Castro underlined the "genuine" nature of the Cuban Revolution and its differences from the Eastern European Communist regimes which, he remarked, were "imposed from without." He added that in Cuba the same thing could never happen, since Cuba had made its own revolution; the people did not ask for new parties because they were already participating through the mass organizations of campesinos, workers, women, students, and the Revolutionary Defense Committees (CDRs) and through the Popular Power system. The most important proposals for laws were discussed in these organizations, starting with their basic units, and Castro maintained a constant dialogue with the people—"direct democracy"—in every corner of the country.

Castro warned that Cuba would not adopt the measures of the so-called representative democracies since they were societies divided between exploiters and the exploited, small groups in which wealth and power were concentrated and the masses of the poorly fed, with abandoned children and beggars, and students who were violently repressed. One could not speak of democracy, he said, where such differences and misery rule.

The capitalist press called the Cuban policies rejecting multiparty "opening" and completely defending socialism "anachronistic" and "retrograde," the Cuban Revolution "fossilized" and "failed," and Castro a "dinosaur."

GORBY IN HAVANA

In April 1989 Gorbachev arrived in Havana on an official visit. He came not as a triumphant victor, in spite of his enormous worldwide popularity, but with a load of uncertainties on his back. It was public knowledge that his reforms were failing, that the Soviet economic situation was in rapid decline, and that internal malaise was growing.

Cuba gave him an overwhelming welcome that could well have been interpreted as an expression of gratitude from the Cuban people for Soviet solidarity, commented *Prensa latina*. As he stepped off the airplane at José Martí Airport, Gorbachev was greeted with a warm embrace by Castro, a military ceremony including a twenty-one-gun salute, greetings from the top Cuban leadership, diplomatic protocol of ambassadors, and a happy crowd waving signs and flags of both countries. More than half a million people, according to official numbers, were awaiting Gorbachev's arrival at the airport and along the route the two leaders were to travel. They were greeted by shouts of "Viva Gorbachev!" and "Viva our Commander-in-Chief!"

Fidel and Gorby traveled the route "shoulder to shoulder" in an open Soviet limousine. The city was decorated with both countries' flags and huge billboards with Gorbachev's image and greetings of welcome for the *compañero*. The country was in a party mood.

Some 500 international journalists came to Havana—more than a hundred from the main papers and television networks of the United States alone—to cover this event, which aroused great expectations because of the evident differences between Castro's and Gorbachev's positions. The visit of the most unpredictable of the Soviet leaders and the one who awakened in Castro the greatest worries began in the "rarefied atmosphere created by the communications transnationals," which were reporting conflicts, distancing, modification of the terms of trade, and punishments of Cuba, noted *Prensa latina*.[62]

Gorbachev arrived in a friendly country but one that was a focus of conflict with the United States. In spite of the eased tensions that already existed between the two superpowers, Washington watched this meeting closely and apprehensively. With numerous forms of pressure it was trying to force Gorbachev to withdraw aid from Cuba and to stop sending arms to Nicaragua. The Soviet Union was critical of the United States military presence in Central America and supported the Contadora peace efforts, which Reagan systematically boycotted. Bush, who had recently been elected president and had not yet defined his foreign policy, declared that he would not change it in regard to Cuba and that he would keep sending "humanitarian aid" to the Nicaraguan contras. Gorbachev warned that he would continue to send arms to Nicaragua for its defense.

The culmination of the Soviet leader's visit was a special session of the national assembly of popular power. Castro defined the Soviet Leader's presence in this forum as a "historic occasion." He called Gorbachev a "real peace crusader" and criticized the United States for not assimilating the "new [international] mentality" set forth by Gorbachev. He paid an emotional homage to the Soviet Union for its "enormous collaboration" with his country over a period of thirty years, without which, he emphasized, the Revolution would never have been able to achieve the "successes on which our people pride themselves." In particular, he pointed to the military aid that had helped Cuba confront the "most powerful empire in human history" and achieve its victory at Playa Girón. "For this, our gratitude shall be eternal."[63]

Gorbachev praised the heroic Cuban people who made the Revolution and enabled Cuba to "repel armed intervention, survive the blockade, and live through the unending aggression by their imperialist neighbor." He emphasized close ties of friendship and cooperation that covered "practically all spheres of social development," demonstrated his intention to extend them, and underlined this wish as the intent of the Friendship and Collaboration Treaty that he and Castro had just signed. He also referred to the transformations his country was undergoing and noted the "change in the climate of social life, by which the people feel freer," but remarked that such an approach and the solutions to Soviet problems were not a "universal formula." He added that the international authority of socialism and its influence on the world "would depend" on developments in his country. He criticized the United States without mentioning it by name. He stated that the international horizon had become brighter in the past two years but that there were still "forces obstinately bound to the stereotypical and outmoded approach of confrontation, of solutions imposed by force . . . of trying to impose their will on others." He reiterated his support for a negotiated peace in Central America "without foreign interference."[64]

Both heads of state disappointed speculations about their disagreements. Castro declared that such differences did not exist in their international policies, nor could they possibly exist in questions of internal policy, since their respective plans for restructuring and rectification proceeded from the identical Marxist-Leninist principles, applied to the concrete conditions of each country. What worked for one did not necessarily work for the other because of the enormous differences in their circumstances. Castro commented that, "the strongest refutation" was the "magnificent" Friendship and Collaboration Treaty that they signed "on Gorbachev's initiative," the first such treaty in the history of the two countries' relations. This treaty, with a term of twenty-five years, laid the groundwork for "enriching" and developing their relations in all areas, including the military, deepening the economic integration of the socialist countries, and assuring the "interaction" of Cuba and the Soviet Union in the international arena.[65]

For appearances' sake, everything seemed ideal in Cuba, but the reality was something else entirely. The Soviet Union could no longer increase its aid or even maintain it at the same level because of its own internal economic decay. Moreover, powerful Soviet parliamentary and media sectors were opposed to this unequal relationship, preponderantly favoring Cuba, in the present circumstance of their own economic crisis.

For the first time Soviet publications criticized relations with Cuba. *Pravda*, the official party newspaper, complained in an editorial about the subsidized prices in trade with Cuba and commented that their relations should be placed on a reciprocal basis. The daily *Izvestia* criticized Cuba for accumulating a foreign debt to the Soviet Union that had risen to 25 billion rubles, not counting the donations of economic and military aid, or the subsidies of the sugar price. The weekly *Moscow News* described Cuba as an "impoverished police state" and wrote that "a change is underway" from "social apathy to a passive and, until now, well hidden discontent." Other papers criticized the Cuban leadership for not following in the footsteps of the "opening," political pluralism and market economy that were being advanced in the Soviet Union.[66]

For the first time in thirty years of close and cordial relations, the Cuban government canceled the distribution of the Soviet publications *Moscow News* and *Sputnik*. In a long editorial *Granma* explained that the Cuban leadership "found itself obliged to reflect on the content of some of the many Soviet pub-lications that circulate in the country," whose points of view in respect to the construction of Soviet socialism were based on interpretations "almost always controversial if not substantially divergent from the criteria and essential ori-entation of our own party," and that the government considered reading them "harmful" to the Cuban people.[67]

A variety of negative factors piled up between Havana and Moscow. In a speech on July 26, 1989, in Camagüey, Castro painted a somber picture but reaffirmed his readiness to fight: "If tomorrow, or on any future day, we awaken to the news that a great civil strife has broken out in the Soviet Union, or even if we awaken to the news that the Soviet Union has disintegrated, some-thing we hope never comes to pass, even under these circumstances Cuba and the Cuban Revolution will keep on fighting and keep on resisting." Castro knew that his strongest ally was a time bomb that would explode sooner or later, and that Cuba would come out of this explosion battered. Two years later it exploded.

DRACULA'S KISS

Gorbachev continued to be praised in the West. He was awarded the Nobel Peace Prize, an outstanding international distinction that meant nothing to the Soviet people or to the Soviet congress, which simply took note of the fact and applauded for thirty seconds. There was bitterness. Yelena Bonner, the widow of Nobel Prize winner Andrei Sakharov, commented, "The blindness of the West to the tragedies our country has experienced in the five years of perestroika led by Gorbachev is alarming." One journalist put his finger on the open sore when he asked Gorbachev, "What do you feel, receiving a prize traditionally given to anti-Communists like Sakharov and Lech Walesa?" Gorbachev did not answer.[68]

The leaders of the Western powers were aware of the serious difficulties Gorbachev was enduring and watched with great concern as his power weak-ened. They applauded the changes he made but demanded greater advances toward a market economy before they would give him the economic aid he asked for and urgently needed. President Bush and British Prime Minister Margaret Thatcher were the most obstinate. Bush treated the high cost of the Soviet defense budget and the millions in "subsidies" that the Soviet Union gave Cuba as obstacles to United States aid. German Chancellor Helmut Kohl offered aid, knowing that reunification of his country depended in large measure on Gorbachev. Gorbachev, politically weakened, accepted, although he wanted Germany neutral and outside the NATO alliance (the West wanted Germany in NATO).

This absence of economic aid for the Soviet Union contrasted sharply with the generous verbal support the West gave Gorbachev. Invitations were sent to their gatherings, honors were lavished on him, and overblown declarations were made about his contribution to the relaxation of world tensions and to the new climate of understanding between the two "formerly antagonistic" blocs. According to the *New York Times*, these grandiose affirmations were to show Gorbachev's critics in the Soviet Union that his conciliatory policies brought good results and "to make it easier" for him to accept a united Germany "within NATO."[69] Gorbachev walked out of these meetings with the great powers with empty hands.

Few could imagine a Soviet political-military alliance with the United States. But such a condition did happen when Iraq invaded Kuwait in August 1990 and Bush assumed the leadership of its "liberation" and began to mount a massive military response to its leader, Saddam Hussein. Bush asked his NATO allies and his new friend "to resist the aggression," free Kuwait, and force Hussein (whom he compared to Hitler) to withdraw his troops. The real objective was to protect the rich oil fields of the Middle East, vital to the Western powers and Japan. Bush decided to insure control of the area though it cost a war. This was how the people in the United States understood it. Large demonstrations in front of the White House showed signs proclaiming: "No Blood for Oil!"

The alliance of the Soviet Union with the West caused profound unease in traditionalist and hard-line sectors of the Soviet leadership. In spite of the soft tone of Gorbachev's support, his gesture was a virtual surrender. He crossed the line that had divided the two politico-military blocs for more than fifty years and broke world equilibrium. "For the first time since the Second World War, we are acting as virtual allies," commented the daily *Izvestia*.[70]

This alliance, and the speed with which the United Nations Security Council supported the United States' use of force against Iraq, were a victory for United States diplomacy, as well as evidence of the weakening of the Soviet colossus in the international arena. It was no longer a contender, much less a threat. The United States was free to exercise its worldwide hegemonic power, one of the fears expressed time and again by Fidel.

The Soviet Union voted with the Western powers in favor of the Security Council resolutions against Iraq presented by the United States. Cuba, a non-permanent Latin America member (the other was Colombia) either abstained or voted no. The final resolution, to authorize the use of "all necessary measures" if Iraq did not withdraw its troops before January 15, 1991, was an ultimatum and a declaration of war. Cuba and Yemen voted against it, and China abstained. The United Nations, created in the name of peace, for the first time declared war.

Castro called Iraq's invasion of Kuwait "a colossal political mistake" and a "flagrant violation of international law." Cuban Chancellor Isidoro Malmierca went to Baghdad to convince Saddam to withdraw his troops and warn him that the United States would wage a "sophisticated and technical war with a minimal loss of American life" and that it had pulled together a "colossal" joint military and political force. Cuba explained this situation to several countries and Iraq "with great frankness and clarity," Castro declared. Iraq did not withdraw, and "the United States takes very good advantage of Iraq's mistakes," he noted.[71]

This was a United States war from start to finish. It was short and brutal, but it was an incomplete victory. When Bush was voted out of the White House, Saddam Hussein, whom he had sworn to oust, was still in power, left with a third of his troops and reorganizing Iraq to withstand the sanctions imposed by the United Nations at the United States' request. "I wonder who won," mused former British Prime Minister Margaret Thatcher five years later.[72]

REQUIEM FOR THE SOVIET UNION

A few olive branches could not wipe out more than seventy years of Marxist-Leninist doctrine, the epicenter of Communism, notable scientific and cultural triumphs, the initiator of the conquest of space (the first satellite and the first cosmonaut were Soviet), the second-greatest world superpower and its anti-imperialist and anticapitalist banners, which kept alive the Soviet people's consciousness of the political and military rivalries, contradictions, and antagonisms with the United States, its greatest enemy. The Soviet Union fell apart. Such was the legacy of glasnost and perestroika.

In the four years of the tortuous perestroika process, the chaotic political scene was shaken by the struggle for power between Gorbachev and Boris Yeltsin, full of their mutual aversion, in which the stability and future of the Communist superpower were at stake. In August 1991, in a coup against Gorbachev, he was arrested and held in his dacha in Foros, Crimea, by order of the self-appointed State Emergency Committee presided over by Prime

Minister Gennadi Yakolev and composed of the highest government officials. Yeltsin was opposed to this coup and defended the constitutional process. His enormous figure, on a truck surrounded by people and Soviet flags, gave the world a shock. Yeltsin led the defense of constitutionality. His prestige within and outside the country grew like wildfire.

The Cuban leadership received word of the Moscow coup as they were celebrating the conclusion of the successful Eleventh Pan-American Games. Havana was in a party mood since its athletes had just won 140 gold medals, and the people were applauding their *Comandante*. In a statement published in the daily *Granma* on August 21, the government expressed its "deep concern," warned of the "incalculable consequences" that there might be for the Soviet people and the rest of the world from any internal conflict in this "multinational country, endowed with powerful nuclear arms," and gave voice to its "fervent desire" that "this great country" should be able to overcome its difficulties in peace, remain unified, and "exercise the international influence it earned as an indispensable counterweight to those who wanted to apply an absolute and hegemonic predominance to the world." The statement went on, "Yankee imperialism, the international policeman that aspires to own the world, has no right to take advantage of this unhappy situation."

Gorbachev returned to Moscow, but Yeltsin was the hero. This ridiculous episode was over, but the chemistry of the country was changed for good. A flood of resignations, arrests, firings, and suicides by those who had supported the coup began at once. The KGB—the secret police—was dismantled (Yeltsin ordered its archives sealed, as well as those of the Interior Ministry and the military), and the CPSU was in agony as the result of mass desertions and paralysis; its activities were prohibited, its headquarters were closed or confiscated by governments of localities and republics, its archives were sealed to prevent the destruction of documents, its newspapers were closed, and a good number of its prominent members were accused and brought up on charges of corruption. Gorbachev's resignation from the post of secretary general of the CPSU, which was urged by Yeltsin, and the resignation of the rest of the Party's leadership, at Gorbachev's request, were the coup de grace. The CPSU, the Soviet regime's backbone, ceased to exist.

The people, euphoric at the disappearance of the "dictatorship" of the party, started to tear down statues of Lenin, the venerable author of the Bolshevik Revolution, creator of the first Communist nation in the world, father of the fatherland, and glory of the Soviet people. These acts of vandalism occurred throughout the country.

Castro called such events inconceivable. They were, he remarked, a lust to destroy the history of the country, deny its values and merits. They ignored the contributions of socialism and the Marxist-Leninist ideas that had given birth to the October Revolution, "one of the greatest events of this century," and denied its leadership in the worldwide struggle of the workers' movement and the societal gains made, in wages and in every other area. It ignored its great influence in international affairs, such as the defeat of fascism, the liberation movements in the former colonies, the disappearance of colonialism, and the liberation struggles of the peoples of all continents. Socialism, he emphasized, had converted the Soviet Union, a poor and backward country, into the second-largest world power. He pointed out the social, military, and scientific achievements, the conquest of space, and its contributions to world culture.[73]

The consequences of the August coup were devastating. One after another, the Soviet republics proclaimed their independence. Yeltsin administered the death blow to Soviet unity on December 8, 1991, when as president of Russia he signed the Commonwealth of Independent States Treaty (CIS) with the presidents of the Ukraine and Belarus republics. Gorbachev denounced the treaty as "illegal and dangerous." His own proposal to create a Union of Sovereign Socialist Republics, led by the Kremlin, was tossed in the trash. Gorbachev warned that the Soviet congress had to ratify this treaty, and he tried to convene it. But the Russian parliament ratified it (188 to 6) and at the same time annulled the 1922 treaty that had first formed the Soviet Union. The Soviet congress decided not to convene.

The dismantling of the Soviet state—a cruel and pathetic process—left Gorbachev with nothing to do, without power, and without a country. Yeltsin, as president of a powerful Russia, nationalized the enormous resources of this immense nation, suspended the Russian contribution to the support of the Soviet government, and issued decrees to put national institutions under Russian control, including eight ministries that the state could no longer maintain for lack of funds. He took possession of the Kremlin, the president's office (he changed the locks so that Gorbachev would be unable to gain access), the ministries of foreign relations and the interior, the KGB, the congress, and all the cash funds of the central government. Analysts called this move another coup d'état against Gorbachev. Yeltsin left the ministry of defense and the atomic power agency under the control of the Supreme Soviet.

On December 21 the CIS spread to the Muslim republics. It was now composed of ten of the fifteen Soviet republics. The three Baltic states, Georgia, and Azerbaijan maintained their complete independence. The CIS replaced the Soviet Union, with Russia at the head, and Boris Yeltsin was leading Russia, with his thumb on the nuclear "button." Russia took the place of the Soviet Union in the United Nations Security Council, including the right to a veto, and the former Soviet republics joined the world organization as independent states.

On December 25, Christmas in the Christian world, the red flag with the hammer and sickle was lowered from the Kremlin dome and the Russian tricolor was raised. With this ceremony, broadcast to the world on CNN, the Soviet Union disappeared from the planet. The following day Gorbachev— pressured by Yeltsin—resigned in a modest ceremony. Yeltsin did not attend because Gorbachev's farewell speech was not to his liking.

From the White House on the other side of the Atlantic, President Bush announced to the nation and to the world this extraordinary development. In a gesture of triumph, he thanked the people of the United States for their help in bringing down the Soviet empire and the Communist world, in ending the Cold War, in the triumph of the West, the free world, democracy, the United States and—though he did not say so—his own. His State of the Union address to Congress in January 1992 was a declaration of victory. Congress reverberated with applause.

The world superpower disappeared. It became a series of independent nations, divided by borders, conflicts, rivalries, and suspicions, with broken economies and enormous domestic problems, some of them with civil wars and fierce struggles for power and wealth—the discreet charm of capitalism—entering the mendicant underdeveloped world.

What Castro had foreseen and feared came to pass. Castro described the Soviet collapse as "an incredible case of self-destruction" for which he blamed its leaders. "Everything they did," he declared, "led to its destruction, the phenomena and tendencies they unleashed led to it. We saw it from the beginning, or very close to the beginning." He remarked that, although Gorbachev had not wanted the dissolution of the Soviet Union—he was trying to improve socialism—he bore the major responsibility for these events.[74]

"Imperialism could not have destroyed the Soviet Union if the Soviets had not destroyed it first," declared Castro. He added that the United States and its allies had helped to destroy socialism and the Soviet Union "by egging on the reactionary forces there." In the West, he added, even the terminology was changed, so that those who wanted to defend the Soviet Union, socialism, and Communism could be termed "conservatives" and those who wanted capitalism and even the disappearance of the Soviet Union could be called "progressive" and "leftist" forces. "All these concepts have deliberately been turned inside out. Western propaganda encouraged this process because the West wanted to force the Soviet Union to its knees. Imperialism did all this, and now it was afraid of what might happen and the possible consequences of this disintegration," he noted.[75]

The world followed the fall of the Soviet colossus with fascination but also with great concern. Its disappearance meant the end of the East-West military standoff, the so-called Cold War, but it also meant the end of a two-power world. The United States remained standing to dominate the world, with Bush at its helm preaching the New World Order (without bothering to explain what that was). "A lone superpower throws the world off balance. It creates the conditions for the hegemony of one single country. It is the worst thing that can happen to the world," declared Castro in an interview with ABC television news anchor Diane Sawyer in Havana, in February 1993. He added, "The hegemonic superpower will not be able to control . . . the world's problems with artillery fire."[76]

BLOWS FROM THE EMPIRE

Ronald Reagan's departure from the White House in January 1989 was a relief to Cuba. The new head of state, George Bush, and his much-hyped "pragmatism" hinted at a favorable change. But he turned out to be worse than Reagan. He turned the economic, commercial, and financial embargo of Cuba into a worldwide blockade, sharpened the psychological warfare, and continued the frenetic military maneuvers in the Caribbean, whose message was a threat to invade the island. In May 1990 Ocean Venture and Solid Shield were carried out simultaneously. The military also carried out exercises at Guantanamo.

Bush was convinced that the winds of perestroika would come to Cuba and that with his "help" the Cuban regime would fall apart and he would get to watch Castro's head roll. In response to Solid Shield, Cuba carried out its own military maneuvers called Cuban Shield, with the deployment of fighter aircraft, a concentration of troops surrounding Guantanamo, and the mobilization of the reserves. If the United States invaded Cuba, warned Castro, "rivers of blood will flow."[77]

Bush maintained his campaign of denigrating Cuba and Castro, continued the "vendetta" of accusations of violations of human rights with even greater determination, and imposed greater restrictions on United States citizens traveling to the island and on Cubans entering the United States, extending them even to members of Cuba's government.

In his annual speech on July 26, 1989, at Camagüey, Castro denounced Bush's aggressive acts. "Never," he declared, "has a United States government, not even Ronald Reagan's, exhibited so triumphalist an attitude. Never has the United States been so threatening as now." He attributed this United States euphoria to Bush's conviction that socialism was on its "death bed."

CHRIST TURNS HIS BACK

The eruption of the worst corruption scandal in the history of the Cuban Revolution, on June 14, 1989, shook the country down to its foundations. The cast of the scandal was composed of elite officers of the armed forces and the ministry of the interior. A sobering statement from the ministry of the revolutionary armed forces, headed by Raúl Castro—the second-most powerful person in the Cuban hierarchy—published in *Granma* stated that it was fulfilling its "unpleasant duty" of reporting the arrest of Divisional General Arnaldo Ochoa Sánchez, accused of serious acts of corruption. "Whatever the merits of any comrade may have been," it added, "the Party and the Revolutionary Armed Forces absolutely could not allow impunity to those who, putting aside the principles of the Revolution, commit serious transgressions against morality and the socialist laws."

Two days later a long editorial in *Granma* reported the arrests of Brigadier General Patricio de la Guardia Font; his twin brother, Colonel Antonio de la Guardia Font; Ochoa's assistant, Captain Jorge Martínez Valdés; an official of the ministry of the interior, Major Amado Padrón Trujillo; and other military officers of lower rank (including one woman), who were all accused of drug trafficking, illicit enrichment, and corruption. The investigators, the paper reported, found no evidence that the arrested officers were involved in any counterrevolutionary activity. It added, "The inexorable weight of justice will fall on them." At that point no connection had been made between Ochoa's arrest and that of the de la Guardia brothers.

The arrest of General Ochoa was a scandal in itself. *Time* compared it to what might have happened in the United States if General Dwight Eisenhower had been arrested. Ochoa was a "Hero of the Republic of Cuba"—a rare honor—for his outstanding performance in international missions (Venezuela was mentioned for the first time in this context) and as commander of the victorious Cuban troops in Ethiopia and Angola. Ochoa was a former fighter in the Sierra Maestra, a member of the central committee, and a deputy to the national assembly, respected by the military hierarchy and admired by the people. He was a friend to Fidel and Raúl. Ochoa was accused of corruption, smuggling marble, diamonds, and precious woods, and dealing on the black market.

Colonel Tony de la Guardia, a special superagent, was respected and enjoyed the friendship of Fidel and Raúl. As Director of the MC Department—responsible for the highly-secret commercial operations that allowed Cuba to thumb its nose at the United States embargo—he traveled freely and carried out business deals of all kinds with very little or no supervision. In May he was dismissed from the MC directorate.

Around the same time, Diócles Torralba, minister of transportation and vice president of the council of ministers, was also arrested, charged with immoral, dissipated, and corrupt conduct—*la dolce vita*, he was sentenced to twenty years in prison. *Granma* claimed that this arrest had nothing to do with Ochoa's, which it described as much more serious and complex. Later General José Abrantes, the minister of the interior, was dismissed and then arrested along with three officials from the ministry, and sentenced to twenty years in prison, where he died of a heart attack in January 1991. "Within less than twenty-four hours the closest circle of officers, connected by family ties, friendship, and common experiences, comes crashing down."[78] They were the officers closest to Castro.

Cuba had opened a Pandora's box without knowing the consequences. "We knew the problem was not a simple one; we knew what happens when a person of this kind must be arrested and tried; we knew what sort of campaign would be unleashed against us," Castro declared. He decided to face the facts, without imagining what might be coming.

The investigations that led to the arrest of the fourteen officers and the testimony in their trials confirmed their activities in the drug traffic and brought to light the involvement of Pablo Escobar, the head of the Medellín cartel and the drug trafficker most wanted by the Colombian and the United States authorities. The connection with Escobar was through Captain Martínez Valdés, Ochoa's assistant, who traveled clandestinely to Colombia using a false Colombian passport. Martínez testified at the trial that Escobar was not interested in money laundering but in being able to count on a Cuban airport, laboratories, and "other things." These other things were ten ground-to-air rocket launchers, an airplane kept in readiness for him, and the construction of a cocaine-processing factory. Major Amado Padrón argued that these "things" were not possible in Cuba.

Between January 1987 and April 1989 there were nineteen "operations," fifteen of them successful. Six tons of cocaine were smuggled into the United States at a profit of $3.4 million. The airplanes took off from Colombia and landed at a military airfield in Varadero. From there the drugs were transported to the Florida keys in fast boats under the command of Marielitos (Cubans who had emigrated to the United States in the Mariel exodus in 1980). In negotiations with the Colombian and Mexican capos, the Cuban officers acted as "envoys" of their government, without revealing the identities of their "bosses." This ambiguity compromised the Cuban government and Fidel and Raúl Castro personally.

The scandal was devastating for Cuba given the importance of the officers implicated and the fact that, since the beginning of the 1980s, Castro had repeatedly, roundly, and vigorously rejected as "calumnies" the United States accusations that Cuban government officials were involved in drug trafficking. He called the charges "infamous propaganda riddled with falsehoods and lies" and described the United States as "a nation in decadence, incapable of overcoming the internal consumption of stupefactants."[79]

"Our first reaction, since we have become accustomed to hearing all sorts of lies, infamies, and calumnies over thirty years, is that this was simply one more invention . . . on the part of the United States, and we paid no particular attention," Castro explained. But a cable from the AP news service on March 6, 1989, put him on his guard because its information coincided with rumors about the drug lords' claims, which friends brought him "by various means" from Colombia.[80] These "means" were members of the guerilla movement M-19.[81]

The cable referred to two Cuban exiles in Miami, Reynaldo Ruíz and his 24-year-old son Rubén, a pilot; both had been arrested by the DEA and charged with drug trafficking. At their trial they pled guilty to transporting more than a ton of cocaine to the United States by way of Cuba, with the help of Cuban officials and officers. They testified that they had many "high level" contacts in Cuba, and they bragged of smoking tobacco from Castro's personal stash. This information, noted the cable, came from the office of the Attorney General in Miami.[82]

Castro ordered the minister of the interior, General Abrantes, to investigate this matter. He had become aware that the United States intelligence services had a great deal of information from as early as mid-1987 about such operations, and that they knew the names of two of the Cuban military officers (one of whom was Tony de la Guardia).

Washington kept this information secret as it prepared to spring on the world a spectacular coup. The plan was to "kidnap" General Abrantes in international waters and take him to a supposed meeting with the drug kingpins. It would be a combined operation by the CIA, the DEA, the Defense Information Agency (DIA), the air force, and the navy, using combat aircraft, AWACS, destroyers, and submarines. The plan did not succeed, however, since the Cuban government revealed the scandal before the United States could act. Besides, a person of Abrantes's standing would not attend a meeting with drug traffickers.[83]

The reports in the Western media on the Ochoa case were biased against Cuba, with constant references to the Havana Cartel, the Cuban Connection, and Castrogate, placing Castro inside the international drug ring. One of the most devastating analyses of this scandal was written by Jean-François Fogel, the former Agence France Presse correspondent in Cuba, in his book, *The End of the Century in Havana* (1992). The United States Congress, the Departments of State and Justice, the Miami anti-Castroites, the dissident Huber Matos and the deserter Rafael del Pino (a former Brigadier General), both living in exile in the United States, all accused the Cuban government, namely Raúl Castro, of drug trafficking. They all claimed that the arrests of the military officers were "purges" to rid Castro of potential rivals, especially Ochoa, asserting that they favored perestroika.

The information war was waged by the powerful United States media and a score of anti-Castro broadcasters in Florida, who also incited the Cuban people to rebel against the government. United States officials claimed that events in Cuba corroborated Washington's old accusations to the effect that high-ranking Cuban officials were involved in the drug trade. A cable from the Spanish-language news agency EFE reported that the suspicions and reports made to Congress by high United States officials had been "confirmed" by two Cuban deserters.[84] The cable was referring to Oscar Valdés, the brother of the former minister of the interior Ramiro Valdés, and Manuel Beúnza, a former Cuban intelligence agent. During testimony before the United States Congress, they accused Raúl Castro of having "organized" the drug traffic in Cuba and the Cuban Embassy in Colombia of being a central connection for the drug lords between 1975 and 1980 (when Fernando Ravelo was ambassador). They also alleged that he had been the central connection for the drug lords. When members of Congress asked for proof of Fidel and Raúl Castro's connection to the drug traffickers, they admitted that "at the moment there is nothing specific."[85]

The Cuban government called this campaign an infamous downpour of accusations and calumnies, difficult to disprove, since Cuba did not have the means to confront the powerful international communications network controlled by the United States. Cuba expelled the Reuters correspondent, the thirty-nine-year-old Frenchman Gilles Trequesser, for transmitting false information. He was taken from his home at dawn and put on a Cuban Airlines flight to Toronto.

The fourteen military officers were tried by a revolutionary armed forces court of honor—made up of forty-four division and brigadier generals and two rear admirals—and later by a three-person military court. But the final word on their sentences came from the council of state, the highest governing body with twenty-nine members, and presided over by Castro. The trials were closed to the national and international press, international observers (several institutions had asked to attend), and the public. Only military officers and the relatives of the accused were allowed to attend. The trial, which the government called summary, took less than a month. Every night, a two-hour edited videotape of the trial was aired on television. The government declared that the tape included the entire proceedings, except matters of morality that could affect innocent persons, or testimony that was too scandalous or might potentially damage Cuba's foreign policies, and which were not decisive factors for the verdicts that had to be passed.[86]

Ochoa, the brightest star in the Cuban military constellation, was the first to be questioned. He confessed his connection with the drug trade since the end of 1987. His intention, however, was not to traffic through Cuba, but to insert himself in the existing network between Colombia and Mexico, make "big deals and get large quantities of money" for "a third party" to invest in Cuban tourism and help Cuba. The drug traffic, he attested, was no more than an incidental consequence. He admitted to authorizing Martínez's trips to Colombia and knowing about the false Colombian passport. "I permitted all of it," he confessed. Several officers testified against him regarding the contraband and the black market. Ochoa pleaded guilty to all charges.[87]

On the television screen he looked profoundly troubled as he made a pathetic statement accepting the seriousness of his crime, his "betrayal" of the Motherland, the Revolution, and Fidel. He confessed to all the charges of which he stood accused and explicitly denied the statements made outside the country about political motives for the trial. "It was to be expected that the enemy would try to exploit this. Nothing could be further from the truth than assigning political motives to my actions." He also denied that Fidel and Raúl Castro were implicated in the drug trade, as was charged outside the country. He declared that he alone was responsible. "I despise myself. . . . A traitor pays for his treason with his life. . . . If my sentence is that I will be shot, my last thought will be for Fidel and for our great Revolution, which he gave to our people."[88]

The second to be tried was Colonel Tony de la Guardia, who admitted to having begun the drug-trafficking operations in 1987 or the end of 1986. "How many officers knew of this business?" asked the prosecutor. "Those who are arrested here," he replied. The prosecutor asked about the meetings of Cubans with Colombian, Mexican, and United States traffickers. He testified that he knew of them but did not participate. The prosecutor asked if he knew that Martínez had traveled to Colombia with a false passport, to which he answered yes. He explained that he did not know the four Colombian drug lords with whom Martínez met. "The only Colombian I met with is Ramiro Lucio." This avowal caused a storm in Colombia and the M-19 guerrilla movement—Lucio was their political spokesman—which was negotiating its return to civilian life with the Colombian government. The Colombian press headlined this information about Lucio to confirm the supposed connections between the guerrillas and the drug lords. United States Ambassador Lewis Tambs had already coined the term "narcoguerrilla." Lucio claimed that the business with Cuba was legitimate trade, that the ministry of defense was informed of his relations with Cuba, and that Tony de la Guardia was the person in the Cuban ministry of the interior who had given permission. Lucio complained that he was one of the most investigated people in Colombia, since his telephones had been tapped and his bank accounts watched for ten years. "I do not know what political intrigue is behind all this. It could be the dark desire to connect M-19 with the dirty business of drug trafficking."[89]

De la Guardia accepted all charges brought against him and admitted that he was the "main person responsible," that none of his superiors knew about his drug activities. "I am completely conscious of how great a mistake I have made, of the damage I have done to Fidel, to the Revolution, to my comrades, my institution, my children—irreparable damage," he stated. The foreign press found his testimony "vacillating" and noted that he did not mention his immediate superior, "to whom he had given part of the drug money," which cast some doubts on the Cuban leadership's knowledge of such activities. "It seemed that he was trying to cover for someone," suggested one diplomat in Havana.[90]

The court of honor and the military court found the officers guilty of treason and ordered them stripped of rank and duties and dishonorably discharged from the army. Former General Ochoa, the former Colonel Tony de la Guardia, former Captain Martínez Valdés and former Major Padrón Trujillo were sentenced to death by firing squad. The others, including the former captain in the ministry of the interior, Rosa María Abierno, were sentenced to thirty, twenty-five, and ten years of prison, according to the seriousness of their crimes. Each member of the council of state, presided over by Castro, corroborated the sentences in brief and emotion-laden statements.

In a long speech delivered at the end of the council of state, Castro stated that the accused had compromised the prestige and security of the state and had dealt a blow to the principles, the dignity, and the honor of the Cuban Revolution. It was "high treason," he noted, since they sold out the country, putting it at serious risk, undermined the morale and prestige of the Revolution, and weakened it in every way. He declared, "The punishment must be exemplary and the sentence the most severe possible."[91]

Demands on Cuba, asking clemency for those condemned to death, and criticisms of the trials and the sentences came from the United States administration and Congress, other governments, Pope John Paul II, politicians, Latin American intellectuals and professionals, and human-rights organizations. Some accused the Cuban government of having manipulated the trials; others claimed that the defense worked not to disprove the charges but to sink the accused even deeper. The defense was in fact poor and extremely limited. Americas Watch stated that the trials of the four who were sentenced to death were "flagrant violations of due process" and questioned how minister of defense Raúl Castro, to whom the accused reported, could have served as a witness. It demanded a "political" decision to commute the sentences.[92]

The American press, international news agencies, Miami anti-Castroites, and "dissidents" in Cuba discounted the confessions of the accused admitting their guilt. They claimed that Ochoa had been brought into court drugged. Ochoa called such accusations calumnies and "shameless lies of imperialism."[93]

In spite of the international pressures, the four officers were shot at dawn on July 13. The following day, in a sober note in *Granma*, the government announced the executions. The allegations by the foreign press, human-rights organizations and activists, anti-Castroites, deserters, and "dissidents" about the manipulation of the trials and the political motives for eliminating Ochoa continued and were played up by the media after the executions. Several "dissidents" and activists were arrested in Cuba and accused of spreading false information and denigrating the trials.

Tony de la Guardia's wife told the foreign press that Castro betrayed them, since he had told them the Revolution had to be saved and led them to believe that they would not get the maximum sentence if they collaborated. Patricio de la Guardia made the same claim in a twenty-page document dated in October 1991, which he managed to smuggle out of prison (addressed to Osmany Cienfuegos and Roberto Robaina, members of the Cuban Communist Party Politburo). The Parisian daily *Le Monde* published some fragments in 1992 in which Patricio claimed that his brother Tony had confessed to having carried out four drug-trafficking operations and personally given $3 million to Minister of the Interior General Abrantes. He also noted that he was "as sure as can be" that Tony was authorized to carry out the clandestine operations for which he was shot. He added that the Cuban government was implicated in "a multitude of illegal activities" and named prominent government figures who were involved in these matters. He did not mention Fidel or Raúl Castro, but *Le Monde* noted that "the text leaves no doubt" about their role in this traffic, whose purpose was to obtain hard currency for the country. De la Guardia mentioned psychological tortures to which he had been submitted and reported that the officer assigned to his defense did not even inquire about his military career and spoke with him for only thirty minutes before the trial.[94] No member of the media mentioned that he had made exactly opposite statements during the trial.[95]

After this devastating scandal Castro proposed to the United States that the two countries carry out joint operations against the drug traffic in the Caribbean. International news agencies reported that the State Department reacted "coldly" to this proposal but that Representative Charles Rangel, the Democrat who chaired the House Select Committee on Narcotics Abuse and Control, criticized Bush's negative reaction as "ridiculous." He accused Bush of "playing at anti-Communist politics" and of putting the success of the war against drugs at risk.[96] Former *New York Times* Latin America correspondent Tad Szulc remarked that for reasons of national interest, Bush ought to have accepted Castro's offer instead of answering him with tired legalisms.

In spite of the drug scandal, the tenacious campaign to discredit the Revolution and Castro, and the "vendetta" on the human-rights theme, Cuba gained some victories in the international arena. In October 1989, two months after the executions, the World Health Organization (WHO) presented Castro with the Health for All Medal in recognition of Cuba's work in this field both at home and abroad. And in spite of pressure from Washington, Cuba was elected a member of the United Nations Security Council (1990–1992) with the highest vote total ever recorded, 146 out of 156 possible votes (for thirty years the United States had prevented this outcome). Cuba was also reelected to the Food and Agriculture Organization Council and to the United Nations Human Rights Commission in Geneva (and reelected in 1992).

Time magazine published an opinion poll sponsored by the State Department in March 1990 that indicated that if elections were held in Cuba then, not only would the Communist Party win, but so would Castro.[97]

Castro also continued to receive emotional demonstrations of support when he attended the ceremonies accompanying changes of government in Latin America. These were minisummits of presidents attended by representatives of the United States government. Again and again national and foreign media headlines proclaimed, "Fidel Steals the Show," "Fidel is the Star," "Fidel Again Center of Attention."

At the United Nations Conference on Environment and Development in Río de Janeiro in 1992, thirty-three years after the triumph of the revolution, and attended by President Bush, Castro received a memorable standing ovation from the thousands of participants and demonstrations of admiration and affection by the Brazilian people. In 1994 in South Africa, when Nelson Mandela was sworn in, Castro was housed and praised by the people and the thousands invited to the ceremony. The press reported that members of the Clinton administration did not conceal their empathy with Castro, that some even greeted him warmly and had their pictures taken with him.

THE CRISIS OF THE EMBASSIES

In July 1990 Havana was caught in another serious diplomatic crisis when Cubans—men, women, and children—pressed into the embassies of Czechoslovakia (where the Communist regime had already fallen), Canada, and various European countries including Spain. The Cuban government accused the United States of instigating this crisis, the fruit of Bush's "feverish obsession" with Cuba. The Cuban government held Jan Domok, the Czech chargé d'affaires, responsible for this incident, and proved that officials of the United States Interests Section and the West German Embassy were participating in the actions. As on earlier occasions, Cuba announced that it would not negotiate with the people barricaded in the embassies and demanded that they leave the premises "unconditionally"; it promised not to exercise reprisals. A few days later the people came out.

The conflict with the Spanish Embassy, however, was long and thorny, lasting fifty days and causing a serious confrontation between Madrid and Havana. There was a fiery exchange of insults between the Cuban authorities and

Spanish Chancellor Francisco Fernández Ordóñez, a raid of the Spanish diplomatic headquarters by Cuban forces (they captured one asylum seeker), protests by the Spanish government against this attack (the Cuban government apologized), the announcement by the Spanish chancellor that the doors of the embassy would remain open to anyone who wanted to seek asylum, and the "indefinite suspension" of Spain's aid to Cuba (around $2.5 million a year).

Castro responded angrily to these announcements. He declared that he "renounced" Spanish aid, which he once termed pyrrhic, and laughed at the chancellor's allegations, which he dismissed as "the responses of an anguished colonial administrator," pointing to the chancellor's "scandalous lack of understanding of matters of international law." He also accused him of wanting to cause "a second Mariel." The infuriated chancellor asked the European Economic Community to suspend aid to Cuba.

On July 26, 1990, the thirty-seventh anniversary of the attack on the Moncada Barracks, Castro dedicated a large part of his three-hour speech to the current crisis, which he described as "a true diplomatic war" and a provocation "planned" by the United States, to which Spain and other European countries lent themselves. He turned the tables on the Europeans, asking them to open an office in Havana for granting entry visas to their countries for Cubans who wanted to leave the island. Castro asked the United States to send ships if it wanted to take in the people who said they were persecuted in Cuba, so that they could leave. He warned that he would not allow those who entered the embassies illegally to leave the country, nor would he accept the pressures from their governments to allow them to leave, since to do so would be acceptance of interference in Cuba's internal affairs. He saved another blow for Spain: he referred to the quinquicentennial of Columbus's "discovery" of America, a pompous celebration to which Spain was allocating millions of dollars, as "the commemoration of the genocide and extermination of those indigenous to the New Continent."

As on previous occasions, the refugees voluntarily left the Spanish Embassy and tensions lifted. Analysts said that Castro put Felipe González's socialist government "up against the wall" by embarrassing Spain, whose ties to Cuba (its last colony in the hemisphere) had remained strong even under Franco's dictatorship, making it appear that Spain was collaborating in a conspiracy against Cuba planned by Washington.

It was obvious that Castro's proposal (more like a challenge) that the European countries open visa offices in Havana fell on deaf ears. None was ready to open its doors to such legal immigration. They continued to give "political asylum" to anyone who made it to their countries (sometimes taking advantage of airlines bearing them to other destinations), turning a blind eye to the fact that, in most cases, the Cubans themselves admitted that they had not been persecuted by the Cuban government.

CHANGING TIMES

On July 26, 1989, during that year's anniversary celebration of the attack on the Moncada Barracks in Camagüey, Castro warned that Soviet aid might dwindle and that austerity and self-sufficiency were necessary. The people must make an effort to produce their own necessities. "If the Soviet oil shipments diminish," he explained, "or if they were to be canceled, Cuba will continue to be socialist, even if we have to return to the oxcart."[98] And Cuba did.

This was the year when the Communist regimes of Eastern Europe began to fall, the Soviet economy was teetering, and Cuban trade with these markets— 85 percent of its total (77 percent with the Soviet Union)—was disappearing. As the Soviet economy was decentralized, many businesses stopped selling to Cuba, others required cash payments, the "clearing" account with Moscow ended, and the oil subsidies dropped. Another casualty for Cuba was the loss of revenues from the resale of excess Soviet oil to other countries—an important agreement between both countries, which represented somewhere between $200 million to $300 million a year.[99] Cuba was left without oil, capital, or credit. Trade with the socialist world was reduced to a minimum—COMECON decided that Cuba was to pay cash for all transactions—and its foreign debt to the Soviet Union and the European banks was enormous. Furthermore, Cuba was under brutal economic aggression from the United States.

Most of Cuban industry had been developed with Soviet-bloc technology, and its economy was integrated with those of the COMECON countries (Cuba was a member), to which it exported the tropical products they wanted. To supply these markets, Cuba developed the sugar and citrus industries at the expense of diversification, an error it later recognized. Trade with the socialist countries, intended to lessen trade in the capitalist arena, actually involved dependency, greater transportation costs, and inferior quality. But no other option was left by the United States blockade. Without markets and no longer receiving the products of primary necessity that those markets exported, the raw materials necessary to its industries, and the oil the country needed, Cuba was more exposed than ever to the rigors of the blockade.[100]

In August 1990, a year and a half before the collapse of the Soviet Union, the Cuban government decreed a Special Period in Time of Peace in preparation for what it called Option Zero: no oil. It imposed great restrictions on the consumption of petroleum fuels and electrical energy. It decreed daily rationing. The mechanization of Cuba—one of the successes of the Revolution—made the lack of oil much more traumatic. This situation forced the country to scale back or suspend important development plans in order to take care of its priorities: food programs and the development of biotechnology (Cuba was one of the world leaders in the field), the pharmaceutical industry, and tourism— important sources of foreign currency. Many businesses closed and industrial projects, including oil exploration, were suspended. Joint ventures with the Soviet Union were reduced, among these the construction of a nickel plant, thermoelectrical and engineering projects, oil refineries, and the nuclear energy plant on Cienfuegos, all vital to Cuba.

The closing of the businesses, cutbacks in working hours, and layoffs at factories and workplaces resulted in high unemployment, leaving "interrupted workers." Some were transferred to other businesses at their old wages, and social security covered the "interruption." Those who did not accept transfers did not receive benefits. Students graduating from the universities were encouraged to continue their studies or accept work in the fields. Agricultural microbrigades were established.

Many basic necessities that had been freely available were now rationed at the same subsidized prices; delays by the Soviet Union in sending cereals, flour, detergent, soap, rice, and other products meant that they had to be rationed. Because of the scarcity of paper pulp, all publications were downsized. Others disappeared. This scarcity of products came to be known as *desabastecimiento* (deprovisioning).

The government increased its agricultural plans and those for the raising of domestic animals, and launched a Victory Garden campaign of home vegetable gardens, for which it distributed seeds and tools. At the end of 1991 the CDRs announced that there were already 796,000 gardens throughout the country. To stimulate production, the government created the Unidades Básicas de Producción Cooperativa (UPBC: Basic Units of Cooperative Production). In the agricultural sector tractors were replaced by oxen. By October 1991, 200,000 animals were already trained and in service. It was harder to replace machines with manual labor in the sugar industry. Given the country's circumstances, Castro noted, it was more difficult to house, feed, and equip thousands of workers than to use oil.

The merchant and fishing fleets were nearly paralyzed. The freight and public transport systems had to be reduced drastically. The government moved to close this gap by importing massive numbers of Chinese bicycles and adapting six factories to bicycle production. By the end of 1991 it distributed more than a million bicycles. Horse-drawn carriages and carts roamed cities and countryside to help out with transport.

Such efforts helped, but they did not pull Cuba out of its economic doldrums. The people suffered because of the lack of basic necessities, the daily power blackouts, the transportation difficulties (getting to work on time was much harder), and the poor communication system, since the telephones often did not work. "Cuba Running on Empty" a Colombian paper headlined. The prophets of doom in the hemisphere predicted violent outcomes.

One of the government's highest priorities was the stimulation of foreign investment. It created joint ventures in the tourist sector and in the citrus and cement industries and signed "high risk" agreements for cooperation in oil exploration and extraction.[101] Was Cuba becoming capitalist? Castro insisted that this was not the case. "Foreign investment does not contradict any principle of socialism or Marxism-Leninism or of the Revolution." Cuba increased its search for new markets in Europe, Latin America, and Canada—difficult and competitive markets—in hard currency and at bargain-basement prices. Or so Castro described the unequal exchange, since the price of sugar (Cuba's main export) in these markets was lower than its production costs. Everywhere Cuba came up against the barriers of the United States blockade—they were not always surmountable—and businesses and investors canceled their agreements with Cuba because of Washington's pressure, threats, and blackmail. This brutal blockade imposed huge hardships on the people. Castro warned that they had not yet seen the worst; greater difficulties were still to come, but that "to resist is to win."

In October 1991, the Fourth Congress of the Cuban Communist Party opened with the slogan "Save the Country, the Revolution, and Socialism." Cuba was in the midst of its most serious and dangerous crisis, barraged by a radio war from Florida urging the Cuban people to rebel and organize protests and by United States military maneuvers at Guantanamo, with simulated evacuations. The government foresaw the danger of an invasion.

This crucial meeting, which had been postponed several times by the increasing deterioration of the socialist world, aroused great expectations within the country and abroad, though Castro warned that there would be no "spectacular" changes, no multiparty system or free market. Outside the island, many believed that this congress offered the last chance for the Cuban regime to transform the country and avoid a violent outcome.

In this situation of external threat, internal anxieties, and uncertainty, the Fourth Congress began. Without invited observers, national or foreign press, the 1,800 delegates from all over the country met for four days. In his five-hour opening speech Castro gave a detailed exposition of Cuba's dramatic situation and the devastating effects of the disappearance of the socialist regimes and the decline of the Soviet Union on Cuba's economy. He described the Soviet situation as a disgrace. The CPSU had been "dissolved by decree." The country was "incredibly weakened and was faced with a serious threat of disintegration." He noted that perestroika awakened sympathies among the Cuban people, since "the first reports were interesting and pleasing about the improvement of socialism," but that its results were disastrous.[102]

The resolutions approved by the party congress hinged on economic and social development plans; restructuring of the party to democratize it and to trim it of its bureaucracy; a new electoral system, with direct, secret, and nonbinding voting; and an easing of restrictions concerning religious beliefs. This final measure was the one that had the greatest impact on public opinion within the country and abroad. "The Cuban Communist Party Receives God" was the headline in one Colombian paper. The Cuban bishops hailed this opening in a pastoral letter but noted that truly democratic changes were necessary.[103] Evangelicals and Protestants applauded the change.

Cuba was forced to adapt to the new international conditions and to refine its government without capitulating to capitalism. Castro pointed to the socialist regimes of Eastern Europe and the consequences of yielding to capitalist pressure: "They gave a finger, later an arm, and finally had their heads ripped off."

In December 1991 the national assembly of popular power took up approval of the reform of the 1976 constitution in the spirit of the socialist system and based on what the Fourth Congress of the CCP had approved. The reform was adopted by unanimous voice vote. The text eliminated reference to the Soviet Union and the socialist world from the preamble and introduced the ideology of José Martí, the apostle of the struggle for Cuban independence, alongside the doctrine of Marx and Lenin, or of the Communist Party as the sole party, the "vanguard" and "main force directing society and the state." It also approved the new electoral law allowing for direct and secret voting. The minimum age to vote or be elected to provincial and municipal assemblies was sixteen, and eighteen (the age of majority in Cuba) for the national assembly. Elections were won with 50 percent of the vote. Proportional representation in the national assembly was maintained at one deputy for every 20,000 people or any fraction over 10,000. In 1991 the number of members grew from 510 to 589. The election of the chief of state and the council of state continued to be a function of the assembly, to "avoid politicking and a war among the candidates," noted Castro.[104]

The new constitution established greater guarantees for foreign investment, broadened religious freedom—the CCP approved the admission of believers to the party—and opened the economic system based on the concept of socialist property to the possibility of transferring state property to private persons or legal entities for economic ends in "exceptional cases."

In its Final Declaration, the assembly condemned the United States aggression against the country and called on the Cuban people to fight counterrevolution, crime, and delinquency. It also rejected "value judgments" on Cuba by foreign governments and parliaments, calling them "unproductive monologues," since they were made at meetings where Cuba had been neither present nor invited. This was criticism of the Río Group (Argentina, Brazil, Colombia, Mexico, Peru, Uruguay, and Venezuela) for having questioned, in a recent meeting at Cartagena, Colombia, the Cuban political system and measures taken by the Cuban government that, in its judgment, constituted an "obstacle" to "real continental coexistence." The Río Group was referring to the detention of twelve activists and dissidents in Cuba, and to Castro's announcement that there would be "no opening" for counterrevolution. The declaration concluded that it was not markets that were on the line but the survival and independence of Cuba, and it called 1992 the year of trial by fire for the Revolution.[105]

In his closing speech Castro promised that Cuba would demonstrate how to make "a revolution with democratic principles and a democracy with one party, though it be under the most difficult conditions," and claimed that Cuba was "the most democratic country in the world." He concluded with the slogan, "Socialism or Death!" to applause and shouts of support for the Revolution and Fidel.[106]

Cuba put its new electoral law to the test in the midst of a hostile and frenetic radio war from Florida, exhorting the people to stay away from the polls, invalidate their vote, or leave their ballots blank. The elections for municipal and provincial assemblies were held in December 1992, and those for the national assembly took place in February 1993; for the first time the people elected their representatives directly. Based on participation (97.2 percent and

99.57 percent, respectively) and the results, the government called the vote a "massive referendum" of support for the government and the Revolution. Most of the votes were for candidates from the slates offered by the mass organizations, as the government recommended. The invalidated votes were 7 percent and 10 percent, and the blank ballots were 3 percent and 4 percent of the total, respectively. No representative of the opposition ran for office, and in the wide-ranging discussions in the 24,215 local assemblies, no proposals of a counter-revolutionary nature were presented.[107]

THE HOME STRETCH

Day by day Cuba's relations with the Soviet Union deteriorated in every way. The Communist power could no longer comply with its export agreements, and Cuba lacked oil. Commercial exchange, now in cash, marked the end of the favorable conditions Cuba had enjoyed for more than thirty years. However, military aid continued. In January 1991 Moscow, disregarding Washington's protests, announced that it was sending MIG-29 fighter planes to Cuba, and in June Soviet Chief of Staff General Mikhail Moiseyev and Rear Admiral Alexander Burgunov arrived in Havana at the head of a naval detachment. They had come to deal with matters pertaining to the two countries' military cooperation. The Soviet ambassador assured Havana that shipments of arms to Cuba would not be reduced, and that such support would cease only when Cuba's relations with the United States improved.

Nevertheless, Cuba began to receive worrisome and contradictory messages from Moscow. High Soviet leaders remarked on the need to establish a "new type" of relations, and there were many items in the Soviet media about the growing opposition in sectors of the parliament to these favorable relations with Cuba at a moment when the Soviet Union was experiencing grave economic difficulties. In June 1991 the Soviet chancellor arrived in Havana to discuss a new five-year economic cooperation agreement. The Soviet Union reduced its exports to Cuba by a third and was importing only a quarter of the Cuban products it once did.

The Soviet Union was weakening internally and throughout the international arena, and Gorbachev, also weakened and depending on United States assistance that did not come, fell into the vortex of Washington's influence. There was a coming and going of officials at the highest levels between Washington and Moscow. Some of the Soviets passed through Havana as they returned from Washington, to "rectify" their agreements. Relations between

Washington and Moscow were going so well that Aeroflot, the Soviet airline, obtained permission to establish a route from Moscow to Miami and
on to another country. Aeroflot dropped its Havana route.

In September 1991, a month after the coup against Gorbachev, Secretary
of State James Baker went to Moscow for consultations. The main topic was
Cuba. He and Gorbachev talked for more than three hours, and at a press
conference the latter announced the "modification" and "modernization" of
relations with Cuba and his decision to withdraw from the island the Soviet
military brigade, which had been there since the missile crisis in 1962. A smiling Baker remarked that this "gesture" was "very significant" and "favorable"
for the relations between their two countries.[108]

Castro learned of the announcement that the brigade would be withdrawn
from international news wires, and he reacted angrily, declaring that this was "an
unprecedented attitude." A long editorial in *Granma* indicated that this "unilateral" Soviet decision was tantamount to "giving the green light" to the United
States to attack Cuba. *Granma* noted that though this brigade (11,000 soldiers)
was unimportant for the defense of Cuba, it held profound significance as an
expression of the friendship and solidarity of the Soviet Union. The article also
stated that the proposals by Soviet Foreign Minister Boris Pankin (Shevardnadze
had resigned) for the "eventual steps" the United States might take in exchange
for the withdrawal of the brigade—he suggested reducing the number of military personnel at Guantanamo—were "extremely modest" and "unimportant."
It was evident, *Granma* declared, that the Soviet Union had negotiated with and
made concessions to the United States with regard to Cuba without having actually spoken with Cuba.[109]

The "eternal friendship" between Cuba and the Soviet Union evaporated.
November 7 was the date on which the Soviet Union commemorated the
October Revolution and the day when its embassy in Havana held grand recep-
tions attended by Fidel and Raúl Castro and high-ranking functionaries and
generals who were seldom seen at diplomatic functions. But on that date in
1991 the embassy remained closed. The Cuban government, on the other
hand, recalled this memorable event with significant ceremonies in Havana
and other cities.

THE GLEE OF THE ANTI-CASTROITES

Bush received the news of the Soviet brigade's withdrawal with particular
enthusiasm and predicted Castro's fall. "It will be sooner than he imagines,"

he declared. Such declarations coincided with the Soviet chancellor's arrival in Havana to negotiate with the Cuban authorities about the withdrawal. In Miami the anti-Castroites hailed it as a "powerful psychological blow" and the beginning of the end of the Castro regime.[110]

So great was the enthusiasm of Mas Canosa, the leader of the United States anti-Castroites and president of CANF, that he left for Moscow within the week. Now he was discovering affinities for the Kremlin leaders. "I feel an emotion I have not been able to transcend," he told a Spanish journalist who called him from Miami. "I, who have fought all my life against the values this country represents . . . have found here a friendly hand. . . . I have received assurances that the subsidies for Cuba will stop, that the Soviet troops will return to their country, and that military aid will be eliminated."[111]

Mas Canosa aspired to replace Castro. His followers addressed him respectfully as "Mr. President," wrote the *New York Times* in an article about him for which he refused to be interviewed. CANF had prepared a new constitution for Cuba, and Mas Canosa had a "Social, Political, and Economic Program for the Reconstruction of Cuba," along capitalist lines.[112] (He died in 1997 of a serious illness, which had been kept secret until the last moment. More than 100,000 people from the Cuban community accompanied his cortege to the cemetery in Miami. Mas Canosa had been the symbol of the United States Cuban exiles' resistance to Fidel Castro.)

The anti-Castro media in Florida exhorted the Cuban people to rebel. The terrorist group Alpha 66 sped up the training of its forces to launch the "liberation" of Cuba, and members of the Cuban-American community (more than 600,000 lived in Florida) put their houses on the market before the expected fall of the government. For when it did fall, there would be an exodus for the island, and prices would drop through the floor. Florida Governor Bob Martínez, a Cuban-American, named a commission to deal with the disturbances that would follow the fall of the Cuban regime. Castro noted sarcastically, "Over there in Miami people are packing their bags."

THE "VENDETTA" CONTINUES

Bush continued the "vendetta" against Cuba in the Human Rights Commission in Geneva, and the CIA kept up its support of activist human-rights groups and Cuban "dissidents" to encourage internal dissatisfactions. When the Eastern European socialist regimes fell, Bush stepped up the aggression, now under the banner of "democratization." He demanded "free" elections, a term that implied a multiparty system and a market economy. Meanwhile, the activities by these small human-rights groups were an irritating problem for the Cuban government, not because they were an internal threat, but because of the campaigns against Cuba organized by Washington and the Miami anti-Castroites and the tensions they created with other governments.

In August 1989 the authorities arrested Elizardo Sánchez, the leader of the Comisión de Derechos Humanos y Reconciliación Nacional (CDHRN: Human Rights and National Reconciliation Commission) and leaders of other Cuban human-rights groups. *Granma* accused them of spreading "calumnies" in their declarations to foreign television networks and anti-Cuban broadcasters sponsored by the United States, with the purpose of discrediting the Cuban courts.[113] They condemned the execution of Ochoa and other officers, calling them "assassinations," and claimed that the Cuban authorities had drugged Ochoa before bringing him to the courtroom, and that all the defendants were victims of mistreatment and psychological torture.

Washington condemned the arrests as "a flagrant violation of human rights in the renewed actions of the Cuban government against activists."[114] Amnesty International and Americas Watch, in separate reports, expressed their concern at the "significant worsening" of this situation in Cuba compared with the previous year.[115]

The criminalization of such groups, the arrests of their members, Castro's declarations that he would not allow counterrevolutionary activities and their occasionally violent harassment of the people invited strong protests from foreign governments and celebrities. They accused Cuba of repression, violating human rights, and failing to honor the civil liberties of freedom of speech and association. The activists claimed that their attackers were transported in government buses and that members of the state security forces dressed in civilian clothes participated. They also alleged that the rapid-action brigades had taken part in the attacks.

The October 1991 arrests of María Elena Cruz Varela and three members of her movement, accused of "defaming state institutions, printing publications, and having secret meetings," brought severe criticism. The Río Group, meeting in Cartagena, Colombia, indicated that these arrests and Castro's declarations were "an obstacle" to Cuba's reintegration into the inter-American system. In a joint statement with four other former Costa Rican presidents, Nobel Peace laureate Óscar Arias asked the Cuban government to free the prisoners. And in Havana, embassies of the European Economic Community countries made clear to the government their concern about the increase of repression in Cuba.[116]

The Cuban government accused Washington of stimulating internal and public opposition and published and circulated among the HRC in Geneva a copy of a communication from the CIA office in Madrid, dated July 1991, urging these groups to become opposition parties. The Cuban government noted that its denunciation was met with silence from the international media. In 1994 it published a top-secret document from the United States Interests Section in Havana to the secretary of state, the CIA, and the INS, which showed the nature of these groups, their activities, and the accusations of repression of which they said they were victims. The document stated that in the applications for visas to leave Cuba, most did not show a real "fear of persecution" but rather a discomfort because of the deterioration of the economic situation. The document reported that "in spite of doing everything possible to work with the human-rights organizations to identify the activists who were being persecuted by the government, the human rights cases represented the weakest part of the refugee program." Rarely did they present reliable evidence of repression, persecution, searches of their homes, interrogations, detentions or arrests, or harassment by state security. It addition, it declared that some were "fraudulent," since there was "a sale of testimonial guarantees." Immigration officials regarded human rights cases as "those most susceptible to fraud," it added.

The United States was beaten three years running in the HRC. It could not win a condemnation of Cuba. Latin America, the socialist countries, and the third world supported the island nation. In 1990 the United States finally succeeded, with the addition of yes votes from Hungary and Bulgaria, whose Communist regimes had already been toppled, and from Panama. The rest of Latin America abstained. Only Mexico voted with Cuba.

The Cuban ambassador, Raúl Roa, noted that the nay votes and the abstentions, all from third world countries, showed that the majority "had not bowed to imperialism." And Castro, furious, accused his former allies of "betrayal" for having voted in favor of this "scurrilous and cynical anti-Cuban motion," since their votes and that of the United States "military occupation government" (he meant Panama) encouraged imperialist aggression. He declared that if Cuba was attacked by military means, "those governments that have been capable of writing such an infamous page of history will be responsible for the blood that is spilled here. Rivers of blood will flow. . . . We have the weapons . . . and our army is composed of all our people."[117]

In 1991 the United States once again managed to get Cuba condemned with the help of formerly socialist countries Argentina and Panama. The resolution asked the HRC to name a "special representative" for Cuba. The 126-page report on human rights in Cuba, presented by Rafael Rivas Posada, the special representative of the United Nations secretary general, accused Cuba of a variety of violations. It singled out the "alarming" increase in cases of political persecution of activists and dissidents. It mentioned abusive "psychiatric treatment," trials without the requisite guarantees, and limitations on the right of free expression and association and it expressed concern at the creation of the rapid-response brigades (civilian groups created by the government to deal with public protest). Rivas Posada's mission was to observe this situation in situ, but because the Cuban government denied him entry, he based his report on declarations by exiled Cubans, human-rights groups outside Cuba, and such organizations as Amnesty International and Americas Watch.

Rivas's report was met with severe criticism from some of the delegates. Roa rejected it as "unilateral" for making value judgments and accepting at face value the "claims of known enemies of the Cuban Revolution," and he questioned the validity of information given by the twenty-one Cuban human-rights groups, since five of these consisted of "one and the same individual."[118]

In 1992 Cuba was again condemned. This time the United States had the support of Russia, Argentina, Chile, Costa Rica, and Uruguay. The rest of Latin America abstained. The resolutions asked that Rivas be named special reporter on Cuba, a particularly serious sanction. Rivas declined the nomination "for personal reasons." *Granma* noted that Washington would have a hard time finding someone of Rivas Posada's prestige to fill the post.

Roa rejected the nomination of special reporter to his country, since such treatment was "discriminatory" and applied only to those countries that "persistently and massively" violated human rights. He pointed out that the report of the HRC mission that had gone to Cuba (Rivas Posada was a member) contradicted Washington's accusations against his country. He warned that his government would not allow the reporter to enter, nor would it cooperate with him.[119]

The Cuban government accused Russia of knuckling under to United States pressures to attack Cuba, and *Granma* called a reception offered by the Russian delegation in the old Soviet Embassy in Geneva a "stateless binge" and commented that the place had been turned into "a Russian dive." The Cuban dissidents Carlos Franky, David Moya, and Ricardo Bofill were guests at this reception and appeared in a *New York Times* photograph, drinks in hand, standing next to the Russians celebrating the "victory."[120] The foreign press played up Russia's "abandonment" of its old ally.

The United States continued to win condemnation of Cuba, with the support of the formerly socialist countries and the abstention of Latin America. The Clinton administration continued this "vendetta." But at the HRC meeting in Geneva in the spring of 1998 the United States suffered its first defeat in seven years. The resolution against Cuba that it presented along with twenty-one other countries did not pass: 19 voted against it, and most of Latin America abstained; the 27-vote majority from the 53 members could not be won. The Cuban delegate celebrated the victory. "Today justice has been done" and a blow had been struck against United States policies against his country, he remarked, and turned the accusation against the United States because of its traditional support for military dictatorships, its economic warfare against his country, and violating human rights with its embargo.[121]

FIDEL'S "CONTRAS"

Within a span of ten days two serious incidents occured in Cuba, both ended by firing squad. On December 28, 1991, a commando composed of three anti-Castroites led by Eduardo Díaz Betancourt entered the island. The others were Daniel Santovenia Fernández and Pedro de la Caridad Álvarez Pedroso. They were captured as they arrived, and their weapons, munitions, explosives, and anti-Castro propaganda were seized.

Some people in Miami believed that Díaz Betancourt, who had left Cuba illegally the year before, was a Cuban government "infiltrator." During long interrogations the captives described how the commando was supposed to be made up of twenty-two combatants but that because of internal conflicts it was reduced to three. They claimed that their relatives knew nothing about the plan, and that the "brains" behind it, considered heroic by some in Miami and stupid by others, was Tony Cuesta (a former Cuban prisoner, the founder of the terrorist organization Alpha 66, and chief of Commando L, another terrorist group of anti-Castro paramilitaries). The objective was to carry out sabotage in movie theaters, dance halls, and recreation areas to create panic among the people, and later to dynamite important economic installations. They reported that they had been assured in Miami that Cuba was on the verge of insurrection. "I now realize," said Santovenia, "that the United States government has used me."[122]

The Cuban government announced that it would impose death sentences, the punishment for terrorist acts against the security of the state. This announcement was met with expressions of rejection and petitions for clemency from Latin American governments and celebrities, anxiety among the relatives, and indignation from the anti-Castroites. In Miami there were public protests, "small in numbers but widely reported by the Florida media," reported the AP. Díaz Betancourt was the only one sentenced to death; the other two were given thirty years of prison.[123]

The other incident came on January 9, 1992, in Tarará, 10 miles from Havana. Three soldiers were killed and one seriously wounded when seven people, including two women who were trying to steal a boat to leave the country, disarmed the soldiers, tied them up, and shot them. This crime, very rare in Cuba, invited profound indignation throughout the nation. Radio stations and *Granma* were overwhelmed by petitions that the perpetrators be given the death penalty. Luis Miguel Almeida Pérez and René Salmerón Pérez, the leaders, were sentenced by the court to death by firing squad for piracy and murder. For two members of the group the sentence was commuted because one was mentally retarded and the other was a minor. They were sentenced to twenty-five and thirty years of prison respectively, and the two women were given ten years. Little is known of what happened to the seventh.

The execution of Díaz Betancourt on January 20 unleashed a persistent campaign against Cuba in Miami. At the funeral for the soldier Pérez Quintosa, who was wounded at Tarará, Fidel classified as "hypocrites" the celebrities (Óscar Arias, Salvadoran President Alfredo Cristiani, the Mexican writer Octavio Paz, and the Vatican spokesman, among others) who demanded clemency for those sentenced to death without condemning their crimes. "They mourn for those who come here to kill, to burn, to plant bombs . . . as if our people had no right to defend themselves from such dirty tricks and such crimes."

Under the Reagan and Bush administrations terrorists and anti-Castro (and anti-Sandinista) paramilitaries had free rein. Their activities, supposedly clandestine, were publicly known, but the authorities did nothing to stop them. They trained at clandestine camps in Florida, and the terrorists, before and after their "secret" missions, announced to the media their plans to assassinate Castro. They succeeded in attacking some supposed "military objectives" from speedboats—they shot up the Hotel Meliá in Varadero—but their attempts to infiltrate agents always failed. They were shot down or arrested.

The United States authorities also collaborated with these terrorist groups. In August 1992 a United States Coast Guard gunboat rescued four agents of

Commando L, led by Cuesta, when their boat sank in Cuban territorial waters. The *Miami Herald* reported that the FBI was investigating the Commando, but no arrests were made.[124]

Gerardo Reyes, the Miami correspondent for *El Tiempo* in Bogotá, referred to the anti-Castro paramilitaries as Fidel's contras. He described them as "dressed in fatigues, dragging themselves through the marshy landscapes of the Everglades to take towns made of four poles, attacking fictitious trenches, disembarking at ghost ports, shooting at the enemy with blanks or making the sounds of gunfire with their voices when they have no bullets."[125] They spent twenty years preparing for war with Cuba.

THE GYPSY'S CURSE

Like Reagan, Bush relied on support from the anti-Castro ultraright in Miami and from CANF, led by Mas Canosa. He tightened the embargo and the sanctions against Cuba even more. The United States Congress was on the same wavelength. This relationship suited everyone for electoral reasons. In 1990, the Senate approved the Mack Amendment (proposed by Republican Senator Connie Mack), which prohibited United States subsidiaries in foreign countries from doing business or investing in Cuba. Faced with strong protests from allied and friendly governments, since the measures proposed by this amendment went beyond United States jurisdiction and compromised other nations' sovereignty and violated international law, Bush vetoed it.

But in February 1992 the Senate and the House approved by wide bipartisan margins the so-called Torricelli Law, the work of Democratic Representatives Robert Torricelli and Bob Graham. They christened it the Cuban Democracy Act. This law included the Mack Amendment and also prohibited ships calling at Cuban ports with passengers or cargo from entering United States ports for a period of 180 days. Such ships could be confiscated and sold and fined up to $50,000. It also imposed sanctions and reprisals on governments; private businesses, whether United States or foreign; domestic and foreign banks; maritime companies and airlines; and individuals from any country who did not comply with it. Further, it mandated the assignment of funds to finance and promote "dissident organizations" within and outside Cuba; in other words, to subvert its internal order.

The Torricelli Law extended United States jurisdiction to the entire world. Faced with a wave of vigorous protests from allied countries, the EEC, foreign parliaments, and criticism from influential United States newspapers, the

State Department signaled the President that it would be "inopportune" to sign the bill. Bush allowed it to languish. However, it being a presidential election year, his reelection hopes weighed more heavily. At a ceremony in one of Miami's central hotels in October, in the presence of hundreds of anti-Castro Cubans and his fellow Republicans, he signed it. Thus he assured himself of Florida's Latino votes.

The signing of the Torricelli Law occasioned angry demonstrations in Miami by those who opposed it—it caused greater hardships and penury for the Cuban people—and they clashed with its anti-Castro supporters, so that the police intervened. The opponents of the law received threats of reprisals and death. A bomb exploded at the *Miami Herald* after it criticized the law in an editorial. In a joint statement, Americas Watch and the Fund for Free Expression denounced the intimidation by counterrevolutionary Cuban exiles in Miami against those who thought differently from them. They also accused the Florida and Miami governments and authorities of fomenting and financing such groups and their police forces of not intervening to prevent these acts of vandalism and making no arrests. Because of this atmosphere of intimidation created by the anti-Castroites, several congressmen decided not to oppose the law, so as not to play it safe during an election year.[126]

Democratic candidate Bill Clinton, who was also hoping to reap the windfall of the Florida Cubans' votes, accused Bush of trying to appropriate this law and called Bush's failure to invite its Democratic authors, Torricelli and Graham, to the signing ceremony cheap politics. He pointed out that without the efforts of the Democrats, the law would never have passed.[127] On March 9, a month after the amendment became law, the *Wall Street Journal* confirmed in an editorial note that Mas Canosa's CANF paid, and Torricelli received, "at least" $26,000, and that Clinton was given $125,000 in a single night by the Cuban exiles after his visit to Miami's Little Havana.

The Cuban government called this law a "monstrosity" and a "diabolic project," intended to starve the Cuban people to death, and a nefarious precedent because it compromised the independence and sovereignty of all nations.[128]

In 1991 Washington became aware that the Cuban government intended to present a resolution to the United Nations General Assembly on the economic blockade of its country. The United States launched an aggressive campaign to prevent this measure. In a statement to the United Nations dated August 21, the State Department maintained that the embargo was a matter of its bilateral relations with another nation, and that in any case, the international organization had no jurisdiction in the matter. It claimed that the

Cuban ambassador was confusing the "embargo" with a "blockade," since a real blockade would mean that the United States would have to take action to prevent other countries from trading with Cuba, which was "clearly" not the case—though clearly it was.

Introducing the matter before the General Assembly, the Cuban ambassador to the United Nations, Ricardo Alarcón, declared that the blockade harmed his country's "right to life and existence" and had a deleterious effect on the purpose and principles of the United Nations Charter and the normal development of international relations. It "seriously impinges on the internal legislation of many nations, institutions and persons of the world." He listed the damage done by the blockade to his country and to foreign business enterprises, including bankruptcies, and declared that governments, businesses, and private individuals were afraid to do business with Cuba because of the law's threats. He called this policy a "criminal aggression" against Cuba, an attack on the sovereignty of other nations, and the source of constant international conflicts.

Alarcón read the pertinent part of a threatening communication Washington had sent to several chancelleries that stated, "The Cubans should understand that their insistence that you support them threatens your good relations with the United States. The American Congress and people will be watching this important issue very closely."[129]

Several governments tried to convince Cuba not to introduce the subject of the blockade in the United Nations. The presidents of the G-3— Colombia, Mexico, and Venezuela—at a meeting in Cozumel, Mexico, to which Castro had been invited, asked him to refrain. Alarcón argued that there was "panic" among governments at the prospect of having to take a position on an issue so irritating to the United States. The president of the United Nations General Assembly was the most eager to make the problem disappear. He offered several options: one, that the debate be limited to hearing Cuba and the United States; two, that Mexico serve as mediator; and three, that the Security Council call on the parties to conduct a dialogue.[130]

Alarcón promised that he would not submit his resolution to a vote, since so many countries felt threatened by Washington, but announced that he would present it the following year. The president of the assembly put the Cuban proposal to a vote, and it was approved by a huge majority. At a press conference after the session, Alarcón said, "This subject will be the 'gypsy's curse' for the United States, for it will continue to be raised here indefinitely."[131]

From this point forward, Cuba defeated the United States in a humiliating fashion in the United Nations General Assembly. The number grew from 59 votes in Cuba's favor in 1992 to 167 in 2000; for the first time Cuba had the support of its former allies from the Soviet bloc. Each year, only Israel and one or two other countries voted with the United States. In an editorial on November 8, 1993, the *New York Times* pointed out that this Washington policy was "domestic politics by proxy," that the "fierce" anti-Castro forces gave their votes and funds to members of Congress, and that Congress therefore added new teeth to the embargo against Cuba. It commented that the Torricelli Law "embarrassingly" isolated the United States, since an "overwhelming" majority supported Cuba in the United Nations for the second time, and it condemned the embargo. "It is hard to recall a comparable humiliation for American diplomacy," it concluded.[132]

In September 1993 the European Economic Community published a declaration of support for Cuba and announced its decision to broaden economic relations with the island. In its turn the European Parliament asked that Cuba be included in the programs of regional cooperation financed by the EEC and recommended that a general agreement of economic and commercial cooperation that "would invigorate bilateral relations and help Cuba to overcome the difficulties it is experiencing" be signed as soon as possible. It questioned United States opposition to the application of foreign laws outside its territory and commercial embargoes imposed by Europe that affected United States interests and its expectation that the rest of the world would respect its embargoes and that foreign enterprises based in Europe would renounce advantageous contracts with Havana.[133]

LATIN AMERICAN "SOLIDARITY"

Given the international obsession with "openness," "representative democracy," the multiparty system and the market economy, some Latin American heads of state thought it opportune to invite Cuba to join this current, so that it could become integrated with the rest of Latin America. Some expressed their "deep concern" at the difficult situation it was enduring and their desire that a "violent outcome" be avoided. The G-3 continued to promote continental integration and closer ties with Cuba but insisted that Cuba make reforms that would "allow" its transition to "the democratic systems that prevail on the continent." What democracy? asked Castro. Democracy, he pointed out, used to mean guaranteeing all of the people's rights to education, health care, social security, employment, protection of children and the old. Respect for these rights is the priority of the Revolution. He pointed to the inequalities, the social injustices, the abandonment of children, and the violence that prevailed throughout Latin America. He called multiparty systems *multiporquería* (multirubbish) and the free market unjust, for it meant the impoverishment of the majorities.[134]

The integrationist wave extended to the "mother countries," Spain and Portugal. Mexican President Carlos Salinas de Gortari invited the Latin American heads of state, including Fidel, the king of Spain, and the president of Portugal, to the first Ibero-American summit. The objective was to lay the foundations for a Latin community of nations. The meeting took place in Guadalajara in June 1991. President Bush was not invited, but in a telephone conversation with Salinas he sent a greeting and his best wishes for a success-ful conference. The White House Press Secretary declared that the United States would be grateful for any move to compel Castro to make internal polit-ical reforms. Gorbachev sent a warm message.

What was to be expected from this first summit? Not much. Venezuelan President Carlos Andrés Pérez announced that there would be discussions, and that no one should expect specific results; this was only a first step. The Latin Community of Nations would be institutionalized at future summits.

In his speech Castro called this summit "historic," since these nations were meeting for the first time at no one else's behest. He provided a rough analy-sis of the economic crisis that had befallen Latin America for ten consecutive years and noted that the situation had worsened. Foreign debt had climbed above $400 billion, transfer of funds to outside Latin America hit $224 billion in just eight years, and inflation rose to unprecedented levels. He criticized the great powers and the international financial organisms under their control for having brought not development, but poverty to 250 million people, for not having brought in capital but promoted its exportation to developed countries. He remarked that Latin America "carries much less weight in the world's econ-omy than twenty years ago" and pointed out that the enormous social and human costs of these realities were expressed "in terms of hunger, sickness, illit-eracy, marginalized communities, and tens of thousands of children homeless, almost half of the population unemployed, underemployed, or malnourished." He added that these "sad realities," (they did not apply to Cuba) "weaken and destabilize" governments "at the speed of light." Ever since independence, he said, "we have been divided, attacked, cut off, interfered with, underdeveloped, looted." If "the total value of all the net convertible cash that leaves Latin America every year" were to be converted "into actual gold" it would be "more than all the gold and silver Spain and Portugal extracted during 500 years. . . . They have imposed on us similar and wasteful dreams and models of consumerism that not only poison and ruin the planet, but which are incompatible with the rational needs of four billion people who live in a third world that is becoming ever poorer. We have never been able to reach our goals through our own efforts, in spite of our immense natural resources and the intelligence of our peoples. We could have been anything, and we are nothing. There is always a new siren song for the eternally wandering navigators we have become. . . . I am not even speaking of blockades, dirty wars, mercenary invasions, or the use of armed force by the strongest military power in the world, all of which has been repeated a scandalous number of times before the eyes of this hemisphere during the past three decades . . . but of illusions like the Alliance for Progress, the Baker Plan, the Brady Plan, and the most recent of these fantasies: the Initiative for the Americas." This last was Bush's plan for economic aid to Latin America. Castro lamented that unity "has been conspicuous for its absence, and especially in the great foreign debt crisis. Where is it? When will it be? How will it be?" He added that the world was marching in an ever worse direction, with "the world political hegemony by one superpower, which has often surpassed itself in the use of force." He recommended unity for Latin America, "not only economic but political," and that it "carry out through acts not words" the will of the people, who dreamed of "a great common homeland, which would be worthy of respect and universal recognition."[135]

The final declaration conveyed the consensus of the heads of state with respect to economic integration, the quality of life of their people, democracy, and diversification of international relations. This was not a new accord but a reaffirmation of the principle of nonintervention and of defense for human rights, which were becoming the subject of "routine litanies" that diluted their power, wrote the Colombian economist Jorge Child.[136] The declaration did not mention the blockade on Cuba and ignored the Bush incentive.

The second Ibero-American summit convened in Spain in 1992, the five hundreth year anniversary of the "discovery" of America—or the Meeting of Two Worlds, as it was called on the other side of the Atlantic—and was celebrated with great splendor. The summit met in Madrid in July. Three presidents did not attend because of serious internal problems: In Venezuela, Carlos Andrés Pérez was shaky after the attempted military coup (headed by Col. Hugo Chavez, subsequently elected president), which was applauded by the people. In Colombia the top drug trafficker, Pablo Escobar, escaped from a "maximum security" prison with eight members of his gang, giving César

Gaviria serious headaches both within the country and with Washington, which was critical of his policy of "submission" to justice. In Peru, Alberto Fujimori was dealing with advances by the terrorist group, Sendero Luminoso (Shining Path).

In his speech, Castro referred to Christopher Columbus's "great accomplishment," but also to the "heroic resistance by the natives" and "by men who, with Bolivar as their leader, were able later to liberate the entire continent." He commented that the commemoration, despite its importance, was not what had brought him to Spain but rather "the consciousness that in Latin America we are still not unified, our independence is still not consolidated, and our full development is yet to be realized." He spoke of the imbalance of forces in the world with the hegemony of a single power, and pointed out that the functions of the United Nations were being "usurped by the Security Council, today manipulated for its own ends by the greatest military power . . . [that] flaunts the anachronistic power of the veto." He criticized a recent decision by the United States Supreme Court that gave its government "the barbarous right to kidnap citizens of any nation in any part of the world," and he denounced the "shameless blockade" the United States had imposed on his country for thirty years. He pointed out the underdevelopment of the immense majority of the countries of Latin America, Africa, and Asia, "which became European colonies starting exactly five hundred years ago," and insisted on the "historic necessity" of union and integration of Latin America.[137] Colombian correspondents noted that these words were the most honest ones of the afternoon.[138]

The final declaration reaffirmed the "commitment to representative democracies and to respect for human rights and fundamental liberties as pillars of our community," mentioned the commemoration of the five hundred years of the "encounter" between two worlds, and noted the end of bipolarity, which opened "new possibilities for consensus" to end the Cold War. Cuba and the blockade once again did not appear in the text.

At the third Ibero-American summit convened by Brazilian President Fernando Collor de Mello in Salvador de Bahía, Brazil, in June 1993, Castro spoke of the crisis of "a world torn apart by ethnic violence, fratricidal wars, the traumatic fragmentation of States, interventionism, the insecurity of all third world countries, and the growing disregard toward the principles of national sovereignty." He noted that there was talk of the beginning of "a decade of hope for Latin America" but that "there have never been more poor and marginalized people on our continent; never have the countries of Latin America suffered greater plunder." He pointed out that when debt service and the losses associated with unequal exchange were counted, more than $700 billion had been shaken out of Latin American pockets, on a debt that amounted $450 billion.[139]

The Latin American majority, which supported Cuba's resolution in the United Nations against the blockade, did not mention it in the final declarations of these summits. In four of the 200 lines of the third summit document, it "noted" that in other international forums there was talk of the "necessity of eliminating the unilateral application, to political ends, of measures with an economic or commercial character, by any state against another state." Mexico and Spain "polished" Cuba's proposed resolution against the blockade in order to make it acceptable to the president of Argentina, Carlos Menem, a vehement opponent of Fidel, and to the Central Americans under Washington's thumb, the biggest opponents of mentioning the embargo.

In June 1994 the fourth summit in Cartagena, Colombia, called by President Gaviria, found the country amidst a presidential campaign, ready to carry out the second round of voting in an atmosphere of confusion and unease. The media were concerned with the internal situation and paid scant attention to the summit, whose mild debates and declarations awakened no interest. Only Castro's presence moved the media.

The final declaration, which had a strong neoliberal bent, maintained that improvement in the quality of life for the people of Latin America lay in "more commercial treaties, more privatizations, and in a greater proportioning of the functions of the State." There was a vague formula—again without mention of Cuba or the blockade—of commitment to "the elimination of coercive measures that affect the free development of international commerce and damage the conditions of life of the people."[140]

Argentina's President Menem remarked that the Cuban government had no other alternative but to change into a democracy and realize "political and economic modifications, which w[ould] allow for its reinsertion into the inter-American system." Castro replied that it would take another summit to define democracy. He pointed to the Revolution's accomplishments in this area, an implicit critique of the deficiencies of the continent's supposed democracies and their policies that work to negate such important rights as health, education, and the right to work. The presidents of Colombia, Chile, and El Salvador and the secretary general of the OAS indicated that Cuba could count on support from the rest of the continent "only with the reestablishment of liberties, respect for human rights, and an economic opening."[141] This was Washington's line, presented in a softer voice. But speaking about respect for human rights while countries such as Colombia and El Salvador were among the world's worst violators was, to say the least, ironic.

In Washington, thirty-five Democratic legislators asked the administration to lift the embargo on Cuba. Charles Rangel, a Democratic representative, called it an anachronism for Washington to promote commercial exchange with such Communist countries as China and Vietnam while refusing to lift the embargo against Cuba. One of Rangel's assistants commented that this embargo cost United States business $6 billion in lost opportunities.[142]

Clinton convoked a hemispheric summit in Miami, to which he invited all the heads of state from Latin America, the Caribbean, and Canada. He did not invite Cuba. Washington announced that the subject of Cuba was to be excluded from the agenda. Castro remarked that this "shows cowardice, mediocrity, and political poverty." Castro noted that the United States' hidden intention was to lay down ground rules for the hemisphere, isolate Cuba and control Latin American and Caribbean markets against Europe, Japan, and the rest of the world.[143]

On December 9, 1994, the Summit of the Americas opened at the Villa Vizcaya on Biscayne Bay in Florida. The subject of Cuba was present inside and outside this forum. The central theme for the summit, free trade, was raised against the backdrop of the blockade and the Torricelli Law, which violated it, demolishing the sovereign rights of all these countries.

Clinton laid out the tasks of the summit in an emotional speech: the opening of new markets, the creation of a hemispheric free trade zone, the strengthening of democracy, and the improvement of quality of life for "all our people." Nevertheless, United States neoprotectionist laws affected products that competed with Cuba's own, and substantially reduced its economic assistance and its programs in Latin America.

Clinton did not speak of human rights, nor did the summit deal with this subject of extreme importance to the people of the Americas. Amnesty International and Human Rights Watch-America (formerly Americas Watch) presented the Declaration of Human Rights—prepared by forty-six organizations in the hemisphere—condemning forced disappearances, extrajudicial executions, torture, and degrading treatment and defending freedom of thought and expression and the rights of political refugees. They did not obtain the support of the presidents.[144]

Clinton spoke of Cuba to placate the vociferous Cuban-American community of Miami. He remarked it was the only nation where democracy was still denied, that he supported the desires of the Cuban people for a peaceful and democratic change, and that he hoped to hold the next summit with the leader of a democratic Cuba. This part of his speech received the loudest applause. The choice of Miami as the seat for this summit conference was yet another concession by the Clinton administration to the anti-Castro community, since it gave it the chance to air its diatribe against the Cuban Revolution and Fidel Castro before the Latin American heads of state. They staged street demonstrations widely announced in the media in which they carried signs against Cuba and Castro. They compared Castro to Hitler and demanded a bigger blockade of Cuba and freedom for the Cuban *balseros* (raft people) confined at Guantanamo. Menem, the "star" of the anti-Castro forces, was invited to speak. Menem expounded at length with accusations against Cuba and Castro amid shouts and deafening applause.

The summit's central theme, commerce, had been proposed by Latin America; the goal of the United States was to lay the foundation for a hemispheric economic bloc that would make the continent a free trade zone by the year 2025, the biggest market in the world—a hemispheric extension of the North American Free Trade Agreement (NAFTA), which included the United States, Canada, and Mexico. (One of the distinguishing acts of this summit was the United States' announcement that Chile had been admitted to NAFTA.) The OAS and the Inter-American Development Bank had a leading role in the development of the plans for achieving the goals. Were these United States proposals advantageous for Latin America? The determining factors were complicated. In the view of Peruvian President Fujimori this economic democracy meant nothing to a people who lived for the most part in absolute poverty, their needs for food, education, health and housing unmet. Many wondered what would happen, given the unequal commercial exchange with the United States, its political manipulation of the commercial exchange, its protectionism, and the Torricelli Law that limited its free trade with Cuba.

LONG, HOT SUMMER

When Clinton arrived in the White House, many people hoped for an improvement in United States relations with Cuba, which had deteriorated under the aggressiveness of the Republican administrations. Clinton was the first head of state to have come of age during the explosive 1960s. His support for the Torricelli Law during the presidential campaign was seen more as a campaigning tactic than an expression of his political position. Few believed that he would lift the blockade, since it would have meant confrontation with the "vehement clique" of anti-Castroites, the powerful Republican ultraright, and the right wing of the Democratic Party. The political costs would have been incalculable.

Clinton's statements on Cuba did not employ the aggressive rhetoric used by Reagan and Bush, but he maintained a hard line and continued the "vendetta" on human rights. The HRC continued to condemn the island nation year after year, and the blockade reached "extreme levels" with Clinton. That was how Roberto Robaina, the Cuban chancellor, phrased it in June 1993 in a letter to United Nations Secretary General Butros Butros-Ghali. He pointed out its "illegal and unjust nature" and detailed United States actions and pressures against foreign governments and businesses to prevent their trading with Cuba and its efforts to block humanitarian aid and donations from reaching the island. Before the General Assembly in 1994 he again referred to the enormous damages the blockade was causing his country and people.

The great economic difficulties Cuba was experiencing, which increased enormously after the disappearance of the Soviet and Eastern-bloc world, led to a growing illegal exodus of Cubans for the United States. In Miami the anti-Castro community, through aggressive radio propaganda, incited them to rebel and leave the country. The legal privileges the United States conceded to this illegal immigration were a powerful incentive. When they arrived on the Florida coast in their fragile craft, they were received as "heroes," and the anti-Castroites and the authorities opened their arms and their doors to them.

Though Bush viewed the growing influx of Cuban *balseros* with alarm, he did nothing to stop it. When he was aiming at a second term, it was politically disadvantageous for him to go against the powerful Cuban-American community. When the Haitian refugees arrived in droves, fleeing the military coup against the Bertrand-Aristide government, his policies were quite different. Bush ordered warships to create a naval cordon and the Coast Guard to prevent the refugees from reaching the United States coasts. In 1991 and 1992 they intercepted some 35,000 Haitians. Some were deported back to Haiti, others were confined at the Guantanamo Naval Base. Human-rights organizations protested. Democratic candidate Clinton criticized this policy as inhumane.

Clinton inherited both problems. He followed Bush's policies on the Haitians and also watched the invasion of Cuban *balseros* with alarm. The invasion was beginning to grow quite large. The Anglos in Florida were protesting, and the refugees were no longer welcome even to many in the Cuban community, according to polls taken in the midst of this crisis. Between

January and August of 1993 more than 6,000 *balseros* arrived, and thirty-six came by helicopter. On December 17, Cubans and Haitians arrived on a boat from the Bahamas. This "joint venture" alarmed Washington. It worried that the Bahamas were becoming a jumping-off point for illegal immigration into the United States. Deeply concerned, Clinton asked Congress for $172 million to stop the growing illegal immigration. Some forty federal agencies and the Coast Guard put an emergency plan into operation.

The summer of 1994 burned hot with tensions for Cuba and the United States. The uncontrolled flow of *balseros* reached proportions that alarmed both governments. Clinton feared a new Mariel. The Cuban government was faced with a new type of violence: the seizure of boats by assault and murder.

On August 4 the tensions between the two governments reached a boiling point when the United States refused to return twenty-five people who had seized a boat in the port of Mariel at Cuba and killed a naval lieutenant. The Cuban government indicted Leonel Macías González for this crime. Macías was a Cuban military recruit, at this point safely in Miami.

The following day, in an attempt to seize a ferry that plied the route between Havana and Regla, a nineteen-year-old policeman was murdered. This was the third seizure in two weeks. The government suspended ferry service to prevent more attacks. The measure produced great anger among the people. Hundreds of people, most of them young, began to gather in the Avenida del Malecón and to protest. When the police appeared, there were clashes and stone-throwing incidents, shots and shouts of protest against the government. The protest turned into massive demonstrations in several streets. The demonstrators broke windows and attacked warehouses, hotels, and "diplomatic stores" where the Cuban public could not shop because they accepted only foreign currency. The daily paper *Juventud Rebelde* (Rebel Youth) reported that thirty-five people were injured, among them ten police officers, and that a "significant" number of arrests had been made. This was the first mass protest against the government and Fidel.

Castro went to the scene of the riots and talked with the crowds. He congratulated those who had helped the police contain the disturbances and stop the attacks. This situation could not continue, he remarked. "Either they [the United States] take serious measures to guard their coasts or we will stop putting obstacles in the way of those who want to leave the country, and we'll stop hindering those who want to come here to look for their relatives. . . . We cannot continue to guard the United States coastline."

The following day, in spite of a heavy rain, there was a gathering of more than half a million people in Havana's Plaza de la Revolución to pay tribute to the policeman killed during the seizure of the tugboat. They carried flags, sang the national anthem, and chanted slogans supporting the Revolution and Fidel. "Until now," said Castro, "the tension has been with countries with few possibilities, which is not the case with Cuba." Cuba was not Haiti.[145]

There was confusion in Washington. Officials complained about the desire they witnessed at the top levels of the government to please the anti-Castro forces for personal reasons. Lawton Chiles, Florida's Democratic governor, had ambitions for another term and needed their votes. But Clinton and Chiles needed to end the influx of refugees. Little by little the Clinton administration hardened its policies aimed at stopping, once and for all, the illegal exodus of Cubans for the United States, provoked by its own policies and the anti-Castroites who supported the illegal emigration. The privileges the United States granted the exiles for three decades as a weapon against the Revolution had now become a harakiri for the United States and an "escape valve" for Cuba. Between January and August a total of 6,000 *balseros* entered Florida in groups of 200, 300, and 500. Fifteen arrived by helicopter.

Clinton ordered a new naval cordon. "Operation Distant Shore" was intended to slow the entry of Cubans and stop the exit of boats to rescue relatives. On August 21, 1,180 Cubans were rescued on the high seas and brought to Florida. The governor declared a "state of emergency" and asked for help from the federal authorities. The *balseros* were installed in military tents at a base 20 miles from Miami, but there was not enough room there. Attorney General Janet Reno warned that those who resorted to violence to hijack boats or planes to leave Cuba would be arrested and charged. Five days later she announced that those who entered illegally would be arrested and sent to the Guantanamo Naval Base, to prevent the Cuban government from using the exodus as an escape valve for its problems. This marked the end of the privileges enjoyed by the Cubans since the Johnson administration.

More than 15,000 Haitians were already confined to the Guantanamo base. The Cubans arrived and were placed in tents in fields surrounded by barbed wire, separated from the Haitians. This base became a concentration camp, alleged Castro. He criticized the measure, which created greater tensions with Cuba.

Leonel Macías González, the Cuban recruit accused of having murdered the navy lieutenant in Mariel, was arrested in Miami. Castro warned that this gesture was not enough, that the problem was "more serious than ever," the crisis much graver, and that the United States must take "rapid, efficient, and serious" measures to change its immigration policies, since they were the reason for the illegal emigrations promoted by "thousands of hours a week of radio warfare." The exodus did not stop.

Clinton called the Florida governor, Mas Canosa, and other Cuban anti-Castro leaders to the White House to study "a series of measures to put pressure on" Cuba. "What have we come to?" asked Castro. The meeting agreed to halve the money that Cuban-Americans were allowed to send to their relatives on the island (which meant $500 million a year to Cuba), to limit the daily charter flights from Miami to Havana to one a week, and to intensify the radio war and the human-rights campaign against Cuba. Castro called Clinton's measures "absurd," since they would only create more internal difficulties and increase the exodus.

White House spokesman Leon Panetta told the ABC-TV network that the administration was looking into a possible blockade of Cuba. The following day Secretary of State Warren Christopher denied this report on CBS News. It would be a warlike move that could lead to a confrontation with Cuba, Christopher said.

The Cuban government opened the escape valve a little. It lowered the age for women and men to be allowed to leave the country to eighteen (it had been twenty), extended the length of temporary absences from six to eleven months, and allowed legal immigrants who had not attacked Cuba to return, with consular documentation. It excluded *balseros*, deserters, those who requested political asylum, and those who stole boats. Washington and the Cuban community in Miami saw an invasion as imminent. Now Radio Martí transmitted messages every ten minutes "begging" Cubans not take to the sea, and for the first time it asked those who wanted to leave Cuba not to risk their lives. José Basulto, president of "Brothers to the Rescue," an organization of anti-Castro Cubans who searched the seas for *balseros* in need of rescue, pleaded with them "please, please" not to try that route, since their resources were limited.[146] In their search for the promised paradise, many men, women, and children drowned.

The Cuban government prohibited the departure of children and adolescents and warned that it would stop "in any way necessary" these irresponsible actions that endangered persons who, because of their age, had "neither the possibility nor the capacity to choose their own actions." That same day, August 23, Clinton announced at a news conference that he was willing to discuss the subject of immigration with Cuba. The dialogue, which would be low-level and limited, was to be held in New York. The embargo would not be discussed. Michael Skol, the assistant undersecretary of state for inter-American affairs, would head the delegation. Cuba designated Ricardo Alarcón, president of the Asamblea Nacional del Poder Popular (ANPP: National Assembly of Popular Power) as its delegate. The spokesman for the Russian chancellery, Gregori Karazin, announced that his government was disposed to "deactivate" the mounting tensions concerning Cuba.

The United States refused to discuss the embargo, even though the Cuban government insisted that it was the very source of the crisis and that to refuse to discuss it was keeping the problem active. The talks took place from September 1 to September 8, 1994. An accord was signed. The United States agreed to issue 20,000 visas per year to Cubans, and Cuba agreed to halt the exodus. (Ten years earlier, Reagan had agreed to issue the same number of visas, but he did not keep his word.)

The Cuban government announced that it would allow departures until noon on September 13. During this brief period, in spite of forecasts of storms and Washington's threat to arrest them and hold them at Guantanamo, many took to the seas.

Guantanamo was not a transitory but a permanent refugee camp. Washington announced that the refugees must return to Cuba and apply for legal immigration papers. Requests for visas would be studied in the usual way, with no obligation to grant them. Several tried to return to Cuban territory by sea or crossing the zone mined by Cuba. Some died in the attempt. In Miami the Cuban community protested, demanding that the *balseros* be admitted to the United States. According to a *Time/CNN* poll in September, 74 percent of United States people did not want Cubans or Haitians to enter the country.[147] The episode ended with the gradual entry of the *balseros* held at Guantanamo. The last 124 entered the United States in February 1996. Most of the Haitians were returned to their country.

THE CESSNA INCIDENT

In February 1996 Cuban MIG fighters shot down two Cessna aircraft belonging to "Brothers to the Rescue," resulting in the deaths of four Cuban-Americans. This incident led to the most heated moment of tension between Cuba and the Clinton administration. The Cuban government claimed that the incident had taken place over its territorial waters. It asserted that on numerous occasions the air traffic control tower in Havana had warned such flights of the danger they were courting in violating Cuban air space, that similar warnings had been sent to Washington. It clearly stated that it would not allow more violations or "provocations," and that if they continued, Cuba would shoot down the airplanes.

The United States accused Cuba of violating international air-traffic laws that prohibited attacks on civilian aircraft, called the downing of the Cessnas a crime, and claimed it took place over international waters. Without waiting for Cuban Chancellor Roberto Robaina's arrival in New York, the United Nations Security Council approved a United States resolution against Cuba, though in terms less harsh than those proposed by its ambassador, Madeleine Albright. China, Russia, and other countries opposed the resolution. It did not condemn Cuba but "strongly deplored" its action. Ambassador Albright accused the Cuban government of cowardice and lack of "*cojones*" (balls). Robaina responded in a press conference that Cuba was overstocked with the latter, and as to the former, it was Cuba's very lack of cowardice that allowed it to face United States aggression. The chancellor asked for a meeting of the General Assembly to explain his government's position, and he received massive support. In a long and substantial speech he detailed the antecedents of the Cessna incident. He gave an accounting of thirty-seven years of United States aggression against the Cuban Revolution and violations of Cuban sovereignty.

The *New York Times* reported that United States intelligence sources claimed that "at least" one of the aircraft and "perhaps" all three—one, piloted by Basulto, escaped—were violating Cuban air space, and that the Cuban authorities did warn them of the danger they were running. These statements were never repeated. What did ensue was a torrent of accusations against Cuba by the administration, Congress, Republican political candidates, and the vociferous and enraged anti-Castroites.

Mas Canosa demanded the harshest sanctions against Cuba and pointed out that this was Clinton's "golden opportunity" to gain the votes of conservative Cuban-Americans. He demanded that relations be severed, that the United States Interests Section office in Havana be closed, and that all telephone communications, charter flights from Miami, and the remittance of dollars to relatives by Cubans in Miami be cut off. "That would be shooting ourselves in the foot," commented Wayne Smith, who had headed the United States Interest Office in Havana during the Carter years, since such measures would go against Clinton's policy of trying to move closer to the Cuban people. One member of the Cuban-American community called such measures illegal because they would cut off the rights to travel and associate freely.[148] Clinton announced that he would limit the movements of Cuban diplomats in the

United States. Cuba warned him that it would do the same with United States personnel in Cuba. Clinton offered to compensate the families of the dead men with frozen Cuban funds, which amounted to $100 million. Following Mas Canosa's line, he suspended charter flights and dollar remittances to relatives in Cuba and ordered an increase in Radio Martí broadcasts to Cuba. Still, he warned that these measures would be reviewed every six months.

The topic of Cuba moved to the forefront of the presidential campaign. The Republicans accused Clinton, who was seeking reelection, of taking "weak and ineffective" measures. Incited by Mas Canosa and company and pressured by Republican criticism, Clinton signed the Cuban Liberty and Democratic Solidarity Act, known as the Helms-Burton Act, though he had announced that he would veto it for fear that it would cause difficulties with allied and friendly countries. Helms-Burton forbade countries and individuals to trade with Cuba. They would be refused visas or not be allowed to trade with the United States. It allowed Cuban-Americans to file suit against foreign businesses and individuals who benefited from properties confiscated from them by the Cuban government. As he had foreseen, this law caused Clinton serious problems among his allies. The EEC warned him that it would take measures in "reprisal" if the act were not overturned. Clinton was unable to apply it fully. In 1998 he continued at half-throttle; he did not want problems with his European allies.

This law also affected United States corporations, and the largest of them registered their complaints. Protests also came from the Chamber of Commerce and the Association of North American Exporters.

In Havana, Ricardo Alarcón claimed that Brothers to the Rescue was a "terrorist" organization, accused Clinton of "pandering" to these groups in Miami, and noted how "pathetic" it was to see a government that aspired to lead the world acting like a gang of Hialeah councilmen. (Hialeah is a Miami suburb overwhelmingly populated by Cubans.)[149]

In 1996 the International Civil Aviation Organization concluded that the Cessnas had been shot down in international air space. The Cuban government rejected this conclusion. The Organization was guided entirely by the United States version of events, Cuba claimed.

THE PARTY'S OVER

Many believed that the collapse of the Communist world would also mean the end of the Cuban Revolution. By 1992 its economy had hit rock bottom.

But in the midst of enormous difficulties and deliberate internal and external pressures, and without making concessions to the West or, as Fidel maintains, endangering the principles of the Revolution, Cuba carries out political changes and modest economic reforms. By the middle of 1996, $2.1 billion flowed into thirty-four economic sectors, especially into the tourist industry.[150] There was talk of the "Chinaization" of Cuba, since it was keeping its socialist system along with a market economy controlled by the government. Fidel traveled to China in the middle of 1995 and was amazed.

In spite of the embargo and the Torricelli and Helms-Burton Laws, Cuba maintained commercial exchanges with United States allies, its own former allies in Eastern Europe, Russia (though considerably diminished and in foreign currency), and with some of the former Soviet Republics. In 1996 Washington threatened to impose sanctions on them if they continued to trade with Cuba. Russia arrived at an agreement with Cuba to finish construction of the nuclear generating plant at Camagüey, which was suspended as the Soviet Union collapsed.

Castro remained strong. Cuba would not make reforms that would weaken the socialist system. Though some areas were weakened, Cuba maintained the great achievements of the Revolution in education, health, sports, culture, and scientific advances, and it distributed its scarce resources equitably among the populace. Year after year the situation had been improving, but it was confronting new internal dangers, noted by Castro. Private business, though small and limited, awakened appetites for the enchantments of capitalism and brought new forms of corruption, which the government was fighting with stern measures.

The United States and world leaders continue to demand that Cuba "democratize," establish a market economy and political pluralism, and make room for activists and dissidents. Fidel has stated again and again that he will not make some capitalist changes, that he will maintain the hegemony of the Communist party, and that he will not allow counterrevolutionary activities. He continues to raise banners in defense of Communism.

Although Cuba is no longer a leader among third world nations or a threat to the stability of Latin America or the security of the United States, Washington continues its aggressive policies against the island. In 1996, pressured by the Republicans and the vociferous anti-Castro Cuban-American community, an important electoral factor in Florida, Clinton approved the Helms-Burton Act, whose objective was to tighten the embargo and strangle the Cuban economy. "The Cold War continues with Cuba," commented

Fidel. This law, with its extraterritorial reach, erased the sovereignty of all States. Clinton did not apply it to its fullest, responding to protests from his European allies, who threatened to take reprisals.

In spite of the difficulties caused by the blockade and United States aggression, the Cuban people did not lose their joy, their creativity, or their enormous dignity. Cuba continues to be an example for many, and Fidel remains one of the great figures of the twentieth century.

THE END OF HISTORY?

The collapse of the Soviet Union and the disappearance of the Communist regimes in Eastern Europe spelled the end of the Cold War—the ever present danger of a confrontation between the two superpowers— and, as a result, the end of the global balance of power. The United States, now the sole military superpower, has secured its global hegemony and promotes NATO's new alliances with countries of the former Soviet block, thereby effecting great changes in the geopolitical map of Europe.

Did the collapse of the Soviet Union signal the end of History as Francis Fukuyama has asserted, guaranteeing that the only viable option for the world are the capitalist system and the liberal democracy? Have Marxist-Leninist doctrines become obsolete, as the West claimed?

Not entirely. China, North Korea, Vietnam, and Cuba remain in the international panorama and, almost immediately after the collapse of the Soviet world, in the former Soviet countries and in Russia the Communists reappeared in the political arena and in the Duma. For many, coming to terms with diminished global prestige was a hard reality to swallow, and facing the end of a life secured by the State and being forced to deal with the great unknown of an emerging capitalist society was a difficult task. Riches, poverty, and class differences began and continue to grow wildly. Small Russian villages held onto their commissaries, statues of Lenin still stood, and the old flag, with its hammer and sickle, remained unfurled; what we had before was better, they said. Although Russia is not a military superpower like the Soviet Union had been, its nuclear stockpiles continue to be a thorn in Washington's side.

Latin America entered the 1990s under political democracies and a neoliberal development model. After decades of internal armed conflicts, the region started to awaken to the new experience of peace and hopes of stability. In the Southern Cone the powerful guerrilla movements have disappeared—having been virtually eliminated—as have the neo-fascist dictatorships of the National Security doctrine. In volatile Central America, the brutal civil wars ended in peaceful negotiations—there were no winners or losers. Salvadoran president Alfredo Cristiani and Guatemalan president Alvaro Arzú, with United Nations assistance, signed peace accords with the FMLN and the URNG guerrillas respectively. These groups then went on to form political parties. In Nicaragua, Reagan's "secret war," carried out by local mercenary militias—the contras, ended with an agreement signed by the Sandinistas and the "rebels." These peace accords were possible only after Reagan had left the White House.

The remaining guerrilla movements in Latin America are the Colombian FARC and ELN, Peru's greatly weakened Sendero Luminoso, and in Mexico the Zapatista National Liberation Army (EZLN), whose spokesperson is the charismatic Subcomandante Marcos. Neither the powerful Colombian groups or Sendero have the chance to take power. They cause great internal problems, but these armed conflicts are far from becoming all-out civil wars.

In 1990, in Nicaragua's presidential election the Sandinistas were defeated by Violeta Barrios de Chamorro, who was openly supported by President Bush. Nonetheless, they gracefully ceded power and aided in reducing the armed forces, in disarming the contras, and in achieving a peaceful transition toward a capitalist democracy. However, unemployment, underemployment, poverty, and unfulfilled promises led to the re-armament of the "recompas" and "recontras." Between 1992 and 1993, they were close to 23,000 in number.[1]

Arnoldo Alemán, who succeeded Chamorro, veered more to the right, embraced Somozism, and negotiated peace with the recompas and recontras. Yet his tenure was plagued by five years of corruption scandals, the peddling of influence, illicit enrichment (his personal fortune ballooned from $26,000 to $260 million and, under unclear circumstances, he acquired fifty-six cattle ranches). His was a life of excesses and extravagance, which left the country's economy in ruins and the people mired in poverty. In 2001, Enrique Bolaños (Alemán's former vice president) was elected despite the unpopularity of his government. Although Daniel Ortega was defeated for the third time, he and the Sandinistas continue to be an important political force. The year 2002 brought new scandals for Alemán: in December the national assembly stripped his immunity as former president to bring him before the court for laundering of $100 million dollars, and for a multi-million-dollar fraud per-petrated against a state television channel.

In El Salvador, almost immediately after the signing of the peace accords that had brought enormous hope to the people, Cristiani decreed a broad amnesty to appease the military elite. That move, which basically served to legitimize impunity, was fiercely rejected by many in the country and by the international community. Nevertheless, the military elite, the main benefici-ary of the amnesty, was unsettled by its loss of power, by the army and budget reductions (agreed upon in the accords), and by the removal of a number of generals, two of whom were former ministers of defense accused by the United Nations Truth Commission of serious human rights violations. Landowners opposed the distribution of land to former guerrillas (also part of the accords). Within two years, there was marked demilitarization and the opening of new democratic space. For the first time in many decades, there was a climate of tolerance in the country.[2]

In 1994 Armando Calderón Sol won the presidential elections and his Arena party gained 39 seats in the national assembly's 84 members. The FMLN, who won 21 seats, became the second most important political force in the coun-try. In 1999 elections, Arena's candidate Francisco Flores won the presidency, with former guerrilla commander, Facundo Guardado, coming in a close sec-ond. In 2002 there were 60 FMLN mayors in the country, including four in the five most important cities, where more than half of the population resides. The FMLN was also the winning party in that election.

In Guatemala in 1996, during the first year of Arzú's presidency, important agreements were signed with the URNG in Mexico City, Oslo, Madrid, and Guatemala City. They contained key elements for a sustainable peace: a cease fire, provisions addressing socioeconomic ills, constitutional and electoral reforms, conditions and formal provisions for the legalization of the URNG, reduction of the army, demobilization of the PACs (paramilitary counterin-surgency mechanism controlled by the army), and the recognition of the rights of indigenous people, among other things. By the end of the year they had signed the Accord for a Firm and Lasting Peace, putting an end to thirty-six years of armed conflict characterized by brutal massacres and other genocidal tactics employed by the army against the indigenous communities. Arzú cleaned up, to some extent, the armed forces and the police, dismantled the PACs, strength-ened democratic institutions, and made important advances toward a new Guatemala—democratic, multiracial, multi-ethnic, and multilingual. These changes brought great hope to the population and the international community.

Nevertheless, Guatemala and El Salvador, which has had the highest rate of homicide in the Western Hemisphere, remain immersed in internal violence and common crime: assassinations, kidnappings, car hijackings, bank robberies, residential burglaries, organized crime in which the military and police are sometimes implicated, and the violence and corruption associated with drug traffic, which permeates all levels of society. Decades of armed conflict have bred cultures of violence, a characteristic of most post-war periods. Many people were born and have grown up in countries at war, where hundreds of thousands of weapons are readily available on the black market. According to official sources, in Guatemala in 2002 there were 1.7 million weapons in the hands of traffickers. In Guatemala, a new aspect of criminality was the public lynching of ordinary delinquents, some of whom were merely targets of personal vendettas.

At the end of the century Guatemala's democracy appeared to be in danger. The growing political prominence of Efraín Ríos Montt and his party, Frente Republicano Guatemalteco (FRG, Guatemalan Republican Front)— also the party of the old military guard—was a significant threat. Ríos Montt was president of the congress, held a majority in parliament, and controlled the government as well as the Supreme Court of Justice. He established new military and economic power groups and his son, General Enrique Ríos, was Chief of the State Military High Command. Ríos Montt's dictatorship (1982 to 1983) was the most bloody period in Guatemala's history: tens of thousands of peasants and indigenous people were killed. However, broad sectors of the population, including regions and provinces victimized by his criminal counterinsurgency strategy, were now supporting him. According to some analysts, this support was due to a general despair in face of the widespread violence that assailed the country and their belief in Rios Montt's promises that he would "establish order."

In 1999 Ríos Montt was running for the presidency, but the Electoral Tribunal annulled his candidacy stating that the constitution (1985) banned the election of anyone who had attempted a coup d'etat. Unable to run, he put forth as candidate Alfonso Portillo, a member of his party. The FRG won an overwhelming victory. Many people feared the plan for the remilitarization of the State and Guatemalan society that Ríos Montt was advancing.[3] That plan was first set into motion during his dictatorship and continued by the military under the civilian governments of Cerezo, Serrano, and de León Carpio. In a report dated in May 2002, MINUGUA, the United Nations office in Guatemala, denounced this campaign: "the present military deployment is similar to the period of the counterinsurgency struggle, not as a function of defense of the nation but in its control of the territory and the people." It also noted that the defense budget exceeded the limits imposed by the peace accords. The Rigoberta Menchú Foundation in October accused Portillo of halting the implementation of the peace accords and the process of transition toward democracy, stepping up the dirty war against human-rights advocates, murders for political reasons, covering up and deflecting the investigations of criminal acts in which agents of the State were involved, and asserted that PACs, dismantled as part of the peace accords, were used as an electoral mechanism for the FRG.[4]

In March 2001, the growing opposition and charges of corruption resulted in a serious crisis; Portillo feared a military coup. The Secretary General of the OAS, César Gaviria, traveled to Guatemala to help mediate in this difficult situation. Gaviria stated that the Guatemalan democracy was at risk and that channels of communication were needed to solve the internal differences. The crisis was provoked in part by the Supreme Court of Justice decision to strip Ríos Montt of his parliamentary immunity and to bring him to court—later he managed to replace the judge before whom he had been summoned and thus exonerate himself from all responsibility and charges. He was freed under parole.

In addition to the CIA's 1954 operation to topple President Jacobo Arbenz, throughout the 1960s the United States used Guatemala as testing ground for its counterinsurgency strategy and supported its military dictatorships despite its human rights record—the worst in the hemisphere. The United States gave it military aid, advisers, arms, trained its armed forces and police officers, while the CIA infiltrated its agents, and paid "assets" and informers—mainly high-ranking military officers. In March 1995 a huge scandal erupted when Jennifer K. Harbury, wife of Everado Bámaca, a member of ORPA guerrilla movement, proved that he was captured in 1992, tortured and assassinated by the army, and that a military intelligence officer, Colonel Julio Roberto Alpírez, was responsible for this crime. She also discovered that Alpírez, who had already been implicated in the 1990 murder of the American citizen Michael DeVine, was a longtime CIA "asset." Her hunger strikes in both Guatemala City and Washington, D.C., received much press attention, including an interview by *60 Minutes* in which she denounced the crime and accused both governments of a cover-up. Democratic Senator Robert Torricelli supported Harbury's denunciations of the CIA's involvement in these crimes, stating that it was not the first time that the agency was working against the United States' national interests. An investigation ordered by President Clinton concluded that Colonel Alpírez was implicated in both crimes and was on the CIA payroll (he received a final payment of $44,000).⁵ Clinton and Secretary of State Madeleine Albright expressed regret for these past "errors." During a four day trip to Central America in 1999, Clinton apologized to the Guatemalan people for the support the United States government had given the military and intelligence forces responsible for the brutal repression. "It was an error that must not be repeated," he stated.⁶ Such declarations, considered "historic" by many—it was the first time the United States recognized the wrongdoings of its foreign policies—were criticized by several Republicans.

Ten years after the amnesties given in the name of national well-being by civilian governments, co-opted by the ever-present military, those benefiting from them were no longer safe. Judges from Spain, France, Belgium, Holland, Germany, Switzerland, and Italy began in 1998 to issue orders for the capture, extradition, and trial of Argentina's former commanders and high ranking officials responsible for the assassination and disappearance of some of their nationals, and against Augusto Pinochet for genocide, kidnapping, and other crimes associated with the notorious "Operation Condor."

The year 1998 would prove to be watershed: In October of that year Scotland Yard arrested Pinochet in a London clinic by order of the Spanish judge Juan Baltazar Garzón. Garzón charged Pinochet for crimes against humanity, for the torture, murder, and disappearance of Spanish citizens during his dictatorship. He asked for Pinochet's extradition in order that he be judged in Spain. Pinochet remained in detention almost two years, while Garzón wrestled with British and Chilean authorities. There were loud protests in the streets from exiled Chileans, children of Pinochet's victims, and anti-Pinochet protesters, demanding his extradition and trial. His supporters also took to the streets, demanding that he be set free. Chilean authorities and Pinochet's lawyers insisted that he must be judged in Chile and argued that his mental conditions could not withstand the pressures of a "just" trial in a language foreign to him. The British authorities released Pinochet for "humanitarian" reasons, he was mentally unfit to stand trial, and the Chilean government whisked him back home in a plane sent from Chile that for months had been waiting at a London airport. Great Britain released Pinochet to avoid tensions with Chile (their commercial relations superseded human rights considerations). His army colleagues, friends, family, and supporters were in a festive mood upon the General's return, meeting him at the airport and giving him a red carpet welcome.

A year later in July 2002, the Chilean Supreme Court, with a vote of four to one, definitively closed the only case brought against Pinochet in Chile—he had been charged with seventy-five murders and kidnappings under the operation called "Caravan of Death." The reason given by the Court was the "deterioration of [Pinochet's] mental faculties." Later Pinochet announced his "resignation" from his post as senator for life "for the good of the country," but kept his immunity as former president and his salary. "If the announcement by the government that 'Justice has been done' has not transformed us into the laughing-stock of the world," wrote Chilean writer Ariel Dorfman, "it is only because the world had already lost any hope that the promise trumpeted when Pinochet returned to Chile would be honored."[7] President Ricardo Lagos came to his defense to avoid confrontations with the aggressive upper echelons of the military and with the right-wing Chileans, both powerful and pro-Pinochet.

Although the 7,500 documents related to Pinochet's dictatorship petitioned by Garzón and declassified by the United States State Department (in response to Clinton's interest in shedding light on the role the United States played in the coup and in the subsequent seventeen years of repression) did not help to bring Pinochet to justice, they will serve, at least to set the records straight and place the responsibility for the crimes committed during that bloody period of Chile's history. Some documents revealed that Henry Kissinger, then secretary of state under Nixon, was the most involved American personality in the coup against Allende, that he withheld information of the atrocities committed during and after the coup, and that since 1974 he, the CIA, and personnel at the United States Embassy in Buenos Aires were abreast of the terrorist activities of Operation Condor and of cases of disappearances.

One document is the transcription of a conversation in La Moneda in June 1976 between Kissinger and Pinochet in which the former said: "We have sympathy for what you are doing" and reassured him that, as far as human rights were concerned, the United States would not take issue with his regime. Other documents strongly suggested egregious human right abuses by Pinochet. Manuel Contreras, former Colonel and former chief of DINA (National Agency Intelligence Directorate), who was sentenced to seven years in prison for assassinations in Chile and abroad, confirmed that all DINA's activity was carried out under Pinochet's orders.[8] In 1999, Garzón learned that Kissinger was in London and requested the British authorities' permission to interrogate him regarding Operation Condor—many pertinent documents carry his signature. His petition was denied after the United States State

Department declared that Kissinger was not authorized to answer questions related to his tenure as secretary of state.[9]

In March 2001 Argentine judge Gabriel Cavallo and in February 2002 Salvadoran lawyer Carlos Urquilla impugned the amnesty laws in their countries and their respective Supreme Courts reviewed them for unconstitutionality. In Guatemala, where the army had been responsible for massive human rights violations during thirty-six years of armed struggle and military rule, for the first time in its history three military officers (and a priest) were condemned for the murder of Bishop Juan Gerardi. This murder took place two days after Monsignor Gerardi made public the archbishopric investigation, "Guatemala: Never Again," which focused on human-rights violations during that war. It accused the army and security forces of 93 percent of all these crimes.

That same year Helen Mack, after a dangerous ten-year penal process, finally succeeded in getting Colonel Juan Valencia condemned by a tribunal to thirty years in prison (two others were acquitted) for the murder of her sister, Myrna Mack, an anthropologist. Valencia was the first of the "untouchable" intelligence military elite to fall.

In Argentina, the Grandmothers of the Plaza de Mayo took to court ten former high-ranking officers. Among these were former generals and Junta Commanders Jorge Videla, Emilio Massera, Leopoldo Galtieri and Carlos Suárez Masón, accused of stealing children (a crime which is neither prescribed as such nor addressed by the amnesty laws) from women taken to detention centers and disappeared. The Grandmothers continue the search for the children kidnapped during seven years of dictatorship who have been given false identities.

Nonetheless, impunity was rampant in Latin America. In November 2002, an Amnesty International report denounced the pressure exercised by the military—and sometimes by governments—to impede the pursuit of justice in cases where the military was implicated. It pointed to the frequent assassinations of and death threats made to judges, public prosecutors, potential witnesses, and human-rights advocates. It further noted that when cases were assigned to military tribunals, the perpetrators were absolved.

The proposal to create an international court to deal with serious human rights abuses by individuals had been on the United Nations agenda since 1948, but it was only after the massacres in Cambodia, Rwanda, and Kosovo in the 1990s that the international community reacted and the idea began to gain popularity. The first step was the Conference of Plenipotentiaries in Rome in 1998, which approved the creation of the International Criminal Court (ICC). With

160 countries represented, the Court statute was approved by a majority of 136 votes, with 21 abstentions and 7 against, including that of the United States. The ICC tribunal will judge individuals—heads of states, soldiers, or civilians—who have committed crimes against humanity whenever the governments cannot or will not judge them. Its action will not be retroactive. Clinton signed the statute in December 2000, one month before leaving office. The ICC was instituted in October 2002, and will become operational in The Hague, Netherlands, in July 2004.

The new millennium has brought with it an avalanche of ultra-right Republicans into the White House under George W. Bush. Like Reagan's team, they arrived engaged in power politics, eager to show the United States' dominance as the world's sole military superpower and its disregard for international treaties and agreements.

Despite the harsh criticism coming from many corners of the world, including its European allies, for abandoning its obligations to the world community, the Bush administration rejected the Kyoto Treaty on the prevention of global warming, and launched a fiery campaign against the International Criminal Court, denying its jurisdiction over United States military and civilian personnel acting on foreign soil. The United States not only withdrew its signature from the ICC Statute, but also cautioned the United Nations Security Council, threatening to withdraw its international peace-keeping missions and to cut its military aid to countries who refused to sign bilateral agreements recognizing the immunity for United States personnel. Only Israel and Romania signed the agreements.

To ensure the "permanent military supremacy" of the United States and prevent the rise of any rival, the Bush administration revived the phantom of nuclear war: it resurrected the ballistic-missile defense program of Reagan's abandoned Star Wars; withdrew from the Anti-Ballistic Missile Treaty signed with the Soviet Union in 1972 (the balancing point in the nuclear arms race); announced the construction of a new nuclear plant to manufacture new arms, and a new defense strategy of "preventive attacks" with eventual use of nuclear weapons, in anticipation of supposed threats from China, Russia, Iraq, Iran, and North Korea (the last three classified by Bush as an "axis of evil").[10] In the global war against terrorism, possible targets also include Libya, Sudan, Syria, and Cuba, as well as myriad terrorist organizations, among them Peru's Sendero Luminoso, Colombia's FARC and ELN, and the Colombian paramilitary AUC.

In order to manage its policy toward Latin America the Bush administration placed in key posts well-known anti-communist warriors and Iran-Contra reprobates, individuals who are highly controversial and widely criticized by the media. John Negroponte was appointed ambassador to the United Nations. He served as ambassador to Honduras (1981–1985) under Reagan, was a central player in the bloody war against Nicaragua, and covered up human rights abuses of the contras (whose bases were in Honduras) and of the CIA-trained and equipped Honduran army Batallion 316—a death squad that he had helped create.

Overriding the Senate confirmation process where the Democrats strongly opposed Cuban-American Otto Reich's nomination, during a Congressional recess Bush appointed him as assistant secretary of state for the western hemisphere. Under Reagan, Reich was the head of the now defunct Office of Public Diplomacy, a contra-support institution whose illegal activities were censored by the House Committee on Foreign Affairs and described by the Comptroller General "as prohibited covert propaganda to influence the media and the public."[11]

Elliot Abrams was placed by Bush in the National Security Council as director of its office for democracy, human rights, and international operations. Abrams played a key role in the Iran-Contra scandal as one of the primary architects of Reagan's illegal Central American foreign policy. He withheld information from Congress, covered up the atrocities committed by the contras and the Salvadoran army, and during the 1991 House hearings, he pleaded guilty to these charges. (In his last day in office, Bush senior pardoned Abrams and many others involved in the scandal, including himself.)[12] And Roger Noriega, protégé of the ultra-right Senator Jesse Helms, was named ambassador to the Organization of American States.[13] These appointments, along with many others, were an appeasement to Florida's Cuban-American community, whose votes represent an important electoral body for the Republicans as has been clearly recognized by the Bush family.

The Bush administration has embarked on a foreign policy that has been questioned by allies and friends for its arrogance, unilateralism, imperialism, and open interference in the internal affairs of other countries. In Latin America in November 2001, Bush's agents were active in Nicaragua to impede the election of Daniel Ortega, a three-time candidate to the presidency. A high-ranking official issued vehement accusations that Ortega and the Sandinistas were having relations with "terrorists," the big word of the moment. For eight years Ortega had been a target of Reagan's secret war. In July 2002, the United States Embassy in La Paz, Bolivia, and Otto Reich, assistant secretary of state for the western hemisphere, were actively campaigning against Evo Morales, the Movimiento al Socialismo (Movement to Socialism) party candidate for the presidency who stood a real chance to win. Morales, who belongs to the indigenous population, was symbol of peasant resistance against the United States' anti-drug policies. Reich announced that if Morales was elected, the United States would never cooperate with him. He was not elected.

The Bush administration's big targets in 2002, however, were Saddam Hussein and Hugo Chávez, presidents of Iraq and Venezuela, two important oil-producing countries (Venezuela is the fourth provider of oil to the United States). Months before the fleeting coup in April, Pedro Carmona, president of Fedecámaras (a powerful union of industrialists connected to multinational capital) orchestrated, with further participation from influential oligarchs, industrialists, intellectuals and some military officials, widespread opposition to Chávez, bolstered by an extremely hostile and inflammatory campaign by the privately owned mass media promoting the coup. The relations of the plotters to the Bush administration started months before the coup. It was no secret that Bush and company wanted Chávez out. They found his populist rhetoric, his friendship with Fidel Castro, and his efforts to secure close relations with Saddam Hussein and Libya's Qaddafi, leaders of two important members of OPEC, unacceptable. Carmona and company went several times to Washington and talked to Otto Reich, Elliot Abrams, and other high officials, and former president Carlos Andres Pérez (target of Chávez's coup) met with Bush. Before and after the coup Carmona and colleagues met with the United States ambassador in Venezuela, Charles Shapiro, and had the support of the National Endowment for Democracy (NED), a quasi official office created by the Reagan administration and Congress to give money "legally" to provisional "assets" willing to do what Washington wanted. In Venezuela NED was distributing money here and there. Two high-ranking military plotters each received $100,000 and the Asociación Civil Consorcio Justicia (Association Civil Justice Consortium)— created to concentrate Chávez's opposition under the banner of promoting democracy—received $84,000.[14] Carmona was chosen president by the military plotters. Within the 48-hour duration of his "government," Carmona dissolved the congress, the Supreme Court of Justice, dismissed the attorney general, governors, and all elected authorities, and embarked on a frantic hunt for ministers and high-ranking officials. But troops loyal to Chávez rescued him from the island to which he had been taken and at 2:49 AM returned him to Miraflores Palace. Masses of enthusiastic followers were waiting for him at the entrance of the Palace since the beginning of the coup demanding his liberation.

On the day Carmona claimed power, Reich summoned Latin American and Caribbean ambassadors to his office to "explain" the version of the events suitable to Washington: the removal of Chávez was not a coup, it was not a rupture of democracy because Chávez had resigned. Reich announced that the United States would now support Carmona. Chávez, however, had not resigned and the coup was a coup. The Bush administration apparently did not mind the political costs for its involvement in the ouster of a democratically elected president. After the Carmona fiasco, Washington announced the creation of an "office of transition" within its embassy in Caracas, still attempting Chávez's overthrow. The violent contradictions between the social and economic elite and the popular sectors galvanized by Chávez has resulted in bloody daily confrontations and extreme violence in the streets.

The United States' aggression against Cuba continues: the economic blockade, its "vendetta" which persists in the guise of human rights concerns, the hostile rhetoric that now fuels threatening and false accusations of Cuba's manufacturing biological weapons and of fomenting terrorism—charges that Cuba vehemently rejects. In response to an offensive speech by George W. Bush in May 2002 to a gathering of anti-Castro Cuban-Americans in Miami, Castro affirmed that Bush's world outlook was ruled by "Nazi methods and concepts" and that by virtue of United States military power, he has "assumed the role of master and gendarme of the world," taken the right to declare a terrorist anyone not supportive of his global "war on terrorism."[15] Meanwhile, Cuba continues to gain support from the United Nations General Assembly in its political struggle against the economic blockade. In the fall of 2002 it received 173 votes in favor of the removal of the blockade, 3 against (including the United States and Israel), and 4 abstentions—a record in the eleven years under the United Nations consideration.[16]

After decades of neo-liberal economic policy embraced by Latin American governments, the resulting economic and social impact on the region has been critical despite the advances in economic sectors and reforms implemented to adapt to that new economic model. Economic growth in the region in 2001 was close to zero. Argentina went bankrupt, and with the exceptions of Chile and Mexico, most of the countries are in a very difficult social and economic situation. The increasingly severe gap between the rich and the poor is widening. According to the Inter-American Development Bank, poverty is affecting 232 million of its 500 million inhabitants, 92 million of whom have reached a point of extreme poverty (in 2002 the number of poor increased by 18 million). The International Labor Organization's November 2001 report evaluates the unemployment situation as critical; at least 160 million—almost a third of the population—is unemployed.[17]

When Luiz Inacio "Lula" da Silva was elected president of Brazil in October 2002, *The Nation* magazine wrote that neo-liberalism had lost the election; the 52.8 million votes for Lula, leader of the working class, reflected that "all social classes [were] tired of depending on the International Monetary Fund." *The Nation* also mentioned Lula's worldwide support and that the "loudest opposition" was coming from Washington.[18] Brazil is the biggest and most influential country in Latin America, and Lula's presidency will affect the whole continent.

Echoing the massive anti-globalization movement that has emerged to counter the implacable advance of multinational corporations, Chávez and Lula have placed anti-neo-liberalism at the top of their agendas, a stance shared by many throughout the continent. They favor the strong role of the government in economic development and social justice rather than that of the private sectors. The election of leftist former Colonel Lucio Gutiérrez (as Chávez responsible for an attempted coup d'etat) as president of Ecuador, reinforces Chávez's and Lula's stances and policies. Impressive anti-global street protests starting in Seattle in 1999 and continuing in Prague and many other cities around the world have begun to make inroads: in July of 2001 G-8 leaders recognized and praised the role that peaceful protest plays in putting issues like debt relief on the international agenda,[19] a promising sign for the highly indebted Latin American countries.

For Latin America this new phase of history, the new millennium—received with so much hope and euphoria around the world—has meant economic crisis, bankruptcies, an astronomical foreign debt ($398 billion), dramatically intensified poverty and social unrest, the faltering of democratic governments, and a new succession of scandals centered around the rampant corruption of a number of presidents. The United States, still stunned by the terrorist attacks of September 11, has been thrust by the Bush administration into a global war on terrorism. Meanwhile, a cascade of scandals—multimillion dollar thefts, fraud, and bankruptcies of powerful corporations—have exposed not only previously unheard of levels of corruption but something far more frightening: the connections between corporations and political higher-ups in Washington as well as the alarming reality of a political world, moved by money under the table, without ethical or moral boundaries. The entire world waits uneasily under the shadow of an amorphous and unpredictable global war against terrorism—an evasive and unknowable enemy. No one knows how far this war will go, how and when it will end, and what sort of victory might be expected, and at what cost.

NOTES

CHAPTER I: Mare Nostrum, Mare Claustrum

1   G. Pierre-Charles, *El Caribe a la hora de Cuba*, Casa de las Américas Prize, Havana, 1980, pp. 19–20.

2   William Appleman Williams, *The Tragedy of American Diplomacy*, Delta Books, New York, 1962, pp. 19–20, 53–54.

3   W. Appleman Williams, *op. cit.*, p. 54.

4   Harold Molineu, *U.S. Policy Toward Latin America*, Westview Press, Boulder and London, 1986, p. 40; William Harbaugh, *The Writings of Theodore Roosevelt*, Bobbs Merrill Co., New York, 1967, p. 32.

5   Jane Franklin, *Cuba and the United States, A Chronological History*, Ocean Press, Melbourne, New York, 1997, pp. 9, 10

6   Héctor Pérez-Brignoli, *A Brief History of Central America*, University of California Press, Berkeley, 1989, p. 124

7   *The Columbia University Encyclopedia*, Columbia University, New York, 1975, pp. 2012–2013

8   H. Pérez-Brignoli, *op. cit.*, p. 124

9   George C. Khon, *Dictionary of Wars*, Anchor Books, New York, 1987, p. 284.

10 Jane Franklin, *The Cuban Revolution and the United States*, Ocean Press, New York, 1992, p. 11.

11 *Instrucción Política*, FAR, Havana, 1973, p. 93.

12 *Lázaro Barredo Medina, Bohemia*, Havana, December 27, 1991.

13 *Instrucción Política*, FAR, *op. cit.*, pp. 84–87.

14 W. Appleman Williams, *op. cit.*, pp. 30–31.

15 *Ibid.*, p. 36.

16 *Instrucción Política*, FAR, *op. cit.*, p. 94.

17 Hubert Herring, *A History of Latin America*, Alfred A. Knopf, New York, 1969, p. 398.

18   *Instrucción Política,* FAR, *op. cit.,* pp. 89–91.
19   J. Franklin, *The Cuban Revolution . . . , op. cit.,* pp. 3, 16.
20   Hugh Thomas, *Cuba,* Ed. Grijalbo, Barcelona, 1973, pp. 587–89.
21   J. Franklin, *op. cit.,* pp. 16–17.
22   *Ibid.,* p. 18.
23   Julio Le Riverend, "Cuba: Del semicolonialismo al socialismo (1933–1975)", in *América Latina: Historia de medio siglo.* Pablo González Casanova, Vol. I, Ed. Siglo XXI, Mexico, 1977, p. 47.
24   Tom Barry, Beth Wood and Deb Preusch, *The Other Side of Paradise: Foreign Control in the Caribbean,* Grove Press Inc., New York, 1984, pp. 238–39.
25   Robert Leiken and Barry Rubin, *Central American Crisis Reader,* Summit Books, New York, 1987, p. 82.
26   A. Aguilar, *Pan Americanism, from Monroe to Present,* M R Press, New York, 1965, pp. 54–55.
27   W. LaFeber, *Inevitable Revolutions,* W. W. Norton Co., New York, 1984, pp. 66–67, 70.
28   Jesús Silva Herzog, quoted by A. Aguilar, *Pan Americanism, op. cit.* p. 70.
29   A. Aguilar, *op. cit.,* p. 72.
30   *Ibid.,* pp. 73–75, 172, 174.
31   *Ibid.,* pp. 76, 174.
32   T. Barry, B. Wood and D. Preusch, *op. cit.,* pp. 197–98.
33   H. Truman, Speech to Congress, March 12, 1947.
34   Edwin R. Bayley, *Joe McCarthy and the Press,* University of Wisconsin Press, Madison, WI, 1981, p. 3.
35   William Fulbright, *The Crippled Giant,* Random House, New York, 1972, pp. 55, 60.
36   A. Aguilar, *op. cit.,* p. 171.

CHAPTER II: Some Come, Some Go

1   Department of State, Memorandum, 1/21/1959
2   Tad Szulc, *Fidel,* William Morrow & Co., New York, p. 457; Martha Harnecker, *Fidel Castro's Political Strategy,* Pathfinder Press, New York, 1987, pp. 49–52.
3   Earl Smith, *The Fourth Floor,* Random House, New York, 1962, p. 188.
4   Hubert Herring, *A History of Latin America,* Alfred A. Knopf, New York, 1968, p. 404
5   Jane Franklin, *The Cuban Revolution and the United States,* Ocean Press, New York, 1992, pp. 19–23.
6   *Instrucción Política de las FAR,* Libro Segundo, Instituto Cubano del Libro, La Habana, 1973, p. 140.
7   *Ibid.,* p. 141.
8   H. Herring, *op. cit.,* pp. 404–405.
9   *Instrucción Política,* FAR, *op. cit.,* pp. 139–41.
10   *Bohemia,* Havana, Oct. 4, 1991
11   M. Harneker, *op. cit.,* pp. 90, 101–103.
12   *Instrucción Política,* FAR, *op. cit.,* p. 210
13   E. Smith, *op. cit.,* pp. 184–85

14   *Ibid.*, p. 185

15   Hugh Thomas, *Cuba*, Ediciones Grijalbo, Barcelona, 1973, p. 1321

16   Guillermo Villaronda, *Bohemia,* Havana, February 15, 1959.

17   *Ibid.*, p. 1321; *Bohemia,* Havana, February 15, 1959.

18   *New York Times,* January 2, 1959.

19   E. Smith, *op. cit.*, p. 186.

20   Ciro Bianchi, *Cuba Internacional*, Havana, December, 1984, p. 27.

21   Robert J. Alexander, *Rómulo Betancourt and the Transformation of Venezuela*, Transaction Books, New Brunswick, 1986, p. 559.

22   Jules Dubois, *Fidel Castro: Rebel-Liberator or Dictator?,* Indianapolis, Bob-Merrill, 1959, pp. 349–50.

23   J. Dubois, op. cit, p. 362

24   Correspondencia diplomática colombiana, February 20, 1959.

25   J. Dubois, *op. cit.*, p. 350.

26   Correspondencia diplomática colombiana, February 20, 1959.

27   *Ibid.*

28   H. Thomas, *op. cit.*, p. 1381.

29   T. Szulc, *op. cit.*, p. 456.

30   *El Tiempo*, Bogotá, December 9, 1958.

31   U.S. Embassy document, Caracas, January 14, 1959.

32   *Ibid.*

33   T. Szulc, *op. cit.*, p.533.

34   *Ibid.*, pp. 531–33.

35   Herbert Matthews, *Fidel Castro*, Touchstone Books, New York, 1969, pp. 139, 145.

36   H. Thomas, *op. cit.*, p. 1401.

37   Todd Gitlin, *The Sixties*, Bantam Books, New York, 1987, pp. 1–2

38   Maurice Halperin, *The Rise and Decline of Fidel Castro*, University of California, Berkeley, 1972, p. 15

39   T. Szulc, *op. cit.*, p. 299.

40   M. Halperin, *op. cit.*, pp. 19–20.

41   *Ibid.*, p. 49.

42   M. Harnecker, *op. cit.*, p. 11.

43   *New York Times*, April 21, 1959.

44   M. Halperin, *op. cit.*, p. 46.

45   Raúl Roa, *Retorno a la alborada*, Editorial Ciencias Sociales, Havana, 1977, pp. 306–307.

46   M. Halperin, *op. cit.*, pp. 52–54.

47   *New York Times*, May 2, 1959.

48   M. Halperin, *op. cit.*, pp. 319–320.

49   *New York Times*, April 28, 1959; May 1, 1959.

50   T. Szulc, *op. cit.*, pp. 541–42.

51   *Ibid.*, p. 541.

52   *Ibid.*, pp. 122–24.

53   Confidential State Department Document, July 30, 1959.

54   State Department Document, April 13, 1959.

55   *New York Times*, April 13, 1959.

56   Confidential Communications of the State Department, September 6, 1959.

57   M. Halperin, *op. cit.*, pp. 69–70.

58   H. Matthews, *op. cit.*, p. 49.

59   *The Cuban Reader*, Ed. Philip Brenner and others, Grove Press, New York, 1989, p. 528.

60   G. Pierre-Charles, *El Caribe a la hora de Cuba*, Casa de las Americas Prize, Havana, 1980, pp. 92n., 114–15.

61   Victor Marchetti and John D. Marks, *The CIA and the Cult of Intelligence*, Dell Books, 1980, p. 268.

62   Jane Franklin, *The Cuban Revolution and the United States*, Ocean, Melbourne, Australia, 1992, pp. 27, 28, 30.

63   Gabriel Molina, *Diario de Girón*, Editora Política, Havana, 1984, p. 7.

64   *Op. cit.*, p. 7.

65   Jon Dennis Cozeau, "The Elite Press and Foreign Policy, The Case of Cuba, 1979" (mimeograph), Library of Congress, Washington, No. BTK 80-0075.

66   Franklin, *op. cit.,* p. 27; Aguilar, *op. cit.*, pp.113–14

67   J. Dubois, *Fidel Castro*, pp. 180–81; T. Szulc, *op.cit.*, p. 451.

68   Townsed Hoopes, *The Devil and John Foster Dulles*, Atlantic Little Brown, Boston, 1973, pp. 498–99.

69   *Op. cit.*, pp. 503–504.

CHAPTER III: The Turbulent 1960s

1   *Time*, July 1980.

2   Theodore C. Sorensen, *Kennedy*, Bantam Books, New York, 1966, p. 15.

3   Jim F. Heath, *Decade of Disillusionment*, Indiana University Press, Bloomington, 1975, pp. 297–98.

4   T. Sorensen, *op. cit.*, p. 589.

5   Leonhard Wolfgang, *Three Faces of Marxism*, Capricorn Books, New York, 1974, pp. 146–147.

6   *Ibid.*, p.257.

7   G. R. Urban, Ed., *Euro-communism*, Universe Books, New York, 1978, pp. 7–8, 17.

8   Edward McNall Burns, *Western Civilizations*, W. W. Norton & Co., New York, 1968, p. 833.

9   Xavier Rynne, *Letters from Vatican City*, Doubleday, Image Books, Garden City, New York, 1964, p. 77.

10   T. Sorensen (1965), *op. cit.*, pp. 514–15

11   T. Sorensen, *op. cit.*, pp. 575, 579.

12   Arthur Schlesinger, *Robert Kennedy and his Times*, Houghton Mifflin Co., Boston, 1978, pp. 550–51; T. Sorensen (1965).

13   Ernest G. Bormann, Ed., *Forerunners of Black Power*, Prentice-Hall, Inc., NJ, 1971, p. 237.

14   Inter-American Economic Affairs, *Government Documents*, Winter, 1961, pp. 79–86.

15   T. Sorensen (1965), *op. cit.*, pp. 533, 536, 537

16   T. Sorensen, op.cit., pp. 600–601.

17   Carlos Sanz de Santamaría, *Alianza para el progreso, revolución silenciosa*, Fondo de Cultura Económica, México, 1971, p. 30.

18   A. Schlesinger, *op. cit.*, p. 576.

19   T. Sorensen (1965), *op. cit.*, pp. 631–33

20   T. Sorensen, *op. cit.*, pp. 712–13.

21   Ana María Bidegain de Urán, *Nacionalismo, militarismo y dominación en América Latina*, Universidad de los Andes, Bogotá, 1983, p. 151; Edwin Lieuwen, *Generales contra presidentes en América Latina*, Siglo XX, Buenos Aires, 1965, pp. 177–79.

22   Claude Heller, *El ejército como agente de cambio*, Fondo de Cultura Económica, México. 1980. pp. 126, 133.

23   Justo Escobar and Sebastián Velásquez, *Examen de la violencia Argentina*, Fondo de Cultura Ecónomica, 1975, p. 125.

24   Alfredo Vázquez Carrizosa, *El poder presidencial en Colombia*, Ediciones Suramérica Ltda., Bogotá, 1979, p. 334.

25   Inter-American Economic Affairs, op. cit, pp. 76–86.

26   Arthur Schlesinger, *A Thousand Days*, Fawcett Premier, New York, 1965, p. 181.

27   T. Sorensen, *op. cit.*, p. 603.

28   T. Sorensen (1965), *op. cit.*, p. 295.

29   A. Schlesinger, *op. cit.*, p. 175–76.

30   T. Sorensen (1965), *op. cit.*, p. 295

31   Gabriel Molina, *Diario de Girón*, Editora Política, Havana, 1984, p. 71.

32   G. Molina, *op. cit.*, pp. 71–72.

33   Peter Wyden, *Bay of Pigs*, Touchstone Books, Simon and Schuster, New York, 1979, pp. 50–53.

34   A. Schlesinger (1965), *op. cit.*, p.242; T. Sorensen (1965), *op. cit.*, pp. 297–8.

35   P. Wyden, *op. cit.*, pp. 99–100.

36   G. Pierre-Charles, *El Caribe a la hora de Cuba*, Casa de las Americas Prize, Havana, 1980, p. 121.

37   A. Schlesinger, quoted by G. Molina, *op. cit.*, p. 135.

38   Maurice Halperin, *The Rise and Decline of Fidel Castro*, University of California Press, Berkeley, 1974, pp. 111–112.

39   T. Sorensen (1965), *op. cit.*, pp. 290, 306–7, 309

40   J. Didion, *Miami*, Simon and Schuster, New York, 1987, pp. 14–15.

41   William Colby, *Honorable Men*, Simon and Schuster, New York, 1978, p. 189.

42   T. Powers, *op. cit.*, pp. 132, 133, 135, 138.

43   Fabián Escalante, *Documentos de la Reunión Tripartita*, Antigua, 1991.

44   John Ranelagh, *The Agency: The Rise and Decline of the CIA*, Touchstone Books, Simon and Schuster, New York, 1987, pp. 345, 357–358, 383, 390; W. Colby, *op. cit.*, pp. 188–190, 428–430, 455.

45   T. Powers, *op. cit.*, p. 155.

46   *Ibid.*, p. 139.

47   A. Aguilar, *op. cit.*, pp. 120–3

48   J. Franklin, *op. cit.*, pp. 120, 176

49   *Segunda Declaration de la Habana*, Asamblea Nacional del Poder Popular, La Habana, February 1962

50   *Ibid.*.

51   Carlos Lechuga, *El ojo de la tormenta*, Ocean Press, Australia, 1995, pp. 55, 65.

52   *Documentos de la Reunión Tripartita*, Moscow, 1989.

53   Victor Marchetti & John D. Markes, *The CIA and the Cult of Intelligence*, Dell Publishing Co., New York, 1980, p. 273.

54   T. Sorensen, *op. cit.*, pp. 767–768; R. McNamara, *Documentos de la Reunión Tripartita*, Moscow, 1989; Ernest R. May & Philip D. Zelikow, Eds., *The Kennedy Tapes, Inside the White House during the Cuban Missile Crisis*, Harvard University Press, Cambridge, MA, 1997, pp. 128, 286.

55   T. Sorensen, *op. cit.*, pp. 753, 756, 777–778.

56   *Ibid.*, pp. 769–770.

57   R. McNamara, *Documentos de la Reunión Tripartita*, Moscow, 1989.

58   T. Sorensen, *op. cit.*, pp. 768–772.

59   *Op. cit.*, pp. 768–772.

60   *Granma*, Havana, November 6, 1991.

61   A. Schlesinger, *A Thousand Days*, *op. cit.*, p. 743.

62   T. Sorensen, *op. cit.*, p. 699.

63   Edwin Lieuwen, *Siglo veinte*, Siglo XXI, Buenos Aires, 1965, p. 176.

64   *UN Yearbook 1963*, New York, pp. 104, 105.

65   May and Zelikow, *op.cit.* p. 390.

66   *UN Yearbook 1962*, New York, pp. 104, 105; *Everyman's United Nations, 1945–1963*, UN, New York, p. 178.

67   J. Franklin *op. cit.*, p. 58.

68   T. Sorensen, pp. 710–11.

69   Jorge Pollo, in *Granma*, October 24, 1991.

70   *Everyman's United Nations*, *op. cit.*, pp. 178–179.

71   May and Zelikow, *op. cit.*, pp. 282, 321, 390, 487, 490.

72   C. Lechuga, *op. cit.*, pp. 125–126.

73   *Ibid.*, pp. 130–132.

74   May and Zelikow, p. 443.

75   Lechuga, pp. 126–130.

76   *Ibid.*, pp. 138–141.

77   *Ibid.*, pp. 146–149.

78   *U.N. Yearbook, 1962*, *op. cit.*, p. 110.

79   *Everman's United Nations, op. cit.*, p. 179.

80   T. Sorensen, *Documentos de la Reunión Tripartita*, Moscow, 1989.

81 James G. Blight, Bruce J. Allyn, and David A. Welch, *Cuba on the Brink, Castro's Missile Crisis and the Soviet Collapse,* Pantheon Books, New York, 1993, pp. 39, 41–42, 249, 376, 477; May and Zelikow, *op. cit.,* p. 321

82 S. Khrushchev, Tripartita, Moscow 1989

83 S. Khrushchev, Tripartita, Antigua, 1991

84 Nikita Khrushchev, *Khrushchev Remembers*, Little, Brown, and Co., Boston, 1970, pp. 493, 494

85 J. Pollo, in *Granma*, Havana, October 30, 1991.

86 Fidel Castro, *Documentos de la Reunión Tripartita*, Havana, 1992

87 Blight, Allyn, and Welch, p. 84.

88 Castro, *op. cit.*

89 S. Mikoyan, *Documentos de la Reunión Tripartita*, Antigua, 1991.

90 T. Sorensen, *op. cit.*, pp. 795–796; H. Thomas, *op. cit.*, pp. 1794–1795.

91 H. Thomas, *op. cit.*, pp. 1794–1795.

92 Maurice Halperin, *op. cit.*, p. 199.

93 Blight, Allyn, and Welch, pp. 23, 214, 248, 485–88

94 Halperin, *op. cit.*, p. 201.

95 *New York Herald Tribune*, October 6, 1963.

96 T. Sorensen, *op. cit.*, p. 601.

97 Tad Szulc, *Fidel*, Avon Books, New York, 1986, pp. 597–598.

98 *Ibid.* pp. 558, 559, 588–89

99 A. Schlesinger, *Robert Kennedy, op. cit.*, pp. 552–553.

100 *Ibid.,* pp. 555–556.

101 *Ibid.*

102 Jim F. Heath, *op. cit.*, p. 11

103 Eric Goldman, *The Tragedy of Lyndon B. Johnson*, Alfred Knopf, New York, 1965, pp. 7, 10, 24–6.

104 Theodore White, *The Making of the President 1964*, Signet Books, New York, 1966, p. 45.

105 Goldman, pp. 29, 165–66

106 Sorensen (1965), p. 489

107 Todd Gitlin, *The Sixties*, Bantam Books, Toronto and New York, 1987, p. 313.

108 A. Schlesinger, *op. cit.*, p. 630.

109 Goldman, *op. cit.*, pp. 76, 395

110 Ellen Ray and William Schaap, "Vernon Walters: Crypto-diplomat and Terrorist", in *Covert Action Information Bulletin*, No. 26, Washington, DC, 1986, pp. 3–8.

111 Goldman, *op.cit.*, p. 73; Heath, pp. 189–90.

112 Aguilar, *op. cit.,* pp. 127–29.

113 Goldman, *op. cit.*, p. 74.

114 A. Schlesinger, *op. cit.*, p. 635.

115 Goldman, *op. cit.,* p. 468

116 Goldman, *op. cit.* p. 382

117 T. Powers, *op. cit.*, p. 171.

118   E. Goldman, *op. cit.*, p. 470.
119   Aguilar, pp. 133–134.
120   E. Goldman, *op. cit.*, p. 470.
121   A. Aguilar, *op. cit.*, pp. 138–139.
122   Goldman, *op. cit.*, p. 75; Heath, *op. cit.*, p. 190
123   A. Schlesinger, *op. cit.*, p. 690.
124   Robert Kennedy, *To Seek a New World*, Bantam Books, New York, 1968, p. 60.
125   Carlos Sanz de Santamaría, *op. cit.*, pp. 148–149, 161–162.
126   Marchetti and Marks, *op. cit.*, p. 269.
127   A. Schlesinger, *op. cit.*, p. 882.
128   E. Goldman, *op. cit.*, p 410.

CHAPTER IV: "The Backyard"

1   R. Leikin and B. Rubin, *op. cit.*, pp. 29–30.
2   Edelberto Torres-Rivas, "Guatemala", in: *América Latina: Historia de medio siglo*, Vol. II, *op. cit.*, p. 141.
3   Héctor Pérez-Brignoli, *A Brief History of Central America*, University of California Press, Berkeley, CA, pp. 118–119.
4   W. LaFeber, *op. cit.*, p. 176
5   Mario Salazar Valiente, "El Salvador", in: *América Latina: . . . medio siglo, op. cit.*, Vol. II, pp. 91–111.
6   Juan Mestre, *Subdesarrollo y Violencia en Guatemala*, I.E.P.A.L., Madrid, 1969, pp. 118–119.
7   Penny Lernoux, *Cry of the People*, Penguin Books, New York, 1979, pp. 107–108.
8   A. Aguilar, *op. cit.*, p. 108.
9   J. Franklin, *op. cit.*, pp. 29, 30.
10   *United Fruit Company: un caso del dominio imperialista en Cuba*, Editorial Ciencias Sociales, Havana, 1978, pp. 14, 67, 78–70.
11   P. Lernoux, *op. cit.*, pp. 107–108.
12   Richard E. Feinberg, Ed., *Central America: International Dimension of the Crisis*, Holmes and Meier Publishers, Inc., New York, 1982, p. 5.
13   Medea Benjamin (Ed.), *Don't be Afraid Gringo*, Harper and Row Publishers, New York, 1987, pp. xv, xvi.
14   P. Lernoux, *op. cit.*, p. 107.
15   W. LaFeber, *op. cit.*, p. 133; G. Molina Chocano, "Honduras", in: *América Latina*, Vol. II, *op. cit.*, pp. 244–245.
16   Mario Rodríguez, *Central America*, Spectrum Books, NJ, 1965, pp. 36–37; W. LaFeber, *op. cit.*, p. 178.
17   *Ibid.*, p. 36.
18   W. LaFeber, *op. cit.*, pp. 179–180.
19   G. Molina Chocano, *op. cit.*, p. 252.
20   W. LaFeber, *op. cit.*, pp. 179–180.
21   G. Molina Chocano, *op. cit.*, p. 254.

22 W. LaFeber, *op. cit.*, pp. 263–264.

23 *Time*, April 24, 1975

24 *Centroamerica, Infopress,* p. H-19; Barry Carr and Steve Ellner, Eds., *The Latin American Left: From the Fall of Allende to Perestroika,* Westview Press, Boulder, CO, 1993, p. 193.

25 M. Salazar Valiente, *op. cit.*, p.88.

26 W. LaFeber, *op. cit.*, pp. 70–71.

27 M. Salazar Valiente, *op. cit.*, p. 93.

28 W. LaFeber, *op. cit.*, pp. 72–74.

29 *Ibid.*, pp. 60; Leiken and Rubin, *op. cit.*, p. 506.

30 Roque Dalton, *Miguel Mármol,* quoted in Mario Salazar Valiente, *"El Salvador", op. cit.,* p. 96.

31 W. LaFeber, *op. cit.*, p. 173; M. Rodríguez, *op. cit.*, pp. 38–39.

32 M. Salazar Valiente, *op. cit.*, pp. 91–111.

33 M. Rodríguez, *op. cit.*, p.39.

34 W. LaFeber, *op. cit.*, p. 172.

35 *Ibid.*, pp. 172–174.

36 M. Salazar Valiente, *op. cit.*, p. 118.

37 Centroamérica, Infopress, *Guatemala,* 1981, p. ES-2.

38 Noam Chomsky, *Turning the Tide,* South End Press, Boston, 1985, p. 98.

39 Tom Barry, *Central America Inside Out,* Grove Winfield, New York, 1991, p. 165.

40 Marvin E. Gettleman et al., eds., *El Salvador,* Grove Press, New York, 1987, pp. 77–79.

41 U.S. Department of State, February, 1979; Leiken and Rubin, *op. cit.*, pp. 337–342.

42 M. Gettleman et al., *op. cit.*, p. 80.

43 *Ibid.*, pp. 188–190.

44 *Ibid.*

45 *Ibid.*, pp. 56, 191.

46 *Alternativa,* Bogotá, No. 235/79; Gettleman et. Al., *op. cit.*, p. 191.

47 M. Gettleman, *op. cit.*, p. 55.

48 Tom Buckley, *Violent Neighbors,* Times Books, New York, 1984, p. 135.

49 Leiken and Rubin, *op. cit.*, pp. 503–504.

50 T, Barry, *op. cit.*, p. 179.

51 Gettleman, *op. cit.*, pp. 90–91, 292.

52 *Ibid.*

53 *Ibid.*, p. 289.

54 Phillip Berryman, *Inside Central America,* Pantheon Books, New York, 1985, pp. 31, 72–73, 123.

55 *Ibid.,* pp. 38, 72–73.

56 M. Gettleman, *op. cit.*, pp. 56, 294; *NACLA Reports,* May-June, 1981, p. 15.

57 Leikin and Rubin, *op. cit.*, pp. 377–380.

58 *NACLA Reports,* May/June, 1981, pp. 16, 23.

59 Leikin and Rubin, *op. cit.*, p. 408.

60 P. Berryman, *op. cit.*, p. 45.

61   M. Gettleman, *op. cit.*, pp. 256–258.

62   W. LaFeber, *op. cit.*, p. 68; M. Rodríguez, *op. cit.*, pp. 125–126.

63   Walter LaFeber, *Inevitable Revolutions*, WW Norton & Co, 1989, p. 69.

64   *Time,* November 15, 1948, p. 43; Peter Rosset (ed.), *The Nicaragua Reader*, Grove Press, New York, 1983, p. 118.

65   Leiken and Rubin, *op. cit.*, pp. 101, 117–118.

66   Stephen Schlesinger and Stephen Kinzer, *Blood of Brothers*, Anchor Books, New York, 1991, p. 32.

67   W. LaFeber, *op. cit.*, p. 162.

68   Manzar Foroohar, *The Catholic Church and Social Change in Nicaragua*, State University of New York Press, New York, 1989, pp. 87–91.

69   Leiken & Rubin, *op. cit.*, pp. 54–55.

70   Tomás Borge, *Paciente impaciencia*, Casa de las Americas Prize, Havana, 1989, p. 146.

71   Leikin and Rubin, *op. cit.*, pp. 149–153.

72   S. Schlesinger and S. Kinzer, *Bitter Fruit*, Anchor Books, New York, 1982, p.42.

73   R. Leikin and B. Rubin, *op. cit.*, pp. 191–192.

74   S. Schlesinger and S. Kinzer, *op. cit.*, p. 40.

75   Leikin and Rubin, *op. cit.*, pp. 186–191.

76   S. Schlesinger and S. Kinzer, *op. cit.*, p. 49.

77   Holly Sklar, *Washington's War on Nicaragua*, South End Press, Boston, MA, pp. 30–32.

78   S. Schlesinger and S. Kinzer, *op. cit.*, p. 70.

79   Leikin and Rubin, *op. cit.*, p. 199.

80   S. Schlesinger and S. Kinzer, *op. cit.*, p. 33; Leikin and Rubin, *op. cit.*, p. 141.

81   Leikin and Rubin, *op. cit.*, p. 199.

82   Anthony Lake, *Somoza Falling: A Case Study of Washington at Work*, University of Massachussets Press, Amherst, 1989, pp. 160–161, 264.

83   S. Schlesinger and S. Kinzer, *op. cit.*, pp. 143–144; Alonso Aguilar, *Pan-Americanism from Monroe to the Present*, MR, 1965, pp. 99–102.

84   John Ranelagh, *The Agency: The Rise and Decline of the CIA*, Simon & Schuster, New York, 1986, pp. 265–269.

85   S. Schlesinger and S. Kinzer, *op. cit.*, pp. 8–9, 108, 122, 192.

86   Kalman H. Silvert, *The Conflict Society: Reaction and Revolution in Latin America*, Harper Colophon Books, New York, 1968, p. 230; Blanche Wiesen Cook, *The Declassified Eisenhower*, Penguin Books, New York, 1984, p. 148; John Ranelagh, *op. cit.*, pp. 265–268.

87   A. Schlesinger, quoted by Susanne Jonas, *The Battle for Guatemala*, West View Press, Boulder and San Francisco, 1989, p. 42.

88   S. Jonas, *op. cit.*, p. 42.

89   S. Schlesinger and S. Kinzer, *op. cit.*, p. 235; Richard H. Immerman, *The CIA in Guatemala*, University of Texas Press, Austin, TX, 1982, p. 200.

90   E. Torres Rivas, *op. cit.*, p. 167.

91   *Ibid.*, p. 167.

92   S. Jonas, *op. cit.*, pp. 70–71.

93 *La amenaza de la guerrilla en América Latina*, Editorial Olimpo, México, 1968, pp. 38–40.

94 W. LaFeber, *op. cit.*, pp. 168–169.

95 J. Mestre, *Subdesarollo y violencia*. Guatemala, I.E.P.A.L., Madrid, 1969, pp. 184–185, 199.

96 S. Jonas, *op. cit.*, p. 70.

97 *Perspectiva Mundial*, New York, June 29, 1981, pp. 14–15.

98 J. Mestre, *op. cit.*, pp. 196–197.

99 *Ibid.*, pp. 191–192, 198.

100 S. Jonas, *op. cit.*, p. 70.

101 J. Mestre, *op. cit.*, pp. 196–197.

102 S. Schlesinger and S. Kinzer, *op. cit.*, p. 244.

103 W. LaFeber, *op. cit.*, p. 170.

104 *Ibid.*

105 J. Mestre, I*op. cit., p. 204.*

106 *Ibid.*, pp. 201–202.

107 W. LaFeber, *op. cit.*, pp. 170–171.

108 *Perspectiva Mundial*, New York, June 29, 1981.

109 S. Schlesinger and S. Kinzer, *op. cit.*, pp. 248–249.

110 S. Jonas, *op. cit.*, p. 95.

111 *Ibid.*, p. 128.

112 *Ibid.*, pp. 124, 128, 137.

113 P. Berryman, *op. cit.*, p. 41.

114 *Perspectiva Mundial*, New York, June 29, 1981.

115 Richard Fagan, *Forging Peace: The Challenge of Central America*, DACCA Books, 1987, p. 91.

116 *Perspectiva Mundial*, New York, June 29, 1981.

CHAPTER V: With Weapons in Hand

1 David Deutschmann, Ed., *Che, a Memoir by Fidel Castro*, Ocean Press, Melbourne, Australia, 1994, p. 84.

2 Rubèn Vásqyez Díaz, *Bolivia a la hora de Che*, Siglo XXI, Mexico, 1978, p. 264.

3 Ernesto Che Guevara, *Diario de Bolivia*, Equipo editorial S. A. Zarauz, Spain, 1968.

4 Gianni Mina, *An Encounter with Fidel*, Ocean Press, Australia, 1991, pp. 215–240.

5 *New York Times*, July 14, 1961.

6 Claudio Heller, Ed., *El ejército como agente de cambio* Fondo de Cultura Económica, Mexico, 1979, p. 126.

7 Ana María Bidegain, *Nacionalismo, militarismo y dominación en América Latina*, Ed. Uniandes, Bogotá, 1983, pp. 150–152.

8 Ximena Ortúzar, *Represión y tortura en el Cono Sur*, Ed. Extemporánea, México, 1977, p. 101.

9 W. J. Pomeroy, *Guerrillas y contraguerrillas*, Ed. Grijalbo, México, 1967, p. 37.

10 C. Heller, *op. cit.*, p. 126.

11 J. Gerassi, *The Great Fear of Latin America*, Collier Books, New York, 1973, pp. 65–66.

12   Mark Kaplan, *Argentina: América Latina: Historia de medio siglo*, Vol I., Siglo XXI, México, 1977, p. 57

13   Tomás Córdoba, *La Argentina, Perón y después*, Ed. Cidal, Caracas, 1975, pp. 126–130.

14   T. Córdoba, *op. cit.*, pp. 132–133.

15   Falange was the fascist party in power in Spain under Franco's regime.

16   M. Kaplan, *op. cit.*, p. 61.

17   T. Córdoba, *op. cit.*, pp. 137–138.

18   Oscar R. Anzorena, *Tiempo*

19   Alain Rouquié, (Comp.), *Argentina hoy*, Siglo XXI, Mexico, 1982, p. 206.

20   O. Anzorena, *op. cit.*, pp. 129–132.

21   A. Rouquié, *op. cit.*, p. 209; O. Anzorena, *op. cit.*, pp. 83–84, 88–89.

22   A. Rouquié, *op. cit.*, pp. 210–211.

23   *Ibid.*, p. 212.

24   O. Anzorena, *op. cit.*, p. 127.

25   *Ibid.*, pp. 52–53.

26   *Ibid.*, p. 53.

27   *Ibid.*, pp. 146–147.

28   A. Rouquié, *op. cit.*, p. 232.

29   O. Anzorena, *op. cit.* pp. 49, 84–86.

30   A. M. Bidegain, *op. cit.*, p. 137.

31   Vania Bambirra and Theotonio Dos Santos, *Brasil: América Latina, Historia de medio Siglo*, Siglo XXI, México, 1977, Vol. I, pp. 151–152.

32   Penny Lernoux, *Cry of the People*, Penguin Books, New York, 1982, p. 169.

33   Eduardo Galeano, *Las venas abiertas de América Latina*, Siglo XXI, México, 1975, pp. 240–241.

34   Marcio Moreira, *Un grano de mostaza*, Casa de las Americas Prize (1972), Ed. Cepe, Buenos Aires, 1973, p. 92.

35   M. Moreira, *op. cit.*, p. 97.

36   P. Lernoux, *op. cit.*, p. 167.

37   A. M. Bidegain, *op.cit.*, pp. 146, 166.

38   M. Moreira, *op. cit.*, p. 108.

39   Thomas E. Skidmore, *The Politics of Military Rule in Brazil, 1964–85*, Oxford University Press, New York, 1988, p. 25.

40   V. Bambirra and Theotonio Dos Santos, *op. cit.*, p. 153.

41   T. Skidmore, *op. cit.*, pp. 24–25.

42   A. M. Bidegain, *op. cit.*, pp. 167–168.

43   M. Moreira, *op. cit.*, p. 95.

44   X. Ortúzar, *op. cit.*, pp. 98–99.

45   Bambirra and Dos Santos, *op. cit.*, p. 159.

46   M. Moreira, *op. cit.*, p. 267.

47   *Ibid.*, pp. 207–210.

48   *Ibid.*, pp. 139, 178–179.

49 Carlos Mariguela, *For the Liberation of Brazil*, Penguin Books, Victoria, Australia, 1971, pp. 19, 183.

50 T. Skidmore, *op. cit.*, pp. 50–51, 78.

51 Informe del Arzobispado de San Pablo, *Torture in Brazil*, (English version), Vintage Books, New York, 1986.

52 P. Lernoux, *op. cit.*, p. 466.

53 Gerónimo Sierra, "Uruguay", in *América Latina: Historia de Medio Siglo*, Siglo XXI, Mexico, 1977, p. 435.

54 G. de Sierra, *op. cit.*, p. 459.

55 Tulio Halperin, *Historia Contemporánea de América Latina*, Alianza Editorial, Madrid, 1986, pp. 534–536.

56 G. de Sierra, *op. cit.*, p. 439.

57 *Ibid.*, pp. 442, 444.

58 *Ibid.*, p. 444.

59 Alain Labrousse, *Los Tupamaros, guerrilla urbana en Uruguay*, Editorial Tiempo Contamporáneo, Buenos Aires, 1971, pp. 83–84.

60 A. Labrousse, *op. cit.*, p. 97.

61 *Ibid.*, pp. 199–200.

62 *Ibid.*, p. 187.

63 *Ibid.*, pp. 161–163.

64 *Ibid.*, pp. 115–118.

65 *Ibid.*, pp. 85–87.

66 *Ibid.*, p. 191.

67 Claudio Trobo, "¿Quién le pone el cascabel a los militares?", in *Nueva Sociedad*, No. 81, 1986, p. 158.

68 A. Labrousse, *op. cit.*, pp. 184–185, 188–190, 194–195, 198.

69 *Ibid.*, pp. 195–199, 203.

70 *Ibid.*, p. 64–66, 69.

71 María Esther Gilio, *La guerra tupamara*, Casa de las Américas Prize (1970), Editorial Prisma, Medellín, Colombia, 1972, pp. 98–99.

72 Maria Ester Gilio, *La guerra tupamara*, *op. cit.* pp. 98–99.

73 Carlos Nuñez, *¿Quiénes son los Tupamaros?*, Ediciones Zureca Ltda., Bogotá, Colombia, 1971, p. 53.

74 Gonzalo Sánchez and Donny Meertens, *Bandoleros, gamonales y campesinos*, Áncora Editores, 1985, pp. 200–201.

75 *Ibid.*, p. 47.

76 Jorge Child, *El MRL, Seminario sobre alternativas populares*, mimeograph, Bogotá, 1987.

77 *Ibid.*; Sánchez and Meertens, *op. cit.*, pp. 94, 212.

78 *State Department Confidential Memos*, September 29 & 30, 1959.

79 Gonzalo Sánchez, (Ed.), *Pasado y presente de la violencia en Colombia*, CEREC, 1986, pp. 398–402.

80   Marta Harnecker, *Entrevista a dirigentes de la Unión Camilista del ELN*, Quimera Ediciones, Ouito, Ecuador, 1988, pp. 9–12, 31.

81   *US State Department Documents*, February, 1959.

82   *Coded cable*, Colombian Chancellery, September 21, 1959.

83   Alfredo Vásquez Carrizosa, *El poder presidencial en Colombia*, Ediciones Suramérica Ltda., Bogotá, 1979, p. 333.

84   Francisco Leal, *Estado y Política en Colombia*, Siglo XXI, Bogotá, 1984, pp. 225–227, 251–253.

85   Gustavo Gallón, (Compilador), *Entre movimientos y caudillos*, Cinep, CEREC, Bogotá, 1989, pp. 247–251, 261.

86   Héctor Béjar Rivera, *Perú 1965, Apuntes sobre una experiencia guerrillera*, Casa de las Américas Prize 1969, Havana, Cuba, pp. 49–50.

87   *Ibid.*, p. 34.

88   J. Gerassi, *op. cit.*, p. 133.

89   Julio Cotler, "Perú", in: *América Latina: Historia de Medio Siglo*, Siglo XXI, México, 1977, pp. 387, 390.

90   Jean Pierre Bernard, Silas Cerqueira, et al., *Tableau des Paris Politiques en Amérique du Sud*, Fondation National de Sciences Politiques, Armand Colan, Paris, 1969, p. 294.

91   Henry Pease García, *El ocaso del poder oligárquico*, Desco, Lima, Perú, 1977, p. 23.

92   J. Cotler, *op. cit.*, p. 395.

93   H. Pease, *op. cit.*, pp. 43–44.

94   H. Béjar, *op. cit.*, pp. 63–65.

95   J. Cotler, *op. cit.*, p. 401.

96   H. Béjar, *op. cit.*, pp. 35–36.

97   *Ibid.*, pp. 34–35.

98   H. Pease, *op. cit.*, pp. 22–26; H. Béjar, *op. cit.*, p. 36.

99   H. Béjar, *op. cit.*, p. 97.

100   *Ibid.*, pp. 98–99.

101   H. Pease G., *op. cit.*, pp. 45–46.

102   *Ibid.*, pp. 46–47, 52–53.

103   *Ibid.*, pp. 49–50.

104   Thomas Dodd, *Latin American Foreign Policies: An Analysis*, Johns Hopkins University Press, Baltimore, 1975, pp. 369–370; J. Cotler, *op. cit.*, pp. 391–392.

105   J. Cotler, *op. cit.*, p. 392.

106   *Ibid.*, p. 391–392.

107   *Ibid.*, p. 405.

108   *Ibid.*, pp. 409–410.

109   *Ibid.*, pp. 419–421.

110   Agustín Blanco Muñoz, *La lucha armada: hablan cinco jefes*, Universidad Central de Venezuela, Caracas, 1981, Vol. 2, p. 86.

111   R. J. Velásquez, *Betancourt en la historia de Venezuela de siglo XX*, Centauro, Caracas, 1980, p. 62.

112   *Ibid.*, p. 67.

113   A. Blanco, *op. cit.*, Vol. 5, pp. 349–350.

114   R. J. Velásquez, *op. cit.*, pp. 86–92.

115   A. Blanco, *op. cit.*, Vol. 2, p.105.

116   Alonso Aguilar, *Pan-Americanism, from Monroe to the Present*, Monthly Review, New York, 1968, pp. 125–126.

117   *Ibid.*, pp. 119, 229.

118   A. Blanco, *op. cit.*, Vol. 3, p. 61.

119   *Ibid.*, pp. 15, 21–25, 68.

120   *Ibid.*, p. 329.

121   *Ibid.*, pp. 349–350.

122   *Ibid.*, pp. 187–188.

123   A. Blanco, *op. cit.*, Vol. 2, pp. 76, 169, 301; Vol. 3, p. 347.

124   *Ibid.*, Vol. 3, p. 306.

125   *Ibid.*, p. 160.

126   *Ibid.*, pp. 60–61.

127   *Ibid.*, Vol. 3, pp. 306–309.

128   *Ibid.*, Vol. 2, p. 228.

129   *Ibid.*, Vol. 3, pp. 308–309.

130   D. F. Maza Zavala, "Venezuela", in: *América Latina: Historia de medio siglo*, Siglo XXI, Mexico, 1977, pp. 527–529.

CHAPTER VI: What About Cuba?

1   Ernesto Che Guevara, *Venceremos, Speeches and Writings*, Simon and Schuster, New York, 1968, pp. 413–424; *Granma*, Prensa Latina, April 16, 1976

2   Carla Ann Robbins, *The Cuban Threat*, Ishi Publications, Philadelphia, 1985, p. 31.

3   *Year Book*, UN, 1966, pp. 211–212.

4   Tad Szulc, *Fidel*, Avon Books, New York, 1986, pp. 522, 525, 602, 610, 612

5   T. Szulc, *op. cit.*, pp. 669–670.

6   Ernesto Che Guevara, *Escritos y Discursos*, Vol. 9, Editorial Ciencias Sociales, Havana, 1977, pp. 358–359; C. A. Robbins, *op. cit.*, pp. 46, 48.

7   T. Szulc, *op. cit.*, p. 683.

8   Anatoly Dobrinin, "In Confidence," Times Books, New York, 1995, p. 96

9   Fidel Castro, *La Revolución de Octubre y la Revolución Cubana, Discursos 1959–1977*, Publication of the PCC, Havana, p. 158.

10   Fidel Castro, *Informe al Segundo Congreso del PCC (1980)*, Publication of the CPC, Havana, 1981 (English Version), p. 32.

11   Fidel Castro, Report, First Congress of Cuban Communist Party, December 17–22, 1975.

12   Jorge Domínguez, *Cuba*, Harvard University Press, Cambridge, 1978.

13   Philip Brenner et al. (Eds.), *The Cuba Reader*, Grove Press, New York, p. 398.

14   Morris H. Morley, *Imperial State and Revolution*, Cambridge University Press, 1987, pp. 249–250.

15   Jane Franklin, *op. cit.*, 1992, p. 111.

16 M. H. Morley, *op. cit.*, p. 252.

17 *Ibid.*, pp. 250–251.

18 *Ibid.*, p. 267.

19 Instituto Cubano del Libro, *El Futuro es el Internacionalismo*, Havana, 1972.

20 J. Franklin, *op. cit.*, p. 114.

21 Fidel Castro, *"XV Aniversario de Playa Girón"*, in: *Granma*, Havana, April, 1976.

22 David Deutschmann, *Changing the History of Africa*, Ocean Press, Victoria, Australia, 1989, p. xvi.

23 *Causa 1/89*, Fin de la Conexion Cubana, Editorial Jose Marti 1989, pp. 443–463

24 J. Franklin, *op. cit.*, p. 253.

25 *Ibid.*, p. 129.

26 H. Morley, *op. cit.*, pp. 260–261.

27 J. Franklin, *op. cit.*, p. 87.

28 H. Morley, *op. cit.*, p. 252.

29 Departamento de orientación revolucionaria del Comité Central del Partido Comunista, "La unión nos dió la victoria", CCPC, Havana, 1976, p. 78.

30 J. Franklin, *op. cit.*, pp. 108–109.

31 *Ibid.*, p. 120.

32 *Ibid.*, pp. 107, 110, 116–117.

33 H. Morley, *op. cit.*, p. 257.

34 J. Franklin, *op. cit.*, pp. 132–133.

35 H. Morley, *op. cit.*, pp. 282–283.

36 F. Castro, *12 de octubre de 1979*, Editorial de Ciencias Sociales, Cuba, 1979.

37 F. Castro, *Informe al Segundo Congreso del PCC*, 1980, pp. 8–9.

38 Author's interview with Pelegrín Torras de la Luz, Vice Minister for Foreign Relations, Havana, September, 1979.

39 F. Castro, *Respuesta del pueblo combatiente*, Editora Política, Havana, 1980. pp. 102, 107.

40 *Granma*, May 11, 1980.

41 *Op. cit.*, p. 106.

42 *Granma*, July 27, 1980.

CHAPTER VII: The Wars Within

1 O. Anzorena, *Tiempo de violencia y de utopía*, Editorial Contrapunto, Buenos Aires, 1988, pp. 162, 168–169.

2 *Ibid.*, p. 182.

3 *Ibid.*, pp. 200, 201.

4 *Ibid.*, pp. 219–222.

5 *Ibid.*, pp. 191–192, 213–214.

6 *Ibid.*, pp. 241–246.

7 Alain Rouquié (Compiler), *Argentina hoy*, Siglo XXI, México, 1982, p. 153.

8 Horacio Verbitsky, quoted by O. Anzorena, *Tiempo de Violencia . . .* , *op. cit.*, p. 259.

9   O. Anzorena, *op. cit.*, pp. 307–311.

10   O. Anzorena, *op. cit.*, p. 355.

11   *Alternativa*, Bogotá, Colombia, No. 76, April, 1976.

12   *Alternativa*, Bogotá, Colombia, No. 93, August, 1976.

13   *Alternativa*, Bogotá, Colombia, No. 106, November, 1976.

14   *Newsweek*, March 30, 1981.

15   *Nunca Más*, Report of the CONADEP, Editorial Universitaria, Buenos Aires, pp. 7–9.

16   *Alternativa*, Bogotá, Colombia, No. 106, November 1976.

17   AFP, *El Tiempo*, Bogotá, Colombia, October 15, 1980.

18   *Alternativa*, Bogotá, Colombia, No. 106, November, 1976.

19   *El Tiempo*, Bogotá, June 13, 1982.

20   *Amnesty International Report*, 1981, pp. 108–109.

21   *Newsweek*, March 30, 1981.

22   Sue Branford and Bernardo Kucinski, *The Debt Squads*, Zed Books, London, 1990, p. 92.

23   *Time*, July 20, 1981.

24   Steven Emerson, *Secret Warriors*, G. P. Putnam's Sons, New York, 1988, p. 121.

25   David Rock, *Argentina, 1516–1987*, University of California Press, Berkeley, 1987, p. 375.

26   *Afrique-Asie*, May 10, 1982.

27   D. Rock, *op. cit.*, p. 391.

28   UPI, *El Tiempo*, Bogotá, Colombia, March 25, 1982.

29   Alfredo Vásquez, *El Tiempo*, Bogotá, May 4, 1982.

30   UPI, *El Tiempo*, Bogotá, May 8, 1982.

31   *Time*, May 9, 1982.

32   Elizabeth Jelin, *The Movement: Eclipsed by Democracy?*, in *NACLA Report on the Americas*, Vol. XXI, No. 4, July/August, 1987, p. 35.

33   UPI, London, *El Tiempo*, Bogotá, May 25, 1982.

34   Alain Rouquié, *International Affairs*, 1983, p. 580.

35   *Time*, May 17, 1982.

36   *An Ocean Apart*, Channel 13, New York, June, 1988.

37   *Time*, May 17, June 7, 1982.

38   *New York Times*, The Week in Review, May 9, 1982.

39   *Time*, November 14, 1983.

40   A. Rouquié, *Argentina Hoy, op. cit.*, p.12.

41   Óscar R. González, "Argentina: la transición alfonsinista", in: *Nueva Sociedad*, No. 82, March/April, 1986, p. 25.

42   Emilio Bignone, "The Ties that Bind", in: *NACLA*, July/August, 1987, p. 20.

43   Document: *La sentencia, fallo de la cámara nacional de apelaciones en lo criminal y correción federal*, Buenos Aires, El fallo: December 9, 1985.

44   *El Espectador*, Bogotá, February 7, 1987.

45   AP, *El Mundo*, Medellín, Colombia, December 7, 1987.

46   *El Espectador*, Bogotá, April 21 & 22, 1987.

47   *New York Times*, April 19, 1982.

48 *El Mundo*, Medellín, Colombia, May 17, 1987.

49 AP, *El Mundo*, Medellín, Colombia, May 15, 1987.

50 E. Bignone, *op. cit.*, p.23.

51 *El Tiempo*, Bogotá, December 11, 1988.

52 *El Tiempo*, Bogotá, December 5, 1988.

53 *Brecha*, Montevideo, Uruguay, February 10, 1989.

54 *Brecha*, Montevideo, Uruguay, March 10, 1989.

55 *Brecha*, Montevideo, Uruguay, July 28, 1989.

56 *Brecha*, Montevideo, Uruguay, November 4, 1988, p. 28.

57 O. R. González, *op. cit.*, p. 26.

58 *Brecha*, Montevideo, Uruguay, December 2, 1988; *Newsweek*, December 12, 1988.

59 *Brecha*, Montevideo, Uruguay, December 2, 1988.

60 AP-Reuter, *El Tiempo*, Bogotá, January 11, 1989; Reuter, *El spectador*, Bogotá, January 14, 1989; *Newsweek*, January 23, 1989.

61 Reuter-AP-AFP, *El Tiempo*, Bogotá, July 10, 1989.

62 AP, *El Espectador*, Bogotá, October 8, 1989.

63 Ximena Ortúzar, *Represión y Tortura en el Cono Sur*, Editorial Extemporánea, México, 1977, pp. 99, 101.

64 B. B. Tyson, *op. cit.*, pp. 237–239.

65 Thomas E. Skidmore, *The Politics of Military Rule in Brazil, 1964–85*, Oxford University Press, New York, 1988, pp. 182, 183.

66 José Serra, *The New Authoritarianism in Latin America*, Editor David Collier, Princeton University Press, NJ, 1979, p. 139.

67 *Alternativa*, Bogotá, No. 34, May, 1975.

68 CINEP, *Brasil: El Fin del Milagro*, Controversia, Bogotá, 1976, pp. 41–42.

69 *Ibid.* p. 59.

70 Helio Jaguaribe, *Sociedad y política en la sociedad brasileña*, Grupo Editores Latinoamericano, Buenos Aires, 1985, p. 39.

71 T. Skidmore, *op. cit.*, pp. 172–173.

72 *Ibid.*, pp. 169, 174–175.

73 *Alternativa*, Bogotá, No. 59, November, 1975.

74 Weil, Comblin, *The Repressive State: The Brazilian National Security Doctrine*, Toronto, 1976, p. 32.

75 T. Skidmore, *op. cit.*, pp. 188, 189, 191.

76 T. Skidmore, *op. cit.*, p. 203.

77 H. Juagaribe, *op. cit.*, p. 40; T. Skidmore, *op. cit.*, pp. 217–218.

78 T. Skidmore, *op. cit.*, p. 217.

79 *Ibid.*, p. 236–239; *Newsweek*, September 26, 1983.

80 H. Jaguaribe, *op. cit.*, p. 42.

81 Newton Carlos, "Brasil: Fatalidad del Destino", in: *Nueva Sociedad*, No. 78, July/August, 1985, pp. 6–7.

82 Nur Dolay, "Brasil: Le Marche du Nouvel Horizon", in: *Asie-Afrique*, August 16–29, 1982, pp. 31–32.

83 Juan Combo, *Bolivia: Bajo el modelo Bánzer*, Cinep, Bogotá, 1977, pp. 28–32.

84 Alain Labrousse, *Los Tupamaros, guerrilla urbana en Uruguay*, Editorial Tiempo Contemporáneo, Buenos Aires, 1971, p. 84n.

85 Gerónimo de Sierra, "Uruguay", in: *América Latina: Historia de Medio Siglo*, Siglo XXI, Mexico, 1977, pp. 441–442.

86 "Uruguay, Nunca más, (English version), *Human Rights Violations, 1972–1985*, Temple University Press, Philadelphia, 1992, pp. 23–25.

87 *Ibid.*, pp. 6–8.

88 G. de Sierra, *op. cit.*, pp. 443–445.

89 *Ibid.*, p. 442.

90 *Ibid.*, p. 446.

91 Andrés Ortiz, *La cuestión de la democracia en Uruguay*, Institutos Latinoamericanos de Investigaciones Sociales, Fundación Friedrich Ebert, 1979, pp. 31–32.

92 G. de Sierra, *op. cit.*, p. 447.

93 *Ibid.*, p. 447.

94 "Uruguay, Nunca más . . .", *op. cit.*, pp. 38, 39.

95 G. de Sierra, *op. cit.*, pp. 446–449.

96 Eduardo Galeano, *Días y noches de amor y guerra*, in: *NACLA*, No. 5, New York, Sept./Oct., 1981, p. 27.

97 E. Galeano, *op. cit.*, pp. 28–29.

98 *Ibid.*, p. 22.

99 *Alternativa*, Bogotá, No. 21, 1974.

100 "Uruguay, Nunca más . . .", *op. cit.*, p. 42.

101 *Ibid.*, pp. 46–47, 51–52.

102 Uruguay, Nunca más . . .", *op. cit.*, p. 57.

103 Tomás Linn, *El Espectador*, Bogotá, September 9, 1988.

104 William Colby, *Honorable Men, My Life in the CIA*, Simon & Schuster, New York, 1978, p. 302; Victor Marchetti & John D. Markes, *The CIA and the Cult of Intelligence*, Dell Publishing Co., New York, 1980, pp. 13–14.

105 Thomas Powers, *The Man Who Kept the Secrets: Richard Helms and the CIA*, Alfred A. Knopf, New York, 1979, pp. 81, 223.

106 T. Powers, *op. cit.*, p. 223.

107 Armando Uribe, *The Black Book of American Intervention in Chile*, Beacon Press, Boston, 1974, pp. 25–26.

108 Marchetti & Marks, *op. cit.*, p. 14, 349; A. Uribe, *op. cit.*, pp. 25–26.

109 A. Uribe, *op. cit.*, pp. 33–34.

110 A. Uribe, *op. cit.*, p. 33.

111 Henry Kissinger, *Years of Upheaval*, Little Brown & Co., Boston, 1982, p. 376.

112 A. Uribe, *op. cit.*, p. 42.

113   Paul E. Sigmund, *The Overthrow of Allende*, University of Pittsburgh Press, Pittsburgh, 1977, pp. 85–87.

114   *Ibid.*, p. 99.

115   *Ibid.*, pp. 121–122.

116   *Ibid.*, pp. 120–121, 123; Genaro Arriagada, *The Politics of Power: Pinochet*, West View Press, Boston, 1988, p. 81.

117   W. Colby, *op. cit.*, p. 304; P. E. Sigmund, *op. cit.*, p. 121.

118   P. E. Sigmund, *op. cit.*, pp. 111–112.

119   Marchetti & Marks, *op. cit.*, pp. 15–16, 309–310.

120   T. Powers, *op. cit.*, pp. 228, 234.

121   A. Uribe, *op. cit.*, pp. 89, 104, 112.

122   P. E. Sigmund, *op. cit.*, p. 162.

123   G. Arriagada, *op. cit.*, p. 92; P. E. Sigmund, *op. cit.*, pp. 225, 228.

124   Salvador Allende, *Las Grandes Alamedas*, Centro Gaitan, Bogotá, 1968

125   G. Arriagada, *op. cit.*, pp. 13, 18.

126   *Ibid.*, pp. 12, 13.

127   *Ibid.*, pp. 15, 16.

128   *Ibid.*, pp. 21, 22.

129   *Ibid.*, p. 33.

130   *Ibid.*, pp. 30–31.

131   Keen Wasserman, *A Short History of Latin America*, Houghton Mifflin Co., Dallas, 1980, p. 348.

132   Amnesty International, *Chile, Informe de 1981*, p. 122.

133   G. Arriagada, *op. cit.*, pp. 50–53.

134   *Ibid.*, pp. 53–54.

135   *Ibid.*, pp. 57, 69.

136   G. Arriagada, *op. cit.*, p. 70.

137   AP-Reuter, *El Tiempo*, Bogotá, October 1, 1988.

138   *El Espectador*, March 3, 1991.

CHAPTER VIII: Reagan's Wars

1   Robert S. Leiken & Barry Rubin, *The Central American Crisis Reader*, Summit Books, New York, 1987, pp. 516–518; Holly Sklar, *Washington's War on Nicaragua*, South End Press, Boston, MA, 1988, p. 58.

2   *Newsweek*, March 16, 1981.

3   Phillip Berryman, *Inside Central-America*, Pantheon Books, New York, 1985, p. 44.

4   Lou Cannon, *President Reagan, the Role of a Lifetime*, Touchstone Books, New York, 1991, p. 344.

5   *Ibid.*, p. 193.

6   AP, *El Tiempo*, Bogotá, March 19, 1981.

7   *El Tiempo*, Bogotá, June 19, 1981.

8   *El Espectador*, Bogotá, June 19, 1981.

9   *Time*, New York, March 16, 1981.

10   Susan Jonas, *The Battle for Guatemala*, Westview Press, Boulder, CO, 1989, pp. 77–78.

11   AP, *El Tiempo*, Bogotá, November 24, 1981.

12   Lilia Bermúdez, *Guerra de baja intensidad, Reagan contra Centroamérica*, Siglo XXI, México, 1987, pp. 66, 68, 70.

13   Richard Fagen, *Forging Peace: The Challenge of Central America*, PACCA, 1987, p. 115.

14   Stephen Kinzer, *Blood of Brothers*, Doubleday, New York, 1991, p. 345.

15   R. Fagen, *op. cit.*, pp. 102–103.

16   L. Bermúdez, *op. cit.*, pp. 66–68.

17   Lars Schoultz, *National Security and United States Policy Toward Latin America*, Princeton University Press, Princeton, NJ, 1987, p. 173.

18   Tom Barry, *Central America Inside Out*, Grove Weidenfield, New York, 1991, p. 333.

19   Sam Dillon, *Commandos: The CIA and Nicaragua's Contra Rebels*, Henry Holt & Co. New York, 1991, pp. 88–90.

20   Prisma, *La Habana*, February, 1983, p. 49.

21   Holly Sklar, *Washington's War on Nicaragua*, South End Press, Boston, MA, 1988, p. 126.

22   Donald Schulz and Deborah Schulz, *The United States, Honduras, and the Crisis in Central America*, Westview Press, Boulder, CO, 1994, p. 81.

23   S. Dillon, *op. cit.*, pp. 99–100.

24   *Ibid.*, p. 327.

25   *Ibid.*, pp. 66, 68.

26   H. Sklar, *op. cit.*, p. 77.

27   S. Dillon, *op. cit.*, p. 64.

28   S. Kinzer, *op. cit.*, pp. 137–138.

29   S. Dillon, *op. cit.*, p. 65.

30   H. Sklar, *op. cit.*, pp. 102, 118, 120.

31   S. Dillon, *op. cit.*, p. 65.

32   H. Sklar, *op. cit.*, pp. 94–95.

33   *Ibid.*, p. 86.

34   L. Cannon, *op. cit.*, p. 353; H. Sklar, *op. cit.*, p. 87.

35   S. Dillon, *op. cit.*, p. 79; H. Sklar, *op. cit.*, p. 87.

36   S. Dillon, *op. cit.*, p. 86.

37   S. Kinzer, *op. cit.*, pp. 230, 232.

38   *Ibid.*, p. 344.

39   S. Dillon, *op. cit.*, pp. 102–103.

40   H. Sklar, *op. cit.*, pp. 102–103.

41   Robert A. Pastor, *Condemned to Repetition*, Princeton University Press, Princeton, NJ, 1987, p. 240; H. Sklar, *Washington's War . . .* , pp. 102–104, 423n; Paul E. Sigmund, *Liberation Theology at the Crossroad, Democracy or Revolution?*, Oxford University Press, New York, 1990, pp. 127–128.

42   H. Sklar, *op. cit.*, p. 113.

43   S. Kinzer, *op. cit.*, p. 97; S. Dillon, *op. cit.*, p. 77.

44   Shirley Christian, *Nicaragua, Revolution in the Family*, Random House, New York, 1985, p. 199.

45   S. Kinzer, *op. cit.*, p. 96.

46   Reed Brody, *Contra Terror in Nicaragua*, South End Press, Boston, MA, 1985, Appendix 3.

47   Peter Rosset, J. Vandermeer, Editors, *Nicaragua, Unfinished Revolution*, Grove Press, New York, 1986, p. 11; H. Sklar, *op. cit.*, p. 113.

48   H. Sklar, *op. cit.*, pp. 124–125.

49   *Ibid.*, pp. 125, 134.

50   S. Dillon, *op. cit.*, p. 75.

51   R. Brody, *op. cit.*, p. 13.

52   *Ibid.*, p. 15.

53   *Ibid.*, pp. 15–16.

54   S. Dillon, *op. cit.*, pp. 119–122, 125–126.

55   *Ibid.*, p. 101.

56   *Ibid.*, pp. 121, 127, 103.

57   *Ibid.*, p. 129.

58   S. Dillon, *op. cit.*, p. 131.

59   *Ibid.*, p. 130.

60   H. Sklar, *op. cit.*, p. 106.

61   P. Rosset, *op. cit.*, pp. 60–61; Phillip Berryman, *Inside Central America*, Pantheon Books, New York, 1985, p. 131.

62   H. Sklar, *op. cit.*, p. 109.

63   P. Berryman, *op. cit.*, p. 131.

64   UPI-AFP, *El Tiempo*, Bogotá, March 15, 1982.

65   P. Berryman, *op. cit.*, p. 131.

66   *Ibid.*, pp. 131–132.

67   *Changing Course . . .*, PACCA, p. 27; R. Brody, *op. cit.*, p. 12; H. Sklar, *op. cit.*, p. 144.

68   Lou Cannon, *President Reagan: The Role of a Lifetime*, (1991), *op. cit.* p. 405.

69   *El Tiempo*, Bogotá, December 6, 1982

70   S. Kinzer, *op. cit.*, p. 98.

71   L. Cannon, *op. cit.*, p. 366.

72   Dario Moreno, *The Struggle for Peace in Central America*, University Press of Florida, 1994, pp. 149–151.

73   D. Moreno, *op. cit.*, pp. 58–59.

74   H. Sklar, *op. cit.*, p. 302.

75   Dario Moreno, *The Struggle for Peace in Central America*, University Press of Florida, 1994, p. 59.

76   *Ibid.*, p. 171.

77   *Ibid.*, p. 117.

78   S. Dillon, *op. cit.*, pp. 81, 84, 93, 124.

79   *Ibid.*, pp. 110–112.

80   *Ibid.*, pp. 112–117; H. Sklar, *op. cit.*, p. 151.

81   Holly Sklar, *Washington's War on Nicaragua*, South End Press, Boston, 1988, p. 151.

82   H. Sklar, *op. cit.*, p. 152.

83   *The Nation*, May 7, 1983.

84   *Ibid.*, pp. 143–144.

85   *Ibid.*, p. 141.

86   *Changing Course: Blueprint for Peace in Central America and the Caribbean*, in: PACCA, Washington, 1984, pp. 30–31; H. Sklar, *op. cit.*, p. 147; S. Dillon, *op. cit.*, p. 96.

87   S. Dillon, *op. cit.*, p. 134.

88   H. Sklar, *op. cit.*, p. 162.

89   Sam Dillon, *Commandos, The CIA and Nicaragua's Contra Rebels*, Henry Holt and Company, New York, 1991, pp. 144–145; H. Sklar, op. cit, p. 238.

90   S. Dillon, *op. cit.*, pp. 143–145; H. Sklar, *op. cit.*, p. 238.

91   S. Dillon, *op. cit.*, pp. 149–150.

92   *Ibid.*, pp. 154–156.

93   Reed, Brody, *Contra Terror in Nicaragua*, South End Press, Boston, MA, 1985, pp. 1–2.

94   *Ibid.*, p. 8.

95   Quoted in the Brody Report, *Contra Terror . . .* , *op. cit.*, p. 9.

96   H. Sklar, *op. cit.*, p. 219; S. Dillon, *op. cit.*, pp. 108–109.

97   S. Kinzer, *op. cit.*, pp. 123–124.

98   H. Sklar, *op. cit.*, p. 132.

99   D. Moreno, *op. cit.*, p. 24.

100   H. Sklar, *op. cit.*, pp. 149–150.

101   *Ibid.*, p. 167.

102   *Ibid.*, p. 165

103   *Ibid.*, p. 168.

104   *Ibid.*, pp. 182–3

105   *Ibid.*, pp. 177–182.

106   *Ibid.*, p. 198.

107   Quoted in the Brody Report, *Contra Terror . . .* , *op. cit.*, p. 16.

108   H. Sklar, *op. cit.*, p. 209.

109   *Ibid.*, p. 209

110   *Ibid.*, p. 367.

111   D. & D. Schulz, *op. cit.*, pp. 147–148.

112   D. Moreno, *op. cit.*, p. 64.

113   *Ibid.*, pp. 64–66.

114   *Ibid.*, pp. 64, 65, 66.

115   D. & D. Schulz, *op. cit.*, p. 146.

116   D. Moreno, *op. cit.*, p. 66.

117   H. Sklar, *op. cit.*, p. 304; D. & D. Schulz, *op. cit.*, pp. 146–147.

118   D. & D. Schulz, *op. cit.*, p. 149.

119   D. Moreno, *op. cit.*, pp. 68–69.

120   *Ibid.*

121   H. Sklar, *op. cit.*, p. 306.

122   S. Dillon, *op. cit.*, p. 128.

123   *Ibid.*, pp. 157–158.

124   *Ibid.*, pp. 156–158.

125   *Ibid.*, pp. 98, 128.

126   S. Dillon, *op. cit.*, p. 158; D. & D. Schulz, *op. cit.*, p. 112.

127   S. Dillon, *op. cit.*, p. 159.

128   *Ibid.*, pp. 158–159.

129   Manzar Foroohar, *The Catholic Church and Social Change in Nicaragua*, State University of New York Press, New York, 1989, p. 104.

130   *Ibid.*, pp. 204–205.

131   *Ibid.*, p. 207; H. Sklar, *op. cit.*, p. 136.

132   Phillip Berryman, *The Religious Roots of Rebellion*, Orbis Books, Maryknoll, New York, 1986, p. 274.

133   M. Foroohar, *op. cit.*, p. 211.

134   *Ibid.*, pp. 210, 211.

135   R. Pastor, *op. cit.*, p. 250.

136   *New York Times*, February 23, 1985.

137   H. Sklar, *op. cit.*, p. 260.

138   D. & D. Schulz, *op. cit.*, pp. 170–171.

139   H. Sklar, *op. cit.*, p. 218.

140   *Ibid.*, p. 263.

141   R. Pastor, *op. cit.*, p. 251.

142   C. Arnson, *op. cit.*, pp. 169, 185, 188.

143   C. Arnson, *op. cit.*, p. 163.

144   *Ibid.*, p. 163.

145   H. Sklar, *op. cit.*, p. 321.

146   H. Sklar, *op. cit.*, pp. 230–231, 246–248.

147   C. Arnson, *op. cit.*, p. 199.

148   H. Sklar, *op. cit.*, p. 327.

149   S. Dillon, *op. cit.*, pp. 182, 205.

150   *Ibid.*, pp. 178–179.

151   *Ibid.*, p. 205.

152   *Ibid.*, pp. 206–209.

153   *Ibid.*, pp. 190, 193–194.

154   D. Moreno, *op. cit.*, p. 87.

155   D. & D. Schulz, *op. cit.*, p. 177.

156   D. Moreno, *op. cit.*, pp. 88–89; H. Sklar, *op. cit.*, pp. 375–76.

157   H. Sklar, *op. cit.*, pp. 377–378.

158   *Ibid.* p. 379

159   *Ibid.* p. 380

160   S. Dillon, *op. cit.*, p. 210.

161 *Ibid.*, pp. 213–214.

162 *Ibid.*, p. 216; D. Moreno, *op. cit.*, p. 2 and Appendix 6.

163 S. Dillon, *op. cit.* pp. 216–217, 218

164 *Ibid.*, p.227.

165 S. Kinzer, *op. cit.*, pp. 384–385; D. Moreno, *op. cit.*, p. 29.

166 Janet Shenk, *El Salvador,* in *NACLA*, May-June, 1981, p. 8.

167 *Ibid.*, pp. 1–10.

168 Robert Armstrong & Janet Shenk, *El Salvador, the Face of Revolution,* South End Press, Boston, MA, 1982, pp. 173–174.

169 L. Cannon, *op. cit.*, p. 195.

170 *State Department Document,* February 23, 1981.

171 Marvin Gettleman et.al., eds., *El Salvador, Central America and the Cold War,* Grove Press, New York, 1986, p. 329 n.

172 *Newsweek*, June 22, 1981; J. Shenk, *op. cit.*, p. 5.

173 *Newsweek*, March 9, 1981.

174 *Ibid.*

175 LeMoyne, quoted in *El Salvador's Decade of Terror,* Americas Watch, Yale University Press, New Haven, CT, 1991, p. 1.

176 *Newsweek*, March 16, 1981.

177 AP, *El Tiempo*, Bogotá, April 7, 1981.

178 Latin Reuter, *El Tiempo*, Bogotá, March 11, 1981.

179 Leiken & Rubin, *op. cit.*, pp. 628–629.

180 AP-AFP, *El Tiempo*, Bogotá, December 7 & 10, 1981; *New York Times*, December 8, 1981.

181 R. Leiken & B. Rubin, *op. cit.*, pp. 409–410.

182 Rufus Jones, *NACLA*, New York, November/December, 1981, p. 36.

183 *El Salvador's Decade of Terror,* Americas Watch, Yale University Press, New Haven CT, 1991, p. 145.

184 R. Fagen, *op. cit.*, p. 72.

185 *Newsweek*, March 9 & 16, 1981.

186 J. Shenk, *No Easy War,* in *NACLA*, New York, May/June, 1981, p. 14.

187 *Time*, February 8, 1982; *Newsweek*, New York, February 8, 1982.

188 AP, *El Tiempo*, Bogotá, January 28, 1982.

189 AP, *El Tiempo*, Bogotá, February 2, 1982.

190 *Time*, February 8, 1982.

191 UPI, *El Tiempo*, Bogotá, February 2, 1982.

192 Rubin & Leiken, *op. cit.*, pp. 426–427.

193 UPI, *El Tiempo*, Bogotá, November 10, 1981.

194 UPI, *El Tiempo*, Bogotá, March 20, 1982.

195 Robert Armstrong, *El Salvador, Beyond Elections,* in: *NACLA*, New York, March/April, 1982, p. 3.

196 *New York Times*, March 30, 1982.

197 Tom Barry, *Roots of Rebellion,* South End Press, Boston, MA, 1987, p. 119.

198 Raymond Bonner, *Weakness and Deceit*, Times Books, New York, 1984, p. 313.

199 M. Gettleman, ed., *op. cit.*, p. 298.

200 UPI, *El Tiempo*, Bogotá, August 23, 1982.

201 *Newsweek*, New York, August 9, 1982.

202 *Time*, July 12, 1982.

203 *Time*, November 8, 1982.

204 UPI, *El Tiempo*, Bogotá, April 15, 1983; Leiken & Rubin, *op. cit.*, pp. 336–337; M.E. Gettleman, *op. cit.*, p. 414.

205 *Time*, February 28, 1983.

206 *Time*, March 28, 1983.

207 Leiken & Rubin, *op. cit.*, pp. 345–346.

208 *Time*, March 21, 1983.

209 *Time*, May 9, 1983.

210 Paul Boyer, Ed., *Reagan as President*, Ivan R. Dee, Publisher, Chicago, IL, 1990, p. 235.

211 *Newsweek*, May 9, 1983.

212 *Time*, July 18, 1983; *Newsweek*, August 15, 1983.

213 Lydia Chávez, "The Odds in El Salvador", *New York Times Magazine*, July 24, 1983.

214 M.E. Gettleman, Ed., *op. cit.*, p. 60.

215 *Time*, December 12, 1983.

216 *Newsweek*, October 17, 1983; *Time*, December 12, 1983.

217 *Bohemia*, Havana, March 30, 1984.

218 Marc Cooper, "Whitewashing Duarte" in *NACLA*, New York, January/March, 1986, p. 8.

219 Gettleman, Ed., *op. cit.*, p. 416.

220 NACLA Report, "Duarte: Prisoner of War" in *NACLA*, New York, January/March, 1986, p. 30.

221 *Bohemia*, Havana, September 28, November 16, 1984; *El Salvador's Decade of . . .* , Americas Watch, *op. cit.*, p. 149.

222 *Newsweek*, July 1, 1985.

223 *Newsweek*, November 4, 1985.

224 *El Tiempo*, Bogotá, January 25, 1987.

225 *New York Times*, November 22 & 23, 1987.

226 *El Salvador's Decade of . . .* , *op. cit.*, pp. 87–88.

227 *Brecha*, Montevideo, March 31, 1989.

228 *New York Times* (International Edition), March 16, 1993.

229 *New York Times*, March 24, 1993.

230 *Perspectiva Mundial*, New York, November 14, 1983.

231 Tom Barry et al., *The Other Side of Paradise*, Grove Press, New York, pp. 307–309.

232 Maurice Bishop, *Discursos Escogidos: 1979–1983*, Casa de las Américas, Havana, 1986, pp. 387–388.

233 AP, *El Tiempo*, Bogotá, March 16, 1983.

234 T. Barry, Ed., *op. cit.*, p. 311.

235 M. Bishop, *op. cit.*, p. 373ss.

236 *Granma*, Havana, April 30, 1983.

237 M. Bishop, *op. cit.*, p. 398.

238 UPI, *El Espectador*, Bogotá, October 26, 1983.

239 *Ibid.*

240 *Ibid.*

241 UPI, *El Espectador*, Bogotá, October 27, 1983.

242 Joseph B. Treaster, *New York Times*, August 21, 1988.

243 Steven Volk, *U.S. Invasion, Grenada Disappeared*, in *NACLA*, New York, January/February, 1984, p. 45.

244 *Time*, November 23, 1987.

245 AP, *El Tiempo*, Bogotá, December 5, 1988.

CHAPTER IX: Panama: "Dead Man Walking . . ."

1   Eduardo Lemaitre, "Panamá y sus tragedias", in: *El Tiempo*, Bogotá, February 8, 1990.

2   John Dinges, *Our Man in Panama*, Times Books, New York, 1990, pp. 82–84.

3   Latin America Update, Washington Office on Latin America, Washington, DC, July/August, 1987.

4   *Newsweek*, June 23, 1986.

5   *Prensa Latina*, July 24, 1986.

6   John Dinges, *op. cit.*, p. 253; AFP, *El Tiempo*, Bogotá, May 11, 1989.

7   Alexander Cockburn, *Noriega fue nuestro compinche, pero no le vamos a tener misericordia ahora*, Tarea, Panamá, p. 96.

8   L. C. Giraldo, in *El Espectador*, Bogotá, September 22, 1991.

9   *El Tiempo*, Bogotá, August 2, 1987.

10   *Time*, June 22, 1987.

11   Document of the OAS, Cp/Inf. 2549, June 30, 1987.

12   *El Espectador*, Bogotá, June 30, 1987.

13   *El Espectador*, Bogotá, July 1, 1987.

14   *El Espectador*, Bogotá, July 15, 1987.

15   *El Tiempo*, Bogotá, August 1, 1987.

16   Reuter, *El Tiempo*, Bogotá, August 6, 1987; *El Espectador*, Bogotá, August 6, 1987.

17   *New York Times*, November 27, December 4, 1987.

18   *Newsweek*, February 1, 1988.

19   *Ibid.*

20   *Time, Newsweek*, February 1, 1988.

21   *Ibid.*

22   *Time*, February 15, 1988.

23   *New York Times*, February 5, 1988.

24   *Time*, February 22, 1988.

25   J. Dinges, *op. cit.*, pp. xx-xxi, xxviii-xxix, 24–25.

26   *New York Times*, February 12, 1988.

27   J. Dinges, *op. cit.*, pp. xxx, 277–279.

28   *Time,* February 22, 1988.

29   *El Espectador,* Bogotá, January 20, 1987.

30   *El Espectador,* Bogotá, July 23, 1987.

31   *New York Times,* February 12, 1988.

32   *El Espectador,* Bogotá, October 19, 1988.

33   David Pitt, in: *New York Times,* April 30, 1988.

34   *Newsweek,* March 14, 1988.

35   Document of IDEN, Tareas No. 74, Panamá, January-April, 1990.

36   *Time,* New York, March 7, 1988.

37   *Ibid.*

38   Uan Eduardo Ritter, Los secretos de la nunciatura, Paneta, Colombia, 1990, p. 44.

39   *New York Times,* March 28, 1988.

40   *NACLA,* New York, July/August, 1988, p. 18.

41   Walter LaFeber, *The Panama Canal,* Oxford University Press, New York, 1989, p. 208.

42   *New York Times,* March 30, 1988.

43   *Time, Newsweek,* March 28, April 11, 1988.

44   *New York Times,* March 21, 1988.

45   *Newsweek,* March 28, April 18, 1988.

46   *Newsweek,* April 18, 1989; *Time,* April 18, 1989

47   *New York Times,* March 21, 1988.

48   *New York Times,* March 26, 1988.

49   *Time,* April 11, 1988.

50   *New York Times,* April 16, 1988.

51   *New York Times,* April 6, 1988.

52   *Newsweek,* March 7, 1988.

53   *Newsweek,* June 6, 1988.

54   *Time,* June 6, 1988.

55   *Newsweek,* June 8, 1988.

56   Anthony Lewis, in the *New York Times,* June 12, 1988.

57   *El Espectador,* Bogotá, August 25, 1988.

58   *Brecha,* Montevideo, October 14, 1988.

59   *U.S. News & World Report,* May 1, 1989.

60   Reuter, *El Tiempo,* Bogotá, April 27, 1989.

61   *Newsweek,* New York, February 6, 1989.

62   *Ibid.*

63   EFE, *El Espectador,* Bogotá, May 2, 1989.

64   AFP, *El Tiempo,* Bogotá, April 29, 1989; G. Selser, in: *Brecha,* Montevideo, May 19, 1989; J. E. Ritter, *op. cit.,* p. 127.

65   *The U.S. Invasion of Panama, Report of the Independent Commission of Inquiry on the U.S. Invasion of Panama,* South End Press, Boston, 1991, pp. 24–25.

66   *Newsweek,* February 6, 1989.

67   AP, United Nations, *El Tiempo,* Bogotá, April 29, 1989.

68 Reuters-AP-AFP, *El Espectador,* Bogotá, May 4, 1989.

69 T. Martinez, *El Espectador,* Bogotá, May 7, 1989.

70 AP, *El Espectador,* Bogotá, May 9, 1989.

71 *El Espectador,* Bogotá, May 11, 1989.

72 *Ibid.*

73 J.E. Ritter, *op. cit.,* p. 127.

74 AP, AFP, Reuter, *El Tiempo,* Bogotá, May 12, 1989.

75 AP, *El Espectador,* Bogotá, May 12, 1989.

76 Raúl Leiss, cited in J.E. Ritter, *op. cit.,* p. 160.

77 AP, AFP, Reuter, *El Tiempo,* Bogotá, May 12, 1989.

78 *El Espectador,* Bogotá, May 11, 1989.

79 T. Martínez, in *El Espectador,* Bogotá, May 13, 1989; Reuter, AP, AFP, *El Tiempo,* Bogotá, May 13, 1989.

80 Reuter, AP, AFP, *El Tiempo,* Bogotá, May 18, 1989.

81 J.E. Ritter, *op. cit.,* pp. 135–136.

82 *Ibid.*

83 *El Tiempo,* Bogotá, May 17, 1989.

84 *El Espectador,* Bogotá, May 17, 1989.

85 AP, UPI, AFP, *El Tiempo,* Bogotá, May 17, 18, 1989

86 AP, AFP, UPI, Ansa, EFE, El País, Madrid, *El Espectador, El Tiempo,* Bogotá, May 18 & 19, 1989.

87 EFE, *El Espectador,* Bogotá, May 20, 1989.

88 *El Tiempo,* Bogotá, May 19, 1989; EFE, *El Espectador,* Bogotá, May 23, 1989.

89 AP-EFE, *El Tiempo,* Bogotá, July 20, 1989; *El Espectador,* Bogotá, July 22, 1989.

90 Reuter-AP-EFE, *El Tiempo,* Bogotá, July 22, 1989.

91 *El Espectador,* Bogotá, July 25, 1989.

92 EFE, Reuter, AP, AFP, *El Tiempo,* Bogotá, August 12, 1989.

93 EFE-Reuter, *El Espectador;* AP, *El Tiempo,* Bogotá, August 23, 1989.

94 AP-EFE-AFP, *El Tiempo,* Bogotá, August 24, 1989.

95 Reuter, *El Espectador,* Bogotá, July 1, 1989.

96 AP-Reuter-EFE, *El Espectador,* Bogotá, August 10, 1989.

97 EFE, *El Espectador,* Bogotá, August 11, 1989.

98 UN, *El Espectador,* Bogotá, August 12, 1989.

99 AP-UN, *El Espectador,* Bogotá, August 12, 1989.

100 EFE-AP, *El Espectador,* Bogotá, August 16, 1989.

101 *Ibid.*

102 Reuter, *El Espectador,* Bogotá, August 19, 1989.

103 *El Espectador,* Bogotá, May 12, 1989.

104 *El Espectador,* Bogotá, July 25 & 28, 1989.

105 EFE-Reuter, *El Espectador,* Bogotá, August 22, 1989.

106 *Newsweek,* May 22, 1989.

107 Reuter, *El Espectador,* Bogotá, September 1, 1989.

108   AP-EFE-Reuter, *El Tiempo*, Bogotá, September 1, 1989; AP, *El Espectador*, Bogotá, September 2, 1989.

109   Reuter-AP, *El Espectador*, Bogotá, September 2, 1989.

110   EFE, *El Tiempo*, Bogotá, September 21, 1989.

111   Reuter-AP-EFE, *El Espectador*, Bogotá, October 5, 1989.

112   *New York Times*, October 9, 1989.

113   EFE-AP-Reuter, *El Tiempo*, Bogotá, October 4 & 10, 1989.

114   EFE, *El Tiempo*, Bogotá, October 6 & 9, 1989.

115   AP, *El Tiempo*, Bogotá, October 5, 1989.

116   AP, *El Tiempo*, Bogotá, October 4, 1989.

117   *El Tiempo*, Bogotá, October 6, 1989.

118   J.E. Ritter, *op. cit.*, pp. 168–169.

119   *Ibid.*, pp. 171–179.

120   *Ibid.*, pp. 163–165.

121   AFP, AP, UPI *El Tiempo*, Bogotá, December 17, 1989; J. Dinges, *op. cit.*, p. 308.

122   AFP, *El Tiempo*, Bogotá, December 18, 1989.

123   *The Independent Commission of Inquiry: The U.S. Invasion of Panama*, South End Press, Boston, 1991, p. 24.

124   Raúl Leis, *The Other Side of Midnight, NACLA,* New York, April, 1990.

125   AP-Reuter, EFE, Ansa, *El Espectador*, Bogotá, December 20 & 21, 1989.

126   Independent Commission . . . , *op. cit.*, p. 46.

127   *Ibid.*, p. 44.

128   *El Espectador*, Bogotá, December 21, 1989.

129   *El Tiempo*, Bogotá, December 23, 1989.

130   Independent Commission . . . , *op. cit.*, p. 41.

131   *Ibid.*

132   *Ibid.*, pp. 2, 3, 41, 43.

133   *Ibid.*, pp. 2, 3, 9–14.

134   *Ibid.*, pp. 41–43.

135   John Weeks & Phillip Gunson, *Panama: Made in the USA,* Latin American Bureau, London, 1991, p. 13.

136   UN Security Council, S/PV 2900, S/PV 2901, December 20, 21, 1989; *New York Times*, James Brook, December 21, 1989, *El Tiempo*, Bogotá, December 21, 1989.

137   OAS Documents.

138   UN Document, S/PV. 2900, December 21, 1989.

139   UN Document, S/21938 Annex.

140   UN Document, S/21048, December 22, 1989.

141   Oscar Ceville, La Invasión Just Cause o la Profecía de Santa Fe II, in: Tareas 75, Panama, May-August, 1990.

142   J. E. Ritter, *op. cit.*, pp. 9–10, 14, 101–102.

143   Carlos Fuentes, Las lecciones de Panamá, in: Tareas 74, Panama, January-April, 1990.

144   J. Weeks & P. Gunson, *op. cit.*, p. 13.

145   UPI, Reuters, *El Espectador*, Bogotá, December 21, 1989

146   J. E. Ritter, *op. cit.*, Annex I, pp. 251–258.

147   *Ibid.*, p. 181–183.

148   *Ibid.*, pp. 182–183.

149   AP, El Espectador, Bogotá, December 22, 1989.

150   Thomas Friedman, *New York Times*, December 28, 1989; J.Dinges, *op. cit.*, pp 313–314.

151   "Harper's Index", in *Harper's*, November, 1991.

152   *New York Times*, April 5, 1992.

153   Peter Eisner, in *El Espectador*, Bogotá, April 5, 1992.

CHAPTER X: The Hurricane Over Cuba

1   *Fidel Castro's Speeches, Cuba's International Foreign Policy, 1975–1980*, Pathfinder Press, New York, 1981, p. 315.

2   Lou Cannon, *President Reagan*, Touchstone, New York, 1991, p. 196.

3   Jane Franklin, *The Cuban Revolution and the United States,* Ocean Press, Melbourne, 1993, p. 155.

4   *New York Times*, April 22, 1981.

5   *Granma,* Havana, October 26, 1981.

6   *El Tiempo*, Bogotá, November 11, 1981.

7   Michael Krinsky & David Golove, *United States Economic Measures Against Cuba,* Aletheia Press, Northampton, MA, 1993, pp. 119–121.

8   *New York Times*, July 9, 1981

9   Krinsky & Golove, pp. 119–121

10   Wayne Smith, *The Closest of Enemies*, W. W. Norton & Co, New York, 1987, pp. 256–257

11   UPI, *El Tiempo*, Bogotá, August 1 & 8, 1981.

12   Morris Morley, *Imperial State and Revolution*, Cambridge University Press, London, 1987, p. 356.

13   *El Tiempo*, Bogotá, October 2, 1981, *New York Times*, October 2, 1981

14   *New York Times*, May 15, 1983

15   Author's interview with DOR officials, Havana, November, 1994.

16   *Ibid.*

17   *El Tiempo*, Bogotá, January, 1982.

18   *Prensa Latina*, Havana, February 23, 1981.

19   *Granma,* Havana, September 11 & 12, 1985.

20   *El Tiempo*, Bogotá, March 24, 1981.

21   *El Tiempo*, Bogotá, April 5, 1981.

22   *El Tiempo*, Bogotá, March 22, 1981.

23   AP, *El Tiempo*, Bogotá, May 12, 1981.

24   UPI, AP, *El Tiempo*, Bogotá, September 17 & 20, 1981.

25   UPI, *El Tiempo*, Bogotá, November 7, 1981.

26   AP, *El Tiempo*, Bogotá, November 6, 1981.

27   M.H. Morley, *op. cit.*, p. 356.

28   David Deutschmann, *Cuba, Socialism and the "New Order,"* Ocean Press, Melbourne, Australia, 1992, p. 13.
29   UPI, *El Tiempo*, Bogotá, January 27 & 28, 1982.
30   UPI, *El Tiempo*, Bogotá, March 17, 1982.
31   UPI, *El Tiempo*, Bogotá, March 27, 1982.
32   J. Franklin, *op. cit.*, pp. 165–166.
33   M.H. Morley, *op. cit.*, pp. 331–332.
34   J. Franklin, *op. cit.*, p. 179, 1997.
35   *Time,* August 15, 1983.
36   Gerardo Reyes, Miami correspondent, *El Tiempo*, Bogotá, February 19, 1989.
37   UN Human Rights Commission, Geneva, March 11, 1987; J. Franklin, *op. cit.*, p. 230.
38   Mikhail Gorbachev, *Perestroika: New Thinking for our Country and for the World,* Harper & Row, New York, 1987, pp. 22–23.
39   UN Human Rights Commission, Geneva, March, 1989
40   *Ibid.*
41   *Ibid.*, p. 121.
42   J. Franklin, *op. cit.*, p. 221.
43   Bernard Gwertzman, ed., *The Decline and Collapse of the Soviet Union,* New York Times Books, 1992, pp. 132–133.
44   *New York Times,* November 8, 1987.
45   F. Castro, *In Defense of Socialism,* Mary-Alice Waters, Ed., New York, Pathfinder, 1989, p. 31.
46   *Ibid.*, pp. 7–18
47   Reuters, *El Espectador,* Bogotá, April 1, 1989.
48   Joseph Threaster, *New York Times,* Week in Review, November 11, 1987.
49   *Granma,* Havana, July 27, 1988.
50   José Ramón Balaguer, Comité Central, Interview with the author, Havana, May, 1994.
51   John B. Dunlop, *The Rise of Russia and the Fall of the Soviet Empire,* Princeton University Press, NJ, 1993, p. 9.
52   Zbigniew Brzizinski, *The Grand Failure,* Collier Books, MacMillan Publishing Co., New York, 1990, p. 87.
53   Luis Rodríguez García, *The Cuban Revolution into the 1990s,* Westview Press, Boulder, CO, 1992, p. 104.
54   Mark Frank, *Cuba Looks to the Year 2000,* International Publishers, New York, 1993, pp. 25–27.
55   *Granma,* December 9, 1989
56   *PL,* Interview with Fidel Castro — L'Humanité, Paris, January, 1989.
57   *Granma,* Havana, November 26, 1990.
58   Fidel Castro, M-A. Waters, Ed., *In Defense of Socialism,* New York, Pathfinder Press 1989, p. 34.
59   *New York Times,* July 31, 1988.
60   *PL,* Havana, April 5, 1989.

61 *Ibid.*

62 *Prensa Latina,* April 2–5, 1989

63 *Ibid.*

64 *Granma,* Havana, August 4, 1989.

65 Bernard Gwertzman & Michal Kaufman, Eds., *op. cit.,* pp. 309–310.

66 *Brecha,* Montevideo, September 1989

67 *Ibid.,* pp. 281–282.

68 *Ibid.,* p. 463.

69 "Presente y futuro de Cuba," *Revista Siempre,* Mexico, 1991, pp. 131–134.

70 *New York Times,* February 4, 1996.

71 Fidel Castro, Interview, Revista Siempre, *op. cit.,* pp. 9–10.

72 Tomás Borge, *Face to Face with Fidel Castro,* Ocean Press, Melbourne, 1993, p. 25.

73 *Ibid.,* pp. 27–28.

74 Reuter-AP, *El Tiempo,* Bogotá, May 4, 1990.

75 Jean-François Fogel & Bertrand Rosenthal, *El Fin de Siglo en La Habana, Los Secretos del Derrumbe de Fidel,* Spanish-language edition, T. M. Editores, 1994, p. 71.

76 *Granma,* February 26, 1993; J. Franklin, *op. cit.,* p. 311

77 Vindicación de Cuba, Editora Política, Havana, 1989, p. 418.

78 *Ibid.,* pp. 418, 422–23, 427.

79 Author's interview with an M-19 Comandante, Bogotá, September, 1996.

80 AP, *El Espectador,* Bogotá, March 7, 1989; Vindicación de Cuba, *op. cit.,* p. 422.

81 Andrés Oppenheimer, *Castro's Final Hour,* Simon & Schuster, New York, 1992, pp. 66–69.

82 EFE, *El Tiempo,* Bogotá, July 28, 1989.

83 Gerardo Reyes, Miami, *El Tiempo,* Bogotá, July 28, 1989.

84 Vindicación . . . , *op. cit.,* pp. 391, 392.

85 Reuters, AFP, *El Tiempo,* Bogotá, June 27, 1989.

86 Vindicación . . . , *op. cit.,* pp. 38–39, 42.

87 *El Tiempo,* Bogotá, June 30, 1989.

88 AP, *El Tiempo,* Bogotá, June 29, 1989.

89 AP-Reuter, *El Tiempo,* Bogotá, July 8, 1989.

90 Vindicación . . . , *op. cit.,* pp. 84–85.

91 *Cause 1/89,* Editorial Jose Marti, Havana, 1989, pp. 423–448

92 EFE, *El Tiempo,* Bogotá, July 31, 1992.

93 Vindicación . . . , *op. cit.,* pp. 259, 265–266.

94 Reuter, *El Espectador,* Bogotá, July, 1989. (Exact date?)

95 *Brecha,* Montevideo, August 23, 1990.

96 Reuter, *El Espectador,* Bogotá, July 28, 1989.

97 Author's interview with José Ramón Balaguer, member of the Central Committee, former Cuban Ambassador to the USSR, Havana, May, 1994.

98 *Ibid.*

99 Carlos Lage, *Estrategia de la economía cubana,* Havana, October, 1993.

100 Gail Reed, *Island in the Storm,* Ocean Press, Melbourne, 1992, p. 35.

101 Author's interview with Msgr. Juan Manuel de Céspedes, Havana, May, 1995.
102 Mirta Muñiz, Ed., *Elecciones en Cuba, ¿Farsa o Democracia?*, Canada, Ocean Press, 1993 pp. 6–8.
103 *Granma*, Havana, September 14, 1991.
104 *Granma Internacional*, January 12, 1992.
105 *Ibid.*
106 *Ibid.*
107 EFE-AP-Reuters, *El Espectador*, Bogotá, September 10, 1991.
108 AP, UPI, Reuters, *El Tiempo*, Bogotá, September 12, 1991
109 Antonio Caño, Miami correspondent, *El Espectador*, Bogotá, September 17, 1991.
110 AP, *El Tiempo*, Bogotá, March 7, 1990; *New York Times*, October 29, 1992.
111 Reuter, *El Tiempo*, Bogotá, August 10, 1989.
112 AP, *El Tiempo*, Bogotá, August 8, 1989.
113 Reuter, *El Tiempo*, Bogotá, February 22, 1990.
114 Cuba Update, New York, March/April, 1992.
115 Fidel Castro, V Congreso de la Federación de Mujeres Cubanas, Havana, March, 1990; Reuter-AP, *El Espectador*, Bogotá, March 10, 1990.
116 EFE-Reuters, *El Espectador*, February 20, 1992; *Granma Internacional*, May 10, 1992.
117 AP, *El Tiempo*, Bogotá, February 27, 1992.
118 UN Human Rights Commission, Geneva, March 8, 1989
119 EFE-Ansa, *El Espectador*,Bogotá, April 22, 1998.
120 *Semana*, Bogotá, January 21, 1992.
121 AP, *El Espectador*, Bogotá, October 15, 1992.
122 Grardo Reyes, *El Tiempo*, Bogotá, January 19, 1992.
123 AP, *El Tiempo*, January 18, 1992
124 Enlace, WOLA, Washington, DC, October, 1992.
125 *El Tiempo*, Bogotá, October 25, 1992
126 Reuter, *El Tiempo*, Bogotá, October 26, 1992.
127 Ricardo Alarcón, UN, New York, November 13, 1991.
128 Author's interview with Ricardo Alarcón, Havana, May, 1994.
129 *Ibid.*
130 *New York Times*, November 9, 1993.
131 J.C. Rincón, Strassbourg correspondent, *El Espectador*, Bogotá, September 17, 1993.
132 Jorge Child, *El Espectador*, Bogotá, July 23, 1991.
133 *El Espectador*, Bogotá, July 24, 1992.
134 *Granma Internacional*, June 29, 1994
135 *Granma Internacional*, July 28, 1991
136 *El Espectador*, Bogotá, June, 1994.
137 *Granma Internacional*, July 28, 1992
138 *El Espectador*, Bogotá, July 17, 1994.
139 *Granma Internacional*, August 2, 1993
140 Reuter, *El Espectador*, Bogotá, July 10, 1994.

141 Fidel Cano, *El Espectador*, Bogotá, December 11, 1994.
142 *New York Times*, August 23, 1994.
143 *El Tiempo*, June 16, 1994
144 *Time*, Septermber 12, 1994.
145 AP, UPI, AFP *El Tiempo*, August 6, 1992.
146 *New York Times*, February 26, 1996.
147 *New York Times*, February 29, 1996.
148 *New York Times*, February 27, 1996.
149 Tad Szulc, *New York Times*, February 29, 1996.

EPILOGUE: The End of History?
1 Cynthia Arnson, *Comparative Peace Processes in Latin America*, Woodrow Wilson Center Press, Washington D.C., 1999, p. 428.
2 *Ibid.* pp. 69–70.
3 Gustavo Meoño, *Guatemala: Fractura en la Transición*, Fundación Rigoberta Menchú, mimeograph, September 10, 2002, pp. 2–3.
4 *Ibid.* p. 3.
5 *New York Times*, May 13, 1995; *Time*, April 10, 1995, *Newsweek*, April 10, 1995.
6 *El Tiempo*, Bogotá, March 13, 1999.
7 Ariel Dorfman, *Exorcising Terror,* Seven Stories Press, New York, 2002, p. 213.
8 *El País*, Madrid, Feb. 24, 1999.
9 *El Tiempo*, Bogotá, May 8, 2002.
10 *The Nation*, June 24, 2002, pgs 3, 13–14; *El Tiempo*, Bogotá, March 12, 2002.
11 *Washington Post*, November 10, 1987.
12 Terry J. Allen, "Scandal? What Scandal?" *Extra*, September/October 2001; pp. 10–14, 21.
13 *Semana*, Bogotá, September 9, 2001.
14 *The Nation*, May 27, 2002.
15 EFE, *El Tiempo*, Bogotá, June 8, 2002.
16 AFP, *El Tiempo*, Bogotá, November 16, 2002.
17 *Granma*, March 30, 2002.
18 *The Nation*, November 26, 2002.
19 *Time*, July 30, 2001.

BIBLIOGRAPHY

Changing Course, Blueprint for Peace in Central America and the Caribbean, PACCA, 1984

Estado, Nuevo Order Económico y Democracia en América, XVIII Congreso de ALAS, Editorial Nueva Sociedad, Venezuela, 1992.

Proyección Internacional de Cuba, Editorial Ciencias Sociales, La Habana, 1975

United Fruit Co.: Un Caso del Dominio Imperialista en Cuba, Editorial Ciencias Sociales, La Habana, 1976

Agresiones de Estados Unidos a Cuba, 1787–1976, Editorial Ciencias Sociales, La Habana, 1978

Agudelo, Carlos, *América Latina: La Libertad Negada*, Cinep, Bogotá, 1981

Aguilar, Alfonso, *Pan-Americanism, from Monroe to the Present,*. Monthly Review, New York, 1965

Allen, James, *The Lesson of Cuba*, New Century Publishers, New York, 1961

Allende, Salvador, *Las Grandes Alamedas*, Centro Gaitan, Bogotá, 1983

Americas Watch Report, *Human Rights in Nicaragua 1986*, New York, 1987

Americas Watch, *El Salvador's Decade of Terror*, Yale University, New Heaven, 1991

Amnesty International, *The 1992 Report on Human Rights Around the World*, Hunter House, London, 1992

Amnistia Internacional, *La Tortura en Chile*, Editorial Fundamentos, Madrid, 1983

Anzorena, Oscar, *Tiempo de Violencia y Utopia, 1966–1976*, Editorial Contrapunto, Buenos Aires, 1988

Appleman Williams, William, *The Tragedy of American Diplomacy*, A Delta Book, New York, 1962

Arbatov, Georgi, *The System: An Insider's Life in Soviet Politics*, Times Books, Random House, New York, 1992

Arbatov, Georgi, *Propaganda Politica Exterior del Imperialismo Moderno*, PCC, La Habana, 1975

Argentina: Del Peronismo a la Dictadura Militar; Bolivia: Bajo el Modelo Banzer, CINEP, Bogotá, 1977

Arnson, Cynthia J., *Crossroad, Congress, the President, and Central America, 1976–1993*, Pennsylvania State University Press, 1993

Arriagada, Genaro, *Politics of Power, Pinochet*, Westview Press, Boulder, 1988

Ayers, Bradley Earl, *The War That Never Was*, Bobb-Merrill Co., Indianapolis, 1976

Barrios de Chungara, Domitila, *Let Me Speak!*, Monthly Review Press, New York, 1978

Barry, Tom, *Central America Inside Out*, Grove Weidenfel, New York, 1991

Barry, Tom, *Roots of Rebellion*, South End Press, Boston, 1987

Bayley, Edwin R., *Joe McCarthy and the Press*, University of Wisconsin Press, Madison, 1981

Bedau, Hugo Adam, ed., *The Death Penalty in America*, Oxford University Press, New York, 1982

Bejar, Hector, *Peru 1965: Apuntes Sobre Una Experiencia Guerrillera*, Premio Casa de las Americas 1969, La Habana

Belfrange, Cedric *The American Inquisition*, Bobb Merrill Co., Indianapolis, 1973

Benjamin, Medea, ed., *Don't Be Afraid Gringo, A Honduran Woman Speaks from the Heart*, Harper and Row Publishers, New York, 1989

Bermudez, Liliana, *Guerra de Baja Intensidad: Reagan Contra Centroamerica*, Siglo XXI, Mexico, 1987

Berryman, Phillip, *Inside Central America*, Pantheon Books. New York, 1985

Berryman, Phillip, *The Religious Roots of Rebellion*, Orbis Books, Maryknoll, New York, 1986

Betto, Frei, *Fidel y la Religion*, Consejo de Estado, Publicaciones, La Habana, 1985

Billington, James H., *Russia Transformed: Breakthrough to Hope*, The Free Press, Macmillan, New York, 1992

Blachman, Morris J. et al., *Confronting Revolution*, Pantheon Books, New York, 1986

Blackman, Morrid J., et al, *Confronting Revolution: Security Through Diplomacy in Central America*, Pantheon Books, New York, 1986

Blanco Munoz, Agustin, *La Lucha Armada*, Universidad Central de Venezuela, Vols. 1–6, Caracas, 1981

Blasier, Cole and Mesa-Lago, Carmelo, *Cuba in the World*, University of Pittsburgh Press, Pittsburgh, 1979

Blight, James G., Allyn, Bruce J., and Welch, David A., *Cuba on the Brink: Castro, the Missile Crisis and the Soviet Collapse*, Pantheon Books, New York, 1993

Boff, Leonardo Clodovis, *Salvation and Liberation*, Orbis Books, Maryland, New York, 1985

Boggs, James, and Grace, Lee, *Revolution and Evolution in the Twentieth Century,* Monthly Review Press, New York, 1974

Boldin, Valery, *Ten Years That Shook the World,* Basic Books, 1994

Bonasso, Miguel, *Recuerdos de la Muerte,* Ediciones Era, Mexico, 1983

Bonner, Raymond, *Weakness and Deceit, U.S. Policy and El Salvador,* Times Books, New York, 1984

Boorstein, Edward, *The Economic Transformation of Cuba,* Modern Reader Paperbacks, New York, 1968

Boorstein, Edward, *An Inside View . . . Allende's Chile,* International Publishers, New York., 1977

Borge, Tomas, *Fidel Face to Face,* Ocean Press, Melbourne, Australia, 1992

Borge, Tomas, *La Paciente Impaciencia,* Premio Casa de las Americas, La Habana, 1989

Borge, Tomas, *La Revolucion Popular Sandinista,* Siglo XXI, Mexico, 1981

Bosch, Juan, *Pentagonismo, Sustituto del Imperialismo,* Guadiana de Publicaciones, Madrid, 1968

Boyer, Paul, ed. *Reagan as President,* Ivan R. Dee, Publisher, Chicago, 1990

Branford, Sue and Kucinski, Bernardo, *The Debt Squads,* Zed Books, London, 1988

Brenner, Philip, *From Confrontation to Negotiation,* Westview Press, Boulder, 1986

Brenner, Philip, Leo Grande, William, and Siegel, Daniel, eds., *The Cuba Reader,* Grove Press, 1989

Brody, Reed, *Contra Terror in Nicaragua,* South End Press, Boston, 1985

Brownlie, Ian, ed., *Basic Documents on Human Rights,* Claderon Press, Oxford, 1981

Brzezinski, Zbigniew, *The Grand Failure,* Collier Books, New York, 1990

Buckley, Kevin, *Panama,* A Touchstone Book, New York, 1992

Burns, E. Bradford, *The Reagan Doctrine and the Politics of Nostalgia,* Perennial Library, New York, 1987

Cabestrero, Teofilo, *Ministros de Dios, Ministros del Pueblo,* Ministerio de Cultura, Nicaragua, 1986

Cabezas, Omar, *La Montana Es Algo Mas Que Una Inmensa Estepa Verde,* Premio Casa de las Americas, La Habana, 1982

Camejo, Pedro, ed., *The Nicaraguan Revolution,* Pathinder Press, New York, 1979

Cannon, Lou, *President Reagan: The Role of a Lifetime,* A Touchstone Book, New York, 1992

Cardoso, Fernando Henrique et al., *The New Authoritarism in Latin America,* Princeton University Press, Princeton, 1979

Carr, Barry and Ellner, Steve, *The Latin American Left: From the Fall of Allende to Perestroika,* Westview Press, Boulder, 1993

Castaneda, Jorge G., *Utopia Unarmed: The Latin American Left After the Cold War,* Alfred A. Knopf, New York, 1993

Castro, Fidel, *La Historia Me Absolvera,* Pcc, La Habana, 1973

Castro, Fidel, *Sobre la Deuda Impagable de America Latina,* Entrevista con Agencia EFE, Editora Politica, La Habana, 1985

Castro, Fidel, *Che,* Ocean, Melbourne, 1994

Castro, Fidel, *Discursos de Fidel,* Vol. I–II, Editorial Ciencias Sociales, La Habana, 1976

Castro, Fidel, *Discursos en Tres Congresos,* Editora Politica, La Habana, 1982

Castro, Fidel, *Fidel Castro Speeches, Cuba's International Foreign Policy 1975–80,* Pathfinder Press, New York, 1981

Castro, Fidel, *In Defense of Socialism,* Pathfinder, New York, 1989

Castro, Fidel, *La Crisis Economica y Social del Mundo,* Consejo de Estado Publicaciones, La Habana, 1983

Castro, Fidel, *La Revolucion de Octubre y la Revolucion Cubana,* Discursos 1959–1977, CCPC, La Habana, 1977

Castro, Fidel, *Nada Podra Detener la Marcha de la Historia,* Editora Politica, La Habana, 1985

Castro, Fidel, *Problemas Actuales de los Paises Subdesarrollados,* Consejo de Estado Publicaciones, La Habana, 1979

Castro, Fidel, *Tomorrow Is Too Late,* Ocean Press, Australia, 1993

Centroamerica 1981, Infopres Centroamericana, Guatemala 1981

Chayes, Abraham, *The Cuban Missile Crisis,* Oxford University Press, New York, 1974

Chomsky, Noam, *Deterring Democracy,* Hill & Wang, New York, 1991

Chomsky, Noam, *Turning the Tide,* U.S. Intervention in Central America and the Struggle for Peace, South End Press, Boston, 1985

Christian, Shirley, *Nicaragua,* Random House, New York, 1985

Cleary, O. P., Edward, L., *Crisis and Change: The Church in Latin America,* Orbis Books, Maryland, New York, 1985

Cleary, O. P., Edward, L., eds., *Born of the Poor,* University of Notre Dame Press, Notre Dame, 1990

Coates, James and Killian, Michael, *Heavy Losses: The Dangerous Decline of American Defense,* Vicking Press, New York, 1985

Cockburn, Leslie, *Out of Control: The Story of the Reagan Administration's Secret War in Nicaragua, the Illegal Arms Pipeline, and the Contra Drug Connection,* Atlantic Monthly Press, New York, 1987

Cohen, Joshua, and Rogers, Joel, *Inequity and Intervention: The Federal Budget and Central America,* South End Press, Boston, 1986

Cohen, Joshua, and Rogers, Joel, *Rules of the Game: American Politics and Central America Movement,* South End Press, Boston, 1986

Colby, William, *Honorable Men, My Life in the Cia,* Simon & Schuster, New York, 1978

Collier, David, *The Authoritarism in Latin America,* Princeton University Press, Princeton, 1979

Constable, Pamela, and Valenzuela, Arturo, *Chile Under Pinochet, A Nation of Enemies,* W. W. Norton, New York, 1991

Cortazar, Julio, *Nicaraguan Sketches,* W.W. Norton & Co., New York, 1989

Dalton, Roque, *Revolucion en la Revolucion? y la Critica de Derecha,* Cuadernos Casa, La Habana, 1970

Daniels, Robert V., ed. *Communism in Russia,* University of Vermont Press, Vermont, 1993

Davis, Harold Eugene, Wilson, Larman C. et al., *Latin American Foreign Policies,* Johns Hopkins University Press, Baltimore, 1975

Debray, Regis, *Prison Writings,* Vintage Books, New York, 1973

Deutschmann, David and Shnookal, Deborah, *With Fidel,* Ocean Press, Australia, 1989

Deutschmann, David, *Changing the History of Africa,* Ocean Press, Melbourne, 1989

Didion, Joan, *Miami,* Simon and Schuster, New York, 1987

Didion, Joan, *Salvador,* Washington Square Press, New York, 1982

Dieterich, Heinz, *Cuba Ante la Razon Cinica,* Editoral Txalaparta, Navarra, Mexico, 1994

Dillon, Sam, *Comandos, The CIA and Nicaragua's Contra Rebels,* Henry Holt and Company, New York, 1991

Dinger, *Our Man in Panama,* Times Books, New York, 1990

Dobrynin, Anatoly, *In Confidence,* Times Books, 1995

Donovan, Hedley *Roosevelt to Reagan,* Harpers and Row Publishers, New York, 1987

Draper, Theodore, *Castro's Cuba,* The New Leader, New York, 1962

Draper, Theodore, *Castro's Cuba, A Revolution Betrayed?,* Frederick A. Praeger, New York, 1963

Draper, Theodore, *A Very Thin Line: The Iran-Contra Affairs,* A Touchstone Book, New York, 1991

Drekonja, Gerard and Tokatlian, Juan, *Teoria y Practica de la Politica Exterior Latinoamericana,* Uniandes, Bogotá, 1983

Dubois, Jules, *Fidel,* New Bobbs-Merrill Co., Indianapolis, 1959

Dunlop, John B., *The Rise of Russia and the Fall of the Soviet Empire,* Princeton University Press, Princeton, N.J., 1993

Eckstein, Susan, ed., *Power and Popular Protest,* Latin American Social Movement, University of California Press, Berkeley, 1989

Eich, Dieter, and Rincon, Carlos, *The Contras,* Interviews with Anti-Sandinistas, Synthesis Publications, San Francisco, 1985

El Futuro Es El Internacionalismo, Visita de Fidel Castro a paises de Africa y Europa Socialista, Instituto Cubano del Libro, La Habana, 1972

El Moncada, Editorial Ciencias Sociales, La Habana, 1975

Elecciones en Cuba: Farsa o Democracia?, Ocean Press, Canada, 1993

Emerson, Steve, *Secret Warriors, Inside the Covert Military Operations of the Reagan Era,* G.P. Putnam's Sons, New York, 1988

Ezcurra, Ana Maria, *Iglesia y Transicion Democratica,* Punto Sur Editore, Buenos Aires, 1988

Fagen, Richard *The Challenge of Central America,* PACCA, New York, 1987

Fagen, Richard R., ed., *Capitalism and the State in U.S.-Latin American Relations,* Stanford University Press, Stanford, 1979

Feinberg, Richard E., ed., *Central America: International Dimension of the Crisis,* Holmes & Meier Publ. Inc., New York, 1982

Feinmann, Jose Pablo, *Estudios sobre el Peronismo,* Editorial Legasa, Buenos Aires, 1983

Fogel, Jean-Francois, and Rosenthal, Bertrand, *Fin de siglo en la Habana,* TM Editores, Bogotá, 1994

Foroohar, Manzar, *The Catholic Church and Social Change in Nicaragua,* State University of New York Press, 1989

Frank, Marc, *Cuba Looks to the Year 2000,* International Publishers, New York, 1993

Frankel, Joseph, *Contemporary International Theory and Behaviour of States,* Oxford Universty Press, New York, 1971

Franklin, Jane, *The Cuban Revolution and the United States,* Ocean Press, Australia, 1992

Franqui, Carlos, *Diary of the Cuban Revolution,* Viking Press, New York, 1976

Franqui, Carlos, *Family Portrait of Fidel,* Random House, New York, 1984

Fried, Jonathan L., Gettleman, Marvin E., Levenson, Deborah T., and Peckenham, Nancy, *Guatemala Rebellion: Unfinished History,* Grove Press, 1983

Fulbright, William *The Crippled Giant,* Random House, New York, 1972

Galeano, Eduardo, *Las Venas Abiertas de America Latina,* Siglo XXI, Mexico, 1971

Garcia Marquez, Gabriel, Galeano, Eduardo, Onetti, Jorge, Fuentes, Carlos, et al., *La Democracia y la Paz en America Latina,* Editorial El Buho, Bogotá, 1986

Gaspar, Edmund, *La Diplomacia y Politica Norteamericana en America Latina,* Editorial del Valle de Mexico, Mexico, 1985

Gerard, Pierre-Charles *El Caribe a la Hora de Cuba,* Casa de las Americas, La Habana, 1980

Gerassi, John, *The Great Fear in Latin America,* Collier Books, New York, 1965

Gettleman, Marvin E. Lacefield, Patrick, Menashe, Louis, Mermelstein, David, eds., *El Salvador, Central America and the New Cold War,* Grove Press, New York, 1986

Gitlin, Todd, *The Sixties, Years of Hope, Days of Rage,* Bantam Books, New York, 1987

Glinkin, A, Martinov, B.and Ykolev, P. *La Evolucion de la Politica de E.U. en America Latina,* Editorial Progreso, Moscu, 1983

Goldman, Eric. F., *The Tragedy of Lyndon Johnson,* Laurel Edition, New York, 1975

Gorbachev, Mikhail, *Perestroika,* New Thinking for Our Country, Harper Row, New York, 1987

Graebner, Norman A. *America as a World Power, a Realist Aprisal from Wilson to Reagan,* Scholary Resource, Willmington, 1984

Graebner, Norman A. *National Security Its Theory and Practice: 1945–1960,* Oxford University Press, New York, 1986

Greog, Robert *International Organization and the Western World*, University of Syracuse Press, Syracuse, 1968

Greog, Robert et al, *After Viet Nam*, Doubleday, New York, 1971

Guevara, Ernesto, *Diario de Bolivia*, Equipo Editorial, S.A., San Sebastian, Espana, 1.968

Guevara, Ernesto, *Discursos y Escritos*, Vols. I–X, Editorial Ciencias Sociales, La Habana, 1977

Guevara, Ernesto, *La guerre de guerilla*, Cahier Libres, Francois Maspero, Paris, 1968

Gunder Frank, Andre, *Latin America: Underdevelopment Or Revolution*, MR, New York, 1969

Gunder Frank, Andre, *Lumpen Bourgeoisie, Lumpen-Development*, MR, New York, 1972

Gunder Frank, Andre, *Capitalismo y Subdesarrollo en America Latina*, Siglo XXI, Mexico, 1976

Gurtov, Melvin and Maghroori, Ray, *Roots of Failure, United States Policy in the World*, Greenwood Press, Westport, Conn., 1984

Gutman, Roy, *Banana Diplomacy: The Making of American Diplomacy in Nicaragua 1981–1987*, Touchstone, New York, 1989

Gwertzman, Bernard and Kaufman, Michael T., *The Decline and Fall of the Soviet Empire*, New York Times Books, New York, 1992

Gwertzman, Bernard, and Kaufman, Michael, eds., *The Collapse of Communism*, New York Times Books, New York, 1991

Halberstam, David, *The Best and the Brightest*, Penguin Books, New York, 1984

Haldeman, H., *The Military Government and the Movement Toward Democracy*, Indiana University Press, Indiana, 1981

Halperin, Maurice, *The Rise and Decline of Fidel Castro*, University of California Press, Berkeley, 1972

Halperin, Tulio, *Historia contemporanea de America Latina*, Alianza Editorial, Madrid, 1986

Harbaugh, William H. *The Writings of Theodore Roosevelt*, Bobbs Merrill Co., Indianapolis, 1967

Harnecker, Martha *Fidel Castro's Political Strategy*, Pathfinder Press, New York, 1987

Hayland, William G., ed., *The Reagan Foreign Policy*, Meridiam Book, New York, 1987

Heath, Jim F., *Decade of Disillusionment: The Kennedy and Johnson Years*, Indiana University Press, Bloomington, 1975

Heller, Claude, *El ejercito como agente de cambio*, Fondo de Cultura Economica, Mexico, 1979

Heyck, Denis, and Daly, Lynn, *Life Stories of the Nicaraguan Revolution*, Routledge, New York, 1990

Hollander, Paul, *Anti-Americanism*, Critics at Home and Abroad, 1965–1990, Oxford University Press, New York, 1992

Hoopes, Townsend, *The Devil and John Foster Dulles*, Atlantic Monthly Press Book, Boston, 1973

Horowitz, Erwing Lewis et al., *Latin American Radicalism*, Vintage Book, New York, 1969

Horowitz, Irving Louis, *Cuban Communism*, Transaction Books, New Brunswick, 1982

Hunt, Michael H. *Roots of Failure, Ideology of U.S. Foreign Policy,* Yale University Press, N.H., 1987

Immerman, Richard H., *The CIA in Guatemala: The Foreign Policy of Intervention,* University of Texas Press, Austin, 1982

Instruccion Politica Far, Libro Segundo, Instituto Cubano del Libro, La Habana, 1973

Isaacson, Walter and Thomas, Evan, *The Wise Men,* Simon and Schuster, New York, 1988

Isaacson, Walter, *Kissinger,* Simon and Schuster, New York, 1992

Jimenez, Eddy E., *La guerra no fue de futbol,* Casa de las Americas, La Habana, 1974

Jonas, Susanne, *The Battle for Guatemala,* Westview Press, Boulder, San Francisco, 1989

Jordan, Amos A. and Taylor, William, *American National Security,* Johns Hopkins University Press, Baltimore, 1984

Kapuscinski, Ryszard, *Another Day of Life: A Haunting Eyewitness Account of Civil War in Angola,* Penguin Books, New York, 1988

Keen/Wasserman, *A Short History of Latin America,* Northern Illinois University, Dallas, 1980

Kennan, George *American Diplomacy 1900–1950,* Merton Books, New York, 1951

Kennedy, J. F. *Strategy of Peace,* Harpers, New York, 1960

Kennedy, Robert, *Thirteen Days: A Memory of the Cuban Missile Crisis,* New American Library, New York, 1969

Kennedy, Robert, *To Seek a Newer World,* Bantam Books, New York, 1968

Kinzer, Stephen, *Blood of Brothers,* Anchor Books, Doubleday, New York, 1991

Kinzer, Stephen, *Blood of Brothers,* G. P. Putnam's Sons, New York, 1991

Kirkpatrick, Jeane, *Dictators and Double Standards,* Simon & Schuster, New York, 1983

Krinsky, Michael and Golove, David, Edit, *United States Economic Measures Against Cuba,* Aketheia Press, Northampton, Mass, 1993

La Union Nos Dio la Victoria, Informe del Primer Congreso del PCC, Publicaciones CCPC, La Habana, 1976

LaFeber, Walter, *Inevitable Revolutions,* W.W. Norton & Co. New York, 1984

LaFeber, Waltert, *The Panama Canal,* Oxford University Press, New York, 1989

Langguth, A. J., *Hidden Terrors: The Truth About U.S. Police Operation in Latin America,* Pantheon Books, New York, 1987

Lawyers Committee for International Human Rights, *Honduras: A Crisis on the Border,* New York, 1985

Leiken, Robert S. and Rubin, Barry, eds., *The Central America Crisis Reader,* Summit Books, New York, 1987

Leke, Anthony, *Somoza Falling,* University of Massachussets Press, Amherst, 1989

Lernoux, Penny, *Cry of the People,* Penguin Books, New York, 1982

Lewis, Oscar, Lewis, Ruth. M., and Rigdon, Susan, *Four Women: An Oral History of Contemporary Cuba,* University of Illinois Press, Urbana, 1977

Main Report, 2nd Congress of the Communist Party of Cuba, Political Publishers, La Habana, 1980

Mankiewcz, Frank and Jones, Kirby, *With Fidel,* Ballantine Books, New York, 1960

Manwarning, Max G., and Prisk, Court, eds., *El Salvador at War,* National Defense University Press, Washington DC, 1988

Marchetti, Victor and Marks, John, *The CIA,* Dell, New York, 1980

Mario, German, *Nicaragua,* Reportaje de la Revolucion, Celadec, Lima, 1982

Martin, Lionel, *El joven Fidel,* Grijalbo, Barcelona, 1982

Martinez, Jose Jesus, *Mi General Torrijos,* Premio Casa de las Americas 1987. La Habana,

Matthews, Herbert, *Fidel Castro,* Simon & Schuster, New York, 1969

Matthews, Herbert, *The Cuban Story,* George Brazilier, New York, 1961

Matthews, Herbert, ed., *The United States and Latin America,* Prentice-Hall Inc., Englewood, 1963

May, Ernest R., and Zelikow, Philip D., *The Kennedy Tapes,* Harvard University Press, Cambridge, 1997

McCarthy, Mary, *The Mask of State: Watergate Portraits,* Harcourt Brace, New York, 1974

Mills, C. Wright, *Listen Yankee,* Ballantine Books, New York, 1960

Mina, Gianni, *An Encounter with Fidel,* Ocean Press, Australia, 1991

Molina, Gabriel, *Diario de Giron,* Editora Politica, La Habana, 1984

Molineu, Harold *U.S. Policy Toward Latin America,* Westview Press, Boulder, 1968

Mommsen, Wolfgang J., *Theories of Imperialism,* Random House, New York, 1980

Moreno, Dario, *The Struggle for Peace in Central America,* University Press of Florida, Miami, 1994

Morley, Morris, *Imperial State and Revolution,* Cambridge University Press, Cambridge, Mass, 1987

Morris, James A. *Honduras, Caudillos, Politics and Military Rule,* Westview Press, Boulder, 1984

Morton Blum, John, *The Republican Roosevelt,* Antheneum, New York, 1974

Munck, Ronald, *Latin America: The Transition to Democracy,* Zed Books Ltd, London, 1989

Murray, Mary, *Cruel and Unusual Punishment,* Ocean Press, Melbourne, 1993

Murray, Mary, *Cuba and the United States: An Interview with Ricardo Alarcon,* Ocean Press, Melbourne, 1992

Netanyahu, Benjamin, ed., *Terrorism, How the West Can Win,* Avon, New York, 1987

Niebuhr, Reinhold and Sigmund, Paul E., *The Democratic Experience,* Frederick Praeger Publ., New York, 1969

Nitze, Paul H., *From Hiroshima to Glasnost,* Grove Weindelfeld, New York, 1989

Nixon, Richard, *1999, Victory Without War,* Simon and Schuster, New York, 1989

Nixon, Richard, *Six Crisis,* Pyramid Books, New York, 1968

Oppenheimer, Andres, *Castro's Final Hour,* Simon and Schuster, New York, 1992

Pages, Beatriz, *Can Cuba Survive? An Interview with Fidel Castro,* Ocean Press, Melbourne, Australia, 1992

Pastror, Robert, *Condemned to Repetition: The United States and Nicaragua,* Princeton University Press, Princeton, 1987

Pereira, Manuel, *Cronicas desde nicaragua,* Casa de las Americas, La Habana, 1981

Perez Valdes, Fernando, *Corresponsales de guerra,* Premio Casa de las Americas, La Habana, 1981

Perez-Brignoli, Hector, *A Brief History of Central America,* University of California Press, Berkeley, California, 1985

Petras, James, *Politics and Social Structure in Latin America,* MR, New York, 1970

Peyeras, Mario, *Los gias de la selva: guerrillas populares en el Quiche,* 1972–1976, Premio Casa de las Americas, 1980, La Habana

Powers, Thomas, *The Man Who Kept the Secrets, Richard Helms and the CIA,* Alfred A. Knopf, New York, 1979

Presente y Futuro de Cuba, Entrevista de Fidel Castro en la Revista "Siempre" de Mexico, Consejo de Estado, Publicaciones, La Habana, 1991

Proyeccion internacional de la revolucion Cubana, PCC, La Habana, 1975

Puente, Rafael, Conde, Alfredo and Segovia, Guillermo, *Procesos politicos en America Latina: Bolivia, Ecuador, El Salvador,* CINEP, Bogotá, 1985

Rama, Angel, *Los Dictadores Latinoamericanos,* Fondo de Cultura Economica, Mexico, 1976

Randall, Margaret, *Woman in Cuba,* Smyrna Press, New York, 1981

Ranelagh, John, *The Agency: The Rise and Decline of the CIA,* Simon & Schuster, New York, 1986

Reckord, Barry, *Does Fidel Eat More Than Your Father?,* New American Library, New York, 1972

Reed, Gail, *Island in the Storm,* Ocean Press, Melbourne, 1992

Remnick, David, *Lenin's Tomb,* Vintage Books, New York, 1994

Revista *Controversia, No. 127,* CINEP, Bogotá, 1978

Revista *Nuestra America,* No. 11, UNAM, Mexico, 1984

Ridenour, Ron, *Back Fire,* Editorial Jos, 1991

Riese, Hans-Peter, ed., *Since the Prague Spring,* Random House, New York, 1979

Ritter, Jorge Eduardo, *Los secretos de la nunciatura,* Planeta, Bogotá, 1991

Roa, Raul, *Retorno a la Alborada,* Editorial Ciencias Sociales, La Habana, 1977

Robbins, Carla Ann *The Cuban Threat,* Ishi Publications, Philadelphia, 1985

Rock, David, *Argentina, 1516–1987,* University of California Press, Berkeley, 1987

Rodriguez, Mario, *Central America,* Prentice-Hall Inc., Englewood, 1965

Roging, Michael, *Ronald Reagan, the Movie,* University of California Press, Berkeley, 1988

Rosset, Peter et al., eds., *Nicaragua: Unfinished Revolution,* Grove Press, New York, 1986

Rosset, Peter, and Vandermerr, John, eds., *The Nicaragua Reader,* Grove Press, New York, 1983

Rouquie, Alain, Comp., *Argentina hoy,* Siglo XXI, Mexico, 1982

Rouquie, Alain, *The Military and the State in Latin America,* University of California Press, Berkeley, 1989

Rovere, Richard H., *Senator Joe McCarthy,* Harper and Row, New York, 1973

Rushdie, Salman, *The Jaguar Smile: A Nicaragua Journey,* Penguin Books, 1988

Sanz de Santamaria, Carlos, *Revolucion Silenciosa,* Fondo de Cultura Economica, Mexico, 1971

Sartre, Jean-Paul, *Huracan Sobre el Azucar,* Merayo Editor, Buenos Aires, 1973

Sartre, Jean-Paul, *Sartre on Cuba,* Ballantine Books, New York, 1961

Schlesinger Jr., Arthur, *The Cycles of American History,* Houghton Mifflin Co., Boston, 1986

Schlesinger, Jr., Arthur M., *A Thousand Days,* Fawcett Premier, New York, 1966

Schlesinger, Jr., Arthur, *The Imperial Presidency,* Popular Library, New York, 1974

Schlesinger, Stephen, and Kinzer, Stephen, *Bitter Fruit: The Untold Story of the American Coup in Guatemala,* Anchor Books, Garden City, 1982

Schoultz, Kars, *National Security and United States Policy Toward Latin America,* Princeton University Press, Princeton, 1987

Schulz Donald, and Sundloff Schulz, Deborah, *The United States, Honduras and the Crisis in Central America,* Westview Press, Boulder, 1994

Seabury, Paul, *Power, Freedom and Diplomacy: The Foreign Policy of the USA,* Vintage Books, New York, 1967

Selser, Gregorio, *Sandino,* Monthly Review Press, New York, 1981

Sherwin, Martin J., *A World Destroyed,* Vintage Books, New York, 1977

Sigmund, Paul E., *Liberation Theology and the Crossroads,* Oxford University Press, New York, 1990

Sigmund, Paul E., *The Overthrow of Allende,* University of Pittsburgh Press, Pittsburgh, 1977

Silverman, Bertram, ed., *Man and Socialism in Cuba,* Atheneum, New York, 1971

Skidmore, Thomas E., and Smith, Peter, *The Modern Latin America,* Oxford University Press, Cambridge, Mass., 1984

Skidmore, Thomas E., *The Politics of Military Rule in Brazil: 1964–85,* Oxford University Press, New York, 1988

Sklar, Holly, *Washington's War on Nicaragua,* South End Press, Boston, 1988

Smith, Earl E. T., *The Four Floor,* Random House, New York, 1962

Smith, Wayne, *The Closest Enemies,* W. W. Norton, New York, 1987

Sorensen, Theodore, *Kennedy,* Bantam Books, New York, 1966

Spear, Joseph C., *Presidents and the Press: The Nixon Legacy,* MIT Press, Cambridge, 1984

Suramerica 76: Modelos de desarrollo (Peru, Brasil, Chile), CINEP, Bogotá, 1976

Szulc, Tad *The Winds of Revolution,* Praeger, New York, 1963

Szulc, Tad, *Fidel: a Critical Portrait,* Avon, New York, 1986

Talbott, Strobe, *The Russians and Reagan,* Vintage Books, New York, 1984

Tannenbaum, Frank, *The Ten Keys to Latin America,* Vintage Books, New York, 1965

Targ, Harry R., *Cuba and the USA: A New World Order?*, International Publishers, New York, 1992

Tazewell, Judy, ed., *The Miskito Question,* Hampton, Virginia, 1984

Tesis y Resoluciones, Primer Congreso del Partido Comunista de Cuba, La Habana, Publicaciones del CC del Partido Comunista de Cuba, 1978

The Cuban Revolution into the 1990s, Edit, Centro de Estudios Sobre America, Westview Press, Boulder, 1992

The Report of the President Commission on Central America, Macmillan Publishing Co., New York, 1983

The Rockefeller Report on Latin America, New York Times Edition, New York, 1969

The U.S. Invasion of Panama: The Independent Commission of Inquiry on the U.S. Invasion of Panama, South End Press, Boston, 1991

Thomas, Hugh, *Cuba,* Grijalbo, Barcelona, 1974

Tokatlian, Juan G., *Cuba-Estados Unidos, Dos Enfoques,* Cerec, Bogotá, 1984

Torture in Brazil, A Report by the Archdiocese of Sao Paulo, Vintage Books, New York,1986

Truman, Harry, *Memoires 1946–1952, Vol. II,* A Signet Book, New York, 1956

Turner, Standfiel, *Secrecy and Democracy: The CIA in Transition,* Harper and Row, New York, 1986

Two Years of Military Dictatorship in Chile, Stockholm, Publication House of Parliament, 1975

Uribe, Armando, *The Black Book of American Intervention in Chile,* Beacon Press, Boston, 1974

Uruguay: Nunca Mas, Human Right Violations, 1972–1985, Servicio Paz y Justicia, Temple University Press, Philadelphia, 1992

Vasquez Diaz, Ruben, *Bolivia a la hora del Che,* Siglo XXI. Mexico 1978

Vindicacion de Cuba, Editora Politica, La Habana, 1989

Volkov, Mai, *La estrategia del neocolonialismo,* Ediciones Estudio, Buenos Aires 1978

von Damm, Helenne, Edit, *Sincerely, Ronald Reagan,* Berkeley Books, New York, 1980

Waddell, Rick, *In War's Shadow: Waging Peace in Central America,* Ivy Books, New York, 1992

Wagley, Charles, *The Latin American Tradition,* Columbia University Press, New York, 1968

Weber, Henry, *Nicaragua: The Sandinista Revolution,* Verso, 1985

Weeks, John, and Guson, Phil, *Panama: Made in the USA,* Latin American Bureau, Londres, 1991

Weisen Cook, Blanche, *The Declassified Eisenhower,* Penguin Books. New York, 1984

White, Theodore, *The Making of the President 1964,* Mentor Books, New York, 1965

Wyden, Peter, *Bay of Pigs,* Simon & Schuster, New York, 1979

Ykolev, Nikolai, *La CIA contra la URSS,* Editorial Progreso, Moscow, 1983

INDEX

ABOUT THE AUTHOR

CLARA NIETO served in the Colombian mission to the United Nations from 1960–1967; was head of the Colombian Delegation at UNESCO, Paris, from 1967–1970; was Colombian Chargé d'Affairs in Yugoslavia until 1976; served as Colombian Ambassador to Cuba from 1977–1980; and from 1984–1986 was Director of UNESCO's regional office for Latin America and the Caribbean stationed in Havana. Her writing has appeared in many newspapers, including *El Tiempo, El Espectador, El Mundo,* and *NACLA.* Nieto lives in New York City and Bogotá, Colombia.